MODERN AMERICAN DRAMAS

NEW EDITION

Edited by

HARLAN HATCHER

VICE PRESIDENT,
OHIO STATE UNIVERSITY

HARCOURT, BRACE AND COMPANY, NEW YORK

CONTENTS

MODERN AMERICAN DRAMA

THE movement that produced the modern drama in Europe, England, and Ireland reached America last of all. In the forty years between the production of a *Doll's House* and *Beyond the Horizon*, the American theatre remained barren and provincial, the American playwrights weak and unaware. A few of the more publicized European and English plays—*A Doll's House, Ghosts, Hedda Gabler, Mrs. Warren's Profession, The Second Mrs. Tanqueray*—had sporadic productions in America. The native plays seem pale and superficial by comparison. They are interesting in a study of American cultural history, and they are important to the student of American drama as an expression of the national life. This period of drama is usually represented on its highest level by William Vaughn Moody's *The Great Divide*, Augustus Thomas's *The Witching Hour*, Percy MacKaye's *The Scarecrow*, Clyde Fitch's *The Truth*, Eugene Walter's *The Easiest Way*, George M. Cohan's *Broadway Jones*, and the work of Bronson Howard, David Belasco, and Edward Sheldon. Ludwig Lewisohn's book *The Modern Drama*, published in 1915, completely ignored these American dramatists, except for an incidental reference to "the decorative sentimentalities of David Belasco." But the critics of a quarter of a century ago were not being merely disrespectful when, in writing about "modern drama," they passed over this American scene without mention. Their judgment was warranted and also inescapable. In a world-wide perspective the American drama as of the year 1915 was not very significant.

While Lewisohn was yet reading the proofs of his essay, the ferment that would revolutionize the American stage was already at work. It was apparent in the talk among the young spirits that were gathering in Greenwich Village; it was manifest in the little theatre groups which they organized. Three of the most important of these—the Washington Square Players (later the Theatre Guild), the Neighborhood Playhouse, and the Provincetown—were all founded in 1915. These coteries were more nearly impromptu than those which founded the Théâtre Libre, Die Freie Bühne, The Moscow Art Theatre, The Abbey, and similar organizations in Europe. Unlike these groups that were mobilized to carry out a clear-cut purpose, the Americans had no well-defined program, no definite artistic creed, no precise goal or theory of drama. They were moved to action by their dissatisfaction with Broadway, its plays and production methods; they vaguely aspired to a richer, more acute dramaturgy and a livelier, more daring, and more experimental stage without knowing quite how these ideals were to be realized. Then the World War brought America and Europe more closely together; the Provincetown, more or less by accident, stumbled upon O'Neill; scenic designers like Lee Simonson, Robert Edmond Jones and his producer-associate Kenneth MacGowan, asserted their fresh genius; and at one giant, ocean-bridging stride American drama not only joined the procession, but rapidly took its place in the vanguard. Nor was it limited to small semi-private or experimental theatres; it immediately became a part of commercial Broadway.

The production of O'Neill's *Beyond the Horizon* on February 2, 1920, was a milestone in the advance of the American drama. One has only to spend a few hours reading the best of the plays we have mentioned above to feel the compelling force of O'Neill's genius. It was as though an unsuspected dimension had been added to the American theatre. It was quick with a bold and trenchant consciousness of life and of the moving drama enmeshed in the experiences of humble men on New England farms, in nameless shops and factories, and on the ships at sea. O'Neill, endowed as he was with the greatest power and scope, was also ably supported in the creation of a new American drama by many gifted playwrights whose work in itself would have given any stage a distinguished elevation.

While O'Neill was striding forward with *The Emperor Jones*, *Anna Christie*, *The Hairy Ape*, *Desire Under the Elms*, *Strange Interlude*, and *Mourning Becomes Electra*, Elmer Rice was offering *The Adding Machine* and *Street Scene*, Maxwell Anderson was writing *What Price Glory?*, *Saturday's Children* and *Elizabeth the Queen*, Sidney Howard was producing *They Knew What They Wanted*, *Lucky Sam McCarver* and *The Silver Cord*, and Robert Sherwood was delighting audiences with *The Road to Rome*, *Waterloo Bridge* and *Reunion in Vienna*. That is in itself a rather imposing list of plays.

The Pulitzer Prizes are also an interesting index to the growth of modern American drama. In the judgment of the committee on the awards the best play for each year was Zona Gale's *Miss Lulu Bett* (1921), O'Neill's *Anna Christie* (1922), Owen Davis' *Icebound* (1923), Hatcher Hughes' *Hell-Bent for Heaven* (1924), Sidney Howard's *They Knew What They Wanted* (1925), George Kelly's *Craig's Wife* (1926), Paul Green's *In Abraham's Bosom* (1927), O'Neill's *Strange Interlude* (1928), Rice's *Street Scene* (1929) and Marc Connelly's *The Green Pastures* (1930).

The new accent of the 1930's is likewise reflected in the Pulitzer awards. The prize went to George S. Kaufman's *Of Thee I Sing* in 1932, to Maxwell Anderson's *Both Your Houses* in 1933, to Sidney Kingsley's *Men in White* in 1934, to Zoe Akins' *The Old Maid* in 1935, to Sherwood's *Idiot's Delight* in 1936, to Hart and Kaufman's *You Can't Take It with You* in 1937, to Thornton Wilder's *Our Town* in 1938, again to a Sherwood play, *Abe Lincoln in Illinois*, in 1939, to William Saroyan's *The Time of Your Life* in 1940, and for the third time to Sherwood for his *There Shall Be No Night* in 1941. These are merely indications of quality, not a complete list or even a cross-section. They do not, for example, reflect the fine work of Clifford Odets in *Waiting for Lefty* (1935), *Awake and Sing* (1935), *Paradise Lost* (1935), *Golden Boy* (1937), etc., plays which dealt with the impact of the depression of the 1930's upon American life and made a profound impression upon their audiences.

The drama during the 1940's has been rather spotty. It may be significant that no Pulitzer award was made in 1942, 1944 (the year of *The Glass Menagerie*, we note), or 1947. Not since 1919 had the committee failed to discover a play worthy, in their opinion, of the award. Wilder received it in 1943 for *The Skin of Our Teeth*, Mary Chase in 1945 for *Harvey*, Crouse and Lindsay in 1946 for *State of the Union*, Tennessee Williams in 1948 for *A Streetcar Named Desire*, and Arthur Miller in 1949 for *Death of a Salesman*. One does not need to concur in the judgment of the committees of award, however, to see in this list an unmistakable index to the high standard maintained by American drama since World War I. And this record is supplemented with notable plays of other greatly talented authors: S. N. Behrman, Philip Barry, Lillian Hellman, Clare Boothe, Mark Reed, Irwin Shaw, John Howard Lawson.

This brief catalogue is only a bare suggestion of the scope, the energy, and the significance of modern American drama in its comparatively brief span of life. We must also bear in mind that all the attendant coordinating arts of the theatre, and an intelligent, constantly expanding audience developed with it, side by side. If we should look more closely into this record season by season we would observe that it has had a succession of phases, or dominant interests, which conveniently divide the decades into periods for simplifying our study. The more outstanding thematic interests of modern American drama and the cyclic mental climate in which American playwrights have worked are reflected in the plays reprinted in this collection.

The collection begins with O'Neill because, in the perspective of modern world drama and the singular phenomenon of its rise as an international movement, O'Neill is the first major playwright in America. The honored writers who preceded him have their own merits, their own interest and importance in our theatre, but not for any outstanding contribution to modern drama.

The older, established playwrights are almost self-selective. When all the criteria are assembled, the names of O'Neill, Anderson, Rice, and Sherwood are not to be evaded. *Winterset* is one of Anderson's best plays and the culmination of American interest in gangster life, in the social implications of the Sacco-Vanzetti case, and the problem of justice. *The Adding Machine* is Rice's most individual triumph and the best expressionistic drama by an American; in the opinion of some, the best play produced by the movement anywhere. *Abe Lincoln in Illinois* is, from the point of view of dramaturgy, Sherwood's best play, and the most notable of the cycle of plays on the new Americanism of the late 1930's.

Tennessee Williams, Arthur Miller, and William Saroyan are among the more notable younger men whose new and individual voices have been heard in more recent seasons. They are most representative of the best of American drama by fresh talent in this decade. Death cut off Thomas Heggen at the beginning of a career that seemed to give great promise, but his *Mister Roberts* is a self-contained delight.

We are still in the lively midst of the developing American drama, and still close to its beginnings. Difference of opinion on the relative merits of individual plays is natural and healthy. The plays here reprinted are themselves rewarding to study quite apart from their place in a larger movement; and they furnish a few solid foundation stones upon which may be erected with assurance fuller understanding of modern American drama. Some of these wider implications are presented in the more detailed critical and biographical introductions to the plays.

EUGENE O'NEILL

AT HOME AND abroad, Eugene O'Neill is America's greatest dramatist. His plays have been translated into most of the important European languages and have been given almost continuous performances in the theatres of the world. No other American has matched him in the scope of his subjects, or in the power and depth of his probings into the tortuous secrets of the inner man. His dramas have produced unrivalled excitement as theatrical experiences, and this same magic intoxicant is still potent on the printed page. Though the plays are American, they are restricted by no national barriers. Wherever the human heart is disturbed and searching out the mystery of its unrest, there is the locale for O'Neill's dramas. Their universality is proclaimed by their success at the same time in America, Russia, Sweden, Germany, and England. Their native quality received the unprecedented, official recognition of three Pulitzer awards (1920, 1922, 1928); their international appeal was formally attested by the Nobel committee when it awarded O'Neill the prize in literature in 1936.

O'Neill brought to the theatre a unique experience. For one with his serious, brooding temperament and dramatic gifts, it was an experience rich in substance. It might have destroyed him, and apparently came close to doing so. But he had enough genius to take command at the right moment and shape his experience into art. A brief chart of his career reads like the outline for an O'Neill play, except that the plays generally end in frustration. He was born October 16, 1888, quite fittingly at the Barrett House on Broadway at Forty-third Street in New York City. His father was a gifted actor who became famous for his long and successful years on the road with his own company in *The Count of Monte Cristo*. O'Neill said that his father cleared fifty thousand dollars a season with this play.

O'Neill immediately began a life that led him alternately in and out of the theatre. During his first seven years, he was carried by his itinerant parents to all the larger towns of the United States. Then until he was thirteen he was placed in various boarding schools. He graduated from Betts Academy at Stamford, Connecticut, in 1906, and entered Princeton the following autumn. Near the end of his freshman year he was suspended for irregularities of conduct— according to the best tradition, for tossing a beer-bottle through the window of the president's campus home. The president was Woodrow Wilson. By the time his suspension had expired, O'Neill was completely alienated from academic life and ready to assault the world on its hardest terms.

O'Neill's college career was ended abruptly, but his education for his future work was just beginning, though he did not know this at the time. It was divided into four episodes which roughly corresponded to the freshman to senior sequence of the university curriculum. After a brief period as secretary for a mail-order jewelry firm, and following his first marriage, O'Neill went gold-

1

hunting in Honduras with a mining engineer—the first of those "beyond the horizon" journeys over the sea in search of himself and the romance which eluded him at home. He found malaria instead, and returned to the United States. He then became assistant manager of the road company starring his father and Viola Allen in *The White Sister*, and stayed with it on tour from St. Louis to Boston. At the end of the season he boarded a Norwegian boat and sailed for sixty-five days to Buenos Aires on his second venture. There he tried again to become mercantile minded successively with Westinghouse, Swift, and Singer, but without success. He went to the water-front to live; he worked occasionally, and saw and heard about life in the raw, unrefined lump. He saw enough characters and heard enough yarns to supply a writer like Jack London with material for a lifetime.

But this life soon palled, and O'Neill shipped as mule-tender on a steamer bound from Buenos Aires to Durban, Africa, where he could not even land because he was destitute. He sailed back to the Argentine, was reduced to beach combing, and finally signed on a British tramp steamer. He got back into New York in 1911. He was turning twenty-three.

O'Neill lived in New York in a three-dollar-a-month room at a vermin-invaded, water-front dive kept by "Jimmy the Priest." He was penniless, and apparently unwilling to be aided or supervised by his family. He finally shipped again for his fourth venture, this time as an able seaman on the American liner *New York*, bound for Southampton. On his return, he joined his father's company in New Orleans, and took a minor part in the ubiquitous *Monte Cristo*, learning his part en route to Ogden,

Utah, where he first became an actor. He had acquired an education somewhat different from that offered him at Princeton.

One other element was needed: the training necessary to give meaning to these experiences through the medium of words. This was supplied to order by Frederick P. Latimer of the New London *Telegraph*, who gave him a job as reporter and printed twenty-four of his verses in a column on the editorial page from August 26 to December 9. He encouraged O'Neill; he was the first man to recognize the possibilities in the wayward boy. The terrific beating O'Neill had given his constitution in his vagabond, drinking, carousing years now claimed its price. He developed a soft spot in his lung, and had to go to Gaylord Farm sanitarium at Wallingford, Connecticut, an account of which appears in the first part of *The Straw*.

O'Neill was now in his twenty-fifth year, and old enough to consider what this furious life of his was all about. The enforced leisure gave him time to ponder, and his resolution and understanding began to take form. He had written just enough to excite his own interest. When he left the sanitarium in the late spring, he went to live with an English family on the Connecticut coast, where he spent more than a year building up his health, and reading intensively the things he had missed that now interested him. He specialized in the great dramatists of Greece and England, in Ibsen, and particularly in Strindberg whose intense psychological plays fascinated him. He also practiced writing and turned out "eleven one-acters, two long plays, and some verse." He was ready for technical training and advice on how to transmute his experience into dramas. The best place for such instruction was the playwriting course at Harvard University.

O'Neill accordingly spent the year 1914–1915 in Professor Baker's 47 Workshop. It is not surprising that a man of O'Neill's age, type, experience, and certainty of direction found the procedure disappointing—another beyond-the-horizon quest. He was somewhat restive under the class routine. He seems to have had the scorn of a socially timid but older and more widely experienced young man for his fellow students in the course. They were trying to make plays without knowledge. When a member of the class went to the blackboard to chart the plot development of a play by Augustus Thomas, O'Neill got up and walked out. It was a characteristic gesture of impatience with the conventional, unimaginative stage techniques and their dull and partial representation of life. O'Neill didn't actually say so, but it seems obvious that he sensed the artificiality and awkwardness of the whole procedure. Everything was backwards. The students were being told how to write before they had anything to say. The exercises did not stem naturally out of a genuine creative problem. O'Neill, on the contrary, was burdened with the raw flesh of what he had seen and lived and known, and he was trying to find an effective way to give it life through the medium of drama. He had great respect for Professor Baker, but he felt that the results of the course were, for him, largely negative.

O'Neill may have carried away more than he could specify at the time; but, fortunately for him, there was at that moment a ferment in the air, and a group of play-conscious intellectuals whose interests were similar to his own. This was the Greenwich Village group who foregathered at Provincetown during the summers, beginning in 1915, and there at the improvised Wharf Theatre played several one-act pieces.

This group of young spirits included George Cram Cook, Susan Glaspell, Mary Heaton Vorse, Wilbur Daniel Steele, Harry Kemp, Hutchins Hapgood, and others. They represented in their fashion the belated arrival in America of the European currents that had produced the Théâtre Libre, the Moscow Art Theatre, and other such organizations for the advancement of the theatre.

O'Neill joined the Provincetown, as they called themselves, in the summer of 1916. Following his year at Harvard he had lived in Greenwich Village where he had learned to criticize the sorry scheme of things, where he had made acquaintance with the radical laborites, the Negroes and Italians, and had added to his collection of characters later to be used in his plays. On invitation from Susan Glaspell, he gave *Bound East for Cardiff* to a gathering of the Provincetown to read. "Then," said Miss Glaspell, "we knew what we were for." They produced this one-act play at the Wharf, and, later in the summer, a second play by O'Neill called *Thirst*. The author acted a small part in each. Both plays created a powerful and original effect on the spectators.

When the group returned to the Village, they opened the Playwright's Theatre at 139 Macdougal Street in November with *Bound East for Cardiff*, in which O'Neill again played the Second Mate. They also produced O'Neill's *Before Breakfast*, *Fog*, and *The Sniper*. In November, 1917, they opened with his *The Long Voyage Home*, and followed on the second bill with his *Ile*, and later with *The Rope*. In the autumn of 1918 they presented his *Where the Cross Is Made*, and *The Moon of the Caribbees;* in 1919 *The Dreamy Kid;* and in 1920 *Exorcism*. Then, on February 2, 1920, at the up-town Morosco Theatre, John D. Williams produced *Beyond the Horizon*, the Pulitzer prize play of the year, the second play to receive that award. On the evening of November 1, 1920, the Provincetown Players presented *The Emperor Jones*. Then came *Diff'rent*, on December 27; *Gold*, June 1, 1921; and a second Pulitzer prize drama, *Anna Christie*, November 2, 1921. Thus with phenomenal timeliness the Provincetown had provided O'Neill with a perfect experimental laboratory theatre, and an assured subscription audience, the like of which no other American playwright ever enjoyed. O'Neill paid tribute to them for their aid. In a few short seasons he emerged as the foremost American dramatist.

The career and achievements of O'Neill since that time have been international news. The Provincetown Players produced *The Hairy Ape* (1922), *All God's Chillun Got Wings* (1924), and *Desire Under the Elms* (1924). The Theatre Guild began its presentations of O'Neill with *Marco Millions* and *Strange Interlude*, both in January, 1928, and has continued to be his producer. He himself has generally stayed away from New York and the theatre. He has lived at Ridgefield, Connecticut; in a chateau in France; in a gleaming white mansion on the water's edge in Bermuda; on an island off the coast of Georgia; and on his present estate, Tao House, in Contra Costa County, California, in the hills back of Berkeley. There he is still at work on his forthcoming cycle of nine plays that will deal with the growth of America since the early days of the nineteenth century.

The closest possible unity and interlinking exist between O'Neill's career as thus briefly sketched and the plays for which he is celebrated. That is a subject for special study in the psychology of creative endeavor in drama. But the effects of O'Neill's natural rebelliousness and prodigality, his dreamy passion, his knowledge of all sorts and conditions of men, and his absorption and synthesis of the discontents and the intellectual interests of Europe and America in the second and third decades of the century are visible in some form in every detail of his work. The plays themselves are so rich in interest from so many points of view that it becomes embarrassing to summarize them or to arrange them into groups.

Their themes and subject matter are extraordinarily varied. The early one-act plays, and certain scenes in the later and longer dramas, were, for the most part, concerned with sailors and the sea realistically presented. The men are rough of manner and of speech; they are violent and hard in action; they are lonely and tormented by some deep-seated malaise; and they have their moments of agitation in the presence of such beauties as life on board ship affords: "the mournful cadence of the song from the shore" that stirs Smitty's memories under the moon of the Caribbees and drives him to drink; Paddy's thoughts in *The Hairy Ape* of "clippers wid tall masts touching the sky" making sail at dawn; of the sound of a chanty song; of a glimpse of the land astern "sinking low and dying out"; or the thrill of a ship scudding south at night under the moon and the stars.

The first five long plays, all individual and searching with an energy new to American drama, were presented in quick succession. *Beyond the Horizon*, a tragedy of fate, illusion, and human frustration, was produced in February, 1920. *The Emperor Jones, Diff'rent, Gold,* and *Anna Christie* were all produced within one year—November 3, 1920, to November 2, 1921. *The Emperor Jones* was a triumph in early American expressionism. It showed O'Neill's technical versatility in flinging on the visible stage in externalized symbols the inner, fear-stricken life, or unconscious, atavistic self of the ex-Pullman porter, the Emperor Jones. The melodramatic devices of the silver bullet and the incessant beat of the tom-tom on Jones's night of penalty and terror, together with the sequence of short, surcharged scenes, built up the entire play to a terrific climax. *Anna Christie* dealt in straightforward style with the redemption of the fallen and bedraggled Anna through the power of a sailor's love and the tradition of the sea. It was set on the fog-drenched water-front that O'Neill knew so well, and it gave a sympathetic character portrayal of Anna's father, Chris, now retired to a barge, but with a full understanding of the sinister power of "old davil sea." The character of the father, who divides the play with Anna, was a remarkable example of how O'Neill salvaged treasure out of the sunken days along the wharfs. He had known the original of Chris at Jimmy the Priest's.

These three plays, with such faults as they have, were genuine achievements. *Diff'rent*, a study of a sex-inhibited New England spinster, is interesting as a forerunner of the greater plays to come on the same subject in the same locale. *The Hairy Ape* was more ambitious in theme and technique. It contained O'Neill's nostalgic tribute to the romance of the sea, and the contrast between the age of sails and the age of steel and steam. It called upon symbols, after the fashion of expressionism, to enlarge its suggestiveness. It presented Yank's concept of "belonging," and the deterioration of the muscular stoker when he lost his conviction of the importance of his place in society. He discovered that he was only a hairy ape, hired and exploited by the idle people represented by fretful Mildred, who called him a "filthy beast" and who fainted when she saw him at work in the stokehole of a transatlantic liner.

As a dramatist O'Neill was more concerned with personal psychological problems in the Strindberg manner than in the social problems that aroused so many of his contemporaries. His somewhat desperate probings of the disturbed inner lives of his characters led him to call still further upon symbolistic methods to transcend the limitations of objective realism on the stage. He wrote four notable plays of this type. They are sharp and clear on certain points, baffling if not confused in others. The most subtle and elusive, as well as the most elaborately symbolic, was *The Great God Brown* (1926). This was the play in which O'Neill introduced his characters with masked faces to represent the personality with which they confront the world; when they lay bare their unspoken thoughts in static soliloquy they remove their masks. The dualism is also represented by the opposed disciplines of Dionysus (pagan acceptance of life) and St. Anthony (the Christian denial of life), in the central character whose name is Dion Anthony; and in the contrasting characters of Marguerite and Cybele, represented by Margaret and Cybel. The symbolism extends through all the details of the play, including the revelation of Brown as "the visionless demi-god of our new materialistic myth —Success," as O'Neill himself explained.

Lazarus Laughed, a literary drama written in 1927, is O'Neill's attempt to do what Browning and others had done before him: to show how a glimpse over the threshold of death affects Lazarus, and how it modified his view of life and his relations with those around him. *Dynamo* (1929) was the beginning of an ambitious, perhaps even pretentious, trilogy on man, God, and the machine age—the new and cruel god (or goddess) here being a dynamo. The play failed and O'Neill abandoned the scheme. Some of its threads of interest were combined with the dual personality theme of *The Great God Brown* to produce *Days Without End*, or John Loving's struggle with his psyche, who stands beside him at all times to represent his demon other-nature. His quest for peace and certainty after the illness of his wife leads him in the final scene to prostrate himself at the foot of the Cross and pour out his soul in faith and surrender; whereupon the corpse of his attendant other-self falls with arms outstretched "like a cripple's testimonial offering in a shrine." These exceedingly interesting and daringly experimental plays were all failures on the stage. Yet they have been among the most widely discussed of O'Neill dramas.

Of the various other plays three represent O'Neill's supreme achievements to date. They are the dramas of sex repressions and psychological involvements so deeply studied as to become genuine tragedies: *Desire Under the Elms* (1924), *Strange Interlude* (1928), and *Mourning Becomes Electra* (1931).

The tragic dignity of *Desire Under the Elms* was somewhat tarnished by the reactions of the sex-obsessed audiences of the 1920's which perverted the play into a *succès de scandale;* but with the passing of the years it has emerged as one of the important tragedies in American drama. Its movement is relentless. It gathers in strength from the thrice-entangled web of human emotions which it weaves and resolves. The character of old Ephraim Cabot is as hard as the stones in the wall around his cow barn. His familiarity with the Scripture does not soften his heart, but merely supports its stubborn granite. Eben and Abbie begin their action against each other motivated by rivalry and thirst for revenge. They are soon caught without warning in the net of mysterious Fate, and are doomed to love. But old Cabot, though victimized, is still able to deliver a mortal blow when he tells Eben that Abbie has merely tricked him in order to get the property for herself and her infant son. Eben, hurt and enraged, cannot believe that this motive of Abbie's has long since yielded to a consuming and unselfish love for him. He precipitates the violent denouément, and the resultant catharsis lifts the play out of tumult into serenity as the small filament of tenderness amid all the stark bitterness lights with Abbie's "I love ye, Eben!" and Eben's "An' I love yew, Abbie!"

Strange Interlude is in nine acts, which require a playing time from late afternoon through an evening. It is the study of the possessive attachment of a father for his daughter. It shows how her own life was frustrated and repressed by a denial of life when her lover went to war, and how, after an aberrant interlude of nervous disorder, she was awakened, and found fulfillment in a collective relationship with her lover, her husband, her son, and the sublimated image of her father in the person of "dear old Charlie." Instead of masks, O'Neill used the ancient device of the monologue to permit the characters to speak to the audience their secret thoughts, which in normal life would be kept in good-mannered concealment.

Mourning Becomes Electra went even further in dramatizing Freudian inner turmoil. O'Neill took an American story about the sinister New England House of Mannon at the close of the Civil War, and modeled it on the outlines of the tragic events in the Greek House of Atreus. He substituted a "modern psychological approximation of the Greek sense of fate" in the belief that this motivation might make real again the force that was lost when "belief in gods and supernatural retribution" was abandoned. He charted with mathematical exactitude the Freudian relationships between wife-husband, mother-son, mother-daughter, woman-lover; between daughter-mother-father-lover; between son-mother-father—etcetera. And out of that gross entanglement came the murders and the penalties that are unfolded with enormous effect in this long tragic trilogy.

The Electra trilogy proved to be the peak in O'Neill's dramatic achievement. He turned to a somewhat nostalgic and successful comedy of the turn-of-the-century American life and manners in *Ah, Wilderness!* (1932), and to a serious and complicated study of multiple personality on a religious theme in *Days Without End* (1933). The play was technically interesting, but it failed to speak forcefully to the public of the depressed 1930's. O'Neill continued to write steadily. The press reported from time to time that he was composing a series of plays about the growth and development of America, and even announced tentative plans for their production. They have not yet reached the public on stage or in print.

There was much excitement in 1946 when O'Neill again produced and published a new play called *The Iceman Cometh* (dated 1939 by the author). It was not one of the series, but a single long play set in Harry Hope's back room and bar, "a cheap ginmill of the five-cent whiskey, last-resort variety situated on the downtown West Side of New York," in the summer 1912. The characters, the mood, and the "beyond the horizon" dreams of the outcast and the defeated suggested the O'Neill of the 1920's. The play was interesting and distinguished, like all of his writings, but not overpowering. *A Moon for the Misbegotten* was given try-out production the following season. It was confusing to audiences, it was severely criticized by reviewers as unformed and unconvincing, and it was withdrawn without a New York performance.

Among his more than a score of plays, plays which have justly made him a world figure in the drama, several stand out as masterpieces in the modern theatre. We have chosen *The Emperor Jones* as one of the most representative. It is full of life, of character, and of poetry, and it is excellent theatre as well as good reading.

THE EMPEROR JONES

CHARACTERS

BRUTUS JONES, *Emperor*

HENRY SMITHERS, *a Cockney trader*

AN OLD NATIVE WOMAN

LEM, *a native chief*

SOLDIERS, *adherents of* LEM

THE LITTLE FORMLESS FEARS; JEFF; THE NEGRO CONVICTS; THE PRISON GUARD; THE PLANTERS; THE AUCTIONEER; THE SLAVES; THE CONGO WITCH DOCTOR; THE CROCODILE GOD

The action of the play takes place on an island in the West Indies as yet not self-determined by white marines. The form of native government is, for the time being, an empire.

SCENE I

The audience chamber in the palace of the Emperor—a spacious, high-ceilinged room with bare, whitewashed walls. The floor is of white tiles. In the rear, to the left of the center, a wide archway giving out on a portico with white pillars. The palace is evidently situated on high ground, for beyond the portico nothing can be seen but a vista of distant hills, their summits crowned with thick groves of palm trees. In the right wall, center, a smaller arched doorway leading to the living quarters of the palace. The room is bare of furniture with the exception of one huge chair made of uncut wood which stands at the center, its back to the rear. This is very apparently the Emperor's throne. It is painted a dazzling, eye-smiting scarlet. There is a brilliant orange cushion on the seat and another smaller one is placed on the floor to serve as a footstool. Strips of matting, dyed scarlet, lead from the foot of the throne to the two entrances.

It is late afternoon, but the sunlight still blazes yellowly beyond the portico and there is an oppressive burden of exhausting heat in the air.

As the curtain rises, a native Negro woman sneaks in cautiously from the entrance on the right. She is very old, dressed in cheap calico, barefooted, a red bandanna handkerchief covering all but a few stray wisps of white hair. A bundle bound in colored cloth is carried over her shoulder on the end of a stick. She hesitates beside the doorway, peering back as if in extreme dread of being discovered. Then she begins to glide noiselessly, a step at a time, toward the doorway in the rear. At this moment, SMITHERS appears beneath the portico.

SMITHERS is a tall, stoop-shouldered man about forty. His bald head, perched on a long neck with an enormous Adam's apple, looks like an egg. The tropics have tanned his naturally pasty face with its small, sharp features to a sickly yellow, and native rum has painted his pointed nose to a startling red. His little, washy-blue eyes are red-rimmed and dart about him like a ferret's. His expression is one of unscrupulous meanness, cowardly and dangerous. He is dressed in a worn riding suit of dirty white drill, puttees, spurs, and wears a white cork helmet. A cartridge belt with an *automatic revolver is around his waist. He carries a riding whip in his hand. He sees the woman and stops to watch her suspiciously. Then, making up his mind, he steps quickly on tiptoe into the room. The woman, looking back over her shoulder continually, does not see him until it is too late. When she does* SMITHERS *springs forward and grabs her firmly by the shoulder. She struggles to get away, fiercely but silently.* 10

SMITHERS (*tightening his grasp—roughly*). Easy! None o' that, me birdie. You can't wriggle out, now I got me 'ooks on yer.

WOMAN (*seeing the uselessness of struggling, gives way to frantic terror, and sinks to the ground, embracing his knees supplicatingly*). No tell him! No tell him, mister! 20

SMITHERS (*with great curiosity*). Tell 'im? (*Then scornfully.*) Oh, you mean 'is bloomin' Majesty. What's the gaime, any'ow? What are you sneakin' away for? Been stealin' a bit, I s'pose. (*He taps her bundle with his riding whip significantly.*)

WOMAN (*shaking her head vehemently*). No, me no steal.

SMITHERS. Bloody liar! But tell me what's 30 up. There's somethin' funny goin' on. I smelled it in the air first thing I got up this mornin'. You blacks are up to some devilment. This palace of 'is is like a bleedin' tomb. Where's all the 'ands? (*The woman keeps sullenly silent.* SMITHERS *raises his whip threateningly.*) Ow, yer won't, won't yer? I'll show yer what's what.

WOMAN (*coweringly*). I tell, mister. You 40 no hit. They go—all go. (*She makes a sweeping gesture toward the hills in the distance.*)

SMITHERS. Run away—to the 'ills?

WOMAN. Yes, mister. Him Emperor— Great Father. (*She touches her forehead to the floor with a quick mechanical jerk.*) Him sleep after eat. Then they go— all go. Me old woman. Me left only. Now me go too.

SMITHERS (*his astonishment giving way to an immense, mean satisfaction*). Ow! So that's the ticket! Well, I know bloody well wot's in the air—when they runs orf to the 'ills. The tom-tom 'll be thumpin' out there bloomin' soon. (*With extreme vindictiveness.*) And I'm bloody glad of it, for one! Serve 'im right! Puttin' on airs, the stinkin' nigger! 'Is Majesty! Gawd blimey! I only 'opes I'm there when they takes 'im out to shoot 'im. (*Suddenly.*) 'E's still 'ere all right, ain't 'e?

WOMAN. Him sleep.

SMITHERS. 'E's bound to find out soon as 'e wakes up. 'E's cunnin' enough to know when 'is time's come. (*He goes to the doorway on the right and whistles shrilly with his fingers in his mouth. The old woman springs to her feet and runs out of the doorway at the rear.* SMITHERS *goes after her, reaching for his revolver.*) Stop or I'll shoot! (*Then, stopping—indifferently.*) Pop orf, then, if yer like, yer black cow. (*He stands in the doorway, looking after her.*)

[JONES *enters from the right. He is a tall, powerfully built, full-blooded Negro of middle age. His features are typically negroid, yet there is something decidedly distinctive about his face—an underlying strength of will, a hardy, self-reliant confidence in himself that inspires respect. His eyes are alive with a keen, cunning intelligence. In manner he is shrewd, suspicious, evasive. He wears a light-blue uniform coat sprayed with brass buttons, heavy gold chevrons on his shoulders, gold braid on the collar, cuffs, etc. His pants are bright-red with a light-blue stripe down the side. Patent-leather laced boots with brass spurs, and a belt with a long-barreled, pearl-*

handled revolver in a holster complete his make-up. Yet there is something not altogether ridiculous about his grandeur. He has a way of carrying it off.]

JONES (*not seeing anyone—greatly irritated and blinking sleepily—shouts*). Who dare whistle dat way in my palace? Who dare wake up de Emperor? I'll git de hide frayled off some o' you niggers sho'!

SMITHERS (*showing himself—in a manner half afraid and half defiant*). It was me whistled to yer. (*As* JONES *frowns angrily.*) I got news for yer.

JONES (*putting on his suavest manner, which fails to cover up his contempt for the white man*). Oh, it's you, Mr. Smithers. (*He sits down on his throne with easy dignity.*) What news you got to tell me?

SMITHERS (*coming close to enjoy his discomfiture*). Don't yer notice nothin' funny today?

JONES (*coldly*). Funny? No. I ain't perceived nothin' of de kind!

SMITHERS. Then yer ain't so foxy as I thought yer was. Where's all your court?—(*Sarcastically.*)—the Generals and the Cabinet Ministers and all?

JONES (*imperturbably*). Where dey mostly runs to minute I closes my eyes—drinkin' rum and talkin' big down in de town. (*Sarcastically.*) How come you don't know dat? Ain't you sousin' with 'em most every day?

SMITHERS (*stung, but pretending indifference—with a wink*). That's part of the day's work. I got ter—ain't I—in my business?

JONES (*contemptuously*). Yo' business!

SMITHERS (*imprudently enraged*). Gawd blimey, you was glad enough for me ter take yer in on it when you landed here first. You didn' 'ave no 'igh and mighty airs in them days!

JONES (*his hand going to his revolver like a flash—menacingly*). Talk polite, white

man! Talk polite, you heah me! I'm boss heah now, is you fergettin'?

[*The Cockney seems about to challenge this last statement with the facts, but something in the other's eyes holds and cows him.*]

SMITHERS (*in a cowardly whine*). No 'arm meant, old top.

JONES (*condescendingly*). I accepts yo' apology. (*Let's his hand fall from his revolver.*) No use'n you rakin' up ole times. What I was den is one thing. What I is now's another. You didn't let me in on yo' crooked work out o' no kind feelin's dat time. I done de dirty work fo' you—and most o' de brainwork, too, fo' dat matter—and I was wu'th money to you, dat's de reason.

SMITHERS. Well, blimey, I give yer a start, didn't I?—when no one else would. I wasn't afraid to 'ire you like the rest was—'count of the story about your breakin' jail back in the States.

JONES. No, you didn't have no s'cuse to look down on me fo' dat. You been in jail you'self more'n once.

SMITHERS (*furiously*). It's a lie! (*Then trying to pass it off by an attempt at scorn.*) Garn! Who told yer that fairy tale?

JONES. Dey's some tings I ain't got to be tole. I kin see 'em in folks' eyes. (*Then after a pause—meditatively.*) Yes, you sho' give me a start. And it didn't take long from dat time to git dese fool woods' niggers right where I wanted dem. (*With pride.*) From stowaway to Emperor in two years! Dat's goin' some!

SMITHERS (*with curiosity*). And I bet you got yer pile o' money 'id safe some place.

JONES (*with satisfaction*). I sho' has! And it's in a foreign bank where no pusson don't ever git it out but me no matter what come. You didn't s'pose I was holdin' down dis Emperor job for de glory in it, did you? Sho'! De fuss and glory part of it, dat's only to turn de heads o' de low-flung bush niggers dat's here. Dey wants de big circus show for deir money. I gives it to 'em an' I gits de money. (*With a grin.*) De long green, dat's me every time! (*Then rebukingly.*) But you ain't got no kick agin me, Smithers. I'se paid you back all you done for me many times. Ain't I pertected you and winked at all de crooked tradin' you been doin' right out in de broad day? Sho' I has —and me makin' laws to stop it at de same time! (*He chuckles.*)

SMITHERS (*grinning*). But, meanin' no 'arm, you been grabbin' right and left yourself, ain't yer? Look at the taxes you've put on 'em! Blimey! You've squeezed 'em dry!

JONES (*chuckling*). No, dey ain't *all* dry yet. I'se still heah, ain't I?

SMITHERS (*smiling at his secret thought*). They're dry right now, you'll find out. (*Changing the subject abruptly.*) And as for me breakin' laws, you've broke 'em all yerself just as fast as yer made 'em.

JONES. Ain't I de Emperor? De laws don't go for him. (*Judicially.*) You heah what I tells you, Smithers. Dere's little stealin' like you does, and dere's big stealin' like I does. For de little stealin' dey gits you in jail soon or late. For de big stealin' dey makes you Emperor and puts you in de Hall o' Fame when you croaks. (*Reminiscently.*) If dey's one thing I learns in ten years on de Pullman ca's listenin' to de white quality talk, it's dat same fact. And when I gits a chance to use it I winds up Emperor in two years.

SMITHERS (*unable to repress the genuine admiration of the small fry for the large*). Yes, yer turned the bleedin' trick, all right. Blimey, I never seen a bloke 'as 'ad the bloomin' luck you 'as.

JONES (*severely*). Luck? What you mean— luck?

SMITHERS. I suppose you'll say as that swank about the silver bullet ain't luck—and that was what first got the fool blacks on yer side the time of the revolution, wasn't it?

JONES (*with a laugh*). Oh, dat silver bullet! Sho' was luck! But I makes dat luck, you heah? I loads de dice! Yessuh! When dat murderin' nigger ole Lem hired to kill me takes aim ten feet away and his gun misses fire and I shoots him dead, what you heah me say?

SMITHERS. You said yer'd got a charm so's no lead bullet 'd kill yer. You was so strong only a silver bullet could kill yer, you told 'em. Blimey, wasn't that swank for yer—and plain, fat-'eaded luck?

JONES (*proudly*). I got brains and I uses 'em quick. Dat ain't luck.

SMITHERS. Yer know they wasn't 'ardly liable to get no silver bullets. And it was luck 'e didn't 'it you that time.

JONES (*laughing*). And dere all dem fool bush niggers was kneelin' down and bumpin' deir heads on de ground like I was a miracle out o' de Bible. Oh Lawd, from dat time on I has dem all eatin' out of my hand. I cracks de whip and dey jumps through.

SMITHERS (*with a sniff*). Yankee bluff done it.

JONES. Ain't a man's talkin' big what makes him big—long as he makes folks believe it? Sho', I talks large when I ain't got nothin' to back it up, but I ain't talkin' wild just de same. I knows I kin fool 'em—I *knows* it— and dat's backin' enough fo' my game. And ain't I got to learn deir lingo and teach some of dem English befo' I kin talk to 'em? Ain't dat wuk? You ain't never learned ary word er it, Smithers, in de ten years you been heah, dough you knows it's money in you' pocket tradin' wid 'em if you does. But you'se too shiftless to take de trouble.

SMITHERS (*flushing*). Never mind about me. What's this I've 'eard about yer really 'avin' a silver bullet molded for yourself?

JONES. It's playin' out my bluff. I has de silver bullet molded and I tells 'em when de times comes I kills myself wid it. I tells 'em dat's 'cause I'm de on'y man in de world big enuff to git me. No use'n deir tryin'. And dey falls down and bumps deir heads. (*He laughs.*) I does dat so's I kin take a walk in peace widout no jealous nigger gunnin' at me from behind de trees.

SMITHERS (*astonished*). Then you 'ad it made—'onest?

JONES. Sho' did. Heah she be. (*He takes out his revolver, breaks it, and takes the silver bullet out of one chamber.*) Five lead an' dis silver baby at de last. Don't she shine pretty? (*He holds it in his hand, looking at it admiringly, as if strangely fascinated.*)

SMITHERS. Let me see. (*Reaches out his hand for it.*)

JONES (*harshly*). Keep yo' hands whar dey b'long, white man. (*He replaces it in the chamber and puts the revolver back on his hip.*)

SMITHERS (*snarling*). Gawd blimey! Think I'm a bleedin' thief, you would.

JONES. No, 'tain't dat. I knows you'se scared to steal from me. On'y I ain't 'lowin' nary body to touch dis baby. She's my rabbit's foot.

SMITHERS (*sneering*). A bloomin' charm, wot? (*Venomously.*) Well, you'll need all the bloody charms you 'as before long, s' 'elp me!

JONES (*judicially*). Oh, I'se good for six months yit 'fore dey gits sick o' my game. Den, when I sees trouble comin', I makes my getaway.

SMITHERS. Ho! You got it all planned, ain't yer?

JONES. I ain't no fool. I knows dis Emperor's time is sho't. Dat why I make hay when de sun shine. Was you thinkin' I'se aimin' to hold down dis job for life? No, suh! What good is gittin' money if you stays back in dis raggedy country? I wants action when I spends. And when I sees dese niggers gittin' up deir nerve to tu'n me out, and I'se got all de money in sight, I resigns on de spot and beats it quick.

SMITHERS. Where to?

JONES. None o' yo' business.

SMITHERS. Not back to the bloody States, I'll lay my oath.

JONES (*suspiciously*). Why don't I? (*Then with an easy laugh.*) You mean 'count of dat story 'bout me breakin' from jail back dere? Dat's all talk.

SMITHERS (*skeptically*). Ho, yes!

JONES (*sharply*). You ain't 'sinuatin' I'se a liar, is you?

SMITHERS (*hastily*). No, Gawd strike me! I was only thinkin' o' the bloody lies you told the blacks 'ere about killin' white men in the States.

JONES (*angered*). How come dey're lies?

SMITHERS. You'd 'ave been in jail if you 'ad, wouldn't yer then? (*With venom.*) And from what I've 'eard, it ain't 'ealthy for a black to kill a white man in the States. They burns 'em in oil, don't they?

JONES (*with cool deadliness*). You mean lynchin' 'd scare me? Well, I tells you, Smithers, maybe I does kill one white man back dere. Maybe I does. And maybe I kills another right heah 'fore long if he don't look out.

SMITHERS (*trying to force a laugh*). I was on'y spoofin' yer. Can't yer take a joke? And you was just sayin' you'd never been in jail.

JONES (*in the same tone—slightly boastful*). Maybe I goes to jail dere for gettin' in an argument wid razors ovah a crap game. Maybe I gits twenty years when dat colored man die. Maybe I gits in 'nother argument wid de prison guard was overseer ovah us when we're wukin' de road. Maybe he hits me wid a whip and I splits his head wid a shovel and runs away and files de chain off my leg and gits away safe. Maybe I does all dat an' maybe I don't. It's a story I tells you so's you knows I'se de kind of man dat if you evah repeats one word of it, I ends yo' stealin' on dis yearth mighty damn quick!

SMITHERS (*terrified*). Think I'd peach on yer? Not me! Ain't I always been yer friend?

JONES (*suddenly relaxing*). Sho' you has— and you better be.

SMITHERS (*recovering his composure—and with it his malice*). And just to show yer I'm yer friend, I'll tell yer that bit o' news I was goin' to.

JONES. Go ahead! Shoot de piece. Must be bad news from de happy way you look.

SMITHERS (*warningly*). Maybe it's gettin' time for you to resign—with that bloomin' silver bullet, wot? (*He finishes with a mocking grin.*)

JONES (*puzzled*). What's dat you say? Talk plain.

SMITHERS. Ain't noticed any of the guards or servants about the place today, I 'aven't.

JONES (*carelessly*). Dey're all out in de garden sleepin' under de trees. When I sleeps, dey sneaks a sleep too, and I pretends I never suspicions it. All I got to do is to ring de bell and dey come flyin', makin' a bluff dey was wukin' all de time.

SMITHERS (*in the same mocking tone*). Ring the bell now an' you'll bloody well see what I means.

JONES (*startled to alertness, but preserving the same careless tone*). Sho' I rings. (*He reaches below the throne and pulls out a big, common dinner bell which is painted the same vivid scarlet as the throne. He rings this vigorously—then stops to listen. Then he goes to both doors, rings again, and looks out.*)

SMITHERS (*watching him with malicious satisfaction, after a pause—mockingly*). The bloody ship is sinkin' an' the bleedin' rats 'as slung their 'ooks.

JONES (*in a sudden fit of anger flings the bell clattering into a corner*). Low-flung woods' niggers! (*Then catching* SMITHERS' *eye on him, he controls himself and suddenly bursts into a low chuckling laugh.*) Reckon I overplays my hand dis once! A man can't take de pot on a bobtailed flush all de time. Was I sayin' I'd sit in six months mo'? Well, I'se changed my mind den. I cashes in and resigns de job of Emperor right dis minute.

SMITHERS (*with real admiration*). Blimey, but you're a cool bird, and no mistake.

JONES. No use'n fussin'. When I knows de game's up I kisses it good-by widout no long waits. Dey've all run off to de hills, ain't dey?

SMITHERS. Yes—every bleedin' man jack of 'em.

JONES. Den de revolution is at de post. And de Emperor better git his feet smokin' up de trail. (*He starts for the door in the rear.*)

SMITHERS. Goin' out to look for your

'orse? Yer won't find any. They steals the 'orses first thing. Mine was gone when I went for 'im this mornin'. That's wot first give me a suspicion of wot was up.

JONES (*alarmed for a second, scratches his head, then, philosophically*). Well, den I hoofs it. Feet, do yo' duty! (*He pulls out a gold watch and looks at it.*) Three-thuty. Sundown's at six-thuty or dere-abouts. (*Puts his watch back—with cool confidence.*) I got plenty o' time to make it easy.

SMITHERS. Don't be so bloomin' sure of it. They'll be after you 'ot and 'eavy. Ole Lem is at the bottom o' this business an' 'e 'ates you like 'ell. 'E'd rather do for you than eat 'is dinner, 'e would!

JONES (*scornfully*). Dat fool no-count nigger! Does you think I'se scared o' him? I stands him on his thick head more'n once befo' dis, and I does it again if he comes in my way—(*Fiercely.*) And dis time I leave him a dead nigger fo' sho'!

SMITHERS. You'll 'ave to cut through the big forest—an' these blacks 'ere can sniff and follow a trail in the dark like 'ounds. You'd 'ave to 'ustle to get through that forest in twelve hours even if you knew all the bloomin' trails like a native.

JONES (*with indignant scorn*). Look-a-heah, white man! Does you think I'se a natural bo'n fool? Give me credit fo' havin' some sense, fo' Lawd's sake! Don't you s'pose I'se looked ahead and made sho' of all de chances? I'se gone out in dat big forest, pretendin' to hunt, so many times dat I knows it high an' low like a book. I could go through on dem trails wid my eyes shut. (*With great contempt.*) Think dese ign'rent bush niggers dat ain't got brains enuff to know deir own names

even can catch Brutus Jones? Huh, I s'pects not! Not on yo' life! Why, man, de white men went after me wid bloodhounds where I come from an' I jes' laughs at 'em. It's a shame to fool dese black trash around heah, dey're so easy. You watch me, man. I'll make dem look sick, I will. I'll be 'cross de plain to de edge of de forest by time dark comes. Once in de woods in de night, dey got a swell chance o' findin' dis baby! Dawn to-morrow I'll be out at de oder side and on de coast whar dat French gun-boat is stayin'. She picks me up, takes me to Martinique when she go dar, and dere I is safe wid a mighty big bank roll in my jeans. It's easy as rollin' off a log.

SMITHERS (*maliciously*). But s'posin' some-thin' 'appens wrong an' they do nab yer?

JONES (*decisively*). Dey don't—dat's de answer.

SMITHERS. But, just for argyment's sake —what 'd you do?

JONES (*frowning*). I'se got five lead bullets in dis gun good enuff fo' common bush niggers—and after dat I got de silver bullet left to cheat 'em out o' gittin' me.

SMITHERS (*jeeringly*). Ho, I was fergettin' that silver bullet. You'll bump your-self orf in style, won't yer? Blimey!

JONES (*gloomily*). You kin bet yo' whole roll on one thing, white man. Dis baby plays out his string to de end and when he quits, he quits wid a bang de way he ought. Silver bullet ain't none too good for him when he go, dat's a fac'! (*Then, shaking off his nervousness—with a confident laugh.*) Sho'! What is I talkin' about? Ain't come to dat yit and I never will—not wid trash niggers like dese yere. (*Boastfully.*) Silver bullet bring me luck anyway. I kin outguess, outrun, outfight, an' outplay de whole lot o' dem all ovah de board any time o' de day er night! You watch me!

[*From the distant hills comes the faint, steady thump of a tom-tom, low and vibrating. It starts at a rate exactly corresponding to normal pulse beat—72 to the minute—and continues at a gradually accelerating rate from this point uninterruptedly to the very* 10 *end of the play.*]

JONES (*starts at the sound; a strange look of apprehension creeps into his face for a moment as he listens; then he asks, with an attempt to regain his most casual manner*): What's dat drum beatin' fo'?

SMITHERS (*with a mean grin*). For you. That means the bleedin' ceremony 'as started. I've 'eard it before and I knows. 20

JONES. Cer'mony? What cer'mony?

SMITHERS. The blacks is 'oldin' a bloody meetin', 'avin' a war dance, gettin' their courage worked up b'fore they starts after you.

JONES. Let dem! Dey'll sho' need it!

SMITHERS. And they're there 'oldin' their 'eathen religious service—makin' no end of devil spells and charms to 'elp 'em against your silver bullet. (*He* 30 *guffaws loudly.*) Blimey, but they're balmy as 'ell!

JONES (*a tiny bit awed and shaken in spite of himself*). Huh! Takes more'n dat to scare dis chicken!

SMITHERS (*scenting the other's feeling— maliciously*). Ternight when it's pitch-black in the forest, they'll 'ave their pet devils and ghosts 'oundin' after you. You'll find yer bloody 'air'll be 40 standin' on end before termorrow mornin'. (*Seriously.*) It's a bleedin' queer place, that stinkin' forest, even in daylight. Yer don't know what might 'appen in there, it's that rotten still. Always sends the cold shivers down my back minute I gets in it.

JONES (*with a contemptuous sniff*). I ain't no chicken-liver like you is. Trees an' me, we'se friends, and dar's a full moon comin' bring me light. And let dem po' niggers make all de fool spells dey'se a min' to. Does yo' s'pect I'se silly enuff to b'lieve in ghosts an' ha'nts an' all dat ole woman's talk? G'long, white man! You ain't talkin' to me. (*With a chuckle.*) Doesn't you know dey's got to do wid a man was member in good standin' o' de Baptist Church? Sho' I was dat when I was porter on de Pullmans, befo' I gits into my little trouble. Let dem try deir heathen tricks. De Baptist Church done pertect me and land dem all in hell. (*Then with more confident satisfaction:*) And I'se got little silver bullet o' my own, don't forgit!

SMITHERS. Ho! You 'aven't give much 'eed to your Baptist Church since you been down 'ere. I've 'eard myself you 'ad turned yer coat an' was takin' up with their blarsted witch doctors, or whatever the 'ell yer calls the swine.

JONES (*vehemently*). I pretends to! Sho' I pretends! Dat's part o' my game from de fust. If I finds out dem niggers believes dat black is white, den I yells it out louder 'n deir loudest. It don't git me nothin' to do missionary work for de Baptist Church. I'se after de coin, an' I lays my Jesus on de shelf for de time bein'. (*Stops abruptly to look at his watch—alertly.*) But I ain't got de time to waste on no more fool talk wid you. I'se gwine away from heah dis secon'. (*He reaches in under the throne and pulls out an expensive panama hat with a bright multicolored band and sets it jauntily on his head.*) So long, white man! (*With a grin.*) See you in jail sometime, maybe!

SMITHERS. Not me, you won't. Well, I

wouldn't be in yer bloody boots for no bloomin' money, but 'ere's wishin' yer luck just the same.

JONES (*contemptuously*). You're de frightenedest man evah I see! I tells you I'se safe's 'f I was in New York City. It takes dem niggers from now to dark to git up de nerve to start somethin'. By dat time, I'se got a head start dey never kotch up wid. 10

SMITHERS (*maliciously*). Give my regards to any ghosts yer meets up with.

JONES (*grinning*). If dat ghost got money, I'll tell him never ha'nt you less'n he wants to lose it.

SMITHERS (*flattered*). Garn! (*Then curiously:*) Ain't yer takin' no luggage with yer?

JONES. I travels light when I wants to move fast. And I got tinned grub 20 buried on de edge o' de forest. (*Boastfully.*) Now say dat I don't look ahead an' use my brains! (*With a wide, liberal gesture.*) I will all dat's left in de palace to you—and you better grab all you kin sneak away wid befo' dey gits here.

SMITHERS (*gratefully*). Righto—and

thanks ter yer. (*As* JONES *walks toward the door in the rear—cautioningly.*) Say! Look 'ere, you ain't goin' out that way, are yer?

JONES. Does you think I'd slink out de back door like a common nigger? I'se Emperor yit, ain't I? And de Emperor Jones leaves de way he comes, and dat black trash don't dare stop him—not yit, leastways. (*He stops for a moment in the doorway, listening to the far-off but insistent beat of the tom-tom.*) Listen to dat roll call, will you? Must be mighty big drum carry dat far. (*Then with a laugh.*) Well, if dey ain't no whole brass band to see me off, I sho' got de drum part of it. So long, white man. (*He puts his hands in his pockets and with studied carelessness, whistling a tune, he saunters out of the doorway and off to the left.*)

SMITHERS (*looks after him with a puzzled admiration*). 'E's got 'is bloomin' nerve with 'im, s'elp me! (*Then angrily.*) Ho—the bleedin' nigger—puttin' on 'is bloody airs! I 'opes they nabs 'im an' gives 'im what's what!

CURTAIN

SCENE II

The end of the plain where the Great Forest begins. The foreground is sandy, level ground 30 dotted by a few stones and clumps of stunted bushes cowering close against the earth to escape the buffeting of the trade wind. In the rear the forest is a wall of darkness dividing the world. Only when the eye becomes accustomed to the gloom can the outlines of separate trunks of the nearest trees be made out, enormous pillars of deeper blackness. A somber monotone of wind lost in the leaves moans in the air. Yet this sound serves but to intensify the impression 40 of the forest's relentless immobility, to form a background throwing into relief its brooding, implacable silence.

JONES *enters from the left, walking rapidly. He stops as he nears the edge of the forest, looks around him quickly, peering into the dark as if searching for some familiar landmark. Then, apparently satisfied that he is where he ought to be, he throws himself on the ground, dog-tired.*

JONES. Well, heah I is. In de nick o' time, too! Little mo' an' it'd be blacker'n de ace of spades heahabouts. (*He pulls a bandanna handkerchief from his hip pocket and mops off his perspiring face.*) Sho'! Gimme air! I'se tuckered out sho' 'nuff. Dat soft Emperor job ain't no trainin' fo' a long hike ovah dat plain in de brilin' sun. (*Then with a chuckle.*) Cheer up, nigger, de worst is yet to come. (*He lifts his head and stares at the forest. His chuckle peters out abruptly. In a tone of awe.*) My goodness, look at dem woods, will you? Dat no-count Smithers said dey'd be black an' he sho' called de turn. (*Turning away from them quickly and looking down at his feet, he snatches at a chance to change the subject—solicitously.*) Feet, you is holdin' up yo' end fine an' I sutinly hopes you ain't blisterin' none. It's time you git a rest. (*He takes off his shoes, his eyes studiously avoiding the forest. He feels of the soles of his feet gingerly.*) You is still in de pink—on'y a little mite feverish. Cool yo'selfs. Remember you done got a long journey yit befo' you. (*He sits in a weary attitude, listening to the rhythmic beating of the tom-tom. He grumbles in a loud tone to cover up a growing uneasiness.*) Bush niggers! Wonder dey wouldn't git sick o' beatin' dat drum. Sound louder, seem like. I wonder if dey's startin' after me? (*He scrambles to his feet, looking back across the plain.*) Couldn't see dem now, no-how, if dey was hundred feet away. (*Then, shaking himself like a wet dog to get rid of these depressing thoughts.*) Sho', dey's miles an' miles behind. What you gittin' fidgety about? (*But he sits down and begins to lace up his shoes in great haste, all the time muttering reassuringly.*)

You know what? Yo' belly is empty, dat's what's de matter wid you. Come time to eat! Wid nothin' but wind on yo' stumach, o' course you feels jiggedy. Well, we eats right heah an' now soon's I gits dese pesky shoes laced up. (*He finishes lacing up his shoes.*) Dere! Now le's see! (*Gets on his hands and knees and searches the ground around him with his eyes.*) White stone, white stone, where is you? (*He sees the first white stone and crawls to it—with satisfaction.*) Heah you is! I knowed dis was de right place. Box of grub, come to me. (*He turns over the stone and feels in under it—in a tone of dismay:*) Ain't heah! Gorry, is I in de right place or isn't I? Dere's 'nother stone. Guess dat's it. (*He scrambles to the next stone and turns it over.*) Ain't heah, neither! Grub, whar is you? Ain't heah. Gorry, has I got to go hungry into dem woods—all de night? (*While he is talking he scrambles from one stone to another, turning them over in frantic haste. Finally, he jumps to his feet excitedly.*) Is I lost de place? Must have! But how dat happen when I was followin' de trail across de plain in broad daylight? (*Almost plaintively.*) I'se hungry, I is! I gotta git my feed. Whar's my strength gonna come from if I doesn't? Gorry, I gotta find dat grub high an' low somehow! Why it come dark so quick like dat? Can't see nothin'. (*He scratches a match on his trousers and peers about him. The rate of the beat of the jar-off tom-tom increases perceptibly as he does so. He mutters in a bewildered voice.*) How come all dese white stones come heah when I only remembers one? (*Suddenly, with a frightened gasp, he flings the match on the ground and stamps on it.*) Nigger, is you gone crazy mad? Is you lightin' matches to show dem whar you is? Fo' Lawd's sake, use yo' haid. Gorry, I'se got to be careful! (*He stares at the plain behind him apprehensively, his hand on his revolver.*) But how come all dese white stones? And whar's dat tin box o' grub I hid all wrapped up in oilcloth?

[*While his back is turned, the* LITTLE FORMLESS FEARS *creep out from the deeper blackness of the forest. They are black, shapeless, only their glittering little eyes can be seen. If they have any describable form at all it is that of a grubworm about the size of a creeping child. They move noiselessly, but with deliberate, painful effort, striving to raise themselves on end, failing and sinking prone again.* JONES *turns about to face the forest. He stares up at the trees, seeking vainly to discover his* 10 *whereabouts by their conformation.*]

Can't tell nothin' from dem trees! Gorry, nothin' 'round heah looks like I evah seed it befo'. I'se done lost de place sho' 'nuff! (*With mournful foreboding.*) It's mighty queer! It's mighty queer! (*With sudden forced defiance—in an angry tone.*) Woods, is you tryin' to put somethin' ovah on me?

[*From the* FORMLESS CREATURES *on the* 20 *ground in front of him comes a tiny gale of low mocking laughter like a rustling of leaves. They squirm upward toward him in twisted attitudes.* JONES *looks down, leaps backward with a yell of terror, yanking out his revolver as he does so—in a quavering voice:*]

What's dat? Who's dar? What is you? Git away from me befo' I shoots you up! You don't?—

[*He fires. There is a flash, a loud report, then silence broken only by the far-off, quickened throb of the tom-tom. The* FORMLESS CREATURES *have scurried back into the forest.* JONES *remains fixed in his position, listening intently. The sound of the shot, the reassuring feel of the revolver in his hand, have somewhat restored his shaken nerve. He addresses himself with renewed confidence.*]

Dey're gone. Dat shot fix 'em. Dey was only little animals—little wild pigs, I reckon. Dey've maybe rooted out yo' grub an' eat it. Sho', you fool nigger, what you think dey is—ha'nts? (*Excitedly.*) Gorry, you give de game away when you fire dat shot. Dem niggers heah dat fo' sutin! Time you beat it in de woods widout no long waits. (*He starts for the forest—hesitates before the plunge—then urging himself in with manful resolution.*) Git in, nigger! What you skeered at? Ain't nothin' dere but de trees! Git in! (*He plunges boldly into the forest.*)

SCENE III

In the forest. The moon has just risen. Its beams, drifting through the canopy of leaves, make a barely perceptible, suffused, eerie glow. A dense low wall of underbrush and creepers is in the nearer foregound, fencing in a small triangular clearing. Beyond this is the massed blackness of the forest like an encompassing barrier. A path is dimly discerned leading down to the clearing from the left rear, and winding away from it again toward the right. As the scene opens nothing can be distinctly made out. Except for the beating of the tom-tom, which is a trifle louder and quicker than at the close of the previous scene, there is silence, broken every few seconds by a queer, clicking sound. Then gradually the figure of the Negro JEFF *can be discerned crouching on his haunches at the rear of the triangle. He is middle-aged, thin, brown in color, is dressed in a Pullman porter's uniform and cap. He is throwing a pair of dice on the ground before him, picking them up, shaking them, casting them out, with the regular, rigid, mechanical movements of an automaton. The heavy, plodding footsteps of someone approaching along the trail from the left are heard and* JONES'S *voice, pitched on a slightly higher key and strained in a cheery effort to overcome its own tremors.*

JONES. De moon's rizen. Does you heah dat, nigger? You gits more light from dis out. No mo' buttin' yo' fool head agin de trunks an' scratchin' de hide off yo' legs in de bushes. Now you sees whar yo'se gwine. So cheer up! From now on you has a snap. (*He steps just to the rear of the triangular clearing and mops off his face on his sleeve. He has lost his panama hat. His face is scratched, his brilliant uniform shows several large rents.*) What time's it gittin' to be, I wonder? 10 I dassent light no match to find out. Phoo'. It's wa'm an' dat's a fac'! (*Wearily.*) How long I been makin' tracks in dese woods? Must be hours an' hours. Seems like fo'evah! Yit can't be, when de moon's jes' riz. Dis am a long night fo' yo', yo' Majesty! (*With a mournful chuckle.*) Majesty! Der ain't much majesty 'bout dis baby now. (*With attempted cheerful-* 20 *ness.*) Never min'. It's all part o' de game. Dis night come to an end like everything else. And when you gits dar safe and has dat bank roll in yo' hands you laughs at all dis. (*He starts to whistle, but checks himself abruptly.*) What yo' whistlin' for, you po' dope! Want all de worl' to heah you? (*He stops talking to listen.*) Heah dat ole drum! Sho' gits nearer from de sound. 30 Dey's packin' it along wid 'em. Time fo' me to move. (*He takes a step forward, then stops—worriedly.*) What's dat odder queer clickety sound I heah? Dere it is! Sound close! Sound like —sound like— Fo' God sake, sound like some nigger was shootin' crap!

(*Frightenedly.*) I better beat it quick when I gits dem notions. (*He walks quickly into the clear space—then stands transfixed as he sees* JEFF—*in a terrified gasp:*) Who dar? Who dat? Is dat you, Jeff? (*Starting toward the other, forgetful for a moment of his surroundings and really believing it is a living man that he sees—in a tone of happy relief.*) Jeff! I'se sho' mighty glad to see you! Dey tol' me you done died from dat razor cut I gives you. (*Stopping suddenly, bewilderedly.*) But how you come to be heah, nigger? (*He stares fascinatedly at the other, who continues his mechanical play with the dice.* JONES's *eyes begin to roll wildly. He stutters.*) Ain't you gwine— look up—can't you speak to me? Is you—is you—a ha'nt? (*He jerks out his revolver in a frenzy of terrified rage.*) Nigger, I kills you dead once. Has I got to kill you agin? You take it den. (*He fires. When the smoke clears away,* JEFF *has disappeared.* JONES *stands trembling— then with a certain reassurance.*) He's gone, anyway. Ha'nt or no ha'nt, dat shot fix him. (*The beat of the far-off tomtom is perceptibly louder and more rapid.* JONES *becomes conscious of it—with a start, looking back over his shoulder.*) Dey's gittin' near! Dey's comin' fast! And heah I is shootin' shots to let 'em know jes' whar I is! Oh, Gorry, I'se got to run. (*Forgetting the path, he plunges wildly into the underbrush in the rear and disappears in the shadow.*)

SCENE IV

In the forest. A wide dirt road runs diagonally from the right front to the left rear. Rising sheer on both sides, the forest walls it in. The moon is now up. Under its light the road glimmers ghastly and unreal. It is as if the forest had stood aside momentarily to let the road pass through and accomplish its veiled purpose. This done, the forest will fold in upon itself again and the road will be no more. JONES *stumbles in from the forest on the right. His uniform is ragged and torn. He looks about him with numbed surprise when he sees the road, his eyes blinking in the bright moonlight. He flops down exhaustedly and pants heavily for a while. Then with sudden anger:*

JONES. I'm meltin' wid heat! Runnin' an' runnin' an' runnin'! Damn dis heah coat! Like a strait jacket! (*He tears off his coat and flings it away from him, revealing himself stripped to the waist.*) Dere! Dat's better! Now I kin breathe! (*Looking down at his feet, the spurs catch his eye.*) And to hell wid dese high-fangled spurs. Dey're what's been a-trippin' me up an' breakin' my neck. (*He unstraps them and flings them away disgustedly.*) Dere! I gits rid o' dem frippety Emperor trappin's an' I travels lighter. Lawd! I'se tired! (*After a pause, listening to the insistent beat of the tom-tom in the distance.*) I must 'a' put some distance between myself an' dem—runnin' like dat—and yit—dat damn drum sounds jes' de same— nearer, even. Well, I guess I a'most holds my lead anyhow. Dey won't never catch up. (*With a sigh.*) If on'y my fool legs stands up. Oh, I'se sorry I evah went in for dis. Dat Emperor job is sho' hard to shake. (*He looks around him suspiciously.*) How'd dis road evah git heah? Good level road, too. I never remembers seein' it befo'. (*Shaking his head apprehensively.*) Dese woods is sho' full o' de queerest things at night. (*With a sudden terror.*) Lawd God, don't let me see no more o' dem ha'nts! Dey gits my goat! (*Then, trying to talk himself into confidence.*) Ha'nts! You fool nigger, dey ain't no such things. Don't de Baptist parson tell you dat many time? Is you civilized, or is you like dese ign'rent black niggers heah? Sho'! Dat was all in yo' own head. Wasn't nothin' dere. Wasn't no Jeff! Know what? You jes' get seein' dem things 'cause yo' belly's empty

and you's sick wid hunger inside. Hunger 'fects yo' head and yo' eyes. Any fool know dat. (*Then, pleading fervently.*) But bless God, I don't come across no more o' dem, whatever dey is! (*Then cautiously.*) Rest! Don't talk! Rest! You needs it. Den you gits on yo' way again. (*Looking at the moon.*) Night's half gone a'most. You hits de coast in de mawning! Den yo's all safe.

[*From the right forward a small gang of Negroes enter. They are dressed in striped convict suits, their heads are shaven, one leg drags limpingly, shackled to a heavy ball and chain. Some carry picks, the others shovels. They are followed by a white man dressed in the uniform of a prison guard. A Winchester rifle is slung across his shoulder and he carries a heavy whip. At a signal from the* GUARD *they stop on the road opposite where* JONES *is sitting.* JONES, *who has been staring up at the sky, unmindful of their noiseless approach, suddenly looks down and sees them. His eyes pop out, he tries to get to his feet and fly, but sinks back, too numbed by fright to move. His voice catches in a choking prayer.*]

Lawd Jesus!

[*The* PRISON GUARD *cracks his whip—noiselessly—and at that signal all the convicts start to work on the road. They swing their picks, they shovel, but not a sound comes from their labor. Their movements, like those of* JEFF *in the preceding scene, are those of automatons—rigid, slow, and mechanical. The* PRISON GUARD *points sternly at* JONES *with his whip, motions him to take his place among the other shovelers.* JONES *gets to his feet in a hypnotized stupor. He mumbles subserviently.*]

Yes, suh! Yes, suh! I'se comin'. (*As he shuffles, dragging one foot, over to his place, he curses under his breath with rage and hatred.*) God damn yo' soul, I gits even wid you yit, some time.

[*As if there were a shovel in his hands he goes through weary, mechanical gestures of digging up dirt, and throwing it to the roadside. Suddenly the* GUARD *approaches him angrily, threateningly. He raises his whip and lashes* JONES *viciously across the shoulders with it.* JONES *winces with pain and cowers abjectly. The* GUARD *turns his back on him and walks away contemptuously. Instantly* JONES *straightens up. With* 10 *arms upraised as if his shovel were a club in his hands, he springs murderously at the unsuspecting* GUARD. *In the act of crashing down his shovel on the white man's skull,* JONES *suddenly becomes aware that his hands are empty. He cries despairingly:*]

Whar's my shovel? Gimme my shovel 'til I splits his damn head! (*Appealing to his fellow convicts.*) Gimme a shovel, one o' you, fo' God sake! 20

[*They stand fixed in motionless attitudes, their eyes on the ground. The* GUARD *seems to wait expectantly, his back turned to the attacker.* JONES *bellows with baffled, terrified rage, tugging frantically at his revolver.*]

I kills you, you white debil, if it's de last thing I evah does! Ghost or debil, I kill you agin!

[*He frees the revolver and fires point-blank at the* GUARD's *back. Instantly the walls of the forest close in from both sides, the road and the figures of the convict gang are blotted out in an enshrouding darkness. The only sounds are a crashing in the underbrush as* JONES *leaps away in mad flight and the throbbing of the tom-tom, still far distant, but increased in volume of sound and rapidity of beat.*]

SCENE V

A large circular clearing, enclosed by the serried ranks of gigantic trunks of tall trees whose tops are lost to view. In the center is a big dead stump worn by time into a curious resemblance to an auction block. The moon floods the clearing with a clear light. JONES *forces his way in through the forest on the left. He looks wildly about the clearing with hunted, fearful glances. His pants are in tatters, his shoes cut and misshapen, flapping* 30 *about his feet. He slinks cautiously to the stump in the center and sits down in a tense position, ready for instant flight. Then he holds his head in his hands and rocks back and forth, moaning to himself miserably.*

JONES. Oh, Lawd, Lawd! Oh, Lawd, Lawd! (*Suddenly he throws himself on his knees and raises his clasped hands to the sky—in a voice of agonized pleading.*) 40 Lawd Jesus, heah my prayer! I'se a po' sinner, a po' sinner! I knows I done wrong, I knows it! When I cotches Jeff cheatin' wid loaded dice my anger overcomes me and I kills him dead! Lawd, I done wrong! When dat guard hits me wid de whip, my anger overcomes me, and I kills him dead. Lawd, I done wrong! And down heah whar dese fool bush niggers raises me up to de seat o' de mighty, I steals all I could grab. Lawd, I done wrong! I knows it! I'se sorry! Forgive me, Lawd! Forgive dis po' sinner! (*Then, beseeching terrifiedly.*) And keep dem away, Lawd! Keep dem away from me! And stop dat drum soundin' in my ears! Dat begin to sound ha'nted, too. (*He gets to his feet, evidently slightly reassured by his prayer—with attempted confidence.*) De Lawd'll preserve me from dem ha'nts after dis. (*Sits down on the stump again.*) I ain't skeered o' real men. Let dem come. But dem odders— (*He shudders —then looks down at his feet, working his toes inside the shoes—with a groan.*) Oh, my po' feet! Dem shoes ain't no use no more 'ceptin' to hurt. I'se better off widout dem. (*He unlaces them and pulls them off—holds the wrecks of the shoes in his hands and regards them mournfully.*) You was real, A-one patin' leather, too. Look at you now. Emperor, you'se gittin' mighty low!

[*He sighs dejectedly and remains with bowed shoulders, staring down at the shoes in his hands as if reluctant to throw them away. While his attention is thus occupied, a crowd of figures silently enter the clearing from all sides. All are dressed in Southern costumes of the period of the fifties of the last century. There are middle-aged men who are evidently well-to-do planters. There is one spruce, authoritative individual—the* AUCTIONEER. *There is a crowd of curious spectators, chiefly young belles and dandies who have come to the slave market for diversion. All exchange courtly greetings in dumb show and chat silently together. There is something stiff, rigid, unreal, marionettish about their movements. They group themselves about the stump. Finally a batch of slaves is led in from the left by an attendant——three men of different ages, two women, one with a baby in her arms, nursing. They are placed to the left of the stump, beside* JONES. *The white planters look them over appraisingly as if they were cattle, and exchange judgments on each. The dandies point with their fingers and make witty remarks. The belles titter bewitchingly. All this in silence save for the ominous throb of the tom-tom. The* AUCTIONEER *holds up his hand, taking his place at the stump. The group strain forward attentively. He touches* JONES *on the shoulder peremptorily, motioning for him to stand on the stump—the auction block.* JONES *looks up, sees the figures on all sides, looks wildly for some opening to escape, sees none, screams, and leaps madly to the top of the stump to get as far away from them as possible. He stands there, cowering, paralyzed with horror. The* AUCTIONEER *begins his silent spiel. He points to* JONES, *appeals to the planters to see for themselves. Here is a good field hand, sound in wind and limb as they can see. Very strong still in spite of his being middle-aged. Look at that back. Look at those shoulders. Look at the muscles in his arms and his sturdy legs. Capable of any amount of hard labor. Moreover, of a good disposition, intelligent, and tractable. Will any gentleman start the bidding? The* PLANTERS *raise their fingers, make their bids. They are apparently all eager to possess* JONES. *The bidding is lively, the crowd interested. While this has been going on,* JONES *has been seized by the courage of desperation. He dares to look down and around him. Over his face abject terror gives way to mystification, to gradual realization —stutteringly.*]

What you all doin', white folks? What's all dis? What you all lookin' at me fo'? What you doin' wid me, anyhow? (*Suddenly convulsed with raging hatred and fear.*) Is dis a auction? Is you sellin' me like dey uster befo' de war? (*Jerking out his revolver just as the* AUCTIONEER *knocks him down to one of the* PLANTERS—*glaring from him to the purchaser.*) And *you* sells me? And *you* buys me? I shows you I'se a free nigger, damn yo' souls!

[*He fires at the* AUCTIONEER *and at the* PLANTER *with such rapidity that the two shots are almost simultaneous. As if this were a signal the walls of the forest fold in. Only blackness remains and silence broken by* JONES *as he rushes off, crying with fear —and by the quickened, ever louder beat of the tom-tom.*]

SCENE VI

A cleared space in the forest. The limbs of the trees meet over it, forming a low ceiling about five feet from the ground. The interlocked ropes of creepers reaching upward to entwine the tree trunks give an arched appearance to the sides. The space thus enclosed is like the dark, noisome hold of some ancient vessel. The moonlight is almost completely shut out and only a vague wan light filters through. There is the noise of someone ap- 10 *proaching from the left, stumbling and crawling through the undergrowth.* JONES'S *voice is heard between chattering moans.*

JONES. Oh Lawd! what I gwine do now? Ain't got no bullet left on'y de silver one. If mo' o' dem ha'nts come after me, how I gwine skeer dem away? Oh Lawd, on'y de silver one left—an' I gotta save dat fo' luck. If I shoots dat 20 one I'm a goner sho'! Lawd, it's black heah! Whar's de moon? Oh Lawd, don't dis night evah come to an end? (*By the sounds, he is feeling his way cautiously forward.*) Dere! Dis feels like a clear space. I gotta lie down an' rest. I don't care if dem niggers does cotch me. I gotta rest.

[*He is well forward now where his figure can be dimly made out. His pants have been so* 30 *torn away that what is left of them is no better than a breechcloth. He flings himself full length, face downward on the ground, panting with exhaustion. Gradually it seems to grow lighter in the enclosed space and two rows of seated figures can be seen behind* JONES. *They are sitting in crumpled, despairing attitudes, hunched, facing one another with their backs touching the forest walls as if they were shackled to them. All are Negroes, naked save for loincloths. At first they are silent and motionless. Then they begin to sway slowly forward toward each and back again in unison, as if they were laxly letting themselves follow the long roll of a ship at sea. At the same time a low, melancholy murmur rises among them, increasing gradually by rhythmic degrees which seem to be directed and controlled by the throb of the tom-tom in the distance, to a long, tremulous wail of despair that reaches a certain pitch, unbearably acute, then falls by slow gradations of tone into silence and is taken up again.* JONES *starts, looks up, sees the figures, and throws himself down again to shut out the sight. A shudder of terror shakes his whole body as the wail rises up about him again. But the next time, his voice, as if under some uncanny compulsion, starts with the others. As their chorus lifts he rises to a sitting posture similar to the others, swaying back and forth. His voice reaches the highest pitch of sorrow, of desolation. The light fades out, the other voices cease, and only darkness is left.* JONES *can be heard scrambling to his feet and running off, his voice sinking down the scale and receding as he moves farther and farther away in the forest. The tom-tom beats louder, quicker, with a more insistent, triumphant pulsation.*]

SCENE VII

The foot of a gigantic tree by the edge of a great river. A rough structure of boulders, like an altar, is by the tree. The raised riverbank is in the nearer background. Beyond this the surface of the river spreads out, brilliant and unruffled in the moonlight, blotted out and merged into a veil of bluish mist in the distance. JONES'S *voice is heard from the left rising and falling in the long, despairing wail of the chained slaves, to the rhythmic beat of the tom-tom. As his voice sinks into silence, he enters the open space. The expression of his face is fixed and stony, his eyes have an obsessed glare, he moves with a strange deliberation like a sleepwalker or one in a trance. He looks around at the tree, the rough stone altar, the moonlit surface of the river beyond, and passes his hand over his head with a vague gesture of puzzled bewilderment. Then, as if in obedience to some obscure impulse, he sinks 10 into a kneeling, devotional posture before the altar. Then he seems to come to himself partly, to have an uncertain realization of what he is doing, for he straightens up and stares about him horrifiedly—in an incoherent mumble:*

JONES. What—what is I doin'? What is— dis place? Seems like I know dat tree —an' dem stones—an' de river. I remember—seems like I been heah 20 befo'. (*Tremblingly.*) Oh, Gorry, I'se skeered in dis place! I'se skeered. Oh Lawd, pertect dis sinner!

[*Crawling away from the altar, he cowers close to the ground, his face hidden, his shoulders heaving with sobs of hysterical fright. From behind the trunk of the tree, as if he had sprung out of it, the figure of the* CONGO WITCH DOCTOR *appears. He is wizened and old, naked except for the fur of* 30 *some small animal tied about his waist, its bushy tail hanging down in front. His body is stained all over a bright red. Antelope horns are on each side of his head, branching upward. In one hand he carries a bone rattle, in the other a charm stick with a bunch of white cockatoo feathers tied to the end. A great number of glass beads and bone ornaments are about his neck, ears, wrists, and ankles. He struts noiselessly with a* 40 *queer prancing step to a position in the clear ground between* JONES *and the altar. Then with a preliminary, summoning stamp of his foot on the earth, he begins to dance and to chant. As if in response to his summons, the beating of the tom-tom grows to a fierce,*

exultant boom whose throbs seem to fill the air with vibrating rhythm. JONES *looks up, starts to spring to his feet, reaches a half-kneeling, half-squatting position and remains rigidly fixed there, paralyzed with awed fascination by this new apparition. The* WITCH DOCTOR *sways, stamping with his foot, his bone rattle clicking the time. His voice rises and falls in a weird, monotonous croon, without articulate word divisions. Gradually his dance becomes clearly one of a narrative in pantomime, his croon is an incantation, a charm to allay the fierceness of some implacable deity demanding sacrifice. He flees, he is pursued by devils, he hides, he flees again. Ever wilder and wilder becomes his flight, nearer and nearer draws the pursing evil, more and more the spirit of terror gains possession of him. His croon, rising to intensity, is punctuated by shrill cries.* JONES *has become completely hypnotized. His voice joins in the incantation, in the cries, he beats time with his hands and sways his body to and fro from the waist. The whole spirit and meaning of the dance has entered into him, has become his spirit. Finally the theme of the pantomime halts on a howl of despair, and is taken up again in a note of savage hope. There is a salvation. The forces of evil demand sacrifice. They must be appeased. The* WITCH DOCTOR *points with his wand to the sacred tree, to the river beyond, to the altar, and finally to* JONES, *with a ferocious command.* JONES *seems to sense the meaning of this. It is he who must offer himself for sacrifice. He beats his forehead abjectly to the ground, moaning hysterically.*]

Mercy, O Lawd! Mercy! Mercy on dis po' sinner.

[*The* WITCH DOCTOR *springs to the riverbank. He stretches out his arms and calls to some god within its depths. Then he starts backward slowly, his arms remaining out. A huge head of a crocodile appears over the bank and its eyes, glittering greenly, fasten upon* JONES. *He stares into them fascinatedly. The* WITCH DOCTOR *prances up to him, touches him with his wand, motions with hideous command toward the waiting monster.* JONES *squirms on his belly nearer and nearer, moaning continually.*]

Mercy, Lawd! Mercy!

[*The crocodile heaves more of his enormous hulk onto the land.* JONES *squirms toward* 10 *him. The* WITCH DOCTOR'S *voice shrills out in furious exultation, the tom-tom beats madly.* JONES *cries out in a fierce, exhausted spasm of anguished pleading.*]

Lawd, save me! Lawd Jesus, heah my prayer!

[*Immediately, in answer to his prayer, comes the thought of the one bullet left him. He snatches at his hip, shouting defiantly.*]

De silver bullet! You don't git me yit!

[*He fires at the green eyes in front of him. The head of the crocodile sinks back behind the riverbank, the* WITCH DOCTOR *springs behind the sacred tree and disappears.* JONES *lies with his face to the ground, his arms outstretched, whimpering with fear as the throb of the tom-tom fills the silence about him with a somber pulsation, a baffled but revengeful power.*]

SCENE VIII

Dawn. Same as Scene II, the dividing line of forest and plain. The nearest tree trunks are dimly revealed, but the forest behind them is still a mass of glooming shadow. The tom- 20 *tom seems on the very spot, so loud and continuously vibrating are its beats.* LEM *enters from the left, followed by a small squad of his soldiers, and by the Cockney trader,* SMITHERS. LEM *is a heavy-set, ape-faced old savage of the extreme African type, dressed only in a loincloth. A revolver and a cartridge belt are about his waist. His soldiers are in different degrees of rag-concealed nakedness. All wear broad palm-leaf hats. Each one carries a rifle.* 30 SMITHERS *is the same as in Scene I. One of the soldiers, evidently a tracker, is peering about keenly on the ground. He points to the spot where* JONES *entered the forest.* LEM *and* SMITHERS *come to look.*

SMITHERS (*after a glance, turns away in disgust*). That's where 'e went in right enough. Much good it'll do yer. 'E's miles orf by this an' safe to the Coast, 40 damn's 'ide! I tole yer yer'd lose 'im, didn't I?—wastin' the 'ole bloomin' night beatin' yer bloody drum and

castin' yer silly spells! Gawd blimey, wot a pack!

LEM (*gutturally*). We cotch him. (*He makes a motion to his soldiers, who squat down on their haunches in a semicircle.*)

SMITHERS (*exasperatedly*). Well, ain't yer goin' in an' 'unt 'im in the woods? What the 'ell's the good of waitin'?

LEM (*imperturbably—squatting down himself*). We cotch him.

SMITHERS (*turning away from him contemptuously*). Aw! Garn! 'E's a better man than the lot o' you put together. I 'ates the sight o' 'im but I'll say that for 'im.

[*A sound comes from the forest. The soldiers jump to their feet, cocking their rifles alertly.* LEM *remains sitting with an imperturbable expression, but listening intently. He makes a quick signal with his hand. His followers creep quickly into the forest, scattering so that each enters at a different spot.*]

SMITHERS. You ain't thinkin' that would be 'im, I 'ope?

LEM (*calmly*). We cotch him.

SMITHERS. Blarsted fat'eads! (*Then after a second's thought—wonderingly:*) Still an' all, it might 'appen. If 'e lost 'is bloody way in these stinkin' woods 'e'd likely turn in a circle without 'is knowin' it.

LEM. (*peremptorily*). Sssh! (*The reports of several rifles sound from the forest, followed a second later by savage, exultant yells. The beating of the tom-tom abruptly ceases.* LEM *looks up at the white man with a grin of satisfaction.*) We cotch him. Him dead.

SMITHERS (*with a snarl*). 'Ow d'yer know it's 'im an' 'ow d'yer know 'e's dead?

LEM. My mens dey got um silver bullets. Lead bullet no kill him. He got um strong charm. I cook um money, make um silver bullet, make um strong charm, too.

SMITHERS (*astonished*). So that's wot you was up to all night, wot? You was scared to put after 'im till you'd molded silver bullets, eh?

LEM (*simply stating a fact*). Yes. Him got strong charm. Lead no good.

SMITHERS (*slapping his thigh and guffawing*). Haw-haw! If yer don't beat all 'ell. (*Then recovering himself—scornfully.*) I'll bet yer it ain't 'im they shot at all, yer bleedin' looney!

LEM (*calmly*). Dey come bring him now.

[*The soldiers come out of the forest, carrying* JONES's *limp body. He is dead. They carry him to* LEM, *who examines his body with great satisfaction.*]

SMITHERS (*leans over his shoulder—in a tone of frightened awe*). Well, they did for yer right enough, Jonesy me lad! Dead as a 'erring! (*Mockingly.*) Where's yer 'igh an' mighty airs now, yer bloomin' Majesty? (*Then with a grin.*) Silver bullets! Gawd blimey, but yer died in the 'eighth o' style, any'ow!

CURTAIN

ELMER RICE

ELMER RICE has been an intermittent storm center of American drama for more than a quarter of a century—intermittent only because he has renounced Broadway from time to time in sorrow over the refusal of the public to respond to his message, and in disgust at what he considered the perversity and the lack of intelligence and understanding on the part of the New York reviewers. In his first play, *On Trial* (1914), the unknown young playwright displayed the talent for technical originality and ingenuity that was to distinguish his career. He introduced a revolving stage in order to cut back swiftly from the courtroom to related earlier scenes in the manner of the cinema. The new device both accelerated the pace and pointed up the melodrama. *On Trial*, with its novel setting and stage economy, was the smash hit of 1914. Its author has never ceased to experiment with theatrical techniques, sometimes, as in the expressionistic masterpiece, *The Adding Machine*, and in the realistic triumph, *Street Scene*, to the permanent enrichment of American drama.

Elmer L. Rice (Reizenstein) was born in New York City, September 28, 1892, and, except for journeys to Europe, he has lived his life near the street scene of his birth. He went through the New York schools; then he tried business, "the highest goal of American manhood," he said, and found it, or himself, wanting. He then turned to the law. He worked at night while attending the New York Law School, from which he was graduated *cum laude* in 1912. After nearly six years of law, he found himself discontented, and longing to try authorship. It might be too much to say that Rice found in writing the contentment for which he was looking, but he has devoted his life to his new profession. And his learning in law came in handy in such plays as *On Trial, For the Defense* (1919), *It Is the Law* (1922), *Counsellor-at-Law* (1931), *Judgment Day* (1934), and incidental scenes in *The Adding Machine* and other plays. His dramatic trial scenes are famous.

Rice had little sympathy with the World War psychology on or off the stage. His own plays of those years were failures, and his collaborations were not very successful. Then, on March 19, 1923, the Theatre Guild produced his *The Adding Machine*. The success of this original play brought Rice to the forefront of the new American drama, but his restless talent was not easily canalized. He did not create an individual type of drama as O'Neill, Anderson, and Odets did. Rice again tried collaboration: with Dorothy Parker in the unsuccessful comedy, *Close Harmony* (1924); with Philip Barry in a mystery, *Cock Robin* (1928), that fared somewhat better in the vogue of the period. Not until the production of *Street Scene* on January 10, 1929, did Rice follow up in his own original way the promise of *The Adding Machine*.

Street Scene, which Rice also staged and cast, was as direct and realistic as *The Adding Machine* was symbolic and fanciful. It was played against the single stark set showing the decayed brown-

27

stone house front in any street on its way down from respectability to become a cheap and overcrowded tenement. Every detail of life on the street that Rice knows so well acquired emphasis and meaning when transferred to this stage: Abraham Kaplan, the Russian Jew, sitting in a window reading a Yiddish newspaper; Greta Fiorentino fanning herself on this hot June evening; Willie Maurrant on roller skates yelling for his "ma" and another nickel for an ice cream cone; the janitor rolling out the ashcans; Emma Jones, home from an errand, pausing on the steps to talk weather with Greta; and so on. This cross section of New York was drawn with such absolute fidelity that it stimulated the response of recognition. But the play passed easily, almost imperceptibly, from this photograph of the street itself to a concentration on a few people. Their personal drama pushed into the background this initial interest in the external aspect of the street scene. The tragedy of the Maurrant household then unfolded with a relentlessness and an inevitability that lifted audiences out of passive witnessing into acute emotional participation as the love of Rose Maurrant and Sam Kaplan, the radical Jewish boy, developed, and her father Frank, the stage hand, returned home unexpectedly to find his wife in the arms of her milkman lover, and shot them both. He was taken to prison, leaving the stricken Rose and Willie among the awed, onlooking tenants. The play was crowded with people and action, yet remained simple, direct, and clear-cut. It was awarded the Pulitzer prize for 1929, and later was made into an effective motion picture.

Two other Elmer Rice plays were produced in 1929. One was called *The Subway*, an expressionistic tragedy in nine scenes about a girl who was betrayed by an artist and threw herself in front of a subway train when she learned that her seducer was about to desert her. The other was *See Naples and Die*, an inconsequential story of the mixed up love affair between a man and his fiancée that began in Paris and ended near Naples after revolutionists shot the titled Russian whom the fiancée was forced to marry. Both plays failed.

In the autumn of 1931 Rice again hit the popular fancy with two plays produced within a few weeks of each other. *The Left Bank* exhibited with great gusto the life of the would-be artists who flocked to Paris in the post-War years, lived in cheap hotels, and talked excitedly of French civilization, art, and good living. Its detailed observations of the Left Bank were as accurate as those of *Street Scene*. *Counsellor-at-Law* was likewise immensely popular. It had action, and accurate observation of the people who pass through an attorney's office, but it was primarily a character study of a moment of crisis in the life of a lawyer who had come up from below to a position of importance. Both of these plays were produced by the author.

The next two plays, also produced by Rice, were stage failures: *Black Sheep* (1932) and *We, the People* (1933). The first was a thin comedy about the homecoming of the black sheep of the family and how the rumor of his importance as a writer altered the family's attitude toward him. *We, the People* brought out the social passion that characterized Rice's work in the thirties. It was a grim indictment of the forces that were wrecking American families in the depths of the depression, and a demand for their eradication. Its powerful and rousing appeal to the social conscience stirred audiences profoundly, but the play was unable to meet the high cost of stage operation.

We, the People indicated the direction of Rice's interest as dramatist, producer, and director. Like other men of the theatre, he had become excited over the extraordinary advances being made by the Russians in designing playhouses, and in directing and staging plays for the masses at the very moment when the American theatre, for example, was languishing. As we have noted in the introduction to Katayev and Soviet Drama, the Russians were attracting to their dramatic festivals the leading producers and critics from all over the world. Rice went to Russia and was impressed by the energy and the vision of the Soviet theatre.

Rice's hopeful enthusiasm inspired him to attempt an experiment of his own. He and Mrs. Rice bought the Belasco Theatre. They proposed to make it the home of Rice's own plays, and a repertory theatre for the people. It opened on September 12, 1934, with Rice's *Judgment Day*, an impassioned and indignant anti-Nazi melodrama, dramatizing the farce-trials and purge that followed the burning of the Reichstag. The response to *Judgment Day* was a disappointment to the producer. A few weeks later, on October 25, he presented a second offering, *Between Two Worlds*. The two worlds were, apparently, those of a society girl and of a Communist who met on board ship, and their drama consisted in her seduction and the effect of the meeting upon her social consciousness. Its failure caused Rice to give up in anger as well as in sorrow and to renounce Broadway for its stupor and its indifference.

Rice's enthusiasm for the theatre is too deep-seated for such easy renuncia-tion. His withdrawals are temporary while he restores his spirit. In 1935 he became the state director of the Federal Theatre Project in New York, only to resign indignantly when his *Living Newspaper* production was censored by the Federal WPA for its too caustic attack on Mussolini. He visited Russia again in 1936, spending several months in studying the Soviet drama and its methods of appealing to the proletariat. He toured the provinces, saw the ballet *Swan Lake* at Odessa, *The Pickwick Club* at the Moscow Art Theatre, *Aristocrats* at the Realistic Theatre, and Afinegenov's *Far Away* that was in repertory in 400 Russian theatres. He was impressed by the fact that plays of sentiment and plays dealing with individual problems and emotional relationships were flourishing along with dramas of social significance and Communistic propaganda. "The Soviet public continues to adore the theatre," he wrote, "and the theatre flourishes."

In 1938, after four years of determined absence from Broadway, Rice joined with Anderson, Sherwood, Behrman, and Howard, to organize the Playwrights' Company for the production of their own plays. Rice directed *Abe Lincoln in Illinois*, and then presented his own *American Landscape* on November 28, 1938. It was a thoughtful play with a message on freedom and the importance of preserving the best elements of the American heritage. It was one of the many plays that started the new vogue of Americanism. It was experimental in its use of ghosts from the past of the Dale family of Connecticut. It made quiet drama out of the problems confronting the family when Captain Dale proposed to sell the factory and the ancestral farm to the new racial elements that were crowding in upon the ancestral tradition. It was told more in speeches than in the drama of life itself, and the audiences were small. It closed on January 7, 1938.

Two on an Island, which Rice wrote and directed, and produced on January 22, 1940, was his second venture with the Playwrights' Company. He had laid aside the almost oppressive message-plays of the thirties to tell the engaging story of a boy and girl whose paths converged in New York; how they rode busses and subways, and were initiated into the life of the city; how they besieged casting offices and were repulsed; and how at last they met at the Statue of Liberty and all came right in the end. The play enjoyed a fairly successful run until April 13.

Through all these plays, uneven as they are, ran in and out one unifying thread. Rice himself said that he had been repeating over and over the simple message "that there is nothing as important in life as freedom," that our dominant concern "should be with the attainment of freedom of body and of mind through liberation from political autocracy, economic slavery, religious superstition, hereditary prejudice and herd psychology and the obtainment of freedom of the soul through liberation from fear, jealousy, hatred, possessiveness and self-delusion." When these noble purposes were expressed in terms of drama, Rice was a playwright of importance. When they were curtain lectures, he failed.

In Elmer Rice's exceedingly varied and crowded career of a quarter of a century in the theatre, *The Adding Machine* stands out in bold relief. Time has not dimmed this brilliant interpretation of a machine-dominated economy reducing the lowly operators to Zeros. On the contrary, as time ravages the merely

spectacular elements in expressionism, the basic soundness of Rice's play in structure and in theme is more clearly revealed. It wedded indissolubly the symbolistic form and the tragedy of Mr. Zero. It is difficult to see how the material and the theme of the play could have been presented so satisfactorily in any other form. It is at the same time both the best example of expressionism, and its justification as a stage device. For it lays hold upon the inner lives of these figures and projects them in dramatic terms visually upon the stage. It comments powerfully on this culminating point in man's struggle upward from the ancient slime in order to press the keys and pull the lever on a "super-hyper-adding machine." The seven scenes are boldly constructed. Each symbol has its immediate interest and its suggestive value; each is sound and right in conception; there is no forcing; each fits into the mood and into the total economy of the play. Their combined force is not dependent on the novelty of the structure. *The Adding Machine* is so freshly imagined and so soundly built that it can eschew the misty obscurity that mars so many expressionistic plays. It is, in fact, sparing in its use of expressionistic paraphernalia. And it even retains the homely American speech, with its salt, its humor, its racy rhythms, and its sharp diction.

Coming, as *The Adding Machine* did, just when European expressionistic drama was enjoying popularity in America, it was only natural for reviewers to link it with such plays as *Liliom, R.U.R., From Morn to Midnight, The World We Live In, Masses and Man,* and *The Hairy Ape.* This note in the reviews led Rice to write a letter to the New York *Times.* He said he could not detect that these plays had anything in common with each other, or with *The Add-ing Machine*, except that each did have an element that might be called "meta-physical." "The author attempts not so much to depict events faithfully as to convey to the spectator what seems to him to be their inner significance. To achieve this end the dramatist often finds it expedient to depart entirely from objective reality and to employ symbols, condensations, and a dozen devices which, to the conservative, must seem arbitrarily fantastic. This, I sup-pose, is what is meant by expressionism."

Rice went on in the letter to make this interesting comment on the writing of the play: "I should like to dispel the notion that *The Adding Machine* is a stunt play. I did not set out with the inten-tion of doing something startling or dar-ing. . . . I wrote the play just as I con-ceived it, without thought of theories of technique, in fact, without rationalizing about it at all.

"As proof of this I may add that from the moment I first conceived the play until the moment the manuscript was completed exactly seventeen days elapsed. And it was this manuscript that the Theatre Guild put into rehearsal. The only changes that were ever made were certain cuts and condensations which Mr. Moeller and I agreed would heighten the dramatic effectiveness of the piece. . . . Whatever the imperfec-tions of *The Adding Machine*, it is an honest piece of work and the recognition of that fact is very gratifying."

THE ADDING MACHINE

CHARACTERS

MR. ZERO

MRS. ZERO

MESSRS. ONE, TWO, THREE, FOUR, FIVE, SIX, *and their respective wives*

DAISY DIANA DOROTHEA DEVORE

THE BOSS

POLICEMAN

TWO ATTENDANTS

JUDY O'GRADY

A YOUNG MAN

SHRDLU

A HEAD

LIEUTENANT CHARLES

JOE

SCENE ONE

A bedroom.

A small room containing an "installment plan" bed, dresser, and chairs. An ugly electric light fixture over the bed with a single glaring naked lamp. One small window with the shade drawn. The walls are papered with sheets of foolscap covered with columns of figures.

MR. ZERO *is lying in the bed, facing the audience, his head and shoulders visible. He is* 10 *thin, sallow, undersized, and partially bald.* MRS. ZERO *is standing before the dresser arranging her hair for the night. She is forty-five, sharp-featured, gray streaks in her hair. She is shapeless in her long-sleeved cotton nightgown. She is wearing her shoes, over which sag her ungartered stockings.*

MRS. ZERO (*as she takes down her hair*). I'm gettin' sick o' them Westerns. All 20 them cowboys ridin' around an' foolin' with them ropes. I don't care

nothin' about that. I'm sick of 'em. I don't see why they don't have more of them stories like *For Love's Sweet Sake.* I like them sweet little love stories. They're nice an' wholesome. Mrs. Twelve was sayin' to me only yesterday, "Mrs. Zero," says she, "what I like is one of them wholesome stories, with just a sweet, simple little love story." "You're right, Mrs. Twelve," I says. "That's what I like, too." They're showin' too many Westerns at the Rosebud. I'm gettin' sick of them. I think we'll start goin' to the Peter Stuyvesant. They got a good bill there Wednesday night. There's a Chubby Delano comedy called *Sea-Sick.* Mrs. Twelve was tellin' me about it. She says it's a scream. They're havin' a picnic in the country and they sit Chubby next to an old maid with a great big mouth. So he gets sore an' when she ain't lookin' he goes and catches a frog and drops it in her clam chowder. An' when she goes to eat the chowder the frog jumps out of it an' right into her mouth. Talk about laugh! Mrs. Twelve was tellin' me she laughed so she nearly passed out. He sure can pull some funny ones. An' they got that big Grace Darling feature, *A Mother's Tears*. 10 She's sweet. But I don't like her clothes. There's no style to them. Mrs. Nine was tellin' me she read in *Pictureland* that she ain't livin' with her husband. He's her second, too. I don't know whether they're divorced or just separated. You wouldn't think it to see her on the screen. She looks so sweet and innocent. Maybe it ain't true. You can't believe all you read. 20 They say some Pittsburgh millionaire is crazy about her and that's why she ain't livin' with her husband. Mrs. Seven was tellin' me her brother-in-law has a friend that used to go to school with Grace Darling. He says her name ain't Grace Darling at all. Her right name is Elizabeth Dugan, he says, an' all them stories about her gettin' five thousand a week is the 30 bunk, he says. She's sweet, though. Mrs. Eight was tellin' me that *A Mother's Tears* is the best picture she ever made. "Don't miss it, Mrs. Zero," she says. "It's sweet," she says. "Just sweet and wholesome. Cry!" she says, "I nearly cried my eyes out." There's one part in it where this big bum of an Englishman—he's a married man, too—an' she's this little 40 simple country girl. An' she nearly falls for him, too. But she's sittin' out in the garden, one day, and she looks up and there's her mother lookin' at her, right out of the clouds. So that night she locks the door of her room.

An' sure enough, when everybody's in bed, along comes this big bum of an Englishman an' when she won't let him in what does he do but go an' kick open the door. "Don't miss it, Mrs. Zero," Mrs. Eight was tellin' me. It's at the Peter Stuyvesant Wednesday night, so don't be tellin' me you want to go to the Rosebud. The Eights seen it downtown at the Strand. They go downtown all the time. Just like us—nit! I guess by the time it gets to the Peter Stuyvesant all that part about kickin' in the door will be cut out. Just like they cut out that big cabaret scene in *The Price of Virtue*. They sure are pullin' some rough stuff in the pictures nowadays. "It's no place for a young girl," I was tellin' Mrs. Eleven, only the other day. An' by the time they get uptown half of it is cut out. But you wouldn't go downtown—not if wild horses was to drag you. You can wait till they come uptown! Well, I don't want to wait, see? I want to see 'em when everybody else is seein' them an' not a month later. Now don't go tellin' me you ain't got the price. You could dig up the price all right, all right, if you wanted to. I notice you always got the price to go to the ball game. But when it comes to me havin' a good time then it's always: "I ain't got the price, I gotta start savin'." A fat lot you'll ever save! I got all I can do now makin' both ends meet an' you talkin' about savin'. (*She seats herself on a chair and begins removing her shoes and stockings.*) An' don't go pullin' that stuff about bein' tired. "I been workin' hard all day. Twice a day in the subway's enough for me." Tired! Where do you get that tired stuff, anyhow? What about me? Where do I come in? Scrubbin' floors an' cookin' your meals an' washin' your dirty clothes. An' you sittin' on a chair all day, just addin' figgers an' waitin' for five-thirty. There's no five-thirty for me. I don't wait for no whistle. I don't get no vacations neither. And what's more I don't get no pay envelope every Saturday night neither. I'd like to know where you'd be without me. An' what have I got to show for it?— slavin' my life away to give you a home. What's in it for me, I'd like to know? But it's my own fault, I guess. I was a fool for marryin' you. If I'd 'a' had any sense, I'd 'a' known what you were from the start. I wish I had it to do over again, I hope to tell you. You was goin' to do wonders, you was! You wasn't goin' to be a book-keeper long—oh, no, not you. Wait till you got started—you was goin' to show 'em. There wasn't no job in the store that was too big for you. Well, I've been waitin'—waitin' for you to get started—see? It's been a good long wait, too. Twenty-five years! An' I ain't seen nothin' happen. Twenty-five years in the same job. Twenty-five years to-morrow! You're proud of it, ain't you? Twenty-five years in the same job an' never missed a day! That's somethin' to be proud of, ain't it? Sittin' for twenty-five years on the same chair, addin' up figures. What about bein' store-manager? I guess you forgot about that, didn't you? An' me at home here lookin' at the same four walls an' workin' my fingers to the bone to make both ends meet. Seven years since you got a raise! An' if you don't get one to-morrow, I'll bet a nickel you won't have the guts to go an' ask for one. I didn't pick much when I picked you, I'll tell the world. You ain't much to be proud of. (*She rises, goes to the window, and raises the shade. A few lighted windows are visible on the other side of the closed court. Looking out for a moment.*) She ain't walkin' around to-night, you can bet your sweet life on that. An' she won't be walkin' around any more nights, neither. Not in this house, anyhow. (*She turns away from the window.*) The dirty bum! The idea of her comin' to live in a house with respectable people. They should 'a' gave her six years, not six months. If I was the judge I'd of gave her life. A bum like that. (*She approaches the bed and stands there a moment.*) I guess you're sorry she's gone. I guess you'd like to sit home every night an' watch her goin's-on. You're somethin' to be proud of, you are! (*She stands on the bed and turns out the light. . . . A thin stream of moonlight filters in from the court. The two figures are dimly visible.* MRS. ZERO *gets into bed.*) You'd better not start nothin' with women, if you know what's good for you. I've put up with a lot, but I won't put up with that. I've been slavin' away for twenty-five years, makin' a home for you an' nothin' to show for it. If you was any kind of a man you'd have a decent job by now an' I'd be gettin' some comfort out of life—instead of bein' just a slave, washin' pots an' standin' over the hot stove. I've stood it for twenty-five years an' I guess I'll have to stand it twenty-five more. But don't you go startin' nothin' with women—(*She goes on talking as the curtain falls.*)

SCENE TWO

An office in a department store. Wood and glass partitions. In the middle of the room, two tall desks back to back. At one desk on a high stool is ZERO. *Opposite him at the other desk, also on a high stool, is* DAISY DIANA DOROTHEA DEVORE, *a plain, middle-aged woman. Both wear green eye-shades and paper sleeve protectors. A pendent electric lamp throws light upon both desks.* DAISY *reads aloud figures from a pile of slips which lie* 10 *before her. As she reads the figures,* ZERO *enters them upon a large square sheet of ruled paper which lies before him.*

DAISY (*reading aloud*). Three ninety-eight. Forty-two cents. A dollar fifty. A dollar fifty. A dollar twenty-five. Two dollars. Thirty-nine cents. Twenty-seven fifty.

ZERO (*petulantly*). Speed it up a little, 20 cancha?

DAISY. What's the rush? To-morrer's another day.

ZERO. Aw, you make me sick.

DAISY. An' you make me sicker.

ZERO. Go on. Go on. We're losin' time.

DAISY. Then quit bein' so bossy. (*She reads.*) Three dollars. Two sixty-nine. Eighty-one fifty. Forty dollars. Eight seventy-five. Who do you think you 30 are, anyhow?

ZERO. Never mind who I think I am. You tend to your work.

DAISY. Aw, don't be givin' me so many orders. Sixty cents. Twenty-four cents. Seventy-five cents. A dollar fifty. Two fifty. One fifty. One fifty. Two fifty. I don't have to take it from you and what's more I won't.

ZERO. Aw, quit talkin'.   40

DAISY. I'll talk all I want. Three dollars. Fifty cents. Fifty cents. Seven dollars. Fifty cents. Two fifty. Three fifty. Fifty cents. One fifty. Fifty cents.

[*She goes bending over the slips and transferring them from one pile to another.* ZERO *bends over his desk, busily entering the figures.*]

ZERO (*without looking up*). You make me sick. Always shootin' off your face about somethin'. Talk, talk, talk. Just like all the other women. Women make me sick.

DAISY (*busily fingering the slips*). Who do you think you are, anyhow? Bossin' me around. I don't have to take it from you, and what's more I won't.

[*They both attend closely to their work, neither looking up.*]

ZERO. Women make me sick. They're all alike. The judge gave her six months. I wonder what they do in the work-house. Peel potatoes. I'll bet she's sore at me. Maybe she'll try to kill me when she gets out. I better be careful. Hello, Girl Slays Betrayer. Jealous Wife Slays Rival. You can't tell what a woman's liable to do. I better be careful.

DAISY. I'm gettin' sick of it. Always pickin' on me about somethin'. Never a decent word out of you. Not even the time o'day.

ZERO. I guess she wouldn't have the nerve at that. Maybe she don't even know it's me. They didn't even put my name in the paper, the big bums. Maybe she's been in the work-house before. A bum like that. She didn't have nothin' on that one time—nothin' but a shirt. (*He glances up quickly, then bends over again.*) You make me sick. I'm sick of lookin' at your face.

DAISY. Gee, ain't that whistle ever goin' to blow? You didn't used to be like that. Not even good mornin' or good evenin'. I ain't done nothin' to you.

It's the young girls. Goin' around without corsets.

ZERO. Your face is gettin' all yeller. Why don't you put some paint on it? She was puttin' on paint that time. On her cheeks and on her lips. And that blue stuff on her eyes. Just sittin' there in a shimmy puttin' on the paint. An' walkin' around the room with her legs all bare.

DAISY. I wish I was dead.

ZERO. I was a goddam fool to let the wife get on to me. She oughta get six months at that. The dirty bum. Livin' in a house with respectable people. She'd be livin' there yet, if the wife hadn't o' got on to me. Damn her!

DAISY. I wish I was dead.

ZERO. Maybe another one'll move in. Gee, that would be great. But the wife's got her eye on me now.

DAISY. I'm scared to do it, though.

ZERO. You oughta move into that room. It's cheaper than where you're livin' now. I better tell you about it. I don't mean to be always pickin' on you.

DAISY. Gas. The smell of it makes me sick.

[ZERO looks up and clears his throat.]

DAISY (looking up, startled). Whadja say?

ZERO. I didn't say nothin'.

DAISY. I thought you did.

ZERO. You thought wrong.

[They bend over their work again.]

DAISY. A dollar sixty. A dollar fifty. Two ninety. One sixty-two.

ZERO. Why the hell should I tell you? Fat chance of you forgettin' to pull down the shade!

DAISY. If I asked for carbolic they might get on to me.

ZERO. Your hair's gettin' gray. You don't wear them shirt-waists any more with the low collars. When you'd bend down to pick somethin' up—

DAISY. I wish I knew what to ask for.

Girl Takes Mercury. After All-Night Party. Woman In Ten-Story Death Leap.

ZERO. I wonder where'll she go when she gets out. Gee, I'd like to make a date with her. Why didn't I go over there the night my wife went to Brooklyn? She never woulda found out.

DAISY. I seen Pauline Frederick do it once. Where could I get a pistol though?

ZERO. I guess I didn't have the nerve.

DAISY. I'll bet you'd be sorry then that you been so mean to me. How do I know, though? Maybe you wouldn't.

ZERO. Nerve! I got as much nerve as anybody. I'm on the level, that's all. I'm a married man and I'm on the level.

DAISY. Anyhow, why ain't I got a right to live? I'm as good as anybody else. I'm too refined, I guess. That's the whole trouble.

ZERO. The time the wife had pneumonia I thought she was goin' to pass out. But she didn't. The doctor's bill was eighty-seven dollars. (Looking up.) Hey, wait a minute! Didn't you say eighty-seven dollars?

DAISY (looking up). What?

ZERO. Was the last you said eighty-seven dollars?

DAISY (consulting the slip). Forty-two fifty.

ZERO. Well, I made a mistake. Wait a minute. (He busies himself with an eraser.) All right. Shoot.

DAISY. Six dollars. Three fifteen. Two twenty-five. Sixty-five cents. A dollar twenty. You talk to me as if I was dirt.

ZERO. I wonder if I could kill the wife without anybody findin' out. In bed some night. With a pillow.

DAISY. I used to think you was stuck on me.

ZERO. I'd get found out, though. They always have ways.

DAISY. We used to be so nice and friendly together when I first came here. You used to talk to me then.

ZERO. Maybe she'll die soon. I noticed she was coughin' this mornin'.

DAISY. You used to tell me all kinds o' things. You were goin' to show them all. Just the same, you're still sittin' here.

ZERO. Then I could do what I damn please. Oh, boy! 10

DAISY. Maybe it ain't all your fault neither. Maybe if you'd had the right kind o' wife—somebody with a lot of common-sense somebody refined—me!

ZERO. At that, I guess I'd get tired of bummin' around. A feller wants some place to hang his hat.

DAISY. I wish she would die. 20

ZERO. And when you start goin' with women you're liable to get into trouble. And lose your job maybe.

DAISY. Maybe you'd marry me.

ZERO. Gee, I wish I'd gone over there that night.

DAISY. Then I could quit workin'.

ZERO. Lots o' women would be glad to get me.

DAISY. You could look a long time be- 30 fore you'd find a sensible, refined girl like me.

ZERO. Yes, sir, they could look a long time before they'd find a steady meal-ticket like me.

DAISY. I guess I'd be too old to have any kids. They say it ain't safe after thirty-five.

ZERO. Maybe I'd marry you. You might be all right, at that. 40

DAISY. I wonder—if you don't want kids —whether—if there's any way—

ZERO (looking up). Hey! Hey! Can't you slow up? What do you think I am— a machine?

DAISY (looking up). Say, what do you want, anyhow? First it's too slow an' then it's too fast. I guess you don't know what you want.

ZERO. Well, never mind about that. Just you slow up.

DAISY. I'm gettin' sick o' this. I'm goin' to ask to be transferred.

ZERO. Go ahead. You can't make me mad.

DAISY. Aw, keep quiet. (She reads.) Two forty-five. A dollar twenty. A dollar fifty. Ninety cents. Sixty-three cents.

ZERO. Marry you! I guess not! You'd be as bad as the one I got.

DAISY. You wouldn't care if I did ask. I got a good mind to ask.

ZERO. I was a fool to get married.

DAISY. Then I'd never see you at all.

ZERO. What chance has a guy got with a woman tied around his neck?

DAISY. That time at the store picnic— the year your wife couldn't come— you were nice to me then.

ZERO. Twenty-five years holdin' down the same job!

DAISY. We were together all day—just sittin' around under the trees.

ZERO. I wonder if the boss remembers about it bein' twenty-five years.

DAISY. And comin' home that night— you sat next to me in the big delivery wagon.

ZERO. I got a hunch there's a big raise comin' to me.

DAISY. I wonder what it feels like to be really kissed. Men—dirty pigs! They want the bold ones.

ZERO. If he don't come across I'm goin' right up to the front office and tell him where he gets off.

DAISY. I wish I was dead.

ZERO. "Boss," I'll say, "I want to have a talk with you." "Sure," he'll say, "sit down. Have a Corona Corona." "No," I'll say, "I don't smoke." "How's that?" he'll say. "Well, boss,"

I'll say, "it's this way. Every time I feel like smokin' I just take a nickel and put it in the old sock. A penny saved is a penny earned, that's the way I look at it." "Damn sensible," he'll say. "You got a wise head on you, Zero."

DAISY. I can't stand the smell of gas. It makes me sick. You coulda kissed me if you wanted to.　　　　　　10

ZERO. "Boss," I'll say, "I ain't quite satisfied. I been on the job twenty-five years now and if I'm gonna stay I gotta see a future ahead of me." "Zero," he'll say, "I'm glad you came in. I've had my eye on you, Zero. Nothin' gets by me." "Oh, I know that, boss," I'll say. That'll hand him a good laugh, that will. "You're a valuable man, Zero," he'll say, "and I 20 want you right up here with me in the front office. You're done addin' figgers. Monday mornin' you move up here."

DAISY. Them kisses in the movies—them long ones—right on the mouth—

ZERO. I'll keep a-goin' right on up after that. I'll show some of them birds where they get off.

DAISY. That one the other night—*The* 30 *Devil's Alibi*—he put his arms around her—and her head fell back and her eyes closed—like she was in a daze.

ZERO. Just give me about two years and I'll show them birds where they get off.

DAISY. I guess that's what it's like—a kinda daze—when I see them like that, I just seem to forget everything.

ZERO. Then me for a place in Jersey. 40 And maybe a little Buick. No tin Lizzie for mine. Wait till I get started—I'll show 'em.

DAISY. I can see it now when I kinda half-close my eyes. The way her head fell back. And his mouth pressed right up against hers. Oh, Gawd! it must be grand!

[*There is a sudden shrill blast from a steam whistle.*]

DAISY *and* ZERO (*together*). The whistle!

[*With great agility they get off their stools, remove their eye-shades and sleeve protectors and put them on the desks Then each produces from behind the desk a hat—*ZERO, *a dusty derby,* DAISY, *a frowsy straw. . . .* DAISY *puts on her hat and turns toward* ZERO *as though she were about to speak to him. But he is busy cleaning his pen and pays no attention to her. She sighs and goes toward the door at the left.*]

ZERO (*looking up*). G'night, Miss Devore.

[*But she does not hear him and exits.* ZERO *takes up his hat and goes left. The door at the right opens and the* BOSS *enters—middle-aged, stoutish, bald, well-dressed.*]

THE BOSS (*calling*). Oh—er—Mister—er—

[ZERO *turns in surprise, sees who it is and trembles nervously.*]

ZERO (*obsequiously*). Yes, sir. Do you want me, sir?

BOSS. Yes. Just come here a moment, will you?

ZERO. Yes, sir. Right away, sir. (*He fumbles his hat, picks it up, stumbles, recovers himself, and approaches the* BOSS, *every fibre quivering.*)

BOSS. Mister—er—er—

ZERO. Zero.

BOSS. Yes, Mr. Zero. I wanted to have a little talk with you.

ZERO (*with a nervous grin*). Yes, sir, I been kinda expectin' it.

BOSS (*staring at him*). Oh, have you?

ZERO. Yes, sir.

BOSS. How long have you been with us, Mister—er—Mister—

ZERO. Zero.

BOSS. Yes, Mister Zero.

ZERO. Twenty-five years to-day.

BOSS. Twenty-five years! That's a long time.

ZERO. Never missed a day.

BOSS. And you've been doing the same work all the time?

ZERO. Yes, sir. Right here at this desk.

BOSS. Then, in that case, a change probably won't be unwelcome to you.

ZERO. No, sir, it won't. And that's the truth. 10

BOSS. We've been planning a change in this department for some time.

ZERO. I kinda thought you had your eye on me.

BOSS. You were right. The fact is that my efficiency experts have recommended the installation of adding machines.

ZERO (*staring at him*). Addin' machines?

BOSS. Yes, you've probably seen them. A 20 mechanical device that adds automatically.

ZERO. Sure. I've seen them. Keys—and a handle that you pull. (*He goes through the motions in the air.*)

BOSS. That's it. They do the work in half the time and a high-school girl can operate them. Now, of course, I'm sorry to lose an old and faithful employee— 30

ZERO. Excuse me, but would you mind sayin' that again?

BOSS. I say I'm sorry to lose an employee who's been with me for so many years—

[*Soft music is heard—the sound of the mechanical player of a distant merry-go-round.*

The part of the floor upon which the desk and stools are standing begins to revolve very slowly.]

BOSS. But, of course, in an organization like this, efficiency must be the first consideration—

[*The music becomes gradually louder and the revolutions more rapid.*]

BOSS. You will draw your salary for the full month. And I'll direct my secretary to give you a letter of recommendation—

ZERO. Wait a minute, Boss. Let me get this right. You mean I'm canned?

BOSS (*barely making himself heard above the increasing volume of sound*). I'm sorry—no other alternative—greatly regret—old employee—efficiency—economy—business—*business*—BUSINESS—

[*His voice is drowned by the music. The platform is revolving rapidly now. ZERO and the BOSS face each other. They are entirely motionless save for the BOSS's jaws, which open and close incessantly. But the words are inaudible. The music swells and swells. To it is added every off-stage effect of the theatre: the wind, the waves, the galloping horses, the locomotive whistle, the sleighbells, the automobile siren, the glass-crash. New Year's Eve, Election Night, Armistice Day, and the Mardi-Gras. The noise deafening, maddening, unendurable. Suddenly it culminates in a terrific peal of thunder. For an instant there is a flash of red and then everything is plunged into blackness.*]

CURTAIN

SCENE THREE

The ZERO dining-room. Entrance door at right. Doors to kitchen and bedroom at left. The walls, as in the first scene, are papered with foolscap sheets covered with columns of figures. In the middle of the room, up-stage, a table set for two. Along each side wall, seven chairs are ranged in symmetrical rows.

[*At the rise of the curtain MRS. ZERO is seen seated at the table looking alternately at the entrance door and a clock on the wall. She wears a bungalow apron over her best dress. After a few moments, the entrance door opens and ZERO enters. He hangs his hat on a rack behind the door and coming over to the table seats himself at the vacant place. His movements throughout are quiet and abstracted.*]

MRS. ZERO (*breaking the silence*). Well, it was nice of you to come home. You're only an hour late and that ain't very much. The supper don't get very cold in an hour. An' of course the part about our havin' a lot of company to-night don't matter. (*They begin to eat.*) Ain't you even got sense enough to come home on time? Didn't I tell you we're goin' to have a lot o' company to-night? Didn't you know the Ones are comin'? An' the Twos? An' the Threes? An' the Fours? An' the Fives? And the Sixes? Didn't I tell you to be home on time? I might as well talk to a stone wall. (*They eat for a few moments in silence.*) I guess you musta had some important business to attend to. Like watchin' the score-board. Or was two kids havin' a fight an' you was the referee? You sure do have a lot of business to attend to. It's a wonder you have time to come home at all. You gotta tough life, you have. Walk in, hang up your hat, an' put on the nose-bag. An' me in the hot kitchen all day, cookin' your supper an' waitin' for you to get good an' ready to come home! (*Again they eat in silence.*) Maybe the boss kept you late to-night. Tellin' you what a big noise you are and how the store couldn't 'a' got along if you hadn't been pushin' a pen for twenty-five years. Where's the gold medal he pinned on you? Did some blind old lady take it away from you or did you leave it on the seat of the boss's limousine when he brought you home? (*Again a few moments of silence.*) I'll bet he gave you a big raise, didn't he? Promoted you from the third floor to the fourth, maybe.

Raise? A fat chance you got o' gettin' a raise. All they gotta do is put an ad in the paper. There's ten thousand like you layin' around the streets. You'll be holdin' down the same job at the end of another twenty-five years—if you ain't forgot how to add by that time.

[*A noise is heard off-stage, a sharp clicking such as is made by the operation of the keys and levers of an adding machine.* ZERO *raises his head for a moment, but lowers it almost instantly.*]

MRS. ZERO. There's the door-bell. The company's here already. And we ain't hardly finished supper. (*She rises.*) But I'm goin' to clear off the table whether you're finished or not. If you want your supper, you got a right to be home on time. Not standin' around lookin' at score-boards. (*As she piles up the dishes,* ZERO *rises and goes toward the entrance door.*) Wait a minute! Don't open the door yet. Do you want the company to see all the mess? An' go an' put on a clean collar. You got red ink all over it. (ZERO *goes toward bedroom door.*) I should think after pushin' a pen for twenty-five years, you'd learn how to do it without gettin' ink on your collar. (ZERO *exits to bedroom.* MRS. ZERO *takes dishes to kitchen talking as she goes.*) I guess I can stay up all night now washin' dishes. You should worry! That's what a man's got a wife for, ain't it? Don't he buy her her clothes an' let her eat with him at the same table? An' all she's gotta do is cook the meals an' do the washin' an' scrub the floor, an' wash the dishes, when the company goes. But, believe me, you're goin' to sling a mean dish-towel when the company goes to-night!

[*While she is talking* ZERO *enters from bedroom. He wears a clean collar and is cramming the soiled one furtively into his pocket.* MRS. ZERO *enters from kitchen. She has removed her apron and carries a table cover which she spreads hastily over the table. The clicking noise is heard again.*]

MRS. ZERO. There's the bell again. Open the door, cancha?

[ZERO *goes to the entrance door and opens it. Six men and six women file into the room in a double column. The men are all shapes and sizes, but their dress is identical with that of* ZERO *in every detail. Each, however, wears a wig of a different color. The women are all dressed alike, too, except that the dress of each is of a different color.*]

MRS. ZERO (*taking the first woman's hand*). How de do, Mrs. One.

MRS. ONE. How de do, Mrs. Zero.

[MRS. ZERO *repeats this formula with each woman in turn.* ZERO *does the same with the men except that he is silent throughout. The files now separate, each man taking a chair from the right wall and each woman one from the left wall. Each sex forms a circle with the chairs very close together. The men—all except* ZERO—*smoke cigars. The women munch chocolates.*]

SIX. Some rain we're havin'.

FIVE. Never saw the like of it.

FOUR. Worst in fourteen years, paper says.

THREE. Y' can't always go by the papers.

TWO. No, that's right, too.

ONE. We're liable to forget from year to year.

SIX. Yeh, come t' think, last year was pretty bad, too.

FIVE. An' how about two years ago?

FOUR. Still this year's pretty bad.

THREE. Yeh, no gettin' away from that.

TWO. Might be a whole lot worse.

ONE. Yeh, it's all the way you look at it. Some rain, though.

MRS. SIX. I like them little organdie dresses.

MRS. FIVE. Yeh, with a little lace trimmin' on the sleeves.

MRS. FOUR. Well, I like 'em plain myself.

MRS. THREE. Yeh, what I always say is the plainer the more refined.

MRS. TWO. Well, I don't think a little lace does any harm.

MRS. ONE. No, it kinda dresses it up.

MRS. ZERO. Well, I always say it's all a matter of taste.

MRS. SIX. I saw you at the Rosebud Movie Thursday night, Mr. One.

ONE. Pretty punk show, I'll say.

TWO. They're gettin' worse all the time.

MRS. SIX. But who was the charming lady, Mr. One?

ONE. Now don't you go makin' trouble for me. That was my sister.

MRS. FIVE. Oho! That's what they all say.

MRS. FOUR. Never mind! I'll bet Mrs. One knows what's what, all right.

MRS. ONE. Oh, well, he can do what he likes—'slong as he behaves himself.

THREE. You're in luck at that, One. Fat chance I got of gettin' away from the frau even with my sister.

MRS. THREE. You oughta be glad you got a good wife to look after you.

THE OTHER WOMEN (*in unison*). That's right, Mrs. Three.

FIVE. I guess I know who wears the pants in your house, Three.

MRS. ZERO. Never mind. I saw them holdin' hands at the movie the other night.

THREE. She musta been tryin' to get some money away from me.

MRS. THREE. Swell chance anybody'd have of gettin' any money away from you.

[*General laughter.*]

FOUR. They sure are a loving couple.

MRS. TWO. Well, I think we oughta change the subject.

MRS. ONE. Yes, let's change the subject.

SIX (*sotto voce*). Did you hear the one about the travellin' salesman?

FIVE. It seems this guy was in a sleeper.

FOUR. Goin' from Albany to San Diego.

THREE. And in the next berth was an old maid.

TWO. With a wooden leg.

ONE. Well, along about midnight—

[*They all put their heads together and whisper.*]

MRS. SIX (*sotto voce*). Did you hear about the Sevens?

MRS. FIVE. They're gettin' a divorce.

MRS. FOUR. It's the second time for him.

MRS. THREE. They're two of a kind, if you ask me.

MRS. TWO. One's as bad as the other.

MRS. ONE. Worse.

MRS. ZERO. They say that she—

[*They all put their heads together and whisper.*]

SIX. I think this woman suffrage is the bunk.

FIVE. It sure is! Politics is a man's business.

FOUR. Woman's place is in the home.

THREE. That's it! Lookin' after the kids, 'stead of hangin' around the streets.

TWO. You hit the nail on the head that time.

ONE. The trouble is they don't know what they want.

MRS. SIX. Men sure get me tired.

MRS. FIVE. They sure are a lazy lot.

MRS. FOUR. And dirty.

MRS. THREE. Always grumblin' about somethin'.

MRS. TWO. When they're not lyin'!

MRS. ONE. Or messin' up the house.

MRS. ZERO. Well, believe me, I tell mine where he gets off.

SIX. Business conditions are sure bad.

FIVE. Never been worse.

FOUR. I don't know what we're comin' to.

THREE. I look for a big smash-up in about three months.

TWO. Wouldn't surprise me a bit.

ONE. We're sure headin' for trouble.

MRS. SIX. My aunt has gall-stones.

MRS. FIVE. My husband has bunions.

MRS. FOUR. My sister expects next month.

MRS. THREE. My cousin's husband has erysipelas.

MRS. TWO. My niece has St. Vitus's dance.

MRS. ONE. My boy has fits.

MRS. ZERO. I never felt better in my life. Knock wood!

SIX. Too damn much agitation, that's at the bottom of it.

FIVE. That's it!—too damn many strikes.

FOUR. Foreign agitators, that's what it is.

THREE. They oughta be run outa the country.

TWO. What the hell do they want, anyhow?

ONE. They don't know what they want, if you ask me.

SIX. America for the Americans is what I say!

ALL (*in unison*). That's it! Damn foreigners! Damn dagoes! Damn Catholics! Damn sheenies! Damn niggers! Jail 'em! shoot 'em! hang 'em! lynch 'em! burn 'em! (*They all rise.*)

ALL (*sing in unison*).

"My country 'tis of thee,
Sweet land of liberty!"

MRS. FOUR. Why so pensive, Mr. Zero?

ZERO (*speaking for the first time*). I'm thinkin'.

MRS. FOUR. Well, be careful not to sprain your mind.

[*Laughter.*]

MRS. ZERO. Look at the poor men all by themselves. We ain't very sociable.

ONE. Looks like we're neglectin' the ladies.

[*The women cross the room and join the men, all chattering loudly. The door-bell rings.*]

MRS. ZERO. Sh! The door-bell!

[*The volume of sound slowly diminishes. Again the door-bell.*]

ZERO (*quietly*). I'll go. It's for me.

[*They watch curiously as* ZERO *goes to the door and opens it, admitting a policeman. There is a murmur of surprise and excitement.*]

POLICEMAN. I'm lookin' for Mr. Zero.

[*They all point to* ZERO.]

ZERO. I've been expectin' you.

POLICEMAN. Come along!

ZERO. Just a minute. (*He puts his hand in his pocket.*)

POLICEMAN. What's he tryin' to pull? (*He draws a revolver.*) I got you covered.

ZERO. Sure, that's all right. I just want to give you somethin'. (*He takes the collar from his pocket and gives it to the* POLICEMAN.)

POLICEMAN (*suspiciously*). What's that?

ZERO. The collar I wore.

POLICEMAN. What do I want it for?

ZERO. It's got blood-stains on it.

POLICEMAN (*pocketing it*). All right, come along!

ZERO (*turning to* MRS. ZERO). I gotta go with him. You'll have to dry the dishes yourself.

MRS. ZERO (*rushing forward*). What are they takin' you for?

ZERO (*calmly*). I killed the boss this afternoon.

[*Quick curtain as the* POLICEMAN *takes him off.*]

SCENE FOUR

A court of justice. Three bare white walls without door or windows except for a single door in the right wall. At the right is a jury-box in which are seated MESSRS. ONE, TWO, THREE, FOUR, FIVE, *and* SIX *and their respective wives. On either side of the jury-box stands a uniformed officer. Opposite the jury-box is a long, bare oak table piled high with law books. Behind the books* ZERO *is seated, his face buried in his hands. There is no other furniture in the room.*

[*A moment after the rise of the curtain, one of the officers rises and, going around the table, taps* ZERO *on the shoulder.* ZERO *rises and accompanies the* OFFICER. *The* OFFICER *escorts him to the great empty space in the middle of the courtroom, facing the jury. He motions to* ZERO *to stop, then points to the jury and resumes his place beside the jury-box.* ZERO *stands there looking at the jury, bewildered and half afraid. The* JURORS *give no sign of having seen him. Throughout they sit with folded arms, staring stolidly before them.*]

ZERO (*beginning to speak; haltingly*). Sure I killed him. I ain't sayin' I didn't, am I? Sure I killed him. Them lawyers! They give me a good stiff pain, that's what they give me. Half the time I don't know what the hell they're talkin' about. Objection sustained. Objection overruled. What's the big idea, anyhow? You ain't heard me do any objectin', have you? Sure not! What's the idea of objectin'? You got a right to know. What I say is if one bird kills another bird, why, you got a right to call him for it. That's what I say. I know all about that. I been on the jury, too. Them lawyers! Don't let 'em fill you full of bunk. All that bull about it bein' red ink on the bill-file. Red ink nothin'! It was blood, see? I want you to get that right. I killed him, see? Right through the heart with the bill-file, see? I want you to get that right—all of you. One, two, three, four, five, six, seven, eight, nine, ten, eleven, twelve. Twelve of you. Six and six. That makes twelve. I figgered it up often enough. Six and six makes twelve. And five is seventeen. And eight is twenty-five. And three is twenty-eight. Eight and carry two. Aw, cut it out! Them damn figgers! I can't forget 'em. Twenty-five years, see? Eight hours a day, exceptin' Sundays. And July and August half-day Saturday. One week's vacation with pay. And another week without pay if you want it. Who the hell wants it? Layin' around the house listenin' to the wife tellin' you where you get off. Nix! An' legal holidays. I nearly forgot them. New Year's, Washington's Birthday, Decoration Day, Fourth o' July, Labor Day, Election Day, Thanksgivin', Christmas. Good Friday if you want it. An' if you're a Jew, Young Kipper an' the other one—I forget what they call it. The dirty sheenies—always gettin' two to the other bird's one. An' when a holiday comes on Sunday, you get Monday off. So that's fair enough. But when the Fourth o' July comes on Saturday, why, you're out o' luck on account of Saturday bein' a half-day anyhow. Get me? Twenty-five years —I'll tell you somethin' funny. Decoration Day an' the Fourth o' July are always on the same day o' the week. Twenty-five years. Never missed a day, and never more'n five minutes late. Look at my time card if you don't believe me. Eight twenty-seven, eight thirty, eight twenty-nine, eight twenty-seven, eight thirty-two. Eight an' thirty-two's forty an'—Goddam them figgers! I can't forget 'em. They're funny things, them figgers. They look like people sometimes. The eights, see? Two dots for the eyes and a dot for the nose. An' a line. That's the mouth, see? An' there's others remind you of other things—but I can't talk about them, on account of there bein' ladies here. Sure I killed him. Why didn't he shut up? If he'd only shut up! Instead o' talkin' an' talkin' about how sorry he was an' what a good guy I was an' this an' that. I felt like sayin' to him: "For Christ's sake, shut up!" But I didn't have the nerve, see? I didn't have the nerve to say that to the boss. An' he went on talkin', sayin' how sorry he was, see? He was standin' right close to me. An' his coat only had two buttons on it. Two an' two makes four an'—aw, can it! An' there was the bill-file on the desk. Right where I could touch it. It ain't right to kill a guy. I know that. When I read all about him in the paper an' about his three kids I felt like a cheap skate, I tell you. They had the kids' pictures in the paper, right next to mine. An' his wife, too. Gee, it must be swell to have a wife like that. Some guys sure is lucky. An' he left fifty thousand dollars just for a rest-room for the girls in the store. He was a good guy, at that. Fifty thousand. That's more'n twice as much as I'd have if I saved every nickel I ever made. Let's see. Twenty-five an' twenty-five an' twenty-five an'—aw, cut it out! An' the ads had a big, black border around 'em; an' all it said was that the store would be closed for three days on account of the boss bein' dead. That nearly handed me a laugh, that did. All them floor-walkers an' buyers an' high-muck-a-mucks havin' me to thank for gettin' three days off. I hadn't oughta killed him. I ain't sayin' nothin' about that. But I thought he was goin' to give me a raise, see? On account of bein' there twenty-five years. He never talked to me before, see? Except one mornin' we happened to come in the store together and I held the door open for him and he said "Thanks." Just like that, see? "Thanks!" That was the only time he ever talked to me. An' when I seen him comin' up to my desk, I didn't know where I got off. A big guy like that comin' up to my desk. I felt like I was chokin' like, and all of a sudden I got a kind o' bad taste in my mouth like when you get up in the mornin'. I didn't have no right to kill him. The district attorney is right about that. He read the law to you, right out o' the book. Killin' a bird—that's wrong. But there was that girl, see? Six months they gave her. It was a dirty trick tellin' the cops on her like that. I shouldn't 'a' done that. But what was I gonna do? The wife wouldn't let up on me. I hadda do it. She used to walk around the room, just in her undershirt, see? Nothin' else on. Just her undershirt. An' they gave her six months. That's the last I'll ever see of her. Them birds—how do they get away with it? Just grabbin' women, the way you see 'em do in the pictures. I've seen lots I'd like to grab like that, but I ain't got the nerve— in the subway an' on the street an' in the store buyin' things. Pretty soft for them shoe-salesmen, I'll say, lookin' at women's legs all day. Them lawyers! They give me a pain, I tell you—a pain! Sayin' the same thing over an' over again. I never said I didn't kill him. But that ain't the same as bein' a regular murderer. What good did it do me to kill him? I didn't make nothin' out of it. Answer yes or no! Yes or no, me elbow! There's some things you can't answer yes or no. Give me the once-over, you guys. Do I look like a murderer? Do I? I never did no harm to nobody.

Ask the wife. She'll tell you. Ask anybody. I never got into trouble. You wouldn't count that one time at the Polo Grounds. That was just fun like. Everybody was yellin', "kill the empire! Kill the empire!" An' before I knew what I was doin' I fired the pop bottle. It was on account of everybody yellin' like that. Just in fun like, see? The yeller dog! Callin' that one a strike—a mile away from the plate. Anyhow, the bottle didn't hit him. An' when I seen the cop comin' up the aisle, I beat it. That didn't hurt anybody. It was just in fun like, see? An' that time in the subway. I was readin' about a lynchin', see? Down in Georgia. They took the nigger an' they tied him to a tree. An' they poured kerosene on him and lit a big fire under him. The dirty nigger! Boy, I'd of liked to been there, with a gat in each hand, pumpin' him full of lead. I was readin' about it in the subway, see? Right at Times Square where the big crowd gets on. An' all of a sudden this big nigger steps right on my foot. It was lucky for him I didn't have a gun on me. I'd of killed him sure, I guess. I guess he couldn't help it all right on account of the crowd, but a nigger's got no right to step on a white man's foot. I told him where he got off all right. The dirty nigger. But that didn't hurt nobody, either. I'm a pretty steady guy, you gotta admit that. Twenty-five years in one job an' I never missed a day. Fifty-two weeks in a year. Fifty-two an' fifty-two an' fifty-two an'—They didn't have t' look for me, did they? I didn't try to run away, did I? Where was I goin' to run to! I wasn't thinkin' about it at all, see? I'll tell you what I was thinkin' about—how I was goin' to break it to the wife about bein' canned. He canned me after twenty-five years, see? Did the lawyers tell you about that? I forget. All that talk gives me a headache. Objection sustained. Objection overruled. Answer yes or no. It gives me a headache. And I can't get the figgers outta my head, neither. But that's what I was thinkin' about—how I was goin' t' 10 break it to the wife about bein' canned. An' what Miss Devore would think when she heard about me killin' him. I bet she never thought I had the nerve to do it. I'd of married her if the wife had passed out. I'd be holdin' down my job yet, if he hadn't o' canned me. But he kept talkin' an' talkin'. An' there was the bill-file right where I could reach it. Do you 20 get me? I'm just a regular guy like anybody else. Like you birds now. (*For the first time the* JURORS *relax, looking indignantly at each other and whispering.*) Suppose you was me, now. Maybe you'd 'a' done the same thing. That's the way you oughta look at it, see? Suppose you was me—

THE JURORS (*rising as one and shouting in unison*). GUILTY!

[ZERO *falls back, stunned for a moment by their vociferousness. The* JURORS *right-face in their places and file quickly out of the jury-box and toward the door in a double column.*]

ZERO (*recovering speech as the* JURORS *pass out at the door*). Wait a minute. Jest a minute. You don't get me right. Jest give me a chance an' I'll tell you how it was. I'm all mixed up, see? On account of them lawyers. And the figgers in my head. But I'm goin' to tell you how it was. I was there twenty-five years, see? An' they gave her six months, see? (*He goes on haranguing the empty jury-box as the curtain falls.*)

SCENE FIVE

A graveyard in full moonlight. It is a second-rate graveyard—no elaborate tombstones or monuments—just simple headstones and here and there a cross. At the back is an iron fence with a gate in the middle. At first no one is visible, but there are occasional 30 sounds throughout: the hooting of an owl, the whistle of a distant whippoorwill, the croaking of a bull-frog, and the yowling of a serenading cat.

[*After a few moments two figures appear outside the gate—a man and a woman. She pushes the gate and it opens with a rusty creak. The couple enter. They are now fully visible in the moonlight—*JUDY O'GRADY *and a* YOUNG MAN.] 40

JUDY (*advancing*). Come on, this is the place.

YOUNG MAN (*hanging back*). This! Why, this here is a cemetery.

JUDY. Aw, quit yer kiddin'!

YOUNG MAN. You don't mean to say—

JUDY. What's the matter with this place?

YOUNG MAN. A cemetery!

JUDY. Sure. What of it?

YOUNG MAN. You must be crazy.

JUDY. This place is all right, I tell you. I been here lots o' times.

YOUNG MAN. Nix on this place for me!

JUDY. Ain't this place as good as another? Whaddya afraid of? They're all dead ones here! They don't bother you. (*With sudden interest.*) Oh, look, here's a new one.

YOUNG MAN. Come on out of here.

JUDY. Wait a minute. Let's see what it says. (*She kneels on a grave in the fore-*

ground and putting her face close to head-stone spells out the inscription.) Z-E-R-O. Z-e-r-o. Zero! Say, that's the guy—

YOUNG MAN. Zero? He's the guy killed his boss, ain't he?

JUDY. Yeh, that's him, all right. But what I'm thinkin' of is that I went to the hoose-gow on account of him.

YOUNG MAN. What for?

JUDY. You know, same old stuff. Tene- 10 ment House Law. (*Mincingly.*) Section blaa-blaa of the Penal Code. Third offense. Six months.

YOUNG MAN. And this bird—

JUDY (*contemptuously*). Him? He was mamma's white-haired boy. We lived in the same house. Across the air-shaft, see? I used to see him lookin' in my window. I guess his wife musta seen him, too. Anyhow, they went 20 and turned the bulls on me. And now I'm out and he's in. (*Suddenly.*) Say— say— (*She bursts into a peal of laughter.*)

YOUNG MAN (*nervously*). What's so funny?

JUDY (*rocking with laughter*). Say, wouldn't it be funny—if—if—(*She explodes again.*) That would be a good joke on him, all right. He can't do nothin' about it now, can he?

YOUNG MAN. Come on out of here. I 30 don't like this place.

JUDY. Aw, you're a bum sport. What do you want to spoil my joke for?

[*A cat yammers mellifluously.*]

YOUNG MAN (*half hysterically*). What's that?

JUDY. It's only the cats. They seem to like it here all right. But come on if you're afraid. (*They go toward the gate. As they go out.*) You nervous men sure 40 are the limit.

[*They go out through the gate. As they disappear, ZERO's grave opens suddenly and his head appears.*]

ZERO (*looking about*). That's funny! I thought I heard her talkin' and

laughin'. But I don't see nobody. Anyhow, what would she be doin' here? I guess I must 'a' been dreamin'. But how could I be dreamin' when I ain't been asleep? (*He looks about again.*) Well, no use goin' back. I can't sleep, anyhow. I might as well walk around a little.

[*He rises out of the ground, very rigidly. He wears a full-dress suit of very antiquated cut and his hands are folded stiffly across his breast.*]

ZERO (*walking woodenly*). Gee! I'm stiff! (*He slowly walks a few steps, then stops.*) Gee, it's lonesome here! (*He shivers and walks on aimlessly.*) I should 'a' stayed where I was. But I thought I heard her laughin'.

[*A loud sneeze is heard.* ZERO *stands motionless, quaking with terror. The sneeze is repeated.*]

ZERO (*hoarsely*). What's that?

A MILD VOICE. It's all right. Nothing to be afraid of.

[*From behind a headstone* SHRDLU *appears. He is dressed in a shabby and ill-fitting cutaway. He wears silver-rimmed spectacles and is smoking a cigarette.*]

SHRDLU. I hope I didn't frighten you.

ZERO (*still badly shaken*). No-o. It's all right. You see, I wasn't expectin' to see anybody.

SHRDLU. You're a newcomer, aren't you?

ZERO. Yeh, this is my first night. I couldn't seem to get to sleep.

SHRDLU. I can't sleep, either. Suppose we keep each other company, shall we?

ZERO (*eagerly*). Yeh, that would be great. I been feelin' awful lonesome.

SHRDLU (*nodding*). I know. Let's make ourselves comfortable.

[*He seats himself easily on a grave.* ZERO *tries to follow his example, but he is stiff in every joint and groans with pain.*]

ZERO. I'm kinda stiff.

SHRDLU. You mustn't mind the stiffness. It wears off in a few days. (*He seats himself on the grave beside* ZERO *and produces a package of cigarettes.*) Will you have a Camel?

ZERO. No, I don't smoke.

SHRDLU. I find it helps keep the mosquitoes away. (*He lights a cigarette.*)

SHRDLU (*suddenly taking the cigarette out of his mouth*). Do you mind if I smoke, Mr.—Mr.—?

ZERO. No, go right ahead.

SHRDLU (*replacing the cigarette*). Thank you. I didn't catch your name.

[ZERO *does not reply.*]

SHRDLU (*mildly*). I say I didn't catch your name.

ZERO. I heard you the first time. (*Hesitantly.*) I'm scared if I tell you who I am and what I done, you'll be off me.

SHRDLU (*sadly*). No matter what your sins may be, they are as snow compared to mine.

ZERO. You got another guess comin'. (*He pauses dramatically.*) My name's Zero. I'm a murderer.

SHRDLU (*nodding calmly*). Oh, yes, I remember reading about you, Mr. Zero.

ZERO (*a little piqued*). And you still think you're worse than me?

SHRDLU (*throwing away his cigarette*). Oh, a thousand times worse, Mr. Zero— a million times worse.

ZERO. What did you do?

SHRDLU. I, too, am a murderer.

ZERO (*looking at him in amazement*). Go on! You're kiddin' me!

SHRDLU. Every word I speak is the truth, Mr. Zero. I am the foulest, the most sinful of murderers! You only murdered your employer, Mr. Zero. But I—I murdered my mother. (*He covers his face with his hands and sobs.*)

ZERO (*horrified*). The hell yer say!

SHRDLU (*sobbing*). Yes, my mother!— my beloved mother!

ZERO (*suddenly*). Say, you don't mean to say you're Mr.—

SHRDLU (*nodding*). Yes. (*He wipes his eyes, still quivering with emotion.*)

ZERO. I remember readin' about you in the papers.

SHRDLU. Yes, my guilt has been proclaimed to all the world. But that would be a trifle if only I could wash the stain of sin from my soul.

ZERO. I never heard of a guy killin' his mother before. What did you do it for?

SHRDLU. Because I have a sinful heart— there is no other reason.

ZERO. Did she always treat you square and all like that?

SHRDLU. She was a saint—a saint, I tell you. She cared for me and watched over me as only a mother can.

ZERO. You mean to say you didn't have a scrap or nothin'?

SHRDLU. Never a harsh or an unkind word. Nothing except loving care and good advice. From my infancy she devoted herself to guiding me on the right path. She taught me to be thrifty, to be devout, to be unselfish, to shun evil companions and to shut my ears to all the temptations of the flesh—in short, to become a virtuous, respectable, and God-fearing man. (*He groans.*) But it was a hopeless task. At fourteen I began to show evidence of my sinful nature.

ZERO (*breathlessly*). You didn't kill anybody else, did you?

SHRDLU. No, thank God, there is only one murder on my soul. But I ran away from home.

ZERO. You did!

SHRDLU. Yes. A companion lent me a profane book—the only profane book

I have ever read, I'm thankful to say. It was called *Treasure Island*. Have you ever read it?

ZERO. No, I never was much on readin' books.

SHRDLU. It is a wicked book—a lurid tale of adventure. But it kindled in my sinful heart a desire to go to sea. And so I ran away from home.

ZERO. What did you do—get a job as a sailor?

SHRDLU. I never saw the sea—not to the day of my death. Luckily, my mother's loving intuition warned her of my intention and I was sent back home. She welcomed me with open arms. Not an angry word, not a look of reproach. But I could read the mute suffering in her eyes as we prayed together all through the night.

ZERO (*sympathetically*). Gee, that must 'a' been tough. Gee, the mosquitoes are bad, ain't they? (*He tries awkwardly to slap at them with his stiff hands.*)

SHRDLU (*absorbed in his narrative*). I thought that experience had cured me of evil and I began to think about a career. I wanted to go in foreign missions at first, but we couldn't bear the thought of the separation. Se we finally decided that I should become a proof-reader.

ZERO. Say, slip me one o' them Camels, will you? I'm gettin' all bit up.

SHRDLU. Certainly (*He hands* ZERO *cigarettes and matches.*)

ZERO (*lighting up*). Go ahead. I'm listenin'.

SHRDLU. By the time I was twenty I had a good job reading proof for a firm that printed catalogues. After a year they promoted me and let me specialize in shoe catalogues.

ZERO. Yeh? That must 'a' been a good job.

SHRDLU. It was a very good job. I was on the shoe catalogues for thirteen years. I'd been on them yet, if I hadn't—(*He chokes back a sob.*)

ZERO. They oughta put a shot o' citronella in that embalmin'-fluid.

SHRDLU (*he sighs*). We were so happy together. I had my steady job. And Sundays we would go to morning, afternoon, and evening service. It was an honest and moral mode of life.

SHRDLU. Then came that fatal Sunday. Dr. Amaranth, our minister, was having dinner with us—one of the few pure spirits on earth. When he had finished saying grace, we had our soup. Everything was going along as usual—we were eating our soup and discussing the sermon, just like every other Sunday I could remember. Then came the leg of lamb —(*He breaks off, then resumes in a choking voice.*) I see the whole scene before me so plainly—it never leaves me—Dr. Amaranth at my right, my mother at my left, the leg of lamb on the table in front of me, and the cuckoo clock on the little shelf between the windows. (*He stops and wipes his eyes.*)

ZERO. Yeh, but what happened?

SHRDLU. Well, as I started to carve the lamb—Did you ever carve a leg of lamb?

ZERO. No, corned beef was our speed.

SHRDLU. It's very difficult on account of the bone. And when there's gravy in the dish there's danger of spilling it. So Mother always used to hold the dish for me. She leaned forward, just as she always did, and I could see the gold locket around her neck. It had my picture in it and one of my baby curls. Well, I raised my knife to carve the leg of lamb—and instead I cut my mother's throat! (*He sobs.*)

ZERO. You must 'a' been crazy!

SHRDLU (*raising his head, vehemently*). No! Don't try to justify me. I wasn't crazy. They tried to prove at the trial that I was crazy. But Dr. Amaranth saw the truth! He saw it from the first! He knew that it was my sinful nature —and he told me what was in store for me.

ZERO (*trying to be comforting*). Well, your troubles are over now.

SHRDLU (*his voice rising*). Over! Do you think this is the end?

ZERO. Sure. What more can they do to us?

SHRDLU (*his tones growing shriller and shriller*). Do you think there can ever be any peace for such as we are— murderers, sinners? Don't you know what awaits us—flames, eternal flames!

ZERO (*nervously*). Keep your shirt on, Buddy—they wouldn't do that to us.

SHRDLU. There's no escape—no escape for us, I tell you. We're doomed! We're doomed to suffer unspeakable torments through all eternity. (*His voice rises higher and higher.*)

[*A grave opens suddenly and a head appears.*]

THE HEAD. Hey, you birds! Can't you shut up and let a guy sleep?

[ZERO *scrambles painfully to his feet.*]

ZERO (*to* SHRDLU). Hey, put on the soft pedal.

SHRDLU (*too wrought up to attend*). It won't be long now! We'll receive our summons soon.

THE HEAD. Are you goin' to beat it or not? (*He calls into the grave.*) Hey, Bill, lend me your head a minute. (*A moment later his arm appears holding a skull.*)

ZERO (*warningly*). Look out! (*He seizes* SHRDLU *and drags him away just as* THE HEAD *throws the skull.*)

THE HEAD (*disgustedly*). Missed 'em. Damn old tabby cats! I'll get 'em next time. (*A prodigious yawn.*) Ho-hum! Me for the worms!

[THE HEAD *disappears as the curtain falls.*]

SCENE SIX

A pleasant place. A scene of pastoral loveliness. A meadow dotted with fine old trees and carpeted with rich grass and field flowers. In the background are seen a number of tents fashioned of gay-striped silks and beyond gleams a meandering river. Clear air and a fleckless sky. Sweet distant music throughout. [*At the rise of the curtain,* SHRDLU *is seen seated under a tree in the foreground in an attitude of deep dejection. His knees are drawn up and his head is buried in his arms. He is dressed as in the preceding scene.*

[*A few minutes later,* ZERO *enters at right. He walks slowly and looks about him with an air of half-suspicious curiosity. He, too, is dressed as in the preceding scene. Suddenly he sees* SHRDLU *seated under the tree. He stands still and looks at him half fearfully. Then, seeing something familiar in him, goes closer.* SHRDLU *is unaware of his presence. At last* ZERO *recognizes him and grins in pleased surprise.*]

ZERO. Well, if it ain't—!(*He claps* SHRDLU *on the shoulder.*) Hello, Buddy!

[SHRDLU *looks up slowly, then, recognizing* ZERO, *he rises gravely and extends his hand courteously.*]

SHRDLU. How do you do, Mr. Zero? I'm very glad to see you again.

ZERO. Same here. I wasn't expectin' to see you, either. (*Looking about.*) This is a kinda nice place. I wouldn't mind restin' here a while.

SHRDLU. You may if you wish.

ZERO. I'm kinda tired. I ain't used to bein' outdoors. I ain't walked so much in years.

SHRDLU. Sit down here, under the tree.

ZERO. Do they let you sit on the grass?

SHRDLU. Oh, yes.

ZERO (*seating himself*). Boy, this feels good. I'll tell the world my feet are sore. I ain't used to so much walkin'. Say, I wonder would it be all right if I took my shoes off; my feet are tired.

SHRDLU. Yes. Some of the people here go barefoot.

ZERO. Yeh? They sure must be nuts. But I'm goin' t' leave 'em off for a while. So long as it's all right. The grass feels nice and cool. (*He stretches out comfortably.*) Say, this is the life of Riley all right, all right. This sure is a nice place. What do they call this place, anyhow?

SHRDLU. The Elysian Fields.

ZERO. The which?

SHRDLU. The Elysian Fields.

ZERO (*dubiously*). Oh! Well, it's a nice place, all right.

SHRDLU. They say that this is the most desirable of all places. Only the most favored remain here.

ZERO. Yeh? Well, that let's me out, I guess. (*Suddenly.*) But what are you doin' here? I thought you'd be burned by now.

SHRDLU (*sadly*). Mr. Zero, I am the most unhappy of men.

ZERO (*in mild astonishment*). Why, because you ain't bein' roasted alive?

SHRDLU (*nodding*). Nothing is turning out as I expected. I saw everything so clearly—the flames, the tortures, an eternity of suffering as the just punishment for my unspeakable crime. And it has all turned out so differently.

ZERO. Well, that's pretty soft for you, ain't it?

SHRDLU (*wailingly*). No, no, no! It's right and just that I should be punished. I could have endured it stoically. All through those endless ages of indescribable torment I should have exulted in the magnificence of divine justice. But this—this is maddening! What becomes of justice? What becomes of morality? What becomes of right and wrong? It's maddening—simply maddening! Oh, if Dr. Amaranth were only here to advise me! (*He buries his face and groans.*)

ZERO (*trying to puzzle it out*). You mean to say they ain't called you for cuttin' your mother's throat?

SHRDLU. No! It's terrible—terrible! I was prepared for anything—anything but this.

ZERO. Well, what did they say to you?

SHRDLU (*looking up*). Only that I was to come here and remain until I understood.

ZERO. I don't get it. What do they want you to understand?

SHRDLU (*despairingly*). I don't know—I don't know! If I only had an inkling of what they meant—(*Interrupting him.*) Just listen quietly for a moment; do you hear anything?

[*They are both silent, straining their ears.*]

ZERO (*at length*). Nope.

SHRDLU. You don't hear any music? Do you?

ZERO. Music? No, I don't hear nothin'.

SHRDLU. The people here say that the music never stops.

ZERO. They're kiddin' you.

SHRDLU. Do you think so?

ZERO. Sure thing. There ain't a sound.

SHRDLU. Perhaps. They're capable of anything. But I haven't told you of the bitterest of my disappointments.

ZERO. Well, spill it. I'm gettin' used to hearin' bad news.

SHRDLU. When I came to this place, my first thought was to find my dear mother. I wanted to ask her forgiveness. And I wanted her to help me to understand.

ZERO. An' she couldn't do it?

SHRDLU (*with a deep groan*). She's not here! Mr. Zero! Here where only the most favoured dwell, that wisest and purest of spirits is nowhere to be found. I don't understand it.

A WOMAN'S VOICE (*in the distance*). Mr. Zero! Oh, Mr. Zero!   10

[ZERO *raises his head and listens attentively.*]

SHRDLU (*going on, unheedingly*). If you were to see some of the people here—the things they do—

ZERO (*interrupting*). Wait a minute, will you? I think somebody's callin' me.

THE VOICE (*somewhat nearer*). Mr. Ze-ro! Oh! Mr. Ze-ro!

ZERO. Who the hell's that now? I wonder if the wife's on my trail already. 20 That would be swell, wouldn't it? An' I figured on her bein' good for another twenty years, anyhow.

THE VOICE (*nearer*). Mr. Ze-ro! Yoo-hoo!

ZERO. No. That ain't her voice. (*Calling, savagely.*) Yoo-hoo. (*To* SHRDLU.) Ain't that always the way? Just when a guy is takin' life easy an' havin' a good time! (*He rises and looks off left.*) Here she comes, whoever she is. (*In* 30 *sudden amazement.*) Well, I'll be—! Well, what do you know about that!

[*He stands looking in wonderment, as* DAISY DIANA DOROTHEA DEVORE *enters. She wears a much-beruffled white muslin dress which is a size too small and fifteen years too youthful for her. She is red-faced and breathless.*]

DAISY (*panting*). Oh! I thought I'd never catch up to you. I've been followin' 40 you for days—callin' an' callin'. Didn't you hear me?

ZERO. Not till just now. You look kinda winded.

DAISY. I sure am. I can't hardly catch my breath.

ZERO. Well, sit down an' take a load off your feet.

[*He leads her to the tree.* DAISY *sees* SHRDLU *for the first time and shrinks back a little.*]

ZERO. It's all right, he's a friend of mine. (*To* SHRDLU.) Buddy, I want you to meet my friend, Miss Devore.

SHRDLU (*rising and extending his hand courteously*). How do you do, Miss Devore?

DAISY (*self-consciously*). How do!

ZERO (*to* DAISY). He's a friend of mine. (*To* SHRDLU.) I guess you don't mind if she sits here a while an' cools off, do you?

SHRDLU. No, no, certainly not.

[*They all seat themselves under the tree.* ZERO *and* DAISY *are a little self-conscious.* SHRDLU *gradually becomes absorbed in his own thoughts.*]

ZERO. I was just takin' a rest myself. I took my shoes off on account of my feet bein' so sore.

DAISY. Yeh, I'm kinda tired, too. (*Looking about.*) Say, ain't it pretty here, though?

ZERO. Yeh, it is at that.

DAISY. What do they call this place?

ZERO. Why—er—let's see. He was tellin' me just a minute ago. The—er—I don't know. Some kind o' fields. I forget now. (*To* SHRDLU.) Say, Buddy, what do they call this place again? (SHRDLU, *absorbed in his thoughts, does not hear him. To* DAISY.) He don't hear me. He's thinkin' again.

DAISY (*sotto voce*). What's the matter with him?

ZERO. Why, he's the guy that murdered his mother—remember?

DAISY (*interested*). Oh, yeh! Is that him?

ZERO. Yeh. An' he had it all figgered out how they was goin' t' roast him or somethin'. And now they ain't goin' to do nothin' to him an' it's kinda got his goat.

DAISY (*sympathetically*). Poor feller!

ZERO. Yeh. He takes it kinda hard.

DAISY. He looks like a nice young feller.

ZERO. Well, you sure are good for sore eyes. I never expected to see you here.

DAISY. I thought maybe you'd be kinda surprised.

ZERO. Surprised is right. I thought you was alive an' kickin'. When did you pass out?

DAISY. Oh, right after you did—a coupla days.

ZERO (*interested*). Yeh? What happened? Get hit by a truck or somethin'?

DAISY. No. (*Hesitantly.*) You see—it's this way. I blew out the gas.

ZERO (*astonished*). Go on! What was the big idea?

DAISY (*falteringly*). Oh, I don't know. You see, I lost my job.

ZERO. I'll bet you're sorry you did it now, ain't you?

DAISY (*with conviction*). No, I ain't sorry. Not a bit. (*Then hesitantly.*) Say, Mr. Zero, I been thinkin'—(*She stops.*)

ZERO. What?

DAISY (*plucking up courage*). I been thinkin' it would be kinda nice—if you an' me—if we could kinda talk things over.

ZERO. Yeh. Sure. What do you want to talk about?

DAISY. Well—I don't know—but you and me—we ain't really ever talked things over, have we?

ZERO. No, that's right, we ain't. Well, let's go to it.

DAISY. I was thinkin' if we could be alone—just the two of us, see?

ZERO. Oh, yeh! Yeh, I get you. (*He turns to* SHRDLU *and coughs loudly.* SHRDLU *does not stir.*)

ZERO (*to* DAISY). He's dead to the world. (*He turns to* SHRDLU.) Say, Buddy! (*No answer.*) Say, Buddy!

SHRDLU (*looking up with a start*). Were you speaking to me?

ZERO. Yeh. How'd you guess it? I was thinkin' that maybe you'd like to walk around a little and look for your mother.

SHRDLU (*shaking his head*). It's no use. I've looked everywhere. (*He relapses into thought again.*)

ZERO. Maybe over there they might know.

SHRDLU. No, no! I've searched everywhere. She's not here.

[ZERO *and* DAISY *look at each other in despair.*]

ZERO. Listen, old shirt, my friend here and me—see?—we used to work in the same store. An' we got somethings to talk over—business, see?—kinda confidential. So if it ain't askin' too much—

SHRDLU (*springing to his feet*). Why, certainly! Excuse me! (*He bows politely to* DAISY *and walks off.* DAISY *and* ZERO *watch him until he has disappeared.*)

ZERO (*with a forced laugh*). He's a good guy at that.

[*Now that they are alone, both are very self-conscious, and for a time they sit in silence.*] DAISY (*breaking the silence*). It sure is pretty here, ain't it?

ZERO. Sure is.

DAISY. Look at the flowers! Ain't they just perfect! Why, you'd think they was artificial, wouldn't you?

ZERO. Yeh, you would.

DAISY. And the smell of them. Like perfume.

ZERO. Yeh.

DAISY. I'm crazy about the country, ain't you?

ZERO. Yeh. It's nice for a change.

DAISY. Them store picnics—remember?

ZERO. You bet. They sure was fun.

DAISY. One time—I guess you don't remember—the two of us—me and you

—we sat down on the grass together under a tree—just like we're doin' now.

ZERO. Sure I remember.

DAISY. Go on! I'll bet you don't.

ZERO. I'll bet I do. It was the year the wife didn't go.

DAISY (*her face brightening*). That's right! I didn't think you'd remember.

ZERO. An' comin' home we sat together 10 in the truck.

DAISY (*eagerly, rather shamefacedly*). Yeh! There's somethin' I've always wanted to ask you.

ZERO. Well, why didn't you?

DAISY. I don't know. It didn't seem refined. But I'm goin' to ask you now, anyhow.

ZERO. Go ahead. Shoot.

DAISY (*falteringly*). Well—while we was 20 comin' home—you put your arm up on the bench behind me—and I could feel your knee kinda pressin' against mine. (*She stops.*)

ZERO (*becoming more and more interested*). Yea—well—what about it?

DAISY. What I wanted to ask you was —was it just kinda accidental?

ZERO (*with a laugh*). Sure it was accidental. Accidental on purpose. 30

DAISY (*eagerly*). Do you mean it?

ZERO. Sure I mean it. You mean to say you didn't know it?

DAISY. No. I've been wantin' to ask you—

ZERO. Then why did you get sore at me?

DAISY. Sore? I wasn't sore! When was I sore?

ZERO. That night. Sure you was sore. If you wasn't sore, why did you move 40 away?

DAISY. Just to see if you meant it. I thought if you meant it, you'd move up closer. An' then when you took your arm away, I was sure you didn't mean it.

ZERO. An' I thought all the time you was sore. That's why I took my arm away. I thought if I moved up you'd holler and then I'd be in a jam, like you read in the paper all the time about guys gettin' pulled in for annoyin' women.

DAISY. An' I was wishin' you'd put your arm around me—just sittin' there wishin' all the way home.

ZERO. What do you know about that? That sure is hard luck, that is. If I'd 'a' only knew! You know what I felt like doin'—only I didn't have the nerve?

DAISY. What?

ZERO. I felt like kissin' you.

DAISY (*fervently*). I wanted you to.

ZERO (*astonished*). You would 'a' let me?

DAISY. I wanted you to! I wanted you to! Oh, why didn't you—why didn't you?

ZERO. I didn't have the nerve. I sure was a dumb-bell.

DAISY. I would 'a' let you all you wanted to. I wouldn't 'a' cared. I know it would 'a' been wrong, but I wouldn't 'a' cared. I wasn't thinkin' about right an' wrong at all. I didn't care— see? I just wanted you to kiss me.

ZERO (*feelingly*). If I'd only knew. I wanted to do it, I swear I did. But I didn't think you cared nothin' about me.

DAISY (*passionately*). I never cared nothin' about nobody else.

ZERO. Do you mean it—on the level? You ain't kiddin' me, are you?

DAISY. No, I ain't kiddin'. I mean it. I'm tellin' you the truth. I ain't never had the nerve to tell you before—but now I don't care. It don't make no difference now. I mean it—every word of it.

ZERO (*dejectedly*). If I'd only knew it.

DAISY. Listen to me. There's somethin'

else I want to tell you. I may as well tell you everything now. It don't make no difference now. About my blowin' out the gas—see? Do you know why I done it?

ZERO. Yeh, you told me—on account o' bein' canned.

DAISY. I just told you that. That ain't the real reason. The real reason is on account o' you.

ZERO. You mean to say on account o' me passin' out—?

DAISY. Yeh. That's it. I didn't want to go on livin'. What for? What did I want to go on livin' for? I didn't have nothin' to live for with you gone. I often thought of doin' it before. But I never had the nerve. An' anyhow I didn't want to leave you.

ZERO. An' me bawlin' you out, about readin' too fast an' readin' too slow.

DAISY (reproachfully). Why did you do it?

ZERO. I don't know, I swear I don't. I was always stuck on you. An' while I'd be addin' them figgers, I'd be thinkin' how, if the wife died, you an' me could get married.

DAISY. I used to think o' that, too.

ZERO. An' then, before I knew it, I was bawlin' you out.

DAISY. Them was the times I'd think o' blowin' out the gas. But I never did till you was gone. There wasn't nothin' to live for then. But it wasn't so easy to do, anyhow. I never could stand the smell o' gas. An' all the while I was gettin' ready, you know, stuffin' up all the cracks, the way you read about in the paper—I was thinkin' of you and hopin' that maybe I'd meet you again. An' I made up my mind if I ever did see you, I'd tell you.

ZERO (taking her hand). I'm sure glad you did. I'm sure glad. (Ruefully.) But it don't do much good now, does it?

DAISY. No, I guess it don't. (Summoning courage.) But there's one thing I'm goin' to ask you.

ZERO. What's that?

DAISY (in a low voice). I want you to kiss me.

ZERO. You bet I will! (He leans over and kisses her cheek.)

DAISY. Not like that. I don't mean like that. I mean really kiss me. On the mouth. I ain't never been kissed like that.

[ZERO puts his arms about her and presses his lips to hers. A long embrace. At last they separate and sit side by side in silence.]

DAISY (putting her hands to her cheeks). So that's what it's like. I didn't know it could be like that. I didn't know anythin' could be like that.

ZERO (fondling her hand). Your cheeks are red. They're all red. And your eyes are shinin'. I never seen your eyes shinin' like that before.

DAISY (holding up her hand). Listen—do you hear it? Do you hear the music?

ZERO. No, I don't hear nothin'!

DAISY. Yeh—music. Listen an' you'll hear it. (They are both silent for a moment.)

ZERO (excitedly). Yeh! I hear it! He said there was music, but I didn't hear it till just now.

DAISY. Ain't it grand?

ZERO. Swell! Say, do you know what?

DAISY. What?

ZERO. It makes me feel like dancin'.

DAISY. Yeh? Me, too.

ZERO (springing to his feet). Come on! Let's dance! (He seizes her hands and tries to pull her up.)

DAISY (resisting laughingly). I can't dance. I ain't danced in twenty years.

ZERO. That's nothin'. I ain't, neither. Come on! I feel just like a kid! (He pulls her to her feet and seizes her about the waist.)

DAISY. Wait a minute! Wait till I fix my skirt.

[*She turns back her skirts and pins them above the ankles.* ZERO *seizes her about the waist. They dance clumsily, but with gay abandon.* DAISY'S *hair becomes loosened and tumbles over her shoulders. She lends herself more and more to the spirit of the dance. But* ZERO *soon begins to tire and dances with less and less zest.*]

ZERO (*stopping at last, panting for breath*). Wait a minute! I'm all winded.

[*He releases* DAISY, *but before he can turn away, she throws her arms about him and presses her lips to his.*]

ZERO (*freeing himself*). Wait a minute! Let me get my wind!

[*He limps to the tree and seats himself under it, gasping for breath.* DAISY *looks after him, her spirits rather dampened.*]

ZERO. Whew! I sure am winded! I ain't used to dancin'. (*He takes off his collar and tie and opens the neckband of his shirt.* DAISY *sits under the tree near him, looking at him longingly. But he is busy catching his breath.*) Gee, my heart's goin' a mile a minute.

DAISY. Why don't you lay down an' rest? You could put your head on my lap.

ZERO. That ain't a bad idea. (*He stretches out, his head in* DAISY'S *lap.*)

DAISY (*fondling his hair*). It was swell, wasn't it?

ZERO. Yeh. But you gotta be used to it.

DAISY. Just imagine if we could stay here all the time—you an' me together—wouldn't it be swell?

ZERO. Yeh. But there ain't a chance.

DAISY. Won't they let us stay?

ZERO. No. This place is only for the good ones.

DAISY. Well, we ain't so bad, are we?

ZERO. Go on! Me a murderer an' you committin' suicide. Anyway, they wouldn't stand for this—the way we been goin' on.

DAISY. I don't see why.

ZERO. You don't! You know it ain't right. Ain't I got a wife?

DAISY. Not any more you ain't. When you're dead, that ends it. Don't they always say "until death do us part?"

ZERO. Well, maybe you're right about that, but they wouldn't stand for us here.

DAISY. It would be swell—the two of us together—we could make up for all them years.

ZERO. Yeh, I wish we could.

DAISY. We sure were fools. But I don't care. I've got you now. (*She kisses his forehead and cheeks and mouth.*)

ZERO. I'm sure crazy about you. I never saw you lookin' so pretty before, with your cheeks all red. An' your hair hangin' down. You got swell hair. (*He fondles and kisses her hair.*)

DAISY (*ecstatically*). We got each other now, ain't we?

ZERO. Yeh. I'm crazy about you. Daisy! That's a pretty name. It's a flower, ain't it? Well—that's what you are—just a flower.

DAISY (*happily*). We can always be together now, can't we?

ZERO. As long as they'll let us. I sure am crazy about you. (*Suddenly he sits upright.*) Watch your step!

DAISY (*alarmed*). What's the matter?

ZERO (*nervously*). He's comin' back.

DAISY. Oh, is that all? Well, what about it?

ZERO. You don't want him to see us layin' around like this, do you?

DAISY. I don't care if he does.

ZERO. Well, you oughta care. You don't want him to think you ain't a refined girl, do you? He's an awful moral bird, he is.

DAISY. I don't care nothin' about him. I don't care nothin' about anybody but you.

ZERO. Sure, I know. But we don't want people talkin' about us. You better fix your hair an' pull down your skirts.

[DAISY *complies rather sadly. They are both silent as* SHRDLU *enters.*]

ZERO (*with feigned nonchalance*). Well, you got back all right, didn't you?

SHRDLU. I hope I haven't returned too soon.

ZERO. No, that's all right. We were just havin' a little talk. You know—about business an' things.

DAISY (*boldly*). We were wishin' we could stay here all the time.

SHRDLU. You may if you like.

ZERO *and* DAISY (*in astonishment*). What!

SHRDLU. Yes. Any one who likes may remain—

ZERO. But I thought you were tellin' me—

SHRDLU. Just as I told you, only the most favored do remain. But any one may.

ZERO. I don't get it. There's a catch in it somewheres.

DAISY. It don't matter as long as we can stay.

ZERO (*to* SHRDLU). We were thinkin' about gettin' married, see?

SHRDLU. You may or not, just as you like.

ZERO. You don't mean to say we could stay if we didn't, do you?

SHRDLU. Yes. They don't care.

ZERO. An' there's some here that ain't married?

SHRDLU. Yes.

ZERO (*to* DAISY). I don't know about this place, at that. They must be kind of a mixed crowd.

DAISY. It don't matter, so long as we got each other.

ZERO. Yeh, I know, but you don't want to mix with people that ain't respectable.

DAISY (*to* SHRDLU). Can we get married

right away? I guess there must be a lot of ministers here, ain't there?

SHRDLU. Not as many as I had hoped to find. The two who seem most beloved are Dean Swift and the Abbé Rabelais. They are both much admired for some indecent tales which they have written.

ZERO (*shocked*). What! Ministers writin' smutty stories! Say, what kind of a dump is this, anyway?

SHRDLU (*despairingly*). I don't know, Mr. Zero. All these people here are so strange, so unlike the good people I've known. They seem to think of nothing but enjoyment or of wasting their time in profitless occupations. Some paint pictures from morning until night, or carve blocks of stone. Others write songs or put words together, day in and day out. Still others do nothing but lie under the trees and look at the sky. There are men who spend all their time reading books and women who think only of adorning themselves. And forever they are telling stories and laughing and singing and drinking and dancing. There are drunkards, thieves, vagabonds, blasphemers, adulterers. There is one—

ZERO. That's enough. I heard enough. (*He seats himself and begins putting on his shoes.*)

DAISY (*anxiously*). What are you goin' to do?

ZERO. I'm goin' to beat it, that's what I'm goin' to do.

DAISY. You said you liked it here.

ZERO (*looking at her in amazement*). Liked it! Say, you don't mean to say you want to stay here, do you, with a lot of rummies an' loafers an' bums?

DAISY. We don't have to bother with them. We can just sit here together an' look at the flowers an' listen to the music.

SHRDLU (*eagerly*). Music! Did you hear music?

DAISY. Sure. Don't you hear it?

SHRDLU. No, they say it never stops. But I've never heard it.

ZERO (*listening*). I thought I heard it before, but I don't hear nothin' now. I guess I must 'a' been dreamin'. (*Looking about.*) What's the quickest way out of this place?

DAISY (*pleadingly*). Won't you stay just a little longer?

ZERO. Didn't yer hear me say I'm goin'? Good-bye, Miss Devore. I'm goin' to beat it. (*He limps off at the right.* DAISY *follows him slowly.*)

DAISY (*to* SHRDLU). I won't ever see him again.

SHRDLU. Are you goin' to stay here?

DAISY. It don't make no difference now. Without him I might as well be alive.

[*She goes off right.* SHRDLU *watches her a moment, then sighs, and, seating himself under the tree, buries his head on his arm. Curtain falls.*]

SCENE SEVEN

Before the curtain rises the clicking of an adding machine is heard. The curtain rises upon an office similar in appearance to that in Scene Two, except that there is a door in the back wall through which can be seen a glimpse of the corridor outside. In the middle of the room ZERO *is seated completely absorbed in the operation of an adding machine. He presses the keys and pulls the lever with mechanical precision. He still wears his full-dress suit, but he has added to it sleeve protectors and a green eye-shade. A strip of white paper-tape flows steadily from the machine as* ZERO *operates. The room is filled with this tape—streamers, festoons, billows of it everywhere. It covers the floor and the furniture, it climbs the walls and chokes the doorways. A few moments later,* LIEUTENANT CHARLES *and* JOE *enter at the left.* LIEUTENANT CHARLES *is middle-aged and inclined to corpulence. He has an air of world-weariness. He is barefooted, wears a Panama hat, and is dressed in bright-red tights which are a very bad fit—too tight in some places, badly wrinkled in others.* JOE *is a youth with a smutty face dressed in dirty blue overalls.*

CHARLES (*after contemplating* ZERO *for a few moments*). All right, Zero, cease firing.

ZERO (*looking up, surprised*). Whaddja say?

CHARLES. I said stop punching that machine.

ZERO (*bewildered*). Stop? (*He goes on working mechanically.*)

CHARLES (*impatiently*). Yes. Can't you stop? Here, Joe, give me a hand. He can't stop.

[JOE *and* CHARLES *each take one of* ZERO'S *arms and with enormous effort detach him from the machine. He resists passively— mere inertia. Finally they succeed and swing him around on his stool.* CHARLES *and* JOE *mop their foreheads.*]

ZERO (*querulously*). What's the idea? Can't you lemme alone?

CHARLES (*ignoring the question*). How long have you been here?

ZERO. Jes' twenty-five years. Three hundred months, ninety-one hundred and thirty-one days, one hundred thirty-six thousand—

CHARLES (*impatiently*). That'll do! That'll do!

ZERO (*proudly*). I ain't missed a day, not an hour, not a minute. Look at all I got done. (*He points to the maze of paper.*)

CHARLES. It's time to quit.

ZERO. Quit? Whaddye mean quit? I ain't goin' to quit!

CHARLES. You've got to.

ZERO. What for? What do I have to quit for?

CHARLES. It's time for you to go back.

ZERO. Go back where? Whaddya talkin' about?

CHARLES. Back to earth, you dub. Where do you think?

ZERO. Aw, go on, Cap, who are you kiddin'?

CHARLES. I'm not kidding anybody. And don't call me Cap. I'm a lieutenant.

ZERO. All right, Lieutenant, all right. But what's this you're tryin' to tell me about goin' back?

CHARLES. Your time's up, I'm telling you. You must be pretty thick. How many times do you want to be told a thing?

ZERO. This is the first time I heard about goin' back. Nobody ever said nothin' to me about it before.

CHARLES. You didn't think you were going to stay here forever, did you?

ZERO. Sure. Why not? I did my bit, didn't I? Forty-five years of it. Twenty-five years in the store. Then the boss canned me and I knocked him cold. I guess you ain't heard about that—

CHARLES (*interrupting*). I know all about that. But what's that got to do with it?

ZERO. Well, I done my bit, didn't I? That oughta let me out.

CHARLES (*jeeringly*). So you think you're all through, do you?

ZERO. Sure, I do. I did the best I could while I was there, and then I passed out. And now I'm sittin' pretty here.

CHARLES. You've got a fine idea of the way they run things, you have. Do you think they're going to all of the trouble of making a soul just to use it once?

ZERO. Once is often enough, it seems to me.

CHARLES. It seems to you, does it? Well, who are you? And what do you know about it? Why, man, they use a soul over and over again—over and over until it's worn out.

ZERO. Nobody ever told me.

CHARLES. So you thought you were all through, did you? Well, that's a hot one, that is.

ZERO (*sullenly*). How was I to know?

CHARLES. Use your brains! Where would we put them all? We're crowded enough as it is. Why, this place is nothing but a kind of repair and service station—a sort of cosmic laundry, you might say. We get the souls in here by the bushelful. Then we get busy and clean them up. And you ought to see some of them. The muck and the slime. Phoo! And as full of holes as a flour-sifter. But we fix them up. We disinfect them and give them a kerosene rub and mend the holes, and back they go—practically as good as new.

ZERO. You mean to say I've been here before—before the last time, I mean?

CHARLES. Been here before! Why, you poor boob—you've been here thousands of times—fifty thousand, at least.

ZERO (*suspiciously*). How is it I don't remember nothin' about it?

CHARLES. Well—that's partly because you're stupid. But it's mostly because that's the way they fix it. (*Musingly.*) They're funny that way—every now and then they'll do something white like that—when you'd least expect it. I guess economy's at the bottom of it, though. They figure that the souls would get worn out quicker if they remembered.

ZERO. And don't any of 'em remember?

CHARLES. Oh, some do. You see there's different types: there's the type that gets a little better each time it goes back—we just give them a wash and send them right through. Then there's another type—the type that gets a little worse each time. That's where 10 you belong!

ZERO (*offended*). Me? You mean to say I'm gettin' worse all the time?

CHARLES (*nodding*). Yes. A little worse each time.

ZERO. Well—what was I when I started? Somethin' big?—A king or somethin'?

CHARLES (*laughing derisively*). A king! That's a good one! I'll tell you what you were the first time—if you want 20 to know so much—a monkey.

ZERO (*shocked and offended*). A monkey!

CHARLES (*nodding*). Yes, sir—just a hairy, chattering, long-tailed monkey.

ZERO. That musta been a long time ago.

CHARLES. Oh, not so long. A million years or so. Seems like yesterday to me.

ZERO. Then look here, whaddya mean by sayin' I'm gettin' worse all the 30 time?

CHARLES. Just what I said. You weren't so bad as a monkey. Of course, you did just what all the other monkeys did, but still it kept you out in the open air. And you weren't women-shy—there was one little red-headed monkey—Well, never mind. Yes, sir, you weren't so bad then. But even in those days there must have been some 40 bigger and brainier monkey that you kow-towed to. The mark of the slave was on you from the start.

ZERO (*sullenly*). You ain't very particular about what you call people, are you?

CHARLES. You wanted the truth, didn't you? If there ever was a soul in the world that was labelled slave, it's yours. Why, all the bosses and kings that there ever were have left their trademarks on your backside.

ZERO. It ain't fair, if you ask me.

CHARLES (*shrugging his shoulders*). Don't tell me about it. I don't make the rules. All I know is you've been getting worse—worse each time. Why, even six thousand years ago you weren't so bad. That was the time you were hauling stones for one of those big pyramids in a place they call Africa. Ever hear of the pyramids?

ZERO. Them big pointy things?

CHARLES (*nodding*). That's it.

ZERO. I seen a picture of them in the movies.

CHARLES. Well, you helped build them. It was a long step down from the happy days in the jungle, but it was a good job—even though you didn't know what you were doing and your back was striped by the foreman's whip. But you've been going down, down. Two thousand years ago you were a Roman galley-slave. You were on one of the triremes that knocked the Carthaginian fleet for a goal. Again the whip. But you had muscles then—chest muscles, back muscles, biceps. (*He feels* ZERO's *arm gingerly and turns away in disgust.*) Phoo! A bunch of mush!

[*He notices that* JOE *has fallen asleep. Walking over, he kicks him in the shin.*]

CHARLES. Wake up, you mutt! Where do you think you are! (*He turns to* ZERO *again.*) And then another thousand years and you were a serf—a lump of clay digging up other lumps of clay. You wore an iron collar then—white ones hadn't been invented yet. Another long step down. But where you dug, potatoes grew and that helped fatten the pigs. Which was something. And now—well, I don't want to rub it in—

ZERO. Rub it in is right! Seems to me I got a pretty healthy kick comin'. I ain't had a square deal! Hard work! That's all I've ever had!

CHARLES (*callously*). What else were you ever good for? 10

ZERO. Well, that ain't the point. The point is I'm through! I had enough! Let 'em find somebody else to do the dirty work. I'm sick of bein' the goat! I quit right here and now!

[*He glares about defiantly. There is a thunder-clap and a bright flash of lightning.*]

ZERO (*screaming*). Ooh! What's that? (*He clings to* CHARLES.)

CHARLES. It's all right. Nobody's going 20 to hurt you. It's just their way of tell-ing you that they don't like you to talk that way. Pull yourself together and calm down. You can't change the rules—nobody can—they've got it all fixed. It's a rotten system—but what are you going to do about it?

ZERO. Why can't they stop pickin' on me? I'm satisfied here—doin' my day's work. I don't want to go back. 30

CHARLES. You've got to, I tell you. There's no way out of it.

ZERO. What chance have I got—at my age? Who'll give me a job?

CHARLES. You big boob, you don't think you're going back the way you are, do you?

ZERO. Sure; how then?

CHARLES. Why, you've got to start all over. 40

ZERO. All over?

CHARLES (*nodding*). You'll be a baby again—a bald, red-faced little ani-mal, and then you'll go through it all again. There'll be millions of others like you—all with their mouths open, squalling for food. And then when you get a little older you'll begin to learn things—and you'll learn all the wrong things and learn them all in the wrong way. You'll eat the wrong food and wear the wrong clothes and you'll live in swarming dens where there's no light and no air! You'll learn to be a liar and a bully and a braggart and a coward and a sneak. You'll learn to fear the sunlight and to hate beauty. By that time you'll be ready for school. There they'll tell you the truth about a great many things that you don't give a damn about and they'll tell you lies about all the things you ought to know—and about all the things you want to know they'll tell you nothing at all. When you get through you'll be equipped for your life-work. You'll be ready to take a job.

ZERO (*eagerly*). What'll my job be? An-other adding machine?

CHARLES. Yes. But not one of these anti-quated adding machines. It will be a superb, super-hyper-adding machine, as far from this old piece of junk as you are from God. It will be some-thing to make you sit up and take no-tice, that adding machine. It will be an adding machine which will be in-stalled in a coal mine and which will record the individual output of each miner. As each miner down in the lower galleries takes up a shovelful of coal, the impact of his shovel will au-tomatically set in motion a graphite pencil in your gallery. The pencil will make a mark in white upon a blackened, sensitized drum. Then your work comes in. With the great toe of your right foot you release a lever which focuses a violet ray on the drum. The ray, playing upon and through the white mark, falls upon a selenium cell which in turn sets the keys of the adding apparatus in motion. In this way the individual output of each miner is recorded without any human effort except the slight pressure of the great toe of your right foot.

ZERO. (in breathless, round-eyed wonder). Say, that'll be some machine, won't it?

CHARLES. Some machine is right. It will be the culmination of human effort— the final triumph of the evolutionary process. For millions of years the nebulous gases swirled in space. For more millions of years the gases cooled and then through inconceivable ages they hardened into rocks. And then came life. Floating green things on the waters that covered the earth. More millions of years and a step upward— an animate organism in the ancient slime. And so on—step by step, down through the ages—a gain here, a gain there—the mollusc, the fish, the reptile, the mammal, man! And all so that you might sit in the gallery of a coal mine and operate the super-hyper-adding machine with the great toe of your right foot!

ZERO. Well, then—I ain't so bad, after all.

CHARLES. You're a failure, Zero, a failure. A waste product. A slave to a contraption of steel and iron. The animal's instincts, but not his strength and skill. The animal's appetites, but not his unashamed indulgence of them. True, you move and eat and digest and excrete and reproduce. But any microscopic organism can do as much. Well—time's up! Back you go—back to your sunless groove—the raw material of slums and wars—the ready prey of the first jingo or demagogue or political ad-

venturer who takes the trouble to play upon your ignorance and credulity and provincialism. You poor, spineless, brainless boob—I'm sorry for you!

ZERO (falling to his knees). Then keep me here! Don't send me back! Let me stay!

CHARLES. Get up. Didn't I tell you I can't do anything for you? Come on, time's up!

ZERO. I can't! I can't! I'm afraid to go through it all again.

CHARLES. You've got to, I tell you. Come on, now!

ZERO. What did you tell me so much for? Couldn't you just let me go, thinkin' everythin' was goin' to be all right?

CHARLES. You wanted to know, didn't you?

ZERO. How did I know what you were goin' to tell me? Now I can't stop thinkin' about it! I can't stop thinkin'! I'll be thinkin' about it all the time.

CHARLES. All right! I'll do the best I can for you. I'll send a girl with you to keep you company.

ZERO. A girl? What for? What good will a girl do me?

CHARLES. She'll help make you forget.

ZERO (eagerly). She will? Where is she?

CHARLES. Wait a minute, I'll call her. (He calls in a loud voice.) Oh! Hope! Yoo-hoo! (He turns his head aside and says in the manner of a ventriloquist imitating a distant feminine voice.) Ye-es. (Then in his own voice.) Come here, will you? There's a fellow who wants you to take him back. (Ventriloquously again.) All right. I'll be right over, Charlie dear. (He turns to ZERO.) Kind of familiar, isn't she? Charlie dear!

ZERO. What did you say her name is?

CHARLES. Hope. H-o-p-e.

ZERO. Is she good-lookin'?

CHARLES. Is she good-looking! Oh, boy, wait until you see her! She's a blonde with big blue eyes and red lips and little white teeth and—

ZERO. Say, that listens good to me. Will she be long?

CHARLES. She'll be here right away. There she is now! Do you see her?

ZERO. No. Where?

CHARLES. Out in the corridor. No, not there. Over farther. To the right. Don't you see her blue dress? And the sunlight on her hair?

ZERO. Oh, sure! Now I see her! What's the matter with me, anyhow? Say, she's some jane! Oh, you baby vamp!

CHARLES. She'll make you forget your troubles.

ZERO. What troubles are you talkin' about?

CHARLES. Nothing. Go on. Don't keep her waiting.

ZERO. You bet I won't. Oh, Hope! Wait for me! I'll be right with you! I'm on my way!

[*He stumbles out eagerly.* JOE *bursts into uproarious laughter.*]

CHARLES (*eyeing him in surprise and anger*). What in hell's the matter with you?

JOE (*shaking with laughter*). Did you get that? He thinks he saw somebody and he's following her! (*He rocks with laughter.*)

CHARLES (*punching him in the jaw*). Shut your face!

JOE (*nursing his jaw*). What's the idea? Can't I even laugh when I see something funny?

CHARLES. Funny! You keep your mouth shut or I'll show you something funny. Go on, hustle out of here and get something to clean up this mess with. There's another fellow moving in. Hurry now.

[*He makes a threatening gesture.* JOE *exits hastily.* CHARLES *goes to a chair and seats himself. He looks weary and dispirited.*]

CHARLES (*shaking his head*). Hell, I'll tell the world this is a lousy job! (*He takes a flask from his pocket, uncorks it, and slowly drains it.*)

CURTAIN

MAXWELL ANDERSON

MAXWELL ANDERSON inherited the position of first American dramatist when Eugene O'Neill temporarily withdrew from the theatre in the early 1930's. He was awarded the Pulitzer prize for *Both Your Houses* in 1933, the year of O'Neill's *Ah, Wilderness!* In 1936 he was given the first Critics' Circle award for *Winterset;* he received the award again in 1937 for *High Tor*. These critical honors merely made official the position which Anderson had already come to occupy in the opinion of the public. They crowned more than a decade of accomplishment in the theatre and in dramatic literature. For Anderson's plays at their best have achieved the rare distinction of being at the same time successful on the competitive New York stage and important contributions to American literature.

Anderson was a minister's son, born on December 15, 1888, in Atlantic, a small railroad village in northwestern Pennsylvania, a few miles from the Ohio border where his father was pastor of the Baptist church. He was much moved about in his youth, chiefly westward, to Ohio and Iowa; and then into North Dakota when Anderson was nineteen and ready for college. He entered the University of North Dakota at Grand Forks, and was graduated in 1911. Dr. Frederick H. Koch, head of the department of dramatic art and director of the Carolina Playmakers at the University of North Carolina, was then an assistant professor at North Dakota, where in 1910 he founded the Dakota Playmakers. Anderson was under good tutelage on the far western plains. After graduation he taught school in North Dakota, and worked on the Grand Forks *Herald* before going on to California. He enrolled in the graduate school at Leland Stanford where he taught English and took an M.A. degree in 1914. He also taught for a brief period at Whittier College, California, but was dismissed, it is reported, for his pacifistic views in the early days of the World War.

It is doubtful in any event if the academic life of a small college in that period could long have nourished the inquiring spirit of Maxwell Anderson. He was ambitious in other and wider directions. He moved into the more animated currents of newspaper work. He wrote editorials for the San Francisco *Bulletin*, but his opinions were too forthright for that nervous time and Anderson moved on, first to the San Francisco *Chronicle*, then straight into New York in 1918. He was an editorial writer on the *New Republic*, then joined the *Evening Globe*, and finally, and more happily, the *Morning World*, where he stayed until 1924. In the meantime he had been working on his first play, *White Desert*. It failed after twelve nights in the autumn of 1923; but on September 3, 1924, his *What Price Glory?*, written in collaboration with Laurence Stallings, was produced with huge success. Thereupon Anderson was both encouraged and enabled to follow his ambition to give his energies to writing for the theatre.

These first two plays had a certain connection with Anderson's thirty-five years of experiences. *White Desert* was set in and around a claim shack on a snow-covered North Dakota prairie in blizzard-lashed mid-winter. It studied the effect of jealousy on Michael Kane. His suspicions of his young wife Mary finally led her in anger and resentment to give them grounds with their neighbor, Sverre Peterson. Michael killed her with a shotgun. The grim tragedy was graced by the careful diction and rhythm which the editorial writer and ex-English instructor employed in the writing of this drama in verse.

Anderson was distressed over the stage failure of *White Desert*, but he was soon absorbed in the collaboration with his colleague, Laurence Stallings. Stallings, a young graduate of Wake Forest College (1915), had left his job as reporter on the Atlantic *Journal* in 1917 to enlist in the U.S. Marines. He served in France, became a captain, and had a leg shattered at Château-Thierry. Completely disillusioned with the romance of war, he enrolled in Georgetown University and took a graduate degree in 1922 with a view toward entering the academic life. He went into newspaper work instead, first in Washington, then as drama critic and book reviewer in "The First Reader" column of the *World*. The views of the two men were one, their experiences and their temperaments in this case perfectly complementary.

What Price Glory? was the fruit of this conjunction of talent. Its success was not only resounding; it was phenomenal. It was the first, and is still among the best, of the American plays dealing with the World War. Its vocabulary was more realistic than any previously spoken on the American stage, and it no doubt helped to break down resistance to the profanity and uncensored words that later became so common in stage dialogue. It forced upon American audiences some understanding of the mud, filth, brutality, and animal horror of war. But it presented its message by implication in a play capably mixed with comic relief, with broad characterizations of Sergeant Quirt and Captain Flagg, and with the manner and salty speech of the soldiers themselves. The play did not go far below the surface aspects of war as a process of life. Later war plays by other authors probed more deeply than Flagg's analysis, expressive of the controlling viewpoint of the play, when he said, "There's something rotten about this profession of arms, some kind of damned religion connected with it that you can't shake. When they tell you to die, you have to do it, even if you're a better man than they are." Yet the debunking of the romantic incitements to war were earnest enough, and *What Price Glory?* was rousing in its own terms as a piece for the theatre.

Anderson worked vigorously at his new calling, but without catching the public fancy again for several seasons. Between September 7 and October 2, 1925, three Anderson plays were produced without commercial success. The first was an adaptation of Jim Tully's novel *Beggars of Life*, called *Outside Looking In*. The other two were romantic-historical plays, written with Laurence Stallings: *First Flight*, about Andrew Jackson in his young duelling days; and *The Buccaneer*, presenting the colorful seventeenth-century pirate who sacked the city of Panama, Captain Henry Morgan. These plays had many good points, and the strong element of individualism and rebellion characteristic of all of Anderson's work; but they were ineffective theatre.

Anderson returned again in January

1927 with a well-made play, *Saturday's Children*, about the contemporary problem of young love and marriage in the American middle class where the standards of living outrun the income. Its comparative success was due in large part to its make-believe device of semiclandestine meetings between the young couple to solve the problem of keeping romance in marriage when the rent is due; and to Ruth Gordon who played the young wife, Bobby. Bobby says, "I think all day how marvelous it's going to be when you come home—and then you get here—and I don't know—it isn't marvelous at all—It's just a house and we're just married people—and—sometimes I hate it. Everything's getting spoiled—" So Bobby takes a room at Mrs. Gorlik's boarding house in East 33rd St. There in the last act her husband slips in to see her, and as the curtain falls on the little comedy of those who work hard for a living, he is fitting a bolt to the door. The play was not very important except as a playable piece with a certain edge to it.

Anderson's heated interest in the issues raised by the execution of Sacco and Vanzetti was expressed in *Gods of the Lightning*, written with Harold Hickerson, and produced in October, 1928. It was a courageous and a zealous play on the miscarriage of justice. Though it was not well received on stage, it pointed toward the triumph of *Winterset* in the next decade. The following January, Anderson's *Gypsy* entered upon a run of two months. This Ibsenish study of a woman who failed to achieve freedom was considered good enough by Burns Mantel, in comparison at least with the other offerings of the season, to be included in his *The Best Plays of 1928–1929*. The public stayed away.

The year 1929 marked an abrupt turning point in Anderson's career as a playwright. His high place in American drama rests almost completely upon the work he has done since *Gypsy*. It began with *Elizabeth the Queen*, produced by the Theatre Guild, November 3, 1930, with Alfred Lunt and Lynn Fontanne. This play was the outgrowth of a general revolution in Anderson's approach to the theatre and to dramatic expression. In an address on "The Essence of Tragedy" delivered at the Modern Language Association at Columbia in 1938 Anderson surveyed his career, noted the failures he had experienced, and said that he had gone back over the history of drama and dramatic theory from the Greeks to the present to see what the immutable laws of tragic drama are. He did not expect to find an infallible recipe for success, but he hoped to discover the principles without which success was at least most unlikely. Read with this purpose, the great plays from the past took on new meaning for him, and he rediscovered Aristotle. He observed the exaltation of language, its cadence and its rhythm in the supreme tragedies. He was impressed by the way noble characters confronted the powers outside themselves, or their own weaknesses, that overwhelmed them, and the paradox of victory in defeat and self-conquest in the face of annihilation. And he saw that, despite the assurance of modern critics that this old concept of tragedy was replaced by that of blind, impersonal social forces crushing to death a poor naturalistic weakling like Falder in *Justice* and Griffiths in *The Case of Clyde Griffiths*, audiences still wanted to leave the theatre believing in something noble and good. The function of the dramatist, as of the poet, is to show man that he is better than he thinks he is.

These mature views on dramatic art coincided with the shift in the public mood from the sophisticated revelry of the 1920's to the sobriety of the perturbed 1930's. Historical themes centering around heroic figures were again acceptable. Even the realistic writers were ready to admit that exact reporting of the objective facts of life in faithfully recorded dialogue had been carried almost as far as it could go, and certainly as far as it was useful. Anderson sensed this temper of the times and gave it expression in a series of plays in verse, or cadenced prose. These plays caught the attention of the 1930's, just as O'Neill's dramas had captured the imagination of the preceding decade. Audiences were surprised and delighted to experience again the pleasure of hearing the language of poetry beautifully spoken on the modern stage. A lost dimension was restored to the theatre. With the exception of the satirical comedy on Congress, *Both Your Houses* (1933), Anderson's output since 1930 has been in conformity with his expressed views on the essence of tragedy.

In *Elizabeth the Queen, Mary of Scotland* (1933), and *Valley Forge* (1934), Anderson had at hand and ready for use historical figures of great stature already firmly supported by their incomparable legends. They were perfectly suited to the purpose of his experiment in poetic tragedy. They were far enough in the past to enjoy a halo of romance, yet near enough in spirit to be integrated with our living present. A studied style, a slightly archaic diction, and a loose blank verse seemed quite appropriate to Elizabeth, Mary, and even George Washington. In choosing these renowned characters, therefore, Anderson was following the recipe which he had formulated after his fresh survey of

world drama: "that poetic tragedy had never been successfully written about its own place and time"; and that "there is not one tragedy by Aeschylus, Sophocles, Euripides, Shakespeare, Corneille or Racine which did not have the advantage of a setting either far away or long ago." And to these remarks in the preface to *Winterset* he adds, "With this admonition in mind I wrote *Elizabeth the Queen* and a succession of historical plays in verse. . . ."

The enthusiastic reception given to *Elizabeth the Queen* and *Mary of Scotland* by critics and theatre goers alike was concrete proof that audiences were willing to grant the author's assumptions. The language had beauty and dignity and at the same time ease and naturalness. In the tense scenes it attained sweep and a lift of power. The comparative failure of *Valley Forge* was not due to its shortcomings as verse drama, for it has some memorable passages in it, but to its decentralization of the potent appeal of Washington himself and hence its structural weakness as a theatre play. The question still remained, however, whether it would be possible to create tragic poetry out of the men and issues among whom the dramatist lives. Anderson had made two attempts with noncontemporary materials which were not exactly heartening—his first play, *White Desert*, and, somewhat more remote, *Night over Taos* (1932), in which he used for a setting the New Mexico of 1847 to portray the overthrow of the Spanish feudal aristocracy, represented by the patriarch Montoya, by the rising capitalistic giant state to the North. But, reassured by the response of later audiences whose taste he had helped to form, and by his growing mastery of the verse play, Anderson decided to attempt the experiment anew, with full knowledge of the fact that "the great masters themselves never tried to make tragic poetry out of the stuff of their own times."

The result of this experiment was *Winterset*, which opened in late September, 1935, with Burgess Meredith as Mio, and with a superlative supporting cast. The play was another triumph for Anderson. In many respects it is his greatest creation. He had no legendary Elizabeth or Mary, no Father of his Country to carry the play. He had only the appeal of a lowly outcast, a restrained indignation against evil, and an exalted sense of human dignity with which to invest with the essence of tragedy these lives in the sombre street beneath the bridge. But nothing more was needed. It was a memorable experience, not easily dimmed, to see the performance of *Winterset;* it is likewise a memorable experience to read the script. Stark Young did not exaggerate when he called *Winterset* "the most notable effort in the poetic dramatic medium that, up to now, we have had in the American theatre."

Winterset was buttressed in its tragic emotion by its indirect use of the Sacco and Vanzetti case which, as we have noted, Anderson had already dramatized in *The Gods of the Lightning*. The emphasis, however, falls not upon the basic melodrama of the swift-paced action, but upon the enduring themes of the nature of abstract justice and its relation to the practical administration of the courts; the study of vengeance; the power of love and the fundamental integrity of the mind to ennoble these dismal lives with a cloak of human dignity; and the exhilaration of victory in the soul through death in the flesh. For a purpose so exalted, language at its peak of intensity, beauty, and expressiveness was not only appropriate, it was compulsory.

Anderson brought to the writing of the play his full resources as a dramatic poet. He created an exact, easy-flowing, cadenced style somewhere between blank verse and economical, realistic speech to give utterance to his themes. In this regard he was following, with the authority of his own developed artistry, the practice of the great tragic dramatists before him. It is incontrovertibly the function of playwrights to record the speech of the time and to reproduce it for the stage on the tongues of characters realistically presented, as *Dead End*, for example, presented them. It is also the responsibility of dramatists to give the fullest possible expression to their characters by lending to them winged words to phrase their dim and halting thoughts and emotions as they would be phrased if the feeling and the words were one. Anderson chose to accept this responsibility in *Winterset*. Of course the vagrant Mio did not speak as Anderson represents him as speaking. His love for Miriamne would, in the *Dead End* realism, have been expressed in a few monosyllables. Anderson gave wisdom and the power of reflection to the bewildered minds, he gave emotion to the disturbed hearts, he gave beauty and precision of language to the inarticulate and the mute.

Something like a meteoric shower of plays by Anderson burst into production after *Winterset: The Wingless Victory* on December 23, 1936; *High Tor* on January 9, 1937; *The Masque of Kings* on February 8, 1937; *The Star-Wagon* on September 29, 1937; *Knickerbocker Holiday* on October 19, 1938; and *Key Largo* on November 27, 1939—the last two produced by the newly organized Playwrights' Producing Company made up of Maxwell Anderson, Robert Sherwood, Elmer Rice, S. N. Behrman, and the late Sidney Howard.

These plays had a kind of Anderson formula but they were remarkably varied in subject and in form; in fact three of them, *High Tor*, *The Star-Wagon*, and *Knickerbocker Holiday*, were novelties. All exploited to the full the fresh popularity of Anderson's free verse rhythm—all except *The Star-Wagon*. This popular comedy, set in a typical small Ohio industrial town somewhere to the west of Anderson's own birthplace, used the device of a time machine "Star-Wagon" to project Steve, his friend Hanus, and his wife Martha, backward some thirty-five years from their arid fifties to the year 1902. "What are you going to do—now you're back here, Steve?" Hanus asks. "I'm going to change everything." But he doesn't. Only one short scene at the close of the second act and Stephen's final speech are in verse. The rest is in realistic, sometimes rather boisterous prose. *Knickerbocker Holiday* was an exuberant, topical libretto-drama, in the Gilbert and Sullivan tradition, accompanied by the music of Kurt Weill. It was set back in 1647, was gay with comedy, but bore at all times a serious overtone of political comment which was made specific in Anderson's preface to the play in such aphorisms as "Men who are fed by their government will soon be driven down to the status of slaves or cattle." The "message," however, was pretty well overshadowed by the tumultuous Pieter Stuyvesant on his silver leg, and by the bold stagebusiness of the comedy.

The other four plays, though evidently done somewhat hastily, and perhaps too facilely, were all serious in purpose and distinguished in whole or in part for their poetic treatment of themes interesting as dramatic material and important in their bearing upon the stresses of contemporary life. *The Wingless Victory* was a study of race hatred, and of human dignity rising to tragic heights in the surcharged emotional impact of the final scene. Its setting in Puritan New England merely lent perspective to a theme of paramount concern to the present day. *High Tor* made good capital of the legend-haunted mountains overhanging the Hudson River near New City where Anderson lives. It dramatized, and brought to bear upon the present moment, the traditional individualism of the Daniel Boone-Henry David Thoreau tradition in conflict with expanding, industrialized America. Its daring combination of the ghosts of Hudson's men, of Van Dorn's love-fantasy, and a modern steam-shovel holding two shyster exploiters suspended in mid-air above the symbolic Tor, made for exhilarating theatre even if it did not contribute greatly to the solution of the economic and philosophic problems which it undertook to discuss.

The Masque of Kings was also an effective stage piece because of the romance and tragedy inherent in the story of the mysterious death of Prince Rudolph of Austria and Mary Vetsera in the shooting lodge at Mayerling. Anderson, however, gave the episode a modern political slant by having Prince Rudolph attempt to found a just government upon revolution, only to abandon it and commit suicide when he saw that he was caught in the same insane processes that lead "fools like myself . . . to power to set men free And hold themselves in power by killing men." *Key Largo* used the disillusion that followed upon the revolution in Spain to study the question whether there is anything important enough to command loyalty even to death in this distraught world of ours. All these plays had moments of passion and great beauty, and all brought into the theatre some of the richness of a poet.

With this series of plays Anderson made the greatest continuous contribution to American drama during the decade of the 1930's. His work in the 1940's has been more uneven. In *Journey to Jerusalem* (1940) Anderson sought an answer to the problem of Hitler and the rule of force. He found it in "the mystery of the emergence of Jesus," and in the belief, through faith, "that there is purpose and pattern in the universe, that man can contribute to this purpose." His play is built around the episode of Jesus in the court of the Sanhedrin, "finding His way to the meaning of the universe as He walks alone among the columns." But even a great dramatist sometimes finds it embarrassing to teach an audience the meaning of the universe in a stage scene. The fundamental source of the play's failure is obvious.

Candle in the Wind (1941) was enhanced on the stage by Helen Hayes. Like *Watch on the Rhine*, it dramatized the terror of the Nazi plague spreading across Europe to threaten England.

Anderson's three plays about World War II show his grave concern over the nature and potential consequences of this global cataclysm. They were *The Eve of St. Mark* (1942), *Storm Operation* (1944), and *Truckline Cafe* (1945). They were deeply felt, and they had their moments of great power as Anderson tried to press home to Americans, removed from the combat theatres of the war, the true nature of the test they were facing and what it was like to the men who were fighting it. The plays were good of their kind and for the occasion.

After the war Anderson took a new direction which has linked his last two plays, *Joan of Lorraine* (1946) and *Anne of the Thousand Days* (1948), with his earlier series on historical subjects in a richly poetic vein. George Bernard Shaw's play about Saint Joan is a masterpiece and lives on undimmed with the passing years. Anderson entered heavy competition when he essayed another play with the same subject matter. It may be argued that he chose the easy approach by framing the story of the Maid as a play within a play instead of creating it boldly as self-contained drama. But an author must be permitted his own choice of method, and in the important test scenes where Joan emerges in her own right she causes one to forget that this is a rehearsal of a play set at a rehearsal. The speeches in which she dedicates her white armor at the altar, answers the Inquisitors, and states the faith she would follow "even to the fire" would distinguish a drama in any setting.

Anne of the Thousand Days seems stronger and more mature than the earlier Elizabeth and Mary plays. It deals in masterly fashion with Henry VIII and Anne Boleyn, the second of his six wives, and the first to be beheaded. The turbulent events of those three years in the early 1530's are always evident, but they are treated as a backdrop to the equally turbulent human relationships between two of the most colorful people in a riotous age.

Anderson has made, and is making, a rich contribution to the American stage. When he fails it is because he attempts too much and is hurrying along too fast; not because he is ever trivial. *Winterset*, in our opinion, shows his extraordinary qualities at their highest effectiveness up to this time.

WINTERSET

CHARACTERS

TROCK	HERMAN
SHADOW	LUCIA
GARTH	PINY
MIRIAMNE	A SAILOR
ESDRAS	STREET URCHIN
THE HOBO	POLICEMAN
1ST GIRL	RADICAL
2ND GIRL	SERGEANT
JUDGE GAUNT	*Non-speaking*
MIO	URCHINS
CARR	TWO MEN IN BLUE SERGE

ACT I

SCENE ONE

The scene is the bank of a river under a bridgehead. A gigantic span starts from the rear of the stage and appears to lift over the heads of the audience and out to the left. At the right rear is a wall of solid supporting masonry. To the left an apartment building abuts against the bridge and forms the left wall of the stage with a dark basement window and a door in the brick wall. To the right, and in the foreground, an outcropping of original rock makes a barricade behind which one may enter through a cleft. To the rear, against the masonry, two sheds have been built by waifs and strays for shelter. The river bank, in the foreground, is black rock worn smooth by years of trampling. There is room for exit and entrance to the left around the apartment house, also around the rock to the right. A single street lamp is seen at the left—and a glimmer of apartment lights in the background beyond. It is an early, dark December morning.

TWO YOUNG MEN IN SERGE *lean against the masonry, matching bills.* TROCK *and* SHADOW *come in from the left.*

TROCK. Go back and watch the car.
[*The* TWO YOUNG MEN *go out.* TROCK *walks to the corner and looks toward the city.*]
 You roost of punks and gulls! Sleep,
  sleep it off,
 whatever you had last night, get down
  in warm,

one big ham-fat against another—
sleep,
cling, sleep and rot! Rot out your
pasty guts
with diddling, you had no brain to begin. If you had
there'd be no need for us to sleep on
iron
who had too much brains for you.

SHADOW. Now look, Trock, look,   10
what would the warden say to talk
like that?

TROCK. May they die as I die!
By God, what life they've left me
they shall keep me well! I'll have that
out of them—
these pismires that walk like men!

SHADOW. Because, look, chief,
it's all against science and penology
for you to get out and begin to cuss 20
that way
before your prison vittles are out of
you. Hell,
you're supposed to leave the pen full
of high thought,
kind of noble-like, loving toward all
mankind,
ready to kiss their feet—or whatever
parts
they stick out toward you. Look at 30
me!

TROCK. I see you.
And even you may not live as long as
you think.
You think too many things are funny.
Well, laugh.
But it's not so funny.

SHADOW. Come on, Trock, you know me.
Anything you say goes, but give me
leave   40
to kid a little.

TROCK. Then laugh at somebody else!
it's a lot safer! They've soaked me
once too often
in that vat of poisoned hell they keep
up-state

to soak men in, and I'm rotten inside,
I'm all
one liquid puke inside where I had
lungs
once, like yourself! And now they
want to get me
and stir me in again—and that'd kill
me—
and that's fine for them. But before
that happens to me
a lot of these healthy boys'll know
what it's like
when you try to breathe and have no
place to put air—
they'll learn it from me!

SHADOW. They've got nothing on you,
chief.

TROCK. I don't know yet. That's what
I'm here to find out.
If they've got what they might have.
It's not a year this time—
no, nor ten. It's screwed down under
a lid.—
I can die quick enough, without help.

SHADOW. You're the skinny kind
that lives forever.

TROCK. He gave me a half a year,
the doc at the gate.

SHADOW. Jesus.

TROCK. Six months I get,
and the rest's dirt, six feet.

[LUCIA, *the street-piano man, comes in right
from behind the rock and goes to the shed
where he keeps his piano.* PINY, *the
apple-woman, follows and stands in the
entrance.* LUCIA *speaks to* ESTRELLA,
who still stands facing SHADOW.]

LUCIA. Morning.

[TROCK *and* SHADOW *go out round the apartment house without speaking.*]

PINY. Now what would you call them?

LUCIA. Maybe someting da river washed
up.

PINY. Nothing ever washed him—that
black one.

LUCIA. Maybe not, maybe so. More like

his pa and ma raise-a heem in da
cellar. (*He wheels out the piano.*)

PINY. He certainly gave me a turn.
(*She lays a hand on the rock.*)

LUCIA. You don' live-a right, ol' gal.
Take heem easy. Look on da
bright-a side. Never say-a die. Me,
every day in every way I getta be
da regular heller. (*He starts out.*)

CURTAIN

SCENE TWO

*A cellar apartment under the apartment
building, floored with cement and roofed with
huge boa constrictor pipes that run slantwise
from left to right, dwarfing the room. An outside door opens to the left and a door at the
right rear leads to the interior of the place. A
low squat window to the left. A table at the
rear and a few chairs and books make up the
furniture.* GARTH, *son of* ESDRAS, *sits alone,
holding a violin upside down to inspect a crack
at its base. He lays the bow on the floor and
runs his fingers over the joint.* MIRIAMNE *enters from the rear, a girl of fifteen.* GARTH
looks up, then down again.

MIRIAMNE. Garth—

GARTH. The glue lets go. It's the steam,
I guess.

It splits the hair on your head.

MIRIAMNE. It can't be mended?

GARTH. I can't mend it.

No doubt there are fellows somewhere

who'd mend it for a dollar—and glad
to do it.

That is if I had a dollar.—Got a dollar?

No, I thought not.

MIRIAMNE. Garth, you've sat at home
here

three days now. You haven't gone out
at all.

Something frightens you.

GARTH. Yes?

MIRIAMNE. And father's frightened.

He reads without knowing where.
When a shadow falls

across the page he waits for a blow to
follow

after the shadow. Then in a little while

he puts his book down softly and goes
out

to see who passed.

GARTH. A bill collector, maybe.

We haven't paid the rent.

MIRIAMNE. No.

GARTH. You're a bright girl, sis.—

You see too much. You run along and
cook.

Why don't you go to school?

MIRIAMNE. I don't like school.

They whisper behind my back.

GARTH. Yes? about what?

MIRIAMNE. What did the lawyer mean

that wrote to you?

GARTH (*rising*).

What lawyer?

MIRIAMNE. I found a letter

on the floor of your room. He said,

"Don't get me wrong,

but stay in out of the rain the next
few days,

just for instance."

GARTH. I thought I burned that letter.

MIRIAMNE. Afterward you did. And then

what was printed

about the Estrella gang—you hid it
from me,

you and father. What is it—about
this murder—?

GARTH. Will you shut up, you fool!

MIRIAMNE. But if you know

why don't you tell them, Garth?

If it's true—what they say—

you knew all the time Romagna
wasn't guilty,

and could have said so—

GARTH. Everybody knew

Romagna wasn't guilty! But they
weren't listening

to evidence in his favor. They didn't
want it.
They don't want it now.

MIRIAMNE. But was that why
they never called on you?—

GARTH. So far as I know
they never'd heard of me—and I can
assure you
I knew nothing about it—

MIRIAMNE. But something's wrong—   10
and it worries father—

GARTH. What could be wrong?

MIRIAMNE. I don't know.
                    [*A pause.*]

GARTH. And I don't know. You're a
good kid, Miriamne,
but you see too many movies. I wasn't
mixed up
in any murder, and I don't mean to
be.   20
If I had a dollar to get my fiddle fixed
and another to hire a hall, by God I'd
fiddle
some of the prodigies back into Sunday School
where they belong, but I won't get
either, and so
I sit here and bite my nails—but if
you hoped
I had some criminal romantic past   30
you'll have to look again!

MIRIAMNE. Oh, Garth, forgive me—
But I want you to be so far above such
things
nothing could frighten you. When you
seem to shrink
and be afraid, and you're the brother
I love,
I want to run there and cry, if there's
any question   40
they care to ask, you'll be quick and
glad to answer,
for there's nothing to conceal!

GARTH. And that's all true—

MIRIAMNE. But then I remember—
how you dim the lights—

and we go early to bed—and speak in
whispers—
and I could think there's a death
somewhere behind us—
an evil death—

GARTH (*hearing a step*).
Now for God's sake, be quiet!

[ESDRAS, *an old rabbi with a kindly face,
enters from the outside. He is hurried
and troubled.*]

ESDRAS. I wish to speak alone with someone here
if I may have this room. Miriamne—

MIRIAMNE (*turning to go*).
Yes, father.

[*The outer door is suddenly thrown open.*
TROCK *appears.*]

TROCK (*after a pause*).
You'll excuse me for not knocking.
(SHADOW *follows* TROCK *in.*)
Sometimes it's best to come in quiet.
Sometimes
it's a good way to go out. Garth's
home, I see.
He might not have been here if I
made a point
of knocking at doors.

GARTH. How are you, Trock?

TROCK. I guess
you can see how I am.
(*To* MIRIAMNE.)
Stay here. Stay where you are.
We'd like to make your acquaintance.
—If you want the facts
I'm no better than usual, thanks. Not
enough sun,
my physician tells me. Too much close
confinement.
A lack of exercise and an overplus
of beans in the diet. You've done well,
no doubt?

GARTH. I don't know what makes you
think so.

TROCK. Who's the family?

GARTH. My father and my sister.

TROCK. Happy to meet you.
  Step inside a minute. The boy and I
  have something to talk about.
ESDRAS. No, no—he's said nothing—
  nothing, sir, nothing!
TROCK. When I say go out, you go—
ESDRAS (*pointing to the door*).
  Miriamne—
GARTH. Go on out, both of you!
ESDRAS. Oh, sir—I'm old—   10
  old and unhappy—
GARTH. Go on!
  [MIRIAMNE *and* ESDRAS *go inside.*]
TROCK. And if you listen
  I'll riddle that door!
  (SHADOW *shuts the door behind them and
  stands against it.*)
  I just got out, you see,
  and I pay my first call on you.
GARTH. Maybe you think   20
  I'm not in the same jam you are.
TROCK. That's what I do think.
  Who started looking this up?
GARTH. I wish I knew,
  and I wish he was in hell! Some
  damned professor
  with nothing else to do. If you saw his
  stuff
  you know as much as I do.
TROCK. It wasn't you
  turning state's evidence?
GARTH. Hell, Trock, use your brain!
  The case was closed. They burned
  Romagna for it
  and that finished it. Why should I
  look for trouble
  and maybe get burned myself?
TROCK. Boy, I don't know,
  but I just thought I'd find out.
GARTH. I'm going straight, Trock.   40
  I can play this thing, and I'm trying
  to make a living.
  I haven't talked and nobody's talked
  to me.
  Christ—it's the last thing I'd want!
TROCK. Your old man knows.

GARTH. That's where I got the money
  that last time
  when you needed it. He had a little
  saved up,
  but I had to tell him to get it. He's as
  safe
  as Shadow there.
TROCK (*looking at* SHADOW).
  There could be people safer
  than that son-of-a-bitch.   10
SHADOW. Who?
TROCK. You'd be safer dead
  along with some other gorillas.
SHADOW. It's beginning to look
  as if you'd feel safer with everybody
  dead,
  the whole god-damn world.
TROCK. I would. These Jesus-bitten
  professors! Looking up their half-ass
  cases!   20
  We've got enough without that.
GARTH. There's no evidence
  to reopen the thing.
TROCK. And suppose they called on you
  and asked you to testify?
GARTH. Why then I'd tell 'em
  that all I know is what I read in the
  papers.
  And I'd stick to that.
TROCK. How much does your sister know? 30
GARTH. I'm honest with you, Trock.
  She read my name
  in the professor's pamphlet, and she
  was scared
  the way anybody would be. She got
  nothing
  from me, and anyway she'd go to the
  chair
  herself before she'd send me there.
TROCK. Like hell.   40
GARTH. Besides, who wants to go to trial
  again
  except the radicals?—You and I
  won't spill
  and unless we did there's nothing to
  take to court

as far as I know. Let the radicals go on
  howling
about getting a dirty deal. They always howl
and nobody gives a damn. This professor's red—
everybody knows it.

TROCK. You're forgetting the judge.
  Where's the damn judge?

GARTH. What judge? 10

TROCK. Read the morning papers.
  It says Judge Gaunt's gone off his nut.
    He's got
  that damn trial on his mind, and been
    going round
  proving to everybody he was right all
    the time
  and the radicals were guilty—stop-
    ping people
  in the street to prove it—and now he's 20
    nuts entirely
  and nobody knows where he is.

GARTH. Why don't they know?

TROCK. Because he's on the loose somewhere! They've got
  the police of three cities looking for
    him.

GARTH. Judge Gaunt?

TROCK. Yes. Judge Gaunt.

SHADOW. Why should that worry 30
  you?
  He's crazy, ain't he? And even if he
    wasn't
  he's arguing on your side. You're jit-
    tery, chief.
  God, all the judges are looney. You've
    got the jitters,
  and you'll damn well give yourself
    away some time
  peeing yourself in public. 40
  (TROCK half turns toward SHADOW in
    anger.)
  Don't jump the gun now,
  I've got pockets in my clothes, too.
  (His hand is in his coat pocket.)

TROCK. All right. Take it easy.

[He takes his hand from his pocket, and
  SHADOW does the same.]
(To GARTH.)
Maybe you're lying to me and maybe
  you're not.
Stay at home a few days.

GARTH. Sure thing. Why not?

TROCK. And when I say stay home I
  mean stay home.
If I have to go looking for you you'll
  stay a long time
wherever I find you.
(To SHADOW.) Come on. We'll get out
  of here.
(To GARTH.) Be seeing you.

[SHADOW and TROCK go out. After a pause
  GARTH walks over to his chair and
  picks up the violin. Then he puts it
  down and goes to the inside door, which
  he opens.]

GARTH. He's gone.

[MIRIAMNE enters, ESDRAS behind her.]

MIRIAMNE (going up to GARTH).
  Let's not stay here.
  (She puts her hands on his arms.)
  I thought he'd come for something—
    horrible.
  Is he coming back?

GARTH. I don't know.

MIRIAMNE. Who is he, Garth?

GARTH. He'd kill me if I told you who he
  is,
  that is, if he knew.

MIRIAMNE. Then don't say it—

GARTH. Yes, and I'll say it! I was with a
  gang one time
  that robbed a pay roll. I saw a murder
    done,
  and Trock Estrella did it. If that got
    out
  I'd go to the chair and so would he—
    that's why
  he was here today—

MIRIAMNE. But that's not true—

ESDRAS. He says it
  to frighten you, child.

GARTH. Oh, no I don't! I say it
because I've held it in too long! I'm
damned
if I sit here forever and look at the
door,
waiting for Trock with his sub-
machine gun, waiting
for police with a warrant!—I say I'm
damned, and I am,
no matter what I do! These piddling 10
scales
on a violin—first position, third, fifth,
arpeggios in E—and what I'm thinking
is Romagna dead for the murder—
dead while I sat here
dying inside—dead for the thing
Trock did
while I looked on—and I could have
saved him, yes—   20
but I sat here and let him die in-
stead of me
because I wanted to live! Well, it's no
life,
and it doesn't matter who I tell, because
I mean to get it over!
MIRIAMNE. Garth, it's not true!
GARTH. I'd take some scum down with
me if I died—   30
that'd be one good deed—
ESDRAS. Son, son, you're mad—
someone will hear—
GARTH. Then let them hear! I've lived
with ghosts too long, and lied too
long. God damn you
if you keep me from the truth!—
(*He turns away.*) Oh, God damn the
world!
I don't want to die!
ESDRAS. I should have known.   40
I thought you hard and sullen,
Garth, my son. And you were a child,
and hurt
with a wound that might be healed.
—All men have crimes,

and most of them are hidden, and
many are heavy
as yours must be to you.
(GARTH *sobs.*)
They walk the streets
to buy and sell, but a spreading crim-
son stain
tinges the inner vestments, touches
flesh,
and burns the quick. You're not
alone.
GARTH. I'm alone
in this.
ESDRAS. Yes, if you hold with the world
that only
those who die suddenly should be re-
venged.
But those whose hearts are cancered,
drop by drop
in small ways, little by little, till
they've borne
all they can bear, and die—these
deaths will go
unpunished now as always. When
we're young
we have faith in what is seen, but
when we're old
we know that what is seen is traced in
air
and built on water. There's no guilt
under heaven,
just as there's no heaven, till men believe it—
no earth, till men have seen it, and
have a word
to say this is the earth.
GARTH. Well, I say there's an earth,
and I say I'm guilty on it, guilty as
hell.
ESDRAS. Yet till it's known you bear no
guilt at all—
unless you wish. The days go by like
film,
like a long written scroll, a figured
veil
unrolling out of darkness into fire

and utterly consumed. And on this
veil,
running in sounds and symbols of
men's minds
reflected back, life flickers and is
shadow
going toward flame. Only what men
can see
exists in that shadow. Why must you
rise and cry out: 10
That was I, there in the ravelled
tapestry,
there, in that pistol flash, when the
man was killed.
I was there, and was one, and am
bloodstained!
Let the wind
and fire take that hour to ashes out of
time
and out of mind! This thing that men 20
call justice,
this blind snake that strikes men down
in the dark,
mindless with fury, keep your hand
back from it,
pass by in silence—let it be forgotten,
forgotten!—
Oh, my son, my son—have pity!

MIRIAMNE. But if it was true
and someone died—then it was more 30
than shadow—
and it doesn't blow away—

GARTH. Well, it was true.

ESDRAS. Say it if you must. If you have
heart to die,
say it, and let them take what's left—
there was little
to keep, even before—

GARTH. Oh, I'm a coward—
I always was. I'll be quiet and live. 40
I'll live
even if I have to crawl. I know.
(*He gets up and goes into the inner room.*)

MIRIAMNE. Is it better
to tell a lie and live?

ESDRAS. Yes, child. It's better.

MIRIAMNE. But if I had to do it—
I think I'd die.

ESDRAS. Yes, child. Because you're
young.

MIRIAMNE. Is that the only reason?

ESDRAS. The only reason.

CURTAIN

SCENE THREE

*Under the bridge, evening of the same day.
When the curtain rises* MIRIAMNE *is sitting
alone on the ledge at the rear of the apartment
house. A spray of light falls on her from a
street lamp above. She shivers a little in her
thin coat, but sits still as if heedless of the
weather. Through the rocks on the other side a*
TRAMP *comes down to the river bank, hunting
a place to sleep. He goes softly to the apple-
woman's hut and looks in, then turns away,
evidently not daring to preëmpt it. He looks at*
MIRIAMNE *doubtfully. The door of the street-
piano man is shut. The vagabond passes it and
picks carefully among some rags and shavings
to the right.* MIRIAMNE *looks up and sees him
but makes no sign. She looks down again, and
the man curls himself up in a makeshift bed in
the corner, pulling a piece of sacking over his
shoulders.* TWO GIRLS *come in round the
apartment house.*

1ST GIRL. Honest, I never heard of anything so romantic. Because you
never liked him.

2ND GIRL. I certainly never did.

1ST GIRL. You've got to tell me how it
happened. You've got to.

2ND GIRL. I couldn't. As long as I live I
couldn't. Honest, it was terrible. It
was terrible.

1ST GIRL. What was so terrible?

2ND GIRL. The way it happened.

1ST GIRL. Oh, please—not to a soul,
never.

2ND GIRL. Well, you know how I hated
him because he had such a big
mouth. So he reached over and

grabbed me, and I began all falling to pieces inside, the way you do— and I said, "Oh no you don't mister," and started screaming and kicked a hole through the windshield and lost a shoe, and he let go and was cursing and growling because he borrowed the car and didn't have money to pay for the windshield, and he started to cry, 10 and I got so sorry for him I let him, and now he wants to marry me.

1ST GIRL. Honest, I never heard of anything so romantic! (*She sees the sleeping* TRAMP.) My God, what you won't see!

[*They give the* TRAMP *a wide berth, and go out right. The* TRAMP *sits up looking about him.* JUDGE GAUNT, *an elderly, quiet man, well dressed but in clothes* 20 *that have seen some weather, comes in uncertainly from the left. He holds a small clipping in his hand and goes up to the* HOBO.]

GAUNT (*tentatively*). Your pardon, sir. Your pardon, but perhaps you can tell me the name of this street.

HOBO. Huh?

GAUNT. The name of this street?

HOBO. This ain't no street. 30

GAUNT. There, where the street lamps are.

HOBO. That's the alley.

GAUNT. Thank you. It has a name, no doubt?

HOBO. That's the alley.

GAUNT. I see. I won't trouble you. You wonder why I ask, I daresay.—I'm a stranger.—Why do you look at me? (*He steps back.*) I—I'm not the man you think. You've mistaken 40 me, sir.

HOBO. Huh?

JUDGE. Perhaps misled by a resemblance. But you're mistaken—I had an errand in this city. It's only by accident that I'm here——

HOBO (*muttering*). You go to hell.

JUDGE (*going nearer to him, bending over him*). Yet why should I deceive you? Before God, I held the proofs in my hands. I hold them still. I tell you the defense was cunning beyond belief, and unscrupulous in its use of propaganda—they gagged at nothing—not even—(*He rises.*) No, no—I'm sorry—this will hardly interest you. I'm sorry. I have an errand.

[*He looks toward the street.* ESDRAS *enters from the basement and goes to* MIRIAMNE. *The* JUDGE *steps back into the shadows.*]

ESDRAS. Come in, my daughter. You'll be cold here.

MIRIAMNE. After a while.

ESDRAS. You'll be cold. There's a storm coming.

MIRIAMNE. I didn't want him to see me crying. That was all.

ESDRAS. I know.

MIRIAMNE. I'll come soon.

[ESDRAS *turns reluctantly and goes out the way he came.* MIRIAMNE *rises to go in, pausing to dry her eyes.* MIO *and* CARR, *road boys of seventeen or so, come round the apartment house. The* JUDGE *has disappeared.*]

CARR. Thought you said you were never coming east again.

MIO. Yeah, but—I heard something changed my mind.

CARR. Same old business?

MIO. Yes, just as soon not talk about it.

CARR. Where did you go from Portland?

MIO. Fishing—I went fishing. God's truth.

CARR. Right after I left?

MIO. Fell in with a fisherman's family on the coast and went after the beautiful mackerel fish that swim in the beautiful sea. Family of Greeks— Aristides Marinos was his lovely name. He sang while he fished. Made the pea-green Pacific ring with his bastard Greek chanties. Then I went to Hollywood High School for a while.

CARR. I'll bet that's a seat of learning.

MIO. It's the hind end of all wisdom. They kicked me out after a time.

CARR. For cause?

MIO. Because I had no permanent ad- 10 dress, you see. That means no- body's paying school taxes for you, so out you go. (*To* MIRIAMNE.) What's the matter, Kid?

MIRIAMNE. Nothing. (*She looks up at him, and they pause for a moment.*) Noth- ing.

MIO. I'm sorry.

MIRIAMNE. It's all right. (*She withdraws her eyes from his and goes out past him.* 20 *He turns and looks after her.*)

CARR. Control your chivalry.

MIO. A pretty kid.

CARR. A baby.

MIO. Wait for me.

CARR. Be a long wait? (MIO *steps swiftly out after* MIRIAMNE, *then returns.*) Yeah?

MIO. She's gone.

CARR. Think of that. 30

MIO. No, but I mean—vanished. Presto —into nothing—prodigioso.

CARR. Damn good thing, if you ask me. The homely ones are bad enough, but the lookers are fatal.

MIO. You exaggerate, Carr.

CARR. I doubt it.

MIO. Well, let her go. This river bank's loaded with typhus rats, too. Might as well die one death as another. 40

CARR. They say chronic alcoholism is nice but expensive. You can always starve to death.

MIO. Not always. I tried it. After the second day I walked thirty miles to Niagara Falls and made a tour of the plant to get the sample of shredded wheat biscuit on the way out.

CARR. Last time I saw you you couldn't think of anything you wanted to do except curse God and pass out. Still feeling low?

MIO. Not much different. (*He turns away, then comes back.*) Talk about the lost generation, I'm the only one fits that title. When the State executes your father, and your mother dies of grief, and you know damn well he was innocent, and the author- ities of your home town politely in- form you they'd consider it a favor if you lived somewhere else—that cuts you off from the world—with a meat-axe.

CARR. They asked you to move? 20

MIO. It came to that.

CARR. God, that was white of them.

MIO. It probably gave them a headache just to see me after all that agita- tion. They knew as well as I did my father never staged a holdup. Any- way, I've got a new interest in life now.

CARR. Yes—I saw her.

MIO. I don't mean the skirt.—No, I got 30 wind of something, out west, some college professor investigating the trial and turning up new evidence. Couldn't find anything he'd writ- ten out there, so I beat it east and arrived on this blessed island just in time to find the bums holing up in the public library for the winter. I know now what the unemployed have been doing since the depres- sion started. They've been catching up on their reading in the main ref- erence room. Man, what a stench! Maybe I stank, too, but a hobo has the stench of ten because his shoes are poor.

CARR. Tennyson.

MIO. Right. Jeez, I'm glad we met up again! Never knew anybody else that could track me through the driven snow of Victorian literature.

CARR. Now you're cribbing from some half-forgotten criticism of Ben Jonson's Roman plagiarisms.

MIO. Where did you get your education, sap? 10

CARR. Not in the public library, sap. My father kept a news-stand.

MIO. Well, you're right again. (*There is a faint rumble of thunder.*) What's that? Winter thunder?

CARR. Or Mister God, beating on His little tocsin. Maybe announcing the advent of a new social order.

MIO. Or maybe it's going to rain coffee and doughnuts. 20

CARR. Or maybe it's going to rain.

MIO. Seems more likely. (*Lowering his voice.*) Anyhow, I found Professor Hobhouse's discussion of the Romagna case. I think he has something. It occurred to me I might follow it up by doing a little sleuthing on my own account.

CARR. Yes?

MIO. I have done a little. And it leads me 30 to somewhere in that tenement house that backs up against the bridge. That's how I happen to be here.

CARR. They'll never let you get anywhere with it, Mio. I told you that before.

MIO. I know you did.

CARR. The State can't afford to admit it was wrong, you see. Not when 40 there's been that much of a row kicked up over it. So for all practical purposes the State was right and your father robbed the pay roll.

MIO. There's still such a thing as evidence.

CARR. It's something you can buy. In fact, at the moment I don't think of anything you can't buy, including life, honor, virtue, glory, public office, conjugal affection and all kinds of justice, from the traffic court to the immortal nine. Go out and make yourself a pot of money and you can buy all the justice you want. Convictions obtained, convictions averted. Lowest rates in years.

MIO. I know all that.

CARR. Sure.

MIO. This thing didn't happen to you.
They've left you your name
and whatever place you can take. For
my heritage
They've left me one thing only, and
that's to be
my father's voice crying up out of the
earth
and quicklime where they stuck him.
Electrocution
doesn't kill, you know. They eviscerate them
with a turn of the knife in the dissecting room.
The blood spurts out. The man was
alive. Then into
the lime pit, leave no trace. Make it
short shrift
and chemical dissolution. That's what
they thought
of the man that was my father. Then
my mother—
I tell you these county burials are
swift
and cheap and run for profit! Out of
the house
and into the ground, you wife of a
dead dog. Wait,
here's some Romagna spawn left.
Something crawls here—
something they called a son. Why
couldn't he die

along with his mother? Well, ease him
out of town,
ease him out, boys, and see you're not
too gentle.
He might come back. And, by their
own living Jesus,
I will go back, and hang the carrion
around their necks that made it!
Maybe I can sleep then.
Or even live.   10
CARR. You have to try it?
MIO. Yes.
Yes. It won't let me alone. I've tried
to live
and forget it—but I was birthmarked
with hot iron
into the entrails. I've got to find out
who did it
and make them see it till it scalds
their eyes   20
and make them admit it till their
tongues are blistered
with saying how black they lied!
[HERMAN, *a gawky shoe salesman, enters from
the left.*]
HERMAN. Hello. Did you see a couple of
girls go this way?
CARR. Couple of girls? Did we see a couple of girls?
MIO. No.
CARR. No. No girls.
[HERMAN *hesitates, then goes out right.*
LUCIA *comes in from the left, trundling
his piano.* PINY *follows him, weeping.*]
PINY. They've got no right to do it——
LUCIA. All right, hell what, no matter, I
got to put him away, I got to put
him away, that's what the hell!
(TWO STREET URCHINS *follow him in.*)
PINY. They want everybody on the relief 40
rolls and nobody making a liv-
ing?
LUCIA. The cops, they do what the big
boss say. The big boss, that's the
mayor, he says he heard it once too
often, the sextette——

PINY. They want graft, that's all. It's a
new way to get graft——
LUCIA. Oh, no, no, no! He's a good man,
the mayor. He's just don't care for
music, that's all.
PINY. Why shouldn't you make a living
on the street? The National Biscuit
Company ropes off Eighth Avenue
—and does the mayor do anything? No, the police hit you over
the head if you try to go through!
LUCIA. You got the big dough, you get
the pull, fine. No big dough, no
pull, what the hell, get off the city
property! Tomorrow I start cooking chestnuts . . . (*He strokes the
piano fondly. The* TWO GIRLS *and* HER-
MAN *come back from the right.*) She's a
good little machine, this baby. Cost
plenty—and two new records I
only played twice. See this one. (*He
starts turning the crank, talking while he
plays.*) Two weeks since they play
this one in a picture house. (*A
SAILOR wanders in from the left. One
of the* STREET URCHINS *begins suddenly
to dance a wild rumba, the others watch.*)
Good boy—see, it's a lulu—it itches
in the feet!
30 [HERMAN, *standing with his girl, tosses the
boy a penny. He bows and goes on dancing; the other* URCHIN *joins him. The
SAILOR tosses a coin.*]
SAILOR. Go it, Cuba! Go it!
[LUCIA *turns the crank, beaming.*]
2ND GIRL. Oh, Herman! (*She throws her
arms round* HERMAN *and they dance.*)
1ST URCHIN. Hey, pipe the professionals!
1ST GIRL. Do your glide, Shirley! Do
your glide!
LUCIA. Maybe we can't play in front,
maybe we can play behind! (*The
HOBO gets up from his nest and comes
over to watch.* A YOUNG RADICAL *wanders in.*) Maybe you don't know,
folks! Tonight we play good-bye to

the piano! Good-bye forever! No more piano on the streets! No more music! No more money for the music-man! Last time, folks! Good-bye to the piano—good-bye forever! (MIRIAMNE *comes out the rear door of the apartment and stands watching. The* SAILOR *goes over to the* 1ST GIRL *and they dance together.*) Maybe you don't know, folks! Tomorrow 10 will be sad as hell, tonight we dance! Tomorrow no more Verdi, no more rumba, no more good time! Tonight we play good-bye to the piano, good-bye forever! (*The* RADICAL *edges up to* MIRIAMNE *and asks her to dance. She shakes her head and he goes to* PINY, *who dances with him. The* HOBO *begins to do a few lonely curvets on the side above.*) Hoy! 20 Hoy! Pick 'em up and take 'em around! Use the head, use the feet! Last time forever! (*He begins to sing to the air.*)

MIO. Wait for me, will you?

CARR. Now's your chance.

[MIO *goes over to* MIRIAMNE *and holds out a hand, smiling. She stands for a moment uncertain, then dances with him.* ESDRAS *comes out to watch.* JUDGE GAUNT 30 *comes in from the left. There is a rumble of thunder.*]

LUCIA. Hoy Hoy! Maybe it rains tonight, maybe it snows tomorrow! Tonight we dance good-bye. (*He sings the air lustily.* A POLICEMAN *comes in from the left and looks on.* TWO OR THREE PEDESTRIANS *follow him.*)

POLICEMAN. Hey you! (LUCIA *goes on sing-* 40 *ing.*) Hey, you!

LUCIA (*still playing*). What you want?

POLICEMAN. Sign off!

LUCIA. What you mean? I get off the street!

POLICEMAN. Sign off!

LUCIA (*still playing*). What you mean? (*The* POLICEMAN *walks over to him.* LUCIA *stops playing and the* DANCERS *pause.*)

POLICEMAN. Cut it.

LUCIA. Is this a street?

POLICEMAN. I say cut it out.

[*The* HOBO *goes back to his nest and sits in it, watching.*]

LUCIA. It's the last time. We dance good-bye to the piano.

POLICEMAN. You'll dance good-bye to something else if I catch you cranking that thing again.

LUCIA. All right.

PINY. I'll bet you don't say that to the National Biscuit Company!

POLICEMAN. Lady, you've been selling apples on my beat for some time now, and I said nothing about it ——

PINY. Selling apples is allowed——

POLICEMAN. You watch yourself—(*He takes a short walk around the place and comes upon the* HOBO.) What are you doing here? (*The* HOBO *opens his mouth, points to it, and shakes his head.*) Oh, you are, are you? (*He comes back to* LUCIA.) So you trundle your so-called musical instrument to wherever you keep it, and don't let me hear it again.

[*The* RADICAL *leaps on the base of the rock at right. The* 1ST GIRL *turns away from the* SAILOR *toward the* 2ND GIRL *and* HERMAN.]

SAILOR. Hey, captain, what's the matter with the music?

POLICEMAN. Not a thing, admiral.

SAILOR. Well, we had a little party going here——

POLICEMAN. I'll say you did.

2ND GIRL. Please, officer, we want to dance.

POLICEMAN. Go ahead. Dance.

2ND GIRL. But we want music!

POLICEMAN (*turning to go*). Sorry. Can't help you.

RADICAL. And there you see it, the perfect example of capitalistic oppression! In a land where music should be free as air and the arts should be encouraged, a uniformed minion of the rich, a guardian myrmidon of the Park Avenue pleasure hunters, steps in and puts a limit on the innocent enjoyments of the poor! We don't go to theatres! Why not? We can't afford it! We don't go to night clubs, where women dance naked and the music drips from saxophones and leaks out of Rudy Vallee—we can't afford that either! —But we might at least dance on the river bank to the strains of a barrel organ—!   20

[GARTH *comes out of the apartment and listens.*]

POLICEMAN. It's against the law!

RADICAL. What law? I challenge you to tell me what law of God or man— what ordinance—is violated by this spontaneous diversion? None! I say none! An official whim of the masters who should be our servants!——   30

POLICEMAN. Get down! Get down and shut up!

RADICAL. By what law, by what ordinance do you order me to be quiet?

POLICEMAN. Speaking without a flag. You know it.

RADICAL (*pulling out a small American flag*). There's my flag! There's the flag of this United States which used to guarantee the rights of man—the rights of man now violated by every statute of the commonweal——   40

POLICEMAN. Don't try to pull tricks on me! I've seen you before! You're

not making any speech, and you're climbing down——

JUDGE GAUNT (*who has come quietly forward*). One moment, officer. There is some difference of opinion even on the bench as to the elasticity of police power when applied in minor emergencies to preserve civil order. But the weight of authority would certainly favor the defendant in any equable court, and he would be upheld in his demand to be heard.

POLICEMAN. Who are you?

GAUNT. Sir, I am not accustomed to answer that question.

POLICEMAN. I don't know you.

GAUNT. I am a judge of some standing, not in your city but in another with similar statutes. You are aware, of course, that the Bill of Rights is not to be set aside lightly by the officers of any municipality——

POLICEMAN (*looking over* GAUNT'S *somewhat bedraggled costume*). Maybe they understand you better in the town you come from, but I don't get your drift.—(*To the* RADICAL.) I don't want any trouble, but if you ask for it you'll get plenty. Get down!

RADICAL. I'm not asking for trouble, but I'm staying right here. (*The* POLICEMAN *moves towards him.*)

GAUNT (*taking the* POLICEMAN'S *arm, but shaken off roughly*). I ask this for yourself, truly, not for the dignity of the law nor the maintenance of precedent. Be gentle with them when their threats are childish—be tolerant while you can—for your least harsh word will return on you in the night—return in a storm of cries!—(*He takes the* POLICEMAN'S *arm again.*) Whatever they may have said or done, let them disperse in peace! It is better that they go softly, lest when they are dead you see their eyes pleading, and their outstretched hands touch you, fingering cold on your heart!—I have been harsher than you. I have sent men down that long corridor into blinding light and blind darkness! (*He suddenly draws himself erect and speaks defiantly.*) And it was well that I did so! I have been an upright judge! They are all liars! Liars!

POLICEMAN (*shaking* GAUNT *off so that he falls*). Why, you fool, you're crazy!

GAUNT. Yes, and there are liars on the force! They came to me with their shifty lies! (*He catches at the* POLICEMAN, *who pushes him away with his foot.*)

POLICEMAN. You think I've got nothing better to do than listen to a crazy fool?

1ST GIRL. Shame, shame!

POLICEMAN. What have I got to be ashamed of? And what's going on here, anyway? Where in hell did you all come from?

RADICAL. Tread on him! That's right! Tread down the poor and the innocent! (*There is a protesting murmur in the crowd.*)

SAILOR (*moving in a little*). Say, big boy, you don't have to step on the guy.

POLICEMAN (*facing them, stepping back*). What's the matter with you! I haven't stepped on anybody!

MIO (*at the right, across from the* POLICEMAN).

Listen now, fellows, give the badge a chance.

He's doing his job, what he gets paid to do,

the same as any of you. They're all picked men,

these metropolitan police, hand picked

for loyalty and a fine up-standing pair of shoulders on their legs—it's not so easy

to represent the law. Think what he does

for all of us, stamping out crime!

Do you want to be robbed and murdered in your beds?

SAILOR. What's eating you?

RADICAL. He must be a capitalist.

MIO. They pluck them fresh,

from Ireland, and a paucity of head-piece

is a prime prerequisite. You from Ireland, buddy?

POLICEMAN (*surly*).

Where are you from?

MIO. Buddy, I tell you flat

I wish I was from Ireland, and could boast

some Tammany connections. There's only one drawback

about working on the force. It infects the brain,

it eats the cerebrum. There've been cases known,

fine specimens of manhood, too, where autopsies,

conducted in approved scientific fashion,

revealed conditions quite incredible

in policemen's upper layers. In some, a trace,

in others, when they've swung a stick too long,

there was nothing there!—but nothing! Oh, my friends,

this fine athletic figure of a man

that stands so grim before us, what will they find

when they saw his skull for the last inspection?

I fear me a little puffball dust will blow away

rejoining earth, our mother—and this
same dust,
this smoke, this ash on the wind, will
represent
all he had left to think with!

THE HOBO. Hooray!

[*The* POLICEMAN *turns on his heel and looks
hard at the* HOBO, *who slinks away.*]

POLICEMAN. Oh, yeah?

MIO. My theme   10
gives ears to the deaf and voice to the
dumb! But now
forgive me if I say you were most unkind
in troubling the officer. He's a simple
man
of simple tastes, and easily confused
when faced with complex issues. He
may reflect
on returning home, that is, so far as he   20
is capable of reflection, and conclude
that he was kidded out of his uniform
pants,
and in his fury when this dawns on
him
may smack his wife down!

POLICEMAN. That'll be about enough
from you, too, professor!

MIO. May I say that I think you have
managed this whole situation   30
rather badly, from the beginning?

POLICEMAN. You may not!

[TROCK *slips in from the background. The*
TWO YOUNG MEN IN SERGE *come with
him.*]

MIO. Oh, but your pardon, sir! It's apparent to the least competent
among us that you should have
gone about your task more subtly—   40
the glove of velvet, the hand of iron,
and all that sort of thing——

POLICEMAN. Shut that hole in your face!

MIO. Sir, for that remark I shall be satisfied with nothing less than an un-
conditional apology! I have an old

score to settle with policemen,
brother, because they're fools and
fat-heads, and you're one of the
most fatuous fat-heads that ever
walked his feet flat collecting graft!
Tell that to your sergeant back in
the booby-hatch.

POLICEMAN. Oh, you want an apology,
do you? You'll get an apology out
of the other side of your mouth!
(*He steps toward* MIO. CARR *suddenly
stands in his path.*) Get out of my
way! (*He pauses and looks round him;
the crowd looks less and less friendly.
He lays a hand on his gun and backs to
a position where there is nobody behind
him.*) Get out of here, all of you!
Get out! What are you trying to
do—start a riot?

MIO. There now, that's better! That's in
the best police tradition. Incite a riot
yourself and then accuse the crowd.

POLICEMAN. It won't be pleasant if I decide to let somebody have it! Get
out!

[*The onlookers begin to melt away. The*
SAILOR *goes out left with the* GIRLS *and*
HERMAN. CARR *and* MIO *go out right,*
CARR *whistling "The Star Spangled
Banner." The* HOBO *follows them. The*
RADICAL *walks past with his head in
the air.* PINY *and* LUCIA *leave the piano
where it stands and slip away to the left.
At the end the* POLICEMAN *is left stand-
ing in the center, the* JUDGE *near him.*
ESDRAS *stands in the doorway.* MIR-
IAMNE *is left sitting half in shadow and
unseen by* ESDRAS.]

JUDGE GAUNT (*to the* POLICEMAN). Yes,
but should a man die, should it be
necessary that one man die for the
good of many, make not yourself
the instrument of death, lest you
sleep to wake sobbing! Nay, it
avails nothing that you are the law
—this delicate ganglion that is the

brain, it will not bear these things
—!

[*The* POLICEMAN *gives the* JUDGE *the once-
over, shrugs, decides to leave him there
and starts out left.* GARTH *goes to his
father—a fine sleet begins to fall
through the street lights.* TROCK *is still
visible.*]

GARTH. Get him in here, quick.

ESDRAS. Who, son?   10

GARTH. The Judge, damn him!

ESDRAS. Is it Judge Gaunt?

GARTH. Who did you think it was? He's
crazy as a bedbug and telling the
world. Get him inside! (*He looks
round.*)

ESDRAS (*going up to* GAUNT). Will you
come in, sir?

GAUNT. You will understand, sir. We
old men know how softly we must 20
proceed with these things.

ESDRAS. Yes, surely, sir.

GAUNT. It was always my practice—always. They will tell you that of me
where I am known. Yet even I am
not free of regret—even I. Would
you believe it?

ESDRAS. I believe we are none of us free
of regret.

GAUNT. None of us? I would it were true. 30
I would I thought it were true.

ESDRAS. Shall we go in, sir? This is sleet
that's falling.

GAUNT. Yes. Let us go in.

[ESDRAS, GAUNT *and* GARTH *enter the basement and shut the door.* TROCK *goes out
with his men. After a pause* MIO *comes
back from the right, alone. He stands at
a little distance from* MIRIAMNE.]

MIO. Looks like rain. (*She is silent.*) You 40
live around here? (*She nods gravely.*)
I guess
you thought I meant it—about waiting here to meet me. (*She nods again.*)
I'd forgotten about it till I got that
winter

across the face. You'd better go inside.
I'm not your kind. I'm nobody's kind
but my own.
I'm waiting for this to blow over.
(*She rises.*)
I lied. I meant it—
I meant it when I said it—but there's
too much black
whirling inside me—for any girl to
know.
So go on in. You're somebody's angel
child
and they're waiting for you.

MIRIAMNE. Yes. I'll go. (*She turns.*)

MIO. And tell them
when you get inside where it's warm,
And you love each other,
and mother comes to kiss her darling,
tell them
to hang on to it while they can, believe while they can
it's a warm safe world, and Jesus finds
his lambs
and carries them in his bosom.—I've
seen some lambs
that Jesus missed. If they ever want
the truth
tell them that nothing's guaranteed in
this climate
except it gets cold in winter, nor on
this earth
except you die sometime.
(*He turns away.*)

MIRIAMNE. I have no mother.
And my people are Jews.

MIO. Then you know something about
it.

MIRIAMNE. Yes.

MIO. Do you have enough to eat?

MIRIAMNE. Not always.

MIO. What do you believe in?

MIRIAMNE. Nothing.

MIO. Why?

MIRIAMNE. How can one?

MIO. It's easy if you're a fool. You see the
words

in books. Honor, it says there, chivalry, freedom,
heroism, enduring love—and these
are words on paper. It's something to
have them there.
You'll get them nowhere else.

MIRIAMNE. What hurts you?

MIO. Just that.
You'll get them nowhere else.

MIRIAMNE. Why should you want them? 10

MIO. I'm alone, that's why. You see those
lights,
along the river, cutting across the
rain—?
those are the hearths of Brooklyn, and
up this way
the love-nests of Manhattan—they
turn their points
like knives against me—outcast of the
world, 20
snake in the streets.—I don't want a
hand-out.
I sleep and eat.

MIRIAMNE. Do you want me to go with
you?

MIO. Where?

MIRIAMNE. Where you go.

[A pause. He goes nearer to her.]

MIO. Why, you god-damned little fool—
what made you say that? 30

MIRIAMNE. I don't know.

MIO. If you have a home
stay in it. I ask for nothing. I've
schooled myself
to ask for nothing, and take what I
can get,
and get along. If I fell for you, that's
my look-out,
and I'll starve it down.

MIRIAMNE. Wherever you go, I'd go. 40

MIO. What do you know about loving?
How could you know?
Have you ever had a man?

MIRIAMNE (after a slight pause). No. But I
know.
Tell me your name.

MIO. Mio. What's yours?

MIRIAMNE. Miriamne.

MIO. There's no such name.

MIRIAMNE. But there's no such name as
Mio!
M.I.O. It's no name.

MIO. It's for Bartolomeo.

MIRIAMNE. My mother's name was
Miriam,
so they called me Miriamne.

MIO. Meaning little Miriam?

MIRIAMNE. Yes.

MIO. So now little Miriamne will go
in
and take up quietly where she
dropped them all
her small housewifely cares.—When I
first saw you,
not a half-hour ago, I heard myself
saying,
this is the face that launches ships for
me—
and if I owned a dream—yes, half a
dream—
we'd share it. But I have no dream.
This earth
came tumbling down from chaos, fire
and rock,
and bred up worms, blind worms that
sting each other
here in the dark. These blind worms
of the earth
took out my father—and killed him,
and set a sign
on me—the heir of the serpent—and
he was a man
such as men might be if the gods were
men—
but they killed him—
as they'll kill all others like him
till the sun cools down to the stabler
molecules,
yes, till men spin their tent-worm
webs to the stars
and what they think is done, even in
the thinking,

and they are the gods, and immortal,
and constellations
turn for them all like mill wheels—
still as they are
they will be, worms and blind. Enduring love,
oh gods and worms, what mockery!—
And yet
I have blood enough in my veins. It
goes like music,
singing, because you're here. My
body turns
as if you were the sun, and warm.
This men called love
in happier times, before the Freudians
taught us
to blame it on the glands. Only go in
before you breathe too much of my
atmosphere
and catch death from me.   20
MIRIAMNE. I will take my hands
and weave them to a little house, and
there
you shall keep a dream——
MIO. God knows I could use a dream
and even a house.
MIRIAMNE. You're laughing at me, Mio!
MIO. The worms are laughing.
I tell you there's death about me
and you're a child! And I'm alone 30
and half mad
with hate and longing. I shall let you
love me
and love you in return, and then, why
then
God knows what happens!
MIRIAMNE. Something most unpleasant?
MIO. Love in a box car—love among the
children.
I've seen too much of it. Are we to live 40
in this same house you make with
your two hands
mystically, out of air?
MIRIAMNE. No roof, no mortgage!
Well, I shall marry a baker out in
Flatbush,

it gives hot bread in the morning! Oh,
Mio, Mio,
in all the unwanted places and waste
lands
that roll up into the darkness out of
sun
and into sun out of dark, there should
be one empty
for you and me.
MIO. No.   10
MIRIAMNE. Then go now and leave me.
I'm only a girl you saw in the tenements,
and there's been nothing said.
MIO. Miriamne.
[*She takes a step toward him.*]
MIRIAMNE. Yes. (*He kisses her lips lightly.*)
MIO. Why, girl, the transfiguration on
the mount
was nothing to your face. It lights
from within—
a white chalice holding fire, a flower
in flame,
this is your face.
MIRIAMNE. And you shall drink the flame
and never lessen it. And round your
head
the aureole shall burn that burns
there now,
forever. This I can give you. And so
forever
the Freudians are wrong.
MIO. They're well-forgotten
at any rate.
MIRIAMNE. Why did you speak to me
when you first saw me?
MIO. I knew then.
MIRIAMNE. And I came back
because I must see you again. And we
danced together
and my heart hurt me. Never, never,
never,
though they should bind me down
and tear out my eyes,
would I ever hurt you now. Take me
with you, Mio,

MIO. What do you know about this?

MIRIAMNE. The other way,
Mio—quick!

[CARR *slips in from the right, in haste.*]

CARR. Look, somebody's just been shot.
He fell in the river. The guys that did
the shooting
ran up the bank.

MIO. Come on.

[MIO *and* CARR *run out right.* MIRIAMNE 10
*watches uncertainly, then slowly turns
and walks to the rear door of the tenement. She stands there a moment, looking
after* MIO, *then goes in, closing the door.*
CARR *and* MIO *return.*]

CARR. There's a rip tide past the point.
You'd never find him.

MIO. No.

CARR. You know a man really ought to
carry insurance living around here. 20
—God, it's easy, putting a fellow
away. I never saw it done before.

MIO (*looking at the place where* MIRIAMNE
stood). They have it all worked
out.

CARR. What are you doing now?

MIO. I have a little business to transact in
this neighborhood.

CARR. You'd better forget it.

MIO. No.

CARR. Need any help?

MIO. Well, if I did I'd ask you first. But
I don't see how it would do any
good. So you keep out of it and
take care of yourself.

CARR. So long, then.

MIO. So long, Carr.

CARR (*looking down-stream*). He was drifting face up. Must be halfway to the
island the way the tide runs. (*He
shivers.*) God, it's cold here. Well
———

[*He goes out to the left.* MIO *sits on the edge of
the rock.* LUCIA *comes stealthily back
from between the bridge and the tenement, goes to the street-piano and wheels
it away.* PINY *comes in. They take a
look at* MIO, *but say nothing.* LUCIA
goes into his shelter and PINY *into hers.*
MIO *rises, looks up at the tenement, and
goes out to the left.*]

CURTAIN

ACT II

*The basement as in Scene Two of Act I.
The same evening.* ESDRAS *sits at the table
reading,* MIRIAMNE *is seated at the left, listening and intent. The door of the inner room
is half open and* GARTH'S *violin is heard. He
is playing the theme from the third movement
of Beethoven's Archduke Trio.* ESDRAS *looks
up.*

ESDRAS. I remember when I came to the
end
of all the Talmud said, and the com-
mentaries,
then I was fifty years old—and it was 40
time
to ask what I had learned. I asked this
question

and gave myself the answer. In all the
Talmud
there was nothing to find but the
names of things,
set down that we might call them by
those names
and walk without fear among things
known. Since then
I have had twenty years to read on
and on
and end with Ecclesiastes. Names of
names,
evanid days, evanid nights and days
and words that shift their meaning.
Space is time,
that which was is now—the men of tomorrow

live, and this is their yesterday. All things
that were and are and will be, have their being
then and now and to come. If this means little
when you are young, remember it. It will return
to mean more when you are old.

MIRIAMNE. I'm sorry—I 10
was listening for something.

ESDRAS. It doesn't matter.
It's a useless wisdom. It's all I have,
but useless. It may be there is no time,
but we grow old. Do you know his name?

MIRIAMNE. Whose name?

ESDRAS. Why, when we're young and listen for a step
the step should have a name—— 20

[MIRIAMNE, *not hearing, rises and goes to the window.* GARTH *enters from within, carrying his violin and carefully closing the door.*]

GARTH (*as* ESDRAS *looks at him*). Asleep.

ESDRAS. He may
sleep on through the whole night—
then in the morning
we can let them know.

GARTH. We'd be wiser to say nothing— 30
let him find his own way back.

ESDRAS. How did he come here?

GARTH. He's not too crazy for that. If he wakes again
we'll keep him quiet and shift him off tomorrow.
Somebody'd pick him up.

ESDRAS. How have I come
to this sunken end of a street, at a life's end——?

GARTH. It was cheaper here—not to be transcendental—
So—we say nothing——?

ESDRAS. Nothing.

MIRIAMNE. Garth, there's no place
in this whole city—not one—

where you would be safer
than here—tonight—or tomorrow.

GARTH (*bitterly*). Well, that may be.
What of it?

MIRIAMNE. If you slipped away and took
a place somewhere where Trock couldn't find you——

GARTH. Yes—
using what for money? and why do you think
I've sat here so far—because I love my home
so much? No, but if I stepped round the corner
it'd be my last corner and my last step.

MIRIAMNE. And yet—
if you're here—they'll find you here—
Trock will come again—
and there's worse to follow——

GARTH. Do you want to get me killed?

MIRIAMNE. No.

GARTH. There's no way out of it. We'll wait
and take what they send us.

ESDRAS. Hush! You'll wake him.

GARTH. I've done it.
I hear him stirring now.

[*They wait quietly.* JUDGE GAUNT *opens the door and enters.*]

GAUNT (*in the doorway*). I beg your pardon—
no, no, be seated—keep your place—
I've made
your evening difficult enough, I fear;
and I must thank you doubly for your kindness,
for I've been ill—I know it.

ESDRAS. You're better, sir?

GAUNT. Quite recovered, thank you. Able, I hope,
to manage nicely now. You'll be rewarded
for your hospitality—though at this moment
(*He smiles.*) I'm low in funds.

(*He inspects his billfold.*) Sir, my embarrassment
is great indeed—and more than mon-
etary,
for I must own my recollection's vague
of how I came here—how we came together—
and what we may have said. My
name is Gaunt,
Judge Gaunt, a name long known in 10
the criminal courts,
and not unhonored there.

ESDRAS. My name is Esdras—
and this is Garth, my son. And Miriamne,
the daughter of my old age.

GAUNT. I'm glad to meet you.
Esdras. Garth Esdras.
(*He passes a hand over his eyes.*)
It's not a usual name.   20
Of late it's been connected with a
case—
a case I knew. But this is hardly the
man.
Though it's not a usual name.
(*They are silent.*) Sir, how I came here,
as I have said, I don't well know.
Such things
are sometimes not quite accident.

ESDRAS. We found you
outside our door and brought you in.

GAUNT. The brain
can be overworked, and weary, even
when the man
would swear to his good health. Sir,
on my word
I don't know why I came here, nor
how, nor when,
nor what would explain it. Shall we
say the machine
begins to wear? I felt no twinge of it.—
You will imagine how much more
than galling
I feel it, to ask my way home—and
where I am—
but I do ask you that.

ESDRAS. This is New York City—
or part of it.

GAUNT. Not the best part, I presume?
(*He smiles grimly.*) No, not the best.

ESDRAS. Not typical, no.

GAUNT. And you—(*To* GARTH.)
you are Garth Esdras?

GARTH. That's my name.

GAUNT. Well, sir, (*To* ESDRAS.)
I shall lie under the deepest obligation
if you will set an old man on his path,
for I lack the homing instinct, if the
truth
were known. North, east and south
mean nothing to me
here in this room.

ESDRAS. I can put you in your way.

GARTH. Only you'd be wiser to wait a
while—
if I'm any judge.——

GAUNT. It happens I'm the judge—
(*With stiff humor.*)
in more ways than one. You'll forgive
me if I say
I find this place and my predicament
somewhat distasteful.
(*He looks round him.*)

GARTH. I don't doubt you do;
but you're better off here.

30 GAUNT. Nor will you find it wise
to cross my word as lightly as you
seem
inclined to do. You've seen me ill
and shaken—
and you presume on that.

GARTH. Have it your way.

GAUNT. Doubtless what information is
required
we'll find nearby.

40 ESDRAS. Yes, sir—the terminal,—
if you could walk so far.

GAUNT. I've done some walking—
to look at my shoes.
(*He looks down, then puts out a hand to
steady himself.*) That—that was why
I came—

never mind—it was there—and it's
gone.
(*To* GARTH.) Professor Hobhouse—
that's the name—he wrote some trash
about you
and printed it in a broadside.
—Since I'm here I can tell you
it's a pure fabrication—lacking facts
and legal import. Senseless and im-
pudent,   10
written with bias—with malicious intent
to undermine the public confidence
in justice and the courts. I knew it
then—
all he brings out about this testimony
you might have given. It's true I
could have called you,
but the case was clear—Romagna
was known guilty,   20
and there was nothing to add. If I've
endured
some hours of torture over their attacks
upon my probity—and in this torture
have wandered from my place, wandered perhaps
in mind and body—and found my
way to face you—
why, yes, it is so—I know it—I beg of
you   30
say nothing. It's not easy to give up
a fair name after a full half century
of service to a state. It may well rock
the surest reason. Therefore I ask of
you
say nothing of this visit.
GARTH. I'll say nothing.
ESDRAS. Nor any of us.
GAUNT. Why, no—for you'd lose, too.
You'd have nothing to gain.
ESDRAS. Indeed we know it.   40
GAUNT. I'll remember you kindly. When
I've returned,
there may be some mystery made of
where I was—
we'll leave it a mystery?

GARTH. Anything you say.
GAUNT. Why, now I go with much more
peace of mind—if I can call you
friends.
ESDRAS. We shall be grateful
for silence on your part, Your Honor.
GAUNT. Sir—
if there were any just end to be served
by speaking out, I'd speak! There is
none. No—
bear that in mind!
ESDRAS. We will, Your Honor.
GAUNT. Then—
I'm in some haste. If you can be my
guide,
we'll set out now.
ESDRAS. Yes, surely.
[*There is a knock at the door. The four look
at each other with some apprehension.*
MIRIAMNE *rises.*]
I'll answer it.
MIRIAMNE. Yes.
[*She goes into the inner room and closes the
door.* ESDRAS *goes to the outer door. The
knock is repeated. He opens the door.*
MIO *is there.*]
ESDRAS. Yes, sir.
MIO. May I come in?
ESDRAS. Will you state your business, sir?
It's late—and I'm not at liberty——
MIO. Why, I might say
that I was trying to earn my tuition
fees
by peddling magazines. I could say
that,
or collecting old newspapers—paying
cash—
highest rates—no questions asked—
(*He looks round sharply.*)
GARTH. We've nothing to sell.
What do you want?
MIO. Your pardon, gentlemen.
My business is not of an ordinary
kind,
and I felt the need of this slight in-
troduction

while I might get my bearings. Your
    name is Esdras,
or they told me so outside.

GARTH. What do you want?

MIO. Is that the name?

GARTH. Yes.

MIO. I'll be quick and brief.
    I'm the son of a man who died many
      years ago
for a pay roll robbery in New Eng- 10
    land. You
should be Garth Esdras, by what I've
    heard. You have
some knowledge of the crime, if one
    can believe
what he reads in the public prints,
    and it might be
that your testimony, if given, would
    clear my father
of any share in the murder. You may 20
    not care
whether he was guilty or not. You
    may not know.
But I do care—and care deeply, and
    I've come
to ask you face to face.

GARTH. To ask me what?

MIO. What do you know of it?

ESDRAS. This man Romagna,
    did he have a son?   30

MIO. Yes, sir, this man Romagna,
    as you choose to call him, had a son,
      and I
am that son, and proud.

ESDRAS. Forgive me.

MIO. Had you known him,
    and heard him speak, you'd know
      why I'm proud, and why
he was no malefactor.

ESDRAS. I quite believe you.   40
    If my son can help he will. But at this
      moment,
    as I told you—could you, I wonder,
      come tomorrow,
    at your own hour?

MIO. Yes.

ESDRAS. By coincidence
we too of late have had this thing in
    mind—
there have been comments printed,
    and much discussion
which we could hardly avoid.

MIO. Could you tell me then
    in a word?—What you know—
is it for him or against him?—
    that's all I need.

ESDRAS. My son knows nothing.

GARTH. No.
    The picture-papers lash themselves to
      a fury
over any rumor—make them up when
      they're short
of bedroom slops.—This is what hap-
    pened. I
had known a few members of a gang
      one time
up there—and after the murder they
      picked me up
because I looked like someone that
      was seen
in what they called the murder car.
      They held me
a little while, but they couldn't iden-
    tify me
for the most excellent reason I wasn't
      there
when the thing occurred. A dozen
      years later now
a professor comes across this, and sees
      red
and asks why I wasn't called on as a
      witness
and yips so loud they syndicate his
      picture
in all the rotos. That's all I know
      about it.
I wish I could tell you more.

ESDRAS. Let me say too
    that I have read some words your
      father said,
    and you were a son fortunate in your
      father,

whatever the verdict of the world.

MIO. There are few
who think so, but it's true, and I
thank you. Then—
that's the whole story?

GARTH. All I know of it.

MIO. They cover their tracks well, the
inner ring
that distributes murder. I came three
thousand miles   10
to this dead end.

ESDRAS. If he was innocent
and you know him so, believe it, and
let the others
believe as they like.

MIO. Will you tell me how a man's
to live, and face his life, if he can't
believe
that truth's like a fire,
and will burn through and be seen   20
though it takes all the years there are?
While I stand up and have breath in
my lungs
I shall be one flame of that fire;
it's all the life I have.

ESDRAS. Then you must live so.
One must live as he can.

MIO. It's the only way
of life my father left me.

ESDRAS. Yes? Yet it's true   30
the ground we walk on is impacted
down
and hard with blood and bones of
those who died
unjustly. There's not one title to land
or life,
even your own, but was built on rape
and murder,
back a few years. It would take a fire
indeed   40
to burn out all this terror.

MIO. Then let it burn down,
all of it!

ESDRAS. We ask a great deal of the world
at first—then less—and then less.
We ask for truth

and justice. But this truth's a thing
unknown
in the lightest, smallest matter—and
as for justice,
who has once seen it done? You loved
your father,
and I could have loved him, for every
word he spoke
in his trial was sweet and tolerant, but
the weight
of what men are and have, rests heavy
on
the graves of those who lost. They'll
not rise again,
and their causes lie there with them.

GAUNT. If you mean to say
that Bartolomeo Romagna was innocent,
you are wrong. He was guilty.
There may have been injustice
from time to time, by regrettable
chance, in our courts,
but not in that case, I assure you.

MIO. Oh, you assure me!
You lie in your scrag teeth, whoever
you are!
My father was murdered!

GAUNT. Romagna was found guilty
by all due process of law, and given
his chance
to prove his innocence.

MIO. What chance? When a court
panders to mob hysterics, and the
jury
comes in loaded to soak an anarchist
and a foreigner, it may be due process
of law
but it's also murder!

GAUNT. He should have thought of that
before he spilled blood.

MIO. He?

GAUNT. Sir, I know too well
that he was guilty.

MIO. Who are you? How do you know?
I've searched the records through, the
trial and what

came after, and in all that million words
I found not one unbiased argument
to fix the crime on him.
GAUNT. And you yourself,
were you unprejudiced?
MIO. Who are you?
ESDRAS. Sir,
    this gentleman is here, as you are
    here,   10
    to ask my son, as you have asked,
    what ground
    there might be for this talk of new evidence
    in your father's case. We gave him the
    same answer
    we've given you.
MIO. I'm sorry. I'd supposed
    his cause forgotten except by myself.
    There's still
    a defense committee then?
GAUNT. There may be. I
    am not connected with it.
ESDRAS. He is my guest,
    and asks to remain unknown.
MIO (*after a pause, looking at* GAUNT).
    The judge at the trial
    was younger, but he had your face.
    Can it be
    that you're the man?—Yes—Yes.—30
    The jury charge—
    I sat there as a child and heard your
    voice,
    and watched that Brahminical
    mouth. I knew even then
    you meant no good to him. And now
    you're here
    to winnow out truth and justice—the
    fountain-head
    of the lies that slew him! Are you 40
    Judge Gaunt?
GAUNT. I am.
MIO. Then tell me what damnation to
    what inferno
    would fit the toad that sat in robes
    and lied

when he gave the charge, and knew
he lied! Judge that,
and then go to your place in that hell!
GAUNT. I know and have known
    what bitterness can rise against a
    court
    when it must say, putting aside all
    weakness,
    that a man's to die. I can forgive you
    that,
    for you are your father's son, and you
    think of him
    as a son thinks of his father. Certain
    laws
    seem cruel in their operation; it's
    necessary
    that we be cruel to uphold them. This
    cruelty
    is kindness to those I serve.
20 MIO. I don't doubt that.
    I know who it is you serve.
GAUNT. Would I have chosen
    to rack myself with other men's despairs,
    stop my ears, harden my heart, and
    listen only
    to the voice of law and light, if I had
    hoped
    some private gain for serving? In all
    my years
    on the bench of a long-established
    commonwealth
    not once has my decision been in
    question
    save in this case. Not once before or
    since.
    For hope of heaven or place on earth,
    or power
    or gold, no man has had my voice, nor
    will
    while I still keep the trust that's laid
    on me
    to sentence and define.
MIO. Then why are you here?
GAUNT. My record's clean. I've kept it
    so. But suppose

with the best intent, among the myr-
iad tongues
that come to testify, I had missed my
way
and followed a perjured tale to a
lethal end
till a man was forsworn to death?
Could I rest or sleep
while there was doubt of this,
even while there was question in a
layman's mind? 10
For always, night and day,
there lies on my brain like a weight,
the admonition:
see truly, let nothing sway you;
among all functions
there's but one godlike, to judge.
Then see to it
you judge as a god would judge, with
clarity,
with truth, with what mercy is found
consonant
with order and law. Without law men
are beasts,
and it's a judge's task to lift and hold
them
above themselves. Let a judge be once
mistaken
or step aside for a friend, and a gap is
made 30
in the dykes that hold back anarchy
and chaos,
and leave men bond but free.
MIO. Then the gap's been made,
and you made it.
GAUNT. I feared that too. May you be a
judge
sometime, and know in what fear,
through what nights long
in fear, I scanned and verified and
compared 40
the transcripts of the trial.
MIO. Without prejudice,
no doubt. It was never in your mind
to prove
that you'd been right.

GAUNT. And conscious of that, too—
that that might be my purpose—
watchful of that,
and jealous as his own lawyer of the
rights
that should hedge the defendant!
And still I found no error,
shook not one staple of the bolts that
linked
the doer to the deed! Still following
on from step to step, I watched all
modern comment,
and saw it centered finally on one
fact—
Garth Esdras was not called. This is
Garth Esdras,
and you have heard him. Would his
deposition
have justified a new trial?
MIO. No. It would not. 20
GAUNT. And there I come, myself. If the
man were still
in his cell, and waiting, I'd have no
faint excuse
for another hearing.
MIO. I've told you that I read
the trial from beginning to end.
Every word you spoke
was balanced carefully to keep the
letter
of the law and still convict—convict,
by Christ,
if it tore the seven veils! You stand
here now
running cascades of casuistry, to
prove
to yourself and me that no judge of
rank and breeding
could burn a man out of hate! But
that's what you did
under all your varnish!
GAUNT. I've sought for evidence,
and you have sought. Have you found
it? Can you cite
one fresh word in defence?
MIO. The trial itself

was shot full of legerdemain, prear-
ranged to lead
the jury astray——
GAUNT. Could you prove that?
MIO. Yes!
GAUNT. And if
the jury were led astray, remember it's
the jury, by our Anglo-Saxon custom,
that finds for guilt or innocence. The
judge   10
is powerless in that matter.
MIO. Not you! Your charge
misled the jury more than the evidence,
accepted every biased meaning, distilled
the poison for them!
GAUNT. But if that were so
I'd be the first, I swear it, to step down
among all men, and hold out both my 20
hands
for manacles—yes, publish it in the
streets,
that all I've held most sacred was de-
filed
by my own act. A judge's brain becomes
a delicate instrument to weigh men's
lives
for good and ill—too delicate to bear 30
much tampering. If he should push
aside
the weights and throw the beam, and
say, this once .
the man is guilty, and I will have it so
though his mouth cry out from the
ground,
and all the world
revoke my word, he'd have a short
way to go   40
to madness. I think you'd find him in
the squares,
stopping the passers-by with arguments,—
see, I was right, the man was guilty
there—

this was brought in against him, this
—and this—
and I was left no choice! It's no light
thing
when a long life's been dedicate to
one end
to wrench the mind awry!
MIO. By your own thesis
you should be mad, and no doubt you
are.
GAUNT. But my madness
is only this—that I would fain look
back
on a life well spent—without one
stain—one breath
of stain to flaw the glass—not in men's
minds
nor in my own. I take my God as witness
I meant to earn that clearness, and
believe
that I have earned it. Yet my name
is clouded
with the blackest, fiercest scandal of
. our age
that's touched a judge. What I can
do to wipe
that smutch from my fame I will. I
think you know
how deeply I've been hated, for no
cause
that I can find there. Can it not be—
and I ask this
quite honestly—that the great injustice lies
on your side and not mine? Time and
time again
men have come before me perfect in
their lives,
loved by all who knew them, loved at
home,
gentle, not vicious, yet caught so ripe
red-handed
in some dark violence there was no
denying
where the onus lay.

MIO. That was not so with my father!

GAUNT. And yet it seemed so to me. To other men
who sat in judgment on him. Can you be sure—
I ask this in humility—that you,
who were touched closest by the tragedy,
may not have lost perspective—may have brooded 10
day and night on one theme—till your eyes are tranced
and show you one side only?

MIO. I see well enough.

GAUNT. And would that not be part of the malady—
to look quite steadily at the drift of things
but see there what you wish—not what is there— 20
not what another man to whom the story
was fresh would say is there?

MIO. You think I'm crazy.
Is that what you meant to say?

GAUNT. I've seen it happen
with the best and wisest men. I but ask the question.
I can't speak for you. Is it not true wherever 30
you walk, through the little town where you knew him well,
or flying from it, inland or by the sea,
still walking at your side, and sleeping only
when you too sleep, a shadow not your own
follows, pleading and holding out its hands
to be delivered from shame? 40

MIO. How you know that
by God I don't know.

GAUNT. Because one spectre haunted you and me—
and haunts you still, but for me it's laid to rest

now that my mind is satisfied. He died
justly and not by error. (*A pause.*)

MIO (*stepping forward*). Do you care to know
you've come so near to death it's miracle
that pulse still beats in your splotchy throat?
Do you know
there's murder in me?

GAUNT. There was murder in your sire,
and it's to be expected! I say he died
justly, and he deserved it!

MIO. Yes, you'd like too well
to have me kill you! That would prove your case
and clear your name, and dip my father's name
in stench forever! You'll not get that from me!
Go home and die in bed, get it under cover,
your lux-et-lex putrefaction of the right thing,
you man that walks like a god!

GAUNT. Have I made you angry
by coming too near the truth?

MIO. This sets him up,
this venomous slug, this sets him up in a gown,
deciding who's to walk above the earth
and who's to lie beneath! And giving reasons!
The cobra giving reasons; I'm a god,
by Buddha, holy and worshipful my fang,
and can I sink it in!
(*He pauses, turns as if to go, then sits.*)
This is no good.
This won't help much.

[*The* JUDGE *and* ESDRAS *look at each other.*]

GAUNT. We should be going.

ESDRAS. Yes. (*They prepare to go.*)
I'll lend you my coat.

GAUNT (*looking at it with distaste*).
No, keep it. A little rain
shouldn't matter to me.
ESDRAS. It freezes as it falls,
and you've a long way to go.
GAUNT. I'll manage, thank you.
[GAUNT *and* ESDRAS *go out,* ESDRAS *obsequious, closing the door.*]
GARTH (*looking at* MIO's *back*). Well?
MIO (*not moving*). Let me sit here a moment. 10
[GARTH *shrugs his shoulders and goes toward the inner door.* MIRIAMNE *opens it and comes out.* GARTH *looks at her, then at* MIO, *then lays his fingers on his lips. She nods.* GARTH *goes out.* MIRIAMNE *sits and watches* MIO. *After a little he turns and sees her.*]
MIO. How did you come here?
MIRIAMNE. I live here. 20
MIO. Here?
MIRIAMNE. My name is Esdras. Garth
is my brother. The walls are thin.
I heard what was said.
MIO (*stirring wearily*). I'm going. This is
no place for me.
MIRIAMNE. What place
would be better?
MIO. None. Only it's better to go.
Just to go. 30
[*She comes over to him, puts her arm around him and kisses his forehead.*]
MIRIAMNE. Mio.
MIO. What do you want?
Your kisses burn me—and your arms.
Don't offer
what I'm never to have! I can have
nothing. They say
they'll cross the void sometime to the
other planets 40
and men will breathe in that air.
Well, I could breathe there,
but not here now. Not on this ball of
mud.
I don't want it.
MIRIAMNE. They can take away so little

with all their words. For you're a king
among them.
I heard you, and loved your voice.
MIO. I thought I'd fallen
so low there was no further, and now a
pit
opens beneath. It was bad enough
that he
should have died innocent, but if he
were guilty—
then what's my life—what have I left
to do—?
The son of a felon—and what they
spat on me
was earned—and I'm drenched with
the stuff.
Here on my hands
and cheeks, their spittle hanging! I
liked my hands
because they were like his. I tell you
I've lived
by his innocence, lived to see it flash
and blind them all—
MIRIAMNE. Never believe them, Mio,
never. (*She looks toward the inner door.*)
MIO. But it was truth I wanted, truth—
not the lies you'd tell yourself, or tell a
woman,
or a woman tells you! The judge with
his cobra mouth
may have spat truth—and I may be
mad! For me—
your hands are too clean to touch me.
I'm to have
the scraps from hotel kitchens—and
instead of love
those mottled bodies that hitch themselves through alleys
to sell for dimes or nickels. Go, keep
yourself chaste
for the baker bridegroom—baker and
son of a baker,
let him get his baker's dozen on you!
MIRIAMNE. No—
say once you love me—say it once;
I'll never

ask to hear it twice, nor for any kindness,
and you shall take all I have!
[GARTH *opens the inner door and comes
out.*]
GARTH. I interrupt
a love scene, I believe. We can do
without
your adolescent mawkishness.
(*To* MIRIAMNE.) You're a child.
You'll both remember that.
MIRIAMNE. I've said nothing to harm
you—
and will say nothing.
GARTH. You're my sister, though,
and I take a certain interest in you.
Where
have you two met?
MIRIAMNE. We danced together.
GARTH. Then   20
the dance is over, I think.
MIRIAMNE. I've always loved you
and tried to help you, Garth. And
you've been kind.
Don't spoil it now.
GARTH. Spoil it how?
MIRIAMNE. Because I love him.
I didn't know it would happen. We
danced together.
And the world's all changed. I see 30
you through a mist,
and our father, too. If you brought
this to nothing
I'd want to die.
GARTH (*to* MIO). You'd better go.
MIO. Yes, I know.
[*He rises. There is a trembling knock at the
door.* MIRIAMNE *goes to it. The* HOBO *is
there shivering.*]
HOBO. Miss, could I sleep under the 40
pipes tonight, miss?
Could I, please?
MIRIAMNE. I think—not tonight.
HOBO. There won't be any more nights

if I don't get warm, miss.

MIRIAMNE. Come in.
[*The* HOBO *comes in, looks round deprecat-
ingly, then goes to a corner beneath a
huge heating pipe, which he crawls un-
der as if he'd been there before.*]
HOBO. Yes, miss, thank you.
GARTH. Must we put up with that?
MIRIAMNE. Father let him sleep there—
last winter.
GARTH. Yes, God, yes.
MIO. Well, good night.
MIRIAMNE. Where will you go?
MIO. Yes, where? As if it mattered.
GARTH. Oh, sleep here, too.
We'll have a row of you under the
pipes.
MIO. No, thanks.
MIRIAMNE. Mio, I've saved a little
money. It's only
some pennies, but you must take it.
(*She shakes some coins out of a box into her
hand.*)
MIO. No, thanks.
MIRIAMNE. And I love you.
You've never said you love me.
MIO. Why wouldn't I love you
when you're clean and sweet,
and I've seen nothing sweet or clean
this last ten years? I love you. I leave
you that
for what good it may do you. It's none
to me.
MIRIAMNE. Then kiss me.
MIO (*looking at* GARTH).
With that scowling over us? No.
When it rains, some spring
on the planet Mercury, where the
spring comes often,
I'll meet you there, let's say. We'll
wait for that.
It may be some time till then.
[*The outside door opens and* ESDRAS *enters
with* JUDGE GAUNT, *then, after a slight
interval,* TROCK *follows.* TROCK *sur-
veys the interior and its occupants one by
one, carefully.*]

TROCK. I wouldn't want to cause you in-
convenience,
any of you, and especially the Judge.
I think you know that. You've all got
things to do——
trains to catch, and so on. But trains
can wait.
Hell, nearly anything can wait, you'll
find,
only I can't. I'm the only one that 10
can't
because I've got no time. Who's all
this here?
Who's that? (*He points to the* HOBO.)

ESDRAS. He's a poor half-wit, sir,
that sometimes sleeps there.

TROCK. Come out. I say come out,
whoever you are.
(*The* HOBO *stirs and looks up.*)
Yes, I mean you. Come out.
(*The* HOBO *emerges.*)
What's your name?

HOBO. They mostly call me Oke.

TROCK. What do you know?

HOBO. No, sir.

TROCK. Where are you from?

HOBO. I got a piece of bread.
(*He brings it out, trembling.*)

TROCK. Get back in there!
(*The* HOBO *crawls back into his corner.*) 30
Maybe you want to know why I'm
doing this.
Well, I've been robbed, that's why—
robbed five or six times;
the police can't find a thing—so I'm
out for myself—
if you want to know.
(*To* MIO.) Who are you?

MIO. Oh, I'm a half-wit,
came in here by mistake. The differ- 40
ence is
I've got no piece of bread.

TROCK. What's your name?

MIO. My name?
Theophrastus Such. That's respectable.

You'll find it all the way from here to
the coast
on the best police blotters.
Only the truth is we're a little touched
in the head,
Oke and me. You'd better ask somebody else.

TROCK. Who is he?

ESDRAS. His name's Romagna. He's the
son.

TROCK. Then what's he doing here?
You said you were on the level.

GARTH. He just walked in. On account
of the stuff in the papers. We didn't
ask him.

TROCK. God, we are a gathering. Now if
we had Shadow we'd be all here,
huh? Only I guess we won't see
Shadow. No, that's too much to ask.

20 MIO. Who's Shadow?

TROCK. Now you're putting questions.
Shadow was just nobody, you see.
He blew away. It might happen to
anyone. (*He looks at* GARTH.) Yes,
anyone at all.

MIO. Why do you keep your hand in
your pocket, friend?

TROCK. Because I'm cold, punk. Because
I've been outside and it's cold as
the tomb of Christ. (*To* GARTH.)
Listen, there's a car waiting up at
the street to take the Judge home.
We'll take him to the car.

GARTH. That's not necessary.

ESDRAS. No.

TROCK. I say it is, see? You wouldn't
want to let the Judge walk, would
you? The Judge is going to ride
where he's going, with a couple of
chauffeurs, and everything done in
style. Don't you worry about the
Judge. He'll be taken care of. For
good.

GARTH. I want no hand in it.

TROCK. Anything happens to me happens to you too, musician.

GARTH. I know that.

TROCK. Keep your mouth out of it then. And you'd better keep the punk here tonight, just for luck. (*He turns toward the door. There is a brilliant lightning flash through the windows, followed slowly by dying thunder.* TROCK *opens the door. The rain begins to pour in sheets.*) Jesus, somebody tipped it over again! (*A cough racks him.*) Wait till it's over. It takes ten days off me every time I step into it. (*He closes the door.*) Sit down and wait.

[*Lightning flashes again. The thunder is fainter.* ESDRAS, GARTH *and the* JUDGE *sit down.*]

GAUNT. We were born too early. Even you who are young
are not of the elect. In a hundred years
man will put his finger on life itself, and then
he will live as long as he likes. For you and me
we shall die soon—one day, one year more or less,
when or where, it's no matter. It's what we call
an indeterminate sentence. I'm hungry.

[GARTH *looks at* MIRIAMNE.]

MIRIAMNE. There was nothing left tonight.

HOBO. I've got a piece of bread.

[*He breaks his bread in two and hands half to the* JUDGE.]

GAUNT. I thank you, sir. (*He eats.*)
This is not good bread. (*He rises.*)
Sir, I am used
to other company. Not better, perhaps, but their clothes
were different. These are what it's the fashion to call
the underprivileged.

TROCK. Oh, hell!
(*He turns toward the door.*)

MIO (*to* TROCK). It would seem that you and the Judge know each other. [TROCK *faces him.*]

TROCK. I've been around.

MIO. Maybe you've met before.

TROCK. Maybe we have.

MIO. Will you tell me where?

TROCK. How long do you want to live?

MIO. How long? Oh, I've got big ideas about that.

TROCK. I thought so. Well, so far I've got nothing against you but your name, see? You keep it that way.

[*He opens the door. The rain still falls in torrents. He closes the door. As he turns from it, it opens again, and* SHADOW, *white, bloodstained and dripping, stands in the doorway.* GARTH *rises.* TROCK *turns.*]

GAUNT (*to the* HOBO). Yet if one were careful of his health, ate sparingly, drank not at all, used himself wisely, it might be that even an old man could live to touch immortality. They may come on the secret sooner than we dare hope. You see? It does no harm to try.

TROCK (*backing away from* SHADOW). By God, he's out of his grave!

SHADOW (*leaning against the doorway, holding a gun in his hands*). Keep your hands where they belong, Trock.
You know me.

TROCK. Don't! Don't! I had nothing to do with it!
(*He backs to the opposite wall.*)

SHADOW. You said the doctor gave you six months to live—well, I don't give you that much. That's what you had, six months, and so you start bumping off your friends to make sure of your damn six months. I got it from you.
I know where I got it.

Because I wouldn't give it to the
   Judge.
So he wouldn't talk.

TROCK. Honest to God—

SHADOW. What God?
   The one that let you put three holes in
      me
   when I was your friend? Well, He let
      me get up again
   and walk till I could find you. That's 10
      as far as I get,
   but I got there, by God! And I can
      hear you
   even if I can't see!
   (*He takes a staggering step forward.*)
      A man needs blood
   to keep going.—I got this far.—And
      now I can't see!
   It runs out too fast—too fast—
   when you've got three slugs
   clean through you.
   Show me where he is, you fools! He's
      here!
   I got here! (*He drops the gun.*)
      Help me! Help me! Oh, God! Oh,
      God!
   I'm going to die! Where does a man
      lie down?
   I want to lie down!

[MIRIAMNE *starts toward* SHADOW. GARTH 30
   and ESDRAS *help him into the next
   room,* MIRIAMNE *following.* TROCK
   *squats in his corner, breathing hard,
   looking at the door.* MIO *stands, watching* TROCK. GARTH *returns, wiping his
   hand with a handkerchief.* MIO *picks up
   and pockets the gun.* MIRIAMNE *comes
   back and leans against the door jamb.*]

GAUNT. You will hear it said that an old
   man makes a good judge, being 40
   calm, clear-eyed, without passion.
   But this is not true. Only the young
   love truth and justice. The old are
   savage, wary, violent, swayed by
   maniac desires, cynical of friend-
   ship or love, open to bribery and
the temptations of lust, corrupt and
   dastardly to the heart. I know
   these old men. What have they left
   to believe, what have they left to
   lose? Whorers of daughters, lickers
   of girls' shoes, contrivers of nasti-
   ness in the night, purveyors of per-
   version, worshippers of possession!
   Death is the only radical. He comes
   late, but he comes at last to put
   away the old men and give the
   young their places. It was time.
   (*He leers.*)
   Here's one I heard yesterday:
      Marmaduke behind the barn
         got his sister in a fix;
      he says damn instead of darn;
         ain't he cute? He's only six!

THE HOBO. He, he, he!

20 GAUNT.
      And the hoot-owl hoots all night,
         and the cuckoo cooks all day,
      and what with a minimum grace of
         God
      we pass the time away.

THE HOBO. He, he, he—I got ya!
   (*He makes a sign with his thumb.*)

GAUNT (*sings*).
      And he led her all around
      and laid her on the ground
      and he ruffled up the feathers of
         her cuckoo's nest!

HOBO. Ho, ho, ho!

GAUNT. I am not taken with the way
   you laugh. You should cultivate
   restraint.

      [ESDRAS *reënters.*]

TROCK. Shut the door.

ESDRAS. He won't come back again.

TROCK. I want the door shut! He was
   dead, I tell you! (ESDRAS *closes the
   door.*) And Romagna was dead,
   too, once! Can't they keep a man
   under ground?

MIO. No. No more! They don't stay
   under ground any more, and they

don't stay under water! Why did
you have him killed?

TROCK. Stay away from me! I know you!

MIO. Who am I, then?

TROCK. I know you, damn you! Your
name's Romagna!

MIO. Yes! And Romagna was dead, too,
and Shadow was dead, but the
time's come when you can't keep
them down, these dead men! They
won't stay down! They come in
with their heads shot off and their
entrails dragging! Hundreds of
them! One by one—all you ever
killed! Watch the door! See!—It
moves!

TROCK (*looking, fascinated, at the door*).
Let me out of here! (*He tries to rise.*)

MIO (*the gun in his hand*). Oh, no! You'll
sit there and wait for them! One by
one they'll come through that
door, pulling their heads out of the
gunny-sacks where you tied them—
glauming over you with their rotten hands! They'll see without
eyes and crawl over you—Shadow
and the paymaster and all the rest
of them—putrescent bones without
eyes! Now! Look! Look! For I'm
first among them!

TROCK. I've done for better men than
you! And I'll do for you!

GAUNT (*rapping on the table*). Order,
gentlemen, order! The witness will
remember that a certain decorum
is essential in the court-room!

MIO. By God, he'll answer me!

GAUNT (*thundering*). Silence! Silence!
Let me remind you of courtesy
toward the witness! What case is
this you try?

MIO. The case of the state against Bartolomeo Romagna for the murder
of the paymaster!

GAUNT. Sir, that was disposed of long
ago!

MIO. Never disposed of, never, not while
I live!

GAUNT. Then we'll have done with it
now! I deny the appeal! I have
denied the appeal before and I do
so again!

HOBO. He, he!—He think's he's in the
moving pictures! (*A flash of lightning.*)

GAUNT. Who set that flash! Bailiff, clear
the court! This is not Flemington,
gentlemen! We are not conducting
this case to make a journalistic holiday! (*The thunder rumbles faintly.*
GARTH *opens the outside door and faces
a solid wall of rain.*) Stop that man!
He's one of the defendants!

[GARTH *closes the door.*]

MIO. Then put him on the stand!

GARTH. What do you think you're
doing?

MIO. Have you any objection?

GAUNT. The objection is not sustained.
We will hear the new evidence.
Call your witness.

MIO. Garth Esdras!

GAUNT. He will take the stand!

GARTH. If you want me to say what I
said before I'll say it!

MIO. Call Trock Estrella then!

GAUNT. Trock Estrella to the stand!

TROCK. No, by God!

MIO. Call Shadow, then! He'll talk! You
thought he was dead, but he'll get
up again and talk!

TROCK (*screaming*). What do you want of
me?

MIO. You killed the paymaster! You!

TROCK. You lie! It was Shadow killed
him!

MIO. And now I know! Now I know!

GAUNT. Again I remind you of courtesy
toward the witness!

MIO. I know them now!
Let me remind you of courtesy toward the dead!

He says that Shadow killed him! If
    Shadow were here
he'd say it was Trock! There were
    three men involved
in the new version of the crime for
    which
my father died! Shadow and Trock
    Estrella
as principals in the murder—Garth
    as witness!—   10
Why are they here together?—and
    you—the Judge—
why are you here? Why, because you
    were all afraid
and you drew together out of that
    fear to arrange
a story you could tell! And Trock
    killed Shadow
and meant to kill the Judge out of
    that same fear—   20
to keep them quiet! This is the thing
    I've hunted
over the earth to find out, and I'd be
    blind
indeed if I missed it now!
(*To* GAUNT.) You heard what he said:
It was Shadow killed him! Now let
    the night conspire
with the sperm of hell! It's plain be-
    yond denial   30
even to this fox of justice—and all his
    words
are curses on the wind! You lied! You
    lied!
You knew this too!
GAUNT (*low*). Let me go. Let me go!
MIO. Then why
    did you let my father die?
GAUNT. Suppose it known,
    but there are things a judge must not 40
        believe
    though they should head and fester
        underneath
    and press in on his brain. Justice once
        rendered
    in a clear burst of anger, righteously,

upon a very common laborer,
confessed an anarchist, the verdict
    found
and the precise machinery of law
invoked to know him guilty—think
    what furor
would rock the state if the court then
    flatly said:
all this was lies—must be reversed?
    It's better,
as any judge can tell you, in such
    cases,
holding the common good to be
    worth more
than small injustice, to let the record
    stand,
let one man die. For justice, in the
    main,
is governed by opinion. Communities
will have what they will have, and
    it's quite as well,
after all, to be rid of anarchists. Our
    rights
as citizens can be maintained as
    rights
only while we are held to be the peers
of those who live about us. A vendor
    of fish
is not protected as a man might be
who kept a market. I own I've some-
    times wished
this was not so, but it is. The man you
    defend
was unfortunate—and his misfortune
    bore
almost as heavily on me.—I'm
    broken—
broken across. You're much too
    young to know
how bitter it is when a worn connec-
    tion chars
and you can't remember—can't re-
    member.
(*He steps forward.*) You
will not repeat this? It will go no fur-
    ther?

MIO. No.

No further than the moon takes the
    tides—no further
than the news went when he died—
when you found him guilty
and they flashed that round the earth.
    Wherever men
still breathe and think, and know
    what's done to them
by the powers above, they'll know. 10
    That's all I ask.
That'll be enough.

[TROCK *has risen and looks darkly at* MIO.]

GAUNT. Thank you. For I've said some
    things
a judge should never say.

TROCK. Go right on talking.

Both of you. It won't get far, I guess.

MIO. Oh, you'll see to that?

TROCK. I'll see to it. Me and some others. 20
    Maybe I lost my grip there just for a
        minute.
    That's all right.

MIO. Then see to it! Let it rain!

What can you do to me now when the
    night's on fire
with this thing I know? Now I could
    almost wish
there was a god somewhere—I could
    almost think   30
there was a god—and he somehow
    brought me here
and set you down before me here in
    the rain
where I could wring this out of you!
    For it's said,
and I've heard it, and I'm free! He
    was as I thought him,
true and noble and upright, even
    when he went   40
to a death contrived because he was
    as he was
and not your kind! Let it rain! Let
    the night speak fire
and the city go out with the tide, for
    he was a man

and I know you now, and I have my
    day!

[*There is a heavy knock at the outside door.*
    MIRIAMNE *opens it, at a glance from*
    GARTH. *The* POLICEMAN *is there in
    oilskins.*]

POLICEMAN. Evening.

(*He steps in, followed by a* SERGEANT,
    similarly dressed.)

We're looking for someone
might be here. Seen an old man
    around
acting a little off?

(*To* ESDRAS.) You know the one
I mean. You saw him out there. Jeez!
    You've got
a funny crowd here!

(*He looks round. The* HOBO *shrinks into
    his corner.*) That's the one I saw.
What do you think?

SERGEANT. That's him. You mean to say
you didn't know him by his pictures?
(*He goes to* GAUNT.) Come on, old man.
You're going home.

GAUNT. Yes, sir. I've lost my way.
I think I've lost my way.

SERGEANT. I'll say you have.
About three hundred miles. Now
    don't you worry.
We'll get you back.

GAUNT. I'm a person of some rank
in my own city.

SERGEANT. We know that. One look at
    you
and we'd know that.

GAUNT. Yes, sir.

POLICEMAN. If it isn't Trock!
Trock Estrella. How are you, Trock?

TROCK. Pretty good,
    Thanks.

POLICEMAN. Got out yesterday again, I
    hear?

TROCK. That's right.

SERGEANT. Hi'ye, Trock?

TROCK. O. K.

SERGEANT. You know we got orders

to watch you pretty close. Be good
now, baby,
or back you go. Don't pull try to anything,
not in my district.

TROCK. No, sir.

SERGEANT. No bumping off.
If you want my advice quit carrying a
gun.
Try earning your living for once.   10

TROCK. Yeah.

SERGEANT. That's an idea.
Because if we find any stiffs on the
river bank
we'll know who to look for.

MIO. Then look in the other room!
I accuse that man of murder! Trock
Estrella!
He's a murderer!

POLICEMAN. Hello. I remember you.   20

SERGEANT. Well, what murder?

MIO. It was Trock Estrella
that robbed the pay roll thirteen years
ago
and did the killing my father died for!
You know
the Romagna case! Romagna was innocent,
and Trock Estrella guilty!

SERGEANT (*disgusted*). Oh, what the hell!   30
That's old stuff—the Romagna case.

POLICEMAN. Hey, Sarge!
(*The* SERGEANT *and* POLICEMAN *come
closer together.*)
The boy's a professional kidder. He
took me over
about half an hour ago. He kids the
police
and then ducks out!

SERGEANT. Oh, yeah?   40

MIO. I'm not kidding now.
You'll find a dead man there in the
next room
and Estrella killed him!

SERGEANT. Thirteen years ago?
And nobody smelled him yet?

MIO (*pointing*). I accuse this man
of two murders! He killed the paymaster long ago
and had Shadow killed tonight. Look,
look for yourself!
He's there all right!

POLICEMAN. Look boy. You stood out
there
and put the booby sign on the dumb
police
because they're fresh out of Ireland.
Don't try it twice.

SERGEANT (*to* GARTH). Any corpses here?

GARTH. Not that I know of.

SERGEANT. I thought so.
(MIO *looks at* MIRIAMNE.)
(*To* MIO.) Think up a better one.

MIO. Have I got to drag him
out here where you can see him?
(*He goes toward the inner door.*) Can't
you scent a murder
when it's under your nose? Look in!

MIRIAMNE. No, no—there's no one—
there's no one there!

SERGEANT (*looking at* MIRIAMNE). Take a
look inside.

POLICEMAN. Yes, sir.
(*He goes into the inside room. The* SER-
GEANT *goes up to the door. The* POLICE-
MAN *returns.*)
He's kidding, Sarge. If there's a ca-
daver
in here I don't see it.

MIO. You're blind then!
(*He goes into the room, the* SERGEANT
following him.)

SERGEANT. What do you mean?
(*He comes out,* MIO *following him.*)
When you make a charge of murder
it's better to have
the corpus delicti, son. You're the
kind puts in
fire alarms to see the engine!

MIO. By God, he was there.
He went in there to die.

SERGEANT. I'll bet he did.

And I'm Haile Selassie's aunt! What's
your name?

MIO. Romagna. (*To* GARTH.) What have
you done with him?

GARTH. I don't know what you mean.

SERGEANT (*to* GARTH). What's he talking
about?

GARTH. I wish I could tell you.
I don't know.

SERGEANT. He must have seen something. 10

POLICEMAN. He's got
the Romagna case on the brain. You
watch yourself,
chump, or you'll get run in.

MIO. Then they're in it together!
All of them!
(*To* MIRIAMNE.) Yes, and you!

GARTH. He's nuts, I say.

MIRIAMNE (*gently*).
You have dreamed something—isn't 20
it true?
You've dreamed—
But truly, there was no one—
(MIO *looks at her comprehendingly.*)

MIO. You want me to say it. (*He pauses.*)
Yes, by God, I was dreaming.

SERGEANT (*to* POLICEMAN). I guess you're
right.
We'd better be going. Haven't you
got a coat?

GAUNT. No, sir.

SERGEANT. I guess I'll have to lend you
mine.
(*He puts his oilskins on* GAUNT.) Come
on, now. It's getting late.

[GAUNT, *the* POLICEMAN *and the* SERGEANT
go out.]

TROCK. They're welcome to him.
His fuse is damp. Where is that walking fool　　　　　　　　40
with the three slugs in him?

ESDRAS. He fell in the hall beyond
and we left him there.

TROCK. That's lucky for some of us. Is he
out this time
or is he still butting around?

ESDRAS. He's dead.

TROCK. That's perfect.
(*To* MIO.) Don't try using your firearms, amigo baby,
the Sarge is outside. (*He turns to go.*)
Better ship that carrion
back in the river! The one that walks
when he's dead;
maybe he'll walk the distance for you.

GARTH. Coming back?

TROCK. Well, if I come back
you'll see me. If I don't, you won't.
Let the punk
go far as he likes. Turn him loose and
let him go.
And may you all rot in hell.

[*He pulls his coat around him and goes to
left.* MIRIAMNE *climbs up to look out
a window.*]

MIRIAMNE. He's climbing up to the street,
along the bridgehead.
(*She turns.*) Quick, Mio! It's safe now!
Quick!

GARTH. Let him do as he likes.

MIRIAMNE. What do you mean? Garth!
He means to kill him!
You know that!

GARTH. I've no doubt Master Romagna
can run his own campaign.

MIRIAMNE. But he'll be killed! 30

MIO. Why did you lie about Shadow?
(*There is a pause.* GARTH *shrugs, walks
across the room, and sits.*) You were
one of the gang!

GARTH. I can take a death if I have to!
Go tell your story,
only watch your step, for I warn you,
Trock's out gunning
and you may not walk very far. Oh,
I could defend it
but it's hardly worth while.
If they get Trock they get me too.
Go tell them. You owe me nothing.

ESDRAS. This Trock you saw,
no one defends him. He's earned his
death so often

there's nobody to regret it. But his
  crime,
his same crime that has dogged you,
  dogged us down
from what little we had, to live here
  among the drains,
where the waterbugs break out like a
  scrofula
on what we eat—and if there's lower
  to go   10
we'll go there when you've told your
  story. And more
that I haven't heart to speak—
MIO (*to* GARTH). My father died
in your place. And you could have
  saved him!
You were one of the gang!
GARTH. Why, there you are.
You certainly owe me nothing.
MIRIAMNE (*moaning*). I want to die.   20
I want to go away.
MIO. Yes, and you lied!
And trapped me into it!
MIRIAMNE. But Mio, he's my brother.
I couldn't give them my brother.
MIO. No. You couldn't.
You were quite right. The gods were
  damned ironic
tonight, and they've worked it out.
ESDRAS. What will be changed   30
if it comes to trial again? More blood
  poured out
to a mythical justice, but your father
  lying still
where he lies now.
MIO. The bright, ironical gods!
What fun they have in heaven! When
  a man prays hard
for any gift, they give it, and then one
  more   40
to boot that makes it useless.
(*To* MIRIAMNE.) You might have
  picked

some other stranger to dance with!
MIRIAMNE. I know.
MIO. Or chosen
some other evening to sit outside in
  the rain.
But no, it had to be this. All my life
  long
I've wanted only one thing, to say to
  the world
and prove it: the man you killed was
  clean and true
and full of love as the twelve-year-old
  that stood
and taught in the temple. I can say
  that now
and give my proofs—and now you
  stick a girl's face
between me and the rites I've sworn
  the dead
shall have of me! You ask too much!
  Your brother
can take his chance! He was ready
  enough to let
an innocent man take certainty for
  him
to pay for the years he's had. That
  parts us, then,
but we're parted anyway, by the same
  dark wind
that blew us together. I shall say what
  I have to say.
(*He steps back.*) And I'm not welcome
  here.
MIRIAMNE. But don't go now! You've
  stayed
too long! He'll be waiting!
MIO. Well, is this any safer?
Let the winds blow, the four winds of
  the world,
and take us to the four winds.
[*The three are silent before him. He turns and
  goes out.*]
                    CURTAIN

ACT III

The river banks ouside the tenement, a lit-
tle before the close of the previous act. The
rain still falls through the street lamps. The
TWO NATTY YOUNG MEN IN SERGE AND
GRAY *are leaning against the masonry in a*
ray of light, concentrating on a game of chance.
Each holds in his hand a packet of ten or fif-
teen crisp bills. They compare the numbers on
the top notes and immediately a bill changes
hands. This goes on with varying fortune until
the tide begins to run toward the 1ST GUNMAN,
who has accumulated nearly the whole supply.
They play on in complete silence, evidently
not wishing to make any noise. Occasionally
they raise their heads slightly to look carefully
about. Luck begins to favor the 2ND GUNMAN,
and the notes come his way. Neither evinces the
slightest interest in how the game goes. They
merely play on, bored, half-absorbed. There is
a slight noise at the tenement door. They put
the bills away and watch. TROCK *comes out,*
pulls the door shut and comes over to them. He
says a few words too low to be heard, and
without changing expression the YOUNG MEN
saunter toward the right. TROCK *goes out to the*
left, and the 2ND PLAYER, *catching that out*
of the corner of his eye, lingers in a glimmer of
light to go on with the game. The 1ST, *with*
an eye on the tenement door, begins to play
without ado, and the bills again shift back and
forth, then concentrate in the hands of the 1ST
GUNMAN. *The* 2ND *shrugs his shoulders,*
searches his pockets, finds one bill, and playing
with it begins to win heavily. They hear the
door opening, and putting the notes away, slip
out in front of the rock. MIO *emerges, closes the*
door, looks around him and walks to the left.
Near the corner of the tenement he pauses,
reaches out his hand to try the rain, looks up
toward the street, and stands uncertainly a
moment. He returns and leans against the
tenement wall. MIRIAMNE *comes out.* MIO
continues to look off into space as if unaware
of her. She looks away.

MIO. This rather takes one off his high
horse.—What I mean, tough
weather for a hegira. You see, this is
my sleeping suit, and if I get it wet
—basta!

MIRIAMNE. If you could only hide here.

MIO. Hide?

MIRIAMNE. Lucia would take you in. The
street-piano man.

MIO. At the moment I'm afflicted with
claustrophobia. I prefer to die in
the open, seeking air.

MIRIAMNE. But you could stay there till
daylight.

MIO. You're concerned about me.

MIRIAMNE. Shall I ask him?

MIO. No. On the other hand there's a
certain reason in your concern. I
looked up the street and our old
friend Trock hunches patiently under the warehouse eaves.

MIRIAMNE. I was sure of that.

MIO. And here I am, a young man on a
cold night, waiting the end of the
rain. Being read my lesson by a boy,
a blind boy—you know the one I
mean. Knee-deep in the salt-marsh,
Miriamne, bitten from within,
fought.

MIRIAMNE. Wouldn't it be better if you
came back in to house?

MIO. You forget my claustrophobia.

MIRIAMNE. Let me walk with you, then.
Please. If I stay beside you he
wouldn't dare.

MIO. And then again he might.—We
don't speak the same language,
Miriamne.

MIRIAMNE. I betrayed you. Forgive me.

MIO. I wish I knew this region. There's
probably a path along the bank.

MIRIAMNE. Yes. Shadow went that way.

MIO. That's true, too. So here I am, a
young man on a wet night, and

blind in my weather eye. Stay and talk to me.

MIRIAMNE. If it happens—it's my fault.

MIO. Not at all, sweet. You warned me to keep away. But I would have it. Now I have to find a way out. It's like a chess game. If you think long enough there's always a way out.— For one or the other.—I wonder why white always wins and black 10 always loses in the problems. White to move and mate in three moves. But what if white were to lose—ah, what then? Why, in that case, obviously black would be white and white would be black.—As it often is.—As we often are.—Might makes white. Losers turn black. Do you think I'd have time to draw a gun?   20

MIRIAMNE. No.

MIO. I'm a fair shot. Also I'm fair game.

[*The door of the tenement opens and* GARTH *comes out to look about quickly. Seeing only* MIO *and* MIRIAMNE *he goes in and comes out again almost immediately carrying one end of a door on which a body lies covered with a cloth. The* HOBO *carries the other end. They go to the right with* 30 *their burden.*]

This is the buriel of Shadow, then;
feet first he dips, and leaves the haunts of men.

Let us make mourn for Shadow, wetly lying,
in elegiac stanzas and sweet crying.

Be gentle with him, little cold waves and fishes;
nibble him not, respect his skin and 40 tissues—

MIRIAMNE. Must you say such things?

MIO. My dear, some requiem is fitting over the dead, even
for Shadow. But the last rhyme was bad.

Whittle him not, respect his dying wishes.

That's better. And then to conclude:

His aromatic virtues, slowly rising
will circumnamb the isle, beyond disguising.   ·
He clung to life beyond the wont of men.
Time and his silence drink us all. Amen.

How I hate these identicals. The French allow them, but the French have no principles anyway. You know, Miriamne, there's really nothing mysterious about human life. It's purely mechanical, like an electric appliance. Stop the engine that runs the generator and the current's broken. When we think the brain gives off a small electrical discharge— quite measurable, and constant within limits. But that's not what makes your hair stand up when frightened.

MIRIAMNE. I think it's a mystery.

MIO. Human life? We'll have to wear veils if we're to keep it a mystery much longer. Now if Shadow and I were made up into sausages we'd probably make very good sausages.

MIRIAMNE. Don't——

MIO. I'm sorry. I speak from a high place, far off, long ago, looking down. The cortège returns. (GARTH *and the* HOBO *return, carrying the door, the cloth lying loosely over it.*) I hope you placed an obol in his mouth to pay the ferryman? Even among the Greeks a little money was prerequisite to Elysium. (GARTH *and the* HOBO *go inside, silent.*) No? It's grim to think of Shadow lingering among lesser shades on the hither side. For lack of a small gratuity.

[ESDRAS *comes out the open door and closes it behind him.*]

ESDRAS. You must wait here, Mio, or go
  inside. I know
you don't trust me, and I haven't
  earned your trust.
You're young enough to seek truth—
and there is no truth;
and I know that—
but I shall call the police and see that
  you
get safely off.   10
MIO. It's a little late for that.
ESDRAS. I shall try.
MIO. And your terms? For I daresay you
  make terms?
ESDRAS. No.
MIO. Then let me remind you what will
  happen.
The police will ask some questions.
When they're answered
they'll ask more, and before they're 20
  done with it
your son will be implicated.
ESDRAS. Must he be?
MIO. I shall not keep quiet.
          [A pause.]
ESDRAS. Still, I'll go.
MIO. I don't ask help, remember. I
  made no truce.
He's not on my conscience, and I'm
  not on yours.   30
ESDRAS. But you
  could make it easier, so easily.
  He's my only son. Let him live.
MIO. His chance of survival's
better than mine, I'd say.
ESDRAS. I'll go.
MIO. I don't urge it.
ESDRAS. No. I put my son's life in your
  hands.
When you're gone,   40
  that may come to your mind.
MIO. Don't count on it.
ESDRAS. Oh,
  I count on nothing.
  (He turns to go. MIRIAMNE runs over to
  him and silently kisses his hands.)

Not mine, not mine, my daughter!
They're guilty hands.
  (He goes out left. GARTH's violin is
  heard within.)
MIO. There was a war in heaven
once, all the angels on one side, and
  all
the devils on the other, and since that
  time
disputes have raged among the
  learned, concerning
whether the demons won, or the
  angels. Maybe
the angels won, after all.
MIRIAMNE. And again, perhaps
there are no demons or angels.
MIO. Oh, there are none.
But I could love your father.
MIRIAMNE. I love him. You see,
he's afraid because he's old. The less
  one has
to lose the more he's afraid.
MIO. Suppose one had
only a short stub end of life, or held
a flashlight with the batteries run
  down
till the bulb was dim, and knew that
  he could live
while the glow lasted. Or suppose one
  knew
that while he stood in a little shelter
  of time
under a bridgehead, say, he could
  live, and then,
from then on, nothing. Then to lie
  and turn
with the earth and sun, and regard
  them not in the least
when the bulb was extinguished or
  he stepped beyond
his circle into the cold? How could
  he live
that last dim quarter-hour, before he
  went,
minus all recollection, to grow in grass
between cobblestones?

MIRIAMNE. Let me put my arms round you, Mio.
Then if anything comes, it's for me, too. (*She puts both arms round him.*)

MIO. Only suppose
this circle's charmed! To be safe until he steps
from this lighted space into dark! Time pauses here
and high eternity grows in one 10 quarter-hour
in which to live.

MIRIAMNE. Let me see if anyone's there—
there in the shadows.
(*She looks toward the right.*)

MIO. It might blast our eternity—
blow it to bits. No, don't go. This is forever,
here where we stand. And I ask you, Miriamne,
how does one spend a forever?

MIRIAMNE. You're frightened?

MIO. Yes.
So much that time stands still.

MIRIAMNE. Why didn't I speak—
tell them—when the officers were here? I failed you
in that one moment!

MIO. His life for mine? Oh, no.
I wouldn't want it, and you couldn't 30 give it.
And if I should go on living we're cut apart
by that brother of yours.

MIRIAMNE. Are we?

MIO. Well, think about it.
A body lies between us, buried in quicklime.
Your allegiance is on the other side of that grave and not to me. 40

MIRIAMNE. No, Mio! Mio, I love you!

MIO. I love you, too, but in case my life went on
beyond that barrier of dark—then Garth
would run his risk of dying.

MIRIAMNE. He's punished, Mio.
His life's been torment to him. Let him go,
for my sake, Mio.

MIO. I wish I could. I wish
I'd never seen him—or you. I've steeped too long
in this thing. It's in my teeth and bones. I can't
let go or forget. And I'll not add my lie
to the lies that cumber his ground. We live our days
in a storm of lies that drifts the truth too deep
for path or shovel; but I've set my foot on a truth
for once, and I'll trail it down!
[*A silence.* MIRIAMNE *looks out to the right.*]
20 MIRIAMNE. There's someone there—
I heard—
[CARR *comes in from the right.*]

MIO. It's Carr.

CARR. That's right. No doubt about it. Excuse me.

MIO. Glad to see you. This is Miriamne. Carr's a friend of mine.

CARR. You're better employed
than when I saw you last.

MIO. Bow to the gentleman,
Miriamne. That's meant for you.

MIRIAMNE. Thank you, I'm sure.
Should I leave you, Mio? You want to talk?

MIO. Oh, no,
we've done our talking.

MIRIAMNE. But—

CARR. I'm the one's out of place—
I wandered back because I got worried about you,
that's the truth.—Oh—those two fellows with the hats
down this way, you know, the ones that ran
after we heard the shooting—they're back again,

lingering or malingering down the
    bank,
revisiting the crime, I guess. They
    may
mean well.
MIO. I'll try to avoid them.
CARR. I didn't care
    for the way they looked at me.—No
        luck, I suppose,
    with that case history? The investiga-
        tion
    you had on hand?
MIO. I can't say. By the way,
    the stiff that fell in the water and we
        saw swirling
    down the eddy, he came trudging up,
        later on,
    long enough to tell his name. His
        name was Shadow
    but he's back in the water now. It's
        all in an evening.
    These things happen here.
CARR. Good God!
MIO. I know.
    I wouldn't believe it if you told it.
CARR. But—
    the man was alive?
MIO. Oh, not for long! He's dunked
    for good this time. That's all that's
        happened.
CARR. Well,
    if you don't need me——
MIRIAMNE. You had a message to send—
    have you forgotten——?
MIO. I?—Yes, I had a message—
    but I won't send it—not now.
MIRIAMNE. Then I will——!
MIO. No.
    Let it go the way it is! It's all ar-
        ranged
    another way. You've been a good
        scout, Carr,
    the best I ever knew on the road.
CARR. That sounds
    like making your will.
MIO. Not yet, but when I do

I've thought of something to leave
    you. It's the view
of Mt. Rainier from the Seattle jail,
snow over cloud. And the rusty chain
    in my pocket from a pair of hand-
    cuffs my father wore. That's all
    the worldly goods I'm seized of.
CARR. Look, Mio—hell—
    if you're in trouble——
MIO. I'm not. Not at all. I have
    a genius that attends me where I go,
    and guards me now. I'm fine.
CARR. Well, that's good news.
    He'll have his work cut out.
MIO. Oh, he's a genius.
CARR. I'll see you then.
    I'll be at the Grand Street place.
        I'm lucky tonight,
    and I can pay. I could even pay for
        two.
MIO. Thanks, I may take you up.
CARR. Good night.
MIO. Right, Carr.
CARR (to MIRIAMNE). Good night.
MIRIAMNE (after a pause). Good night.
    [CARR goes out to the left.]
    Why did you do that? He's your
        genius, Mio,
    and you let him go.
MIO. I couldn't help it.
MIRIAMNE. Call him.
    Run after him and call him!
MIO. I tried to say it
    and it strangled in my throat. I
        might have known
    you'd win in the end.
MIRIAMNE. Is it for me?
MIO. For you?
    It stuck in my throat, that's all I
        know.
MIRIAMNE. Oh, Mio,
    I never asked for that! I only hoped
    Garth could go clear.
MIO. Well, now he will.
MIRIAMNE. But you—
    It was your chance!

MIO. I've lost
my taste for revenge if it falls on you.
Oh, God,
deliver me from the body of this death
I've dragged behind me all these
years! Miriamne!
Miriamne!
MIRIAMNE. Yes!
MIO. Miriamne, if you love me
teach me a treason to what I am, and have been,
till I learn to live like a man! I think
I'm waking
from a long trauma of hate and fear
and death
that's hemmed me from my birth—
and glimpse a life
to be lived in hope—but it's young in
me yet, I can't
get free, or forgive! But teach me
how to live
and forget to hate!
MIRIAMNE. He would have forgiven.
MIO. He?
MIRIAMNE. Your father. (*A pause.*)
MIO. Yes. (*Another pause.*)
You'll think it strange, but I've never
remembered that.
MIRIAMNE. How can I help you?
MIO. You have.
MIRIAMNE. If I were a little older—if I
knew
the things to say! I can only put out
my hands
and give you back the faith you
bring to me
by being what you are. Because to
me
you are all hope and beauty and
brightness drawn   40
across what's black and mean!
MIO. He'd have forgiven—
Then there's no more to say—I've
groped long enough
through this everglades of old re-
venges—here

the road ends.—Miriamne, Miri-
amne,
the iron I wore so long—it's eaten
through
and fallen from me. Let me have
your arms.
They'll say we're children—Well—
the world's made up of children.
MIRIAMNE. Yes.
MIO. But it's too late for me.
MIRIAMNE. No.
(*She goes into his arms, and they kiss for
the first time.*)
Then we'll meet again?
MIO. Yes.
MIRIAMNE. Where?
MIO. I'll write—
or send Carr to you.
MIRIAMNE. You won't forget?
MIO. Forget?
Whatever streets I walk, you'll walk
them, too,
from now on, and whatever roof or
stars
I have to house me, you shall share
my roof
and stars and morning. I shall not
forget.
MIRIAMNE. God keep you!
MIO. And keep you. And this to remember!
if I should die, Miriamne, this half-
hour
is our eternity. I came here seeking
light in darkness, running from the
dawn,
and stumbled on a morning.
[*One of the* YOUNG MEN IN SERGE *strolls in
casually from the right, looks up and
down without expression, then, seemingly
having forgotten something, retraces his
steps and goes out.* ESDRAS *comes in
slowly from the left. He has lost his hat,
and his face is bleeding from a slight
cut on the temple. He stands abjectly
near the tenement.*]

MIRIAMNE. Father—what is it?
(*She goes toward* ESDRAS.)

ESDRAS. Let me alone.
(*He goes nearer to* MIO.)
He wouldn't let me pass.
The street's so icy up along the bridge
I had to crawl on my knees—he
kicked me back
three times—and then he held me
there—I swear   10
what I could do I did! I swear to you
I'd save you if I could.

MIO. What makes you think
that I need saving?

ESDRAS. Child, save yourself if you can!
He's waiting for you.

MIO. Well, we knew that before.

ESDRAS. He won't wait much longer.
He'll come here—
he told me so. Those damned six 20
months of his—
he wants them all—and you're to die
—you'd spread
his guilt—I had to listen to it——

MIO. Wait—
(*He walks forward and looks casually to
the right, then returns.*)
There must be some way up through
the house and out
across the roof——

ESDRAS. He's watching that. But come
in—
and let me look.——

MIO. I'll stay here, thanks. Once in
and I'm a rat in a deadfall—I'll
stay here—
look for me if you don't mind.

ESDRAS. Then watch for me—
I'll be on the roof——
(*He goes in hurriedly.*)   40

MIO (*looking up*). Now all you silent
powers
that make the sleet and dark, and
never yet
have spoken, give us a sign, let the
throw be ours

this once, on this longest night, when
the winter sets
his foot on the threshold leading up
to spring
and enters with remembered cold—
let fall
some mercy with the rain. We are
two lovers
here in your night, and we wish to
live.

MIRIAMNE. Oh, Mio—
if you pray that way, nothing good
will come!
You're bitter, Mio.

MIO. How many floors has this building?

MIRIAMNE. Five or six. It's not as high
as the bridge.

MIO. No, I thought not. How many
pomegranate seeds did you eat,
Persephone?

MIRIAMNE. Oh, darling, darling,
if you die, don't die alone.

MIO. I'm afraid I'm damned
to hell, and you're not damned at
all. Good God,
how long he takes to climb!

MIRIAMNE. The stairs are steep.
(*A slight pause.*)

MIO. I'll follow him.

MIRIAMNE. He's there—at the window
—now.
He waves you to go back, not to go in.
Mio, see, that path between the
rocks—
they're not watching that—they're
out at the river—
I can see them there—they can't
watch both—
it leads to a street above.

MIO. I'll try it, then.
Kiss me. You'll hear. But if you never
hear—
then I'm the king of hell, Persephone,
and I'll expect you.

MIRIAMNE. Oh, lover, keep safe.

MIO. Good-bye.

[*He slips out quickly between the rocks. There is a quick machine gun rat-tat. The violin stops.* MIRIAMNE *runs toward the path.* MIO *comes back slowly, a hand pressed under his heart.*]
It seems you were mistaken.

MIRIAMNE. Oh, God, forgive me!
(*She puts an arm around him. He sinks to his knees.*) 10
Where is it, Mio? Let me help you
in! Quick, quick, let me help you!

MIO. I hadn't thought to choose—this
—ground—
but it will do. (*He slips down.*)

MIRIAMNE. Oh, God, forgive me!

MIO. Yes?
The king of hell was not forgiven
then,
Dis is his name and Hades is his 20
home—
and he goes alone——

MIRIAMNE. Why does he bleed so? Mio,
if you go
I shall go with you.

MIO. It's better to stay alive.
I wanted to stay alive—because of
you—
I leave you that—and what he said
to me dying: 30
I love you, and will love you after I die.
Tomorrow, I shall still love you, as
I've loved
the stars I'll never see, and all the
mornings
that might have been yours and mine.
Oh, Miriamne,
you taught me this.

MIRIAMNE. If only I'd never seen you
then you could live—— 40

MIO. That's blasphemy—Oh, God,
there might have been some easier
way of it.
You didn't want me to die, did you,
Miriamne—?
You didn't send me away——?

MIRIAMNE. Oh, never, never——

MIO. Forgive me—kiss me—I've got
blood on your lips—
I'm sorry—it doesn't matter—I'm
sorry——
[ESDRAS *and* GARTH *come out.*]

MIRIAMNE. Mio—
I'd have gone to die myself—you
must hear this, Mio,
I'd have died to help you—you must
listen, sweet,
you must hear it—(*She rises.*)
I can die, too, see! You! There!
You in the shadows!—You killed
him to silence him!
(*She walks toward the path.*)
But I'm not silenced! All that he
knew I know,
and I'll tell it tonight! Tonight—
tell it and scream it
through all the streets—that Trock's
a murderer
and he hired you for this murder!
Your work's not done—
and you won't live long! Do you
hear?
You're murderers, and I know who
you are!

[*The machine gun speaks again. She sinks to her knees.* GARTH *runs to her.*]

GARTH. You little fool!
(*He tries to lift her.*)

MIRIAMNE. Don't touch me!
(*She crawls toward* MIO.)
Look, Mio! They killed me, too.
Oh, you can believe me
now, Mio. You can believe I wouldn't
hurt you,
because I'm dying! Why doesn't he
answer me?
Oh, now he'll never know!

[*She sinks down, her hand over her mouth, choking.* GARTH *kneels beside her, then rises, shuddering. The* HOBO *comes out.* LUCIA *and* PINY *look out.*]

ESDRAS. It lacked only this.

GARTH. Yes.

[ESDRAS *bends over* MIRIAMNE, *then rises
    slowly.*]

Why was the bastard born? Why did
    he come here?

ESDRAS.   Miriamne—Miriamne—yes,
    and Mio,

one breath shall call you now—for-
    give us both—

forgive the ancient evil of the earth   10
that brought you here——

GARTH. Why must she be a fool?

ESDRAS. Well, they were wiser than you
    and I. To die

when you are young and untouched,
    that's beggary

to a miser of years, but the devils
    locked in synod

shake and are daunted when men set
    their lives   20

at hazard for the heart's love, and
    lose. And these,

who were yet children, will weigh
    more than all

a city's elders when the experiment

is reckoned up in the end. Oh,
    Miriamne,

and Mio—Mio, my son—know this
    where you lie,

this is the glory of earth-born men 30
    and women,

not to cringe, never to yield, but
    standing,

take defeat implacable and defiant,

die unsubmitting. I wish that I'd
    died so,

long ago; before you're old you'll wish

that you had died as they have. On
    this star,

in this hard star-adventure, knowing
    not

what the fires mean to right and left,
    nor whether

a meaning was intended or presumed,

man can stand up, and look out blind,
    and say:

in all these turning lights I find no clue,

only a masterless night, and in my
    blood

no certain answer, yet is my mind my
    own,

yet is my heart a cry toward some-
    thing dim

in distance, which is higher than I am

and makes me emperor of the endless
    dark

even in seeking! What odds and ends
    of life

men may live otherwise, let them live,
    and then

go out, as I shall go, and you. Our
    part

is only to bury them. Come, take her
    up.

They must not lie here.

[LUCIA *and* PINY *come near to help.* ESDRAS
    and GARTH *stoop to carry* MIRIAMNE.]

CURTAIN

ROBERT E. SHERWOOD

ROBERT E. SHERWOOD emerged in the late 1930's as the chief dramatic spokesman against the demiurgic threat of brute barbarity completely to destroy such civilization as man in his enlightened moments has achieved. From the concocter of comedies of intrigue for the sophisticated, he has become a man tense with a message for his time. He is intimately in touch with the uncertainty and the worries of free men everywhere. He is sensitive to the vital issues that harass this age. His attitudes are representative of the struggling course of American opinion toward enlightenment and effective action. He has not originated these views, but he has usually been among the first to give them currency. He has not been too far from their origin to invest them with the power of freshness; yet he has been far enough in the vanguard of this opinion to give to his voice the ring of prophecy before the mass mind of a theatrical audience. He has an extraordinary talent for stating in terms of effective, often exciting, theatre the issues insistently before the community of democratic minds. His statements are starkly realistic, but not drained of hope. His work is the epitome of the modern form of the topical thesis drama; the production of his plays has added life to the useful theatre.

Robert E. Sherwood was born at New Rochelle, N. Y. in 1896. The E. is for Emmet, the family name of his mother, Rosina Emmet Sherwood, a well-known New York artist. Robert Sherwood prepared for college at Mil-

ton Academy, and entered Harvard University in 1914. The World War caught him up in 1917. In the spirit of the times, he enlisted as a common soldier in the Canadian Black Watch and saw service in the Canadian Expeditionary Force. He has written of himself at this period in the illuminating preface to *There Shall Be No Night* (1940). He says that he had been brought up to believe in his superiority to lesser mortals because he was a 100 per cent American and a Harvard man, but that the elemental experiences at the Front, in the training camps, hospitals, and clinks, with men from all over the United States and the British Empire, revealed to him the common unity of men and the narrowness of his previous views. Looking back over his career, he roots in these harsh experiences the beginning of his growth into the Sherwood we now know.

Sherwood left the army in February 1919 almost on the eve of his twenty-second birthday. He reentered civilian life with two years of warfare as a substitute for the upper-class years at peaceful Harvard. Those years had taught him to hate war; and they had made him an internationalist because he believed that only by eliminating blind, local patriotisms and by developing in their stead peaceful international co-operation could war be banished and human dignity restored. But under the tutelage of George Harvey and Senator Henry Cabot Lodge, he denounced the League of Nations, and, as he confesses "with deep shame," cast his first vote for Warren G. Harding, and "did my bit for the great betrayal."

But back in the 1920's, Sherwood was a man of his day and of his circle, not a lone, far-sighted prophet of the coming disasters. He plunged into the New York of the post-armistice era. He was dramatic editor of smart *Vanity Fair* in 1919–1920, with young Dorothy Parker and Robert Benchley as associates. He was successively motion picture critic, associate editor, and editor of *Life* from 1920–1928, and also for a time motion picture critic on the New York *Herald*. He wrote his first play in 1926, primarily because, so he said, he was nearing thirty, and as a newspaper man he was impressed with the importance of getting that promised novel written before he reached thirty, or like other newspaper men, he would never get it done. He didn't have time for a novel, he said, so he wrote a play; and that sounds quite in key with the insouciance so characteristic of the year 1926.

The play was called *The Road to Rome*. It was modelled for its day and public, and it was a hit of the season. It treated cavalierly the historical episode of Hannibal's march on Rome. It made Amytis, the wife of the Roman Fabius Maximus, into a daring and modernized Monna Vanna. She knew how to handle the susceptible Carthaginian conqueror, how to twist him with her shrewd wit, and how to bargain her favors for the preservation of the Roman capital. Her character, her nimble comment, her barbed thrusts at both Fabius and Hannibal gayly carried the play to success. Sherwood gently deprecates this first piece as a mixture of all styles of writing and dramaturgy, with only one memorable line and that Hannibal's farewell double-entendre to the Roman dictator Fabius about his pro-

spective sons. In this opinion the author is wrong; for present day readers going back to the play come upon Amytis's words to Hannibal: "I want you to believe that every sacrifice in the name of war is wasted. When you believe that you will be a great man." And Amytis was there speaking for her creator Sherwood.

The Road to Rome launched Sherwood on his new career as playwright; he has worked industriously at it ever since. He dramatized Ring Lardner's story, *The Love Nest*, which had a short run beginning December 22, 1927. *The Queen's Husband*, an inconsequential comedy on the same basic formula as *The Road to Rome*, opened on January 25, 1928, but did only fairly well. He made other attempts that were unsuccessful. One of these, he reports, was called *Marching as to War;* it dealt with a conscientious objector at the time of the Crusades. In January 1930, his *Waterloo Bridge* was produced. Sherwood, who had been living in England, cast this play on the sentimental side to tell how an American chorus girl in London helped a young soldier compatriot to keep his faith in the purity of womanhood. The author regards the play as "almost good" but not coherent. The following November he tried again with a rather tough little melodrama, *This Is New York*, culminating in a scandal involving a western Senator, his daughter, and her worthless New York friend. Its run was short.

We mention these plays as an interesting exhibit illustrating how a gifted playwright was trying hard to define his interests and to find his individual manner of expression. His next play discovered one region in which his spirit was at home—bright theatrical comedy with an undertone of serious comment on the modern world. It was called *Reunion in Vienna*. It was produced by the Theatre Guild in November 1931, and became on the stage with Alfred Lunt and Lynn Fontanne, and on the screen with John Barrymore, one of the big successes of the period. In its calculated manipulation of character and incident it was expert theatre. It was styled in the smart continental fashion set by Molnar and Schnitzler and popularized in New York by the Theatre Guild. It capitalized on the universal feeling of nostalgia for old Vienna, the romantic city once gay with laughter and waltzes and charming intrigue, but now shabby and middleclass amid the ruins of war. It hinted strongly at the always popular Admirable Crichton theme in the persons of the dispossessed Hapsburgs, notably Prince Rudolph Maximilian who, deprived of the artificial support of his royal background and thrust solely upon his personal worth, has reached his present status as a taxi driver on the Riviera. Sherwood brought the Hapsburgs to this reunion, and drove his comedy along on the meeting between Rudolph and his favorite former mistress Elena, who is now married to, of all people, a psychoanalyst. The play centers in the renewal of their amour.

Sherwood wrote that "I went into this play with what seemed to me an important if not strikingly original idea—science hoist with its own petard—and came out with a gay, romantic comedy." This is a correct description of the end product. Sherwood wrote a somewhat pretentious preface to the play setting forth not too coherently his ideas on the failure of man in his utilization of science. The ideas in the preface, though important, have only the most tenuous relationship to the stage play,

and certainly the audiences who kept it running for nearly three hundred performances did not go to the Martin Beck to learn about the shortcomings of science but to see the wild young fallen Hapsburg overcome the reluctance of Elena.

Up to this point in his career, and perhaps a little further, Sherwood concentrated more effort upon devising entertaining theatrical situations than upon his expanding sense of the message behind his plays. The concentration is, of course, perfectly legitimate. In this first period of his work as a dramatist, he was a man of the twenties. But as the sobering years of the thirties advanced, Sherwood shifted his brittle comedies until the dominant became the incidental, the center the periphery. The message that was crowded out altogether in *Reunion in Vienna* became the heart of the later plays.

Sherwood's plays since *Reunion in Vienna* have been of one piece, though of varying success and power. Of the five plays written in the following two years, four were discarded by the author, and one, *Acropolis*, was produced in London at a financial loss. Sherwood considered it the best play he had written up to that time, no doubt because the message was coming in clearer. One of its passages of hope taken from Pericles was used in part by Dr. Valkonen in his letter to his wife near the close of *There Shall Be No Night*.

The Petrified Forest opened in January 1935 with Leslie Howard playing the lead. Its success was instantaneous. Again Sherwood had accurately sensed the interest of the moment and had dramatized the plight of the Second Lost Generation at the nadir of the great depression. Its tense situation involving the itinerant, lost intellectual, the aspiring girl in the filling station, the desperate gangsters, and their clash of values was pretty well obscured by the fireworks, but the author points out that, though it was a "negative, inconclusive sort of play," he had attempted to speak out directly and for the first time about his own country in his own period. Its thesis was stated and acted out by Alan Squire, the intellectual who perished at the hands of the gangsters, when he said that Nature was hitting back at man, "taking the world away from the intellectuals and giving it back to the brutes" and to chaos. Squire and the murderous outlaws were intended to symbolize the two contending forces, and the brute was victorious.

Sherwood was by this time moving rapidly toward the thesis play. *Idiot's Delight* was written in 1935, and produced in March 1936, again with Alfred Lunt and Lynn Fontanne, as international relations deteriorated toward the second World War within a period of only two decades. The play was characterized by its author as representative of himself and "completely American in that it represented a compound of blank pessimism and desperate optimism, of chaos and jazz." This summary is apt. *Idiot's Delight* was a gripping spectacle merely as an evening at the theatre, what with the vaudeville antics of Harry Van and his naughty chorus girls, his coincidental meeting with an Omaha hotel friend, now a fake Russian and mistress to a munitions magnate; and all the coming in and going out in the cocktail lounge of the Hotel Monte Gabriele on the Swiss-Austrian-Italian border. But it was much more than this, and the spectator was not permitted to take the thesis or leave it as he was in *The Petrified Forest*. For the bombs of the second

World War burst upon the scene, and the shattering destruction is the grim laughter of the supreme Idiot who delights in War. And in the postscript to the published play, Sherwood eloquently voiced his faith in a greater destiny than death in a bomb cellar, in the power of "awareness and remembrance" of "the persistent validity of the Sermon on the Mount" to resist the unleashed forces of destruction.

Then came *Abe Lincoln in Illinois*, written in 1937 and presented in October 1938 with Raymond Massey as Lincoln. Sherwood had written even better than he knew, and the time was ripe for this dramatization of a great American hero. The country was emotionally deep in the rediscovery of Americanism. A wave of novels and plays had broken over the Republic resurrecting its great men and its common citizens alike in all the crucial periods of our history. *Abe Lincoln in Illinois* soon was recognized as a triumph in this movement to set up the American way of peace and good will against the totalitarian glorification of war and brutal power for the enslavement of free peoples. It utilized the full force of the Lincoln legend, already firmly planted in American minds and hearts, to fill out to heroic size the figure of this reluctant Illinois man forced into great place and distasteful action in a time of national crisis.

Sherwood stated the core of the dramatic thrust when he said that *Abe Lincoln in Illinois* "was the story of a man of peace who had to face the issue of appeasement or war. He faced it." The striking similarity between the issues confronting Lincoln at the close of the play, and those before the America and the world of 1938–1940 was obvious enough to extend the dimensions of the play, but not too insistent to disturb its historical accuracy or the harmony of its picture. The authentic tragic lift of the drama came when the hesitant Lincoln ceased to run away from his destiny and turned at last with all the force of his great character to confront the menace and the challenge.

It is faulty criticism to object, as John Mason Brown objected, that "Mr. Sherwood does not prepare us for Lincoln's greatness. His greatness overtakes him during an intermission." It is wrong on two counts. First, because, in an important sense, Lincoln's greatness did overtake him. And, second, because a biographical play of this kind, highlighting in a single evening's performance the life of a man, must succeed, as this play succeeds, by creating scenes that call up in the spectator's mind the full stature of the completed man and his legend. The powerful effect of this technique is illustrated in the closing scene. Lincoln is on the threshold of his supreme test. He makes a simple speech to his fellow townsmen, and the train pulls out while his friends and neighbors sing, "His soul goes marching on." But at that point the spectator or the reader leaps on down the years, reviewing the heroic labors and tragic death of the President, and involuntarily he surrounds this ending of the play with the banked-up emotions released by the thought of Lincoln's sacrifice for our democracy and the Union. This ending is also the final device for linking the threat of those days with the problem of our own future in this democracy.

Abe Lincoln in Illinois was a complete triumph on stage and screen. It was in rehearsal during the Munich crisis in September 1938. It ran while Europe fell into war under Nazi pressure. Sherwood, like all thinking men, was in "a frenzy of uncertainty." But he was not ready to surrender the civilized world to the fiends of darkness. Even the shock of the Russian attack on Finland failed to divest him of hope. It provoked him instead to a ringing, and at times heartbreaking, cry against the drift toward insanity and the obliteration of the good by evil as symbolized by the crushing of Finland. He cast his eloquent testimonial into a drama, and gave it the title of his faith: *There Shall Be No Night*. With Alfred Lunt and Lynn Fontanne in the leading parts, it crowded the theatres in New York and across the country. By the device of broadcasting a speech by Dr. Valkonen on his researches into the nature and causes of mental disease, of having him voice his hope in a schoolroom just before his death, and of reproducing his last letter to his wife, Sherwood has dramatized the point of view of the civilized man who, like Lincoln before him, hates war and yet must fight, who sees the present evils, but yet believes "that man, in his new-found consciousness, can find the means of his redemption."

Sherwood gave his energy and talent to the war as one of the inner circle around President Roosevelt. The story of that period of his life and of the men who led the western world through the conflict is told in his Pulitzer Prize-winning book, *Roosevelt and Hopkins*—in one important sense his greatest drama. With that record completed, Sherwood turned his attention once more to the theatre. With Irving Berlin he produced *Miss Liberty*, which had a long try-out run in Philadelphia before opening in New York on July 15, 1949. It was Sherwood's first venture into musical extravaganza. It revealed still another facet in the vast capabilities of this American dramatist.

ABE LINCOLN IN ILLINOIS

CHARACTERS

MENTOR GRAHAM	MARY TODD
ABE LINCOLN	THE EDWARDS' MAID
ANN RUTLEDGE	JIMMY GALE
BEN MATTLING	AGGIE GALE
JUDGE BOWLING GREEN	GOBEY
NINIAN EDWARDS	STEPHEN A. DOUGLAS
JOSHUA SPEED	WILLIE LINCOLN
TRUM COGDAL	TAD LINCOLN
JACK ARMSTRONG	ROBERT LINCOLN
BAB	THE LINCOLNS' MAID
FEARGUS	CRIMMIN
JASP	BARRICK
SETH GALE	STURVESON
NANCY GREEN	JED
WILLIAM HERNDON	KAVANAGH
ELIZABETH EDWARDS	Major

Soldiers, railroad men, townspeople

ACT I

SCENE I

MENTOR GRAHAM'S *cabin near New Salem, Illinois. Late at night.*

There is one rude table, piled with books and papers. Over it hangs an oil lamp, the only source of light.

At one side of the table sits MENTOR GRAHAM, *a sharp but patient schoolteacher.*

Across from him is ABE LINCOLN— *young, gaunt, tired but intent, dressed in the ragged clothes of a backwoodsman. He speaks with the drawl of southern Indiana— an accent which is more Kentuckian than* 10 *middle-western.*

MENTOR *is leaning on the table.* ABE'S *chair is tilted back, so that his face is out of the light.* MENTOR *turns a page in a grammar book.*

MENTOR. The moods. (MENTOR *closes the book and looks at* ABE.) Every one of us has many moods. You yourself have more than your share of them, Abe. They express the various aspects of your character. So it is with the English language—and you must try to consider this language as if it were a living person, who may be awkward and stumbling, or pompous and pretentious, or simple and direct. Name me the five moods.

ABE. The Indicative, Imperative, Potential, Subjunctive and Infinitive.

MENTOR. And what do they signify?

ABE. The Indicative Mood is the easy one. It just indicates a thing—like "He loves," "He is loved"—or, when you put it in the form of a question, "Does he love?" or "Is he loved?" The Imperative Mood is used for commanding, like "Get out and be 10 damned to you."

MENTOR (*smiling*). Is that the best example you can think of?

ABE. Well—you can put it in the Bible way—"Go thou in peace." But it's still imperative.

MENTOR. The mood derives its name from the implication of command. But you can use it in a very different sense—in the form of the humblest 20 supplication.

ABE. Like "Give us this day our daily bread and forgive us our trespasses."

MENTOR (*reaching for a newspaper in the mess on the table*). I want you to read this—it's a speech delivered by Mr. Webster before the United States Senate. A fine document, and a perfect usage of the Imperative Mood in its hortatory sense. Here it 30 is. Read this—down here. (*He leans back to listen.*)

ABE (*takes paper, leans forward into the light and reads*). "Sir," the Senator continued, in the rich deep tones of the historic church bells of his native Boston, "Sir—I have not allowed myself to look beyond the Union, to see what might be hidden in the dark recess behind. While the Union 40 lasts . . ." (ABE *has been reading in a monotone, without inflection.*)

MENTOR (*testily*). Don't read it off as if it were an inventory of Denton Offut's groceries. Imagine that *you're* making the speech before the Senate,

with the fate of your country at stake. Put your own life into it!

ABE. I couldn't use words as long as Dan'l Webster.

MENTOR. That's what you're here for—to learn! Go ahead.

ABE (*reading slowly, gravely*). "While the Union lasts, we have high prospects spread out before us, for us and our children. Beyond that, I seek not to penetrate the veil. God grant that in my day, at least, the curtain may not rise."

MENTOR. Notice the use of verbs from here on.

ABE (*reads*). "When my eyes shall be turned to behold for the last time the sun in heaven, may I not see him shining on the broken and dishonored fragments of a once glorious Union; on States dissevered, discordant, belligerent; on a land rent with civil feuds, or drenched, it may be, in fraternal blood! Let their last feeble glance rather behold the glorious ensign of the republic, now known and honored throughout the earth, not a single star of it obscured, bearing for its motto no such miserable interrogatory . . ." (*He stumbles over the pronunciation.*)

MENTOR. Interrogatory.

ABE (*continuing*). ". . . interrogatory as 'What is all this worth?' Nor, those other words of delusion and folly, 'Liberty first and Union afterwards'; but everywhere, spread all over in characters of living light, that other sentiment, dear to every true American heart—Liberty and Union . . ."

MENTOR. Emphasize the "*and.*"

ABE. "Liberty *and* Union, now and forever, one and inseparable!" (*He puts the paper back on the table.*) He must have had 'em up on their feet cheering with *that*, all right.

MENTOR. Some cheered, and some spat, depending on which section they came from.

ABE. What was he talking about?

MENTOR. It was in the debate over the right of any state to secede from the Union. Hayne had pleaded South Carolina's cause—pleaded it ably. He said that just as we have liberty as individuals—so have we liberty as 10 states—to go as we please. Which means, if we don't like the Union, as expressed by the will of its majority, then we can leave it, and set up a new nation, or many nations—so that this continent might be as divided, as Europe. But Webster answered him, all right. He proved that without Union, we'd have precious little liberty left. Now—go 20 on with the Potential Mood.

ABE. That signifies possibility—usually of an unpleasant nature. Like, "If I ever get out of debt, I will probably get right back in again."

MENTOR (smiles). Why did you select that example, Abe?

ABE. Well—it just happens to be the thought that's always heaviest on my mind.

MENTOR. Is the store in trouble again?

ABE (calmly). Yes. Berry's drunk all the whiskey we ought to have sold, and we're going to have to shut up any day now. I guess I'm my father's own son. Give me a steady job, and I'll fail at it.

MENTOR. You haven't been a failure here, Abe. There isn't a manjack in this community that isn't fond of you 40 and anxious to help you get ahead.

ABE (with some bitterness). I know— just like you, Mentor, sitting up late nights, to give me learning, out of the goodness of your heart. And now, Josh Speed and Judge Green and some of the others I owe money to want to get me the job of post-master, thinking that maybe I can handle that, since there's only one mail comes in a week. I've got friends, all right—the best friends. But they can't change my luck, or maybe it's just my nature.

MENTOR. What you want to do is get out of New Salem. This poor little forgotten town will never give any one any opportunity.

ABE. Yes—I've thought about moving, think about it all the time. My family have always been movers, shifting about, never knowing what they were looking for, and whatever it was, never finding it. My old father ambled from Virginia, to one place after another in Kentucky, where I was born, and then into Indiana, and then here in Illinois. About all I can remember of when I was a boy was hitching up, and then unhitching, and then hitching up again.

MENTOR. Then get up and go, Abe. Make a new place for yourself in a new world.

ABE. As a matter of fact, Seth Gale and me have been talking a lot about moving—out to Kansas or Nebraska territory. But—wherever I go—it'll be the same story—more friends, more debts.

MENTOR. Well, Abe—just bear in mind that there are always two professions open to people who fail at everything else: there's school-teaching, and there's politics.

ABE. Then I'll choose school-teaching. You go into politics, and you may get elected.

MENTOR. Yes—there's always that possibility.

ABE. And if you get elected, you've

got to go to the city. I don't want none of that.

MENTOR. What did I say about two negatives?

ABE. I meant, any of that.

MENTOR. What's your objection to cities, Abe? Have you ever seen one?

ABE. Sure. I've been down river twice to New Orleans. And, do you know, every minute of the time I was there, 10 I was scared?

MENTOR. Scared of what, Abe?

ABE. Well—it sounds kind of foolish—I was scared of people.

MENTOR (laughs). Did you imagine they'd rob you of all your gold and jewels?

ABE (serious). No. I was scared they'd kill me.

MENTOR (also serious). Why? Why should 20 they want to kill you?

ABE. I don't know.

MENTOR (after a moment). You think a lot about death, don't you?

ABE. I've had to, because it has always seemed to be so close to me—always —as far back as I can remember. When I was no higher than this table, we buried my mother. The milksick got her, poor creature. I helped Paw 30 make the coffin—whittled the pegs for it with my own jackknife. We buried her in a timber clearing beside my grandmother, old Betsy Sparrow. I used to go there often and look at the place—used to watch the deer running over her grave with their little feet. I never could kill a deer after that. One time I catched hell from Paw because when he was 40 taking aim I knocked his gun up. And I always compare the looks of those deer with the looks of men— like the men in New Orleans—that you could see had murder in their hearts.

MENTOR (after a moment). You're a hopeless mess of inconsistency, Abe Lincoln.

ABE. How do you mean, Mentor?

MENTOR. I've never seen any one who is so friendly and at the same time so misanthropic.

ABE. What's that?

MENTOR. A misanthrope is one who distrusts men and avoids their society.

ABE. Well—maybe that's how I am. Oh—I like people, well enough— when you consider 'em one by one. But they seem to look different when they're put into crowds, or mobs, or armies. But I came here to listen to you, and then I do all the talking.

MENTOR. Go right on, Abe. I'll correct you when you say things like "catched hell."

ABE (grins). I know. Whenever I get talking about Paw, I sort of fall back into his language. But—you've got your own school to teach tomorrow. I'll get along. (He stands up.)

MENTOR. Wait a minute. . . . (He is fishing about among the papers. He takes out a copy of an English magazine.) There's just one more thing I want to show you. It's a poem. (He finds the place in the magazine.) Here it is. You read it, Abe. (He hands ABE the magazine.)

[ABE seats himself on the edge of the table, and holds the magazine under the light.]

ABE (reads). " 'On Death,' written at the age of nineteen by the late John Keats:

'Can death be sleep, when life is but a dream,

And scenes of bliss pass as a phantom by?

The transient (He hesitates on that word.) pleasures as a vision seem,

And yet we think the greatest pain's to die. (He moves closer to the light.)

How strange it is that man on earth
should roam,
And lead a life of woe, but not forsake
His rugged path—nor dare he view
alone
His future doom—which is but to
awake.' "
(*He looks at* MENTOR.) That sure is good,
Mentor. It's *fine!* (*He is reading it
again, to himself, when the lights fade.*)

SCENE II

*The Rutledge Tavern, New Salem. Noon
on the Fourth of July.*

*It is a large room, with log walls, but with
curtains on the windows and pictures on the
walls to give it an air of dressiness. The
pictures include likenesses of all the presi-
dents from Washington to Jackson, and
there is also a picture (evidently used for
campaign purposes) of Henry Clay.*

*At the left is a door leading to the kitchen.
At the back, toward the right, is the main
entrance, which is open. The sun is shining
brightly.*

*The furniture of the room consists of two
tables, two benches, and various chairs and
stools.*

BEN MATTLING *is seated on a bench at
the rear of the room. He is an ancient,
paunchy, watery-eyed veteran of the Revolution, and he wears a cocked hat and the
tattered but absurd semblance of a Colonial
uniform.* JUDGE BOWLING GREEN *and*
NINIAN EDWARDS *come in, followed by*
JOSHUA SPEED. BOWLING *is elderly, fat,
gentle.* NINIAN *is young, tall, handsome,
prosperous.* JOSH *is quiet, mild, solid,
thoughtful, well-dressed.*

BOWLING (*as they come in*). This is the
Rutledge Tavern, Mr. Edwards.
It's not precisely a gilded palace of
refreshment.
NINIAN. Make no apologies, Judge
Green. As long as the whiskey is wet.

[JOSH *has crossed to the door at the left. He
calls off.*]
JOSH. Miss Rutledge.
ANN (*appearing at the door*). Yes, Mr.
Speed?
JOSH. Have you seen Abe Lincoln?
ANN. No. He's probably down at the
foot races. (*She goes back into the kitchen.*
JOSH *turns to* BOWLING.)
JOSH. I'll find Abe and bring him here.
NINIAN. Remember, Josh, we've got
to be back in Springfield before
sundown.
[JOSH *has gone out.*]
BOWLING (*to* MATTLING). Ah, good day,
Uncle Ben. Have a seat, Mr. Ed-
wards.
[*They cross to the table at the right.*]
BEN. Good day to you, Bowling.
[ANN *comes in from the kitchen.*]
ANN. Hello, Judge Green.
BOWLING. Good morning, Ann. We'd
be grateful for a bottle of your
father's best whiskey.
ANN. Yes, Judge. (*She starts to go off.*)
BEN (*stopping her*). And git me another
mug of that Barbadoes rum.
ANN. I'm sorry, Mr. Mattling, but I've
given you one already and you know
my father said you weren't to have
any more till you paid for . . .
BEN. Yes, wench—I know what your
father said. But if a veteran of the
Revolutionary War is to be denied
so much as credit, then this country
has forgot its gratitude to them that
made it.
BOWLING. Bring him the rum, Ann. I'll
be happy to pay for it.
[TRUM COGDAL *comes in. He is elderly,
persnicketty.*]
BEN (*reluctantly*). I have to say thank
you, Judge.
TRUM. Ann, bring me a pot of Sebago tea.
ANN. Yes, Mr. Cogdal. (*She goes out at
the left.* TRUM *sits down at the table.*)

BOWLING. Don't say a word, Ben.

TRUM. Well, Mr. Edwards—what's your impression of our great and enterprising metropolis?

NINIAN. Distinctly favorable, Mr. Cogdal. I could not fail to be impressed by the beauty of your location, here on this hilltop, in the midst of the prairie land.

TRUM. Well, we're on the highroad to the West—and when we get the rag, tag and bobtail cleaned out of here, we'll grow. Yes, sir—we'll grow!

NINIAN (*politely*). I'm sure of it.

[ANN *has returned with the whiskey, rum and tea.*]

BOWLING. Thank you, Ann.

ANN. Has the mud-wagon come in yet?

TRUM. No. I been waiting for it.

BOWLING. Not by any chance expecting a letter, are you, Ann?

ANN. Oh, no—who'd be writing to *me*, I'd like to know?

BOWLING. Well—you never can tell what might happen on the Fourth of July. (*He and* NINIAN *lift their glasses.*) But I beg to wish you all happiness, my dear. And let me tell you that Mr. Edwards here is a married man, so you can keep those lively eyes to yourself.

ANN (*giggles*). Oh, Judge Green—you're just joking me! (*She goes to the kitchen.*)

NINIAN. A mighty pretty girl.

TRUM. Comes of good stock, too.

NINIAN. With the scarcity of females in these parts, it's a wonder some one hasn't snapped her up.

BOWLING. Some one has. The poor girl promised herself to a man who called himself McNiel—it turned out his real name's McNamar. Made some money out here and then left town, saying he'd return soon. She's still waiting for him. But your time is short, Mr. Edwards, so if you tell us just what it is you want in New Salem, we'll do our utmost to . . .

NINIAN. I'm sure you gentlemen know what I want.

TRUM. Naturally, you want votes. Well —you've got mine. Anything to frustrate that tyrant, Andy Jackson. (*He shakes a finger at the picture of Andrew Jackson.*)

NINIAN. I assure you that I yield to none in my admiration for the character of our venerable president, but when he goes to the extent of ruining our banking structure, destroying faith in our currency and even driving sovereign states to the point of secession, then, gentlemen, it is time to call a halt.

BOWLING. We got two more years of him—if the old man lives that long. You can't make headway against his popularity.

NINIAN. But we can start now to drive out his minions here in the government of the state of Illinois. We have a great battle cry, "End the reign of Andrew Jackson."

[JACK ARMSTRONG *and three others of the Clary's Grove boys have come in during this speech. The others are named* BAB, FEARGUS *and* JASP. *They are the town bullies—boisterous, good-natured but tough.*]

JACK (*going to the door at the left*). Miss Rutledge!

ANN (*appearing in the doorway*). What do *you* want, Jack Armstrong?

JACK. Your humble pardon, Miss Rutledge, and we will trouble you for a keg of liquor.

BAB. And we'll be glad to have it quick, because we're powerful dry.

ANN. You get out of here—you get out of here right now—you low *scum!*

JACK. I believe I said a keg of liquor. Did you hear me say it, boys?

FEARGUS. That's how it sounded to me, Jack.

JASP. Come along with it, Annie——

ANN. If my father were here, he'd take a gun to you, just as he would to a pack of prairie wolves.

JACK. If your Paw was here, he'd be scareder than you. 'Cause he knows 10 we're the wildcats of Clary's Grove, worse'n any old wolves, and we're a-howlin', and a-spittin' for drink. So get the whiskey, Miss Annie, and save your poor old Paw a lot of expenses for damages to his property. [ANN *goes.*]

TRUM (*in an undertone to* NINIAN). That's the rag, tag and bobtail I was . . .

JACK. And what are you mumblin' 20 about, old measely-weasely Trum Cogdal—with your cup of tea on the Fourth of July?

BAB. He's a cotton-mouthed traitor and I think we'd better whip him for it.

FEARGUS (*at the same time*). Squeeze that air tea outen him, Jack.

JASP (*shouting*). Come on you, Annie, with that liquor!

JACK. And you, too, old fat-pot Judge 30 Bowling Green that sends honest men to prison—and who's the stranger? Looks kind of damn elegant for New Salem.

BOWLING. This is Mr. Ninian Edwards of Springfield, Jack—and for the Lord's sake, shut up, and sit down, and behave yourselves.

JACK. Ninian Edwards, eh! The Governor's son, I presume. Well—well!

NINIAN (*amiably*). You've placed me.

JACK. No wonder you've got a New Orleans suit of clothes and a gold fob and a silver-headed cane. I reckon you can buy the best of everything with that steamin' old pirate land-grabber for a Paw. I guess them fancy pockets of yourn are pretty well stuffed with the money your Paw stole from us tax-payers— eh, Mr. Edwards?

BAB. Let's take it offen him, Jack.

FEARGUS. Let's give him a lickin', Jack.

JACK (*still to* NINIAN). What you come here for anyway? Lookin' for a fight? Because if that's what you're a-cravin', I'm your man—wrasslin', clawin', bitin', and tearin'.

ANN (*coming in*). Jack Armstrong, here's your liquor! Drink it and go away. (ANN *carries four mugs.*)

JASP. He told you to bring a keg!

JACK (*contemplating the mugs*). One little noggin apiece? Why—that ain't enough to fill a hollow tooth! Get the keg, Annie.

FEARGUS. Perhaps she can't tote it. I'll get it, Jack. (*He goes out into the kitchen.*)

ANN (*desperate*). Aren't there any of you men can do anything to protect decent people from these ruffians?

NINIAN. I'll be glad to do whatever I . . . (*He starts to rise.*)

BOWLING (*restraining him*). I'd be rather careful, Mr. Edwards.

JACK. That's right, Mr. Edwards. You be careful. Listen to the old Squire. He's got a round pot but a level head. He's seen the Clary's Grove boys in action, and he can tell you you might get that silver-headed cane rammed down your gullet. Hey, Bab—you tell him what we did to Hank Spears and Gus Hocheimer. Just tell him!

40 BAB. Jack nailed the two of 'em up in a barr'l and sent 'em rollin' down Salem hill and it jumped the bank and fotched up in the river and when we opened up the barr'l they wasn't inclined to move much.

JACK. Of course, it'd take a bigger

barr'l to hold you and your friend here, Squire, but I'd do it for you and I'd do it for any by God rapscallions and sons of thieves that come here a-preachin' treachery and disunion and pisenin' the name of Old Hickory, the people's friend.

[FEARGUS *returns with the keg.*]

BEN. Kill him, boys! You're the only *real* Americans we got left!

NINIAN (*rising*). If you gentlemen will step outside, I'll be glad to accommodate you with the fight you seem to be spoiling for.

TRUM. You're committing suicide, Mr. Edwards.

JACK. Oh, no—he ain't. We ain't killers—we're just bone crushers. After a few months, you'll be as good as new, which ain't saying much. 20 You bring that keg, Feargus.

[*They are about to go when* ABE *appears in the door. He now is slightly more respectably dressed, wearing a battered clawhammer coat and pants that have been "foxed" with buckskin. He carries the mail. Behind him is* JOSH SPEED.]

ABE. The mud-wagon's in! Hello, Jack. Hello, boys. Ain't you fellers drunk yet? Hello, Miss Ann. Got a letter for you. (*There is a marked shyness in his attitude toward* ANN.)

ANN. Thank you, Abe. (*She snatches the letter and runs out with it.*)

BEN. Abe, there's goin' to be a fight!

NINIAN (*to* JACK). Well—come on, if you're coming.

JACK. All right, boys.

ABE. Fight? Who—and why?

JACK. This is the son of Ninian Edwards, 40 Abe. Come from Springfield lookin' for a little crotch hoist and I'm aimin' to oblige.

[ABE *looks* NINIAN *over.*]

BOWLING. Put a stop to it, Abe. It'd be next door to murder.

JACK. You shut your trap, Pot Green. Murder's too good for any gooselivered enemy of Andy Jackson. Come on, boys!

ABE. Wait a minute, boys. Jack, have you forgotten what day it is?

JACK. No, I ain't! But I reckon the Fourth is as good a day as any to whip a politician!

10 ABE (*amiably*). Well, if you've just got to fight, Jack, you shouldn't give preference to strangers. Being postmaster of this thriving town, I can rate as a politician, myself, so you'd better try a fall with me—(*He thrusts* JACK *aside and turns to* NINIAN.) And as for you, sir, I haven't the pleasure of your acquaintance; but my name's Lincoln, and I'd like to shake hands with a brave man.

NINIAN (*shaking hands with* ABE). I'm greatly pleased to know you, Mr. Lincoln.

ABE. You should be. Because I come here just in time to save you quite some embarrassment, not to mention injury. Oh, got a couple of letters for you, Bowling. And here's your *Cincinnati Journal*, Trum.

30 JACK. Look here, Abe—you're steppin' into something that ain't none of your business. This is a private matter of patriotic honor . . .

ABE. Everything in this town is my business, Jack. It's the only kind of business I've got. And besides—I saw Hannah down by the grove and she says to tell you to come on to the picnic and that means *now* or she'll give the cake away to the Straders children and you and the boys'll go hungry. So get moving.

FEARGUS (*to* JACK). Are you goin' to let Abe talk you out of it?

ABE. Sure he is. (*He turns to* TRUM.) Say, Trum—if you ain't using that

Journal for a while, would you let me have a read?

TRUM. By all means, Abe. Here you are. (*He tosses the paper to* ABE.)

ABE. Thanks. (*He turns again to* JACK.) You'd better hurry, Jack, or *you'll* get a beating from Hannah. (*He starts to take the wrapper off, as he goes over to a chair at the left.* JACK *looks at* ABE *for a moment, then laughs.*) 10

JACK (*to* NINIAN). All right! Abe Lincoln's saved your hide. I'll consent to callin' off the fight just because he's a friend of mine.

ABE (*as he sits*). And also because I'm the only one around here you can't lick.

JACK. But I just want to tell you, Mr. Ninian Edwards, Junior, that the next time you come around here a-spreadin' pisen and . . . 20

ABE. Go on, Jack. Hannah's waiting.

JACK (*walking over to* ABE). I'm going, Abe. But I warn you—you'd better stop this foolishness of readin'—readin'—readin', mornin', noon and night, or you'll be gettin' soft and you won't be the same fightin' man you are now—and it would break my heart to see you licked by anybody, includin' me! (*He laughs, slaps* 30 ABE *on the back, then turns to go.*) Glad to have met you, Mr. Edwards.

[*He goes out, followed by* BAB *and* JASP. FEARGUS *picks up the keg and starts after them.*]

NINIAN (*to* JACK). It's been a pleasure.

ABE. Where'd you get that keg, Feargus?

FEARGUS (*nervously*). Jack told me to take it outen Mis' Rutledge's kitchen and I . . . 40

ABE. Well—put it down. . . . If you see Seth Gale, tell him I've got a letter for him.

FEARGUS. I'll tell him, Abe. (FEARGUS *puts down the keg and goes.* JOSH SPEED *laughs and comes up to the table.*)

JOSH. Congratulations, Ninian. I shouldn't have enjoyed taking you home to Mrs. Edwards after those boys had done with you.

NINIAN (*grinning*). I was aware of the certain consequences, Josh. (*He turns to* ABE.) I'm deeply in your debt, Mr. Lincoln.

ABE. Never mind any thanks, Mr. Edwards. Jack Armstrong talks big but he means well.

NINIAN. Won't you join us in a drink?

ABE. No, thank you. (*He's reading the paper.* BOWLING *fills the glasses.*)

BOWLING. *I'm* going to have another! I don't mind telling you, I'm still trembling. (*He hands a glass to* NINIAN, *then drinks himself.*)

TRUM. You see, Mr. Edwards. It's that very kind of lawlessness that's holding our town back.

NINIAN. You'll find the same element in the capital of our nation, and everywhere else, these days. (*He sits down and drinks.*)

ABE. Say, Bowling! It says here that there was a riot in Lyons, France. (*He reads.*) "A mob of men, deprived of employment when textile factories installed the new sewing machines, re-enacted scenes of the Reign of Terror in the streets of this prosperous industrial center. The mobs were suppressed only when the military forces of His French Majesty took a firm hand. The rioters carried banners inscribed with the incendiary words, 'We will live working or die fighting!'" (ABE *looks at the group at the right.*) That's Revolution!

BOWLING. Maybe, but it's a long way off from New Salem.

JOSH. Put the paper down, Abe. We want to talk to you.

ABE. Me? What about? (*He looks curiously at* JOSH, BOWLING *and* NINIAN.)

JOSH. I brought Mr. Edwards here for the sole purpose of meeting you—and with his permission, I shall tell you why.

NINIAN. Go right ahead, Josh.

[*All are looking intently at* ABE.]

JOSH. Abe—how would you like to run for the State Assembly?

ABE. When?

JOSH. Now—for the election in the fall. 10

ABE. Why?

NINIAN. Mr. Lincoln, I've known you for only a few minutes, but that's long enough to make me agree with Josh Speed that you're precisely the type of man we want. The whole Whig organization will support your candidacy.

ABE. This was all your idea, Josh?

JOSH (*smiling*). Oh, no, Abe—you're the 20 people's choice!

TRUM. What do *you* think of it, Bowling?

BOWLING (*heartily*). I think it's as fine a notion as I ever heard. Why, Abe—I can hear you making speeches, right and left, taking your stand on all the issues—secession, Texas, the National Bank crisis, abolitionism—it'll be more fun than we ever had in our lives! 30

ABE (*rising*). Isn't anybody going to ask what *I* think?

JOSH (*laughs*). All right, Abe—*I'll* ask you.

ABE (*after a moment's pause*). It's a comical notion, all right—and I don't know if I can give you an answer to it, off-hand. But my first, hasty impression is that I don't think much of it.

BOWLING. Don't overlook the fact that, if elected, your salary would be 40 three whole dollars a day.

ABE. That's fine money. No doubt of that. And I see what you have in mind, Bowling. I owe you a considerable sum of money; and if I stayed in the legislature for, say, twenty years, I'd be able to pay off—let me see—two dollars and a half a day. . . . (*He is figuring it up on his fingers.*)

BOWLING. I'm not thinking about the debts, Abe.

ABE. I know you ain't, Bowling. But I've got to. And so should you, Mr. Edwards. The Whig party is the party of sound money and God save the National Bank, ain't it?

NINIAN. Why, yes—among other things. . . .

ABE. Well, then—how would it look if you put forward a candidate who has demonstrated no earning power but who has run up the impressive total of fifteen hundred dollars of debts?

BOWLING (*to* NINIAN). I can tell you something about those debts. Abe started a grocery store in partnership with an unfortunate young man named Berry. Their stock included whiskey, and Berry started tapping the keg until he had consumed all the liquid assets. So the store went bankrupt—and Abe voluntarily assumed all the obligations. That may help to explain to you, Mr. Edwards, why we think pretty highly of him around here.

NINIAN. It's a sentiment with which I concur most heartily.

ABE. I thank you one and all for your kind tributes, but don't overdo them, or I'll begin to think that three dollars a day ain't enough!

JOSH. What's the one thing that you want most, Abe? You want to learn. This will give you your chance to get at a good library, to associate with the finest lawyers in the State.

ABE. I've got a copy of Blackstone, already. Found it in an old junk barrel. And how can I tell that the finest lawyers would welcome association with *me?*

NINIAN. You needn't worry about that. I saw how you dealt with those ruffians. You quite obviously know how to handle men.

ABE. I can handle the Clary's Grove boys because I can outwrassle them —but I can't go around Sangamon County throwing *all* the voters.

BOWLING (*laughing*). I'll take a chance on that, Abe. 10

ABE (*to* NINIAN). Besides—how do you know that my political views would agree with yours? How do you know I wouldn't say the wrong thing?

NINIAN. What *are* your political leanings, Mr. Lincoln?

ABE. They're all toward staying out. . . . What sort of leanings did you want?

NINIAN. We have a need for good con- 20 servative men to counteract all the radical firebrands that have swept over this country in the wake of Andrew Jackson. We've got to get this country back to first principles!

ABE. Well—I'm conservative, all right. If I got into the legislature you'd never catch me starting any movements for reform or progress. I'm pretty certain I wouldn't even have the 30 nerve to open my mouth.

JOSH (*laughs*). I told you, Ninian—he's just the type of candidate you're looking for.

[NINIAN *laughs too, and rises.*]

NINIAN (*crossing towards* ABE). The fact is, Mr. Lincoln, we want to spike the rumor that ours is the party of the more privileged classes. That is why we seek men of the plain people for 40 candidates. As post-master, you're in an excellent position to establish contacts. While delivering letters, you can also deliver speeches and campaign literature, with which our headquarters will keep you supplied.

ABE. Would you supply me with a suit of store clothes? A candidate mustn't look *too* plain.

NINIAN (*smiling*). I think even that could be arranged, eh, Judge?

BOWLING. I think so.

NINIAN (*pompously*). So—think it over, Mr. Lincoln, and realize that this is opportunity unlimited in scope. Just consider what it means to be starting up the ladder in a nation which is now expanding southward, across the vast area of Texas; and westward, to the Empire of the Californias on the Pacific Ocean. We're becoming a continent, Mr. Lincoln—and all that we need is men! (*He looks at his watch.*) And now, gentlemen, if you will excuse me—I must put in an appearance at the torch-light procession in Springfield this evening, so I shall have to be moving on. Good-bye, Mr. Lincoln. This meeting has been a happy one for me.

ABE (*shaking hands*). Good-bye, Mr. Edwards. Good luck in the campaign.

NINIAN. And the same to you.

[*All at the right have risen and are starting to go, except* BEN MATTLING, *who is still sitting at the back, drinking.*]

ABE. Here's your paper, Trum.

TRUM. Go ahead and finish it, Abe. I won't be looking at it yet awhile.

ABE. Thanks, Trum. I'll leave it at your house.

[TRUM *and* NINIAN *have gone.*]

BOWLING. I'll see you later, Abe. Tell Ann I'll be back to pay for the liquor.

ABE. I'll tell her, Bowling.

[BOWLING *goes.* JOSH *is looking at* ABE, *who, after a moment, turns to him.*]

ABE. I'm surprised at you, Josh. I thought you were my friend.

JOSH. I know, Abe. But Ninian Edwards asked me is there anybody in that

God-forsaken town of New Salem that stands a chance of getting votes, and the only one I could think of was you. I can see you're embarrassed by this—and you're annoyed. But—whether you like it or not—you've got to grow; and here's your chance to get a little scrap of importance.

ABE. Am I the kind that wants importance?

JOSH. You'll deny it, Abe—but you've got a funny kind of vanity—which is the same as saying you've got some pride—and it's badly in need of nourishment. So, if you'll agree to this—I don't think you'll be sorry for it or feel that I've betrayed you.

ABE (*grins*). Oh—I won't hold it against you, Josh. (*He walks away and looks out the door.*) But that Mr. Ninian Edwards—he's rich and he's prominent and he's got a high-class education. Politics to him is just a kind of a game. And maybe I'd like it if I could play it *his* way. (*He turns to* JOSH.) But when you get to reading Blackstone, not to mention the Bible, you can't help feeling maybe there's some serious responsibility in the giving of laws—and maybe there's something more important in the business of government than just getting the Whig Party back into power.

[SETH GALE *comes in. He is a young, husky frontiersman, with flashes of the sun of Western empire in his eyes.*]

SETH. Hey, Abe—Feargus said you've got a letter for me.

ABE (*fishing in his mail pouch*). Yes.

SETH. Hello, Mr. Speed.

JOSH. How are you, Mr. Gale?

ABE. Here you are, Seth. (*He hands him a letter.* SETH *takes it to the right, sits down and starts to read.*)

JOSH. I've got to get home to Spring-

field, Abe, but I'll be down again in a week or so.

ABE. I'll be here, Josh.

[JOSH *goes.* ABE *sits down again at the right, picks up his paper, but doesn't read it.* BEN *stands up and comes down a bit unsteadily.*]

BEN (*angrily*). Are you going to do it, Abe? Are you goin' to let them make you into a *candidate?*

ABE. I ain't had time to think about it yet.

BEN. Well—I tell you to stop thinkin' before it's too late. Don't let 'em get you. Don't let 'em put you in a store suit that's the uniform of degradation in this miserable country. You're an honest man, Abe Lincoln. You're a good-for-nothin', debt-ridden loafer—but you're an honest man. And you have no place in that den of thieves that's called gov'ment. They'll corrupt you as they've corrupted the whole damn United States. Look at Washington, look at Jefferson, and John Adams—(*He points grandly to the pictures.*)—where are they today? Dead! And everything they stood for and fought for and *won*—that's dead too. (ANN *comes in to collect the mugs from the table at the left.* ABE *looks at her.*) Why—we'd be better off if we was all black niggers held in the bonds of slavery. *They* get fed—*They* get looked after when they're old and sick. (ANN *goes.*) But *you* don't care—you ain't listenin' to me, neither . . . (*He starts slowly toward the door.*)

ABE. Of course I'm listening, Ben.

BEN. No, you ain't. *I* know. You're goin' to the assembly and join the wolves who're feedin' off the carcass of Liberty. (*He goes out.*)

ABE. You needn't worry. I'm not going.

[ANN *comes in. She crosses to the right to pick*

up the glasses. She seems extremely sub-dued. ABE *looks at her, curiously.*]

ABE. Bowling Green said to tell you he'd be back later, to pay you what he owes.

ANN (*curtly*). That's all right. (ANN *puts the glasses and bottle on a tray and picks it up.* ABE *jumps to his feet.*)

ABE. Here, Ann. Let me take that.

ANN (*irritably*). No—leave it alone! I can carry it! (*She starts across to the left.*)

ABE. Excuse me, Ann. . . .

ANN (*stopping*). Well?

ABE. Would you come back after you're finished with that? I—I'd like to talk to you.

[SETH *has finished the letter. Its contents seem to have depressed him.*]

ANN. All right. I'll talk to you—if you want.

[*She goes out.* SETH *crosses toward* ABE, *who, during the subsequent dialogue, is continu-ally looking toward the kitchen.*]

SETH. Abe . . . Abe—I got a letter from my folks back in Maryland. It means—I guess I've got to give up the dream we had of moving out into Nebraska territory.

ABE. What's happened, Seth?

SETH (*despondently*). Well—for one thing, the old man's took sick, and he's pretty feeble.

ABE. I'm sorry to hear that.

SETH. So am I. They've sent for me to come back and work the farm. Measly little thirty-six acres—sandy soil. I tell you, Abe, it's a bitter dis-appointment to me, when I had my heart all set on going out into the West. And the worst of it is—I'm let-ting *you* down on it, too.

ABE (*with a glance toward the kitchen*). Don't think about that, Seth. Maybe I won't be able to move for a while myself. And when your father gets to feeling better, you'll come back . . .

SETH. He won't get to feeling better. Not at his age. I'll be stuck there, just like he was. I'll be pushed in and cramped all the rest of my life, till the malaria gets me, too. . . . Well —there's no use crying about it. If I've got to go back East, I've got to go. (ANN *comes back.*) I'll tell you good-bye, Abe, before I leave.

[*He goes.* ABE *turns and looks at* ANN, *and she at him.*]

ANN. Well—what is it, Abe?

ABE (*rising*). I just thought—you might like to talk to me.

ANN (*sharply*). What about?

ABE. That letter you got from New York State.

ANN. What do *you* know about that letter?

ABE. I'm the postmaster. I know more than I ought to about people's private affairs. I couldn't help seeing that that was the handwriting of Mr. McNiel. And I couldn't help seeing, from the look on your face, that the bad news you've been afriad of has come.

[ANN *looks at him with surprise. He is a lot more observant than she had thought.*]

ANN. Whatever the letter said, it's no concern of yours, Abe.

ABE. I know that, Ann. But—it appears to me that you've been crying—and it makes me sad to think that some-thing could have hurt you. The thing is—I think quite a lot of you—always have—ever since I first came here, and met you. I wouldn't mention it, only when you're distressed about something it's a comfort sometimes to find a pair of ears to pour your troubles into—and the Lord knows my ears are big enough to hold a lot.

[*Her attitude of hostility softens and she re-wards him with a tender smile.*]

ANN. You're a Christian gentleman, Abe Lincoln. (*She sits down.*)

ABE. No, I ain't. I'm a plain, common sucker with a shirt-tail so short I can't sit on it.

ANN (*laughs*). Well—sit down, anyway, Abe—here, by me.

ABE. Why—it'd be a pleasure. (*He crosses and sits near her.*)

ANN. You can always say something to make a person laugh, can't you?

ABE. Well—I don't even have to *say* anything. A person just has to *look* at me.

ANN. You're right about that letter, Abe. It's the first I've heard from him in months—and now he says he's delayed by family troubles and doesn't know when he'll be able to get to New Salem again. By which he probably means—never.

ABE. I wouldn't say that, Ann.

ANN. I would. (*She looks at him.*) I reckon you think I'm a silly fool for ever having promised myself to Mr. McNiel.

ABE. I think no such thing. I liked him myself, and still do, and whatever reasons he had for changing his name I'm sure were honorable. He's a smart man, and a handsome one—and I—I wouldn't blame any girl for —loving him.

ANN (*too emphatically*). I guess I don't love him, Abe. I guess I couldn't love anybody that was as—as faithless as that.

ABE (*trying to appear unconcerned*). Well, then. There's nothing to fret about. Now—poor Seth Gale—he got some *really* bad news. His father's sick and he has to give up his dream which was to go and settle out West.

ANN (*looks at him*). I don't believe you know much about females, Abe.

ABE. Probably I don't—although I certainly spend enough time thinking about 'em.

ANN. You're a big man, and you can lick anybody, and you can't understand the feelings of somebody who is weak. But—I'm a female, and I can't help thinking what they'll be saying about me—all the old gossips, all over town. They'll make it out that he deserted me; I'm a rejected woman. They'll give me their sympathy to my face, but they'll snigger at me behind my back. (*She rises and crosses toward the right.*)

ABE. Yes—that's just about what they would do. But—would you let *them* disturb you?

ANN (*rising*). I told you—it's just weakness—it's just vanity. It's something you couldn't understand, Abe. (*She has crossed to the window and is staring out.* ABE *twists in his chair to look at her.*)

ABE. Maybe I can understand it, Ann. I've got a kind of vanity myself. Josh Speed said so, and he's right. . . . It's—it's nothing but vanity that's kept me from declaring my inclinations toward you. (*She turns, amazed, and looks at him.*) You see, I don't like to be sniggered at, either. I know what I am—and I know what I look like—and I know that I've got nothing to offer any girl that I'd be in love with.

ANN. Are you saying that you're in love with me, Abe?

ABE (*with deep earnestness*). Yes—I am saying that. (*He stands up, facing her. She looks intently into his eyes.*) I've been loving you—a long time—with all my heart. You see, Ann—you're a particularly fine girl. You've got sense, and you've got bravery—those are two things that I admire particularly. And you're powerful good to look at, too. So—it's only natural I should have a great regard for you. But—I don't mean to worry you about it, Ann. I only mentioned it because—if you would do me the honor of keeping company with me for a while, it might shut the old gossips' mouths. They'd figure you'd chucked McNiel for—for some one else. Even me.

ANN (*going to him*). I thought I knew you pretty well, Abe. But I didn't.

ABE (*worried*). Why do you say that? Do you consider I was too forward, in speaking out as I did?

ANN (*gravely*). No, Abe. . . . I've always thought a lot of you—the way I thought you were. But—the idea of love between you and me—I can't say how I feel about that, because now you're like some other person, that I'm meeting for the first time.

ABE (*quietly*). I'm not expecting you to feel anything for me. I'd never dream of expecting such a thing.

ANN. I know that, Abe. You'd be willing to give everything you have and never expect anything in return. Maybe you're different in that way from any man I've ever heard of. And I can tell you this much—now, and truthfully—if I ever do love you, I'll be happy about it—and lucky, to be loving a good, decent man. . . . If you just give me time—to think about it. . . .

ABE (*unable to believe his eyes and ears*). You mean—if you took time—you might get in your heart something like the feeling I have for you?

ANN (*with great tenderness*). I don't know, Abe. (*She clutches his lapel.*) But I do know that you're a man who could fill any one's heart—yes, fill it and warm it and make it glad to be living. [ABE *covers her hand with his.*]

ABE. Ann—I've always tried hard to believe what the orators tell us—that this is a land of equal opportunity for all. But I've never been able to credit it, any more than I could agree that God made all men in his own image. But—if I could win you, Ann—I'd be willing to disbelieve everything I've ever seen with my own eyes, and have faith in everything wonderful that I've ever read in poetry books. (*Both are silent for a moment. Then* ANN *turns away.*) But—I'm not asking you to say anything now. And I won't ask you until the day comes when I know I've got a right to. (*He turns and walks quickly toward the door, picking up his mail pouch.*)

ANN. Abe! Where are you going?

ABE. I'm going to find Bowling Green and tell him a good joke. (*He grins. He is standing in the doorway.*)

ANN. A *joke?* What about?

ABE. I'm going to tell him that I'm a candidate for the assembly of the State of Illinois. (*He goes.*)
[*The light fades.*]

SCENE THREE

BOWLING GREEN'S *house near New Salem. It is a small room, but the walls are lined with books and family pictures. In the center is a table with a lamp on it. Another light—a candle in a glass globe—is on a bureau at the right. There are comfortable chairs on either side of the table, and a sofa at the left.*

At the back, toward the left, is the front door. A rifle is leaning against the wall by the door. There is another door in the right wall. Toward the right, at the back, is a ladder fixed against the wall leading up through an opening to the attic.

It is late in the evening, a year or so after Scene II. A storm is raging outside.

BOWLING *is reading aloud from a sort of pamphlet. His comfortable wife,* NANCY, *is listening and sewing.*

BOWLING. "And how much more interesting did the spectacle become when, starting into full life and animation, as a simultaneous call for 'Pickwick' burst from his followers, that illustrious man slowly mounted into the Windsor chair, on which he had been previously seated, and addressed the club himself had founded." (BOWLING *chuckles.* NANCY *laughs.*)

NANCY. He sounds precisely like *you*, Bowling.

[*There is a knock at the door.*]

NANCY (*nervous*). That's not Abe's knock. Who can it be?

BOWLING (*rising*). We don't know yet, my dear.

NANCY. It's a strange hour for any one to be calling. You'd better have that gun ready.

[BOWLING *unbolts and opens the door. It is* JOSH SPEED.]

BOWLING. Why—Josh Speed!

JOSH. Good evening, Bowling.

BOWLING. We haven't seen you in a coon's age.

NANCY. Good evening, Mr. Speed.

JOSH. Good evening, Mrs. Green. And I beg you to forgive me for this untimely intrusion.

NANCY. We're delighted to see you. Take your wrap off.

JOSH. Thank you. I've just come down from Springfield. I heard Abe Lincoln was in town and I was told I might find him here.

BOWLING. He's been sleeping here, up in the attic.

NANCY. But he's out now at the Rutledge Farm, tending poor little Ann.

JOSH. Miss Rutledge? What's the matter with her?

NANCY. She's been taken with the brain sickness. It's the most shocking thing. People have been dying from it right and left.

BOWLING. But Ann's young. She'll pull through, all right. Sit down, Josh.

JOSH. Thank you. (*He sits.* BOWLING *places the pamphlet on the top of the bookcase and stands there, filling his pipe.*)

NANCY. I suppose you know that Abe came rushing down from Vandalia the moment he heard she was taken. He's deeply in love with her.

BOWLING. Now, Nancy—don't exaggerate.

[JOSH *is listening to all this, intently.*]

JOSH. So Abe is in love. I wondered what has been the matter with him lately.

NANCY. Why, it's written all over his poor, homely face.

JOSH. The last time I saw him, he seemed pretty moody. But when I asked him what was wrong, he said it was his liver.

BOWLING (*laughing*). That sounds more likely. Has he been getting on well in the Assembly?

JOSH. No. He has just been sitting there—drawing his three dollars a day—and taking no apparent interest in the proceedings. Do you fancy that Miss Rutledge cares anything for him?

NANCY. Indeed she does! She broke her promise to that Mr. McNiel because of her feelings for Abe!

JOSH. Has he any notion of marrying her?

NANCY. It's the only notion of his life right now. And the sooner they are married, the better for both of them.

BOWLING (*seating himself*). Better for her, perhaps—but the worse for him.

NANCY (*finishing her sewing*). And why? The Rutledges are fine people, superior in every way to those riff-raff Hankses and Lincolns that are Abe's family!

BOWLING. I think you feel as I do, Josh. Abe has his own way to go and— sweet and pretty as Ann undoubtedly is—she'd only be a hindrance to him.

JOSH. I guess it wouldn't matter much if she could give him a little of the happiness he's never had.

NANCY (*rising*). That's just it! I think as much of Abe as you do, Bowling. But we can't deny that he's a poor man, and he's failed in trade, and he's been in the legislature for a year without accomplishing a blessed thing . . . (*She goes to the bookcase to put her sewing-basket away.*)

BOWLING. He could go to Springfield and set up a law practice and make a good thing of it. Ninian Edwards would help him to get started. And he'd soon forget little Ann. He has just happened to fasten on her his own romantic ideal of what's beautiful and unattainable. Let him ever attain her, and she'd break his heart.

NANCY (*seating herself*). Do you agree with Bowling on that, Mr. Speed?

JOSH (*sadly*). I can't say, Mrs. Green. I've abandoned the attempt to predict anything about Abe Lincoln. The first time I ever saw him was when he was piloting that steamboat, the *Talisman*. You remember how she ran into trouble at the dam. I had a valuable load of goods aboard for my father's store, and I was sure that steamboat, goods and all were a total loss. But Abe got her through. It was a great piece of work. I thought, "Here is a reliable man." So I cultivated his acquaintance, believing, in my conceit, that I could help him to fame and fortune. I soon learned differently. I found out that he has plenty of strength and courage in his body—but in his mind he's a hopeless hypochondriac. He can split rails, push a plough, crack jokes, all day—and then sit up all night reading "Hamlet" and brooding over his own fancied resemblance to that melancholy prince. Maybe he's a great philosopher—maybe he's a great fool. I don't know what he is.

BOWLING (*laughs*). Well—if only Ann had sense enough to see all the things *you* saw, Josh, she'd be so terrified of him she'd run all the way back to York State and find McNiel. At least, *he's* not complicated.

NANCY (*with deeper emotion*). You're talking about Abe Lincoln as if he were some problem that you found in a book, and it's interesting to try to figure it out. Well—maybe he is a problem—but he's also a man, and a miserable one. And what do you do for his misery? You laugh at his comical jokes and you vote for him on election day and give him board and lodging when he needs it. But all that doesn't give a scrap of satisfaction to Abe's soul—and never will. Because the one thing he needs is a woman with the will to face life for him.

BOWLING. You think he's afraid to face it himself?

NANCY. He is! He listens too much to the whispers, that he heard in the forest where he grew up, and where he always goes now when he wants to be alone. They're the whispers of the women behind him—his dead mother—and *her* mother, who was no better than she should be. He's got that awful fear on him, of not knowing what the whispers mean, or where they're directing him. And none of your back-slapping will knock that fear out of him. Only a woman can free him—a woman who loves him truly, and believes in him. . . .

[*There is a knock on the door.*]

BOWLING. That's Abe now. (*He gets up and opens it.*)

[ABE *is there, bareheaded, wet by the storm. He now wears a fairly respectable dark suit of clothes. He looks older and grim-mer.*]

BOWLING. Why, hello, Abe! We've been sitting up waiting for you. Come on in out of the wet!

[ABE *comes in.* BOWLING *shuts the door behind him.*]

NANCY. We were reading The Post-humous Papers of the Pickwick Club when Mr. Speed came in.   10

ABE. Hello, Josh. Glad to see you.

JOSH. Hello, Abe.

[ABE *turns to* NANCY.]

ABE. Nancy . . .

NANCY. Yes, Abe?

ABE. She's dead.

BOWLING. Ann? She's dead?

ABE. Yes. Tonight, the fever suddenly got worse. They couldn't seem to do anything for it.   20

[NANCY *gives* BOWLING *a swift look, then goes quickly to* ABE *and takes his hand.*]

NANCY. Oh, Abe—I'm so sorry. She was such a dear little girl. Every one who knew her will join in mourning for her.

ABE. I know they will. But it won't do any good. She's dead.

BOWLING. Sit down, Abe, and rest yourself.   30

ABE. No—I'm not fit company for anybody. I'd better be going. (*He turns toward the door.*)

JOSH (*stopping him*). No, you don't, Abe. You'll stay right here.

BOWLING. You better do what Josh tells you.

NANCY. Come here, Abe. Please sit down.

[ABE *looks from one to the other, then obedi-* 40 *ently goes to a chair and sits.*]

Your bed is ready for you upstairs when you want it.

ABE (*dully*). You're the best friends I've got in the world, and it seems a pretty poor way to reward you for all that you've given me, to come here now, and inflict you with a corpse.

BOWLING. This is your home, Abe. This is where you're loved.

ABE. Yes, that's right. And I love you, Bowling and Nancy. But I loved her more than everything else that I've ever known.

NANCY. I know you did, Abe. I know it.

ABE. I used to think it was better to be alone. I was always most contented when I was alone. I had queer notions that if you got too close to people, you could see the truth about them, that behind the surface, they're all insane, and they could see the same in you. And then—when I saw her, I knew there could be beauty and purity in people—like the purity you sometimes see in the sky at night. When I took hold of her hand, and held it, all fear, all doubt, went out of me. I believed in God. I'd have been glad to work for her until I die, to get for her everything out of life that she wanted. If she thought I could do it, then I could. That was my belief. . . . And then I had to stand there, as helpless as a twig in a whirlpool; I had to stand there and watch her die. And her father and mother were there, too, praying to God for her soul. The Lord giveth, and the Lord taketh away, blessed be the name of the Lord! That's what they kept on saying. But I couldn't pray with them. I couldn't give any devotion to one who has the power of death, and uses it. (*He has stood up, and is speaking with more passion.*) I'm making a poor exhibition of myself—and I'm sorry —but—I can't stand it. I can't live with myself any longer. I've got to die and be with her again, or I'll go crazy! (*He goes to the door and opens it.*

The storm continues.) I can't bear to think of her out there alone!

[NANCY *looks at* BOWLING *with frantic appeal. He goes to* ABE, *who is standing in the doorway, looking out.*]

BOWLING (*with great tenderness*). Abe . . . I want you to go upstairs and see if you can't get some sleep. . . . Please, Abe—as a special favor to Nancy and me.

ABE (*after a moment*). All right, Bowling. (*He turns and goes to the ladder.*)

NANCY. Here's a light for you, dear Abe. (*She hands him the candle.*)

ABE. Thank you, Nancy. . . . Good night. (*He goes up the ladder into the attic.*)

    [*They all look up after him.*]

NANCY (*tearful*). Poor, lonely soul.

    [BOWLING *cautions her to be quiet.*]

JOSH. Keep him here with you, Mrs. Green. Don't let him out of your sight.

BOWLING. We won't, Josh.

JOSH. Good night. (*He picks up his hat and cloak and goes.*)

BOWLING. Good night, Josh. (*He closes and bolts the door, then comes down to the table and picks up the lamp.*)

[NANCY *looks up once more, then goes out at the right.* BOWLING *follows her out, carrying the lamp with him. He closes the door behind him, so that the only light on the stage is the beam from the attic.*]

        CURTAIN

ACT II

SCENE IV

Law office of Stuart and Lincoln on the second floor of the Court House in Springfield, Ill. A sunny summer's afternoon, some five years after the preceding scene.

The room is small, with two windows and one door, upstage, which leads to the hall and staircase.

At the right is a table and chair, at the left an old desk, littered with papers. At the back is a ramshackle bed, with a buffalo robe thrown over it. Below the windows are some rough shelves, sagging with law books. There is an old wood stove.

On the wall above the desk is hung an American flag, with 26 stars. Between the windows is an election poster, for Harrison and Tyler, with a list of Electors, the last of whom is Ab'm Lincoln, of Sangamon.

    BILLY HERNDON *is working at the table. He is young, slight, serious-minded, smouldering. He looks up as* ABE *comes in.* ABE *wears a battered plug hat, a light alpaca coat, and carries an ancient, threadbare carpet-bag. He is evidently not in a talkative*

mood. His boots are caked in mud. He is only thirty-one years old, but his youth was buried with Ann Rutledge.

He leaves the office door open, and lettered on it we see the number, 4, and the firm's name—Stuart & Lincoln, Attorneys & Counsellors at Law.

BILLY. How de do, Mr. Lincoln. Glad to see you back.

ABE. Good day, Billy. (*He sets down the carpet-bag, takes off his hat and puts it on his desk.*)

BILLY. How was it on the circuit, Mr. Lincoln?

ABE. About as usual.

BILLY. Have you been keeping in good health?

ABE. Not particularly. But Doc Henry dosed me enough to keep me going. (*He sits down at the desk and starts looking at letters and papers that have accumulated during his absence. He takes little interest in them, pigeonholing some letters unopened.*)

BILLY. Did you have occasion to make any political speeches?

ABE. Oh—they got me up on the stump a couple of times. Ran into Stephen Douglas—he was out campaigning, of course—and we had some arguments in public.

BILLY (*greatly interested*). That's good! What issues did you and Mr. Douglas discuss?

ABE. Now—don't get excited, Billy. We weren't taking it serious. There was no blood shed. . . . What's the news here?

BILLY. Judge Stuart wrote that he arrived safely in Washington and the campaign there is getting almost as hot as the weather. Mrs. Fraim stopped in to say she couldn't possibly pay your fee for a while.

ABE. I should hope not. I ought to be paying her, seeing as I defended her poor husband and he hanged.

[BILLY *hands him a letter and watches him intently, while he reads it.*]

BILLY. That was left here by hand, and I promised to call it especially to your attention. It's from the Elijah P. Lovejoy League of Freemen. They want you to speak at an Abolitionist rally next Thursday evening. It'll be a very important affair.

ABE (*reflectively*). It's funny, Billy—I was thinking about Lovejoy the other day—trying to figure what it is in a man that makes him glad to be a martyr. I was on the boat coming from Quincy to Alton, and there was a gentleman on board with twelve Negroes. He was shipping them down to Vicksburg for sale—had 'em chained six and six together. Each of them had a small iron clevis around his wrist, and this was chained to the main chain, so that those Negroes were strung together precisely like fish on a trot line. I gathered they were being separated forever from their homes—mothers, fathers, wives, children—whatever families the poor creatures had got—going to be whipped into perpetual slavery, and no questions asked. It was quite a shocking sight.

BILLY (*excited*). Then you will give a speech at the Lovejoy rally?

ABE (*wearily*). I doubt it. That Freemen's League is a pack of hell-roaring fanatics. Talk reason to them and they scorn you for being a mealy-mouth. Let 'em make their own noise. (ABE *has opened a letter. He starts to read it.*)

[BILLY *looks at him with resentful disappointment, but he knows too well that any argument would be futile. He resumes his work. After a moment,* BOWLING GREEN *comes in, followed by* JOSH SPEED.]

BOWLING. Are we interrupting the majesty of the Law?

ABE (*heartily*). Bowling! (*He jumps up and grasps* BOWLING'S *hand.*) How are you, Bowling?

BOWLING. Tolerably well, Abe—and glad to see you.

ABE. This is Billy Herndon—Squire Green, of New Salem. Hello, Josh.

JOSH. Hello, Abe.

BILLY (*shaking hands with* BOWLING). I'm proud to know you, sir. Mr. Lincoln speaks of you constantly.

BOWLING. Thank you, Mr. Herndon. Are you a lawyer, too?

BILLY (*seriously*). I hope to be, sir. I'm serving here as a clerk in Judge Stuart's absence.

BOWLING. So now you're teaching others, Abe?

ABE. Just providing a bad example.

BOWLING. I can believe it. Look at the mess on that desk. Shameful!

ABE. Give me another year of law practise and I'll need a warehouse for the overflow. . . . But—sit yourself down, Bowling, and tell me what brings you to Springfield.

[BOWLING *sits.* JOSH *has sat on the couch, smoking his pipe.* BILLY *is again at the table.*]

BOWLING. I've been up to Lake Michigan—fishing—came in today on the steam-cars—scared me out of a year's growth. But how are you doing, Abe? Josh says you're still broke, but you're a great social success.

ABE. True—on both counts. I'm greatly in demand at all the more elegant functions. You remember Ninian Edwards?

BOWLING. Of course.

ABE. Well, sir—I'm a guest at his mansion regularly. He's got a house so big you could race horses in the parlor. And his wife is one of the Todd family from Kentucky. Very high-grade people. They spell their name with two D's—which is pretty impressive when you consider that one was enough for God.

JOSH. Tell Bowling whom you met over in Rochester.

ABE. The President of the United States!

BOWLING. You don't tell me so!

ABE. Do you see that hand? (*He holds out his right hand, palm upward.*)

BOWLING. Yes—I see it.

ABE. It has shaken the hand of Martin Van Buren!

BOWLING (*laughing*). Was the President properly respectful to you, Abe?

ABE. Indeed he was! He said to me, "We've been hearing great things of you in Washington." I found out later he'd said the same thing to every other cross-roads politician he'd met. (*He laughs.*) But Billy Herndon there is pretty disgusted with me for associating with the wrong kind of people. Billy's a firebrand—a real, radical abolitionist—and he can't

stand anybody who keeps his mouth shut and abides by the Constitution. If he had his way, the whole Union would be set on fire and we'd all be burned to a crisp. Eh, Billy?

BILLY (*grimly*). Yes, Mr. Lincoln. And if you'll permit me to say so, I think you'd be of more use to your fellow-men if you allowed some of the same incendiary impulses to come out in you.

ABE. You see, Bowling? He wants me to get down into the blood-soaked arena and grapple with all the lions of injustice and oppression.

BOWLING. Mr. Herndon—my profound compliments.

BILLY (*rising and taking his hat*). Thank you, sir. (*He shakes hands with* BOWLING, *then turns to* ABE.) I have the writ prepared in the Willcox case. I'll take it down to the Clerk of Court to be attested.

ABE. All right, Billy.

BILLY (*to* BOWLING). Squire Green—Mr. Lincoln regards you and Mr. Speed as the best friends he has on earth, and I should like to beg you, in his presence, for God's sake drag him out of this stagnant pool in which he's rapidly drowning himself. Good day, sir—good day, Mr. Speed.

JOSH. Good day, Billy.

[BILLY *has gone.*]

BOWLING. That's a bright young man, Abe. Seems to have a good grasp of things.

ABE (*looking after* BILLY). He's going downstairs to the Clerk's office, but he took his hat. Which means that before he comes back to work, he'll have paid a little visit to the Chenery House saloon.

BOWLING. Does the boy drink?

ABE. Yes. He's got great fires in him, but he's putting 'em out fast. . . .

Now—tell me about New Salem. (*He leans against the wall near the window.*)

BOWLING. Practically nothing of it left.

ABE. How's that blessed wife of yours?

BOWLING. Nancy's busier than ever, and more than ever concerned about your innermost thoughts and yearnings. In fact, she instructed me expressly to ask what on earth is the matter with you?

ABE (*laughs*). You can tell her there's nothing the matter. I've been able to pay off my debts to the extent of some seven cents on the dollar, and I'm sound of skin and skeleton.

BOWLING. But why don't we hear more from you and of you?

ABE. Josh can tell you. I've been busy.

BOWLING. What at?

ABE. I'm a candidate.   20

JOSH (*pointing to the poster*). Haven't you noticed his name? It's here—at the bottom of the list of Electors on the Whig ticket.

ABE. Yes, sir—if old Tippecanoe wins next fall, I'll be a member of the Electoral College.

BOWLING. The Electoral College! And is that the best you can do?

ABE. Yes—in the limited time at my dis- 30 posal. I had a letter from Seth Gale—remember—he used to live in New Salem and was always aiming to move West. He's settled down in Maryland now and has a wife and a son. He says that back East they're powerful worried about the annexation of Texas.

BOWLING. They have reason to be. It would probably mean extending slav- 40 ery through all the territories, from Kansas and Nebraska right out to Oregon and California. That would give the South absolute rule of the country—and God help the rest of us in the free states.

JOSH. It's an ugly situation, all right. It's got the seeds in it of nothing more nor less than civil war.

ABE. Well, if so, it'll be the abolitionists' own fault. They know where this trouble might lead, and yet they go right on agitating. They ought to be locked up for disturbing the peace, all of them.

10 BOWLING. I thought you were opposed to slavery, Abe. Have you changed your mind about it?

ABE (*ambles over to the couch and sprawls on it*). No. I am opposed to slavery. But I'm even more opposed to going to war. And, on top of that, I know what you're getting at, both of you. (*He speaks to them with the utmost good nature.*) You're following Billy Herndon's lead—troubling your kind hearts with concerns about me and when am I going to amount to something. Is that it?

BOWLING. Oh, no, Abe. Far be it from me to interfere in your life.

JOSH. Or me, either. If we happen to feel that, so far, you've been a big disappointment to us, we'll surely keep it to ourselves.

30 ABE (*laughs*). I'm afraid you'll have to do what I've had to do—which is, learn to accept me for what I am. I'm no fighting man. I found that out when I went through the Black Hawk War, and was terrified that I might have to fire a shot at an Indian. Fortunately, the Indians felt the same way, so I never saw one of them. Now, I know plenty of men who like to fight; they're willing to kill, and not scared of being killed. All right. Let them attend to the battles that have to be fought.

BOWLING. Peaceable men have sometimes been of service to their country.

ABE. They may have been peaceable

when they started, but they didn't remain so long after they'd become mixed in the great brawl of politics. (*He sits up.*) Suppose I ran for Congress, and got elected. I'd be right in the thick of that ugly situation you were speaking of. One day I might have to cast my vote on the terrible issue of war or peace. It might be war with Mexico over Texas; or war with England over Oregon; or even war with our own people across the Ohio River. What attitude would I take in deciding which way to vote? "The Liberal attitude," of course. And what is the Liberal attitude? To go to war, for a tract of land, or a moral principle? Or to avoid war at all costs? No, sir. The place for me is in the Electoral College, where all I have to do is vote for the President whom everybody else elected four months previous.

BOWLING. Well, Abe—you were always an artful dodger—and maybe you'll be able to go on to the end of your days avoiding the clutch of your own conscience.

[NINIAN EDWARDS *comes in. He is a little stouter and more prosperous.*]

ABE *and* JOSH. Hello, Ninian.

NINIAN. Hello. I saw Billy Herndon at the Chenery House and he said you were back from the circuit. (*He sees* BOWLING.) Why—it's my good friend Squire Green. How de do, and welcome to Springfield. (*He shakes hands with* BOWLING.)

BOWLING. Thank you, Mr. Edwards.

NINIAN. I just called in, Abe, to tell you you must dine with us. And, Squire, Mrs. Edwards would be honored to receive you, if your engagements will permit—and you, too, Josh.

JOSH. Delighted!

NINIAN. We're proudly exhibiting my sister-in-law, Miss Mary Todd, who has just come from Kentucky to grace our home. She's a very gay young lady—speaks French like a native, recites poetry at the drop of a hat, and knows the names and habits of all the flowers. I've asked Steve Douglas and some of the other eligibles to meet her, so you boys had better get in early.

BOWLING. My compliments to Mrs. Edwards, but my own poor wife awaits me impatiently, I hope.

NINIAN. I appreciate your motives, Squire, and applaud them. You'll be along presently, Abe?

ABE. I wouldn't be surprised.

NINIAN. Good. You'll meet a delightful young lady. And I'd better warn you she's going to survey the whole field of matrimonial prospects and select the one who promises the most. So you'd better be on your guard, Abe, unless you're prepared to lose your standing as a free man.

ABE. I thank you for the warning, Ninian.

NINIAN. Good day to you, Squire. See you later, Josh. (*He goes out.*)

ABE. There, Bowling—you see how things are with me. Hardly a day goes by but what I'm invited to meet some eager young female who has all the graces, including an ability to speak the language of diplomacy.

BOWLING. I'm sorry, Abe, that I shan't be able to hear you carrying on a flirtation in French. (ABE *looks at him, curiously.*)

ABE. I'm not pretending with you, Bowling—or you, Josh. I couldn't fool you any better than I can fool myself. I know what you're thinking about me, and I think so, too. Only I'm not so merciful in considering my own shortcomings, or so ready to forgive them, as you are. But—you talk about civil war—there seems to be one going on inside me all the time. Both sides are right and both are wrong and equal in strength. I'd like to be able to rise superior to the struggle—but—it says in the Bible that a house divided against itself cannot stand, so I reckon there's not much hope. One of these days, I'll just split asunder, and part company with 10 myself—and it'll be a good riddance from both points of view. However— come on. (*He takes his hat.*) You've got to get back to Nancy, and Josh and I have got to make a good impression upon Miss Mary Todd, of Kentucky. (*He waves them to the door. As they go out, the light fades.*)

SCENE V   20

Parlor of the Edwards house in Springfield. An evening in November, some six months after the preceding scene.

There is a fireplace at the right, a heavily curtained bay window at the left, a door at the back leading into the front hall.

At the right, by the fireplace, are a small couch and an easy chair. There is another couch at the left, and a table and chairs at the back. There are family portraits on the walls. 30 *It is all moderately elegant.*

NINIAN *is standing before the fire, in conversation with* ELIZABETH, *his wife. She is high-bred, ladylike—excessively so. She is, at the moment, in a state of some agitation.*

ELIZABETH. I cannot believe it! It is an outrageous reflection on my sister's good sense.
NINIAN. I'm not so sure of that. Mary 40 has known Abe for several months, and she has had plenty of chance to observe him closely.
ELIZABETH. She has been entertained by him, as we all have. But she has been far more attentive to Edwin Webb

and Stephen Douglas and many others who are distinctly eligible.
NINIAN. Isn't it remotely possible that she sees more in Abe than you do?
ELIZABETH. Nonsense! Mr. Lincoln's chief virtue is that he hides no part of his simple soul from any one. He's a most amiable creature, to be sure; but as the husband of a high-bred, high-spirited young lady . . .
NINIAN. Quite so, Elizabeth. Mary *is* high-spirited! That is just why she set her cap for him. (ELIZABETH *looks at him sharply, then laughs.*)
ELIZABETH. You're making fun of me, Ninian. You're deliberately provoking me into becoming excited about nothing.
NINIAN. No, Elizabeth—I am merely trying to prepare you for a rude shock. You think Abe Lincoln would be overjoyed to capture an elegant, cultivated girl, daughter of the President of the Bank of Kentucky, descendant of a long line of English gentlemen. Well, you are mistaken . . .

[MARY TODD *comes in. She is twenty-two— short, pretty, remarkably sharp. She stops short in the doorway, and her suspecting eyes dart from* ELIZABETH *to* NINIAN.]
MARY. What were you two talking about?
NINIAN. I was telling your sister about the new song the boys are singing: "What is the great commotion, motion,
Our country through?
It is the ball a-rolling on
For Tippecanoe and Tyler, too—for Tippecanoe . . ."
MARY (*with a rather grim smile*). I compliment you for thinking quickly, Ninian. But you were talking about *me!* (*She looks at* ELIZABETH, *who quails a little before her sister's determination.*) Weren't you?

ELIZABETH. Yes, Mary, we were.

MARY. And quite seriously, I gather.

NINIAN. I'm afraid that our dear Elizabeth has become unduly alarmed . . .

ELIZABETH (*snapping at him*). Let me say what I have to say! (*She turns to* MARY.) Mary—you must tell me the truth. Are you—have you ever given one moment's serious thought to the possibility of marriage with Abraham Lincoln? (MARY *looks at each of them, her eyes flashing.*) I promise you, Mary, that to me such a notion is too far beyond the bounds of credibility to be . . .

MARY. But Ninian has raised the horrid subject, hasn't he? He has brought the evil scandal out into the open, and we must face it, fearlessly. Let us do so at once, by all means. I shall answer you, Elizabeth: I have given more than one moment's thought to the possibility you mentioned—and I have decided that I shall be Mrs. Lincoln. (*She seats herself on the couch.*)

[NINIAN *is about to say,* "*I told you so,*" *but thinks better of it.* ELIZABETH *can only gasp and gape.*]

MARY. I have examined, carefully, the qualifications of all the young gentlemen, and some of the old ones, in this neighborhood. Those of Mr. Lincoln seem to me superior to all others, and he is my choice.

ELIZABETH. Do you expect me to congratulate you upon this amazing selection?

MARY. No! I ask for no congratulations, nor condolences, either.

ELIZABETH (*turning away*). Then I shall offer none.

NINIAN. Forgive me for prying, Mary— but have you as yet communicated your decision to the gentleman himself?

MARY (*with a slight smile at* NINIAN). Not yet. But he is coming to call this evening, and he will ask humbly for my hand in marriage; and, after I have displayed the proper amount of surprise and confusion, I shall murmur, timidly, "Yes!"

ELIZABETH (*pitiful*). You make a brave jest of it, Mary. But as for me, I am deeply and painfully shocked. I don't know what to say to you. But I urge you, I beg you, as your elder sister, responsible to our father and our dead mother for your welfare . . .

MARY (*with a certain tenderness*). I can assure you, Elizabeth—it is useless to beg or command. I have made up my mind.

NINIAN. I admire your courage, Mary, but I should like . . .

ELIZABETH. I think, Ninian, that this is a matter for discussion solely between my sister and myself!

MARY. No! I want to hear what Ninian has to say. (*To* NINIAN.) What is it?

NINIAN. I only wondered if I might ask you another question.

MARY (*calmly*). You may.

NINIAN. Understand, my dear—I'm not quarreling with you. My affection for Abe is eternal—but—I'm curious to know—what is it about him that makes you choose him for a husband?

MARY (*betraying her first sign of uncertainty*). I should like to give you a plain, simple answer, Ninian. But I cannot.

ELIZABETH (*jumping at this*). Of course you cannot! You're rushing blindly into this. You have no conception of what it will mean to your future.

MARY. You're wrong about that, Elizabeth. This is not the result of wild, tempestuous infatuation. I have not been swept off my feet. Mr. Lincoln is a Westerner, but that is his only point of resemblance to Young Lochinvar. I simply feel that of all the men I've ever known, he is the one whose life and destiny I want most to share.

ELIZABETH. Haven't you sense enough to know you could never be happy with him? His breeding—his background—his manner—his whole point of view . . . ?

MARY (*gravely*). I could not be content with a "happy" marriage in the accepted sense of the word. I have no craving for comfort and security.

ELIZABETH. And have you a craving for the kind of life you would lead? A miserable cabin, without a servant, without a stitch of clothing that is fit for exhibition in decent society?

MARY (*raising her voice*). I have not yet 20 tried poverty, so I cannot say how I should take to it. But I might well prefer it to anything I have previously known—so long as there is forever before me the chance for high adventure—so long as I can know that I am always going forward, with my husband, along a road that leads across the horizon. (*This last is said with a sort of mad intensity.*)

ELIZABETH. And how far do you think you will go with any one like Abe Lincoln, who is lazy and shiftless and prefers to stop constantly along the way to tell jokes?

MARY (*rising; furious*). He will *not* stop, if I am strong enough to make him go on! And I am strong! I know what *you* expect of me. You want me to do precisely as you have done—and 40 marry a man like Ninian—and I know many, that are *just* like him! But with all due respect to my dear brother-in-law—I don't want that— and I won't have it! Never! You live in a house with a fence around it—

presumably to prevent the common herd from gaining access to your sacred precincts—but really to prevent you, yourselves, from escaping from your own narrow lives. In Abraham Lincoln I see a man who has split rails for other men's fences, but who will never build one around himself!

10 ELIZABETH. What are you *saying*, Mary? You are talking with a degree of irresponsibility that is not far from sheer madness . . .

MARY (*scornfully*). I imagine it does seem like insanity to you! You married a man who was settled and established in the world, with a comfortable inheritance, and no problems to face. And you've never made a move to change your condition, or improve it. You consider it couldn't be improved. To you, all this represents perfection. But it doesn't to me! I want the chance to *shape* a new life, for myself, and for my husband. Is that irresponsibility?

[*A* MAID *appears.*]

MAID. Mr. Lincoln, ma'am.

ELIZABETH. He's here.

30 MARY (*firmly*). I shall see him!

MAID. Will you step in, Mr. Lincoln?

[ABE *comes in, wearing a new suit, his hair nearly neat.*]

ABE. Good evening, Mrs. Edwards. Good evening, Miss Todd. Ninian, good evening.

ELIZABETH. Good evening.

MARY. Good evening, Mr. Lincoln. (*She sits on the couch at the left.*)

40 NINIAN. Glad to see you, Abe.

[ABE *sees that there is electricity in the atmosphere of this parlor. He tries hard to be affably casual.*]

ABE. I'm afraid I'm a little late in arriving, but I ran into an old friend of mine, wife of Jack Armstrong, the champion rowdy of New Salem. I believe you have some recollection of him, Ninian.

NINIAN (*smiling*). I most certainly have. What's he been up to now?

ABE (*stands in front of the fireplace*). Oh, he's all right, but Hannah, his wife, is in fearful trouble because her son Duff is up for murder and she wants me to defend him. I went over to the 10 jail to interview the boy and he looks pretty tolerably guilty to me. But I used to give him lessons in the game of marbles while his mother foxed my pants for me. (*He turns to* ELIZABETH.) That means, she sewed buckskin around the legs of my pants so I wouldn't tear 'em to shreds going through underbrush when I was surveying. Well—in view of old times, I 20 felt I had to take the case and do what I can to obstruct the orderly processes of justice.

NINIAN (*laughs, with some relief*). And the boy will be acquitted. I tell you, Abe —this country would be law-abiding and peaceful if it weren't for you lawyers. But—if you will excuse Elizabeth and me, we must hear the children's prayers and see them safely 30 abed.

ABE. Why—I'd be glad to hear their prayers, too.

NINIAN. Oh, no! You'd only keep them up till all hours with your stories. Come along, Elizabeth.

[ELIZABETH *doesn't want to go, but doesn't know what to do to prevent it.*]

ABE (*to* ELIZABETH). Kiss them good night, for me.

NINIAN. We'd better not tell them you're in the house, or they'll be furious.

ELIZABETH (*making one last attempt*). Mary! Won't you come with us and say good night to the children?

NINIAN. No, my dear. Leave Mary here

—to keep Abe entertained. (*He guides* ELIZABETH *out, following her.*)

MARY (*with a little laugh*). I don't blame Ninian for keeping you away from those children. They all adore you.

ABE. Well—I always seemed to get along well with children. Probably it's because they never want to take me seriously.

MARY. You understand them—that's the important thing . . . But—do sit down, Mr. Lincoln. (*She indicates that he is to sit next to her.*)

ABE. Thank you—I will. (*He starts to cross to the couch to sit beside* MARY. *She looks at him with melting eyes. The lights fade.*)

SCENE VI

Again the Law Office. It is afternoon of New Year's Day, a few weeks after the preceding scene.

ABE *is sitting, slumped in his chair, staring at his desk. He has his hat and overcoat on. A muffler is hanging about his neck, untied.*

JOSH SPEED *is half-sitting on the table at the right. He is reading a long letter, with most serious attention. At length he finishes it,* 30 *refolds it very carefully, stares at the floor.*

ABE. Have you finished it, Josh?

JOSH. Yes.

ABE. Well—do you think it's all right?

JOSH. No, Abe—I don't. (ABE *turns slowly and looks at him.*) I think the sending of this letter would be a most grave mistake—and that is putting it mildly and charitably.

40 ABE. Have I stated the case too crudely?

(ABE *is evidently in a serious state of distress, although he is making a tremendous effort to disguise it by speaking in what he intends to be a coldly impersonal tone. He is struggling mightily to hold himself back from the brink of nervous collapse.*)

JOSH. No—I have no quarrel with your choice of words. None whatever. If anything, the phraseology is too correct. But your method of doing it, Abe! It's brutal, it's heartless, it's so unworthy of you that I—I'm at a loss to understand how you ever thought you could do it this way.

ABE. I've done the same thing before with a woman to whom I seemed to 10 have become attached. She approved of my action.

JOSH. This is a different woman. (*He walks over to the window, then turns again toward* ABE.) You cannot seem to accept the fact that women are human beings, too, as variable as we are. You act on the assumption that they're all the same one—and that one is a completely unearthly being of 20 your own conception. This letter isn't written to Mary Todd—it's written to yourself. Every line of it is intended to provide salve for your own conscience.

ABE (*rising; coldly*). Do I understand that you will not deliver it for me?

JOSH. No, Abe—I shall not.

ABE (*angrily*). Then some one else will!

JOSH (*scornfully*). Yes. You could give it 30 to the minister, to hand to the bride when he arrives for the ceremony. But—I hope, Abe, you won't send it till you're feeling a little calmer in your mind. . . .

ABE (*vehemently, turning to* JOSH). How can I ever be calm in my mind until this thing is settled, and out of the way, once and for all? Have you got eyes in your head, Josh? Can't you 40 see that I'm desperate?

JOSH. I can see that plainly, Abe. I think your situation is more desperate even than you imagine, and I believe you should have the benefit of some really intelligent medical advice.

ABE (*seating himself at* BILLY's *table*). The trouble with me isn't anything that a doctor can cure.

JOSH. There's a good man named Dr. Drake, who makes a specialty of treating people who get into a state of mind like yours, Abe . . .

ABE (*utterly miserable*). So that's how you've figured it! I've done what I've threatened to do many times before: I've gone crazy. Well—you know me better than most men, Josh—and perhaps you're not far off right. I just feel that I've got to the end of my rope, and I must let go, and drop—and where I'll land, I don't know, and whether I'll survive the fall, I don't know that either. . . . But—this I *do* know: I've got to get out of this thing—I can't go through with it—I've got to have my release!

[JOSH *has turned to the window. Suddenly he turns back, toward* ABE.]

JOSH. Ninian Edwards is coming up. Why not show this letter to him and ask for his opinion. . . .

ABE (*interrupting, with desperation*). No, no! Don't say a word of any of this to him! Put that letter in your pocket. I can't bear to discuss this business with him, now.

[JOSH *puts the letter in his pocket and crosses to the couch.*]

JOSH. Hello, Ninian.

NINIAN (*heartily, from off*). Hello, Josh! Happy New Year! (NINIAN *comes in. He wears a handsome, fur-trimmed great-coat, and carries two silver-headed canes, one of them in a baize bag, which he lays down on the table at the right.*)

NINIAN. And Happy New Year, Abe—in fact, the happiest of your whole life!

ABE. Thank you, Ninian. And Happy New Year to you.

NINIAN (*opening his coat*). That didn't

sound much as if you meant it. (*He goes to the stove to warm his hands.*) However, you can be forgiven today, Abe. I suppose you're inclined to be just a wee bit nervous. (*He chuckles and winks at* JOSH.) God—but it's cold in here! Don't you ever light this stove?

ABE. The fire's all laid. Go ahead and light it, if you want.

NINIAN (*striking a match*). You certainly are in one of your less amiable moods today. (*He lights the stove.*)

JOSH. Abe's been feeling a little under the weather.

NINIAN. So it seems. He looks to me as if he'd been to a funeral.

ABE. That's where I have been.

NINIAN (*disbelieving*). What? A funeral on your wedding day?

JOSH. They buried Abe's oldest friend, Bowling Green, this morning.

NINIAN (*shocked*). Oh—I'm mighty sorry to hear that, Abe. And—I hope you'll forgive me for—not having known about it.

ABE. Of course, Ninian.

NINIAN. But I'm glad you were there, Abe, at the funeral. It must have been a great comfort to his family.

ABE. I wasn't any comfort to any one. They asked me to deliver an oration, a eulogy of the deceased—and I tried—and I couldn't say a thing. Why do they expect you to strew a lot of flowery phrases over anything so horrible as a dead body? Do they think that Bowling Green's soul needs quotations to give it peace? All that mattered to me was that he was a good, just man—and I loved him—and he's dead.

NINIAN. Why didn't you say that, Abe?

ABE (*rising*). I told you—they wanted an oration.

NINIAN. Well, Abe—I think Bowling himself would be the first to ask you to put your sadness aside in the prospect of your own happiness, and Mary's—and I'm only sorry that our old friend didn't live to see you two fine people married. (*He is making a gallant attempt to assume a more cheerily nuptial tone.*) I've made all the arrangements with the Reverend Dresser, and Elizabeth is preparing a bang-up dinner—so you can be sure the whole affair will be carried off handsomely *and* painlessly.

[BILLY HERNDON *comes in. He carries a bottle in his coat pocket, and is already more than a little drunk and sullen, but abnormally articulate.*]

NINIAN. Ah, Billy—Happy New Year!

BILLY. The same to you, Mr. Edwards. (*He puts the bottle down on the table and takes his coat off.*)

NINIAN. I brought you a wedding present, Abe. Thought you'd like to make a brave show when you first walk out with your bride. It came from the same place in Louisville where I bought mine. (*He picks up one of the canes and hands it proudly to* ABE, *who takes it and inspects it gravely.*)

ABE. It's very fine, Ninian. And I thank you. (*He takes the cane over to his desk and seats himself.*)

NINIAN. Well—I'll frankly confess that in getting it for you, I was influenced somewhat by consideration for Mary and her desire for keeping up appearances. And in that connection—I know you'll forgive me, Josh, and you, too, Billy, if I say something of a somewhat personal nature?

BILLY (*truculent*). If you want me to leave you, I shall be glad to. . . .

NINIAN. No, please, Billy—I merely want to speak a word or two as another of Abe's friends; it's my last chance before the ceremony. Of course, the fact that the bride is my sister-in-law gives me a little added responsibility in wishing to promote the success of this marriage. (*He crosses to* ABE.) And a success it will be, Abe . . . if only you will bear in mind one thing: you must keep a tight rein on her ambition. My wife tells me that even as a child, she had delusions of grandeur—she predicted to one and all that the man she 10 would marry would be President of the United States. (*He turns to* JOSH.) You know how it is—every boy in the country plans some day to be president, and every little girl plans to marry him. (*Again to* ABE.) But Mary is one who hasn't entirely lost those youthful delusions. So I urge you to beware. Don't let her talk you into any gallant crusades or wild goose 20 chases. Let her learn to be satisfied with the estate to which God hath brought her. With which, I shall conclude my pre-nuptial sermon. (*He buttons his coat.*) I shall see you all at the house at five o'clock, and I want you to make sure that Abe is looking his prettiest.

JOSH. Good-bye, Ninian.

[NINIAN *goes out.* ABE *turns again to the desk* 30 *and stares at nothing.* BILLY *takes the bottle and a cup from his desk and pours himself a stiff drink. He raises the cup toward* ABE.]

BILLY (*huskily*). Mr. Lincoln, I beg leave to drink to your health and happiness . . . and to that of the lady who will become your wife. (ABE *makes no response.* BILLY *drinks it down, then puts the cup back on the table.*) You 40 don't want to accept my toast because you think it wasn't sincere. And I'll admit I've made it plain that I've regretted the step you've taken. I thought that in this marriage, you were lowering yourself—you were trading your honor for some exalted family connections. . . . I wish to apologize for so thinking. . . .

ABE. No apologies required, Billy.

BILLY. I doubt that Miss Todd and I will ever get along well together. But I'm now convinced that our aims are the same—particularly since I've heard the warnings delivered by her brother-in-law. (*A note of scorn colors his allusion to* NINIAN.) If she really is ambitious for you—if she will never stop driving you, goading you—then I say, God bless her, and give her strength!

[*He has said all this with* ABE'S *back to him.* BILLY *pours himself another drink, nearly emptying the large bottle.* ABE *turns and looks at him.*]

ABE. Have you had all of that bottle today?

BILLY. This bottle? Yes—I have.

JOSH. And why not? It's New Year's Day!

BILLY (*looking at* JOSH). Thank you, Mr. Speed. Thank you for the defense. And I hope you will permit me to propose one more toast. (*He takes a step toward* ABE.) To the President of the United States, and Mrs. Lincoln! (*He drinks.*)

ABE (*grimly*). I think we can do without any more toasts, Billy.

BILLY. Very well! That's the last one—until after the wedding. And then, no doubt, the Edwards will serve us with the costliest champagne. And, in case you're apprehensive, I shall be on my best behavior in that distinguished gathering!

ABE. There is not going to be a wedding. (BILLY *stares at him, and then looks at* JOSH, *and then again at* ABE.) I have a letter that I want you to deliver to Miss Todd.

BILLY. What letter? What is it?

ABE. Give it to him, Josh. (JOSH *takes the*

letter out of his pocket, and puts it in the stove. ABE *jumps up.*) You have no right to do that!

JOSH. I know I haven't! But it's done. (ABE *is staring at* JOSH.) And don't look at me as if you were planning to break my neck. Of course you could do it, Abe—but you won't. (JOSH *turns to* BILLY.) In that letter, Mr. Lincoln asked Miss Todd for his release. He told her that he had made a mistake in his previous protestations of affection for her, and so he couldn't go through with a marriage which could only lead to endless pain and misery for them both.

ABE (*deeply distressed*). If that isn't the truth, what is?

JOSH. I'm not disputing the truth of it. I'm only asking you to tell her so, to her face, in the manner of a man.

ABE. It would be a more cruel way. It would hurt her more deeply. For I couldn't help blurting it *all* out—all the terrible things I didn't say in that letter. (*He is speaking with passion.*) I'd have to tell her that I have hatred for her infernal ambition—that I don't want to be ridden and driven, upward and onward through life, with her whip lashing me, and her spurs digging into me! If her poor soul craves importance in life, then let her marry Stephen Douglas. He's ambitious, too. . . . I want only to be left alone! (*He sits down again and leans on the table.*)

JOSH (*bitterly*). Very well, then—tell her all that! It will be more gracious to admit that you're afraid of her, instead of letting her down flat with the statement that your ardor, such as it was, has cooled.

[BILLY *has been seething with a desire to get into this conversation. Now, with a momentary silence, he plunges.*]

BILLY. May I say something?

ABE. I doubt that you're in much of a condition to contribute. . . .

JOSH. What is it, Billy?

BILLY (*hotly*). It's just this. Mr. Lincoln, you're not abandoning Miss Mary Todd. No! You're only using her as a living sacrifice, offering her up, in the hope that you will thus gain forgiveness of the gods for your failure to do your own great duty!

ABE (*smoldering*). Yes! My own great duty. Every one feels called upon to remind me of it, but no one can tell me what it is.

BILLY (*almost tearful*). I can tell you! I can tell you what is the duty of every man who calls himself an American! It is to perpetuate those truths which were once held to be self-evident: that all men are created equal—that they are endowed with certain inalienable rights—that among these are the right to life, liberty and the pursuit of happiness.

ABE (*angrily*). And are those rights denied to *me*?

BILLY. Could you ever enjoy them while your mind is full of the awful knowledge that two million of your fellow beings in this country are slaves? Can you take any satisfaction from looking at that flag above your desk, when you know that ten of its stars represent states which are willing to destroy the Union—rather than yield their property rights in the flesh and blood of those slaves? And what of all the States of the future? All the territories of the West—clear out to the Pacific Ocean? Will they be the homes of free men? Are you answering *that* question to your own satisfaction? That is your flag, Mr. Lincoln, and you're proud of it. But what are you doing to save it from being ripped into shreds?

[ABE *jumps to his feet, towers over* BILLY, *and speaks with temper restrained, but with great passion.*]

ABE. I'm minding my own business—that's what I'm doing! And there'd be no threat to the Union if others would do the same. And as to slavery—I'm sick and tired of this righteous talk about it. When you know more about law, you'll know that those property rights you mentioned are guaranteed by the Constitution. And if the Union can't stand on the Constitution, then let it fall!

BILLY. The hell with the Constitution! This is a matter of the rights of living men to freedom—and those came before the Constitution! When the Law denies those rights, then the Law is wrong, and it must be changed, if not by moral protest, then by force! There's no course of action that isn't justified in the defense of freedom! And don't dare to tell me that any one in the world knows that better than you do, Mr. Lincoln. You, who honor the memory of Elijah Lovejoy and every other man who ever died for that very ideal!

ABE (*turning away from him*). Yes—I honor them—and envy them—because they could believe that their ideals are *worth* dying for. (*He turns to* JOSH *and speaks with infinite weariness.*) All right, Josh—I'll go up now and talk to Mary—and then I'm going away. . . .

JOSH. Where, Abe?

ABE (*dully*). I don't know.

[*He goes out and closes the door after him. After a moment,* BILLY *rushes to the door, opens it, and shouts after* ABE.]

BILLY. You're quitting, Mr. Lincoln! As surely as there's a God in Heaven, He knows that you're running away from your obligations to Him, and to your fellow-men, and your own immortal soul!

JOSH (*drawing* BILLY *away from the door*). Billy—Billy—leave him alone. He's a sick man.

BILLY (*sitting down at the table*). What can we do for him, Mr. Speed? What can we do? (BILLY *is now actually in tears.*)

JOSH. I don't know, Billy. (*He goes to the window and looks out.*) He'll be in such a state of emotional upheaval, he'll want to go away by himself, for a long time. Just as he did after the death of poor little Ann Rutledge. He'll go out and wander on the prairies, trying to grope his way back into the wilderness from which he came. There's nothing we can do for him, Billy. He'll have to do it for himself.

BILLY (*fervently*). May God be with him!

SCENE VII

On the prairie, near New Salem. It is a clear, cool, moonlit evening, nearly two years after the preceding scene.

In the foreground is a campfire. Around it are packing cases, blanket rolls and one ancient trunk. In the background is a covered wagon, standing at an angle, so that the opening at the back of it is visible to the audience.

SETH GALE *is standing by the fire, holding his seven-year-old son,* JIMMY, *in his arms. The boy is wrapped up in a blanket.*

JIMMY. I don't want to be near the fire, Paw. I'm burning up. Won't you take the blanket offen me, Paw?

SETH. No, son. You're better off if you keep yourself covered.

JIMMY. I want some water, Paw. Can't I have some water?

SETH. Yes! Keep quiet, Jimmy! Gobey's getting the water for you now. (*He looks off to the right, and sees* JACK ARM-

STRONG *coming*.) Hello, Jack, I was afraid you'd got lost.

JACK (*coming in*). I couldn't get lost anywhere's around New Salem. How's the boy?

SETH (*with a cautionary look at* JACK). He—he's a little bit thirsty. Did you find Abe?

JACK. Yes—it took me some time because he'd wandered off—went out to the old cemetery across the river to visit Ann Rutledge's grave.

SETH. Is he coming here?

JACK. He said he'd better go get Doc Chandler who lives on the Winchester Road. He'll be along in a while. (*He comes up to* JIMMY.) How you feelin', Jimmy?

JIMMY. I'm burning . . .

[AGGIE *appears, sees* JACK.]

AGGIE. Oh—I'm glad you're back, Mr. Armstrong.

JACK. There'll be a doctor here soon, Mrs. Gale.

AGGIE. Thank God for that! Bring him into the wagon, Seth. I got a nice, soft bed all ready for him.

SETH. You hear that, Jimmy? Your ma's fixed a place where you can rest comfortable.

[AGGIE *retreats into the wagon*.]

JIMMY. When'll Gobey come back? I'm thirsty. When'll he bring the water?

SETH. Right away, son. You can trust Gobey to get your water. (*He hands* JIMMY *into the wagon*.)

JACK. He's worse, ain't he?

SETH (*in a despairing tone*). Yes. The fever's been raging something fierce since you left. It'll sure be a relief when Abe gets here. He can always do something to put confidence in you.

JACK. How long since you've seen Abe, Seth?

SETH. Haven't laid eyes on him since I left here—eight—nine years ago. We've corresponded some.

JACK. Well—you may be surprised when you see him. He's changed plenty since he went to Springfield. He climbed up pretty high in the world, but he appears to have slipped down lately. He ain't much like his old comical self.

SETH. Well, I guess we all got to change. (*He starts up, hearing* GOBEY *return*.) Aggie!

[GOBEY, *a Negro, comes in from the left, carrying a bucket of water*. AGGIE *appears from the wagon*.]

SETH. Here's Gobey with the water.

GOBEY. Yes, Miss Aggie. Here you are. (*He hands it up*.)

AGGIE. Thanks, Gobey. (*She goes back into the wagon*.)

GOBEY. How's Jimmy now, Mr. Seth?

SETH. About the same.

GOBEY (*shaking his head*). I'll get some more water for the cooking. (*He picks up a kettle and a pot and goes*.)

SETH (*to* JACK). It was a bad thing to have happen, all right—the boy getting sick—when we were on an expedition like this. No doctor—no way of caring for him.

JACK. How long you been on the road, Seth?

SETH. More than three months. Had a terrible time in the Pennsylvania Mountains, fearful rains and every stream flooded. I can tell you, there was more than one occasion when I wanted to turn back and give up the whole idea. But—when you get started—you just can't turn . . . (*He is looking off right*.) Say! Is that Abe coming now?

JACK (*rising*). Yep. That's him.

SETH (*delighted*). My God, look at him! Store clothes and a plug hat! Hello—Abe!

ABE. Hello, Seth. (*He comes on and shakes hands, warmly*) I'm awful glad to see you again, Seth.

SETH. And me, too, Abe.

ABE. It did my heart good when I heard you were on your way West. Where's your boy?

SETH. He's in there—in the wagon. . . . [AGGIE *has appeared from the wagon.*]

AGGIE. Is that the doctor? 10

SETH. No, Aggie—this is the man I was telling you about I wanted so much to see. This is Mr. Abe Lincoln—my wife, Mrs. Gale.

ABE. Pleased to meet you, Mrs. Gale.

AGGIE. Pleased to meet you, Mr. Lincoln.

ABE. Doc Chandler wasn't home. They said he was expected over at the Boger farm at midnight. I'll go there 20 then and fetch him.

SETH. It'll be a friendly act, Abe.

AGGIE. We'll be in your debt, Mr. Lincoln.

ABE. In the meantime, Mrs. Gale, I'd like to do whatever I can. . . .

SETH. There's nothing to do, Abe. The boy's got the swamp fever, and we're just trying to keep him quiet.

AGGIE (*desperately*). There's just one 30 thing I would wish—is—is there any kind of a preacher around this God-forsaken place?

SETH (*worried*). Preacher?

ABE. Do you know of any, Jack?

JACK. No. There ain't a preacher within twenty miles of New Salem now.

AGGIE. Well—I only thought if there was, we might get him here to say a prayer for Jimmy. (*She goes back into* 40 *the wagon.* SETH *looks after her with great alarm.*)

SETH. She wants a preacher. That looks as if she'd given up, don't it?

JACK. It'd probably just comfort her.

ABE. Is your boy very sick, Seth?

SETH. Yes—he is.

JACK. Why don't *you* speak a prayer, Abe? You could always think of somethin' to say.

ABE. I'm afraid I'm not much of a hand at praying. I couldn't think of a blessed thing that would be of any comfort.

SETH. Never mind. It's just a—a religious idea of Aggie's. Sit down, Abe.

ABE (*looking at the wagon*). So you've got your dream at last, Seth. You're doing what you and I used to talk about—you're moving.

SETH. Yes, Abe. We got crowded out of Maryland. The city grew up right over our farm. So—we're headed for a place where there's more room. I wrote you—about four months back —to tell you we were starting out, and I'd like to meet up with you here. I thought it was just possible you might consider joining in this trip.

ABE. It took a long time for your letter to catch up with me, Seth. I've just been drifting—down around Indiana and Kentucky where I used to live. (*He sits down on a box.*) Do you aim to settle in Nebraska?

SETH. No, we're not going to stop there. We're going right across the continent—all the way to Oregon.

ABE (*deeply impressed*). Oregon?

JACK. Sure. That's where they're all headin' for now.

SETH. We're making first for a place called Westport Landing—that's in Kansas right on the frontier—where they outfit the wagon trains for the far West. You join up there with a lot of others who are like-minded, so you've got company when you're crossing the plains and the mountains.

ABE. It's staggering—to think of the distance you're going. And you'll be taking the frontier along with you.

SETH. It may seem like a fool-hardy thing to do—but we heard too many tales of the black earth out there, and the balance of rainfall and sunshine.

JACK. Why don't you go with them, Abe? That country out west is gettin' settled fast. Why—last week alone, I counted more than two hundred wagons went past here—people from all over—Pennsylvania, Connecticut, Vermont—all full of jubilation at the notion of gettin' land. By God, I'm goin' too, soon as I can get me a wagon. They'll need men like me to fight the Indians for 'em—and they'll need men with brains, like you, Abe, to tell 'em how to keep the peace.

ABE (*looking off*). It's a temptation to go, I can't deny that.

JACK. Then what's stoppin' you from doin' it? You said yourself you've just been driftin'.

ABE. Maybe that's it—maybe I've been drifting too long. . . . (*He changes the subject.*) Is it just the three of you, Seth?

SETH. That's all. The three of us and Gobey, the nigger.

ABE. Is he your slave?

SETH. Gobey? Hell, no! He's a free man! My father freed his father twenty years ago. But we've had to be mighty careful about Gobey. You see, where we come from, folks are pretty uncertain how they feel about the slave question, and lots of good free niggers get snaked over the line into Virginia and then sold down river before you know it. And when you try to go to court and assert their legal rights, you're beaten at every turn by the damned, dirty shyster lawyers. That's why we've been keeping well up in free territory on this trip.

ABE. Do you think it will be free in Oregon?

SETH. Of course it will! It's got to——

ABE (*bitterly*). Oh no, it hasn't, Seth. Not with the politicians in Washington selling out the whole West piece by piece to the slave traders.

SETH (*vehemently*). That territory has got to be free! If this country ain't strong enough to protect its citizens from slavery, then we'll cut loose from it and join with Canada. Or, better yet, we'll make a *new* country out there in the far west.

ABE (*gravely*). A new country?

SETH. Why not?

ABE. I was just thinking—old Mentor Graham once said to me that some day the United States might be divided up into many hostile countries, like Europe.

SETH. Well—let it be! Understand—I love this country and I'd fight for it. And I guess George Washington and the rest of them loved England and fought for it when they were young—but they didn't hesitate to cut loose when the government failed to play fair and square with 'em. . . .

JACK. By God, if Andy Jackson was back in the White House, he'd run out them traitors with a horsewhip!

ABE. It'd be a bad day for us Americans, Seth, if we lost you, and your wife, and your son.

SETH (*breaking*). My son!—Oh—I've been talking big—but it's empty talk. If he dies—there won't be enough spirit left in us to push on any further. What's the use of working for a future when you know there won't be anybody growing up to enjoy it. Excuse me, Abe—but I'm feeling pretty scared.

ABE (*suddenly rises*). You mustn't be scared, Seth. I know I'm a poor one to be telling you that—because I've been scared all my life. But—seeing you now—and thinking of the big thing you've set out to do—well, it's made me feel pretty small. It's made me feel that I've got to do something, too; to keep you and your kind in the United States of America. You mustn't quit, Seth! Don't let anything beat you—don't you ever give up!

[AGGIE *comes out of the wagon. She is very frightened.*]

AGGIE. Seth!

SETH. What is it, Aggie?

AGGIE. He's worse, Seth! He's moaning in his sleep, and he's grosping for breath. . . . (*She is crying.* SETH *takes her in his arms.*)

SETH. Never mind, honey. Never mind. When the doctor gets here, he'll fix him up in no time. It's all right, honey. He'll get well.

ABE. If you wish me to, Mrs. Gale—I'll try to speak a prayer.

[*They look at him.*]

JACK. That's the way to talk, Abe!

SETH. We'd be grateful for anything you might say, Abe.

[ABE *takes his hat off. As he starts speaking,* GOBEY *comes in from the left and stops reverently to listen.*]

ABE. Oh God, the father of all living, I ask you to look with gentle mercy upon this little boy who is here, lying sick in this covered wagon. His people are travelling far, to seek a new home in the wilderness, to do your work, God, to make this earth a good place for your children to live in. They can see clearly where they're going, and they're not afraid to face all the perils that lie along the way. I humbly beg you not to take their child from them. Grant him the freedom of life. Do not condemn him to the imprisonment of death. Do not deny him his birthright. Let him know the sight of great plains and high mountains, of green valleys and wide rivers. For this little boy is an American, and these things belong to him, and he to them. Spare him, that he too may strive for the ideal for which his fathers have labored, so faithfully and for so long. Spare him and give him his fathers' strength—give us all strength, oh God, to do the work that is before us. I ask you this favor, in the name of *your* son, Jesus Christ, who died upon the Cross to set men free. Amen.

GOBEY (*with fervor*). Amen!

SETH AND AGGIE (*murmuring*). Amen!

[ABE *puts his hat on.*]

ABE. It's getting near midnight. I'll go over to the Boger farm and get the doctor. (*He goes out.*)

SETH. Thank you, Abe.

AGGIE. Thank you—thank you, Mr. Lincoln.

GOBEY. God bless you, Mr. Lincoln!

[*The lights fade quickly.*]

SCENE VIII

Again the parlor of the Edwards house. A few days after preceding scene.

MARY *is seated, reading a book.*

After a moment, the MAID *enters.*

MAID. Miss Mary—Mr. Lincoln is here.

MARY. Mr. Lincoln! (*She sits still a moment in an effort to control her emotions, then sharply closes the book and rises.*)

MAID. Will you see him, Miss Mary?

MARY. Yes—in one moment. (*The* MAID *goes off.* MARY *turns, drops her book on the sofa, then moves over toward the right, struggling desperately to compose herself. At the fireplace, she stops and turns to face* ABE *as he enters.*) I'm glad to see you again, Mr. Lincoln.

[*There is considerable constraint between them. He is grimly determined to come to the point with the fewest possible words; she is making a gallant, well-bred attempt to observe the social amenities.*]

ABE. Thank you, Mary. You may well wonder why I have thrust myself on your mercy in this manner.

MARY (*quickly*). I'm sure you're always welcome in Ninian's house.

ABE. After my behavior at our last meeting here, I have not been welcome company for myself.

MARY. You've been through a severe illness. Joshua Speed has kept us informed of it. We've been greatly concerned.

ABE. It is most kind of you.

MARY. But you're restored to health now—you'll return to your work, and no doubt you'll be running for the assembly again—or perhaps you have larger plans?

ABE. I have no plans, Mary. (*He seems to brace himself.*) But I wish to tell you that I am sorry for the things that I said on that unhappy occasion which was to have been our wedding day.

MARY. You need not say anything about that, Mr. Lincoln. Whatever happened then, it was my own fault.

ABE (*disturbed by this unforeseen avowal*). *Your* fault! It was my miserable cowardice——

MARY. I was blinded by my own self-confidence! I—I loved you. (*For a moment her firm voice falters, but she immediately masters that tendency toward weakness.*) And I believed I could make you love me. I believed we might achieve a real communion of spirit, and the fire of my determination would burn in you. You would become a man and a leader of men! But you didn't wish that. (*She turns away.*) I knew you had strength—but I did not know you would use it, all of it, to resist your own magnificent destiny.

ABE (*deliberately*). It is true, Mary—you once had faith in me which I was far from deserving. But the time has come, at last, when I wish to strive to deserve it. (MARY *looks at him, sharply.*) When I behaved in that shameful manner toward you, I did so because I thought that our ways were separate and could never be otherwise. I've come to the conclusion that I was wrong. I believe that our destinies are together, for better or for worse, and I again presume to ask you to be my wife. I fully realize, Mary, that taking me back now would involve humiliation for you.

MARY (*flaring*). I am not afraid of humiliation, if I know it will be wiped out by ultimate triumph! But there can be no triumph unless you yourself are sure. What was it that brought you to this change of heart and mind?

ABE. On the prairie, I met an old friend of mine who was moving West, with his wife and child, in a covered wagon. He asked me to go with him, and I was strongly tempted to do so. (*There is great sadness in his tone—but he seems to collect himself, and turns to her again, speaking with a sort of resignation.*) But then I knew that was not my direction. The way I must go is the way you have always wanted me to go.

MARY. And you will promise that never again will you falter, or turn to run away?

ABE. I promise, Mary—if you will have me—I shall devote myself for the rest of my days to trying—to do what is right—as God gives me power to see what is right.

[*She looks at him, trying to search him. She would like to torment him, for a while, with artful indecision. But she can not do it.*]

MARY. Very well then—I shall be your wife. I shall fight by your side—till death do us part. (*She runs to him and clutches him.*) Abe! I love you—oh, I love you! Whatever becomes of the two of us, I'll die loving you!

[*She is sobbing wildly on his shoulder. Awkwardly, he lifts his hands and takes hold of her in a loose embrace. He is staring down at the carpet, over her shoulder.*]

CURTAIN

ACT III

SCENE IX

A speakers' platform in an Illinois town. It is a summer evening in the year 1858.

A light shines down on the speaker at the front of the platform.

At the back of the platform are three chairs. At the right sits JUDGE STEPHEN A. DOUGLAS—at the left, ABE, who has his plug hat on and makes occasional notes on a piece of paper on his knee. The chair in the middle is for NINIAN, acting as Moderator, who is now at the front of the platform.

NINIAN. We have now heard the leading arguments from the two candidates for the high office of United States Senator from Illinois—Judge Stephen A. Douglas and Mr. Abraham Lincoln. A series of debates between these two eminent citizens of Illinois has focussed upon our state the attention of the entire nation, for here are being discussed the vital issues which now affect the lives of all Americans and the whole future history of our beloved country. According to the usual custom of debate, each of the candidates will now speak in rebuttal. . . . Judge Douglas.

[NINIAN *retires and sits, as* DOUGLAS *comes forward. He is a brief but magnetic man, confident of his powers.*]

DOUGLAS. My fellow citizens: My good friend, Mr. Lincoln, has addressed you with his usual artless sincerity, his pure, homely charm, his perennial native humor. He has even devoted a generously large portion of his address to most amiable remarks upon my fine qualities as a man, if not as a statesman. For which I express deepest gratitude. But—at the same time—I most earnestly beg you not to be deceived by his seeming innocence, his carefully cultivated spirit of good will. For in each of his little homilies lurk concealed weapons. Like Brutus, in Shakespeare's immortal tragedy, Mr. Lincoln is an honorable man. But, also like Brutus, he is an adept at the art of inserting daggers between an opponent's ribs, just when said opponent least expects it. Behold me, gentlemen—I am covered with scars. And yet—somehow or other—I am still upright. Perhaps because I am supported by that sturdy prop called "Truth." Truth—which, crushed to earth by the assassin's blades, doth rise again! Mr. Lincoln makes you laugh with his pungent anecdotes. Then he draws tears from your eyes with his dramatic pictures of the plight of the black slave labor in the South. Always, he guides you skilfully to the threshold of truth, but then, as you are about to cross it, diverts your attention elsewhere. For one thing—he never, by any mischance, makes reference to the condition of labor here in the North! Oh, no! Perhaps New England is so far beyond the bounds of his parochial ken that he does not know that tens of thousands of working men and women in the textile industry are now on STRIKE! And why are they on strike? Because from early morning to dark of night—fourteen hours a day —those "free" citizens must toil at shattering looms in soulless factories 10 and never see the sun; and then, when their fearful day's work at last comes to its exhausted end, these ill-clad and undernourished laborers must trudge home to their foul abodes in tenements that are not fit habitations for rats! What kind of Liberty is this? And if Mr. Lincoln has not heard of conditions in Massachusetts —how has it escaped his attention 20 that here in our own great state no wheels are now turning on that mighty railroad, the Illinois Central? Because its oppressed workers are also on STRIKE! Because they too demand a living wage! So it is throughout the North. Hungry men, marching through the streets in ragged order, promoting riots, because they are not paid enough to keep the flesh 30 upon the bones of their babies! What kind of Liberty is *this?* And what kind of equality? Mr. Lincoln harps constantly on this subject of equality. He repeats over and over the argument used by Lovejoy and other abolitionists: to wit, that the Declaration of Independence having declared all men free and equal, by divine law, thus Negro equality is an inalienable 40 right. Contrary to this absurd assumption stands the verdict of the Supreme Court, as it was clearly stated by Chief Justice Taney in the case of Dred Scott. The Negroes are established by this decision as an inferior race of beings, subjugated by the dominant race, enslaved and, therefore, *property*—like all other property! But Mr. Lincoln is inclined to dispute the constitutional authority of the Supreme Court. He has implied, if he did not say so outright, that the Dred Scott decision was a prejudiced one, which must be over-ruled by the voice of the people. Mr. Lincoln is a lawyer, and I presume, therefore, that he knows that when he seeks to destroy public confidence in the integrity, the inviolability of the Supreme Court, he is preaching *revolution!* He is attempting to stir up odium and rebellion in this country against the constituted authorities; he is stimulating the passions of men to resort to violence and to mobs, instead of to the law. He is setting brother against brother! There can be but one consequence of such inflammatory persuasion—and that is *Civil War!* He asks me to state my opinion of the Dred Scott Decision, and I answer him unequivocally by saying, "I take the decisions of the Supreme Court as the law of the land, and I intend to obey them as such!" Nor will I be swayed from that position by all the rantings of all the fanatics who preach "racial equality," who ask us to vote, and eat, and sleep, and marry with Negroes! And I say further—Let each State mind its own business and leave its neighbors alone. If we will stand by that principle, then Mr. Lincoln will find that this great republic can exist forever divided into free and slave states. We can go on as we have done, increasing in wealth, in population, in power, until we shall be the admiration and the terror of the world! (*He glares at the audience, then turns, mopping his brow, and resumes his seat.*)

NINIAN (*rising*). Mr. Lincoln.

[ABE *glances at his notes, takes his hat off, puts the notes in it, then rises slowly and comes forward. He speaks quietly, reasonably. His words come from an emotion so profound that it needs no advertisement.*]

ABE. Judge Douglas has paid tribute to my skill with the dagger. I thank him for that, but I must also admit that he can do more with that weapon than I 10 can. He can keep ten daggers flashing in the air at one time. Fortunately, he's so good at it that none of the knives ever falls and hurts anybody. The Judge can condone slavery in the South and protest hotly against its extension to the North. He can crowd loyalty to the Union and defense of states' sovereignty into the same breath. Which reminds me—and I 20 hope the Judge will allow me one more homely little anecdote, because I'd like to tell about a woman down in Kentucky. She came out of her cabin one day and found her husband grappling with a ferocious bear. It was a fight to the death, and the bear was winning. The struggling husband called to his wife, "For heaven's sake, *help* me!" The wife asked what could 30 *she* do? Said the husband, "You could at least *say* something encouraging." But the wife didn't want to seem to be taking sides in this combat, so she just hollered, "Go it husband—go it bear!" Now, you heard the Judge make allusion to those who advocate voting and eating and marrying and sleeping with Negroes. Whether he meant me specifically, I do not know. 40 If he did, I can say that just because I do not want a colored woman for a slave, I don't necessarily want her for a wife. I need not have her for either. I can just leave her alone. In some respects, she certainly is not my equal, any more than I am the Judge's equal, in some respects; but in her natural right to eat the bread she earns with her own hands without asking leave of some one else, she is my equal, and the equal of all others. And as to sleeping with Negroes—the Judge may be interested to know that the slave states have produced more than four hundred thousand mulattoes—and I don't think many of them are the children of abolitionists. That word "abolitionists" brings to mind New England, which also has been mentioned. I assure Judge Douglas that I have been there, and I have seen those cheerless brick prisons called factories, and the workers trudging silently home through the darkness. In those factories, cotton that was picked by black slaves is woven into cloth by white people who are separated from slavery by no more than fifty cents a day. As an American, I cannot be proud that such conditions exist. But—as an American—I can ask: would any of those striking workers in the North elect to change places with the slaves in the South? Will they not rather say, "The remedy is in *our* hands!" And, still as an American, I can say—thank God we live under a system by which men have the *right* to strike! I am not preaching rebellion. I don't have to. This country, with its institutions, belongs to the people who inhabit it. Whenever they shall grow weary of the existing government, they can exercise their constitutional right of amending it, or their revolutionary right to dismember or overthrow it. If the founding fathers gave us anything, they gave us that. And I am not preaching disrespect for the Supreme Court. I am only saying that the decisions of mortal men are often influenced by unjudicial bias—and the Supreme Court is composed of mortal men, most of whom, it so happens, come from the privileged class in the South. There is an old saying that judges are just as honest as other men, and not more so; and in case some of you are wondering who said that, it was Thomas Jefferson. (*He has* 10 *half turned to* DOUGLAS.) The purpose of the Dred Scott Decision is to make property, and nothing but property, of the Negro in all states of the Union. It is the old issue of property rights versus human rights—an issue that will continue in this country when these poor tongues of Judge Douglas and myself shall long have been silent. It is the eternal struggle between 20 two principles. The one is the common right of humanity, and the other the divine right of kings. It is the same spirit that says, "You toil and work and earn bread, and I'll eat it." Whether those words come from the mouth of a king who bestrides his people and lives by the fruit of their labor, or from one race of men who seek to enslave another race, it is the 30 same tyrannical principle. As a nation, we began by declaring, "All men are created equal." There was no mention of any exceptions to the rule in the Declaration of Independence. But we now practically read it, "All men are created equal except Negroes." If we accept this doctrine of race or class discrimination, what is to stop us from decreeing in the future 40 that "All men are created equal except Negroes, foreigners, Catholics, Jews, or—just poor people?" That is the conclusion toward which the advocates of slavery are driving us. Many good citizens, North and

South, agree with the Judge that we should accept that conclusion—don't stir up trouble—"Let each State mind its own business." That's the safer course, for the time being. But— I advise you to watch out! When you have enslaved any of your fellow beings, dehumanized him, denied him all claim to the dignity of manhood, placed him among the beasts, among the damned, are you quite sure that the demon you have thus created, will not turn and rend *you?* When you begin qualifying freedom, watch out for the consequences to *you!* And I am not preaching civil war. All I am trying to do—now, and as long as I live—is to state and restate the fundamental virtues of our democracy, which have made us great, and which can make us greater. I believe most seriously that the perpetuation of those virtues is now endangered, not only by the honest proponents of slavery, but even more by those who echo Judge Douglas in shouting, "Leave it alone!" This is the complacent policy of indifference to evil, and that policy I cannot but hate. I hate it because of the monstrous injustice of slavery itself. I hate it because it deprives our republic of its just influence in the world; enables the enemies of free institutions everywhere to taunt us as hypocrites; causes the real friends of freedom to doubt our sincerity; and especially because it forces so many good men among ourselves into an open war with the very fundamentals of civil liberty, denying the good faith of the Declaration of Independence, and insisting that there is no right principle of action but *self-interest.* . . . In his final words tonight, the Judge said that we may be "the terror of the world." I don't think we want to be that. I think we would prefer to be the encouragement of the world, the proof that man is at last worthy to be free. But—we shall provide no such encouragement, unless we can establish our ability as a nation to live and grow. And we shall surely do neither if these states fail to remain *united*. There can be no distinction in the definitions of liberty as between one section and another, one race and another, one class and another. "A house divided against itself cannot stand." This government can not endure permanently, half slave and half free! (*He turns and goes back to his seat.*)

[*The lights fade.*]

SCENE X

Parlor of the Edwards home, now being used by the Lincolns. Afternoon of a day in the early Spring of 1860.

ABE *is sitting on the couch at the right, with his seven-year-old son,* TAD, *on his lap. Sitting beside them is another son,* WILLIE, *aged nine. The eldest son,* ROBERT, *a young Harvard student of seventeen, is sitting by the window, importantly smoking a pipe and listening to the story* ABE *has been telling the children.* JOSHUA SPEED *is sitting at the left.*

ABE. You must remember, Tad, the roads weren't much good then— mostly nothing more than trails—and it was hard to find my way in the darkness. . . .

WILLIE. Were you scared?

ABE. Yes—I was scared.

WILLIE. Of Indians?

ABE. No—there weren't any of them left around here. I was afraid I'd get lost, and the boy would die, and it would be all my fault. But, finally, I found the doctor. He was very tired,

and wanted to go to bed, and he grumbled a lot, but I made him come along with me then and there.

WILLIE. Was the boy dead?

ABE. No, Willie. He wasn't dead. But he was pretty sick. The doctor gave him a lot of medicine.

TAD. Did it taste bad, Pa?

ABE. I presume it did. But it worked. I never saw those nice people again, but I've heard from them every so often. That little boy was your age, Tad, but now he's a grown man with a son almost as big as you are. He lives on a great big farm, in a valley with a river that runs right down from the tops of the snow mountains. . . .

[MARY *comes in.*]

MARY. Robert! You are smoking in my parlor!

ROBERT (*wearily*). Yes, Mother. (*He rises.*)

MARY. I have told you that I shall not tolerate tobacco smoke in my parlor or, indeed, in any part of my house, and I mean to . . .

ABE. Come, come, Mary—you must be respectful to a Harvard man. Take it out to the woodshed, Bob.

ROBERT. Yes, Father.

MARY. And this will not happen again!

ROBERT. No, Mother. (*He goes out.*)

ABE. I was telling the boys a story about some pioneers I knew once.

MARY. It's time for you children to make ready for your supper.

[*The* CHILDREN *promptly get up to go.*]

WILLIE. But what happened after that, Pa?

ABE. Nothing. Everybody lived happily ever after. Now run along.

[WILLIE *and* TAD *run out.*]

JOSH. What time *is* it, Mary?

MARY. It's nearly half past four. (*She is shaking the smoke out of the curtains.*)

JOSH. Half past four, Abe. Those men will be here any minute.

ABE (*rising*). Good Lord!

MARY (*turning sharply to* ABE). What men?

ABE. Some men from the East. One of them's a political leader named Crimmin—and there's a Mr. Sturveson—he's a manufacturer—and . . .

MARY (*impressed*). Henry D. Sturveson?

ABE. That's the one—and also the Rev- 10 erend Dr. Barrick from Boston.

MARY (*sharply*). What are they coming here for?

ABE. I don't precisely know—but I suspect that it's to see if I'm fit to be a candidate for President of the United States.

[MARY *is, for the moment, speechless.*]

I suppose they want to find out if we still live in a log cabin and keep pigs 20 under the bed. . . .

MARY (*in a fury*). And you didn't *tell* me!

ABE. I'm sorry, Mary—the matter just slipped my . . .

MARY. You forgot to tell me that we're having the most important guests who ever crossed the threshold of my house!

ABE. They're not guests. They're only here on business. 30

MARY (*bitterly*). Yes! Rather important business, it seems to me. They want to see us as we *are*—crude, sloppy, vulgar Western barbarians, living in a house that reeks of foul tobacco smoke.

ABE. We can explain about having a son at Harvard.

MARY. If I'd only *known!* If you had only given me a little time to prepare for 40 them. Why didn't you put on your best suit? And those filthy old boots!

ABE. Well, Mary, I clean forgot. . . .

MARY. I declare, Abraham Lincoln, I believe you would have treated me with much more consideration if I

had been your slave, instead of your wife! You have never, for one moment, stopped to think that perhaps I have some interests, some concerns, in the life we lead together. . . .

ABE. I'll try to clean up my boots a little, Mary.

[*He goes out, glad to escape from this painful scene.* MARY *looks after him. Her lip is quivering. She wants to avoid tears.*]

MARY (*seating herself; bitterly*). You've seen it all, Joshua Speed. Every bit of it—courtship, if you could call it that, change of heart, change back again, and marriage, eighteen years of it. And you probably think just as all the others do—that I'm a bitter, nagging woman, and I've tried to kill his spirit, and drag him down to my level. . . .

[JOSH *rises and goes over to her.*]

JOSH (*quietly*). No, Mary. I think no such thing. Remember, I know Abe, too.

MARY. There never could have been another man such as he is! I've read about many that have gone up in the world, and all of them seemed to have to fight to assert themselves every inch of the way, against the opposition of their enemies and the lack of understanding in their own friends. But he's never had any of that. He's never had an enemy, and every one of his friends has always been completely confident in him. Even before I met him, I was told that he had a glorious future, and after I'd known him a day, I was sure of it myself. But he didn't believe it—or, if he did, secretly, he was so afraid of the prospect that he did all in his power to avoid it. He had some poem in his mind, about a life of woe, along a rugged path, that leads to some future doom, and it has been an obsession with him. All these years, I've tried and tried to stir him out of it, but all my efforts have been like so many puny waves, dashing against the Rock of Ages. And now, opportunity, the greatest opportunity, is coming here, to him, right into his own house. And what can I do about it? He *must* take it! He *must* see that this is what he was meant for! But I can't persuade him of it! I'm tired—I'm tired to death! (*The tears now come.*) I thought I could help to shape him, as I knew he should be, and I've succeeded in nothing—but in breaking myself. . . . (*She sobs bitterly.*)

[JOSH *sits down beside her and pats her hand.*]

JOSH (*tenderly*). I know, Mary. But—there's no reason in heaven and earth for you to reproach yourself. Whatever becomes of Abe Lincoln is in the hands of a God who controls the destinies of all of us, including lunatics, and saints.

[ABE *comes back.*]

ABE (*looking down at his boots*). I think they look all right now, Mary. (*He looks at* MARY, *who is now trying hard to control her emotion.*)

MARY. You can receive the gentlemen in here. I'll try to prepare some refreshment for them in the dining-room.

[*She goes out.* ABE *looks after her, miserably. There are a few moments of silence. At length,* ABE *speaks, in an off-hand manner.*]

ABE. I presume these men *are* pretty influential.

JOSH. They'll have quite a say in the delegations of three states that may swing the nomination away from Seward.

ABE. Suppose, by some miracle, or fluke, they did nominate me; do you think I'd stand a chance of winning the election?

JOSH. An excellent chance, in my opinion. There'll be four candidates in the field, bumping each other, and opening up the track for a dark horse.

ABE. But the dark horse might run in the wrong direction.

JOSH. Yes—you can always do that, Abe. I know *I* wouldn't care to bet two cents on you.

ABE (*grinning*). It seems funny to be comparing it to a horserace, with an old, spavined hack like me. But I've had some mighty energetic jockeys—Mentor Graham, Bowling Green, Bill Herndon, you, and Mary—most of all, Mary.

JOSH (*looking at* ABE). They don't count now, Abe. You threw 'em all, long ago. When you finally found yourself running against poor little Douglas, you got the bit between your teeth and went like greased lightning. You'd do the same thing to him again, if you could only decide to get started, which you probably won't . . .

[*The doorbell jangles.* JOSH *gets up.*]

ABE. I expect that's them now.

JOSH. I'll go see if I can help Mary. (*He starts for the door but turns and looks at* ABE, *and speaks quietly.*) I'd just like to remind you, Abe—there are pretty nearly thirty million people in this country; most of 'em are common people, like you. They're in serious trouble, and they need somebody who understands 'em, as you do. So—when these gentlemen come in—try to be a *little* bit polite to them. (ABE *grins.* JOSH *looks off.*) However—you won't listen to any advice from me.

[JOSH *goes. The door is opened by a* MAID *and* STURVESON, BARRICK, *and* CRIMMIN *come in.* STURVESON *is elderly, wealthy and bland.* BARRICK *is a soft Episcopalian dignitary.* CRIMMIN *is a shrewd, humorous fixer.*]

ABE. Come right in, gentlemen. Glad to see you again, Mr. Crimmin. (*They shake hands.*)

CRIMMIN. How de do, Mr. Lincoln. This is Dr. Barrick of Boston, and Mr. Sturveson, of Philadelphia.

DR. BARRICK. Mr. Lincoln.

STURVESON. I'm honored, Mr. Lincoln.

LINCOLN. Thank you, sir. Pray sit down, gentlemen.

STURVESON. Thank you. (*They sit.*)

CRIMMIN. Will Mrs. Lincoln seriously object if I light a seegar?

LINCOLN. Go right ahead! I regret that Mrs. Lincoln is not here to receive you, but she will join us presently. (*He sits down.*)

BARRICK (*with great benignity*). I am particularly anxious to meet Mrs. Lincoln, for I believe, with Mr. Longfellow, that "as unto the bow the cord is, so unto the man is woman."

STURVESON (*very graciously*). And we are here dealing with a bow that is stout indeed. (ABE *bows slightly in acknowledgment of the compliment.*) And one with a reputation for shooting straight. So you'll forgive us, Mr. Lincoln, for coming directly to the point.

ABE. Yes, sir. I understand that you wish to inspect the prairie politician in his native lair, and here I am.

STURVESON. It is no secret that we are desperately in need of a candidate— one who is sound, conservative, safe— and clever enough to skate over the thin ice of the forthcoming campaign. Your friends—and there's an increasingly large number of them throughout the country—believe that you are the man.

ABE. Well, Mr. Sturveson, I can tell you that when first I was considered for political office—that was in New Salem, twenty-five years ago—I assured my sponsors of my conserva-

tism. I have subsequently proved it, by never progressing anywhere.

BARRICK (*smiling*). Then you agree that you are the man we want?

ABE. I'm afraid I can't go quite that far in self-esteem, Dr. Barrick, especially when you have available a statesman and gentleman as eminent as Mr. Seward who, I believe, is both ready and willing.

STURVESON. That's as may be. But please understand that this is not an inquisition. We merely wish to know you better, to gain a clearer idea of your theories on economics, religion and national affairs, in general. To begin with—in one of your memorable debates with Senator Douglas, your opponent indulged in some of his usual demagoguery about industrial conditions in the North, and you replied shrewdly that whereas the slaves in the South . . .

ABE. Yes, I remember the occasion. I replied that I was thankful that laborers in free states have the right to strike. But that wasn't shrewdness, Mr. Sturveson. It was just the truth.

STURVESON. It has gained for you substantial support from the laboring classes, which is all to the good. But it has also caused a certain amount of alarm among business men, like myself.

ABE. I cannot enlarge on the subject. It seems obvious to me that this nation was founded on the supposition that men have the right to protest, violently if need be, against authority that is unjust or oppressive. (*He turns to* BARRICK.) The Boston Tea Party was a kind of strike. So was the Revolution itself. (*Again to* STURVESON.) So was Nicholas Biddle's attempt to organize the banks against the Jackson administration.

STURVESON. Which is all perfectly true—but—the days of anarchy are over. We face an unprecedented era of industrial expansion—mass production of every conceivable kind of goods—railroads and telegraph lines across the continent—all promoted and developed by private enterprise. In this great work, we must have a free hand, and a firm one, Mr. Lincoln. 10 To put it bluntly, would you, if elected, place the interests of labor above those of capital?

ABE. I cannot answer that, bluntly, or any other way; because I cannot tell what I should do, if elected.

STURVESON. But you must have inclinations toward one side or the other. . . .

ABE. I think you know, Mr. Sturveson, 20 that I am opposed to slavery.

BARRICK. And we of New England applaud your sentiments! We deplore the inhumanity of our Southern friends in . . .

ABE (*to* BARRICK). There are more forms of slavery than that which is inflicted upon the Negroes in the South. I am opposed to all of them. (*He turns again to* STURVESON.) I believe in our demo- 30 cratic system—the just and generous system which opens the way to all—gives hope to all, and consequent energy and progress and improvement of condition to all, including employer and employee alike.

BARRICK. We support your purpose, Mr. Lincoln, in steadfastly proclaiming the rights of men to resist unjust authority. But I am most anxious to 40 know whether you admit One Authority to whom devotion is unquestioned?

ABE. I presume you refer to the Almighty?

BARRICK. I do.

ABE. I think there has never been any doubt of my submission to His will.

BARRICK. I'm afraid there is a great deal of doubt as to your devotion to His church.

ABE. I realize that, Doctor. They say I'm an atheist, because I've always refused to become a church member.

BARRICK. What have been the grounds of your refusal?

ABE. I have found no churches suitable for my own form of worship. I could not give assent without mental reservations to the long, complicated statements of Christian doctrine which characterize their Articles of Belief and Confessions of Faith. But I can promise you, Dr. Barrick—I shall gladly join any church at any time if its sole qualification for membership is obedience to the Saviour's statement of Law and Gospel: "Thou shalt love the Lord thy God with all thy heart and with all thy soul and with all thy mind, and thou shalt love thy neighbor as thyself." . . . But—I beg you gentlemen to excuse me for a moment. I believe Mrs. Lincoln is preparing a slight collation, and I must see if I can help with it. . . .

CRIMMIN. Certainly, Mr. Lincoln. (ABE *goes, closing the door behind him.* CRIMMIN *looks at the door, then turns to the others.*) Well?

BARRICK. The man is unquestionably an infidel. An idealist—in his curious, primitive way—but an infidel!

STURVESON. And a radical!

CRIMMIN. A radical? Forgive me, gentlemen, if I enjoy a quiet laugh at that.

STURVESON. Go ahead and enjoy yourself, Crimmin—but I did not like the way he evaded my direct question. I tell you, he's as unscrupulous a demagogue as Douglas. He's a rabble rouser!

CRIMMIN. Of course he is! As a dealer in humbug, he puts Barnum himself to shame.

STURVESON. Quite possibly—but he is not *safe!*

CRIMMIN. Not safe, eh? And what do you mean by that?

STURVESON. Just what I say. A man who devotes himself so whole-heartedly to currying favor with the mob develops 10 the mob mentality. He becomes a preacher of discontent, of mass unrest. . . .

CRIMMIN. And what about Seward? If we put him up, he'll start right in demanding liberation of the slaves—and then there *will* be discontent and unrest! I ask you to believe me when I tell you that this Lincoln *is* safe—in economics and theology and every- 20 thing else. After all—what is the essential qualification that we demand of the candidate of our party? It is simply this: that he be able to get himself elected! And there is the man who can do that. (*He points off-stage.*)

STURVESON (*smiling*). I should like to believe you!

BARRICK. So say we all of us!

CRIMMIN. Then just keep faith in the 30 eternal stupidity of the voters, which is what *he* will appeal to. In that uncouth rail splitter you may observe one of the smoothest, slickest politicians that ever hoodwinked a yokel mob! You complain that he evaded your questions. Of course he did, and did it perfectly. Ask him about the labor problem, and he replies, "I believe in democracy." Ask his views on 40 religion, and he says, "Love thy neighbor as thyself." Now—you know you couldn't argue with that, either of you. I tell you, gentlemen, he's a vote-getter if I ever saw one. His very name is right—Abraham Lincoln!

Honest Old Abe! He'll play the game with us now, and he'll go right on playing it when we get him into the White House. He'll do just what we tell him. . . .

DR. BARRICK (*cautioning him*). Careful, Mr. Crimmin. . . .

[ABE *returns.*]

ABE. If you gentlemen will step into the dining-room, Mrs. Lincoln would be pleased to serve you with a cup of tea.

BARRICK. Thank you.

STURVESON. This is most gracious. (*He and BARRICK move off toward the door.*)

ABE. Or perhaps something stronger for those who prefer it.

[STURVESON *and* BARRICK *go.* CRIMMIN *is looking for a place to throw his cigar.*]

ABE (*heartily*). Bring your seegar with you, Mr. Crimmin!

CRIMMIN. Thank you—thank you!

[*He smiles at* ABE, *gives him a slap on the arm, and goes out,* ABE *following. The lights fade.*]

SCENE XI

Lincoln campaign headquarters in the Illinois State House. The evening of Election Day, November 6, 1860.

It is a large room with a tall window opening out on to a wide balcony. There are doors upper right and upper left. At the left is a table littered with newspapers and clippings. There are many chairs about, and a liberal supply of spittoons.

At the back is a huge chart of the thirty-three states, with their electoral votes, and a space opposite each side for the posting of bulletins. A short ladder gives access to Alabama and Arkansas at the top of the list.

On the wall at the left is an American flag. At the right is a map of the United States, on which each state is marked with a red, white or blue flag.

ABE *is sitting at the table, with his back to*

the audience, reading newspaper clippings.
He wears his hat and has spectacles on.
MRS. LINCOLN *is sitting at the right of the*
table, her eyes darting nervously from ABE,
to the chart, to the map. She wears her bon-
net, tippet and muff.

ROBERT LINCOLN *is standing near her,*
studying the map. NINIAN EDWARDS *is sit-*
ting at the left of the table and JOSH SPEED *is*
standing near the chart. They are both smok- 10
ing cigars and watching the chart.

The door at the left is open, and through it
the clatter of telegraph instruments can be
heard. The window is partly open, and we
can hear band music from the square below,
and frequent cheers from the assembled mob,
who are watching the election returns flashed
from a magic lantern on the State House bal-
cony.

Every now and then, a telegraph operator 20
named JED *comes in from the left and tacks a*
new bulletin up on the chart. Another man
named PHIL *is out on the balcony taking bul-*
letins from JED.

ROBERT. What do those little flags mean,
stuck into the map?
JOSH. Red means the state is sure for us.
White means doubtful. Blue means
hopeless.
[ABE *tosses the clipping he has been reading*
on the table and picks up another. JED
comes in and goes up to pin bulletins op-
posite Illinois, Maryland and New York.]
NINIAN (*rising to look*). Lincoln and Douglas neck and neck in Illinois.
[JOSH *and* ROBERT *crowd around the chart.*]
JOSH. Maryland is going all for Breckenridge and Bell. Abe—you're nowhere
in Maryland.   40
MARY (*with intense anxiety*). What of New
York?
JED (*crossing to the window*). Say, Phil—
when you're not getting bulletins,
keep that window closed. We can't
hear ourselves think.

PHIL. All right. Only have to open 'er up
again. (*He closes the window.*)
MARY. What does it say about New
York?
[JED *goes.*]
NINIAN. Douglas a hundred and seven-
teen thousand—Lincoln a hundred
and six thousand.
MARY (*desperately, to* ABE). He's winning
from you in New York, Abe!
JOSH. Not yet, Mary. These returns so
far are mostly from the city where
Douglas is bound to run the strongest.
ABE (*interested in a clipping*). I see the
New York *Herald* says I've got the
soul of a Uriah Heep encased in the
body of a baboon. (*He puts the clipping*
aside and starts to read another.)
NINIAN (*who has resumed his seat*). You'd
better change that flag on Rhode Island from red to white, Bob. It looks
doubtful to me.
[ROBERT, *glad of something to do, changes*
the flag as directed.]
MARY. What does it look like in Pennsylvania, Ninian?
NINIAN. There's nothing to worry about
there, Mary. It's safe for Abe. In fact,
you needn't worry at all.
MARY (*very tense*). Yes. You've been saying that over and over again all
evening. There's no need to worry.
But how can we help worrying when
every new bulletin shows Douglas
ahead.
JOSH. But every one of them shows Abe
gaining.
NINIAN (*mollifying*). Just give them time
to count all the votes in New York
and then you'll be on your way to the
White House.
MARY. Oh, why don't they hurry with
it? Why don't those returns come in?
ABE (*preoccupied*). They'll come in—soon
enough.
[BILLY HERNDON *comes in from the right.*

He has been doing a lot of drinking but has hold of himself.]

BILLY. That mob down there is sickening! They cheer every bulletin that's flashed on the wall, whether the news is good or bad. And they cheer every picture of every candidate, including George Washington, with the same, fine, ignorant enthusiasm.

JOSH. That's logical. They can't tell 'em apart.

BILLY (*to* ABE). There are a whole lot of reporters down there. They want to know what will be your first official action after you're elected.

NINIAN. What do you want us to tell 'em, Abe?

ABE (*still reading*). Tell 'em I'm thinking of growing a beard.

JOSH. A beard?

NINIAN (*amused*). Whatever put that idea into your mind?

ABE (*picking up another clipping*). I had a letter the other day from some little girl. She said I ought to have whiskers, to give me more dignity. And I'll need it—if elected.

[JED *arrives with new bulletins.* BILLY, NINIAN, JOSH *and* ROBERT *huddle around* JED, *watching him post the bulletins.*]

MARY. What do they say now?

[JED *goes to the window and gives some bulletins to* PHIL.]

MARY. Is there anything new from New York?

NINIAN. Connecticut—Abe far in the lead. That's eleven safe electoral votes anyway. Missouri—Douglas thirty-five thousand—Bell thirty-three—Breckenridge sixteen—Lincoln, eight. . . .

[*Cheers from the crowd outside until* PHIL *closes the window.* JED *returns to the office at the left.*]

MARY. What are they cheering for?

BILLY. They don't know!

ABE (*with another clipping*). The Chicago *Times* says, "Lincoln breaks down! Lincoln's heart fails him! His tongue fails him! His legs fail him! He fails all over! The people refuse to support him! They laugh at him! Douglas is champion of the people! Douglas skins the living dog!" (*He tosses the clipping aside.* MARY *stands up.*)

MARY (*her voice is trembling*). I can't stand it any longer!

ABE. Yes, my dear—I think you'd better go home. I'll be back before long.

MARY (*hysterical*). I won't go home! You only want to be rid of me. That's what you've wanted ever since the day we were married—and before that. Anything to get me out of your sight, because you hate me! (*Turning to* JOSH, NINIAN *and* BILLY.) And it's the same with all of you—all of his friends—you hate me—you wish I'd never come into his life.

JOSH. No, Mary.

[ABE *has stood up, quickly, at the first storm signal. He himself is in a fearful state of nervous tension—in no mood to treat* MARY *with patient indulgence. He looks sharply at* NINIAN *and at the others.*]

ABE. Will you please step out for a moment?

NINIAN. Certainly, Abe.

[*He and the others go into the telegraph office.* JOSH *gestures to* ROBERT *to go with them.* ROBERT *casts a black look at his mother and goes.* . . . ABE *turns on* MARY *with strange savagery.*]

ABE. Damn you! Damn you for taking every opportunity you can to make a public fool of me—and yourself! It's bad enough, God knows, when you act like that in the privacy of our own home. But here—in front of people! You're not to do that again. Do you hear me? You're never to do that again!

[MARY *is so aghast at this outburst that her*

hysterical temper vanishes, giving way to blank terror.]

MARY (*in a faint, strained voice*). Abe! You cursed at me. Do you realize what you did? You cursed at me.

[ABE *has the impulse to curse at her again, but with considerable effort, he controls it.*]

ABE (*in a strained voice*). I lost my temper, Mary. And I'm sorry for it. But I still think you should go home rather than 10 endure the strain of this—this Death Watch.

[*She stares at him, uncomprehendingly, then turns and goes to the door.*]

MARY (*at the door*). This is the night I dreamed about, when I was a child, when I was an excited young girl, and all the gay young gentlemen of Springfield were courting me, and I fell in love with the least likely of 20 them. This is the night when I'm waiting to hear that my husband has become President of the United States. And even if he does—it's ruined, for me. It's too late. . . .

[*She opens the door and goes out.* ABE *looks after her, anguished, then turns quickly, crosses to the door at the left and opens it.*]

ABE (*calling off*). Bob! (ROBERT *comes in.*) Go with your Mother.

ROBERT. Do I have to?

ABE. Yes! Hurry! Keep right with her till I get home.

[ROBERT *has gone.* ABE *turns to the window.* PHIL *opens it.*]

PHIL. Do you think you're going to make it, Mr. Lincoln?

ABE. Oh—there's nothing to worry about.

CROWD OUTSIDE (*singing*).

Old Abe Lincoln came out of the wil- 40 derness

Out of the wilderness

Out of the wilderness

Old Abe Lincoln came out of the wilderness

Down in Illinois!

[NINIAN, JOSH, BILLY, *and* JED *come in, the latter to post new bulletins. After* JED *has communicated these,* PHIL *again closes the window.* JED *goes.*]

NINIAN. It looks like seventy-four electoral votes sure for you. Twenty-seven more probable. New York's will give you the election.

[ABE *walks around the room.* JOSH *has been looking at* ABE.]

JOSH. Abe, could I get you a cup of coffee?

ABE. No, thanks, Josh.

NINIAN. Getting nervous, Abe?

ABE. No. I'm just thinking what a blow it would be to Mrs. Lincoln if I should lose.

NINIAN. And what about me? I have ten thousand dollars bet on you.

BILLY (*scornfully*). I'm afraid that the loss to the nation would be somewhat more serious than that.

JOSH. How would you feel, Abe?

ABE (*sitting on the chair near the window*). I guess I'd feel the greatest sense of relief of my life.

[JED *comes in with a news despatch.*]

JED. Here's a news despatch. (*He hands it over and goes.*)

NINIAN (*reads*). "Shortly after nine o'clock this evening, Mr. August Belmont stated that Stephen A. Douglas has piled up a majority of fifty thousand votes in New York City and carried the state."

BILLY. Mr. Belmont be damned!

[CRIMMIN *comes in, smoking a cigar, looking contented.*]

CRIMMIN. Good evening, Mr. Lincoln. Good evening, gentlemen—and how are you all feeling *now*?

[*They all greet him.*]

NINIAN. Look at this, Crimmin. (*He hands the despatch to* CRIMMIN.)

CRIMMIN (*smiles*). Well—Belmont is going to fight to the last ditch, which is just what he's lying in now. I've been in Chicago and the outlook there is cloudless. In fact, Mr. Lincoln, I came down tonight to protect you from the office-seekers. They're lining up downstairs already. On the way in I counted four Ministers to Great Britain and eleven Secretaries of State.

[JED *has come in with more bulletins to put on the chart and then goes to the window to give* PHIL *the bulletins.*]

BILLY (*at the chart*). There's a bulletin from New York! Douglas a hundred and eighty-three thousand—Lincoln a hundred and eighty-*one* thousand!
                    [JED *goes.*]

JOSH. Look out, Abe. You're catching up!

CRIMMIN. The next bulletin from New York will show you winning. Mark my words, Mr. Lincoln, this election is all wrapped up tightly in a neat bundle, ready for delivery on your doorstep tonight. We've fought the good fight, and we've won!

ABE (*pacing up and down the room*). Yes— we've fought the good fight—in the dirtiest campaign in the history of corrupt politics. And if I have won, then I must cheerfully pay my political debts. All those who helped to nominate and elect me must be paid off. I have been gambled all around, bought and sold a hundred times. And now I must fill all the dishonest pledges made in my name.

NINIAN. We realize all that, Abe—but the fact remains that you're winning. Why, you're even beating the coalition in Rhode Island!

ABE. I've got to step out for a moment. (*He goes out at the right.*)

NINIAN (*cheerfully*). Poor Abe.

CRIMMIN. You gentlemen have all been close friends of our Candidate for a long time so perhaps you could answer a question that's been puzzling me considerably. Can I possibly be correct in supposing that he doesn't want to win?

JOSH. The answer is—yes.

CRIMMIN (*looking toward the right*). Well— I can only say that, for me, this is all a refreshingly new experience.

BILLY (*belligerently*). Would *you* want to become President of the United States at this time? Haven't you been reading the newspapers lately?

CRIMMIN. Why, yes—I try to follow the events of the day.

BILLY (*in a rage*). Don't you realize that they've raised ten thousand volunteers in South Carolina? They're arming them! The Governor has issued a proclamation saying that if Mr. Lincoln is elected, the State will secede tomorrow, and every other state south of the Dixon line will go with it. Can you see what that means? War! Civil War! And *he'll* have the whole terrible responsibility for it—a man who has never wanted anything in his life but to be let alone, in peace!

NINIAN. Calm down, Billy. Go get yourself another drink.
                    [JED *rushes in.*]

JED. Mr. Edwards, here it is! (*He hands a news despatch to* NINIAN, *then rushes to the window to attract* PHIL'S *attention and communicate the big news.*)

NINIAN (*reads*). "At 10:30 tonight the New York *Herald* conceded that Mr. Lincoln has carried the state by a majority of at least twenty-five thousand and has won the election!" (*He tosses the despatch in the air.*) He's won! He's won! Hurrah!

[*All on the stage shout, cheer, embrace and slap each other.*]

BILLY. God be praised! God be praised!

CRIMMIN. I knew it! I never had a doubt of it!

[JED *is on the balcony, shouting through a megaphone.*]

JED. Lincoln is elected! Honest Old Abe is our next President!

[*A terrific cheer ascends from the crowd below.* ABE *returns. They rush at him.* BILLY *shakes hands with him, too deeply moved to speak.*] 10

NINIAN. You've carried New York, Abe! You've won! Congratulations!

CRIMMIN. My congratulations, Mr. President. This is a mighty achievement for all of us!

[JED *comes in and goes to* ABE.]

JED. My very best, Mr. Lincoln!

ABE (*solemnly*). Thank you—thank you all very much. (*He comes to the left.* JOSH *is the last to shake his hand.*)

JOSH. I congratulate you, Abe.

ABE. Thanks, Josh.

NINIAN. Listen to them, Abe. Listen to that crazy, howling mob down there.

CRIMMIN. It's all for you, Mr. Lincoln.

NINIAN. Abe, get out there and let 'em see you!

ABE. No. I don't want to go out there. I—I guess I'll be going on home, to tell Mary. (*He starts toward the door.*)

[*A short, stocky officer named* KAVANAGH 30 *comes in from the right. He is followed by two soldiers.*]

CRIMMIN. This is Captain Kavanagh, Mr. *President.*

KAVANAGH (*salutes*). I've been detailed to accompany you, Mr. Lincoln, in the event of your election.

ABE. I'm grateful, Captain. But I don't need you. 40

KAVANAGH. I'm afraid you've got to have us, Mr. Lincoln. I don't like to be alarming, but I guess you know as well as I do what threats have been made.

ABE (*wearily*). I see . . . Well—Good

night, Josh—Ninian—Mr. Crimmin—Billy. Thank you for your good wishes. (*He starts for the door. The others bid him good night, quietly.*)

KAVANAGH. One moment, Sir. With your permission, I'll go first.

[*He goes out,* ABE *after him, the two other soldiers follow. The light fades.*]

SCENE XII

The yards of the railroad station at Springfield. The date is February 11, 1861. At the right, at an angle toward the audience, is the back of a railroad car. From behind this, off to the upper left, runs a ramp. Flags and bunting are draped above. In a row downstage are soldiers, with rifles and bayonets fixed, and packs on their backs, standing at ease. Off to the left is a large 20 *crowd, whose excited murmuring can be heard.*

KAVANAGH *is in the foreground. A* BRAKEMAN *with a lantern is inspecting the wheels of the car, at the left. A* WORKMAN *is at the right, polishing the rails of the car.* KAVANAGH *is pacing up and down, chewing a dead cigar. He looks at his watch. A swaggering* MAJOR *of militia comes down the ramp from the left.*

MAJOR. I want you men to form up 30 against this ramp. (*To* KAVANAGH; *with a trace of scorn.*) You seem nervous, Mr. Kavanagh.

KAVANAGH. Well—I am nervous. For three months I've been guarding the life of a man who doesn't give a damn what happens to him. I heard today that they're betting two to one in Richmond that he won't be alive to take the oath of office on March the 4th.

MAJOR. I'd like to take some of that money. The State Militia is competent to protect the person of our Commander-in-Chief.

KAVANAGH. I hope the United States

Army is competent to help. But those Southerners are mighty good shots. And I strongly suggest that your men be commanded to keep watch through every window of every car, especially whenever the train stops—at a town, or a tank, or anywhere. And if any alarm is sounded, at any point along the line . . .

MAJOR (*a trifle haughty*). There's no need to command my men to show courage in an emergency.

KAVANAGH. No slur was intended, Major—but we must be prepared in advance for everything.

[*A brass band off to the left strikes up the campaign song, "Old Abe Lincoln came out of the wilderness." The crowd starts to sing it, more and more voices taking it up. A* CONDUCTOR *comes out of the car and looks at his watch. There is a commotion at the left as* NINIAN *and* ELIZABETH EDWARDS, *and* JOSH, BILLY *and* CRIMMIN *come in and are stopped by the soldiers. The* MAJOR *goes forward, bristling with importance.*]

MAJOR. Stand back, there! Keep the crowd back there, you men!

NINIAN. I'm Mr. Lincoln's brother-in-law.

MAJOR. What's your name?

KAVANAGH. I know him, Major. That's Mr. and Mrs. Edwards, and Mr. Speed and Mr. Herndon with them. I know them all. You can let them through.

MAJOR. Very well. You can pass.

[*They come down to the right. The* MAJOR *goes off at the left.*]

CRIMMIN. How is the President feeling today? Happy?

NINIAN. Just as gloomy as ever.

BILLY (*emotionally*). He came down to the office, and when I asked him what I should do about the sign, "Lincoln and Herndon," he said,

"Let it hang there. Let our clients understand that this election makes no difference to the firm. If I live, I'll be back some time, and then we'll go right on practising just as if nothing had happened."

ELIZABETH. He's always saying that— "If I live" . . .

[*A tremendous cheer starts and swells offstage at the left. The* MAJOR *comes on, briskly.*]

MAJOR (*to* KAVANAGH). The President has arrived! (*To his men.*) Attention! (*The* MAJOR *strides down the platform and takes his position by the car, looking off to the left.*)

KAVANAGH (*to* NINIAN *and the others*). Would you mind stepping back there? We want to keep this space clear for the President's party.

[*They move upstage, at the right. The cheering is now very loud.*]

MAJOR. Present—Arms!

[*The soldiers come to the Present. The* MAJOR *salutes. Preceded by soldiers who are looking sharply to the right and left,* ABE *comes in from the left, along the platform. He will be fifty-two years old tomorrow. He wears a beard. Over his shoulders is his plaid shawl. In his right hand, he carries his carpet-bag; his left hand is leading* TAD. *Behind him are* MARY, ROBERT *and* WILLIE, *and the* MAID. *All, except* MARY, *are also carrying bags. She carries a bunch of flowers. When they come to the car,* ABE *hands his bag up to the* CONDUCTOR, *then lifts* TAD *up.* MARY, ROBERT, WILLIE *and the* MAID *get on board, while* ABE *steps over to talk to* NINIAN *and the others. During this, there is considerable commotion at the left, as the crowd tries to surge forward.*]

MAJOR (*rushing forward*). Keep 'em back! Keep 'em back, men!

[*The* SOLDIERS *have broken their file on the platform and are in line, facing the crowd.* KAVANAGH *and his men are close to* ABE.

*Each of them has his hand on his revolver,
and is keeping a sharp lookout.*]

KAVANAGH. Better get on board,
Mr. President.

[ABE *climbs up on to the car's back platform.
There is a great increase in the cheering
when the crowd sees him. They shout:
"Speech! Speech! Give us a speech, Abe!
Speech, Mr. President! Hurray for Old
Abe!" Etc. . . . ABE turns to the
crowd, takes his hat off and waves it with a
half-hearted gesture. The cheering dies
down.*]

NINIAN. They want you to say something, Abe.

[*For a moment,* ABE *stands still, looking off
to the left.*]

ABE. My dear friends—I have to say
good-bye to you. I am going now to
Washington, with my new whiskers—of which I hope you ap-
prove.

[*The crowd roars with laughter at that.
More shouts of "Good Old Abe!" In its
exuberant enthusiasm, the crowd again
surges forward, at and around the* SOL-
DIERS, *who shout, "Get back, there! Stand
back, you!"*]

ABE (*to the* MAJOR). It's all right—let
them come on. They're all old friends
of mine.

[*The* MAJOR *allows his men to retreat so that
they form a ring about the back of the car.*
KAVANAGH *and his men are on the car's
steps, watching. The crowd—an assortment of townspeople, including some
Negroes—fills the stage.*]

ABE. No one, not in my situation, can
appreciate my feelings of sadness at
this parting. To this place, and the
kindness of you people, I owe everything. I have lived here a quarter of a
century, and passed from a young to
an old man. Here my children have
been born and one is buried. I now
leave, not knowing when or whether

ever I may return. I am called upon
to assume the Presidency at a time
when eleven of our sovereign states
have announced their intention to
secede from the Union, when threats
of war increase in fierceness from day
to day. It is a grave duty which I now
face. In preparing for it, I have tried
to enquire: what great principle or
ideal is it that has kept this Union so
long together? And I believe that it
was not the mere matter of separation of the colonies from the mother-
land, but that sentiment in the Declaration of Independence which gave
liberty to the people of this country
and hope to all the world. This sentiment was the fulfillment of an ancient dream, which men have held
through all time, that they might one
day shake off their chains and find
freedom in the brotherhood of life.
We gained democracy, and now there
is the question whether it is fit to survive. Perhaps we have come to the
dreadful day of awakening, and the
dream is ended. If so, I am afraid it
must be ended forever. I cannot believe that ever again will men have
the opportunity we have had. Perhaps we should admit that, and con-
cede that our ideals of liberty and
equality are decadent and doomed. I
have heard of an eastern monarch
who once charged his wise men to
invent him a sentence which would
be true and appropriate in all times
and situations. They presented him
the words, "And this too shall pass
away." That is a comforting thought
in time of affliction—"And this too
shall pass away." And yet—(*Suddenly he speaks with quiet but urgent
authority.*)—let us believe that it is not
true! Let us live to prove that we can
cultivate the natural world that is

about us, and the intellectual and moral world that is within us, so that we may secure an individual, social and political prosperity, whose course shall be forward, and which, while the earth endures, shall not pass away. . . . I commend you to the care of the Almighty, as I hope that in your prayers you will remember me. . . . Good-bye, my friends and 10 neighbors.

[*He leans over the railing of the car platform to say good-bye to* NINIAN, ELIZABETH, JOSH, BILLY *and* CRIMMIN, *shaking each by the hand. The band off-stage strikes up "John Brown's Body." The cheering swells. The* CONDUCTOR *looks at his watch and speaks to the* MAJOR, *who gets on board the train. The crowd on stage is shouting "Good-bye, Abe," "Good-bye, 20 Mr. Lincoln," "Good luck, Abe," "We trust you, Mr. Lincoln."*

[*As the band swings into the refrain, "Glory, Glory, Hallelujah," the crowd starts to* sing, *the number of voices increasing with each word.*

[KAVANAGH *tries to speak to* ABE *but can't be heard. He touches* ABE'S *arm, and* ABE *turns on him, quickly.*]

KAVANAGH. Time to pull out, Mr. President. Better get inside the car.

[*These words cannot be heard by the audience in the general uproar of singing.* NINIAN, ELIZABETH, JOSH *and* BILLY *are up on the station platform. The* SOLDIERS *are starting to climb up on to the train.* ABE *gives one last wistful wave of his hat to the crowd, then turns and goes into the car, followed by* KAVANAGH, *the* MAJOR *and the* SOLDIERS. *The band reaches the last line of the song.*]

ALL (*singing*). His soul goes marching on.

[*The* BRAKEMAN, *downstage, is waving his lantern. The* CONDUCTOR *swings aboard. The crowd is cheering, waving hats and handkerchiefs. The shrill screech of the engine whistle sounds from the right.*]

CURTAIN

WILLIAM SAROYAN

THE O. HENRY MEMORIAL AWARD for the best short story of 1934 was given to William Saroyan, a lively and vocal young Armenian-American from California, for his story entitled "The Daring Young Man on the Flying Trapeze." The award committee spoke of him as "the most widely discussed discovery" of 1934. The year was one of the darker periods of the great depression. Jobless men lengthened the bread lines, and young men ready for labor could find no place. Saroyan captured newspaper headlines with this artistic, restrained, and beautifully realized impressionistic story of one of the unemployed young men who starved to death in a San Francisco rooming house. On the table beside him was a bright penny polished to underscore "In God We Trust, Liberty, 1923," and some sheets of YMCA stationery on which he had penned an "Application for Permission to Live." Saroyan's use of the stream of consciousness and the symbolism of the title made the story something of a tour de force.

At the end of the year 1934 Random House published a collection of twenty-six Saroyan pieces under the title *The Daring Young Man on the Flying Trapeze*. It was a best seller. The "greatly unpublished writer" from the Fresno vineyards became a figure in American letters. The "stories" were unique. Saroyan had poured them out in a stream. They were formless, poignant collections of sentences held together by the warmth of their perception and by the personality of Saroyan. They were deeply personal. They were written with such abandon at such breathless speed that if the author ran out of something to say he went right on tapping at his typewriter to say that he had nothing to say except that he was sitting there in his room tapping at his typewriter and this is what he had written.

He flooded the magazines with his stories, more than two hundred, and collected them into several volumes with singular titles—*Inhale and Exhale*, *Three Times Three*, *The Trouble with Tigers*. They contained a detailed autobiography, for they were chiefly about William Saroyan, how he grew and what the personal experience and the spectacle were like to one Whitmanesque young man in these times. He was born in Fresno, California, of Armenian immigrant parents, in 1908. He learned more from selling newspapers, sneaking into picture shows, reading books and plays that fell into his hands than he learned formally at school. In the classroom he took pride in being a problem child. He is still brashly scornful of all formal education, especially any school or university course on the art of playwriting.

A part of his virtue is a naive and poetic immediacy, a passion for bringing together as closely and intimately as possible the experience of living and the art which captures it in words. He has been unusually successful in this in his writing about childhood and adolescence, with their unaccountable melancholy and loneliness and idle, bewildering tears. He has talked much about this theme of being alive. In his piece called "A Cold Day" he said it in its tersest form: "The man you write of need not perform some heroic or monstrous deed in order to make your prose great. Let him do what he has always done, day in and day out, continuing to live. Let him walk and talk and think and sleep and dream and awaken and walk again and talk again and move and be alive. It is enough. There is nothing else to write about. . . . Your own consciousness is the only form you need."

These words might have been penned as a rationale of the Saroyan plays. They have been poured forth breathlessly in much the same quantity as the "stories": *My Heart's in the Highlands*, 1939; *The Time of Your Life*, 1939; *Love's Old Sweet Song*, 1939; *The Beautiful People*, 1941; *Across the Board on Tomorrow Morning*, 1941; *Jim Dandy*, 1941; *Razzle Dazzle*, short plays, 1942; *The Human Comedy*, movie, 1942; *Get Away, Old Man*, 1943. Of these plays, *The Time of Your Life* is the best, and presents rather completely the singular contribution of Saroyan to modern drama.

It is as wayward and formless as life itself. Compared to one of Somerset Maugham's tightly constructed comedies like *The Circle*, it seems less like a play than a set of random Saroyan jottings about some folks who drift in and out of Nick's honky-tonk bar on the San Francisco waterfront. The curtain might go up or down on it at any point, for the division into five acts is arbitrary. The scene was going on before the curtain rose and it continued after the lights went out. Yet it is held together by a kind of Saroyan magic, a childlike enthusiasm for the illusion of Santa Claus. Perhaps Tennessee Williams came as near to its nerve center as anyone when he said, in his preface to *The Glass Menagerie*, "William Saroyan wrote a great play on this theme, that purity of heart is the one success worth having. 'In the time of your life—live!' That time is short and it doesn't return again." Saroyan himself added his own characteristic sentence, "In the time of your life live—so that in that wondrous time you shall not add to the misery and sorrow of the world, but shall smile to the infinite delight and mystery of it." Joe is the agent for bringing out the dreams that haunt these distressed souls. The play bears comparison with the same general concept in the plays of Arthur Miller and Tennessee Williams. Like them it was immensely successful on stage with Eddie Dowling as Joe and Julie Haydon as Kitty Duval—the two actors who, with Laurette Taylor, created the parts in *The Glass Menagerie*.

The Time of Your Life received the Critics' Circle award and also the Pulitzer Prize, though the latter was rejected by the unpredictable Saroyan, who always mentions the fact that the play *was* given this prize and that it was rejected. Whether he ever equals or surpasses the achievement of this play is of little moment in view of the fact that *The Time of Your Life* is complete Saroyan. He, in common with other, more objective, observers believes it is good. We have his own word for this: "Like *My Heart's in the Highlands*, *The Time of Your Life* will very likely take an important place in the development of the new American theater. I know why, but I am going to leave the full details to the critics, as I believe in the right of every profession to function."

THE TIME OF YOUR LIFE

In the time of your life, live—so that in that good time there shall be no ugliness or death for yourself or for any life your life touches. Seek goodness everywhere, and when it is found, bring it out of its hiding place and let it be free and unashamed. Place in matter and in flesh the least of the values, for these are the things that hold death and must pass away. Discover in all things that which shines and is beyond corruption. Encourage virtue in whatever heart it may have been driven into secrecy and sorrow by the shame and terror of the world. Ignore the obvious, for it is unworthy of the clear eye and the kindly heart. Be the inferior of no man, nor of any man be the superior. Remember that every man is a variation of yourself. No man's guilt is not yours, nor is any man's innocence a thing apart. Despise evil and ungodliness, but not men of ungodliness or evil. These, understand. Have no shame in being kindly and gentle, but if the time comes in the time of your life to kill, kill and have no regret. In the time of your life, live—so that in that wondrous time you shall not add to the misery and sorrow of the world, but shall smile to the infinite delight and mystery of it.

THE PEOPLE

JOE, *a young loafer with money and a good heart*

TOM, *his admirer, disciple, errand boy, stooge, and friend*

KITTY DUVAL, *a young woman with memories*

NICK, *owner of Nick's Pacific Street Saloon, Restaurant, and Entertainment Palace*

ARAB, *an Eastern philosopher and harmonica-player*

KIT CARSON, *an old Indian-fighter*

MCCARTHY, *an intelligent and well-read longshoreman*

KRUPP, *his boyhood friend, a water-front cop who hates his job but doesn't know what else to do instead*

HARRY, *a natural-born hoofer who wants to make people laugh but can't*

WESLEY, *a colored boy who plays a mean and melancholy boogie-woogie piano*

DUDLEY, *a young man in love*

ELSIE, *a nurse, the girl he loves*

LORENE, *an unattractive woman*

MARY L., *an unhappy woman of quality and great beauty*

WILLIE, *a marble-game maniac*

BLICK, *a heel*

MA, *Nick's mother*

A KILLER

HER SIDE KICK

A COP

ANOTHER COP

A SAILOR

A SOCIETY GENTLEMAN

A SOCIETY LADY

THE DRUNKARD

THE NEWSBOY

ANNA, *Nick's daughter*

THE PLACE: *Nick's Pacific Street Saloon, Restaurant, and Entertainment Palace at the foot of Embarcadero, in San Francisco. A suggestion of Room 21 at The New York Hotel, upstairs, around the corner.*

THE TIME: *Afternoon and night of a day in October 1939.*

ACT ONE

Nick's is an American place: a San Francisco water-front honky-tonk. At a table, JOE: *always calm, always quiet, always thinking, always eager, always bored, always superior. His expensive clothes are casually and youthfully worn and give him an almost boyish appearance. He is thinking. Behind the bar,* NICK: *a big redheaded young Italian-American with an enormous naked woman tattooed in red on the inside of his right arm. He is* 10 *studying* The Racing Form.

The ARAB, *at his place at the end of the bar. He is a lean old man with a rather ferocious old-country mustache, with the ends twisted up. Between the thumb and forefinger of his left hand is the Mohammedan tattoo indicating that he has been to Mecca. He is sipping a glass of beer.*

It is about eleven-thirty in the morning. SAM *is sweeping out. We see only his back. He* 20 *disappears into the kitchen. The* SAILOR *at the bar finishes his drink and leaves, moving thoughtfully, as though he were trying very hard to discover how to live. The* NEWSBOY *comes in.*

NEWSBOY (*cheerfully*). Good morning, everybody. •(*No answer. To* NICK.) Paper, mister? (NICK *shakes his head, no. The* NEWSBOY *goes to* JOE.) Paper, 30 mister?

[JOE *shakes his head, no. The* NEWSBOY *walks away, counting papers.*]

JOE (*noticing him*). How many you got?

NEWSBOY. Five.

[JOE *gives him a quarter, takes all the papers, glances at the headlines with irritation, throws them away. The* NEWSBOY *watches carefully, then goes.*]

ARAB (*picks up a paper, looks at the headlines, shakes his head as if rejecting everything else a man might say about the world*). No foundation. All the way down the line.

[*The* DRUNK *comes in. Walks to the telephone, looks for a nickel in the chute, sits down at* JOE's *table.* NICK *takes the* DRUNK *out. The* DRUNK *returns.*]

DRUNK (*champion of the Bill of Rights*). This is a free country, ain't it?

[WILLIE, *the marble-game maniac, explodes through the swinging doors and lifts the forefinger of his right hand comically, indicating one beer. He is a very young man, not more than twenty. He is wearing heavy shoes, a pair of old and dirty corduroys, a light-green turtle-neck jersey with a large letter F on the chest, an oversize two-button tweed coat, and a green hat, with the brim up.* NICK *sets out a glass of beer for him, he drinks it, straightens up vigorously, saying "Aaah," makes a solemn face, gives* NICK *a one-finger salute of adieu, and begins to leave, refreshed and restored in spirit. He walks by the marble game, halts suddenly, turns, studies the*

*contraption, gestures as if to say, "Oh no."
Turns to go, stops, returns to the machine,
studies it, takes a handful of small coins
out of his pants pocket, lifts a nickel, indicates with a gesture, One game, no more.
Puts the nickel in the slot, pushes in the
slide, making an interesting noise.*]

NICK. You can't beat that machine.

WILLIE. Oh yeah?

[*The marbles fall, roll, and take their place.* 10
*He pushes down the lever, placing one
marble in position. Takes a very deep
breath, walks in a small circle, excited at
the beginning of great drama. Stands
straight and pious before the contest. Himself vs. the machine. Willie vs. Destiny.
His skill and daring vs. the cunning and
trickery of the novelty industry of America,
and the whole challenging world. He is the
last of the American pioneers, with nothing* 20
*more to fight but the machine, with no other
reward than lights going on and off, and six
nickels for one. Before him is the last
champion, the machine. He is the last chal-
lenger, the young man with nothing to do
in the world.* WILLIE *grips the knob delicately, studies the situation carefully,
draws the knob back, holds it a moment,
and then releases it. The first marble rolls
out among the hazards, and the contest is* 30
*on. At the very beginning of the play "The
Missouri Waltz" is coming from the
phonograph. The music ends here.*]

*This is the signal for the beginning of the
play.*

[JOE *suddenly comes out of his reverie. He
whistles the way people do who are calling
a cab that's about a block away, only he
does it quietly.* WILLIE *turns around, but*
JOE *gestures for him to return to his work.* 40
NICK *looks up from* The Racing Form.]

JOE (*calling*). Tom. (*To himself.*) Where
the hell is he, every time I need him?
(*He looks around calmly: the nickel-in-the-
slot phonograph in the corner; the open
public telephone; the stage; the marble*

*game; the bar; and so on. He calls again,
this time very loud.*) Hey, Tom.

NICK (*with morning irritation*). What do
you want?

JOE (*without thinking*). I want the boy to
get me a watermelon, that's what *I*
want. What do *you* want? Money, or
love, or fame, or what? You won't
get them studying *The Racing Form*.

NICK. I like to keep abreast of the times.

[TOM *comes hurrying in. He is a great big
man of about thirty or so who appears to
be much younger because of the childlike
expression of his face: handsome, dumb, innocent, troubled, and a little bewildered by
everything. He is obviously adult in years,
but it seems as if by all rights he should
still be a boy. He is defensive as clumsy,
self-conscious, overgrown boys are. He is
wearing a flashy cheap suit.* JOE *leans back
and studies him with casual disapproval.*
TOM *slackens his pace and becomes clumsy
and embarrassed, waiting for the bawling-
out he's pretty sure he's going to get.*]

JOE (*objectively, severely, but a little amused*).
Who saved your life?

TOM (*sincerely*). You did, Joe. Thanks.

JOE (*interested*). How'd I do it?

TOM (*confused*). What?

JOE (*even more interested*). How'd I do it?

TOM. Joe, you know how you did it.

JOE (*softly*). I want you to answer me.
How'd I save your life? I've forgotten.

TOM (*remembering, with a big sorrowful
smile*). You made me eat all that
chicken soup three years ago when I
was sick and hungry.

JOE (*fascinated*). *Chicken soup?*

TOM (*eagerly*). Yeah.

JOE. Three years? Is it that long?

TOM (*delighted to have the information*).
Yeah, sure. 1937. 1938. 1939. This
is 1939, Joe.

JOE (*amused*). Never mind what year it
is. Tell me the whole story.

TOM. You took me to the doctor. You

gave me money for food and clothes, and paid my room rent. Aw, Joe, you know all the different things you did.

[JOE *nods, turning away from* TOM *after each question.*]

JOE. You in good health now?

TOM. Yeah, Joe.

JOE. You got clothes?

TOM. Yeah, Joe.

JOE. You eat three times a day. Sometimes four?

TOM. Yeah, Joe. Sometimes five.

JOE. You got a place to sleep?

TOM. Yeah, Joe.

[JOE *nods. Pauses. Studies* TOM *carefully.*]

JOE. Then where the hell have you been?

TOM (*humbly*). Joe, I was out in the street listening to the boys. They're talking about the trouble down here on the water front.

JOE (*sharply*). I want you to be around when I need you.

TOM (*pleased that the bawling-out is over*). I won't do it again. Joe, one guy out there says there's got to be a revolution before anything will ever be all right.

JOE (*impatient*). I know all about it. Now, here. Take this money. Go up to the Emporium. You know where the Emporium is?

TOM. Yeah, sure, Joe.

JOE. All right. Take the elevator and go up to the fourth floor. Walk around to the back, to the toy department. Buy me a couple of dollars' worth of toys and bring them here.

TOM (*amazed*). Toys? What *kind* of toys, Joe?

JOE. Any kind of toys. Little ones that I can put on this table.

TOM. What do you want toys for, Joe?

JOE (*mildly angry*). What?

TOM. All right, all right. You don't have to get sore at *everything*. What'll people think, a big guy like me buying toys?

JOE. What people?

TOM. Aw, Joe, you're always making me do crazy things for you, and *I'm* the guy that gets embarrassed. You just sit in this place and make me do all the dirty work.

JOE (*looking away*). Do what I tell you.

TOM. O.K., but I wish I knew *why*. (*He makes to go.*)

JOE. Wait a minute. Here's a nickel. Put it in the phonograph. Number seven. I want to hear that waltz again.

TOM. Boy, I'm glad *I* don't have to stay and listen to it. Joe, what do you hear in that song anyway? We listen to that song ten times a day. Why can't we hear number six, or two, or nine? There are a lot of other numbers.

JOE (*emphatically*). Put the nickel in the phonograph. (*Pause.*) Sit down and wait till the music's over. Then go get me some toys.

TOM. O.K. O.K.

JOE (*loudly*). Never mind being a martyr about it, either. The cause isn't worth it.

[TOM *puts the nickel into the machine, with a ritual of impatient and efficient movement which plainly shows his lack of sympathy or enthusiasm. His manner also reveals, however, that his lack of sympathy is spurious and exaggerated. Actually, he is fascinated by the music, but is so confused by it that he pretends he dislikes it.*

[*The music begins. It is another variation of "The Missouri Waltz," played dreamily and softly, with perfect orchestral form, and with a theme of weeping in the horns repeated a number of times. At first* TOM *listens with something close to irritation, since he can't understand what is so attractive in the music to* JOE, *and what is so painful and confusing in it to himself. Very soon, however, he is carried away by the melancholy story of grief and nostalgia of the song. He stands, troubled by the poetry and confusion in himself.*

[JOE, *on the other hand, listens as if he were not listening, indifferent and unmoved. What he's interested in is* TOM. *He turns and glances at* TOM.

[KITTY DUVAL, *who lives in a room in the New York Hotel, around the corner, comes beyond the swinging doors quietly, and walks slowly to the bar, her reality and* 10 *rhythm a perfect accompaniment to the sorrowful American music, which is her music, as it is* TOM's. *Which the world drove out of her, putting in its place brokenness and all manner of spiritually crippled forms. She seems to understand this, and is angry. Angry with herself, full of hate for the poor world, and full of pity and contempt for its tragic, unbelievable, confounded people. She is a small, powerful girl, with* 20 *that kind of delicate and rugged beauty which no circumstance of evil or ugly reality can destroy. This beauty is that element of the immortal which is in the seed of good and common people, and which is kept alive in some of the female of our kind, no matter how accidentally or pointlessly they may have entered the world.* KITTY DUVAL *is somebody. There is an angry purity, and a fierce pride, in her. In her stance, and way* 30 *of walking, there is grace and arrogance.* JOE *recognizes her as a great person immediately. She goes to the bar.*]

KITTY. Beer.

[NICK *places a glass of beer before her mechanically. She swallows half the drink, and listens to the music again.* TOM *turns and sees her. He becomes dead to everything in the world but her. He stands like a lump, fascinated and undone by his almost re-* 40 *ligious adoration for her.* JOE *notices* TOM.]

JOE (*gently*). Tom. (TOM *begins to move toward the bar, where* KITTY *is standing. Loudly.*) Tom. (TOM *halts, then turns, and* JOE *motions to him to come over to the*

table. TOM *goes over. Quietly.*) Have you got everything straight?

TOM (*out of the world*). What?

JOE. What do you mean, what? I just gave you some instructions.

TOM (*pathetically*). What do you want, Joe?

JOE. I want you to come to your senses.

[*He stands up quietly and knocks* TOM's *hat off.* TOM *picks up his hat quickly.*]

TOM. I got it, Joe. I got it. The Emporium. Fourth floor. In the back. The toy department. Two dollars' worth of toys. That you can put on a table.

KITTY (*to herself*). Who the hell is he to push a big man like that around?

JOE. I'll expect you back in a half hour. Don't get sidetracked anywhere. Just do what I tell you.

TOM (*pleading*). Joe? Can't I bet four bits on a horse race? There's a long shot—Precious Time—that's going to win by ten lengths. I got to have money.

[JOE *points to the street.* TOM *goes out.* NICK *is combing his hair, looking in the mirror.*]

NICK. I thought you wanted him to get you a watermelon.

JOE. I forgot. (*He watches* KITTY *a moment. To* KITTY, *clearly, slowly, with great compassion.*) What's the dream?

KITTY (*moving to* JOE, *coming to*). What?

JOE (*holding the dream for her*). What's the dream, *now?*

KITTY (*coming still closer*). What dream?

JOE. What dream! The dream you're dreaming.

NICK. Suppose he did bring you a watermelon? What the hell would you do with it?

JOE (*irritated*). I'd put it on this table. I'd look at it. Then I'd eat it. What do you *think* I'd do with it, sell it for a profit?

NICK. How should I know what *you'd* do with *anything?* What I'd like to know is, where do you get your money from? What work do you do?

JOE (*looking at* KITTY). Bring us a bottle of champagne.

KITTY. Champagne?

JOE (*simply*). Would you rather have something else?

KITTY. What's the big idea?

JOE. I thought you might like some champagne. I myself am very fond of it.

KITTY. Yeah, but what's the big idea? You can't push *me* around.

JOE (*gently but severely*). It's not in my nature to be unkind to another human being. I have only contempt for wit. Otherwise I might say something obvious, therefore cruel, and perhaps untrue.

KITTY. You be careful what you think about me.

JOE (*slowly, not looking at her*). I have only the noblest thoughts for both your person and your spirit.

NICK (*having listened carefully and not being able to make it out*). What are you talking about?

KITTY. You shut up. You——

JOE. He owns this place. He's an important man. All kinds of people come to him looking for work. Comedians. Singers. Dancers.

KITTY. I don't care. He can't call me names.

NICK. All right, sister.

KITTY (*furiously*). Don't you dare call me names. I used to be in burlesque.

NICK. If you were ever in burlesque, I used to be Charlie Chaplin.

KITTY (*angry and a little pathetic*). I *was* in burlesque. I played the burlesque circuit from coast to coast. I've had flowers sent to me by European royalty. I've had dinner with young men of wealth and social position.

NICK. You're dreaming.

KITTY (*to* JOE). *I was in burlesque.* Kitty Duval. That was my name. Life-size photographs of me in costume in front of burlesque theaters all over the country.

JOE (*gently, coaxingly*). I believe you. Have some champagne.

NICK (*going to the table with champagne bottle and glasses*). There he goes again.

JOE. Miss Duval?

KITTY (*sincerely, going over*). That's not my *real* name. That's my *stage* name.

JOE. I'll call you by your stage name.

NICK (*pouring*). All right, sister, make up your mind. Are you going to have champagne with him, or not?

JOE. Pour the lady some wine.

NICK. O.K., Professor. Why you come to this joint instead of one of the high-class dumps uptown is more than I can understand. Why don't you have champagne at the St. Francis? Why don't you drink with a lady?

KITTY (*furiously*). Don't you call me names—you dentist.

JOE. Dentist?

NICK (*amazed, loudly*). What kind of cussing is that? (*Pause. Looking at* KITTY, *then at* JOE, *bewildered.*) This guy doesn't belong here. The only reason I've got champagne is because *he* keeps ordering it all the time. (*To* KITTY.) Don't think you're the only one he drinks champagne with. He drinks with *all* of them. (*Pause.*) He's crazy. Or something.

JOE (*confidentially*). Nick, I think you're going to be all right in a couple of centuries.

NICK. I'm sorry, I don't understand your English.

[JOE *lifts his glass.* KITTY *slowly lifts hers, not quite sure of what's going on.*]

JOE (*sincerely*). To the spirit, Kitty Duval.

KITTY (*beginning to understand, and very grateful, looking at him*). Thank you. [*They drink.*]

JOE (*calling*). Nick.

NICK. Yeah?

JOE. Would you mind putting a nickel in the machine again? Number——

NICK. Seven. I know. I know. I don't mind at all, your Highness, although, personally, I'm not a lover of music. 10 (*Going to the machine.*) As a matter of fact I think Tchaikowsky was a dope.

JOE. Tchaikowsky? Where'd you ever hear of Tchaikowsky?

NICK. He was a dope.

JOE. Yeah. Why?

NICK. They talked about him on the radio one Sunday morning. He was a sucker. He let a woman drive him crazy.   20

JOE. I see.

NICK. I stood behind that bar listening to the goddamn stuff and cried like a baby. *None but the lonely heart!* He was a dope.

JOE. What made you cry?

NICK. What?

JOE (*sternly*). What made you cry, Nick?

NICK (*angry with himself*). I don't know.

JOE. I've been underestimating you, 30 Nick. Play number seven.

NICK. They get everybody worked up. They give everybody stuff they shouldn't have.

[NICK *puts the nickel into the machine and the waltz begins again. He listens to the music, then studies* The Racing Form.]

KITTY (*to herself, dreaming*). I like champagne, and everything that goes with it. Big houses with big porches, and 40 big rooms with big windows, and big lawns, and big trees, and flowers growing everywhere, and big shepherd dogs sleeping in the shade.

NICK. I'm going next door to Frankie's to make a bet. I'll be right back.

JOE. Make one for me.

NICK (*going to* JOE). Who do you like?

JOE (*giving him money*). Precious Time.

NICK. *Ten dollars?* Across the board?

JOE. No. On the nose.

NICK. O.K. (*He goes.*)

[DUDLEY R. BOSTWICK, *as he calls himself, breaks through the swinging doors, and practically flings himself upon the open telephone beside the phonograph.*

[DUDLEY *is a young man of about twenty-four or twenty-five, ordinary and yet extraordinary. He is smallish, as the saying is, neatly dressed in bargain clothes, overworked and irritated by the routine and dullness and monotony of his life, apparently nobody and nothing, but in reality a great personality. The swindled young man. Educated, but without the least real understanding. A brave, dumb, salmon-spirit struggling for life in weary, stupefied flesh, dueling ferociously with a banal mind which has been only irritated by what it has been taught. He is a great personality because, against all these handicaps, what he wants is simple and basic: a woman. This urgent and violent need, common yet miraculous enough in itself, considering the unhappy environment of the animal, is the force which elevates him from nothingness to greatness. A ridiculous greatness, but in the nature of things beautiful to behold. All that he has been taught, and everything he believes, is phony, and yet he himself is real, almost super-real, because of this indestructible force in himself. His face is ridiculous. His personal rhythm is tense and jittery. His speech is shrill and violent. His gestures are wild. His ego is disjointed and epileptic. And yet deeply he possesses the same wholeness of spirit, and directness of energy, that is in all species of animals. There is little innate or cultivated spirit in him, but there is no absence of innocent animal force. He is a young man who has been taught that he has a chance, as a per-*

son, and believes it. As a matter of fact, he hasn't a chance in the world, and should have been told by somebody, or should not have had his natural and valuable ignorance spoiled by education, ruining an otherwise perfectly good and charming member of the human race.

[At the telephone he immediately begins to dial furiously, hesitates, changes his mind, stops dialing, hangs up furiously, and sud- 10 denly begins again.

[Not more than half a minute after the firecracker arrival of DUDLEY R. BOSTWICK, occurs the polka-and-waltz arrival of HARRY.

[HARRY is another story. He comes in timidly, turning about uncertainly, awkward, out of place everywhere, embarrassed and encumbered by the contemporary costume, sick at heart, but determined to fit in somewhere. 20 His arrival constitutes a dance. His clothes don't fit. The pants are a little too large. The coat, which doesn't match, is also a little too large, and loose. He is a dumb young fellow, but he has ideas. A philosophy, in fact. His philosophy is simple and beautiful. The world is sorrowful. The world needs laughter. HARRY is funny. The world needs HARRY. HARRY will make the world laugh. He has probably had 30 a year or two of high school. He has also listened to the boys at the poolroom. He's looking for NICK. He goes to the ARAB, and says, "Are you Nick?" The ARAB shakes his head. He stands at the bar, waiting. He waits very busily.]

HARRY (as NICK returns). You Nick?

NICK (very loudly). I am Nick.

HARRY (acting). Can you use a great
· comedian? 40

NICK (behind the bar). Who, for instance?

HARRY (almost angry). Me.

NICK. You? What's funny about you?

[DUDLEY, at the telephone, is dialing. Because of some defect in the apparatus the dialing is very loud.]

DUDLEY. Hello. Sunset 7349? May I speak to Miss Elsie Mandelspiegel? (Pause.)

HARRY (with spirit and noise, dancing). I dance and do gags and stuff.

NICK. In costume? Or are you wearing your costume?

DUDLEY. All I need is a cigar.

KITTY (continuing the dream of grace). I'd walk out of the house, and stand on the porch, and look at the trees, and smell the flowers, and run across the lawn, and lie down under a tree, and read a book. (Pause.) A book of poems, maybe.

DUDLEY (very, very clearly). Elsie Mandelspiegel. (Impatiently.) She has a room on the fourth floor. She's a nurse at the Southern Pacific Hospital. Elsie Mandelspiegel. She works at night. Elsie. Yes.

[He begins waiting again. WESLEY, a colored boy, comes to the bar and stands near HARRY, waiting.]

NICK. Beer?

WESLEY. No, sir. I'd like to talk to you.

NICK (to HARRY). All right. Get funny.

HARRY (getting funny, an altogether different person, an actor with great energy, both in power of voice, and in force and speed of physical gesture). Now I'm standing on the corner of Third and Market. I'm looking around. I'm figuring it out. There it is. Right in front of me. The whole city. The whole world. People going by. They're going somewhere. I don't know where, but they're going. I ain't going anywhere. Where the hell can you go? I'm figuring it out. All right, I'm a citizen. A fat guy bumps his stomach into the face of an old lady. They were in a hurry. Fat and old. They bumped. Boom. I don't know. It may mean war. War. Germany.

England. Russia. I don't know for sure. (*Loudly, dramatically, he salutes, about-faces, presents arms, aims, and fires.*) WAAAAAR.

[*He blows a call to arms.* NICK *gets sick of this, indicates with a gesture that* HARRY *should hold it, and goes to* WESLEY.]

NICK. What's on your mind?

WESLEY (*confused*). Well——

NICK. Come on. Speak up. Are you hungry, or what?

WESLEY. Honest to God, I ain't hungry. All I want is a job. I don't want no charity.

NICK. Well, what can you do, and how good are you?

WESLEY. I can run errands, clean up, wash dishes, anything.

DUDLEY (*on the telephone, very eagerly*). Elsie? Elsie, this is Dudley. Elsie, I'll jump in the bay if you don't marry me. Life isn't worth living without you. I can't sleep. I can't think of anything but you. All the time. Day and night and night and day. Elsie, I love you. I love you. What? (*Burning up.*) Is this Sunset 7-3-4-9? (*Pause.*) 7943? (*Calmly, while* WILLIE *begins making a small racket.*) Well, what's your name? *Lorene?* Lorene Smith? I thought you were Elsie Mandelspiegel. What? Dudley. Yeah. Dudley R. Bostwick. Yeah. R. It stands for Raoul, but I never spell it out. I'm pleased to meet *you*, too. What? There's a lot of noise around here. (WILLIE *stops hitting the marble game.*) Where am I? At Nick's, on Pacific Street. I work at the S. P. I told them I was sick and they gave me the afternoon off. Wait a minute. I'll ask them. I'd like to meet *you*, too. Sure. I'll ask them. (*Turns around to* NICK.) What's this address?

NICK. Number 3 Pacific Street, you cad.

DUDLEY. Cad? You don't know how I've been suffering on account of Elsie. I take things too ceremoniously. I've got to be more lackadaisical. (*Into telephone.*) Hello, Elenore? I mean Lorene. It's Number 3 Pacific Street. Yeah. Sure. I'll wait for you. How'll you know me? You'll *know* me. I'll recognize *you*. Good-by, now. (*He hangs up.*)

HARRY (*continuing his monologue, with gestures, movements, and so on*). I'm standing there. I didn't do anything to anybody. Why should *I* be a soldier? (*Sincerely, insanely.*) BOOOOOOOOOM. *WAR!* O.K. War. *I* retreat. *I* hate war. I move to Sacramento.

NICK (*shouting*). All right, comedian. Lay off a minute.

HARRY (*brokenhearted, going to* WILLIE). Nobody's got a sense of humor any more. The world's dying for comedy like never before, but nobody knows how to *laugh*.

NICK (*to* WESLEY). Do you belong to the union?

WESLEY. What union?

NICK. For the love of Mike, where've you been? Don't you know you can't come into a place and ask for a job and get one and go to work, just like that. You've got to belong to one of the unions.

WESLEY. I didn't know. I got to have a job. Real soon.

NICK. Well, you've got to belong to a union.

WESLEY. I don't want any favors. All I want is a chance to earn a living.

NICK. Go on into the kitchen and tell Sam to give you some lunch.

WESLEY. Honest, I ain't hungry.

DUDLEY (*shouting*). What I've gone through for Elsie.

HARRY. I've got all kinds of funny ideas in my head to help make the world happy again.

NICK (*holding* WESLEY). No, he isn't hungry.

[WESLEY *almost faints from hunger.* NICK *catches him just in time. The* ARAB *and* NICK *go off with* WESLEY *into the kitchen.*]

HARRY (*to* WILLIE). See if you think this is funny. It's my own idea. I created this dance myself. It comes after the monologue.

[HARRY *begins to dance.* WILLIE *watches a moment, and then goes back to the game. It's a goofy dance, which* HARRY *does with great sorrow, but much energy.*]

DUDLEY. Elsie. Aw, gee, Elsie. What the hell do I want to see Lorene Smith for? Some girl I don't know.

[JOE *and* KITTY *have been drinking in silence. There is no sound now except the soft-shoe shuffling of* HARRY *the comedian.*] 20

JOE. What's the dream now, Kitty Duval?

KITTY (*dreaming the words and pictures*). I dream of home. Christ, I always dream of home. I've no *home.* I've no place. But I always dream of all of us together again. We had a farm in Ohio. There was nothing good about it. It was always sad. There was always trouble. But I always dream 30 about it as if I could go back and Papa would be there and Mamma and Louie and my little brother Stephen and my sister Mary. I'm Polish. Duval! My name isn't Duval, it's Koranovsky. Katerina Koranovsky. We lost everything. The house, the farm, the trees, the horses, the cows, the chickens. Papa died. He was old. He was thirteen years older 40 than Mamma. We moved to Chicago. We tried to work. We tried to stay together. Louie got in trouble. The fellows he was with killed him for something. I don't know what. Stephen ran away from home. Sev-

enteen years old. I don't know where he is. Then Mamma died. (*Pause.*) What's the dream? I dream of home.

[NICK *comes out of the kitchen with* WESLEY.]

NICK. Here. Sit down here and rest. That'll hold you for a *while.* Why didn't you tell me you were hungry? You all right now?

10 WESLEY (*sitting down in the chair at the piano*). Yes, I am. Thank you. I didn't know I was *that* hungry.

NICK. Fine. (*To* HARRY, *who is dancing.*) Hey. What the hell do you think you're doing?

HARRY (*stopping*). That's my own idea. I'm a natural-born dancer and comedian.

[WESLEY *begins slowly, one note, one chord, at a time, to play the piano.*]

NICK. You're no good. Why don't you try some other kind of work? Why don't you get a job in a store, selling something? What do you want to be a comedian for?

HARRY. I've got something for the world and they haven't got sense enough to let me give it to them. Nobody knows me.

30 DUDLEY. Elsie. Now I'm waiting for some dame I've never seen before. Lorene Smith. Never saw her in my life. Just happened to get the wrong number. She turns on the personality and I'm a cooked Indian. Give me a beer, please.

HARRY. Nick, you've got to see my act. It's the greatest thing of its kind in America. All I want is a chance. No salary to begin. Let me try it out tonight. If I don't wow 'em, O.K., I'll go home. If vaudeville wasn't dead, a guy like me would have a chance.

NICK. You're not funny. You're a sad young punk. What the hell do you want to try to be funny for? You'll break everybody's heart. What's there for you to be funny about? You've been poor all your life, haven't you?

HARRY. I've been poor all right, but don't forget that some things count more than some other things.

NICK. What counts more, for instance, than what else, for instance?

HARRY. Talent, for instance, counts more than money, for instance, that's what, and I've got talent. I get new ideas night and day. Everything comes natural to me. I've got style, but it'll take me a little time to round it out. That's all.

[By now WESLEY is playing something of his own which is very good and out of the world. He plays about half a minute, after which HARRY begins to dance.]

NICK (watching). I run the lousiest dive in Frisco, and a guy arrives and makes me stock up with champagne. The streetwalkers come in and holler at me that they're ladies. Talent comes in and begs me for a chance to show itself. Even society people come here once in a while. I don't know what for. Maybe it's liquor. Maybe it's the location. Maybe it's my personality. Maybe it's the crazy personality of the joint. The old honky-tonk. (Pause.) Maybe they can't feel at home anywhere else.

[By now WESLEY is really playing, and HARRY is going through a new routine. DUDLEY grows sadder and sadder.]

KITTY. Please dance with me.

JOE (loudly). I never learned to dance.

KITTY. Anybody can dance. Just hold me in your arms.

JOE. I'm very fond of you. I'm sorry. I can't dance. I wish to God I could.

KITTY. Oh, please.

JOE. Forgive me. I'd like to very much.

[KITTY dances alone. TOM comes in with a package. He sees KITTY and goes gaga again. He comes out of the trance and puts the bundle on the table in front of JOE.]

JOE (taking the package). What'd you get?

TOM. Two dollars' worth of toys. That's what you sent me for. The girl asked me what I wanted with toys. I didn't know what to tell her. (He stares at KITTY, then back at JOE.) Joe? I've got to have some money. After all you've done for me, I'll do anything in the world for you, but, Joe, you got to give me some money once in a while.

JOE. What do you want it for?

[TOM turns and stares at KITTY dancing.]

JOE (noticing). Sure. Here. Here's five. (Shouting.) Can you dance?

TOM (proudly). I got second prize at the Palomar in Sacramento five years ago.

JOE (loudly, opening the package). O.K., dance with her.

TOM. You mean her?

JOE (loudly). I mean Kitty Duval, the burlesque queen. I mean the queen of the world burlesque. Dance with her. She wants to dance.

TOM (worshipping the name Kitty Duval, helplessly). Joe, can I tell you something?

JOE (he brings out a toy and winds it). You don't have to. I know. You love her. You really love her. I'm not blind. I know. But take care of yourself. Don't get sick that way again.

NICK (looking at and listening to WESLEY with amazement). Comes in here and wants to be a dishwasher. Faints from hunger. And then sits down and plays better than Heifetz.

JOE. Heifetz plays the violin.

NICK. All right, don't get careful. He's good, ain't he?

TOM (to KITTY). Kitty.

JOE (he lets the toy go, loudly). Don't talk. Just dance.

[TOM and KITTY dance. NICK is at the bar,

watching everything. HARRY *is dancing.* DUDLEY *is grieving into his beer.* LORENE SMITH, *about thirty-seven, very overbearing and funny-looking, comes to the bar.*]

NICK. What'll it be, lady?

LORENE (*looking about and scaring all the young men*). I'm looking for the young man I talked to on the telephone. Dudley R. Bostwick.

DUDLEY (*jumping, running to her, stopping, shocked*). Dudley R. (*Slowly.*) Bostwick? Oh yeah. He left here ten minutes ago. You mean Dudley Bostwick, that poor man on crutches?

LORENE. Crutches?

DUDLEY. Yeah. Dudley Bostwick. That's what he *said* his name was. He said to tell you not to wait.

LORENE. Well. (*She begins to go, turns around.*) Are you sure *you're* not Dudley Bostwick?

DUDLEY. Who—me? (*Grandly.*) My name is Roger Tenefrancia. I'm a French Canadian. I never saw the poor fellow before.

LORENE. It seems to me your voice is like the voice I heard over the telephone.

DUDLEY. A coincidence. An accident. A quirk of fate. One of those things. Dismiss the thought. That poor cripple hobbled out of here ten minutes ago.

LORENE. He said he was going to commit suicide. I only wanted to be of help. (*She goes.*)

DUDLEY. Be of help? What kind of help could she be of? (DUDLEY *runs to the telephone in the corner.*) Gee whiz, Elsie. Gee whiz. I'll never leave you again. (*He turns the pages of a little address book.*) Why do I always forget the number? I've tried to get her on the phone a hundred times this week and I still forget the number. She won't come to the phone, but I keep trying

anyway. She's out. She's not in. She's working. I get the wrong number. Everything goes haywire. I can't sleep. (*Defiantly.*) She'll come to the phone one of these days. If there's anything to true love at all, she'll come to the phone. Sunset 7349.

[*He dials the number as* JOE *goes on studying the toys. They are one big mechanical toy, whistles, and a music box.* JOE *blows into the whistles, quickly, by way of getting casually acquainted with them.* TOM *and* KITTY *stop dancing.* TOM *stares at her.*]

DUDLEY. Hello. Is this Sunset 7349? May I speak to Elsie? Yes. (*Emphatically, and bitterly.*) No, this is *not* Dudley Bostwick. This is Roger Tenefrancia of Montreal, Canada. I'm a childhood friend of Miss Mandelspiegel. We went to kindergarten together. (*His hand over the phone.*) God damn it. (*Into the phone.*) Yes. I'll wait, thank you.

TOM. I love you.

[TOM *embraces her. They go.* JOE *watches. Goes back to the toy.*]

JOE. Where's that longshoreman, McCarthy?

NICK. He'll be around.

JOE. What do you think he'll have to say today?

NICK. Plenty, as usual. I'm going next door to see who won that third race at Laurel.

JOE. Precious Time won it.

NICK. That's what you think. (*He goes.*)

JOE (*to himself*). A horse named McCarthy is running in the sixth race today.

DUDLEY (*on the phone*). Hello. Hello, Elsie? Elsie? (*His voice weakens, also his limbs.*) My God. She's come to the phone. Elsie, I'm at Nick's on Pacific Street. You've got to come here and talk to me. Hello. Hello, Elsie? (*Amazed.*) Did she hang up? Or was

I disconnected? (*He hangs up and goes to the bar.*)

[WESLEY *is still playing the piano.* HARRY *is still dancing.* JOE *has wound up the big mechanical toy and is watching it work.* NICK *returns.*]

NICK (*watching the toy*). Say. That's some gadget.

JOE. How much did I win?

NICK. How do you know you *won?* 10

JOE. Don't be silly. He said Precious Time was going to win by ten lengths, didn't he? He's in love, isn't he?

NICK. O.K. I don't know why, but Precious Time won. You got eighty for ten. How do you do it?

JOE (*roaring*). Faith. Faith. How'd he win?

NICK. By a nose. Look him up in *The Racing Form.* The slowest, the cheap- 20 est, the worst horse in the race, and the worst jockey. What's the matter with my luck?

JOE. How much did you lose?

NICK. Fifty cents.

JOE. You should never gamble.

NICK. Why not?

JOE. You always bet fifty cents. You've got no more faith than a flea, that's why. 30

HARRY (*shouting*). How do you like this, Nick? (*He is really busy now, all legs and arms.*)

NICK (*turning and watching*). Not bad. Hang around. You can wait table. (*To* WESLEY.) Hey. Wesley. Can you play that again tonight?

WESLEY (*turning, but still playing the piano*). I don't know for sure, Mr. Nick. I can play *something.* 40

NICK. Good. *You* hang around, too. (*He goes behind the bar.*)

[*The atmosphere is now one of warm, natural, American ease; every man innocent and good; each doing what he believes he should do, or what he must do. There is deep* American naïveté and faith in the behavior of each person. No one is competing with anyone else. No one hates anyone else. Every man is living, and letting live. Each man is following his destiny as he feels it should be followed; or is abandoning it as he feels he must, by now, be abandoned; or is forgetting it for the moment as he feels he should forget it. Although everyone is dead serious, there is unmistakable smiling and humor in the scene; a sense of the human body and spirit emerging from the world-imposed state of stress and fretfulness, fear and awkwardness, to the more natural state of casualness and grace. Each person belongs to the environment, in his own person, as himself: WESLEY *is playing better than ever.* HARRY *is hoofing better than ever.* NICK *is behind the bar shining glasses.* JOE *is smiling at the toy and studying it.* DUDLEY, *although still troubled, is at least calm now and full of melancholy poise.* WILLIE, *at the marble game, is happy. The* ARAB *is deep in his memories, where he wants to be.*

[*Into this scene and atmosphere comes* BLICK. BLICK *is the sort of human being you dislike at sight. He is no different from anybody else physically. His face is an ordinary face. There is nothing obviously wrong with him, and yet you know that it is impossible, even by the most generous expansion of understanding, to accept him as a human being. He is the strong man without strength—strong only among the weak—the weakling who uses force on the weaker.* BLICK *enters casually, as if he were a customer, and immediately* HARRY *begins slowing down.*]

BLICK (*oily, and with mock friendliness*). Hello, Nick.

NICK (*stopping his work and leaning across the bar*). What do you want to come here for? You're too big a man for a little honky-tonk.

BLICK (*flattered*). Now, Nick.

NICK. Important people never come here. *Here.* Have a drink. (*Whisky bottle.*)

BLICK. Thanks, I don't drink.

NICK (*drinking the drink himself*). Well, why don't you?

BLICK. I have responsibilities.

NICK. You're head of the lousy Vice Squad. There's no vice here.

BLICK (*sharply*). Streetwalkers are work- 10 ing out of this place.

NICK (*angry*). What do you want?

BLICK (*loudly*). I just want you to know that it's got to *stop.*

[*The music stops. The mechanical toy runs down. There is absolute silence, and a strange fearfulness and disharmony in the atmosphere now.* HARRY *doesn't know what to do with his hands or feet.* WESLEY'S *arms hang at his sides.* JOE *quietly* 20 *pushes the toy to one side of the table, eager to study what is happening.* WILLIE *stops playing the marble game, turns around, and begins to wait.* DUDLEY *straightens up very, very vigorously, as if to say: "Nothing can scare me. I know love is the only thing."* *The* ARAB *is the same as ever, but watchful.* NICK *is arrogantly aloof. There is a moment of this silence and tension, as though* BLICK *were waiting for everybody* 30 *to acknowledge his presence. He is obviously flattered by the acknowledgment of* HARRY, DUDLEY, WESLEY, *and* WILLIE, *but a little irritated by* NICK'S *aloofness and unfriendliness.*]

NICK. Don't look at me. I can't tell a streetwalker from a lady. You married?

BLICK. You're not asking *me* questions. *I'm* telling *you.* 40

NICK (*interrupting*). You're a man of about forty-five or so. You *ought* to know better.

BLICK (*angry*). Streetwalkers are working out of this place.

NICK (*beginning to shout*). Now don't start any trouble with me. People come here to drink and loaf around. I don't care who they are.

BLICK. Well, I do. Any more of it, and I'll have your joint closed.

NICK (*very casually, without ill will*). Listen. I've got no use for you, or anybody like you. You're out to change the world from something bad to something worse. Something like yourself.

BLICK (*furious pause, and contempt*). I'll be back tonight. (*He begins to go.*)

NICK (*very angry but very calm*). Do yourself a big favor and don't come back tonight. Send somebody else. I don't like your personality.

BLICK (*casually, but with contempt*). Don't break any laws. I don't like yours, either. (*He looks the place over, and goes.*)

[*There is a moment of silence. Then* WILLIE *turns and puts a new nickel in the slot and starts a new game.* WESLEY *turns to the piano and rather falteringly begins to play. His heart really isn't in it.* HARRY *walks about, unable to dance.* DUDLEY *lapses into his customary melancholy, at a table.* NICK *whistles a little, suddenly stops.* JOE *winds the toy.*]

JOE (*comically*). Nick. You going to kill that man?

NICK. I'm disgusted.

JOE. Yeah? Why?

NICK. Why should I get worked up over a guy like that? Why should I hate *him.* He's nothing. He's nobody. He's a mouse. But every time he comes into this place I get burned up. He doesn't want to drink. He doesn't want to sit down. He doesn't want to take things easy. Tell me one thing?

JOE. Do my best.

NICK. What's a punk like *that* want to go out and try to change the world for?

JOE (*amazed*). Does *he* want to change the world, too?

NICK (*irritated*). You know what I mean. What's he want to bother people for? He's *sick*.

JOE (*almost to himself, reflecting on the fact that* BLICK *too wants to change the world*). I guess he wants to change the world at that.

NICK. So I go to work and hate him.

JOE. It's not him, Nick. It's everything.

NICK. Yeah, *I know*. But I've still got no use for him. He's no good. You know what I mean? He hurts little people. (*Confused.*) One of the girls tried to commit suicide on account of him. (*Furiously.*) I'll break his head if he hurts anybody around here. This is *my* joint. (*Afterthought.*) Or anybody's *feelings*, either.

JOE. He may not be so bad, deep down underneath.

NICK. I know all about him. He's no good.

[*During this talk* WESLEY *has really begun to play the piano, the toy is rattling again, and little by little* HARRY *has begun to dance.* NICK *has come around the bar, and now, very much like a child—forgetting all his anger—is watching the toy work. He begins to smile at everything: turns and listens to* WESLEY; *watches* HARRY; *nods at the* ARAB; *shakes his head at* DUDLEY; *and gestures amiably about* WILLIE. *It's his joint all right. It's a good, low-down, honky-tonk American place that lets people alone.*]

NICK. I've got a good joint. There's nothing wrong here. Hey. Comedian. Stick to the dancing tonight. I think you're O.K. Wesley? Do some more of that tonight. That's fine!

HARRY. Thanks, Nick. Gosh, I'm on my way at last. (*On the telephone.*) Hello, Ma? Is that you, Ma? Harry. I got the job. (*He hangs up and walks around, smiling.*)

NICK (*watching the toy all this time*). Say, that really is something. What is that, anyway?

[MARY L. *comes in.*]

JOE (*holding it toward* NICK, *and* MARY L.). Nick, this is a toy. A contraption devised by the cunning of man to drive boredom, or grief, or anger out of children. A noble gadget. A gadget, I might say, infinitely nobler than any other I can think of at the moment. (*Everybody gathers around* JOE's *table to look at the toy. The toy stops working.* JOE *winds the music box. Lifts a whistle, blows it, making a very strange, funny and sorrowful sound.*) Delightful. Tragic, but delightful.

[WESLEY *plays the music-box theme on the piano.* MARY L. *takes a table.*]

NICK. Joe. That girl, Kitty. What's she mean, calling me a dentist? I wouldn't hurt anybody, let alone a tooth.

[NICK *goes to* MARY L.'s *table.* HARRY *imitates the toy. Dances. The piano music comes up, the light dims slowly, while the piano solo continues.*]

CURTAIN

ACT TWO

An hour later. All the people who were at Nick's when the curtain came down are still there. JOE *at his table, quietly shuffling and turning a deck of cards, and at the same time watching the face of the woman, and looking at the initials on her handbag, as though they were the symbols of the lost glory of the world. The woman, in turn, very casually regards* JOE *occasionally. Or rather senses him; has sensed him in fact the whole hour. She is mildly tight on beer, and* JOE *himself is tight, but as always completely under control, simply sharper. The others are about, at tables, and so on.*

JOE. Is it Madge—Laubowitz?

MARY. Is what *what?*

JOE. Is the name Mabel Lepescu?

MARY. What name?

JOE. The name the initials M. L. stand for. The initials on your bag.

MARY. No.   10

JOE (*after a long pause, thinking deeply what the name might be, turning a card, looking into the beautiful face of the woman*). Margie Longworthy?

MARY (*all this is very natural and sincere, no comedy on the part of the people involved: they are both solemn, being drunk*). No.

JOE (*his voice higher-pitched, as though he were growing a little alarmed*). Midge 20 Laurie? (MARY *shakes her head.*) My initials are J. T.

MARY (*pause*). John?

JOE. No. (*Pause.*) Martha Lancaster?

MARY. No. (*Slight pause.*) Joseph?

JOE. Well, not exactly. That's my first name, but everybody calls me Joe. The last name is the tough one. I'll help you a little. I'm Irish. (*Pause.*) Is it just plain Mary?

MARY. Yes, it is. I'm Irish, too. At least on my father's side. English on my mother's side.

JOE. I'm Irish on both sides. Mary's one of my favorite names. I guess that's why I didn't think of it. I met a girl in Mexico City named Mary once. She was an American from Philadelphia. She got married there. In Mexico City, I mean. While I was 40 *there.* We were in love, too. At least *I* was. You never know about anyone else. They were engaged, you see, and her mother was with her, so they went through with it. Must have been six or seven years ago. She's probably got three or four children by this time.

MARY. Are you still in love with her?

JOE. Well—no. To tell you the truth, I'm not sure. I guess I am. I didn't even know she was engaged until a couple of days before they got married. I thought *I* was going to marry her. I kept thinking all the time about the kind of kids we would be likely to have. My favorite was the third one. The first two were fine. Handsome and fine and intelligent, but that third one was different. Dumb and goofy-looking. I liked *him* a lot. When she told me she was going to be married, I didn't feel so bad about the first two, it was that dumb one.

MARY (*after a pause of some few seconds*). What do you do?

JOE. Do? To tell you the truth, nothing.

MARY. Do you always drink a great deal?

JOE (*scientifically*). Not *always.* Only when I'm awake. I sleep seven or eight hours every night, you know.

MARY. How nice. I mean to drink when you're awake.

JOE (*thoughtfully*). It's a privilege.

MARY. Do you really *like* to drink?

JOE (*positively*). As much as I like to breathe.

MARY (*beautifully*). Why?

JOE (*dramatically*). Why do I like to drink? (*Pause.*) Because I don't like to be gypped. Because I don't like to be dead most of the time and just a little alive every once in a long while. (*Pause.*) If I don't drink, I become fascinated by unimportant things— like everybody else. I get busy. Do things. All kinds of little stupid things, for all kinds of little stupid reasons. Proud, selfish, *ordinary* things. I've done them. Now I don't do anything. *I live all the time.* Then I go to sleep. (*Pause.*)

MARY. Do you sleep well?

JOE (*taking it for granted*). Of course.

MARY (*quietly, almost with tenderness*). What are your plans?

JOE (*loudly, but also tenderly*). Plans? I haven't *got* any. *I just get up.*

MARY (*beginning to understand everything*). Oh yes. Yes, of course.

[DUDLEY *puts a nickel in the phonograph.*]

JOE (*thoughtfully*). Why do I drink? (*Pause, while he thinks about it. The thinking appears to be profound and complex, and has the effect of giving his face a very comical and naïve expression.*) That question calls for a pretty complicated answer. (*He smiles abstractly.*)

MARY. Oh, I didn't mean——

JOE (*swiftly, gallantly*). No. No. I *insist.* I *know* why. It's just a matter of finding words. Little ones.

MARY. It really doesn't matter.

JOE (*seriously*). Oh yes it does. (*Clinically.*) Now, why do I drink? (*Scientifically.*) No. Why does *anybody* drink? (*Working it out.*) Every day has twenty-four hours.

MARY (*sadly, but brightly*). Yes, that's true.

JOE. Twenty-four hours. Out of the twenty-four hours at *least* twenty-three and a half are—my God, I don't know why—dull, dead, boring, empty, and murderous. Minutes on the clock, *not time of living.* It doesn't make any difference who you are or what you do, twenty-three and a half hours of the twenty-four are spent *waiting.*

MARY. Waiting?

JOE (*gesturing, loudly*). And the more you wait, the less there is to wait *for.*

MARY (*attentively, beautifully his student*). Oh?

JOE (*continuing*). That goes on for days and days, and weeks and months and years and years, and the first thing you know *all* the years are dead. All the minutes are dead. You yourself are dead. There's nothing to wait for any more. Nothing except *minutes* on the *clock.* No time of life. Nothing but minutes, and idiocy. Beautiful, bright, intelligent idiocy. (*Pause.*) Does that answer your question?

MARY (*earnestly*). I'm afraid it does. Thank you. You shouldn't have gone to all the trouble.

JOE. No trouble at all. (*Pause.*) You have children?

MARY. Yes. Two. A son and a daughter.

JOE (*delighted*). How swell. Do they look like you?

MARY. Yes.

JOE. Then why are you sad?

MARY. I was always sad. It's just that after I was married I was allowed to drink.

JOE (*eagerly*). Who are you waiting for?

MARY. No one.

JOE (*smiling*). I'm not waiting for anybody, either.

MARY. My husband, of course.

JOE. Oh, sure.

MARY. He's a lawyer.

JOE (*standing, leaning on the table*). He's a great guy. I like him. I'm very fond of him.

MARY (*listening*). You have responsibilities?

JOE (*loudly*). *One,* and *thousands.* As a matter of fact, I feel responsible to everybody. At least to everybody I meet. I've been trying for three years to find out if it's possible to live what I think is a civilized life. I mean a life that can't hurt any other life.

MARY. You're famous?

JOE. Very. Utterly unknown, but very famous. Would you like to dance?

MARY. All right.

JOE (*loudly*). I'm sorry. I don't dance. I didn't think you'd like to.

MARY. To tell you the truth, I don't like to dance at all.

JOE (*proudly. Commentator*). I can hardly walk.

MARY. You mean you're tight?

JOE (*smiling*). *No.* I mean *all* the time.

MARY (*looking at him closely*). Were you ever in Paris?

JOE. In 1929, and again in 1934.

MARY. What month of 1934?

JOE. Most of April, all of May, and a little of June.

MARY. I was there in November and December that year.

JOE. We were there almost at the same time. You were married?

MARY. Engaged. (*They are silent a moment, looking at one another. Quietly and with great charm.*) Are you *really* in love with me?

JOE. Yes.

MARY. Is it the champagne?

JOE. Yes. Partly, at least. (*He sits down.*)

MARY. If you don't see me again, will you be very unhappy?

JOE. Very.

MARY (*getting up*). I'm so pleased. (*JOE is deeply grieved that she is going. In fact, he is almost panic-stricken about it, getting up in a way that is full of furious sorrow and regret.*) I must go now. Please don't get up. (*JOE is up, staring at her with amazement.*) Good-by.

JOE (*simply*). Good-by.

[*The woman stands looking at him a moment, then turns and goes. JOE stands staring after her for a long time. Just as he is slowly sitting down again, the NEWSBOY enters, and goes to JOE's table.*]

NEWSBOY. Paper, mister?

JOE. How many you got this time?

NEWSBOY. Eleven.

[*JOE buys them all, looks at the lousy headlines, throws them away. The NEWSBOY looks at JOE, amazed. He walks over to NICK at the bar.*]

NEWSBOY (*troubled*). Hey, mister, do you own this place?

NICK (*casually but emphatically*). I own this place.

NEWSBOY. Can you use a great lyric tenor?

NICK (*almost to himself*). Great lyric tenor? (*Loudly.*) Who?

NEWSBOY (*loud and the least bit angry*). Me. I'm getting too big to sell papers. I don't want to holler headlines all the time. I want to *sing.* You can use a great lyric tenor, can't you?

NICK. What's lyric about you?

NEWSBOY (*voice high-pitched, confused*). My voice.

NICK. Oh. (*Slight pause, giving in.*) All right, then—sing!

[*The NEWSBOY breaks into swift and beautiful song: "When Irish Eyes Are Smiling." NICK and JOE listen carefully, NICK with wonder, JOE with amazement and delight.*]

NEWSBOY (*singing*).

When Irish eyes are smiling,
Sure 'tis like a morn in spring.
In the lilt of Irish laughter,
You can hear the angels sing.
When Irish hearts are happy,
All the world seems bright and gay.
But when Irish eyes are smiling——

NICK (*loudly, swiftly*). Are you Irish?

NEWSBOY (*speaking swiftly, loudly, a little impatient with the irrelevant question*). No. I'm Greek. (*He finishes the song, singing louder than ever.*)

Sure they steal your heart away.

[*He turns to NICK dramatically, like a vaudeville singer begging his audience for applause. NICK studies the boy eagerly. JOE gets to his feet, and leans toward the boy and NICK.*]

NICK. Not bad. Let me hear you again about a year from now.

NEWSBOY (*thrilled*). Honest?

NICK. Yeah. Along about November seventh, 1940.

NEWSBOY (*happier than ever before in his life, running over to* JOE). Did you hear it too, mister?

JOE. Yes, and it's great. What part of Greece?

NEWSBOY. Salonica. Gosh, mister. Thanks.

JOE. Don't wait a year. Come back with some papers a little later. You're a great singer.

NEWSBOY (*thrilled and excited*). Aw, thanks, mister. So long. (*Running, to* NICK). Thanks, mister.

[*He runs out.* JOE *and* NICK *look at the swinging doors.* JOE *sits down.* NICK *laughs.*]

NICK. Joe, people are so wonderful. Look at that kid.

JOE. Of course they're wonderful. Every one of them is wonderful.

[MCCARTHY *and* KRUPP *come in, talking.* MCCARTHY *is a big man in work clothes, which make him seem very young. He is wearing black jeans, and a blue workman's shirt. No tie. No hat. He has broad shoulders, a lean intelligent face, thick black hair. In his right back pocket is the longshoreman's hook. His arms are long and hairy. His sleeves are rolled up to just below his elbows. He is a casual man, easy-going in movement, sharp in perception, swift in appreciation of charm or innocence or comedy, and gentle in spirit. His speech is clear and full of warmth. His voice is powerful, but modulated. He enjoys the world, in spite of the mess it is, and he is fond of people, in spite of the mess they are.* KRUPP *is not quite as tall or broad-shouldered as* MCCARTHY. *He is physically encumbered by his uniform, club, pistol, belt, and cap. And he is plainly not at home in the role of policeman. His movement is stiff and unintentionally pompous. He is a naïve man, essentially good. His understanding is less than* MCCARTHY'S, *but he is honest and he doesn't try to bluff.*]

KRUPP. You don't understand what I mean. Hi-ya, Joe.

JOE. Hello, Krupp.

MCCARTHY. Hi-ya, Joe.

JOE. Hello, McCarthy.

KRUPP. Two beers, Nick. (*To* MCCARTHY.) All I do is carry out orders, carry out orders. I don't know what the idea is behind the order. Who it's for, or who it's against, or why. All I do is carry it out.

[NICK *gives them beer.*]

MCCARTHY. You don't read enough.

KRUPP. I do read. I read the *Examiner* every morning. The *Call-Bulletin* every night.

MCCARTHY. And carry out orders. What are the orders now?

KRUPP. To keep the peace down here on the water front.

MCCARTHY. Keep it for who? (*To* JOE.) Right?

JOE (*sorrowfully*). Right.

KRUPP. How do I know for who? The peace. Just keep it.

MCCARTHY. It's got to be kept for somebody. Who would you suspect it's kept for?

KRUPP. For citizens!

MCCARTHY. I'm a citizen!

KRUPP. All right, I'm keeping it for you.

MCCARTHY. By hitting me over the head with a club? (*To* JOE.) Right?

JOE (*melancholy, with remembrance*). I don't know.

KRUPP. Mac, you know I never hit you over the head with a club.

MCCARTHY. But you will if you're on duty at the time and happen to stand on the opposite side of myself, on duty.

KRUPP. We went to Mission High together. We were always good friends. The only time we ever fought was that time over Alma Haggerty. Did *you* marry Alma Haggerty? (*To* JOE.) Right?

JOE. Everything's right.

MCCARTHY. No. Did you? (*To* JOE.) Joe, are you with me or against me?

JOE. I'm with everybody. One at a time.

KRUPP. No. And that's just what I mean.

MCCARTHY. You mean neither one of us is going to marry the thing we're fighting for?

KRUPP. *I don't even know what it is.*

MCCARTHY. You don't read enough, I tell you.

KRUPP. Mac, you don't know what you're fighting for, either.

MCCARTHY. It's so simple it's fantastic.

KRUPP. All right, what are you fighting for?

MCCARTHY. For the rights of the inferior. Right?

JOE. Something like that.

KRUPP. The who?

MCCARTHY. The inferior. The world full of Mahoneys who haven't got what it takes to make monkeys out of everybody else, near by. The men who were created equal. Remember?

KRUPP. Mac, you're not inferior.

MCCARTHY. I'm a longshoreman. And an idealist. I'm a man with too much brawn to be an intellectual, exclusively. I married a small, sensitive, cultured woman so that my kids would be sissies instead of suckers. A strong man with any sensibility has no choice in this world but to be a heel, or a *worker*. I haven't the heart to be a heel, so I'm a worker. I've got a son in high school who's already thinking of being a writer.

KRUPP. I wanted to be a writer once.

JOE. Wonderful. (*He puts down the paper, looks at* KRUPP *and* MCCARTHY.)

MCCARTHY. They *all* wanted to be writers. Every maniac in the world

that ever brought about the murder of people through war started out in an attic or a basement writing poetry. It stank. So they got even by becoming important heels. And it's still going on.

KRUPP. Is it really, Joe?

JOE. Look at today's paper.

MCCARTHY. Right now on Telegraph Hill is some punk who is trying to be Shakespeare. Ten years from now he'll be a Senator. Or a communist.

KRUPP. Somebody ought to do something about it.

MCCARTHY (*mischievously, with laughter in his voice*). The thing to do is to have more magazines. Hundreds of them. *Thousands*. Print everything they write, so they'll believe they're immortal. That way keep them from going haywire.

KRUPP. Mac, you ought to be a writer yourself.

MCCARTHY. I hate the tribe. They're mischief-makers. Right?

JOE (*swiftly*). Everything's right. Right and wrong.

KRUPP. Then why do you read?

MCCARTHY (*laughing*). It's relaxing. It's soothing. (*Pause.*) The lousiest people born into the world are writers. Language is all right. It's the people who use language that are lousy. (*The* ARAB *has moved a little closer, and is listening carefully. To the* ARAB.) What do you think, brother?

ARAB (*after making many faces, thinking very deeply*). No foundation. All the way down the line. What. What-not. Nothing. I go walk and look at sky. (*He goes.*)

KRUPP. What? What-not? (*To* JOE.) What's that mean?

JOE (*slowly, thinking, remembering*). What? What-not? That means this side, that side. Inhale, exhale. What: birth.

What-not: death. The inevitable, the astounding, the magnificent seed of growth and decay in all things. Beginning, and end. That man, in his own way, is a prophet. He is one who, with the help of *beer*, is able to reach that state of deep understanding in which what and what-not, the reasonable and the unreasonable, are *one*.

McCARTHY. Right.

KRUPP. If you can understand that kind of talk, how can you be a longshoreman?

McCARTHY. I come from a long line of McCarthys who never married or slept with anything but the most powerful and quarrelsome flesh. (*He drinks beer.*)

KRUPP. I could listen to you two guys for hours, but I'll be damned if I know what the hell you're talking about.

McCARTHY. The consequence is that all the McCarthys are too great and too strong to be heroes. Only the weak and unsure perform the heroic. They've *got* to. The more heroes you have, the worse the history of the world becomes. Right?

JOE. Go outside and look at it.

KRUPP. You sure can philos—philosoph—— Boy, you can talk.

McCARTHY. I wouldn't talk this way to anyone but a man in uniform, and a man who couldn't understand a word of what I was saying. The party I'm speaking of, my friend, is *YOU*.

[*The phone rings.* HARRY *gets up from his table suddenly and begins a new dance.*]

KRUPP (*noticing him, with great authority*). Here. Here. What do you think you're doing?

HARRY (*stopping*). I just got an idea for a new dance. I'm trying it out. Nick. Nick, the phone's ringing.

KRUPP (*to* McCARTHY). Has he got a right to do that?

McCARTHY. The living have danced from the beginning of time. I might even say the dance and the life have moved along together, until now we have—— (*To* HARRY.) Go into your dance, son, and show us what we have.

HARRY. I haven't got it worked out completely yet, but it starts out like this. (*He dances.*)

NICK (*on the phone*). Nick's Pacific Street Restaurant, Saloon, and Entertainment Palace. Good afternoon. Nick speaking. (*Listens.*) Who? (*Turns around.*) Is there a Dudley Bostwick in the joint?

[DUDLEY *jumps to his feet and goes to the phone.*]

DUDLEY (*on the phone*). Hello. Elsie? (*Listens.*) You're coming down? (*Elated. To the saloon.*) She's coming down. (*Pause.*) No. I won't drink. Aw, gosh, Elsie.

[*He hangs up, looks about him strangely, as if he were just born, walks around touching things, putting chairs in place, and so on.*]

McCARTHY (*to* HARRY). Splendid. Splendid.

HARRY. Then I go into this little routine. (*He demonstrates.*)

KRUPP. Is that good, Mac?

McCARTHY. It's awful, but it's honest and ambitious, like everything else in this great country.

HARRY. Then I work along into this. (*He demonstrates.*) And *this* is where I really get going. (*He finishes the dance.*)

McCARTHY. Excellent. A most satisfying demonstration of the present state of the American body and soul. Son, you're a genius.

HARRY (*delighted, shaking hands with* McCARTHY). I go on in front of an audience for the first time in my life tonight.

McCARTHY. They'll be delighted. Where'd you learn to dance?

HARRY. Never took a lesson in my life. I'm a natural-born dancer. And *comedian*, too.

McCARTHY (*astounded*). You can make people *laugh?*

HARRY (*dumbly*). I can be funny, but they won't laugh.

McCARTHY. That's odd. Why not?

HARRY. I don't know. They just won't laugh.

McCARTHY. Would you care to be funny now?

HARRY. I'd like to try out a new monologue I've been thinking about.

McCARTHY. Please do. I promise you if it's funny I shall *roar* with laughter.

HARRY. This is it. (*Goes into the act, with much energy.*) I'm up at Sharkey's on 20 Turk Street. It's a quarter to nine, daylight-saving. Wednesday, the eleventh. What I've got is a headache and a 1918 nickel. What I *want* is a cup of coffee. If I buy a cup of coffee with the nickel, I've got to walk home. I've got an eight-ball problem. George the Greek is shooting a game of snooker with Pedro the Filipino. I'm in rags. They're wearing thirty- 30 five dollar suits, made to order. I haven't got a cigarette. They're smoking Bobby Burns panatelas. I'm thinking it over, like I always do. George the Greek is in a tough spot. If I buy a cup of coffee, I'll want another cup. What happens? My *ear* aches! My ear. George the Greek takes the cue. Chalks it. Studies the table. Touches the cue ball delicately. 40 Tick. What happens? He makes the three-ball! What do I do? I get confused. *I go out and buy a morning paper.* What the hell do I want with a morning paper? What I *want* is a cup of coffee, and a good used car. I go

out and buy a morning paper. Thursday, the twelfth. Maybe the headline's about *me*. I take a quick look. *No. The headline is not about me.* It's about Hitler. Seven thousand miles away. I'm here. Who the hell is Hitler? Who's behind the eight-ball? I turn around. *Everybody's behind the eight-ball!*

[*Pause.* KRUPP *moves toward* HARRY *as if to make an important arrest.* HARRY *moves to the swinging doors.* McCARTHY *stops* KRUPP.]

McCARTHY (*to* HARRY). It's the funniest thing I've ever heard. Or *seen*, for that matter.

HARRY (*coming back to* McCARTHY). Then why don't you laugh?

McCARTHY. I don't know, *yet*.

HARRY. I'm always getting funny ideas that nobody will laugh at.

McCARTHY (*thoughtfully*). It may be that you've stumbled headlong into a new kind of comedy.

HARRY. Well, what good is it if it doesn't make anybody laugh?

McCARTHY. There are *kinds* of laughter, son. I must say, in all truth, that I *am* laughing, although not *out loud*.

HARRY. I want to *hear* people laugh. *Out loud.* That's why I keep thinking of funny things to say.

McCARTHY. Well. They may catch on in time. Let's go, Krupp. So long, Joe.

[McCARTHY *and* KRUPP *go.*]

JOE. So long. (*After a moment's pause.*) Hey, Nick.

NICK. Yeah.

JOE. Bet McCarthy in the last race.

NICK. You're crazy. That horse is a double-crossing, no-good——

JOE. Bet everything you've got on McCarthy.

NICK. I'm not betting a nickel on him. You bet everything you've got on McCarthy.

JOE. I don't need money.

NICK. What makes you think McCarthy's going to win?

JOE. McCarthy's name's McCarthy, isn't it?

NICK. Yeah. So what?

JOE. The *horse* named McCarthy is going to win, *that's all*. Today.

NICK. Why?

JOE. You do what I tell you and everything will be all right.

NICK. McCarthy likes to talk, that's all. (*Pause.*) Where's Tom?

JOE. He'll be around. He'll be miserable, but he'll be around. Five or ten minutes more.

NICK. You don't believe that Kitty, do you? About being in burlesque?

JOE (*very clearly*). I believe dreams sooner than statistics.

NICK (*remembering*). She sure is somebody. Called me a dentist.

[TOM, *turning about, confused, troubled, comes in, and hurries to* JOE's *table*.]

JOE. What's the matter?

TOM. Here's your five, Joe. I'm in trouble again.

JOE. If it's not organic, it'll cure itself. If it is organic, science will cure it. What is it, organic or nonorganic?

TOM. Joe, I don't know—— (*He seems to be completely broken-down.*)

JOE. What's eating you? I want you to go on an errand for me.

TOM. It's Kitty.

JOE. What about her?

TOM. She's up in her room, crying.

JOE. Crying?

TOM. Yeah, she's been crying for over an hour. I been talking to her all this time, but she won't stop.

JOE. What's she crying about?

TOM. I don't know. I couldn't understand anything. She kept crying and telling me about a big house and collie dogs all around and flowers and one of her brothers's dead and the other one lost somewhere. Joe, I can't stand Kitty crying.

JOE. You want to marry the girl?

TOM (*nodding*). Yeah.

JOE (*curious and sincere*). Why?

TOM. I don't know why, exactly, Joe. (*Pause.*) Joe, I don't like to think of Kitty out in the streets. I guess I love her, that's all.

JOE. She's a nice girl.

TOM. She's like an angel. She's not like those other streetwalkers.

JOE (*swiftly*). Here. Take all this money and run next door to Frankie's and bet it on the nose of McCarthy.

TOM (*swiftly*). All this money, Joe? McCarthy?

JOE. Yeah. Hurry.

TOM (*going*). Ah, Joe. If McCarthy wins we'll be rich.

JOE. Get going, will you?

[TOM *runs out and nearly knocks over the* ARAB *coming back in.* NICK *fills him a beer without a word.*]

ARAB. No foundation, anywhere. Whole world. No foundation. All the way down the line.

NICK (*angry*). McCarthy! Just because you got a little lucky this morning, you have to go to work and throw away eighty bucks.

JOE. He wants to marry her.

NICK. Suppose she doesn't want to marry *him?*

JOE (*amazed*). Oh yeah. (*Thinking.*) Now, why wouldn't she want to marry a nice guy like Tom?

NICK. She's been in burlesque. She's had flowers sent to her by European royalty. She's dined with young men of quality and social position. She's above Tom.

[TOM *comes running in.*]

TOM (*disgusted*). They were running when I got there. Frankie wouldn't take the bet. McCarthy didn't get a call till the stretch. I thought we were going to save all this money. Then McCarthy won by *two* lengths.

JOE. What'd he pay, fifteen to one?

TOM. Better, but Frankie wouldn't take the bet.

NICK (*throwing a dish towel across the room*). Well, for the love of Mike.

JOE. Give me the money.

TOM (*giving back the money*). We would have had about a thousand five hundred dollars.

JOE (*bored, casually, inventing*). Go up to Schwabacher-Frey and get me the biggest Rand-McNally map of the nations of Europe they've got. On your way back stop at one of the pawnshops on Third Street and buy me a good revolver and some car- 20 tridges.

TOM. She's up in her room crying, Joe.

JOE. Go get me those things.

NICK. What are you going to do, study the map and then go out and shoot somebody?

JOE. I want to read the names of some European towns and rivers and valleys and mountains.

NICK. What do you want with the re- 30 volver?

JOE. I want to study it. I'm interested in things. Here's twenty dollars, Tom. Now go get them things.

TOM. A big map of Europe. And a revolver.

JOE. Get a good one. Tell the man you don't know anything about firearms and you're trusting him not to fool you. Don't pay more than ten 40 dollars.

TOM. Joe, you got something on your mind. Don't go fool with a revolver.

JOE. Be sure it's a good one.

TOM. Joe.

JOE (*irritated*). What, Tom?

TOM. Joe, what do you send me out for crazy things for all the time?

JOE (*angry*). They're not crazy, Tom. Now get going.

TOM. What about Kitty, Joe?

JOE. Let her cry. It'll do her good.

TOM. If she comes in here while I'm gone, talk to her, will you, Joe? Tell her about me.

10 JOE. O.K. Get going. Don't load that gun. Just buy it and bring it here.

TOM (*going*). You won't catch me loading any gun.

JOE. Wait a minute. Take these toys away.

TOM. Where'll I take them?

JOE. Give them to some kid. (*Pause.*) No. Take them up to Kitty. Toys stopped me from crying once. That's the reason I had you buy them. I wanted to see if I could find out *why* they stopped me from crying. I remember they seemed awfully stupid at the time.

TOM. Shall I, Joe? Take them up to Kitty? Do you think they'd stop *her* from crying?

JOE. They might. You get curious about the way they work and you forget whatever it is you're remembering that's making you cry. That's what they're for.

TOM. Yeah. Sure. The girl at the store asked me what I wanted with toys. I'll take them up to Kitty. (*Tragically.*) She's like a little girl. (*He goes.*)

WESLEY. Mr. Nick, can I play the piano again?

NICK. Sure. Practice all you like—until I tell you to stop.

WESLEY. You going to pay me for playing the piano?

NICK. Sure. I'll give you enough to get by on.

WESLEY (*amazed and delighted*). Get money for playing the piano?

[*He goes to the piano and begins to play quietly.* HARRY *goes up on the little stage and listens to the music. After a while he begins a soft-shoe dance.*]

NICK. What were you crying about?

JOE. My mother.

NICK. What about her?

JOE. She was dead. I stopped crying when they gave me the toys.

[NICK'S MOTHER, *a little old woman of sixty or so, dressed plainly in black, her face shining, comes in briskly, chattering loudly in Italian, gesturing.* NICK *is delighted to see her.*]

NICK'S MOTHER (*in Italian*). Everything all right, Nickie?

NICK (*in Italian*). Sure, Mamma.

[NICK'S MOTHER *leaves as gaily and as noisily as she came, after half a minute of loud Italian family talk.*]

JOE. Who was that?

NICK (*to* JOE, *proudly and a little sadly*). My mother. (*Still looking at the swinging doors.*)

JOE. What'd she say?

NICK. Nothing. Just wanted to see me. (*Pause.*) What do you want with that gun?

JOE. I study things, Nick.

[*An old man who looks as if he might have been Kit Carson at one time walks in importantly, moves about, and finally stands at* JOE'S *table.*]

KIT CARSON. Murphy's the name. Just an old trapper. Mind if I sit down?

JOE. Be delighted. What'll you drink?

KIT CARSON (*sitting down*). Beer. Same as I've been drinking. And thanks.

JOE (*to* NICK). Glass of beer, Nick.

[NICK *brings the beer to the table,* KIT CARSON *swallows it in one swig, wipes his big white mustache with the back of his right hand.*]

KIT CARSON (*moving in*). I don't suppose you ever fell in love with a midget weighing thirty-nine pounds?

JOE (*studying the man*). Can't say I have, but have another beer.

KIT CARSON (*intimately*). Thanks, thanks. Down in Gallup, twenty-years ago. Fellow by the name of Rufus Jenkins came to town with six white horses and two black ones. Said he wanted a man to break the horses for him because his left leg was wood and he couldn't do it. Had a meeting at Parker's Mercantile Store and finally came to blows, me and Henry Walpal. Bashed his head with a brass cuspidor and ran away to Mexico, but he didn't die.

Couldn't speak a word. Took up with a cattle-breeder named Diego, educated in California. Spoke the language better than you and me. Said, "Your job, Murph, is to feed them prize bulls." I said, "Fine, what'll I feed them?" He said, "Hay, lettuce, salt, beer, and aspirin." Came to blows two days later over an accordion he claimed I stole. I had *borrowed* it. During the fight I busted it over his head; ruined one of the finest accordions I ever saw. Grabbed a horse and rode back across the border. Texas. Got to talking with a fellow who looked honest. Turned out to be a Ranger who was looking for me.

JOE. Yeah. You were saying, a thirty-nine-pound midget.

KIT CARSON. Will I ever forget that lady? Will I ever get over that Amazon of small proportions?

JOE. Will you?

KIT CARSON. If I live to be sixty.

JOE. Sixty? You look more than sixty now.

KIT CARSON. That's trouble showing in my face. Trouble and complications. I was fifty-eight three months ago.

JOE. That accounts for it, then. Go ahead, tell me more.

KIT CARSON. Told the Texas Ranger my name was Rothstein, mining engineer from Pennsylvania, looking for something worth while. Mentioned two places in Houston. Nearly lost an eye early one morning, going down the stairs. Ran into a six-footer with an iron claw where his right hand was [10] supposed to be. Said, "You broke up my home." Told him I was a stranger in Houston. The girls gathered at the top of the stairs to see a fight. Seven of them. Six feet and an iron claw. That's bad on the nerves. Kicked him in the mouth when he swung for my head with the claw. Would have lost an eye except for quick thinking. He rolled into the gutter and pulled a [20] gun. Fired seven times. I was back upstairs. Left the place an hour later, dressed in silk and feathers, with a hat swung around over my face. Saw him standing on the corner, waiting. Said, "Care for a wiggle?" Said he didn't. I went on down the street and left town. I don't suppose you ever had to put a dress on to save your skin, did you?

JOE. No, and I never fell in love with a [30] midget weighing thirty-nine pounds. Have another beer?

KIT CARSON. Thanks. (*Swallows a glass of beer.*) Ever try to herd cattle on a bicycle?

JOE. No. I never got around to that.

KIT CARSON. Left Houston with sixty cents in my pocket, gift of a girl named Lucinda. Walked fourteen [40] miles in fourteen hours. Big house with barb wire all around, and big dogs. One thing I never could get around. Walked past the gate, anyway, from hunger and thirst. Dogs jumped up and came for me. Walked right into them, growing older every second. Went up to the door and knocked. Big Negress opened the door, closed it quick. Said, "On your way, white trash." Knocked again. Said, "On your way." Again. "On your way." Again. This time the old man himself opened the door, ninety, if he was a day. Sawed-off shotgun, too. Said, "I ain't looking for trouble, Father. I'm hungry and thirsty, name's Cavanaugh." Took me in and made mint juleps for the two of us. Said, "Living here alone, Father?" Said, "Drink and ask no questions. Maybe I am and maybe I ain't. You saw the lady. Draw your own conclusions." I'd heard of that, but didn't wink out of tact. If I told you that old Southern gentleman was my grandfather, you wouldn't believe me, would you?

JOE. I might.

KIT CARSON. Well, it so happens he wasn't. Would have been romantic if he had been, though.

JOE. Where did you herd cattle on a bicycle?

KIT CARSON. Toledo, Ohio, 1918.

JOE. Toledo, Ohio? They don't herd cattle in Toledo.

KIT CARSON. They don't any more. They did in 1918. One fellow did, leastaways. Bookkeeper named Sam Gold. Straight from the East Side, New York. Sombrero, lariats, Bull Durham, two head of cattle and two bicycles. Called his place The Gold Bar Ranch, two acres, just outside the city limits. That was the year of the war, you'll remember.

JOE. Yeah, I remember, but how about herding them two cows on a bicycle? How'd you do it?

KIT CARSON. Easiest thing in the world. Rode no hands. Had to, otherwise couldn't lasso the cows. Worked for Sam Gold till the cows ran away. Bicycles scared them. They went into Toledo. Never saw hide nor hair of them again. Advertised in every paper, but never got them back. Broke his heart. Sold both bikes and returned to New York. Took four aces from a deck of red cards and walked to town. Poker. Fellow in the game named Chuck Collins, liked to gamble. Told him with a smile I didn't suppose he'd care to bet a hundred dollars I wouldn't hold four aces the next hand. Called it. My cards were red on the blank side. The other cards were blue. Plumb forgot all about it. Showed him four aces. Ace of spades, ace of clubs, ace of diamonds, ace of hearts. I'll remember them four cards if I live to be sixty. Would have been killed on the spot except for the hurricane that year.

JOE. Hurricane?

KIT CARSON. You haven't forgotten the Toledo hurricane of 1918, have you?

JOE. No. There was no hurricane in Toledo in 1918, or any other year.

KIT CARSON. For the love of God, then what do you suppose that commotion was? And how come I came to in Chicago, dream-walking down State Street?

JOE. I guess they scared you.

KIT CARSON. No, that wasn't it. You go back to the papers of November 1918 and I think you'll find there was a hurricane in Toledo. I remember sitting on the roof of a two-story house, floating northwest.

JOE (*seriously*). Northwest?

KIT CARSON. Now, son, don't tell me *you* don't believe me, either?

JOE (*Pause. Very seriously, energetically and sharply*). Of course I believe you.

Living is an art. It's not bookkeeping. It takes a lot of rehearsing for a man to get to be himself.

KIT CARSON (*thoughtfully, smiling, and amazed*). You're the first man I've ever met who believes me.

JOE (*seriously*). Have another beer.

[TOM *comes in with the Rand-McNally book, the revolver, and the box of cartridges.* KIT *goes to the bar.*]

JOE (*to* TOM). Did you give her the toys?

TOM. Yeah, I gave them to her.

JOE. Did she stop crying?

TOM. No. She started crying harder than ever.

JOE. That's funny. I wonder why.

TOM. Joe, if I was a minute earlier, Frankie would have taken the bet and now we'd have about a thousand five hundred dollars. How much of it would you have given me, Joe?

JOE. If she'd marry you—*all* of it.

TOM. Would you, Joe?

JOE (*opening the packages, examining the book first, and the revolver next*). Sure. In this realm there's only one subject, and you're it. It's my duty to see that my subject is happy.

TOM. Joe, do you think we'll ever have eighty dollars for a race sometime again when there's a fifteen-to-one shot that we like, weather good, track fast, they get off to a good start, our horse doesn't get a call till the stretch, we think we're going to lose all that money, and then it wins, by a nose?

JOE. I didn't quite get that.

TOM. You know what I mean.

JOE. You mean the impossible. No, Tom, we won't. We were just a little late, that's all.

TOM. We might, Joe.

JOE. It's not likely.

TOM. Then how am I ever going to make enough money to marry her?

JOE. I don't know, Tom. Maybe you aren't.

TOM. Joe, I got to marry Kitty. (*Shaking his head.*) You ought to see the crazy room she lives in.

JOE. What kind of a room is it?

TOM. It's little. It crowds you in. It's bad, Joe. Kitty don't belong in a place like that.

JOE. You want to take her away from there?

TOM. Yeah. I want her to live in a house where there's room enough to live. Kitty ought to have a garden, or something.

JOE. You want to take care of her?

TOM. Yeah, sure, Joe. I ought to take care of somebody good that makes me feel like *I'm* somebody.

JOE. That means you'll have to get a job. What can you do?

TOM. I finished high school, but I don't know what I can do.

JOE. Sometimes when you think about it, what do you think you'd like to do?

TOM. Just sit around like you, Joe, and have somebody run errands for me and drink champagne and take things easy and never be broke and never worry about money.

JOE. That's a noble ambition.

NICK (*to* JOE). How do you do it?

JOE. I really don't know, but I think you've got to have the full co-operation of the Good Lord.

NICK. I can't understand the way you talk.

TOM. Joe, shall I go back and see if I can get her to stop crying?

JOE. Give me a hand and I'll go with you.

TOM (*amazed*). What! You're going to get up already?

JOE. She's crying, isn't she?

TOM. She's crying. Worse than ever now.

JOE. I thought the toys would stop her.

TOM. I've seen you sit in one place from four in the morning till two the next morning.

JOE. At my best, Tom, I don't travel by foot. That's all. Come on. Give me a hand. I'll find some way to stop her from crying.

TOM (*helping* JOE). Joe, I never did tell you. You're a different kind of a guy.

JOE (*swiftly, a little angry*). Don't be silly. I don't understand things. I'm trying to understand them.

[JOE *is a little drunk. They go out together. The lights go down slowly, while* WESLEY *plays the piano, and come up slowly on:*]

ACT THREE

A cheap bed in Nick's to indicate Room 21 of the New York Hotel, upstairs, around the corner from Nick's. The bed can be at the center of Nick's, or up on the little stage. Everything in Nick's is the same, except that all the people are silent, immobile, and in darkness except WESLEY, *who is playing the piano softly and sadly.* KITTY DUVAL, *in a dress she has carried around with her from the early days in Ohio, is seated on the bed, tying a ribbon in her hair. She looks at herself in a hand mirror. She is deeply grieved at the change she sees in herself. She takes off the ribbon, angry and hurt. She lifts a book from the bed and tries to read. She begins to sob again. She picks up an old picture of herself and looks at it. Sobs harder than ever, falling on the bed and burying her face. There is a knock, as if at the door.*

KITTY (*sobbing*). Who is it?

TOM'S VOICE. Kitty, it's me. Tom. Me and Joe.

[JOE, *followed by* TOM, *comes to the bed*

quietly. JOE *is holding a rather large toy carousel.* JOE *studies* KITTY *a moment. He sets the toy carousel on the floor, at the foot of* KITTY's *bed.*]

TOM (*standing over* KITTY *and bending down close to her*). Don't cry any more, Kitty.

KITTY (*not looking, sobbing*). I don't like this life.

[JOE *starts the carousel, which makes a* 10 *strange, sorrowful, tinkling music. The music begins slowly, becomes swift, gradually slows down, and ends.* JOE *himself is interested in the toy, watches and listens to it carefully.*]

TOM (*eagerly*). Kitty. Joe got up from his chair at Nick's just to get you a toy and come here. This one makes music. We rode all over town in a cab to get it. Listen. 20

[KITTY *sits up slowly, listening, while* TOM *watches her. Everything happens slowly and somberly.* KITTY *notices the photograph of herself when she was a little girl. Lifts it, and looks at it again.*]

TOM (*looking*). Who's that little girl, Kitty?

KITTY. That's me. When I was seven.
  [KITTY *hands the photo to* TOM.]

TOM (*looking, smiling*). Gee, you're 30 pretty, Kitty.

[JOE *reaches up for the photograph, which* TOM *hands to him.* TOM *returns to* KITTY, *whom he finds as pretty now as she was at seven.* JOE *studies the photograph.* KITTY *looks up at* TOM. *There is no doubt that they really love one another.* JOE *looks up at them.*]

KITTY. Tom?

TOM (*eagerly*). Yeah, Kitty. 40

KITTY. Tom, when you were a little boy what did you want to be?

TOM (*a little bewildered, but eager to please her*). What, Kitty?

KITTY. Do you remember when you were a little boy?

TOM (*thoughtfully*). Yeah, I remember sometimes, Kitty.

KITTY. What did you want to be?

TOM (*looks at* JOE. JOE *holds* TOM's *eyes a moment. Then* TOM *is able to speak*). Sometimes I wanted to be a locomotive engineer. Sometimes I wanted to be a policeman.

KITTY. I wanted to be a great actress. (*She looks up into* TOM's *face.*) Tom, didn't you ever want to be a doctor?

TOM (*looks at* JOE. JOE *holds* TOM's *eyes again, encouraging* TOM *by his serious expression to go on talking*). Yeah, now I remember. Sure, Kitty. I wanted to be a doctor—*once.*

KITTY (*smiling sadly*). I'm so glad. Because I wanted to be an actress and have a young doctor come to the theater and see me and fall in love with me and send me flowers.

[JOE *pantomimes to* TOM, *demanding that he go on talking.*]

TOM. I would do that, Kitty.

KITTY. I wouldn't know who it was, and then one day I'd see him in the street and fall in love with him. I wouldn't know *he* was the one who was in love with me. I'd think about him all the time. I'd dream about him. I'd dream of being near him the rest of my life. I'd dream of having children that looked like him. I wouldn't be an actress all the time. Only until I found him and fell in love with him. After that we'd take a train and go to beautiful cities and see the wonderful people everywhere and give money to the poor and whenever people were sick he'd go to them and make them well again.

[TOM *looks at* JOE, *bewildered, confused, and full of sorrow.* KITTY *is deep in memory, almost in a trance.*]

JOE (*gently*). Talk to her, Tom. Be the wonderful young doctor she dreamed about and never found. Go ahead. Correct the errors of the world.

TOM. Joe. (*Pathetically.*) I don't know what to say.

[*There is rowdy singing in the hall. A loud young* VOICE *sings:* "*Sailing, sailing, over the bounding main.*"]

VOICE. Kitty. Oh, Kitty! (KITTY *stirs, shocked, coming out of the trance.*) Where the hell are you? Oh, Kitty. 10

[TOM *jumps up, furiously.*]

TOM (*to* JOE). Joe, I'll kill him.

KITTY (*fully herself again, terribly frightened*). Who is it?

[*She looks long and steadily at* TOM *and* JOE. TOM *is standing, excited and angry.* JOE *is completely at ease, his expression full of pity.* KITTY *buries her face in the bed.*]

JOE (*gently*). Tom. Just take him away.

VOICE. Here it is. Number 21. Three 20 naturals. Heaven. My blue heaven. The west, a nest, and you. Just Molly and me. (*Tragically.*) Ah, to hell with everything.

[*A young* SAILOR, *a good-looking boy of no more than twenty or so, who is only drunk and lonely, comes to the bed, singing sadly.*]

SAILOR. Hi-ya, Kitty. (*Pause.*) Oh. Visitors. Sorry. A thousand apologies. (*To* KITTY.) I'll come back later. 30

TOM (*taking him by the shoulders, furiously*). If you do, I'll kill you.

[JOE *holds* TOM. TOM *pushes the frightened boy away.*]

JOE (*somberly*). Tom. You stay here with Kitty. I'm going down to Union Square to hire an automobile. I'll be back in a few minutes. We'll ride out to the ocean and watch the sun go down. Then we'll ride down the Great Highway to Half Moon Bay. We'll have supper down there, and you and Kitty can dance.

TOM (*stupefied, unable to express his amazement and gratitude*). Joe, you mean you're going to go on an errand for me? You mean you're not going to send me?

JOE. That's right.

[*He gestures toward* KITTY, *indicating that* TOM *shall talk to her, protect the innocence in her which is in so much danger when* TOM *isn't near, which* TOM *loves so deeply.* JOE *leaves.* TOM *studies* KITTY, *his face becoming childlike and somber. He sets the carousel into motion, listens, watching* KITTY, *who lifts herself slowly, looking only at* TOM. TOM *lifts the turning carousel and moves it slowly toward* KITTY, *as though the toy were his heart. The piano music comes up loudly and the lights go down, while* HARRY *is heard dancing swiftly.*]

BLACKOUT

ACT FOUR

A little later. WESLEY, *the colored boy, is at the piano.* HARRY *is on the little stage, dancing.* NICK *is behind the bar. The* ARAB *is in his place.* KIT CARSON *is asleep on his folded arms. The* DRUNKARD *comes in. Goes to the telephone for the nickel that might be in the return chute.* NICK *comes to take him out. He gestures for* NICK *to hold on a minute. Then produces a half dollar.* NICK *goes behind the bar to serve the* DRUNKARD *whisky.*

THE DRUNKARD. To the old, God bless them. (*Another.*) To the new, God love them. (*Another.*) To—children and small animals, like little dogs that don't bite. (*Another. Loudly.*) To reforestation. (*Searches for money. Finds some.* To—President Taft. (*He goes out.*)

[*The telephone rings.*]

KIT CARSON (*jumping up, fighting*). Come

on, *all* of you, if you're looking for trouble. I never asked for quarter and I always gave it.

NICK (*reproachfully*). Hey, Kit Carson.

DUDLEY (*on the phone*). Hello. Who? Nick? Yes. He's here. (*To* NICK.) It's for you. I think it's important.

NICK (*going to the phone*). Important! *What's* important?

DUDLEY. He sounded like big shot. 10

NICK. Big *what?* (*To* WESLEY *and* HARRY.) Hey, you. Quiet. I want to hear this important stuff.

[WESLEY *stops playing the piano.* HARRY *stops dancing.* KIT CARSON *comes close to* NICK.]

KIT CARSON. If there's anything I can do, name it. I'll do it for you. I'm fifty-eight years old; been through three wars; married four times; the 20 father of countless children whose *names* I don't even know. I've got no money. I live from hand to mouth. But if there's anything I can do, name it. I'll do it.

NICK (*patiently*). Listen, Pop. For a moment, please sit down and go back to sleep—*for me.*

KIT CARSON. I can do that, too.

[*He sits down, folds his arms, and puts his* 30 *head into them. But not for long. As* NICK *begins to talk, he listens carefully, gets to his feet,* and *then begins to express in pantomime the moods of each of* NICK's *remarks.*]

NICK (*on phone*). Yeah? (*Pause.*) Who? Oh, I see. (*Listens.*) Why don't you leave them alone? (*Listens.*) The church people? Well, to hell with the church people. I'm a Catholic my- 40 self. (*Listens.*) All right. I'll send them away. I'll tell them to lay low for a couple of days. Yeah, I know how it is. (NICK's *daughter* ANNA *comes in shyly, looking at her father, and stands un-*

noticed by the piano.) What? (*Very angry.*) Listen. I don't like that Blick. He was here this morning, and I told him not to come back. I'll keep the girls out of here. You keep Blick out of here. (*Listens.*) I know his brother-in-law is important, but I don't want him to come down here. He looks for trouble everywhere, and he always finds it. I don't break any laws. I've got a dive in the lousiest part of town. Five years nobody's been robbed, murdered, or gypped. I leave people alone. Your swanky joints uptown make trouble for you every night. (NICK *gestures to* WESLEY—*keeps listening on the phone—puts his hand over the mouthpiece. To* WESLEY *and* HARRY.) Start playing again. My ears have got a headache. Go into your dance, son. (WESLEY *begins to play again.* HARRY *begins to dance.* NICK, *into the mouthpiece.*) Yeah. I'll keep them out. Just see that Blick doesn't come around and start something. (*Pause.*) O.K. (*He hangs up.*)

KIT CARSON. Trouble coming?

NICK. That lousy Vice Squad again. It's that gorilla Blick.

KIT CARSON. Anybody at all. You can count on me. What kind of a gorilla is this gorilla Blick?

NICK. Very dignified. Toenails on his fingers.

ANNA (*to* KIT CARSON, *with great, warm, beautiful pride, pointing at* NICK). That's my father.

KIT CARSON (*leaping with amazement at the beautiful voice, the wondrous face, the magnificent event*). Well, bless your heart, child. Bless your lovely heart. I had a little daughter point me out in a crowd once.

NICK (*surprised*). Anna. What the hell are you doing here? Get back home where you belong and help Grandma cook me some supper.

[ANNA *smiles at her father, understanding him, knowing that his words are words of love. She turns and goes, looking at him all the way out, as much as to say that she would cook for him the rest of her life.* NICK *stares at the swinging doors.* KIT CARSON *moves toward them, two or three steps.* ANNA *pushes open one of the doors* 10 *and peeks in, to look at her father again. She waves to him. Turns and runs.* NICK *is very sad. He doesn't know what to do. He gets a glass and a bottle. Pours himself a drink. Swallows some. It isn't enough, so he pours more and swallows the whole drink.*]

NICK (*to himself*). My beautiful, beautiful baby. Anna, she is you again. (*He brings out a handkerchief, touches his eyes,* 20 *and blows his nose.* KIT CARSON *moves close to* NICK, *watching* NICK'S *face.* NICK *looks at him. Loudly, almost making* KIT *jump.*) You're broke, aren't you?

KIT CARSON. Always. Always.

NICK. All right. Go into the kitchen and give Sam a hand. Eat some food and when you come back you can have a couple of beers.

KIT CARSON (*studying* NICK). Anything 30 at all. I know a good man when I see one. (*He goes.*)

[ELSIE MANDELSPIEGEL *comes into Nick's. She is a beautiful, dark girl, with a sorrowful, wise, dreaming face, almost on the verge of tears, and full of pity. There is an aura of dream about her. She moves softly and gently, as if everything around her were unreal and pathetic.* DUDLEY *doesn't notice her for a moment or two. When he* 40 *does finally see her, he is so amazed he can barely move or speak. Her presence has the effect of changing him completely. He gets up from his chair, as if in a trance, and walks toward her, smiling sadly.*]

ELSIE (*looking at him*). Hello, Dudley.

DUDLEY (*brokenhearted*). Elsie.

ELSIE. I'm sorry. (*Explaining.*) So many people are sick. Last night a little boy died. I love you, but—— (*She gestures, trying to indicate how hopeless love is. They sit down.*)

DUDLEY (*staring at her, stunned and quieted*). Elsie. You'll never know how glad I am to see you. Just to *see* you. (*Pathetically.*) I was afraid I'd never see you again. It was driving me crazy. I didn't want to live. Honest. (*He shakes his head mournfully, with dumb and beautiful affection. Two streetwalkers come in, and pause near* DUDLEY, *at the bar.*) I know. You told me before, but I can't help it, Elsie. I love you.

ELSIE (*quietly, somberly, gently, with great compassion*). I know you love me, and I love you, but don't you see love is impossible in this world?

DUDLEY. Maybe it isn't, Elsie.

ELSIE. Love is for birds. They have wings to fly away on when it's time for flying. For tigers in the jungle because they don't know their end. We know *our* end. Every night I watch over poor, dying men. I hear them breathing, crying, talking in their sleep. Crying for air and water and love, for mother and field and sunlight. We can never know love or greatness. We *should* know both.

DUDLEY (*deeply moved by her words*). Elsie, I love you.

ELSIE. You want to live. *I* want to live, too, but where? Where can we escape our poor world?

DUDLEY. Elsie, we'll find a place.

ELSIE (*smiling at him*). All right. We'll try again. We'll go together to a room in a cheap hotel, and dream that the world is beautiful, and that living is full of love and greatness. But in the morning, can we forget debts, and duties, and the cost of ridiculous things?

DUDLEY (*with blind faith*). Sure we can, Elsie.

ELSIE. All right, Dudley. Of course. Come on. The time for the new pathetic war has come. Let's hurry, before they dress you, stand you in line, hand you a gun, and have you kill and be killed.   10

[ELSIE *looks at him gently, and takes his hand.* DUDLEY *embraces her shyly, as if he might hurt her. They go, as if they were a couple of young animals. There is a moment of silence. One of the streetwalkers bursts out laughing.*]

KILLER. Nick, what the hell kind of a joint are you running?

NICK. Well, it's not out of the world. It's on a street in a city, and people   20 come and go. They bring whatever they've got with them and they say what they must say. (*Remembering.*) Oh yeah. Finnegan telephoned.

KILLER. That mouse in elephant's body?

THE OTHER STREETWALKER. What the hell does *he* want?

NICK. Spend your time at the movies for the next couple of days.

KILLER. They're all lousy. (*Mocking.*)   30 All about love.

NICK. Lousy or not lousy, for a couple of days the flatfoots are going to be romancing you, so stay out of here, and lay low.

KILLER. I always was a pushover for a man in uniform, with a badge, a club and a gun.

[KRUPP *comes into the place. The girls put down their drinks.*]   40

NICK. O.K., get going.

[*The girls begin to leave and meet* KRUPP.]

THE OTHER STREETWALKER. We was just going.

KILLER. We was formerly models at Magnin's.

[*They go.*]

KRUPP (*at the bar*). The strike isn't enough, so they've got to put us on the tails of the girls, too. I don't know. I wish to God I was back in the Sunset holding the hands of kids going home from school, where I belong. I don't like trouble. Give me a beer. (NICK *gives him a beer. He drinks some.*) Right now, McCarthy, my best friend, is with sixty strikers who want to stop the finks who are going to try to unload the *Mary Luckenbach* tonight. Why the hell McCarthy ever became a longshoreman instead of a professor of some kind is something I'll never know.

NICK. Cowboys and Indians, cops and robbers, longshoremen and finks.

KRUPP. They're all guys who are trying to be happy—trying to make a living, support a family, bring up children, enjoy sleep. Go to a movie, take a drive on Sunday. They're all good guys, so out of nowhere comes trouble. All they want is a chance to get out of debt and relax in front of a radio while Amos and Andy go through their act. What the hell do they always want to make trouble for? I been thinking everything over, Nick, and you know what I think?

NICK. No. What?

KRUPP. I think we're all crazy. It came to me while I was on my way to Pier 27. All of a sudden it hit me like a ton of bricks. A thing like that never happened to me before. Here we are in this wonderful world, full of all the wonderful things—here we are—all of us, and look at us. Just look at us. We're crazy. We're nuts. We've got everything, but we always feel lousy and dissatisfied just the same.

NICK. Of course we're crazy. Even so, we've got to go on living together.

(*He waves at the people in his joint.*)

KRUPP. There's no hope. I don't suppose it's right for an officer of the law to feel the way I feel, but, by God, right or not right, that's how I feel. Why are we all so lousy? This is a good world. It's wonderful to get up in the morning and go out for a little walk and smell the trees and see the streets and the kids going to school and the clouds in the sky. It's wonderful just to be able to move around and whistle a song if you feel like it, or maybe try to sing one. This is a nice world. So why do they make all the trouble?

NICK. I don't know. Why?

KRUPP. We're crazy, that's why. We're no good any more. All the corruption everywhere. The poor kids selling themselves. A couple of years ago they were in grammar school. Everybody trying to get a lot of money in a hurry. Everybody betting the horses. Nobody going quietly for a little walk to the ocean. Nobody taking things easy and not wanting to make some kind of a killing. Nick, I'm going to quit being a cop. Let somebody else keep law and order. The stuff I hear about at headquarters. I'm thirty-seven years old, and I still can't get used to it. The only trouble is, the wife'll raise hell.

NICK. Ah, the wife.

KRUPP. She's a wonderful woman, Nick. We've got two of the swellest boys in the world. Twelve and seven years old.

[*The* ARAB *gets up and moves closer to listen.*]

NICK. I didn't know that.

KRUPP. Sure. But what'll I do? I've wanted to quit for seven years. I wanted to quit the day they began putting me through the school. I didn't quit. What'll I do if I quit? Where's money going to be coming in from?

NICK. That's one of the reasons we're all crazy. We don't know where it's going to be coming in from, except from wherever it happens to be coming in from at the time, which we don't usually like.

KRUPP. Every once in a while I catch myself being mean, hating people just because they're down and out, broke and hungry, sick or drunk. And then when I'm with the stuffed shirts at headquarters, all of a sudden I'm nice to them, trying to make an impression. On who? People I don't like. And I feel disgusted. (*With finality.*) I'm going to quit. That's all. Quit. Out. I'm going to give them back the uniform and the gadgets that go with it. I don't want any part of it. This is a good world. What do they want to make all the trouble for all the time?

ARAB (*quietly, gently, with great understanding*). No foundation. All the way down the line.

KRUPP. What?

ARAB. No foundation. No foundation.

KRUPP. I'll say there's no foundation.

ARAB. All the way down the line.

KRUPP (*to* NICK). Is that all he ever says?

NICK. That's all he's been saying *this* week.

KRUPP. What is he, anyway?

NICK. He's an Arab, or something like that.

KRUPP. No, I mean what's he do for a living?

NICK (*to* ARAB). What do you do for a living, brother?

ARAB. Work. Work all my life. All my life, work. From small boy to old man, work. In old country, work. In new country, work. In New York.

Pittsburgh. Detroit. Chicago. Imperial Valley. San Francisco. Work. No beg. Work. For what? Nothing. Three boys in old country. Twenty years, not see. Lost. Dead. Who knows? What. What-not. No foundation. All the way down the line.

KRUPP. What'd he say last week?

NICK. Didn't say anything. Played the harmonica.

ARAB. Old country song, I play. (*He brings a harmonica from his back pocket.*)

KRUPP. Seems like a nice guy.

NICK. Nicest guy in the world.

KRUPP (*bitterly*). But crazy. Just like all the rest of us. Stark raving mad.

[WESLEY *and* HARRY *long ago stopped playing and dancing. They sat at a table together and talked for a while, then began playing casino or rummy. When the* ARAB *begins his solo on the harmonica, they stop their game to listen.*]

WESLEY. You hear that?

HARRY. That's *something*.

WESLEY. That's crying. That's crying.

HARRY. I want to make people laugh.

WESLEY. That's deep, deep crying. That's crying a long time ago. That's crying a thousand years ago. Some place five thousand miles away.

HARRY. Do you think you can play to that?

WESLEY. I want to *sing* to that, but I can't *sing*.

HARRY. You try and play to that. I'll try to dance.

[WESLEY *goes to the piano, and after closer listening, he begins to accompany the harmonica solo.* HARRY *goes to the little stage and after a few efforts begins to dance to the song. This keeps up quietly for some time.* KRUPP *and* NICK *have been silent, and deeply moved.*]

KRUPP (*softly*). Well, anyhow, Nick.

NICK. Hmmmmmmm?

KRUPP. What I said. Forget it.

NICK. Sure.

KRUPP. It gets me down once in a while.

NICK. No harm in talking.

KRUPP (*the policeman again, loudly*). Keep the girls out of here.

NICK (*loud and friendly*). Take it easy.

[*The music and dancing are now at their height.*]

CURTAIN

ACT FIVE

That evening. Foghorns are heard throughout the scene. A man in evening clothes and a top hat, and his woman, also in evening clothes, are entering.

WILLIE *is still at the marble game.* NICK *is behind the bar.* JOE *is at his table, looking at the book of maps of the countries of Europe. The box containing the revolver and the box containing the cartridges are on the table, beside his glass. He is at peace, his hat tilted back on his head, a calm expression on his face.* TOM *is leaning against the bar, dreaming of love and* KITTY. *The* ARAB *is gone.* WESLEY *and* HARRY *are gone.* KIT CARSON *is watching the boy at the marble game.*

LADY. Oh, come on, please.

[*The gentleman follows miserably. The* SOCIETY MAN *and* WIFE *take a table.* NICK *gives them a menu. Outside, in the street, the Salvation Army people are playing a song. Big drum, tambourines, cornet, and singing. They are singing "The Blood of the Lamb." The music and words come into the place faintly and comically. This is followed by an old sinner testifying. It is the* DRUNKARD. *His words are not intelligible, but his message is unmistakable. He is saved. He wants to sin no more. And so on.*]

DRUNKARD (*testifying, unmistakably drunk*).

Brothers and sisters. I was a sinner. I chewed tobacco and chased women. Oh, I sinned, brothers and sisters. And then I was saved. Saved by the Salvation Army, God forgive me.

JOE. Let's see now. Here's a city. Pribor. Czechoslovakia. Little, lovely, lonely Czechoslovakia. I wonder what kind of a place Pribor was? (*Calling.*) Pribor! *Pribor!*   10

[TOM *leaps.*]

LADY. What's the matter with him?

MAN (*crossing his legs, as if he ought to go to the men's room*). Drunk.

TOM. Who you calling, Joe?

JOE. Pribor.

TOM. Who's Pribor?

JOE. He's a Czech. And a Slav. A Czechoslovakian.

LADY. How interesting.   20

MAN (*uncrosses his legs*). He's drunk.

JOE. Tom, Pribor's a city in Czechoslovakia.

TOM. Oh. (*Pause.*) You sure were nice to her, Joe.

JOE. Kitty Duval? She's one of the finest people in the world.

TOM. It sure was nice of you to hire an automobile and take us for a drive along the ocean front and down to 30 Half Moon Bay.

JOE. Those three hours were the most delightful, the most somber, and the most beautiful I have ever known.

TOM. Why, Joe?

JOE. Why? I'm a student (*Lifting his voice.*), Tom. (*Quietly.*) I'm a student. I study all things. All. All. And when my study reveals something of beauty in a place or in a person where by all 40 rights only ugliness or death should be revealed, then I know how full of goodness this life is. And that's a good thing to know. That's a truth I shall always seek to verify.

LADY. Are you *sure* he's drunk?

MAN (*crossing his legs*). He's either drunk or just naturally crazy.

TOM. Joe?

JOE. Yeah.

TOM. You won't get sore or anything?

JOE (*impatiently*). What is it, Tom?

TOM. Joe, where do you get all that money? You paid for the automobile. You paid for supper and the two bottles of champagne at the Half Moon Bay Restaurant. You moved Kitty out of the New York Hotel around the corner to the St. Francis Hotel on Powell Street. I saw you pay her rent. I saw you give her money for new clothes. Where do you get all that money, Joe? Three years now and I've never asked.

JOE (*looking at TOM sorrowfully, a little irritated, not so much with TOM as with the world and himself, his own superiority. He speaks clearly, slowly and solemnly*). Now don't be a fool, Tom. Listen carefully. If anybody's got any money—to hoard or to throw away—you can be sure he stole it from other people. Not from rich people who can spare it, but from poor people who can't. From their lives and from their dreams. I'm no exception. I *earned* the money I throw away. I stole it like everybody else does. I hurt people to get it. Loafing around this way, I *still* earn money. The money itself earns *more*. I *still* hurt people. I don't know who they are, or where they are. If I did, I'd feel worse than I do. I've got a Christian conscience in a world that's got no conscience at all. The world's trying to get some sort of a *social* conscience, but it's having a devil of a time trying to do *that*. I've got money. I'll always have money, as long as this world stays the way it is. I don't work. I don't make anything. (*He sips.*) I drink, I worked when I was a kid. I worked *hard*. I mean hard, Tom. People are supposed to enjoy living. I got tired. (*He lifts the gun and looks at it while he talks.*) I decided to get even on the world. Well, you can't enjoy living unless you work. Unless you do something. I don't do anything. I don't *want* to do anything any more. There isn't anything I can do that won't make me feel embarrassed. Because I can't do simple, good things. I haven't the patience. And I'm too smart. Money is the guiltiest thing in the world. It stinks. Now, don't ever bother me about it again.

TOM. I didn't mean to make you feel bad, Joe.

JOE (*slowly*). Here. Take this gun out in the street and give it to some worthy holdup man.

LADY. What's he saying?

MAN (*uncrosses his legs*). You wanted to visit a honky-tonk. Well, *this* is a honky-tonk. (*To the world.*) Married twenty-eight years and she's still looking for adventure.

TOM. How should I know who's a hold-up man?

JOE. Take it away. Give it to somebody.

TOM (*bewildered*). Do I *have* to *give* it to somebody?

JOE. Of course.

TOM. Can't I take it back and get some of our money?

JOE. Don't talk like a businessman. Look around and find somebody who appears to be in need of a gun and give it to him. It's a good gun, isn't it?

TOM. The man said it was, but how can I tell who needs a gun?

JOE. Tom, you've seen good people who needed guns, haven't you?

TOM. I don't remember. Joe, I might

give it to the wrong kind of guy. He might do something crazy.

JOE. All right. I'll find somebody myself. (TOM *rises*.) Here's some money. Go get me this week's *Life, Liberty, Time,* and six or seven packages of chewing gum.

TOM (*swiftly, in order to remember each item*). *Life, Liberty, Time,* and six or seven packages of chewing gum?

JOE. That's right.

TOM. All that chewing gum? What kind?

JOE. Any kind. Mix 'em up. All kinds.

TOM. Licorice, too?

JOE. Licorice, by all means.

TOM. Juicy Fruit?

JOE. Juicy Fruit.

TOM. Tutti-Frutti?

JOE. Is there such a gum?

TOM. I think so.

JOE. All right. Tutti-Frutti, too. Get *all* the kinds. Get as many kinds as they're selling.

TOM. *Life, Liberty, Time,* and all the different kinds of gum. (*He begins to go.*)

JOE (*calling after him loudly*). Get some jelly beans too. All the different colors.

TOM. All right, Joe.

JOE. And the longest panatela cigar you can find. Six of them.

TOM. Panatela. I got it.

JOE. Give a news kid a dollar.

TOM. O.K., Joe.

JOE. Give some old man a dollar.

TOM. O.K., Joe.

JOE. Give them Salvation Army people in the street a couple of dollars and ask them to sing that song that goes—— (*He sings loudly.*) Let the lower lights be burning, send a gleam across the wave.

TOM (*swiftly*). Let the lower lights be burning, send a gleam across the wave.

JOE. That's it. (*He goes on with the song,*

very loudly and religiously.) Some poor, dying, struggling seaman, you may rescue, you may save. (*Halts.*)

TOM. O.K., Joe. I got it. *Life, Liberty, Time,* all the kinds of gum they're selling, jelly beans, six panatela cigars, a dollar for a news kid, a dollar for an old man, two dollars for the Salvation Army. (*Going.*) Let the lower lights be burning, send a gleam 10 across the wave.

JOE. That's it.

LADY. He's absolutely insane.

MAN (*wearily crossing his legs*). You asked me to take you to a honky-tonk instead of to the Mark Hopkins. You're *here* in a honky-tonk. I can't help it if he's crazy. Do you want to go back to where people *aren't* crazy?

LADY. No, not just yet. 20

MAN. Well, all right then. Don't be telling me every minute that he's crazy.

LADY. You needn't be huffy about it.

[*The* MAN *refuses to answer, uncrosses his legs. When* JOE *began to sing,* KIT CARSON *turned away from the marble game and listened. While the man and woman are arguing he comes over to* JOE'*s table.*]

KIT CARSON. Presbyterian?

JOE. I attended a Presbyterian Sunday 30 school.

KIT CARSON. Fond of singing?

JOE. On occasion. Have a drink?

KIT CARSON. Thanks.

JOE. Get a glass and sit down.

[KIT CARSON *gets a glass from* NICK, *returns to the table, sits down.* JOE *pours him a drink, they touch glasses just as the Salvation Army people begin to fulfill the request. They sip some champagne, and at* 40 *the proper moment begin to sing the song together, sipping champagne, raising hell with the tune, swinging it, and so on. The* SOCIETY LADY *joins them, and is stopped by her husband.*]

JOE. Always was fond of that song. Used

to sing it at the top of my voice. Never saved a seaman in my life.

KIT CARSON (*flirting with the* SOCIETY LADY, *who loves it*). I saved a seaman once. Well, he wasn't exactly a seaman. He was a darky named Wellington. Heavy-set sort of a fellow. Nice personality, but no friends to speak of. Not until I came along, at any rate. In New Orleans. In the summer of the year 1899. No. Ninety-eight. I was a lot younger of course, and had no mustache, but was regarded by many people as a man of means.

JOE. Know anything about guns?

KIT CARSON (*flirting*). All there is to know. Didn't fight the Ojibways for nothing. Up there in the Lake Takalooca Country, in Michigan. (*Remembering.*) Along about in 1881 or two. Fought 'em right up to the shore of the Lake. Made 'em swim for Canada. One fellow in particular, an Indian named Harry Daisy.

JOE (*opening the box containing the revolver*). What sort of a gun would you say this is? Any good?

KIT CARSON (*at sight of the gun, leaping*). Yep. That looks like a pretty nice hunk of shooting iron. That's a six-shooter. Shot a man with a six-shooter once. Got him through the palm of his right hand. Lifted his arm to wave to a friend. Thought it was a bird. Fellow named, I believe, Carroway. Larrimore Carroway.

JOE. Know how to work one of these things? (*He offers* KIT CARSON *the revolver, which is old and enormous.*)

KIT CARSON (*laughing at the absurd question*). Know how to work it? Hand me that little gun, son, and I'll show you all about it. (JOE *hands* KIT *the revolver. Importantly.*) Let's see now. This is probably a new kind of six-shooter. After my time. Haven't nicked an Indian in years. I believe this here place is supposed to move out. (*He fools around and gets the barrel out for loading.*) That's it. There it is.

JOE. Look all right?

KIT CARSON. It's a good gun. You've got a good gun there, son. I'll explain it to you. You see these holes? Well, that's where you put the cartridges. 10

JOE (*taking some cartridges out of the box*). Here. Show me how it's done.

KIT CARSON (*a little impatiently*). Well, son, you take 'em one by one and put 'em in the holes, like this. There's one. Two. Three. Four. Five. Six. Then you get the barrel back in place. Then cock it. Then all you got to do is aim and fire.

[*He points the gun at the* LADY *and* GENTLE- 20 MAN, *who scream and stand up, scaring* KIT CARSON *into paralysis. The gun is loaded, but uncocked.*]

JOE. It's all set?

KIT CARSON. Ready to kill.

JOE. Let me hold it.

[KIT *hands* JOE *the gun. The* LADY *and* GENTLEMAN *watch, in terror.*]

KIT CARSON. Careful now, son. Don't cock it. Many a man's lost an eye 30 fooling with a loaded gun. Fellow I used to know named Danny Donovan lost a nose. Ruined his whole life. Hold it firm. Squeeze the trigger. Don't snap it. Spoils your aim.

JOE. Thanks. Let's see if I can unload it. (*He begins to unload it.*)

KIT CARSON. Of course you can.

[JOE *unloads the revolver, looks at it very closely, puts the cartridges back into the* 40 *box.*]

JOE (*looking at the gun*). I'm mighty grateful to you. Always wanted to see one of those things close up. Is it really a good one?

KIT CARSON. It's a beaut, son.

JOE (*aims the empty gun at a bottle on the bar*). Bang!

WILLIE (*at the marble game, as the machine groans*). Oh boy! (*Loudly, triumphantly.*) There you are, Nick. Thought I couldn't do it, hey? *Now*, watch. (*The machine begins to make a special kind of noise. Lights go on and off. Some red, some green. A bell rings loudly six times.*) One. Two. Three. Four. Five. Six. (*An American flag jumps up.* WILLIE *comes to attention. Salutes.*) Oh boy, what a beautiful country. (*A loud music-box version of the song "America."* JOE, KIT, *and the* LADY *get to their feet. Singing.*) My country, 'tis of thee, sweet land of liberty, of thee I sing. (*Everything quiets down. The flag goes back into the machine.* WILLIE *is thrilled, amazed, delighted. Everybody has watched the performance of the defeated machine from wherever he happened to be when the performance began.* WILLIE, *looking around at everybody, as if they had all been on the side of the machine.*) O.K. How's that? I knew I could do it. (*To* NICK.) Six nickels. (NICK *hands him six nickels.* WILLIE *goes over to* JOE *and* KIT.) Took me a little while, but I finally did it. It's scientific, really. With a little skill a man can make a modest living beating the marble games. Not that that's what I want to do. I just don't like the idea of anything getting the best of me. A machine or anything else. Myself, I'm the kind of a guy who makes up his mind to do something, and then goes to work and does it. There's no other way a man can be a success at anything. (*Indicating the letter F on his sweater.*) See that letter? That don't stand for some little-bitty high school somewhere. That stands for *me*. Faroughli. Willie Faroughli. I'm an Assyrian. We've got a civilization six or seven centuries old, I think.

Somewhere along in there. Ever hear of Osman? Harold Osman? He's an Assyrian, too. He's got an orchestra down in Fresno. (*He goes to the* LADY *and* GENTLEMAN.) I've never seen you before in my life, but I can tell from the clothes you wear and the company you keep (*Graciously indicating the* LADY.) that you're a man who looks every problem straight in the 10 eye, and then goes to work and *solves* it. I'm that way myself. Well. (*He smiles beautifully, takes the* GENTLEMAN's *hand furiously.*) It's been wonderful talking to a nicer type of people for a change. Well. I'll be seeing you. So long. (*He turns, takes two steps, returns to the table. Very politely and seriously.*) Good-by, lady. You've got a good man there. Take good care of him. 20

[WILLIE *goes, saluting* JOE *and the world.*]

KIT CARSON (*to* JOE). By God, for a while there I didn't think that young Assyrian was going to do it. That fellow's got something.

[TOM *comes back with the magazines and other stuff.*]

JOE. Get it all?

TOM. Yeah. I had a little trouble finding the jelly beans.

JOE. Let's take a look at them.

TOM. These are the jelly beans.

[JOE *puts his hand into the cellophane bag and takes out a handful of the jelly beans, looks at them, smiles, and tosses a couple into his mouth.*]

JOE. Same as ever. Have some. (*He offers the bag to* KIT.)

KIT CARSON (*flirting*). Thanks! I remember the first time I ever ate jelly beans. 40 I was six, or at the most seven. Must have been in (*Slowly.*) eighteen— seventy-seven. Seven or eight. Baltimore.

JOE. Have some, Tom.

[TOM *takes some.*]

TOM. Thanks, Joe.

JOE. Let's have some of that chewing gum. (*He dumps all the packages of gum out of the bag onto the table.*)

KIT CARSON (*flirting*). Me and a boy named Clark. Quinton Clark. Became a Senator.

JOE. Yeah. Tutti-Frutti all right. (*He opens a package and folds all five pieces into his mouth.*) Always wanted to see how many I could chew at one time. Tell you what, Tom. I'll bet I can chew more at one time than you can.

TOM (*delighted*). All right.

[*They both begin to fold gum into their mouths.*]

KIT CARSON. I'll referee. Now, one at a time. How many you got?

JOE. Six.

KIT CARSON. All right. Let Tom catch up with you.

JOE (*while* TOM's *catching up*). Did you give a dollar to a news kid?

TOM. Yeah, sure.

JOE. What'd he say?

TOM. Thanks.

JOE. What sort of a kid was he?

TOM. Little, dark kid. I guess he's Italian.

JOE. Did he seem pleased?

TOM. Yeah.

JOE. That's good. Did you give a dollar to an old man?

TOM. Yeah.

JOE. Was he pleased?

TOM. Yeah.

JOE. Good. How many you got in your mouth?

TOM. Six.

JOE. All right. I got six, too. (*Folds one more in his mouth.* TOM *folds one too.*)

KIT CARSON. Seven. Seven each. (*They each fold one more into their mouths, very solemnly, chewing them into the main hunk of gum.*) Eight. Nine. Ten.

JOE (*delighted*). Always wanted to do this.

(*He picks up one of the magazines.*) Let's see what's going on in the world. (*He turns the pages, and keeps folding gum into his mouth and chewing.*)

KIT CARSON. Eleven. Twelve.

[KIT *continues to count while* JOE *and* TOM *continue the contest. In spite of what they are doing, each is very serious.*]

TOM. Joe, what'd you want to move Kitty into the St. Francis Hotel for? 10

JOE. She's a better woman than any of them tramp society dames that hang around that lobby.

TOM. Yeah, but do you think she'll feel at home up there?

JOE. Maybe not at first, but after a couple of days she'll be all right. A nice big room. A bed for sleeping in. Good clothes. Good food. She'll be all right, Tom. 20

TOM. I hope so. Don't you think she'll get lonely up there with nobody to talk to?

JOE (*looking at* TOM *sharply, almost with admiration, pleased but severe*). There's nobody *anywhere* for *her* to talk to— except *you*.

TOM (*amazed and delighted*). *Me*, Joe?

JOE (*while* TOM *and* KIT CARSON *listen carefully*, KIT *with great appreciation*). 30 Yes, you. By the grace of God, you're the other half of that girl. Not the angry woman that swaggers into this water-front dive and shouts because the world has kicked her around. *Anybody* can have *her*. You belong to the little kid in Ohio who once dreamed of living. Not with her carcass, for *money*, so she can have food and clothes, and pay rent. With *all* of her. 40 I put her in that hotel so she can have a chance to gather herself together again. She can't do that in the New York Hotel. You saw what happens there. There's nobody anywhere for her to talk to, except you. They all

make her talk like a streetwalker. After a while, she'll *believe* them. Then she won't be able to remember. She'll get lonely. Sure. People can get lonely for *misery*, even. I want her to go on being lonely for *you*, so she can come together again the way she was meant to be from the beginning. Loneliness is good for people. Right now it's the only thing for Kitty. Any more licorice?

TOM (*dazed*). What? Licorice? (*Looking around busily.*) I guess we've chewed all the licorice in. We still got Clove, Peppermint, Doublemint, Beechnut, Teaberry, and Juicy Fruit.

JOE. Licorice used to be my favorite. Don't worry about her, Tom, she'll be all right. You really want to marry her, don't you?

TOM (*nodding*). Honest to God, Joe. (*Pathetically.*) Only I haven't got any money.

JOE. Couldn't you be a prize fighter or something like that?

TOM. Naaaah. I couldn't hit a man if I wasn't sore at him. He'd have to do something that made me hate him.

JOE. You've got to figure out something to do that you won't mind doing very much.

TOM. I wish I could, Joe.

JOE (*thinking deeply; suddenly*). Tom, would you be embarrassed driving a truck?

TOM (*hit by a thunderbolt*). Joe, I never thought of that. I'd like that. Travel. Highways. Little towns. Coffee and hot cakes. Beautiful valleys and mountains and streams and trees and daybreak and sunset.

JOE. There *is* poetry in it, at that.

TOM. Joe, that's just the kind of work I *should* do. Just sit there and travel, and look, and smile, and bust out laughing. Could Kitty go with me, sometimes?

JOE. I don't know. Get me the phone book. Can you drive a truck?

TOM. Joe, you know I can drive a truck, or any kind of thing with a motor and wheels.

[TOM *takes* JOE *the phone book.* JOE *turns the pages.*]

JOE (*looking*). Here! Here it is. Tuxedo 10 7900. Here's a nickel. Get me that number.

[TOM *goes to telephone, dials the number.*]

TOM. Hello.

JOE. Ask for Mr. Keith.

TOM (*mouth and language full of gum*). I'd like to talk to Mr. Keith. (*Pause.*) Mr. Keith.

JOE. Take that gum out of your mouth for a minute. 20

[TOM *removes the gum.*]

TOM. Mr. Keith. Yeah. That's right. Hello, Mr. Keith?

JOE. Tell him to hold the line.

TOM. Hold the line, please.

JOE. Give me a hand, Tom. (TOM *helps* JOE *to the telephone. At the phone, wad of gum in his fingers delicately.*) Keith? Joe. Yeah. Fine. Forget it. (*Pause.*) Have you got a place for a good 30 driver? (*Pause.*) I don't think so. (*To* TOM.) You haven't got a driver's license, have you?

TOM (*worried*). No. But I can get one, Joe.

JOE (*at the phone*). No, but he can get one easy enough. To hell with the union. He'll join later. All right, call him a vice-president and say he drives for relaxation. Sure. What do you mean? Tonight? I don't know why not. San 40 Diego? All right, let him start driving without a license. What the hell's the difference? Yeah. Sure. Look him over. Yeah. I'll send him right over. Right. (*He hangs up.*) Thanks. (*To the telephone.*)

TOM. Am I going to get the job?

JOE. He wants to take a look at you.

TOM. Do I look all right, Joe?

JOE (*looking at him carefully*). Hold up your head. Stick out your chest. How do you feel?

[TOM *does these things.*]

TOM. Fine.

JOE. You *look* fine, too. (JOE *takes his wad of gum out of his mouth and wraps the Liberty magazine around it.*) You win, Tom. Now, look. (*He bites off the tip of a very long panatela cigar, lights it, and hands one to* TOM, *and another to* KIT.) Have yourselves a pleasant smoke. Here. (*He hands two more to* TOM.) Give those slummers one each. (*He indicates the* SOCIETY LADY *and* GENTLEMAN.)

[TOM *goes over and without a word gives a cigar each to the* MAN *and the* LADY. *The* MAN *is offended; he smells and tosses aside his cigar. The* WOMAN *looks at her cigar a moment, then puts the cigar in her mouth.*]

MAN. What do you think you're doing?

LADY. Really, dear. I'd like to.

MAN. Oh, this is too much.

LADY. I'd *really*, really like to, dear.

[*She laughs, puts the cigar in her mouth. Turns to* KIT. *He spits out tip. She does the same.*]

MAN (*loudly*). The mother of five grown men, and she's still looking for *romance*. (*Shouts as* KIT *lights her cigar.*) No. I forbid it.

JOE (*shouting*). What's the matter with you? Why don't you leave her alone? What are you always pushing your women around for? (*Almost without a pause.*) Now, look, Tom. (*The* LADY *puts the lighted cigar in her mouth, and begins to smoke, feeling wonderful.*) Here's ten bucks.

TOM. Ten bucks?

JOE. He may want you to get into a

truck and begin driving to San Diego tonight.

TOM. Joe, I got to tell Kitty.

JOE. I'll tell her.

TOM. Joe, take care of her.

JOE. She'll be all right. Stop worrying about her. She's at the St. Francis Hotel. Now look. Take a cab to Townsend and Fourth. You'll see the big sign. Keith Motor Transport 10 Company. He'll be waiting for you.

TOM. O.K., Joe. (*Trying hard.*) Thanks, Joe.

JOE. Don't be silly. Get going.

[TOM *goes. The* LADY *starts puffing on the cigar. As* TOM *goes*, WESLEY *and* HARRY *come in together.*]

NICK. Where the hell have you been? We've got to have some entertainment around here. Can't you see 20 them fine people from uptown? (*He points at the* SOCIETY LADY *and* GEN-TLEMAN.)

WESLEY. You said to come back at ten for the second show.

NICK. Did I say that?

WESLEY. Yes, sir, Mr. Nick, that's exactly what you said.

HARRY. Was the first show all right?

NICK. That wasn't a show. There was 30 no one here to see it. How can it be a show when no one sees it? People are afraid to come down to the water front.

HARRY. Yeah. We were just down to Pier 27. One of the longshoremen and a cop had a fight and the cop hit him over the head with a blackjack. We saw it happen, didn't we?

WESLEY. Yes, sir, we was standing there 40 looking when it happened.

NICK. (*a little worried*). Anything else happen?

WESLEY. They was all talking.

HARRY. A man in a big car came up and said there was going to be a meeting right away and they hoped to satisfy everybody and stop the strike.

WESLEY. Right away. *Tonight.*

NICK. Well, it's about time. Them poor cops are liable to get nervous and— shoot somebody. (*To* HARRY, *suddenly.*) Come back here. I want you to tend bar for a while. I'm going to take a walk over to the pier.

HARRY. Yes, sir.

NICK (*to the* SOCIETY LADY *and* GENTLE-MAN). You society people made up your minds yet?

LADY. Have you champagne?

NICK (*indicating* JOE). What do you think he's pouring out of that bottle, water or something?

LADY. Have you a chill bottle?

NICK. I've got a dozen of them chilled. He's been drinking champagne here all day and all night for a month now.

LADY. May we have a bottle?

NICK. It's six dollars.

LADY. I think we can manage.

MAN. I don't know. I *know* I don't know.

[NICK *takes off his coat and helps* HARRY *into it.* HARRY *takes a bottle of champagne and two glasses to the* LADY *and the* GENTLE-MAN, *dancing, collects six dollars, and goes back behind the bar, dancing.* NICK *gets his coat and hat.*]

NICK (*to* WESLEY). Rattle the keys a little, son. Rattle the keys.

WESLEY. Yes, sir, Mr. Nick.

[NICK *is on his way out. The* ARAB *enters.*]

NICK. Hi-ya, Mahmed.

ARAB. No foundation.

NICK. All the way down the line. (*He goes.*)

[WESLEY *is at the piano, playing quietly. The* ARAB *swallows a glass of beer, takes out his harmonica, and begins to play.* WESLEY *fits his playing to the* ARAB'S. KITTY DUVAL, *strangely beautiful, in new clothes, comes in. She walks shyly, as if she were embarrassed by the fine clothes, as if she had no right to wear them. The* LADY *and* GENTLEMAN *are very impressed.* HARRY *looks at her with amazement.* JOE *is reading* Time *magazine.* KITTY *goes to his table.* JOE *looks up from the magazine, without the least amazement.*]

JOE. Hello, Kitty.

KITTY. Hello, Joe.

JOE. It's nice seeing you again.

KITTY. I came in a cab.   10

JOE. You been crying again? (KITTY *can't answer. To* HARRY.) Bring a glass. [HARRY *comes over with a glass.* JOE *pours* KITTY *a drink.*]

KITTY. I've got to talk to you.

JOE. Have a drink.

KITTY. I've never been in burlesque. We were just poor.

JOE. Sit down, Kitty.

KITTY (*sits down*). I tried other things. 20

JOE. Here's to you, Katerina Koranovsky. Here's to you. And Tom.

KITTY (*sorrowfully*). Where *is* Tom?

JOE. He's getting a job tonight driving a truck. He'll be back in a couple of days.

KITTY (*sadly*). I told him I'd marry him.

JOE. He wanted to see you and say good-by.

KITTY. He's too good for me. He's like 30 a little boy. (*Wearily.*) I'm—— Too many things have happened to me.

JOE. Kitty Duval, you're one of the few truly innocent people I have ever known. He'll be back in a couple of days. Go back to the hotel and wait for him.

KITTY. That's what I mean. I can't stand being alone. I'm no good. I tried very hard. I don't know what it 40 is. I miss—— (*She gestures.*)

JOE (*gently*). Do you really want to come back here, Kitty?

KITTY. I don't know. I'm not sure. Everything *smells* different. I don't know how to feel, or what to think.

(*Gesturing pathetically.*) I know I don't belong there. It's what I've wanted all my life, but it's too *late*. I try to be happy about it, but all I can do is remember everything and cry.

JOE. I don't know what to tell you, Kitty. I didn't mean to hurt you.

KITTY. You haven't hurt me. You're the only person who's ever been good to me. I've never known anybody like you. I'm not sure about love any more, but I know I love you, and I know I love Tom.

JOE. I love you too, Kitty Duval.

KITTY. He'll want babies. I know he will. I know *I* will, too. Of course I will. I can't—— (*She shakes her head.*)

JOE. Tom's a baby himself. You'll be very happy together. He wants you to ride with him in the truck. Tom's good for you. You're good for Tom.

KITTY (*like a child*). Do you want me to go back and wait for him?

JOE. I can't *tell* you what to do. I think it would be a good idea, though.

KITTY. I wish I could tell you how it makes me feel to be alone. It's almost worse.

JOE. It might take a whole week, Kitty. (*He looks at her sharply, at the arrival of an idea.*) Didn't you speak of reading a book? A book of poems?

KITTY. I didn't know what I was saying.

JOE (*trying to get up*). Of course you knew. I think you'll like poetry. Wait here a minute, Kitty. I'll go see if I can find some books.

KITTY. All right, Joe.

[*He walks out of the place, trying very hard not to wobble. Foghorn. Music. The* NEWSBOY *comes in. Looks for* JOE. *Is brokenhearted because* JOE *is gone.*]

NEWSBOY (*to the* SOCIETY GENTLEMAN). Paper?

MAN (*angry*). No.

[*The* NEWSBOY *goes to the* ARAB.]

NEWSBOY. Paper, mister?

ARAB (*irritated*). No foundation.

NEWSBOY. What?

ARAB (*very angry*). No foundation.

[*The* NEWSBOY *starts out, turns, looks at the* ARAB, *shakes his head.*]

NEWSBOY. No foundation? How do you figure?

[BLICK *and* TWO COPS *enter.*]

NEWSBOY (*to* BLICK). Paper, mister? 10

[BLICK *pushes him aside. The* NEWSBOY *goes.*]

BLICK (*walking authoritatively about the place, to* HARRY). Where's Nick?

HARRY. He went for a walk.

BLICK. Who are you?

HARRY. Harry.

BLICK (*to the* ARAB *and* WESLEY). Hey, you. Shut up. (*The* ARAB *stops playing the harmonica,* WESLEY *the piano.* BLICK 20 *studies* KITTY.) What's your name, sister?

KITTY (*looking at him*). Kitty Duval. What's it to you?

[KITTY's *voice is now like it was at the beginning of the play: tough, independent, bitter, and hard.*]

BLICK (*angry*). Don't give me any of your gutter lip. Just answer my questions.

KITTY. You go to hell, you. 30

BLICK (*coming over, enraged*). Where do you live?

KITTY. The New York Hotel. Room 21.

BLICK. Where do you work?

KITTY. I'm not working just now. I'm looking for work.

BLICK. What kind of work? (KITTY *can't answer.*) What kind of work? (KITTY *can't answer. Furiously.*) WHAT KIND OF WORK? 40

[KIT CARSON *comes over.*]

KIT CARSON. You can't talk to a lady that way in *my* presence.

[BLICK *turns and stares at* KIT. *The* COPS *begin to move from the bar.*]

BLICK (*to the* COPS). It's all right, boys.

I'll take care of this. (*To* KIT.) What'd you say?

KIT CARSON. You got no right to hurt people. Who are *you?*

[BLICK, *without a word, takes* KIT *to the street. Sounds of a blow and a groan.* BLICK *returns, breathing hard.*]

BLICK (*to the* COPS). O.K., boys. You can go now. Take care of him. Put him on his feet and tell him to behave himself from now on. (*To* KITTY *again.*) Now answer my question. What kind of work?

KITTY (*quietly*). You know what kind of work I do. And I know what kind you do.

MAN (*shocked and really hurt*). Excuse me, officer, but it seems to me that your attitude——

BLICK. Shut up.

MAN (*quietly*). ——is making the poor child say things that are not true.

BLICK. Shut up, I said.

LADY. Well. (*To the* MAN.) Are you going to stand for such insolence?

BLICK (*to the* MAN, *who is standing*). Are you?

MAN (*taking the woman's arm*). I'll get a divorce. I'll start life all over again. (*Pushing the woman.*) Come on. Get the hell out of here!

[*The* MAN *hurries his woman out of the place,* BLICK *watching them go.*]

BLICK (*to* KITTY). Now. Let's begin again, and see that you tell the truth. What's your name?

KITTY. Kitty Duval.

BLICK. Where do you live?

KITTY. Until this evening I lived at the New York Hotel. Room 21. This evening I moved to the St. Francis Hotel.

BLICK. Oh. To the St. Francis Hotel. Nice place. Where do you work?

KITTY. I'm looking for work.

BLICK. What kind of work do you do?

KITTY. I'm an actress.

BLICK. I see. What movies have I seen you in?

KITTY. I've worked in burlesque.

BLICK. You're a liar.

[WESLEY *stands, worried and full of dumb resentment.*]

KITTY (*pathetically, as at the beginning of the play*). It's the truth.

BLICK. What are you doing here?

KITTY. I came to see if I could get a job here.

BLICK. Doing what?

KITTY. Singing—and—dancing.

BLICK. You can't sing or dance. What are you lying for?

KITTY. I can. I sang and danced in burlesque all over the country.

BLICK. You're a liar.

KITTY. I said lines, too.

BLICK. So you danced in burlesque?

KITTY. Yes.

BLICK. All right. Let's see what you did.

KITTY. I can't. There's no music, and I haven't got the right clothes.

BLICK. There's music. (*To* WESLEY.) Put a nickel in that phonograph. (WESLEY *can't move.*) Come on. Put a nickel in that phonograph. (WESLEY *does so. To* KITTY.) All right. Get up on that stage and do a hot little burlesque number. (KITTY *stands. Walks slowly to the stage, but is unable to move.* JOE *comes in, holding three books.*) Get going, now. Let's see you dance the way you did in burlesque, all over the country.

[KITTY *tries to do a burlesque dance. It is beautiful in a tragic way.*]

BLICK. All right, start taking them off!

[KITTY *removes her hat and starts to remove her jacket.* JOE *moves closer to the stage, amazed.*]

JOE (*hurrying to* KITTY). Get down from there. (*He takes* KITTY *into his arms. She is crying. To* BLICK.) What the hell do you think you're doing!

WESLEY (*like a little boy, very angry*). It's that man, Blick. *He* made her take off her clothes. He beat up the old man, too.

[BLICK *pushes* WESLEY *off as* TOM *enters.* BLICK *begins beating up* WESLEY.]

TOM. What's the matter, Joe? What's happened?

JOE. Is the truck out there?

TOM. Yeah, but what's happened? Kitty's crying again!

JOE. You driving to San Diego?

TOM. Yeah, Joe. But what's he doing to that poor colored boy?

JOE. Get going. Here's some money. Everything's O.K. (*To* KITTY.) Dress in the truck. Take these books.

WESLEY'S VOICE. You can't hurt me. You'll get yours. You wait and see.

TOM. Joe, he's hurting that boy. I'll kill him!

JOE (*pushing* TOM). Get out of here! Get married in San Diego. I'll see you when you get back. (TOM *and* KITTY *go.* NICK *enters and stands at the lower end of bar.* JOE *takes the revolver out of his pocket. Looks at it.*) I've always wanted to kill somebody, but I never knew who it should be.

[*He cocks the revolver, stands real straight, holds it in front of him firmly, and walks to the door. He stands a moment watching* BLICK, *aims very carefully, and pulls the trigger. There is no shot.* NICK *runs over and grabs the gun, and takes* JOE *aside.*]

NICK. What the hell do you think you're doing?

JOE (*casually, but angry*). That dumb Tom. Buys a six-shooter that won't even shoot once.

[JOE *sits down, dead to the world.* BLICK *comes out, panting for breath.* NICK *looks at him. He speaks slowly.*]

NICK. Blick! I told you to stay out of here! Now get out of here. (*He takes* BLICK *by the collar, tightening his grip as he speaks, and pushing him out.*) If you come back again, I'm going to take you in that room where you've been beating up that colored boy, and I'm going to murder you—slowly—with my hands. Beat it! (*He pushes* BLICK *out. To* HARRY.) Go take care of the colored boy.

[HARRY *runs out.* WILLIE *returns and doesn't sense that anything is changed.* WILLIE *puts another nickel into the machine, but he does so very violently. The consequence of this violence is that the flag comes up again.* WILLIE, *amazed, stands at attention and salutes. The flag goes down. He shakes his head.*]

WILLIE (*thoughtfully*). As far as I'm concerned, this is the *only* country in the world. If you ask me, *nuts* to Europe! (*He is about to push the slide in again when the flag comes up again. Furiously, to* NICK, *while he salutes and stands at attention, pleadingly.*) Hey, Nick. This machine is out of order.

NICK (*somberly*). Give it a whack on the side.

[WILLIE *does so. A hell of a whack. The result is, the flag comes up and down, and* WILLIE *keeps saluting.*]

WILLIE (*saluting*). Hey, Nick. Something's wrong.

[*The machine quiets down abruptly.* WILLIE *very stealthily slides a new nickel in, and starts a new game. From a distance two pistol shots are heard, each carefully timed.* NICK *runs out. The* NEWSBOY *enters, crosses to* JOE'S *table, senses something is wrong.*]

NEWSBOY (*softly*). Paper, mister?

[JOE *can't hear him. The* NEWSBOY *backs away, studies* JOE, *wishes he could cheer* JOE *up. Notices the phonograph, goes to it and puts a coin in it, hoping music will make* JOE *happier. The* NEWSBOY *sits down. Watches* JOE. *The music begins. "The Missouri Waltz." The* DRUNKARD *comes in and walks around. Then sits down.* NICK *comes back.*]

NICK (*delighted*). Joe, Blick's dead! Somebody just shot him, and none of the cops are trying to find out who.

[JOE *doesn't hear.* NICK *steps back, studying* JOE.]

NICK (*shouting*). Joe.

JOE (*looking up*). What?

NICK. Blick's dead.

JOE. Blick? Dead? Good! That goddamn gun wouldn't go off. I *told* Tom to get a good one.

NICK (*picking up the gun and looking at it*). Joe, you wanted to kill that guy! (HARRY *returns.* JOE *puts the gun in his coat pocket.*) I'm going to buy you a bottle of champagne.

[NICK *goes to the bar.* JOE *rises, takes his hat from the rack, puts his coat on. The* NEWSBOY *jumps up, helps* JOE *with the coat.*]

NICK. What's the matter, Joe?

JOE. Nothing. Nothing.

NICK. How about the champagne?

JOE. Thanks. (*Going.*)

NICK. It's not eleven yet. Where you going, Joe?

JOE. I don't know. Nowhere.

NICK. Will I see you tomorrow?

JOE. I don't know. I don't think so.

[KIT CARSON *enters, walks to* JOE. JOE *and* KIT *look at one another knowingly.*]

JOE. Somebody just shot a man. How are you feeling?

KIT. Never felt better in my life. (*Loudly, bragging, but somber.*) I shot a man once. In San Francisco. Shot him two times. In 1939, I think it was. In October. Fellow named Blick or Glick or something like that. Couldn't stand the way he talked to ladies. Went up to my room and got my old pearl-handled revolver and waited for him on Pacific Street. Saw him walking, and let him have it, two

times. Had to throw the beautiful revolver into the Bay.

[HARRY, NICK, *the* ARAB, *and the* DRUNK-
ARD *close in around him.* JOE *searches his
pockets, brings out the revolver, puts it in*
KIT'S *hand, looks at him with great admiration and affection.* JOE *walks slowly
to the stairs leading to the street, turns and
waves.* KIT, *and then one by one everybody
else, waves, and the marble game goes into
its beautiful American routine again: flag,
lights, and music. The play ends.*]

CURTAIN

TENNESSEE WILLIAMS

A NEW and distinctive talent was introduced to the American theatre in *The Glass Menagerie*. It had opened in Chicago the night after Christmas, 1944, to critical acclaim but a sparse audience. The critics refused to let the play die. Their insistence soon had Chicago people flocking to see it, and it played for three months before capacity crowds. It moved on to the Playhouse in New York, March 31, 1945, and ran for a year and a half. It was selected for the Drama Critics' Circle award as the best play written by an American and produced in New York in the season 1944–45. In Williams' own words, "I was snatched out of virtual oblivion and thrust into sudden prominence." He has sustained that prominence by the unique quality of his art and his perception of some of the more illusive values in the national life.

Williams came up the rough road and hammered out his art from his own unremitting struggles. His career fits the legendary pattern of an artist's development through obstacles, disappointment, frustration, and perseverance. He was born Thomas Lanier Williams at Columbus, Miss., March 26, 1914. He was reared in St. Louis, where his father held a position with a shoe company. He began writing poetry and short stories at the University of Missouri, which he attended from 1931–33. When the depression forced him to give up college, he went to work with the shoe company. He was temperamentally unfit for this kind of employment. He solaced himself after work-

hours by writing. His health broke down, and he took time off to recuperate. Then he got forward with his college work at Washington University in 1936–37, went on to the University of Iowa, and received his A.B., with a major in drama, in 1938.

No enchanted doors into the theatre opened to him. He waited tables in a New Orleans French Quarter restaurant, and worked on a pigeon ranch in California. He kept on writing. His one-act plays, distilled from this hard-won but valuable experience, caught the notice of a New York agent. He was given a scholarship to the playwrights' seminar directed by Theresa Hepburn and John Gassner at the New School for Social Research. He won a Rockefeller Foundation Fellowship in 1940, and a thousand dollar grant for work in drama. These subsidies provided him with food and shelter while he worked at perfecting his art. His first play, *Battle of Angels*, produced by the Theatre Guild, was abandoned after its opening in Boston on December 30, 1940. The next few years were a well-nigh desperate contest with drama and destitution. He resorted to odd jobs to keep going. Finally, while on a Hollywood contract, he wrote *The Glass Menagerie*. This was it. He adopted his pen name, Tennessee Williams, to symbolize his metamorphosis into a new period of professional life.

The hard, astringent facts of living which he had seen and experienced might well have induced him to compose plays of the genre of *The Lower*

Depths. But instead, like Anton Chekhov, whose work he admires, his compassion and his perception have allowed him to see behind the repellent facts to the dreams and illusions by which men live and sustain their spirits while they endure the assault of these facts. The mother, Amanda, in *The Glass Menagerie*, one of his best creations, lives in a world of sentimental illusion of her own creation; if she accepted the alley in St. Louis at its real value with all its devastating drabness and absence of hope, she would perish. She lives where she dreams, and tomorrow will be better. Her daughter Laura, crippled in body and withdrawn from the world in spirit, lives in a world of make-believe more delicate and tenuous than her mother could ever perceive. She becomes another fragile piece in the collection of the glass menagerie. And the son Tom, narrator of the play, works in a warehouse but escapes intermittently and desperately into a poet's dream world. "I give you truth," he says, "in the pleasant disguise of illusion."

Williams' problem is to catch this gossamer world in the setting of the alley apartment and to make the audience share the illusion by suspending their disbelief. The technique is designed to facilitate this adventure. It calls upon the narrator to speak directions to his listeners, and to help them philosophize about the significance of memory and reality; it uses music, recurring themes, gauze curtains, special lighting effects, and symbolic lantern slides to help create the mood. Opinion is divided as to whether these devices are merely superficial "literary" tricks external to the play, or whether they are an inherent part of the total structure. To this spectator and reader they are so skillfully handled that they are absorbed into the living tissue of the play.

A Streetcar Named Desire, which began its sensational run at the Barrymore Theater on December 3, 1947, dispensed with the devices and the external symbols of make-believe to root itself in a gross and turbulent segment of New Orleans life. It is written "straight," and the make-believe world of Blanche DuBois is conveyed from within the play itself through the power of its character creation. It relies on no external stage tricks to achieve its ultimately tender and tragic effect. It was awarded the Pulitzer Prize in 1948. *Summer and Smoke* (1948) is touched by the peculiar warmth and compassion characteristic of Tennessee Williams. Margo Jones had given it a sensitive production in Dallas, but it failed as a stage venture in New York when it opened at the Music Box on October 6, 1948.

The Glass Menagerie remains representative of Williams' best work in dramatic theme and technique. What he called, in his preface to the play, "the obsessive interest in human affairs, plus a certain amount of compassion and moral conviction," is here translated into moving drama.

THE GLASS MENAGERIE

CHARACTERS

TOM WINGFIELD

AMANDA WINGFIELD, *his mother*

LAURA WINGFIELD, *his sister*

JIM O'CONNOR

SCENE: *An alley in St. Louis.*

PART I: *Preparation for a Gentleman Caller.*

PART II: *The Gentleman Calls.*

TIME: *Now and the Past.*

ACT I

SCENE I

The Wingfield apartment is in the rear of the building, one of those vast hivelike conglomerations of cellular living units that flower as warty growths in overcrowded urban centers of lower-middle-class population and are symptomatic of the impulse of this largest and fundamentally enslaved section of American society to avoid fluidity and differentiation and to exist and function as one interfused mass of automatism.

The apartment faces an alley and is entered by a fire escape, a structure whose name is a touch of accidental poetic truth, for all of these huge buildings are always burning with the slow and implacable fires of human desperation. The fire escape is included in the set— that is, the landing of it and steps descending from it. (*Note that the stage left alley may be entirely omitted, since it is never used except for* TOM'S *first entrance, which can take place at the stage right.*)

The scene is memory and is therefore nonrealistic. Memory takes a lot of poetic license. It omits some details; others are exaggerated, according to the emotional value of the articles it touches, for memory is seated predominantly in the heart. The interior is therefore rather dim and poetic.

As soon as the house lights dim, dance-hall music is heard on stage right. Old popular music of, say, 1915–1920 period. This continues until TOM is at the fire-escape landing, having lighted a cigarette, and begins speaking.

At the rise of the house curtain, the audience is faced with the dark, grim rear wall of the Wingfield tenement. (*The stage set proper is screened out by a gauze curtain, which suggests the front part, outside, of the building.*) This building, which runs parallel to the footlights, is flanked on both sides by dark, narrow alleys which run into murky canyons of tangled clotheslines, garbage cans, and the sinister latticework of neighboring fire escapes. (*The alleys are actually in darkness, and the objects just mentioned are not visible.*) It is up and down these side alleys that exterior entrances and exits are made during the play. At the end of TOM'S opening commentary, the dark tenement wall slowly reveals (*by means* of a transparency) the interior of the ground-floor Wingfield apartment. (*A gauze curtain, which suggests the front part of the building, rises on the interior set.*) Downstage is the living room, which also serves as a sleeping room for LAURA, the day bed unfolding to make her bed. Just above this is a small stool or table on which is a telephone. Upstage, center, and divided by a wide arch or second proscenium with transparent faded portieres 10 (or second curtain; "*second curtain*" is actually the inner gauze curtain between the living room and the dining room, which is upstage of it), is the dining room. In an old-fashioned whatnot in the living room are seen scores of transparent glass animals. A blown-up photograph of the father hangs on the wall of the living room, facing the audience, to the left of the archway. It is the face of a very handsome young man in a doughboy's First World War 20 cap. He is gallantly smiling, ineluctably smiling, as if to say, "*I will be smiling forever.*" (*Note that all that is essential in connection with the dance hall is that the window be shown lighting the lower part of the alley. It is not necessary to show any considerable part of the dance hall.*)

The audience hears and sees the opening scene in the dining room through both the transparent fourth wall (this is the gauze 30 curtain which suggests the outside of the building) of the building and the transparent gauze portieres of the dining-room arch. It is during this revealing scene that the fourth wall slowly ascends, out of sight. This transparent exterior wall is not brought down again until the very end of the play, during TOM's final speech.

The narrator is an undisguised convention of the play. He takes whatever license with 40 dramatic convention is convenient to his purposes.

TOM enters dressed as a merchant sailor from the alley, stage left (i.e., stage right if the left alley is omitted), and strolls across the front of the stage to the fire escape. (TOM may lean against the grillwork of this as he lights his cigarette.) There he stops and lights a cigarette. He addresses the audience.

TOM. I have tricks in my pocket—I have things up my sleeve—but I am the opposite of the stage magician. He gives you illusion that has the appearance of truth. I give you truth in the pleasant disguise of illusion. I take you back to an alley in St. Louis. The time, that quaint period when the huge middle class of America was matriculating from a school for the blind. Their eyes had failed them, or they had failed their eyes, and so they were having their fingers pressed forcibly down on the fiery Braille alphabet of a dissolving economy.—In Spain there was revolution.—Here there was only shouting and confusion and labor disturbances, sometimes violent, in otherwise peaceful cities such as Cleveland—Chicago—Detroit. . . . That is the social background of this play. . . . The play is memory. (*Music cue No. 2.*) Being a memory play, it is dimly lighted, it is sentimental, it is not realistic.—In memory everything seems to happen to music.—That explains the fiddle in the wings. I am the narrator of the play, and also a character in it. The other characters in the play are my mother, Amanda, my sister, Laura, and a gentleman caller who appears in the final scenes. He is the most realistic character in the play, being an emissary from a world that we were somehow set apart from.—But having a poet's weakness for symbols, I am using this character as a symbol —as the long-delayed but always expected something that we live for.— There is a fifth character who doesn't appear other than in a photograph hanging on the wall. When you see the picture of this grinning gentleman, please remember this is our father, who left us a long time ago. He was a telephone man who fell in love with long distance—so he gave up his job with the telephone company and skipped the light fantastic out of town. . . . The last we heard of him was a picture post card from the Pacific coast of Mexico, containing a message of two words: 'Hello—Goodby!', and no address. I think the rest of the play will explain itself.

[*Lights up in the dining room.*]

[TOM *exits at the right. He goes off downstage, takes off his sailor overcoat and skull-fitting knitted cap, and remains off stage by the dining-room right door for his entrance cue.*]

[AMANDA'S *voice becomes audible through the portieres—i.e., gauze curtains separating the dining room from living room.* AMANDA *and* LAURA *are seated at a dropleaf table.* AMANDA *is sitting in the center chair and* LAURA *in the left chair. Eating is indicated by gestures without food or utensils.* AMANDA *faces the audience. The interior of the dining room has lit up softly and through the scrim—gauze curtains— we see* AMANDA *and* LAURA *seated at the table in the upstage area.*]

AMANDA. You know, Laura, I had the funniest experience in church last Sunday. The church was crowded except for one pew way down front, and in that was just one little woman. I smiled very sweetly at her and said, "Excuse me, would you mind if I shared this pew?" "I certainly would," she said. "This space is rented." Do you know that is the first time that I ever knew that the Lord rented space. (*The dining-room gauze curtains open automatically.*) These Northern Episcopalians! I can understand the Southern Episcopalians, but these Northern ones, no. (TOM *enters the dining room by the right, slips over to the table, and sits in the chair at the right.*) Honey, don't push your food with your fingers. If you have to push your food with something, the thing to use is a crust of bread. You must chew your food. Animals have secretions in their stomachs which enable them to digest their food without mastication, but human beings must chew their food before they swallow it down, and chew, chew. Oh, eat leisurely. Eat leisurely. A well-cooked meal has many delicate flavors that have to be held in the mouth for appreciation, not just gulped down. Oh, chew, chew—chew! (*At this point the scrim curtain—if the director decides to use it— the one suggesting the exterior wall—rises here and does not come down again until just before the end of the play.*) Don't you want to give your salivary glands a chance to function?

TOM. Mother, I haven't enjoyed one bite of my dinner because of your constant directions on how to eat it. It's you that makes me hurry through my meals with your hawklike attention to every bite I take. It's disgusting—all this discussion of animals' secretion— salivary glands—mastication! (*Comes down to the armchair in the living room at the right, lights a cigarette.*)

AMANDA. Temperament like a Metropolitan star! You're not excused from this table.

TOM. I'm getting a cigarette.

AMANDA. You smoke too much.

LAURA (*rising*). Mother, I'll bring in the coffee.

AMANDA. No, no, no, no. You sit down. I'm going to be the colored boy today and you're going to be the lady.

LAURA. I'm already up.

AMANDA. Resume your seat. Resume your seat. You keep yourself fresh and pretty for the gentlemen callers.

[LAURA *sits.*]

LAURA. I'm not expecting any gentlemen callers.

AMANDA (*who has been gathering the dishes from the table and loading them on a tray*). Well, the nice thing about them is they come when they're least ex- 10 pected. Why, I remember one Sunday afternoon in Blue Mountain when your mother was a girl . . . (*Goes out for coffee, up right.*)

TOM. I know what's coming now!

[LAURA *rises.*]

LAURA. Yes. But let her tell it. (*Crosses to the left of the day bed, sits.*)

TOM. Again?

LAURA. She loves to tell it. 20

AMANDA (*entering from the right in the dining room and coming down into the living room with the tray and coffee*). I remember one Sunday afternoon in Blue Mountain when your mother was a girl she received—seventeen— gentlemen callers!

[AMANDA *crosses to* TOM *at the armchair to the right, gives him coffee, and crosses to the center.* LAURA *comes to her, takes the cup,* 30 *resumes her place on the left of the day bed.* AMANDA *puts the tray on the small table at the right of the day bed, sits at the right on day bed. The inner curtain closes, the light dims out.*]

AMANDA. Why, sometimes there weren't chairs enough to accommodate them all, and we had to send the colored boy over to the parish house to fetch the folding chairs. 40

TOM. How did you entertain all those gentlemen callers?

[TOM *finally sits in the armchair at the right.*]

AMANDA. I happened to understand the art of conversation!

TOM. I bet you could talk!

AMANDA. Well, I could. All the girls in my day could, I tell you.

TOM. Yes?

AMANDA. They knew how to entertain their gentlemen callers. It wasn't enough for a girl to be possessed of a pretty face and a graceful figure— although I wasn't slighted in either respect. She also needed to have a nimble wit and a tongue to meet all occasions.

TOM. What did you talk about?

AMANDA. Why, we'd talk about things of importance going on in the world! Never anything common or coarse or vulgar. My callers were gentlemen— all! Some of the most prominent men on the Mississippi Delta—planters and sons of planters! There was young Champ Laughlin. (*Music cue No. 3.*) He later became vice-president of the Delta Planters' Bank. And Hadley Stevenson; he was drowned in Moon Lake.—My goodness, he certainly left his widow well provided for—a hundred and fifty thousand dollars in government bonds. And the Cutrere Brothers—Wesley and Bates. Bates was one of my own bright particular beaus! But he got in a quarrel with that wild Wainwright boy and they shot it out on the floor of Moon Lake Casino. Bates was shot through the stomach. He died in the ambulance on his way to Memphis. He certainly left his widow well provided for, too —eight or ten thousand acres, no less. He never loved that woman; she just caught him on the rebound. My picture was found on him the night he died. Oh, and that boy, that boy that every girl in the Delta was setting her cap for! That beautiful (*Music fades out.*) brilliant young Fitzhugh boy from Greene County!

TOM. What did he leave his widow?

AMANDA. He never married! What's the matter with you—you talk as though all my old admirers had turned up their toes to the daisies!

TOM. Isn't this the first you've mentioned that still survives?

AMANDA. He made an awful lot of money. He went North to Wall Street and made a fortune. He had the Midas touch—everything that boy 10 touched just turned to gold! (*Gets up.*) And I could have been Mrs. J. Duncan Fitzhugh—mind you! (*Crosses left center.*) But—what did I do?—I just went out of my way and picked your father! (*Looks at the picture on the left wall. Goes to small table to the right of the day bed for the tray.*)

LAURA (*rises from the day bed*). Mother, let me clear the table. 20

AMANDA (*crossing left for* LAURA's *cup, then crossing right for* TOM's). No, dear, you go in front and study your typewriter chart. Or practice your shorthand a little. Stay fresh and pretty! It's almost time for our gentlemen callers to start arriving. How many do you suppose we're going to entertain this afternoon?

[TOM *opens the curtains between the dining* 30 *room and the living room for her. These close behind her, and she exits into the kitchen by the right.* TOM *stands up center in the living room.*]

LAURA (*to* AMANDA, *off stage*). I don't believe we're going to receive any, Mother.

AMANDA (*off stage*). Not any? Not one? Why, you must be joking! Not one gentleman caller? What's the matter? 40 Has there been a flood or a tornado?

LAURA (*crossing to the typing table*). It isn't a flood. It's not a tornado, Mother. I'm just not popular like you were in Blue Mountain. Mother's afraid that I'm going to be an old maid.

(*Music cue No. 4.*)

[*The lights dim out.* TOM *exits up center in the blackout.* LAURA *crosses to the menagerie at the right.*]

SCENE II

SCENE *is the same. The lights dim up on the living room.*

LAURA *is discovered by the menagerie, polishing the glass. Crosses to the phonograph, plays a record.[1] She times this business so as to put the needle on the record as Music cue No. 4 ends.*

Enter AMANDA *down the alley to the right. Rattles the key in the lock.* LAURA *crosses guiltily to the typewriter and types. (A small typewriter table with a typewriter on it is still on stage in the living room at the left.)* AMANDA *comes into the room by the right,* 20 *closing the door. Crosses to the armchair, putting her hat, purse, and gloves on it.*

Something has happened to AMANDA. *It is written in her face: a look that is grim and hopeless and a little absurd. She has on one of those cheap or imitation velvety-looking cloth coats with an imitation fur collar. Her hat is five or six years old, one of those dreadful cloche hats that were worn in the late twenties, and she is clasping an enormous* 30 *black patent-leather pocketbook with nickel clasps and initials. This is her full-dress outfit, the one she usually wears to the D.A.R.*

She purses her lips, opens her eyes very wide, rolls them upward, and shakes her head. Seeing her mother's expression, LAURA *touches her lips with a nervous gesture.*

LAURA. Hello, Mother, I was just . . .

AMANDA. I know. You were just practicing your typing, I suppose. (*Behind* 40 *the chair at the right.*)

LAURA. Yes.

[1] While "Dardanella" was used in the professional production, any other popular record of the 20's may be substituted. It should be a worn record.

AMANDA. Deception, deception, deception!

LAURA (*shakily*). How was the D.A.R. meeting, Mother?

AMANDA (*crosses to* LAURA). D.A.R. meeting!

LAURA. Didn't you go to the D.A.R. meeting, Mother?

AMANDA (*faintly, almost inaudibly*). No, I didn't go to any D.A.R. meeting. 10 (*Then more forcibly:*) I didn't have the strength—I didn't have the courage. I just wanted to find a hole in the ground and crawl in it and stay there the rest of my entire life. (*Tears the type charts, throws them on the floor.*)

LAURA (*faintly*). Why did you do that, Mother?

AMANDA (*sits on the right end of the day bed.*) Why? Why? How old are you, Laura? 20

LAURA. Mother, you know my age.

AMANDA. I was under the impression that you were an adult, but evidently I was very much mistaken. (*She stares at* LAURA.)

LAURA. Please don't stare at me, Mother!

[AMANDA *closes her eyes and lowers her head. Pause.*]

AMANDA. What are we going to do? 30 What is going to become of us? What is the future? (*Pause.*)

LAURA. Has something happened, Mother? Mother, has something happened?

AMANDA. I'll be all right in a minute. I'm just bewildered—by life . . .

LAURA. Mother, I wish that you would tell me what's happened!

AMANDA. I went to the D.A.R. this 40 afternoon, as you know; I was to be inducted as an officer. I stopped off at Rubicam's Business College to tell them about your cold and to ask how you were progressing down there.

LAURA. Oh . . .

AMANDA. Yes, oh—oh—oh. I went straight to your typing instructor and introduced myself as your mother. She didn't even know who you were. Wingfield, she said? We don't have any such scholar enrolled in this school. I assured her she did. I said my daughter Laura's been coming to classes since early January. "Well, I don't know," she said, "unless you mean that terribly shy little girl who dropped out of school after a few days' attendance?" No, I said, I don't mean that one. I mean my daughter, Laura, who's been coming here every single day for the past six weeks! "Excuse me," she said. And she took down the attendance book and there was your name, unmistakable, printed, and all the dates you'd been absent. I still told her she was wrong. I still said, "No, there must have been some mistake! There must have been some mix-up in the records!" "No," she said, "I remember her perfectly now. She was so shy and her hands trembled so that her fingers couldn't touch the right keys! When we gave a speed test—she just broke down completely —was sick at the stomach and had to be carried to the washroom! After that she never came back. We telephoned the house every single day and never got any answer." (*Rises from the day bed, crosses right center.*) That was while I was working all day long down at that department store, I suppose, demonstrating those— (*With her hands indicates a brassière.*) Oh! I felt so weak I couldn't stand up! (*Sits in the armchair.*) I had to sit down while they got me a glass of water! (LAURA *crosses up to the phonograph.*) Fifty dollars' tuition. I don't care about the money so much, but all my hopes for any kind of future for you—gone up the spout, just gone up the spout like that. (LAURA *winds the phonograph up.*) Oh, don't *do* that, Laura!— Don't play that Victrola!

LAURA. Oh! (*Stops the phonograph, crosses to the typing table, sits.*)

AMANDA. What have you been doing every day when you've gone out of the house pretending that you were going to business college? 10

LAURA. I've just been going out walking.

AMANDA. That's not true!

LAURA. Yes it is, Mother, I just went walking.

AMANDA. Walking? Walking? In winter? Deliberately courting pneumonia in that light coat? Where did you walk to, Laura?

LAURA. All sorts of places—mostly in the park. 20

AMANDA. Even after you'd started catching that cold?

LAURA. It was the lesser of two evils, Mother. I couldn't go back. I threw up on the floor!

AMANDA. From half-past seven till after five every day you mean to tell me you walked around in the park, because you wanted to make me think that you were still going to Rubicam's 30 Business College?

LAURA. Oh, Mother, it wasn't as bad as it sounds. I went inside places to get warmed up.

AMANDA. Inside where?

LAURA. I went in the art museum and the birdhouses at the Zoo. I visited the penguins every day! Sometimes I did without lunch and went to the movies. Lately I've been spending 40 most of my afternoons in the Jewel Box, that big glass house where they raise the tropical flowers.

AMANDA. You did all that to decieve me, just for deception! Why? Why? Why? Why?

LAURA. Mother, when you're disappointed, you get that awful suffering look on your face, like the picture of Jesus' mother in the Museum! (*Rises.*)

AMANDA. Hush!

LAURA (*crosses right to the menagerie*). I couldn't face it. I couldn't.

[*Music cue No. 5.*]

AMANDA (*rising from the day bed*). So what are we going to do now, honey, the rest of our lives? Just sit down in this house and watch the parades go by? Amuse ourselves with the glass menagerie? Eternally play those worn-out records you father left us as a painful reminder of him? (*Slams the phonograph lid.*) We can't have a business career. (*End of Music cue No. 5.*) No, we can't do that—that just gives us indigestion. (*Around right of the day bed.*) What is there left for us now but dependency all our lives? I tell you, Laura, I know so well what happens to unmarried women who aren't prepared to occupy a position in life. (*Crosses left, sits on the day bed.*) I've seen such pitiful cases in the South— barely tolerated spinsters living on some brother's wife or a sister's husband—tucked away in some mousetrap of a room—encouraged by one in-law to go on and visit the next in-law—little birdlike women—without any nest—eating the crust of humility all their lives! Is that the future that we've mapped out for ourselves? I swear I don't see any other alternative. And I don't think that's a very pleasant alternative. Of course—some girls *do* marry. My goodness, Laura, haven't you ever liked some boy?

LAURA. Yes, Mother, I liked one once.

AMANDA. You did?

LAURA. I came across his picture awhile ago.

AMANDA. He gave you his picture, too?

(*Rises from the day bed, crosses to the chair at the right.*)

LAURA. No, it's in the yearbook.

AMANDA (*sits in the armchair*). Oh—a high-school boy.

LAURA. Yes. His name was Jim. (*Kneeling on the floor, gets a yearbook from under the menagerie.*) Here he is in *The Pirates of Penzance.*

AMANDA (*absently*). The what?

LAURA. The operetta the senior class put on. He had a wonderful voice. We sat across the aisle from each other Mondays, Wednesdays, and Fridays in the auditorium. Here he is with a silver cup for debating! See his grin?

AMANDA. So he had a grin, too! (*Looks at the picture of the father on the wall behind the phonograph.[1] Hands the yearbook back.*)

LAURA. He used to call me—Blue Roses.

AMANDA. Blue Roses? What did he call you a silly name like that for?

LAURA (*still kneeling*). When I had that attack of pleurosis—he asked me what was the matter when I came back. I said pleurosis—he thought that I said "Blue Roses." So that's what he always called me after that. Whenever he saw me, he'd holler, "Hello, Blue Roses!" I didn't care for the girl that he went out with. Emily Meisenbach. Oh, Emily was the best-dressed girl at Soldan. But she never struck me as being sincere. . . . I read in a newspaper once that they were engaged. (*Puts the yearbook back on a shelf of the glass menagerie.*) That's a long time ago—they're probably married by now.

AMANDA. That's all right, honey, that's all right. It doesn't matter. Little girls who aren't cut out for business careers sometimes end up married to very nice young men. And I'm just going to see that you do that, too!

LAURA. But, Mother——

AMANDA. What is it now?

LAURA. I'm—crippled!

AMANDA. Don't say that word! (*Rises, crosses to the center. Turns to LAURA.*) How many times have I told you never to say that word! You're not crippled, you've just got a slight defect. (LAURA *rises.*) If you lived in the days when I was a girl and they had long graceful skirts sweeping the ground, it might have been considered an asset. When you've got a slight disadvantage like that, you've just got to cultivate something else to take its place. You have to cultivate charm—or vivacity—or *charm!* (*Spotlight on the photograph. Then dim out.*) That's the only thing your father had plenty of—charm!

[AMANDA *sits on the day bed.* LAURA *crosses to the armchair and sits. Music cue No. 6. Blackout.*]

SCENE III

SCENE: *The same. The lights up again, but only on the right alley and the fire-escape landing; the rest of the stage dark. (The typewriter table and typewriter have been taken off stage.) Enter* TOM, *again wearing the merchant-sailor overcoat and knitted cap, in the alley at the right. As Music cue No. 6 ends,* TOM *begins to speak.*

TOM (*leans against the grill of the fire escape, smoking*). After the fiasco at Rubicam's Business College, the idea of getting a gentleman caller for my sister Laura began to play a more and more important part in my mother's calculations. It became an obsession. Like some archetype of the universal

---

[1] In the original production this photo was a life-sized head. It lights up from time to time as indicated. The illumination may, if desired, be omitted. If used, it lights here.

unconscious, the image of the gentleman caller haunted our small apartment. An evening at home rarely passed without some allusion to this image, this specter, this hope. . . . And even when he wasn't mentioned, his presence hung in my mother's preoccupied look and in my sister's frightened, apologetic manner. It hung like a sentence passed upon the Wingfields! But my mother was a woman of action as well as words. (*Music cue No. 7.*) She began to take logical steps in the planned direction. Late that winter and in the early spring—realizing that extra money would be needed to properly feather the nest and plume the bird—she began a vigorous campaign on the telephone, roping in subscribers to one of those magazines for matrons called *The Homemaker's Companion*, the type of journal that features the serialized sublimations of ladies of letters who think in terms of delicate cuplike breasts, slim, tapering waists, rich creamy thighs, eyes like wood smoke in autumn, fingers that soothe and caress like soft, soft strains of music. Bodies as powerful as Etruscan sculpture.

[*He exits down right into the wings. The light in the alley at the right is blacked out, and a head spot falls on* AMANDA, *at the phone in the living room. Music cue No. 7 ends as* TOM *stops speaking.*]

AMANDA. Ida Scott? (*During this speech* TOM *enters the dining room up right unseen by the audience, not wearing overcoat or hat. There is an unlighted reading lamp on the table. Sits at the center of the dining-room table with writing materials.*) This is Amanda Wingfield. We missed you at the D.A.R. last Monday. Oh, first I want to know how's your sinus condition? You're just a Christian martyr. That's what you are. You're just a Christian martyr. Well, I was just going through my little red book, and I saw that your subscription to the *Companion* is about to expire just when that wonderful new serial by Bessie Mae Harper is starting. It's the first thing she's written since *Honeymoon for Three*. Now, that was unusual, wasn't it? Why, Ida, this one is even lovelier. It's all about the horsy set on Long Island and a debutante is thrown from her horse while taking him over the jumps at the—regatta. Her spine—her spine is injured. That's what the horse did—he stepped on her. Now there is only one surgeon in the entire world that can keep her from being completely paralyzed, and that's the man she's engaged to be married to and he's tall and he's blond and he's handsome. That's unusual, too, huh? Oh, he's not perfect. Of course he has a weakness. He has the most terrible weakness in the entire world. He just drinks too much. What? Oh, no, honey, don't let them burn. You go take a look in the oven and I'll hold on. . . . Why, that woman! Do you know what she did? She hung up on me. (*Dining-room and living-room lights dim in. The reading lamp lights up at the same time.*)

LAURA. Oh, Mother, Mother, Tom's trying to write. (*Rises from the armchair where she was left at the curtain of the previous scene, goes to the curtain between the dining room and the living room, which is already open.*)

AMANDA. Oh! So he is. So he is. (*Crosses from the phone, goes to the dining room and up to* TOM.)

TOM (*at table*). Now what are you up to?

AMANDA. I'm trying to save your eyesight. (*Business with the lamp.*) You've only got one pair of eyes and you've got to take care of them. Oh, I know that Milton was blind, but that's not what made him a genius.

TOM. Mother, will you please go away and let me finish my writing?

AMANDA (*squares his shoulders*). Why can't you sit up straight? So your shoulders don't stick through like sparrows' wings?

TOM. Mother, please go busy yourself with something else. I'm trying to write.

AMANDA (*business with* TOM). Now I've seen a medical chart, and I know what that position does to your internal organs. You sit up and I'll show you. Your stomach presses against your lungs, and your lungs press against your heart, and that poor little heart gets discouraged because it hasn't got any room left to go on beating for you.

TOM. What in hell——

[*The inner curtains between the living room and the dining room close. The lights dim down in the dining room.* LAURA *crosses, stands at the center of the curtains in the living room listening to the following scene between* TOM *and* AMANDA.]

AMANDA.[1] Don't you talk to me like that——

TOM. ——am I supposed to do?

AMANDA. What's the matter with you? Have you gone out of your senses?

TOM. Yes, I have. You've driven me out of them.

AMANDA. What is the matter with you lately, you big—big—idiot?

TOM. Look, Mother—I haven't got a thing, not a single thing, left in this house that I can call my own.

AMANDA. Lower your voice!

[1] TOM and AMANDA remain in the dining room throughout their argument.

TOM. Yesterday you confiscated my books! You had the nerve to——

AMANDA. I did. I took that horrible novel back to the library—that awful book by that insane Mr. Lawrence. I cannot control the output of a diseased mind or people who cater to them, but I won't allow such filth in my house. No, no, no, no, no!

TOM. House, house! Who pays the rent on the house, who makes a slave of himself to——!

AMANDA. Don't you dare talk to me like that!

[LAURA *crosses down left to the back of the armchair.*]

TOM. No, I mustn't say anything! *I've* just got to keep quiet and let you do all the talking.

AMANDA. Let me tell you something!

TOM. I don't want to hear any more.

AMANDA. You will hear more——

[LAURA *crosses to the phonograph.*]

TOM (*crossing through the curtains between the dining room and the living room. Goes upstage of the door at the right where, in a dark spot, there is supposedly a closet*). Well, I'm not going to listen. I'm going out. (*Gets out a coat.*)

AMANDA (*coming through the curtains into the living room, stands at the center*). You are going to listen to me, Tom Wingfield. I'm tired of your impudence.— And another thing—I'm right at the end of my patience!

TOM (*putting his overcoat on the back of the armchair and crossing back to* AMANDA). What do you think I'm at the end of, Mother? Aren't I supposed to have any patience to reach the end of? I know, I know. It seems unimportant to you, what I'm *doing*—what I'm trying to do—having a difference between them! You don't think that.

AMANDA. I think you're doing things

that you're ashamed of, and that's why you act like this. (TOM *crosses to the day bed and sits*.) I don't believe that you go every night to the movies. Nobody goes to the movies night after night. Nobody in their right minds goes to the movies as often as you pretend to. People don't go to the movies at nearly midnight and movies don't let out at two A.M. Come in stumbling, muttering to yourself like a maniac. You get three hours' sleep and then go to work. Oh, I can picture the way you're doing down there. Moping, doping, because you're in no condition.

TOM. That's true—that's very, very true. I'm in no condition!

AMANDA. How dare you jeopardize your job? Jeopardize our security? How do you think we'd manage——? (*Sits in the armchair at the right*.)

TOM. Look, Mother, do you think I'm *crazy* about the *warehouse?* You think I'm in love with the Continental Shoemakers? You think I want to spend fifty-five years of my life down there in that—*celotex interior!* with—*fluorescent tubes?!* Honest to God, I'd rather somebody picked up a crowbar and battered out my brains than go back mornings! But I *go!* Sure, every time you come in yelling that bloody *Rise and shine!* Rise and shine!! I think how lucky dead people are! But I get up. (*Rises from the day bed*.) I *go!* For sixty-five dollars a month I give up all that I dream of doing and being *ever!* And you say that is all I think of. Oh God! Why, Mother, if self is all I ever thought of, Mother, *I'd* be where *he* is—GONE! (*Crosses to get his overcoat on the back of the armchair*.) As far as the system of transportation reaches! (AMANDA *rises,*

crosses to him and grabs his arm.) Please don't grab at me, Mother!

AMANDA (*following him*). I'm not grabbing at you. I want to know where you're going now.

TOM (*taking his overcoat, starts crossing to door at the right*). I'm going to the movies!

AMANDA (*crosses center*). I don't believe that lie!

TOM (*crosses back to* AMANDA). No? Well, you're right. For once in your life you're right. I'm not going to the movies. I'm going to opium dens! Yes, Mother, opium dens, dens of vice and criminals' hangouts, Mother. I've joined the Hogan gang. I'm a hired assassin, I carry a tommy gun in a violin case! I run a string of cathouses in the valley! They call me Killer, Killer Wingfield, I'm really leading a double life. By day I'm a simple, honest warehouse worker, but at night I'm a dynamic czar of the underworld. Why, I go to gambling casinos and spin away a fortune on the roulette table! I wear a patch over one eye and a false mustache, sometimes I wear green whiskers. On those occasions they call me—El Diablo! Oh, I could tell you things to make you sleepless! My enemies plan to dynamite this place some night! Some night they're going to blow us all sky-high. And will I be glad! Will I be happy! And so will you be. You'll go up—up—over Blue Mountain on a broomstick! With seventeen gentlemen callers! You ugly babbling old witch!

[*He goes through a series of violent, clumsy movements, seizing his overcoat, lunging to the right door, pulling it fiercely open. The women watch him, aghast. His arm catches in the sleeve of the coat as he strug-*

gles to pull it on. *For a moment he is pinioned by the bulky garment. With an outraged groan he tears the coat off again, splitting the shoulder of it, and hurls it across the room. It strikes against the shelf of* LAURA's *glass collection; there is a tinkle of shattering glass.* LAURA *cries out as if wounded.*]

LAURA. My glass—menagerie . . . (*She covers her face and turns away.*) 10

AMANDA (*in an awful voice*). I'll never speak to you again as long as you live unless you apologize to me!

[AMANDA *exits through the living-room curtains.* TOM *is left with* LAURA. *He stares at her stupidly for a moment. Then he crosses to the shelf holding the glass menagerie. Drops awkwardly on his knees to collect the fallen glass, glancing at* LAURA *as if he would speak, but couldn't.*] 20

[*Blackout.* TOM, AMANDA, *and* LAURA *exit in the blackout.*]

SCENE IV

The interior is dark. Faint light in the alley at the right. A deep-voiced bell in a church is tolling the hour of five as the scene commences.

TOM *appears at the top of the right alley. After each solemn boom of the bell in the* 30 *tower he shakes a little toy noisemaker or rattle as if to express the tiny spasm of man in contrast to the sustained power and dignity of the Almighty. This and the unsteadiness of his advance make it evident that he has been drinking.*

As he climbs the few steps to the fire-escape landing light steals up inside. LAURA *appears in a nightdress, entering the living room from the left door of the dining room, observing* 40 TOM's *empty bed* (*day bed*) *in the living room.*

TOM *fishes in his pockets for his door key, removing a motley assortment of articles in the search, including a perfect shower of movie-ticket stubs and an empty bottle. At last he finds the key, but just as he is about to insert*

it, *it slips from his fingers. He strikes a match and crouches below the door.*

TOM (*bitterly*). One crack—and it falls through!

[LAURA *opens the door at the right.*][1]

LAURA. Tom, Tom, what are you doing?

TOM. Looking for a door key.

LAURA. Where have you been all this time?

TOM. I have been to the movies.

LAURA. All this time at the movies?

TOM. There was a very long program. There was a Garbo picture and a Mickey Mouse and a travelogue and a newsreel and a preview of coming attractions. And there was an organ solo and a collection for the milk fund —simultaneously—which ended up in a terrible fight between a fat lady and an usher!

LAURA (*innocently*). Did you have to stay through everything?

TOM. Of course! And oh, I forgot! There was a big stage show! The headliner on this stage show was Malvolio the Magician. He performed wonderful tricks, many of them, such as pouring water back and forth between pitchers. First it turned to wine and then it turned to beer and then it turned to whisky. I know it was whisky it finally turned into because he needed somebody to come up out of the audience to help him, and I came up—both shows! It was Kentucky Straight Bourbon. A very generous fellow, he gave souvenirs. (*He pulls from his back pocket a shimmering rainbow-colored scarf.*) He gave me this. This is his magic scarf. You can have it, Laura. You wave it over a canary cage and you get a bowl of goldfish. You wave it over the goldfish bowl

[1] The next few speeches are spoken on the fire-escape landing.

and they fly away canaries. . . . But the wonderfulest trick of all was the coffin trick. We nailed him into a coffin and he got out of the coffin without removing one nail. (*They enter.*) There is a trick that would come in handy for me—get me out of this two-by-four situation! (*Flops onto the day bed and starts removing his shoes.*)

LAURA. Tom—Shhh!   10

TOM. What're you shushing me for?

LAURA. You'll wake up Mother.

TOM. Goody goody! Pay 'er back for all those "Rise an' shines." (*Lies down groaning.*) You know it don't take much intelligence to get yourself into a nailed-up coffin, Laura. But who in hell ever got himself out of one without removing one nail?

[*As if in answer, the father's grinning photo-*   20
graph lights up.]

[LAURA *exits up left. The lights fade except for a blue glow in the dining room. A pause after the lights fade, then the clock chimes six times. This is followed by the alarm clock. Dim in forestage.*]

SCENE V

SCENE *is the same. Immediately following. The church bell is heard striking six. At the*   30
sixth stroke the alarm clock goes off in AMANDA's *room off to the right of the dining room and after a few moments we hear her calling, "Rise and shine! Rise and shine! Laura, go tell your brother to rise and shine!"*

TOM (*sitting up slowly in the day bed*). I'll rise—but I won't shine.

[*The light increases.*]

AMANDA (*off stage*). Laura, tell your   40
brother his coffee is ready.

[LAURA, *fully dressed, a cape over her shoulders, slips into the living room.* TOM *is still in bed, covered with a blanket, having taken off only shoes and coat.*]

LAURA. Tom!—It's nearly seven. Don't

make Mother nervous. (*He stares at her stupidly. Beseechingly:*) Tom, speak to Mother this morning. Make up with her, apologize, speak to her!

TOM (*putting on his shoes*). She won't to me. It's her that started not speaking.

LAURA. If you just say you're sorry she'll start speaking.

TOM. Her not speaking—is that such a tragedy?

LAURA. Please—please!

AMANDA (*calling off stage at the right from the kitchen*). Laura, are you going to do what I asked you to do, or do I have to get dressed and go out myself?

LAURA. Going, going—soon as I get on my coat! (*She rises and crosses to the door at the right.*) Butter and what else? (*To* AMANDA.)

AMANDA (*off stage*). Just butter. Tell them to charge it.

LAURA. Mother, they make such faces when I do that.

AMANDA (*off stage*). Sticks and stones can break our bones, but the expression on Mr. Garfinkel's face won't harm us! Tell your brother his coffee is getting cold.

LAURA (*at the door to the right*). Do what I asked you, will you, will you, Tom? (*He looks sullenly away.*)

AMANDA. Laura, go now or just don't go at all!

LAURA (*rushing out by the right*). Going— going!

[*A second later she cries out. Falls on the fire-escape landing.* TOM *springs up and crosses to the door at the right.* AMANDA *rushes anxiously in from the dining room, puts dishes on the dining-room table.* TOM *opens the door at the right.*]

TOM. Laura?

LAURA. I'm all right. I slipped, but I'm all right. (*Goes up the right alley, out of sight.*)

AMANDA (*on the fire escape*). I tell you if

anybody falls down and breaks a leg on those fire-escape steps, the landlord ought to be sued for every cent he—— (*Sees* TOM.) Who are you? (*Leaves the fire-escape landing, crosses to the dining room, and returns with bowls, coffee cup, cream, etc. Puts them on a small table to the right of the day bed, crosses to the armchair, sits. Count 3.*)

[*Music cue No. 9.*]

[*As* TOM *re-enters from the right, listlessly, for his coffee, she turns her back to him as she sits in the armchair. The light on her face with its aged but childish features is cruelly sharp, satirical as a Daumier print.*

[TOM *glances sheepishly but sullenly at her averted figure and sits on the day bed next to the food. The coffee is scalding hot; he sips it and gasps and spits it back into the cup. At his gasp,* AMANDA *catches her breath and half turns, then catches herself and turns away.*

[TOM *blows on his coffee, glancing sidewise at his mother. She clears her throat.* TOM *clears his. He starts to rise. Sinks back down again, scratches his head, clears his throat again.* AMANDA *coughs.* TOM *raises his cup in both hands to blow on it, his eyes staring over the rim of it at his mother for several moments. Then he slowly sets the cup down and awkwardly and hesitantly rises from the day bed.*]

TOM (*hoarsely*). I'm sorry, Mother. I'm sorry for all those things I said. I didn't mean it. I apologize.

AMANDA (*sobbingly*). My devotion has made me a witch and so I make myself hateful to my children!

TOM. No you don't.

AMANDA. I worry so much, I don't sleep, it makes me nervous!

TOM (*gently*). I understand that.

AMANDA. You know I've had to put up a solitary battle all these years. But you're my right-hand bower! Now don't fail me. Don't fall down.

TOM (*gently*). I try, Mother.

AMANDA (*with great enthusiasm*). That's all right! You just keep on trying and you're bound to succeed. Why, you're —you're just full of natural endowments! Both my children are—they're very precious children and I've got an awful lot to be thankful for; you just must promise me one thing.

[*Music cue No. 9 stops.*]

TOM. What is it, Mother?

AMANDA. Promise me you're never going to become a drunkard!

TOM. I promise, Mother. I won't ever become a drunkard, Mother.

AMANDA. That's what frightened me so, that you'd be drinking! Eat a bowl of Purina.

TOM. Just coffee, Mother.

AMANDA. Shredded Wheat Biscuit?

TOM. No, no, Mother, just coffee.

AMANDA. You can't put in a day's work on an empty stomach. You've got ten minutes—don't gulp! Drinking too-hot liquids makes cancer of the stomach. . . . Put cream in.

TOM. No, thank you.

AMANDA. To cool it.

TOM. No! No, thank you, I want it black.

AMANDA. I know, but it's not good for you. We have to do all that we can to build ourselves up. In these trying times we live in, all that we have to cling to is—each other. . . . That's why it's so important to—— Tom, I—I sent out your sister so I could discuss something with you. If you hadn't spoken I would have spoken to you. (*Sits down.*)

TOM (*gently*). What is it, Mother, that you want to discuss?

AMANDA. Laura!

[TOM *puts his cup down slowly. Music cue No. 10.*]

TOM. —Oh.—Laura . . .

AMANDA (*touching his sleeve*). You know

how Laura is. So quiet but—still water runs deep! She notices things and I think she—broods about them. (TOM *looks up.*) A few days ago I came in and she was crying.

TOM. What about?

AMANDA. You.

TOM. Me?

AMANDA. She has an idea that you're not happy here.   10

[*Music cue No. 10 stops.*]

TOM. What gave her that idea?

AMANDA. What gives her any idea? However, you do act strangely. (TOM *slaps his cup down on the small table.*) I—I'm not criticizing, understand that! I know your ambitions do not lie in the warehouse, that like everybody in the whole wide world—you've had to—make sacrifices, but—Tom—Tom— 20 life's not easy, it calls for—Spartan endurance! There's so many things in my heart that I cannot describe to you! I've never told you but I—loved your father . . .

TOM (*gently*). I know that, Mother.

AMANDA. And you—when I see you taking after his ways! Staying out late—and—well, you had been drinking the night you were in that—ter- 30 rifying condition! Laura says that you hate the apartment and that you go out nights to get away from it! Is that true, Tom?

TOM. No. You say there's so much in your heart that you can't describe to me. That's true of me, too. There's so much in my heart that I can't describe to you! So let's respect each other's——

AMANDA. But, why—why, Tom—are you always so restless? Where do you go to, nights?

TOM. I—go to the movies.

AMANDA. Why do you go to the movies so much, Tom?

TOM. I go to the movies because—I like adventure. Adventure is something I don't have much of at work, so I go to the movies.

AMANDA. But, Tom, you go to the movies entirely too much!

TOM. I like a lot of adventure. (AMANDA *looks baffled, then hurt. As the familiar inquisition resumes he becomes hard and impatient again.* AMANDA *slips back into her querulous attitude toward him.*)

AMANDA. Most young men find adventure in their careers.

TOM. Then most young men are not employed in a warehouse.

AMANDA. The world is full of young men employed in warehouses and offices and factories.

TOM. Do all of them find adventure in their careers?

AMANDA. They do or they do without it! Not everybody has a craze for adventure.

TOM. Man is by instinct a lover, a hunter, a fighter, and none of those instincts are given much play at the warehouse!

AMANDA. Man is by instinct! Don't quote instinct to me! Instinct is something that people have got away from! It belongs to animals! Christian adults don't want it!

TOM. What do Christian adults want, then, Mother?

AMANDA. Superior things! Things of the mind and the spirit! Only animals have to satisfy instincts! Surely your aims are somewhat higher than theirs! Than monkeys—pigs——

TOM. I reckon they're not.

AMANDA. You're joking. However, that isn't what I wanted to discuss.

TOM (*rising*). I haven't much time.

AMANDA (*pushing his shoulders*). Sit down.

TOM. You want me to punch in red at the warehouse, Mother?

AMANDA. You have five minutes. I want to talk about Laura.

TOM. All right! What about Laura?

AMANDA. We have to be making some plans and provisions for her. She's older than you, two years, and nothing has happened. She just drifts along doing nothing. It frightens me terribly how she just drifts along.

TOM. I guess she's the type that people call home girls.

AMANDA. There's no such type, and if there is, it's a pity! That is unless the home is hers, with a husband!

TOM. What?

AMANDA (*crossing down right to the armchair*). Oh, I can see the handwriting on the wall as plain as I see the nose in front of my face! It's terrifying! More and more you remind me of your father! He was out all (*Sits in the armchair.*) hours without explanation! —Then left! Good-by! And me with the bag to hold. I saw that letter you got from the Merchant Marine. I know what you're dreaming of. I'm not standing here blindfolded. Very well, then. Then do it! But not till there's somebody to take your place.

TOM. What do you mean?

AMANDA. I mean that as soon as Laura has got somebody to take care of her, married, a home of her own, independent—why, then you'll be free to go wherever you please (*Rises, crosses to* TOM.)—on land, on sea, whichever way the wind blows you! But until that time you've got to look out for your sister. (*Crosses right behind the armchair.*) I don't say me because I'm old and don't matter! I say for your sister because she's young and dependent. I put her in business college—a dismal failure! Frightened her so it made her sick at the stomach. I took her over to the Young People's League at the church. Another fiasco. She spoke to nobody, nobody spoke to her. (*Sits in the armchair.*) Now all she does is fool with those pieces of glass and play those worn-out records. What kind of a life is that for a girl to lead?

TOM. What can I do about it?

AMANDA. Overcome selfishness! Self, self, self is all that you ever think of! (TOM *springs up and crosses right to get his coat and put it on. It is ugly and bulky. He pulls on a cap with earmuffs.*) Where is your muffler? Put your wool muffler on! (*He snatches it angrily from the hook and tosses it around his neck and pulls both ends tight.*) Tom! I haven't said what I had in mind to ask you.

TOM. I'm too late to——

AMANDA (*catching his arm—very importunately, then shyly*). Down at the warehouse, aren't there some—nice young men?

TOM. No!

AMANDA. There must be—some——

TOM. Mother—— (*Gesture.*)

AMANDA. Find out one that's clean-living—doesn't drink and—ask him out for sister!

TOM. What?

AMANDA. For sister! To meet! Get acquainted!

TOM (*stamping to the door at the right*). Oh, my go-osh!

AMANDA. Will you? (*He opens the door. Imploringly:*) Will you? (*He starts out.*) Will you? Will you, dear? (TOM *exits up the alley to the right.* AMANDA *is on the fire-escape landing.*)

TOM (*calling back*). Yes!

AMANDA (*re-entering by the right and crossing to the phone. Music cue No. 11.*) Ella Cartwright? Ella, this is Amanda Wingfield. First, first, how's that kidney trouble? Oh, it has? It has come back? Well, you're just a Christian martyr, you're just a Christian martyr. I was noticing in my little red book that your subscription to the *Companion* has run out just when that wonderful new serial by Bessie Mae Harper was starting. It's all about the horsy set on Long Island. Oh, you have? You have read it? Well, how do you think it turns out? 10 Oh no. Bessie Mae Harper never lets you down. Oh, of course we have to have complications. You have to have complications—oh, you can't have a story without them—but Bessie Mae Harper always leaves you with such an uplift. What's the matter, Ella? You sound so mad. Oh, because it's seven o'clock in the morning. Oh, Ella, I forgot that you never got up 20 until nine. I forgot that anybody in the world was allowed to sleep as late as that. I can't say any more than I'm sorry, can I? Oh, you will? You're going to take that subscription from me anyhow? Well, bless you, Ella, bless you, bless you, bless you.

[*Music cue No. 11 fades into dance music and continues into the next scene. Dim out the* 30 *lights. Music cue No. 11-A.*]

SCENE VI

SCENE: *The same.—Only the right alley lighted, with a dim light.*

TOM (*enters down right and stands as before, leaning against the grillwork, with a cigarette, wearing the merchant-sailor coat and cap*). Across the alley was the 40 Paradise Dance Hall. Evenings in spring they'd open all the doors and windows and the music would come outside. Sometimes they'd turn out all the lights except for a large glass sphere that hung from the ceiling. It would turn slowly about and filter the dusk with delicate rainbow colors. Then the orchestra would play a waltz or a tango, something that had a slow and sensuous rhythm. The young couples would come outside, to the relative privacy of the alley. You could see them kissing behind ash pits and telephone poles. This was the compensation for lives that passed like mine, without change or adventure. Changes and adventure, however, were imminent this year. They were waiting around the corner for all these dancing kids. Suspended in the mist over Berchtesgaden, caught in the folds of Chamberlain's umbrella.—In Spain there was Guernica! Here there was only hot swing music and liquor, dance halls, bars, and movies, and sex that hung in the gloom like a chandelier and flooded the world with brief, deceptive rainbows. . . . While these unsuspecting kids danced to "Dear One, The World is Waiting for the Sunrise." All the world was really waiting for bombardments.

[*Music cue No. 11-A stops. Dim in the dining room: faint glow.* AMANDA *is seen in the dining room.*]

AMANDA. Tom, where are you?

TOM (*standing as before*). I came out to smoke. (*Exits by the right into the wings, where he again changes coats, and leaves his hat.*)

AMANDA. (TOM *re-enters and stands on the fire-escape landing, smoking. He opens the door for* AMANDA, *who sits on the hassock on the landing.*) Oh, you smoke too much. A pack a day at fifteen cents a pack. How much would that be in a month? Thirty times fifteen? It wouldn't be very much? Well, it would be enough to help towards a night-school course in accounting at the Washington U! Wouldn't that be lovely?

TOM. I'd rather smoke.

AMANDA. I know! That's the tragedy of you. This fire-escape landing is a poor excuse for the porch we used to have. What are you looking at?

TOM. The moon.

AMANDA. Is there a moon this evening?

TOM. It's rising over Garfinkel's deli- 10 catessen.

AMANDA. Oh! So it is! Such a little silver slipper of a moon. Have you made a wish on it?

TOM. Um-mm.

AMANDA. What did you wish?

TOM. That's a secret.

AMANDA. All right, I won't tell you what I wished, either. I can keep a secret, too. I can be just as mysterious as 20 you.

TOM. I bet I can guess what you wished.

AMANDA. Why, is my head transparent?

TOM. You're not a sphinx.

AMANDA. No, I don't have secrets. I'll tell you what I wished for on the moon. Success and happiness for my precious children. I wish for that whenever there's a moon, and when there isn't a moon, I wish for it too. 30

TOM. I thought perhaps you wished for a gentleman caller.

AMANDA. Why do you say that?

TOM. Don't you remember asking me to fetch one?

AMANDA. I remember suggesting that it would be nice for your sister if you brought home some nice young man from the warehouse. I think that I've made that suggestion more than 40 once.

TOM. Yes, you have made it repeatedly.

AMANDA. Well?

TOM. We are going to have one.

AMANDA. *What?*

TOM. A gentleman caller!

AMANDA. You mean you have asked some nice young man to come over? (*Rising from the stool, facing* TOM.)

TOM. I've asked him to dinner.

AMANDA. You really did?

TOM. I did.

AMANDA. And did he—accept?

TOM. He did!

AMANDA. He did?

TOM. He did. 10

AMANDA. Well, isn't that lovely!

TOM. I thought that you would be pleased.

AMANDA. It's definite, then?

TOM. Oh, very definite.

AMANDA. How soon?

TOM. Pretty soon.

AMANDA. How soon?

TOM. Quite soon.

AMANDA. How soon? 20

TOM. Very, very soon.

AMANDA. Every time I want to know anything you start going on like that.

TOM. What do you want to know?

AMANDA. Go ahead and guess. Go ahead and guess.

TOM. All right, I'll guess. You want to know when the gentleman caller's coming—he's coming tomorrow.

AMANDA. Tomorrow? Oh no, I can't do 30 anything about tomorrow. I can't do anything about tomorrow.

TOM. Why not?

AMANDA. That doesn't give me any time.

TOM. Time for what?

AMANDA. Time for preparations. Oh, you should have phoned me the minute you asked him—the minute he accepted!

TOM. You don't have to make any fuss. 40

AMANDA. Of course I have to make a fuss! I can't have a man coming into a place that's all sloppy. It's got to be thrown together properly. I certainly have to do some fast thinking by tomorrow night, too.

TOM. I don't see why you have to think at all.

AMANDA. That's because you just don't know. (*Enter the living room, crosses to the center. Dim in the living room.*) You just don't know, that's all. We can't have a gentleman caller coming into a pigsty! Now, let's see. Oh! I've got those three pieces of wedding silver left. I'll polish that up. I wonder how that old lace tablecloth is holding up all these years? We can't wear anything. We haven't got it. We haven't got anything to wear. We haven't got it. (*Goes back to door at the right.*)

TOM. Mother! This boy is no one to make a fuss over.

AMANDA (*crossing to the center*). I don't know how you can say that when this is the first gentleman caller your little sister's ever had! I think it's pathetic that that little girl has never had a single gentleman caller! Come on inside! Come on inside!

TOM. What for?

AMANDA. I want to ask you a few things.

TOM (*from the doorway at the right*). If you're going to make a fuss, I'll call the whole thing off. I'll call the boy up and tell him not to come.

AMANDA. No! You mustn't ever do that. People hate broken engagements. They have no place to go. Come on inside. Come on inside. Will you come inside when I ask you to come inside? Sit down. (*TOM comes into the living room.*)

TOM. Any particular place you want me to sit?

AMANDA. Oh! Sit anywhere. (*TOM sits in the armchair at the right.*) Look! What am I going to do about that? (*Looking at the day bed.*) Did you ever see anything look so sad? I know, I'll get a bright piece of cretonne. That won't cost much. And I made payments on a floor lamp. So I'll have that sent out! And I can put a bright cover on the chair. I wish I had time to paper the walls. What's his name?

TOM. His name is O'Connor.

AMANDA. O'Connor—he's Irish and tomorrow's Friday—that means fish. Well, that's all right, I'll make a salmon loaf and some mayonnaise dressing for it. Where did you meet him? (*Crosses to the day bed and sits.*)

TOM. At the warehouse, of course. Where else would I meet him?

AMANDA. Well, I don't know. Does he drink?

TOM. What made you ask me that?

AMANDA. Because your father did.

TOM. Now don't get started on that!

AMANDA. He drinks, then.

TOM. No, not that I know of.

AMANDA. You have to find out. There's nothing I want less for my daughter than a man who drinks.

TOM. Aren't you being a little bit premature? After all, poor Mr. O'Connor hasn't even appeared on the scene yet.

AMANDA. But he will tomorrow. To meet your sister. And what do I know about his character? (*Rises and crosses to* TOM, *who is still in the armchair, smooths his hair.*)

TOM (*submitting grimly*). Now what are you up to?

AMANDA. I always did hate that cowlick. I never could understand why it won't sit down by itself.

TOM. Mother, I want to tell you something and I mean it sincerely, right straight from my heart. There's a lot of boys who meet girls which they don't marry!

AMANDA. You know you always had me worried because you could never stick to a subject. (*Crosses to the day bed.*) What I want to know is, what's his position at the warehouse?

TOM. He's a shipping clerk.

AMANDA. Oh! Shipping clerk! Well, that's fairly important. That's where you'd be if you had more get-up. How much does he earn? (*Sits on the day bed.*)

TOM. I have no way of knowing that for sure. I judge his salary to be approximately eighty-five dollars a month.

AMANDA. Eighty-five dollars? Well, that's not princely.

TOM. It's twenty dollars more than I make.

AMANDA. I know that. Oh, how well I know that! How well I know that! Eighty-five dollars a month. No. It can't be done. A family man can never get by on eighty-five dollars a month.

TOM. Mother, Mr. O'Connor is not a family man.

AMANDA. Well, he might be some time in the future, mightn't he?

TOM. Oh, I see. . . . Plans and provisions.

AMANDA. You are the only young man that I know of who ignores the fact that the future becomes the present, the present the past, and the past turns into everlasting regret if you don't plan for it.

TOM. I will think that over and see what I can make of it!

AMANDA. Don't be supercilious with your mother! Tell me some more about this.—What do you call him? Mr. O'Connor, Mr. O'Connor. He must have another name besides Mr.——?

TOM. His full name is James D. O'Connor. The D. is for Delaney.

AMANDA. Delaney? Irish on both sides and he doesn't drink?

TOM (*rises from the armchair*). Shall I call

him up and ask him? (*Starts toward the phone.*)

AMANDA (*crossing to the phone*). No!

TOM. I'll call him up and tell him you want to know if he drinks. (*Picks up the phone.*)

AMANDA (*taking the phone away from him*). No, you can't do that. You have to be discreet about that subject. When I was a girl in Blue Mountain if it was (TOM *sits on the right of the day bed.*) suspected that a young man was drinking and any girl was receiving his attentions—if any girl *was* receiving his attentions, she'd go to the minister of his church and ask about his character—or her father, if her father was living, then it was his duty to go to the minister of his church and ask about his character, and that's how young girls in Blue Mountain were kept from making tragic mistakes, (*Picture dims in and out.*)

TOM. How come you made such a tragic one?

AMANDA. Oh, I don't know how he did it, but that face fooled everybody. All he had to do was grin and the world was bewitched. (*Behind the day bed crosses to the armchair.*) I don't know of anything more tragic than a young girl just putting herself at the mercy of a handsome appearance, and I hope Mr. O'Connor is *not* too good-looking.

TOM. As a matter of fact he isn't. His face is covered with freckles and he has a very large nose.

AMANDA. He's not right-down homely?

TOM. No. I wouldn't say right-down homely—medium homely, I'd say.

AMANDA. Well, if a girl had any sense she'd look for character in a man anyhow.

TOM. That's what I've always said, Mother.

AMANDA. You've always said it—you've always said it! How could you've always said it when you never even thought about it?

TOM. Aw, don't be so suspicious of me.

AMANDA. I am. I'm suspicious of every word that comes out of your mouth when you talk to me, but I want to know about this young man. Is he up and coming?

TOM. Yes. I really do think he goes in for self-improvement.

AMANDA. What makes you think it?

TOM. He goes to night school.

AMANDA. Well, what does he do there at night school?

TOM. He's studying radio engineering and public speaking.

AMANDA. Oh! Public speaking! Oh, that shows, that shows that he intends to be an executive some day— and radio engineering. Well, that's coming . . . huh?

TOM. I think it's here.

AMANDA. Well, those are all very illuminating facts. (*Crosses to the back of the armchair.*) Facts that every mother should know about any young man calling on her daughter, seriously or not.

TOM. Just one little warning, Mother. I didn't tell him anything about Laura. I didn't let on we had dark ulterior motives. I just said, "How about coming home to dinner sometime?" and he said, "Fine," and that was the whole conversation.

AMANDA. I bet it was, too. I tell you, sometimes you can be as eloquent as an oyster. However, when he sees how pretty and sweet that child is, he's going to be—well, he's going to be very glad he was asked over here to have some dinner. (*Sits in the armchair.*)

TOM. Mother, just one thing. You won't expect too much of Laura, will you?

AMANDA. I don't know what you mean.

[TOM *crosses slowly to* AMANDA. *He stands for a moment, looking at her. Then:*]

TOM. Well, Laura seems all those things to you and me because she's ours and we love her. We don't even notice she's crippled any more.

AMANDA. Don't use that word.

TOM. Mother, you have to face the facts; she is, and that's not all.

AMANDA. What do you mean "that's not all"?

[TOM *kneels by her chair.*]

TOM. Mother—you know that Laura is very different from other girls.

AMANDA. Yes, I do know that, and I think that difference is all in her favor, too.

TOM. Not quite all—in the eyes of others —strangers—she's terribly shy. She lives in a world of her own, and those things make her seem a little peculiar to people outside the house.

AMANDA. Don't use that word "peculiar."

TOM. You have to face the facts.—She is.

AMANDA. I don't know in what way she's peculiar.

[*Music cue No. 12, till curtain.* TOM *pauses a moment for the music, then:*]

TOM. Mother, Laura lives in a world of little glass animals. She plays old phonograph records—and—that's about all—— (TOM *rises slowly, goes quietly out the door at the right, leaving it open, and exits slowly up the alley.* AMANDA *rises, goes onto the fire-escape landing at the right, looks at the moon.*)

AMANDA. Laura! Laura!

[LAURA *answers from the kitchen at the right.*]

LAURA. Yes, Mother.

AMANDA. Let those dishes go and come in front! (LAURA *appears with a dish* towel. *Gaily:*) Laura, come here and make a wish on the moon!

LAURA (*entering from the kitchen at the right, comes down to the fire-escape landing*). Moon—moon?

AMANDA. A little silver slipper of a moon. Look over your left shoulder, Laura, and make a wish! (LAURA *looks faintly puzzled as if called out of sleep.* AMANDA *seizes her shoulders and turns her at an angle on the fire-escape landing.*) Now! Now, darling, wish!

LAURA. What shall I wish for, Mother?

AMANDA (*her voice trembling and her eyes suddenly filling with tears*). Happiness! Good fortune!

[*The stage dims out.*]

CURTAIN

ACT II

SCENE VII

SCENE: *The same.*

The inner curtains are closed between the dining room and the living room. The interiors of both rooms are dark as at the beginning of the play. (*Music cue No. 13.*) TOM *has on the same jacket and cap as at first. Same music as cue No. 1, fading as* TOM *begins.*

TOM (*discovered leaning against the grill on the fire-escape landing, as before, and smoking*). And so the following evening I brought Jim home to dinner. I had known Jim slightly in high school. In high school, Jim was a hero. He had tremendous Irish good nature and vitality, with the scrubbed and polished look of white chinaware. He seemed to move in a continual spotlight. He was a star in basketball, captain of the debating club, president of the senior class and the glee club, and he sang the male lead in the annual light opera. He was forever running or bounding, never just walking. He seemed always just at the point of defeating the law of gravity. He was shooting with such velocity through his adolescence that you would just logically expect him to arrive at nothing short of the White House by the time he was thirty. But

Jim apparently ran into more interference after his graduation from high school, because his speed had definitely slowed. And so, at this particular time in our lives he was holding a job that wasn't much better than mine.

He was the only one at the warehouse with whom I was on friendly terms. I was valuable to Jim as someone who could remember his former glory, who had seen him win basketball games and the silver cup in debating. He knew of my secret practice of retiring to a cabinet of the washroom to work on poems whenever business was slack in the warehouse. He called me Shakespeare. And while the other boys in the warehouse regarded me with suspicious hostility, Jim took a humorous attitude toward me. Gradually his attitude began to affect the other boys and their hostility wore off. And so, after a time they began to smile at me too, as people smile at some oddly fashioned dog that trots across their path at some distance. I knew that Jim and Laura had known each other in high school, because I had heard my sister Laura speak admiringly of Jim's voice. I didn't know if Jim would remember her or not. Because in high school Laura had been as unobtrusive as Jim had been astonishing. And if he did remember Laura, it was not as my sister, for when I asked him home to dinner, he smiled and said, "You know, a funny thing, Shakespeare, I never thought of you as having folks!"

Well, he was about to discover that I did. . . .

[*Music cue No. 13-A.* TOM *exits by the right. The interior living-room lights dim in.* AMANDA *is sitting at the small table at the right of the day bed sewing on the hem of* LAURA'S *dress.* LAURA *stands facing the door at the right.*

[AMANDA *has worked like a Turk in preparation for the gentleman caller. The results are astonishing. The new floor lamp with its rose-silk shade is in place, at the right of the living room next to the wall, a colored paper lantern conceals the broken light fixture in the ceiling, chintz covers are on the chairs and sofa, a pair of new sofa pillows make their initial appearance.*

[LAURA *stands in the middle of the room with lifted arms while* AMANDA *crouches before her, adjusting the hem of the new dress, devout and ritualistic. The dress is colored, and designed by memory. The arrangement of* LAURA'S *hair is changed; it is softer and more becoming. A fragile, unearthly prettiness has come out in* LAURA: *she is like a piece of translucent glass touched by light, given a momentary radiance, not actual, not lasting.*

[AMANDA, *still seated, is sewing* LAURA'S *dress.* LAURA *is standing at the right of* AMANDA.]

AMANDA. Why are you trembling so, Laura?

LAURA. Mother, you've made me so nervous!

AMANDA. Why, how have I made you nervous?

LAURA. By all this fuss! You make it seem so important.

AMANDA. I don't understand you at all, honey. Every time I try to do anything for you that's the least bit different you just seem to set yourself against it. Now take a look at yourself. (LAURA *starts for the door at the right.*) No, wait! Wait just a minute—I forgot something. (*Picks two powder puffs from the day bed.*)

LAURA. What is it?

AMANDA. A couple of improvements. (*Business with powder puffs.*) When I was a girl we had round little lacy things like that and we called them "gay deceivers."

LAURA. I won't wear them!

AMANDA. Of course you'll wear them.

LAURA. Why should I?

AMANDA. Well, to tell you the truth, honey, you're just a little bit flatchested.

LAURA. You make it seem like we were setting a trap.

AMANDA. We are. All pretty girls are a trap and men expect them to be traps. Now look at yourself in that glass. (LAURA *crosses right. Looks at the mirror, invisible to the audience, which is in darkness up right of the right door.*) See? You look just like an angel on a post card. Isn't that lovely? Now you just wait. I'm going to dress myself up. You're going to be astonished at your mother's appearance.

[*The end of the music cue leads into dance music, which then leads in Music cue No. 14 a few lines below, at the stage direction.* AMANDA *exits through the curtains upstage off left in the dining room.* LAURA *looks in the mirror for a moment. Removes the "gay deceivers," hides them under the mattress of the day bed. Sits at the small table at the right of the day bed for a moment, goes out to the fire-escape landing, listens to the dance music, until* AMANDA'S *entrance.*]

AMANDA (*off*). I found an old dress in the

trunk. But what do you know? I had to do a lot to it, but it broke my heart when I had to let it out. Now, Laura, just look at your mother. Oh no! Laura, come look at me now! (*Enters the dining room left door. Comes down through the living-room curtain to the living room center.*)

[*Music cue No. 14-A.*]

LAURA (*re-enters from the fire-escape landing. Sits on the left arm of the armchair.*) Oh, Mother, how lovely!

[AMANDA *wears a girlish frock. She carries a bunch of jonquils.*]

AMANDA (*standing center, holding the flowers*). It used to be. It used to be. It had a lot of flowers on it, but they got awful tired, so I had to take them all off. I led the cotillion in this dress years ago. I won the cake walk twice at Sunset Hill, and I wore it to the Governor's ball in Jackson. You should have seen your mother. You should have seen your mother, how she just sashayed around (*Crossing around left of the day bed back to the center.*) the ballroom, just like that. I had it on the day I met your father. I had malaria fever, too. The change of climate from East Tennessee to the Delta weakened my resistance. Not enough to be dangerous, just enough to make me restless and giddy. Oh, it was lovely. Invitations poured in from all over. My mother said, "You can't go any place because you have a fever. You have to stay in bed." I said I wouldn't and I took quinine and kept on going and going. Dances every evening and long rides in the country in the afternoon and picnics. That country— that country—so lovely—so lovely in May, all lacy with dogwood and simply flooded with jonquils. My mother said, "You can't bring any more jonquils in this house." I said, "I will," and I kept on bringing them in anyhow. Whenever I saw them I said, "Wait a minute, I see jonquils," and I'd make my gentlemen callers get out of the carriage and help me gather some. To tell you the truth, Laura, it got to be a kind of a joke. "Look out," they'd say, "here comes that girl and we'll have to spend the afternoon picking jonquils." My mother said, "You can't bring any more jonquils in the house, there aren't any more vases to hold them." "That's quite all right," I said, "I can hold some myself." Malaria fever, your father and jonquils. (AMANDA *puts the jonquils in* LAURA's *lap and goes out onto the fire-escape landing. Music cue No. 14 stops. Thunder heard.*) I hope they get here before it starts to rain. I gave your brother a little extra change so he and Mr. O'Connor could take the service car home.

[LAURA *puts the flowers on the armchair at the right, and crosses to the door at the right.*]

LAURA. Mother!

AMANDA. What's the matter now? (*Re-entering the room.*)

LAURA. What did you say his name was?

AMANDA. O'Connor. Why?

LAURA. What is his first name?

AMANDA (*crosses to the armchair at the right*). I don't remember—— Oh, yes, I do too—it was—Jim! (*Picks up the flowers.*)

LAURA. Oh, Mother, not Jim O'Connor!

AMANDA. Yes, that was it, it was Jim! I've never known a Jim that wasn't nice. (*Crosses left, behind the day bed, puts the flowers in a vase.*)

LAURA. Are you sure his name was Jim O'Connor?

AMANDA. Why, sure I'm sure. Why?

LAURA. Is he the one that Tom used to know in high school?

AMANDA. He didn't say so. I think he just got to know him (*Sits on the day bed*) at the warehouse.

LAURA. There was a Jim O'Connor we both knew in high school. If that is the one that Tom is bringing home to dinner—oh, Mother, you'd have to 10 excuse me, I wouldn't come to the table!

AMANDA. What's this now? What sort of silly talk is this?

LAURA. You asked me once if I'd ever liked a boy. Don't you remember I showed you this boy's picture?

AMANDA. You mean the boy in the year-book?

LAURA. Yes, that boy.

AMANDA. Laura, Laura, were you in love with that boy?

LAURA (*crosses to the right of the armchair*). I don't know, Mother. All I know is that I couldn't sit at the table if it was him.

AMANDA (*rises, crosses left and works up left of the day bed*). It won't be him! It isn't the least bit likely. But whether it is or not, you will come to the table 30 —you will not be excused.

LAURA. I'll have to be, Mother.

AMANDA (*behind the day bed*). I don't intend to humor your silliness, Laura. I've had too much from you and your brother, both. So just sit down and compose yourself till they come. Tom has forgotten his key, so you'll *have* to let them in when they arrive.

LAURA. Oh, Mother—*you* answer the 40 door! (*Sits in the chair at the right.*)

AMANDA. How can I when I haven't even finished making the mayonnaise dressing for the salmon?

LAURA. Oh, Mother, please answer the door, don't make me do it!

[*Thunder heard offstage.*]

AMANDA. Honey, do be reasonable! What's all this fuss about—just one gentleman caller—that's all—just one!

[*Exits through the living-room curtains. TOM and JIM enter the alley at the right, climb the fire-escape steps to the landing, and wait outside of the closed door. Hearing them approach, LAURA rises with a panicky gesture. She retreats to the living-room curtains. The doorbell rings. LAURA catches her breath and touches her throat. More thunder heard offstage.*]

AMANDA (*offstage*). Laura, sweetheart, the door!

LAURA. Mother, please, you go to the door! (*Starts for the door at the right, then back.*)

AMANDA (*offstage, in a fierce whisper*). What is the matter with you, you silly thing? (*Enters through the living-room curtains, and stands by the day bed.*)

LAURA. Please, you answer it, please.

AMANDA. Why have you chosen this moment to lose your mind? You go to that door.

LAURA. I can't.

AMANDA. Why can't you?

LAURA. Because I'm sick. (*Crosses to the left end of the day bed and sits.*)

AMANDA. You're sick! Am I sick? You and your brother have me puzzled to death. You can never act like normal children. Will you give me one good reason why you should be afraid to open a door? You go to that door. Laura Wingfield, you march straight to that door!

LAURA (*crosses to the door at the right*). Yes, Mother.

AMANDA (*stopping LAURA*). I've got to put courage in you, honey, for living.

[*Exits through the living-room curtains, and exits right into the kitchen. LAURA opens the door. TOM and JIM enter. LAURA re-*

mains hidden in the hall behind the door.]

TOM. Laura—(LAURA *crosses center.*)— this is Jim. Jim, this is my sister Laura.

JIM. I didn't know that Shakespeare had a sister! How are you, Laura?

LAURA (*retreating stiff and trembling, shakes hands*). How—how do you do?

JIM. Well, I'm okay! Your hand's *cold*, Laura! (TOM *puts their hats on the phone table.*)

LAURA. Yes, well—I've been playing the Victrola. . . .

JIM. Must have been playing classical music on it. You ought to play a little hot swing music to warm you up.

[LAURA *crosses to the phonograph.* TOM *crosses up to* LAURA. LAURA *starts phonograph* [1]—*looks at* JIM. *Exits through the living-room curtains and goes off by the left.*]

JIM. What's the matter?

TOM. Oh—Laura? Laura is—is terribly shy. (*Crosses and sits on the day bed.*)

JIM (*crosses down center*). Shy, huh? Do you know it's unusual to meet a shy girl nowadays? I don't believe you ever mentioned you had a sister.

TOM. Well, now you know I have one. You want a piece of the paper?

JIM (*crosses to* TOM). Uh-huh.

TOM. Comics?

JIM. Comics? Sports! (*Takes the paper. Crosses, sits in the chair at the right.*) I see that Dizzy Dean is on his bad behavior.

TOM (*starts to the door at the right! goes out*). Really?

JIM. Yeah. Where are *you* going? (*As* TOM *reaches the steps at the right of the fire-escape landing.*)

TOM (*calling from the fire-escape landing*). Out on the terrace to smoke.

JIM (*rises, leaving the newspaper in the arm-*

[1] A worn record of "Dardanella" or some other popular tune of the 1920's.

chair, goes over to turn off the Victrola. Crosses right. Exits to the fire-escape landing.) You know, Shakespeare—I'm going to sell you a bill of goods!

TOM. What goods?

JIM. A course I'm taking.

TOM. What course?

JIM. A course in public speaking! You know you and me, we're not the warehouse type.

TOM. Thanks—that's good news. What has public speaking got to do with it?

JIM. It fits you for—executive positions!

TOM. Oh.

JIM. I tell you it's done a helluva lot for me.

TOM. In what respect?

JIM. In all respects. Ask yourself: What's the difference between you and me and the guys in the office down front? Brains?—No!—Ability? —No! Then what? Primarily, it amounts to just one single thing——

TOM. What is that one thing?

JIM. Social poise! The ability to square up to somebody and hold your own on any social level!

AMANDA (*offstage*). Tom?

TOM. Yes, Mother?

AMANDA. Is that you and Mr. O'Connor?

TOM. Yes, Mother.

AMANDA. Make yourselves comfortable.

TOM. We will.

AMANDA. Ask Mr. O'Connor if he would like to wash his hands.

JIM. No thanks, ma'am—I took care of that down at the warehouse. Tom?

TOM. Huh?

JIM. Mr. Mendoza was speaking to me about you.

TOM. Favorably?

JIM. What do you think?

TOM. Well——

JIM. You're going to be out of a job if you don't wake up.

TOM. I'm waking up——

JIM. Yeah, but you show no signs.

TOM. The signs are interior. I'm just about to make a change. I'm right at the point of committing myself to a future that doesn't include the warehouse or Mr. Mendoza, or even a night-school course in public speaking.

JIM. Now what are you gassing about? 10

TOM. I'm tired of the movies.

JIM. The movies!

TOM. Yes, movies! Look at them. (*He waves his hands.*) All of those glamorous people—having adventures—hogging it all, gobbling the whole thing up! You know what happens? People go to the *movies* instead of *moving.* Hollywood characters are supposed to have all the adventures 20 for everybody in America while everybody in America sits in a dark room and watches them having it! Yes, until there's a war. That's when adventure becomes available to the masses! Everyone's dish, not only Gable's! Then the people in the dark room come out of the dark room to have some adventures themselves— goody—goody! It's our turn now to 30 go to the South Sea Islands—to make a safari—to be exotic, far off! . . . But I'm not patient. I don't want to wait till then. I'm tired of the movies and I'm about to move!

JIM (*incredulously*). Move?

TOM. Yes.

JIM. When?

TOM. Soon!

JIM. Where? Where? 40

TOM. I'm starting to boil inside. I know I seem dreamy, but inside—well, I'm boiling! Whenever I pick up a shoe I shudder a little, thinking how short life is, and what I am doing!—Whatever that means, I know it doesn't mean shoes—except as something to wear on a traveler's feet! (*Gets a card from his inside coat pocket.*) Look!

JIM. What?

TOM. I'm a member.

JIM (*reading*). The Union of Merchant Seamen.

TOM. I paid my dues this month, instead of the electric-light bill.

JIM. You'll regret it when they turn off the lights.

TOM. I won't be here.

JIM. Yeah, but how about your mother?

TOM. I'm like my father. The bastard son of a bastard. See how he grins? And he's been absent going on sixteen years.

JIM. You're just talking, you drip. How does your mother feel about it?

TOM. Sh! Here comes Mother! Mother's not acquainted with my plans!

AMANDA (*offstage*). Tom!

TOM. Yes, Mother?

AMANDA (*offstage*). Where are you all?

TOM. On the terrace, Mother.

AMANDA (*enters through the living-room curtain and stands at the center*). Why don't you come in?

[*They start inside. She advances to them. TOM is distinctly shocked at her appearance. Even JIM blinks a little. He is making his first contact with girlish Southern vivacity, and in spite of the night-school course in public speaking is somewhat thrown off the beam by the unexpected outlay of social charm.*]

[*Certain responses are attempted by JIM but are swept aside by AMANDA's gay laughter and chatter. TOM is embarrassed, but after the first shock JIM reacts very warmly. Grins and chuckles, is altogether won over.*]

[*TOM and JIM come in, leaving the door open.*]

TOM. Mother, you look so pretty.

AMANDA. You know, that's the first compliment you ever paid me. I wish you'd look pleasant when you're about to say something pleasant, so I could expect it. Mr. O'Connor?

[JIM *crosses to* AMANDA.]

JIM. How do you do?

AMANDA. Well, well, well, so this is Mr. O'Connor? Introduction's entirely unnecessary. I've heard so much about you from my boy. I finally said to him, "Tom, good gracious, why don't you bring this paragon to supper finally? I'd like to meet this nice young man at the warehouse! Instead of just hearing you sing his praises so much." I don't know why my son is so stand-offish—that's not Southern behavior. Let's sit down. (TOM *closes the door, crosses up right, stands.* JIM *and* AMANDA *sit on the day bed,* JIM *right,* AMANDA *left.*) Let's sit down, and I think we could stand a little more air in here. Tom, leave the door open. I felt a nice fresh breeze a moment ago. Where has it gone to? Mmmm, so warm already! And not quite summer, even. We're going to burn up when summer really gets started. However, we're having—we're having a very light supper. I think light things are better fo'—for this time of year. The same as light clothes are. Light clothes and light food are what warm weather calls fo'. You know our blood gets so thick during th' winter—it takes a while fo' us to adjust ou'selves!—when the season changes. . . . It's come so quick this year. I wasn't prepared. All of a sudden—heavens! Already summer!—I ran to the trunk an'— pulled out this light dress—terribly old! Historical almost! But feels so good—so good and cool, why, y' know——

TOM. Mother, how about our supper?

AMANDA (*rises, crosses right to* TOM). Honey, you go ask Sister if supper is ready! You know that Sister is in full charge of supper. Tell her you hungry boys are waiting for it. (TOM *exits through the curtains and off by the left.* AMANDA *turns to* JIM.) Have you met Laura?

JIM. Well, she came to the door.

AMANDA. She let you in?

JIM. Yes, ma'am.

AMANDA (*crossing to the armchair and sitting*). She's very pretty.

JIM. Oh yes, ma'am.

AMANDA. It's rare for a girl as sweet an' pretty as Laura to be domestic! But Laura is, thank heaven, not only pretty but also very domestic. I'm not at all. I never was a bit. I never could make a thing but angel-food cake. Well, in the South we had so many servants. Gone, gone, gone. All vestige of gracious living! Gone completely! I wasn't prepared for what the future brought me. All of my gentlemen callers were sons of planters and so of course I assumed that I would be married to one and raise my family on a large piece of land with plenty of servants. But man proposes—and woman accepts the proposal!—To vary that old, old saying a little bit.—I married no planter! I married a man who worked for the telephone company!—That gallantly smiling gentleman over there! (*Points to the picture.*) A telephone man who—fell in love with long distance!—Now he travels and I don't even know where!—But what am I going on for about my—tribulations? Tell me yours—I hope you don't have any! Tom?

TOM (*re-enters through the living-room curtains from off left*). Yes, Mother.

AMANDA. What about that supper?

TOM. Why, supper is on the table.

[*The inner curtains between the living room and the dining room open. The lights dim up in the dining room, dim out in the living room.*]

AMANDA. Oh, so it is. (*Rises, crosses up to the table at the center in the dining room and the chair at the center.*) How lovely. Where is Laura?

TOM (*going to the chair at the left and standing*). Laura is not feeling too well and thinks maybe she'd better not come to the table.

AMANDA. Laura!

LAURA (*offstage, faintly*). Yes, Mother?
          [TOM *gestures re:* JIM.]

AMANDA. Mr. O'Connor.

[JIM *crosses up left to the table and to the chair at the left and stands.*]

JIM. Thank you, ma'am.

AMANDA. Laura, we can't say grace till you come to the table.

LAURA (*enters up left, obviously quite faint, lips trembling, eyes wide and staring. Moves unsteadily toward the dining-room table.*) Oh, Mother, I'm so sorry.

[TOM *catches her as she feels faint. He takes her to the day bed in the living room.*]

AMANDA (*as* LAURA *lies down*). Why, Laura, you are sick, darling! Laura— rest on the sofa. Well! (*To* JIM.) Standing over the hot stove made her ill!—I told her that it was just too warm this evening, but—— (*To* TOM.) Is Laura all right now?

TOM. She's better, Mother. (*Sits in the chair to the left in the dining room.*)
          [*Thunder off stage.*]

AMANDA (*returning to the dining room and sitting at the table, as* JIM *does*). My goodness, I suppose we're going to have a little rain! Tom, you say grace.

TOM. What?

AMANDA. What do we generally do before we have something to eat? We say grace, don't we?

TOM. For these and all Thy mercies— God's Holy Name be praised.

[*The lights dim out. Music cue No. 15.*]

SCENE VIII

SCENE: *The same. A half hour later. Dinner is coming to an end in the dining room.*

AMANDA, TOM, *and* JIM *are sitting at the table as at the end of the last scene.*

The lights dim up in both rooms, and Music cue No. 15 ends.

AMANDA (*laughing, as* JIM *laughs too*). You know, Mr. O'Connor, I haven't had such a pleasant evening in a very long time.

JIM (*rises*). Well, Mrs. Wingfield, let me give you a toast. Here's to the old South.

AMANDA. The old South.
          [*Blackout in both rooms.*]

JIM. Hey, Mr. Light Bulb!

AMANDA. Where was Moses when the lights went out? Do you know the answer to that one, Mr. O'Connor?

JIM. No, ma'am, what's the answer to that one?

AMANDA. Well, I heard one answer, but it wasn't very nice. I thought you might know another one.

JIM. No, ma'am.

AMANDA. It's lucky I put those candles on the table. I just put them on for ornamentation, but it's nice when they prove useful, too.

JIM. Yes, ma'am.

AMANDA. Now, if one of you gentlemen can provide me with a match we can have some illumination.

JIM (*lighting the candles; dim in glow for the candles*). I can, ma'am.

AMANDA. Thank you.

JIM (*crosses back to the right of the dining-room table*). Not at all, ma'am.

AMANDA. I guess it must be a burnt-out fuse. Mr. O'Connor, do you know anything about a burnt-out fuse?

JIM. I know a little about them, ma'am, but where's the fuse box?

AMANDA. Must you know that, too? Well, it's in the kitchen. (JIM *exits by the right into the kitchen*.) Be careful. It's dark. Don't stumble over any- 10 thing. (*Sound of a crash off stage*.) Oh, my goodness, wouldn't it be awful if we lost him! Are you all right, Mr. O'Connor?

JIM (*off stage*). Yes, ma'am, I'm all right.

AMANDA. You know, electricity is a very mysterious thing. The whole uni- verse is mysterious to me. Wasn't it Benjamin Franklin who tied a key to 20 a kite? I'd like to have seen that—he might have looked mighty silly. Some people say that science clears up all the mysteries for us. In my opinion they just keep on adding more. Haven't you found it yet?

JIM (*re-enters from the right*). Yes, ma'am. I found it all right, but them fuses look okay to me. (*Sits as before*.)

AMANDA. Tom.   30

TOM. Yes, Mother?

AMANDA. That light bill I gave you several days ago. The one I got the notice about?

TOM. Oh—yeah. You mean last month's bill?

AMANDA. You didn't neglect it by any chance?

TOM. Well, I——

AMANDA. You did! I might have known 40 it!

JIM. Oh, maybe Shakespeare wrote a poem on that light bill, Mrs. Wing- field.

AMANDA. Maybe he did, too. I might have known better than to trust him

with it! There's such a high price for negligence in this world today.

JIM. Maybe the poem will win a ten- dollar prize.

AMANDA. We'll just have to spend the rest of the evening in the nineteenth century, before Mr. Edison found that Mazda lamp!

JIM. Candlelight is my favorite kind of light.

AMANDA. That shows you're romantic! But that's no excuse for Tom. How- ever, I think it was very nice of them to let us finish our dinner before they plunged us into everlasting darkness. Tom, as a penalty for your careless- ness you can help me with the dishes.

JIM (*rising; TOM rises*). Can I be of some help, ma'am?

AMANDA (*rising*). Oh no, I couldn't al- low that.

JIM. Well, I ought to be good for *some- thing*.

AMANDA. What did I hear?

JIM. I just said, "I ought to be good for something."

AMANDA. That's what I thought you said. Well, Laura's all by her lone- some out front. Maybe you'd like to keep her company. I can give you this lovely old candelabrum for light. (JIM *takes the candles*.) It used to be on the altar at the Church of the Heavenly Rest, but it was melted a little out of shape when the church burned down. The church was struck by lightning one spring, and Gypsy Jones, who was holding a revival meeting in the village, said that the church was struck by lightning be- cause the Episcopalians had started to have card parties right in the church.

JIM. Is that so, ma'am?

AMANDA. I never say anything that isn't so.

JIM. I beg your pardon.

AMANDA (*pouring wine into a glass, hands it to* JIM). I'd like Laura to have a little dandelion wine. Do you think you can hold them both?

JIM. I can try, ma'am.

AMANDA (*exits up right into the kitchen*). Now Tom, you get into your apron.

TOM. Yes, Mother.

[*Follows* AMANDA. JIM *looks around, puts* 10 *the wine-glass down, takes a swig from the wine decanter, replaces it with a thud, takes the wine-glass—enters the living room. The inner curtains close as the dining room dims out.*

[LAURA *sits up nervously as* JIM *enters. Her speech at first is low and breathless from the almost intolerable strain of being alone with a stranger. In her speeches in this scene, before* JIM'S *warmth overcomes her* 20 *paralyzing shyness,* LAURA'S *voice is thin and breathless as though she has just run up a steep flight of stairs.*]

JIM (*entering holding the candelabra with lighted candles in one hand and the glass of wine in the other, stands*). How are you feeling now? Any better? (JIM'S *attitude is gently humorous. In playing this scene it should be stressed that while the incident is apparently unimportant, it is to* 30 LAURA *the climax of her secret life.*)

LAURA. Yes, thank you.

JIM (*gives her the glass of wine*). Oh, here, this is for you. It's a little dandelion wine.

LAURA. Thank you.

JIM (*crosses center*). Well, drink it—but don't get drunk. (*He laughs heartily.*) Say, where'll I put the candles?

LAURA. Oh, anywhere . . .

JIM. Oh, how about right here on the floor? You got any objections?

LAURA. No.

JIM. I'll just spread a newspaper under it to catch the drippings. (*Gets the newspaper from the armchair. Puts the candelabra down on the floor at the center.*) I like to sit on the floor. (*Sits on the floor.*) Mind if I do?

LAURA. Oh no.

JIM. Would you give me a pillow?

LAURA. What?

JIM. A pillow!

LAURA. Oh . . . (*Puts the wine-glass on the telephone table, hands him a pillow, sits left on the day bed.*)

JIM. How about you? Don't you like to sit on the floor?

LAURA. Oh yes.

JIM. Well, why don't you?

LAURA. I—will.

JIM. Take a pillow! (*Throws a pillow as she sits on the floor.*) I can't see you sitting way over there. (*Sits on the floor again.*)

LAURA. I can—see you.

JIM. Yeah, but that's not fair. I'm right here in the limelight. (LAURA *moves a little closer to him.*) Good! Now I can see you! Are you comfortable?

LAURA. Yes. Thank you.

JIM. So am I. I'm comfortable as a cow! Say, would you care for a piece of chewing gum? (*Offers gum.*)

LAURA. No, thank you.

JIM. I think that I will indulge. (*Musingly unwraps it and holds it up.*) Gee, think of the fortune made by the guy that invented the first piece of chewing gum! It's amazing, huh? Do you know that the Wrigley Building is one of the sights of Chicago?—I saw it summer before last at the Century of Progress.—Did you take in the Century of Progress?

40 LAURA. No, I didn't.

JIM. Well, it was a wonderful exposition, believe me. You know what impressed me most? The Hall of Science. Gives you an idea of what the future will be like in America. Oh, it's more wonderful than the present time is!

Say, your brother tells me you're shy. Is that right, Laura?

LAURA. I—don't know.

JIM. I judge you to be an old-fashioned type of girl. Oh, I think that's a wonderful type to be. I hope you don't think I'm being too personal—do you?

LAURA. Mr. O'Connor?

JIM. Huh?

LAURA. I believe I *will* take a piece of 10 gum, if you don't mind. (JIM *peels the gum, gets on his knees, hands it to* LAURA. *She breaks off a tiny piece.* JIM *looks at what remains, puts it in his mouth, and sits again.*) Mr. O'Connor, have you— kept up with your singing?

JIM. Singing? Me?

LAURA. Yes, I remember what a beautiful voice you had.

JIM. You heard me sing?   20

LAURA. Oh, yes! Very often. . . . I— don't suppose—you remember me— at all?

JIM (*smiling doubtfully*). You know, as a matter of fact I did have an idea I'd seen you before. Do you know it seemed almost like I was about to remember your name. But the name I was about to remember—wasn't a name! So I stopped myself before I 30 said it.

LAURA. Wasn't it—Blue Roses?

JIM (*grinning*). Blue Roses! Oh my gosh, yes—Blue Roses! You know, I didn't connect you with high school somehow or other. But that's where it was, it was high school. Gosh, I didn't even know you were Shakespeare's sister! Gee, I'm sorry.

LAURA. I didn't expect you to.—You— 40 barely knew me!

JIM. But we did have a speaking acquaintance.

LAURA. Yes, we—spoke to each other.

JIM. Say, didn't we have a class in something together?

LAURA. Yes, we did.

JIM. What class was that?

LAURA. It was—singing—chorus!

JIM. Aw!

LAURA. I sat across the aisle from you in the auditorium. Mondays, Wednesdays, and Fridays.

JIM. Oh yeah! I remember now—you're the one who always came in late.

LAURA. Yes, it was so hard for me, getting upstairs. I had that brace on my leg then—it clumped so loud!

JIM. I never heard any clumping.

LAURA (*wincing at the recollection*). To me it sounded like—thunder!

JIM. I never even noticed.

LAURA. Everybody was seated before I came in. I had to walk in front of all those people. My seat was in the back row. I had to go clumping up the aisle with everyone watching!

JIM. Oh gee, you shouldn't have been self-conscious.

LAURA. I know, but I was. It was always such a relief when the singing started.

JIM. I remember now. And I used to call you Blue Roses. How did I ever get started calling you a name like that?

LAURA. I was out of school a little while with pleurosis. When I came back you asked me what was the matter. I said I had pleurosis and you thought I said Blue Roses. So that's what you always called me after that!

JIM. I hope you didn't mind?

LAURA. Oh, no—I liked it. You see, I wasn't acquainted with many— people. . . .

JIM. Yeah. I remember you sort of stuck by yourself.

LAURA. I never did have much luck at making friends.

JIM. Well, I don't see why you wouldn't.

LAURA. Well, I started out badly.

JIM. You mean being——?

LAURA. Well, yes, it—sort of—stood between me . . .

JIM. You shouldn't have let it!

LAURA. I know, but it did, and I——

JIM. You mean you were shy with people!

LAURA. I tried not to be but never could——

JIM. Overcome it?

LAURA. No, I—never could!

JIM. Yeah. I guess being shy is something you have to work out of kind of gradually.

LAURA. Yes—I guess it——

JIM. Takes time!

LAURA. Yes.

JIM. Say, you know something, Laura? (*Rises to sit on the day bed at the right.*) People are not so dreadful when you know them. That's what you have to remember! And everybody has problems, not just you but practically everybody has problems. You think of yourself as being the only one who is disappointed. But just look around you and what do you see—a lot of people just as disappointed as you are. You take me, for instance. Boy, when I left high school I thought I'd be a lot further along at this time than I am now. Say, you remember that wonderful write-up I had in *The Torch?*

LAURA. Yes, I do! (*She gets the yearbook from under a pillow at the left of the day bed.*)

JIM. Said I was bound to succeed in anything I went into! Holy Jeez! *The Torch!*

[*She opens the book, shows it to him, and sits next to him on the day bed.*]

LAURA. Here you are in *The Pirates of Penzance!*

JIM. *The Pirates!* "Oh, better far to live and die under the brave black flag I fly!" I sang the lead in that operetta.

LAURA. So beautifully!

JIM. Aw . . .

LAURA. Yes, yes—beautifully—beautifully!

JIM. You heard me then, huh?

LAURA. I heard you all three times!

JIM. No!

LAURA. Yes!

JIM. You mean all three performances?

LAURA. Yes.

JIM. What for?

LAURA. I—wanted to ask you to—autograph my program. (*Takes a program from the book.*)

JIM. Why didn't you ask me?

LAURA. You were always surrounded by your own friends so much that I never had a chance.

JIM. Aw, you should have just come right up and said, Here is my——

LAURA. Well, I—thought you might think I was——

JIM. Thought I might think you was—what?

LAURA. Oh——

JIM (*with reflective relish*). Oh! Yeah, I was beleaguered by females in those days.

LAURA. You were terribly popular!

JIM. Yeah. . . .

LAURA. You had such a—friendly way——

JIM. Oh, I was spoiled in high school.

LAURA. Everybody liked you!

JIM. Including you?

LAURA. I—why, yes, I—I did, too. . . .

JIM. Give me that program, Laura. (*She does so, and he signs it.*) There you are—better late than never!

LAURA. My—what a—surprise!

JIM. My signature's not worth very much right now. But maybe someday—it will increase in value! You know, being disappointed is one thing and being discouraged is something else. Well, I may be disappointed but I am not discouraged. Say, you finished high school?

LAURA. I made bad grades in my final examinations.

JIM. You mean you dropped out?

LAURA (*rises*). I didn't go back. (*Crosses right to the menagerie. JIM lights a cigarette, still sitting on the day bed. LAURA puts the yearbook under the menagerie. Rises, picks up a unicorn—a small glass object—her back to JIM. When she touches the unicorn, Music cue No. 16.*) How is—Emily Meisenbach getting along?

JIM. That kraut-head!

LAURA. Why do you call her that?

JIM. Because that's what she was.

LAURA. You're not still—going with her?

JIM. Oh, I never even see her.

LAURA. It said in the Personal section that you were—engaged!

JIM. Uh-huh, I know, but I wasn't impressed by that—propaganda!

LAURA. It wasn't—the truth?

JIM. It was only true in Emily's optimistic opinion!

LAURA. Oh . . .

[*Turns to the right of JIM. JIM lights a cigarette and leans indolently back on his elbows, smiling at LAURA with a warmth and charm which lights her inwardly with altar candles. She remains by the glass-menagerie table and turns in her hands a piece of glass to cover her tumult.*]

[*Cut Music cue No. 16.*]

JIM. What have you done since high school? Huh?

LAURA. What?

JIM. I said what have you done since high school?

LAURA. Nothing much.

JIM. You must have been doing something all this time.

LAURA. Yes.

JIM. Well, then, such as what?

LAURA. I took a business course at business college . . .

JIM. You did? How did that work out?

LAURA (*turns back to JIM*). Well, not very —well . . . I had to drop out, it gave me—indigestion. . . .

JIM (*laughs gently*). What are you doing now?

LAURA. I don't do anything—much. . . . Oh, please don't think I sit around doing nothing! My glass collection takes a good deal of time. Glass is something you have to take good care of.

JIM. What did you say—about glass?

LAURA (*she clears her throat and turns away again, acutely shy*). Collection, I said— I have one.

JIM (*puts out his cigarette; abruptly*). Say! You know what I judge to be the trouble with you? (*Rises from the day bed and crosses right.*) Inferiority complex! You know what that is? That's what they call it when a fellow low-rates himself! Oh, I understand it, because I had it, too. Uh-huh! Only my case was not as aggravated as yours seems to be. I had it until I took up public speaking and developed my voice, and learned that I had an aptitude for science. Do you know that until that time I never thought of myself as being outstanding in any way whatsoever!

LAURA. Oh my!

JIM. Now I've never made a regular study of it—(*Sits in the armchair at the right.*)—mind you, but I have a friend who says I can analyze people better than doctors that make a profession of it. I don't claim that's necessarily true, but I can sure guess a person's psychology. Excuse me, Laura. (*Takes out his gum.*) I always take it out when the flavor is gone. I'll just wrap it in a piece of paper. (*Tears a piece of paper off the newspaper under the candelabrum, wraps the gum in it, crosses to the day bed, looks to see if* LAURA *is watching. She isn't. Crosses around the day bed.*) I know how it is when you get it stuck on a shoe. (*Throws the gum under the day bed, crosses around left of the day bed. Crosses right to* LAURA.) Yep—that's what I judge to be your principal trouble. A lack of confidence in yourself as a person. Now I'm basing that fact on a number of your remarks and on certain observations I've made. For instance, that clumping you thought was so awful in high school. You say that you dreaded to go upstairs? You see what you did? You dropped out of school, you gave up an education, all because of a little clump, which as far as I can see is practically non-existent! Oh, a little physical defect is all you have. It's hardly noticeable even! Magnified a thousand times by your imagination! You know what my strong advice to you is? You've got to think of yourself as *superior* in some way! (*Crosses left to the small table to the right of the day bed. Sits.* LAURA *sits in the armchair.*)

LAURA. In what way would I think?

JIM. Why, man alive, Laura! Look around you a little and what do you see? A world full of common people! All of 'em born and all of 'em going to die! Now, which of them has one-tenth of your strong points! Or mine! Or anybody else's for that matter? You see, everybody excels in some one thing. Well—some in many! You take me, for instance. My interest happens to lie in electrodynamics. I'm taking a course in radio engineering at night school, on top of a fairly responsible job at the warehouse. I'm taking that course *and* studying public speaking.

LAURA. Ohhhh. My!

JIM. Because I believe in the future of television! I want to be ready to go right up along with it. (*Rises, crosses right.*) I'm planning to get in on the ground floor. Oh, I've already made the right connections. All that remains now is for the industry itself to get under way—full steam! You know, *knowledge*—ZSZZppp! *Money*—— Zzzzzzpp! *POWER!* Wham! That's the cycle democracy is built on! (*Pause.*) I guess you think I think a lot of myself!

LAURA. No—o-o-o, I don't.

JIM (*kneels at the armchair to the right*). Well, now how about you? Isn't there some one thing that you take more interest in than anything else?

LAURA. Oh—yes . . .

JIM. Well, then, such as what?

LAURA. Well, I do—as I said—have my —glass collection . . .

[*Music cue No. 16-A.*]

JIM. Oh, you do. What kind of glass is it?

LAURA (*takes a glass ornament off the shelf*). Little articles of it, ornaments mostly. Most of them are little animals made out of glass, the tiniest little animals in the world. Mother calls them the glass menagerie! Here's an example of one, if you'd like to see it! This is one of the oldest, it's nearly thirteen. (*Hands it to* JIM.) Oh, be careful—if you breathe, it breaks!

[*The Bell Solo should begin here. This is the last part of cue No. 16-A and should play to the end of the record.*]

JIM. I'd better not take it. I'm pretty clumsy with things.

LAURA. Go on, I trust you with him! (JIM *takes the horse.*) There—you're holding him gently! Hold him over the light, he loves the light! (JIM *holds the horse up to the light.*) See how the light shines through him?

JIM. It sure does shine!

LAURA. I shouldn't be partial, but he is my favorite one.

JIM. Say, what kind of a thing is this one supposed to be?

LAURA. Haven't you noticed the single horn on his forehead?

JIM. Oh, a unicorn, huh?

LAURA. Mmmm-hmmmmm!

JIM. Unicorns, aren't they extinct in the modern world? 10

LAURA. I know!

JIM. Poor little fellow must feel kind of lonesome.

LAURA. Well, if he does he doesn't complain about it. He stays on a shelf with some horses that don't have horns and they all seem to get along nicely together.

JIM. They do. Say, where will I put him? 20

LAURA. Put him on the table. (JIM *crosses to the small table to the right of the day bed, puts the unicorn on it.*) They all like a change of scenery once in a while!

JIM (*center, facing upstage, stretching his arms*). They do. (*Music cue No. 16-B: dance music.*) Hey! Look how big my shadow is when I stretch.

LAURA (*crossing to the left of the day bed.*) 30 Oh, oh yes—it stretched across the ceiling!

JIM (*crosses to the door at the right, exits, leaving the door open, and stands on the fire-escape landing. Sings to the music.* (*Popular record of the day for a dance hall.*) *When JIM opens the door, the music swells.*) It's stopped raining. Where does the music come from?

LAURA. From the Paradise Dance Hall 40 across the alley.

JIM (*re-entering the room, closing the door at the right, crosses to LAURA*). How about cutting the rug a little, Miss Wing-field? Or is your program filled up? Let me take a look at it. (*Crosses back center. Music, in the dance hall, goes into a waltz. Business here with an imaginary dance-program card.*) Oh say! Every dance is taken! I'll just scratch some of them out. Ahhhh, a waltz! (*Crosses to LAURA.*)

LAURA. I—can't dance!

JIM. There you go with that inferiority stuff!

LAURA. I've never danced in my life!

JIM. Come on, try!

LAURA. Oh, but I'd step on you!

JIM. Well, I'm not made out of glass.

LAURA. How—how do we start?

JIM. You hold your arms out a little.

LAURA. Like this?

JIM. A little bit higher. (*Takes LAURA in his arms.*) That's right. Now don't tighten up, that's the principal thing about it—just relax.

LAURA. It's hard not to.

JIM. Okay.

LAURA. I'm afraid you can't budge me.

JIM (*dances around to the left of the day bed slowly*). What do you bet I can't?

LAURA. Goodness, yes, you can!

JIM. Let yourself go, now, Laura, just let yourself go.

LAURA. I'm——

JIM. Come on!

LAURA. Trying!

JIM. Not so stiff now—easy does it!

LAURA. I know, but I'm——!

JIM. Come on! Loosen your backbone a little! (*When they get to the upstage corner of the day bed—so that the audience will not see him lift her—JIM's arm tightens around her waist and he swings her around to the center with her feet off the floor about three complete turns before they hit the small table at the right of the day bed. The music swells as JIM lifts her.*) There we go! (*JIM knocks the glass horse off the table.*)

[*Music fades.*]

LAURA. Oh, it doesn't matter——

JIM (*picks the horse up*). We knocked the little glass horse over.

LAURA. Yes.

JIM (*hands the unicorn to* LAURA). Is he broken?

LAURA. Now he's just like all the other horses.

JIM. You mean he lost his——?

LAURA. He's lost his horn. It doesn't matter. Maybe it's a blessing in disguise.

JIM. Gee, I bet you'll never forgive me. I bet that was your favorite piece of glass.

LAURA. Oh, I don't have favorites— (*Pause.*)—much. It's no tragedy. Glass breaks so easily. No matter how careful you are. The traffic jars the shelves and things fall off them.

JIM. Still, I'm awfully sorry that I was the cause of it.

LAURA. I'll just imagine he had an operation. The horn was removed to make him feel less—freakish! (*Crosses left, sits at the small table.*) Now he will feel more at home with the other horses, the ones who don't have horns. . . .

JIM (*sits on the arm of the armchair at the right, faces* LAURA). I'm glad to see that you have a sense of humor. You know—you're—different than anybody else I know? (*Music cue No. 17.*) Do you mind me telling you that? I mean it. You make me feel sort of—I don't know how to say it! I'm usually pretty good at expressing things, but—this is something I don't know how to say! Did anybody ever tell you that you were pretty? (*Rises, crosses to* LAURA.) Well, you are! And in a different way from anyone else. And all the nicer because of the difference. Oh boy, I wish that you were my sister! I'd teach you to have confidence in yourself. Being different is nothing to be ashamed of. Because other people aren't such wonderful people. They're a hundred times one thousand. You're one times one! They walk all over the earth. You just stay here. They're as common as— weeds, but—you, well you're—*Blue Roses!*

LAURA. But blue is—wrong for—roses. . . .

JIM. It's right for you!—You're pretty!

LAURA. In what respect am I pretty?

JIM. In all respects—your eyes—your hair. Your hands are pretty! You think I'm saying this because I'm invited to dinner and have to be nice. Oh, I could do that! I could say lots of things without being sincere. But I'm talking to you sincerely. I happened to notice you had this inferiority complex that keeps you from feeling comfortable with people. Somebody ought to build your confidence up—way up! and make you proud instead of shy and turning away and—blushing—— (JIM *lifts* LAURA *up on the small table on the "way up."*) Somebody—ought to—— (*Lifts her down.*) Somebody ought to— kiss you, Laura! (*They kiss.* JIM *releases her and turns slowly away, crossing a little down right. Then, quietly, to himself: As* JIM *turns away, the music ends.*) Gee, I shouldn't have done that—that was way off the beam. (*Gives way down right. Turns to* LAURA. LAURA *sits at the small table.*) Would you care for a cigarette? You don't smoke, do you? How about a mint? Peppermint— Life-Saver? My pocket's a regular drugstore. . . . Laura, you know, if I had a sister like you, I'd do the same thing as Tom. I'd bring fellows home to meet you. Maybe I shouldn't be saying this. That may not have been the idea in having me over. But what if it was? There's nothing wrong with that.—The only trouble is that in my case—I'm not in a position to —I can't ask for your number and say I'll phone. I can't call up next week end—ask for a date. I thought I had better explain the situation in case you—misunderstood and I hurt your feelings. . . .

LAURA (*faintly*). You—won't—call again?

JIM (*crossing to the right of the day bed, and sitting*). No, I can't. You see, I've—got strings on me. Laura, I've—been going steady! I go out all the time with a girl named Betty. Oh, she's a nice quiet home girl like you, and Catholic and Irish, and in a great many ways we—get along fine. I met her last summer on a moonlight boat trip up the river to Alton, on the *Majestic*. Well—right away from the start it was—love! Oh boy, being in love has made a new man of me! The power of love is pretty tremendous! Love is something that—changes the whole world. It happened that Betty's aunt took sick and she got a wire and had to go to Centralia. So naturally when Tom asked me to dinner— naturally I accepted the invitation, not knowing—I mean—not knowing. I wish that you would—say something. (LAURA *gives* JIM *the unicorn.*) What are you doing that for? You mean you want me to have him? What for?

LAURA. A—souvenir. (*She crosses right to the menagerie.* JIM *rises.*)

AMANDA (*offstage*). I'm coming, children. (*She enters into the dining room from the kitchen at the right.*) I thought you'd like some liquid refreshment. (*Puts a tray on the small table. Lifts a glass.*) Mr. O'Connor, have you heard that song about lemonade? It's

"Lemonade, lemonade,
  Made in the shade and stirred
    with a spade—
  And then it's good enough for
    any old maid!"

JIM. No, ma'am, I never heard it.

AMANDA. Why are you so serious, honey? (*To* LAURA.)

JIM. Well, we were having a serious conversation.

AMANDA. I don't understand modern young people. When I was a girl I was gay about everything.

JIM. You haven't changed a bit, Mrs. Wingfield.

AMANDA. I suppose it's the gaiety of the occasion that has rejuvenated me. Well, here's to the gaiety of the occasion! (*Spills the lemonade on her dress.*) Oooo! I baptized myself. (*Puts the glass on the small table at the right of the day bed.*) I found some cherries in the kitchen, and I put one in each glass.

JIM. You shouldn't have gone to all that trouble, ma'am.

AMANDA. It was no trouble at all. Didn't you hear us cutting up in the kitchen? I was so outdone with Tom for not bringing you over sooner, but now you've found your way I want you to come all the time—not just once in a while—but all the time. Oh, I think I'll go back in that kitchen. (*Starts to exit up center.*)

JIM. Oh no, ma'am, please don't go, ma'am. As a matter of fact, I've got to be going.

AMANDA. Oh, Mr. O'Connor, it's only the shank of the evening!

[JIM *and* AMANDA *stand up center.*]

JIM. Well, you know how it is.

AMANDA. You mean you're a young workingman and have to keep workingmen's hours?

JIM. Yes, ma'am.

AMANDA. Well, we'll let you off early this time, but only on the condition that you stay later next time, much later—What's the best night for you? Saturday?

JIM. Well, as a matter of fact, I have a couple of time clocks to punch, Mrs. Wingfield, one in the morning and another one at night!

AMANDA. Oh, isn't that nice, you're so ambitious! You work at night, too?

JIM. No, ma'am, not work but—Betty!

AMANDA (crosses left below the day bed). Betty? Who's Betty?

JIM. Oh, just a girl. The girl I go steady with!

AMANDA. You mean it's serious? (Crosses down left.)

JIM. Oh, yes, ma'am. We're going to be married the second Sunday in June.

AMANDA (sits on the day bed). Tom didn't say anything at all about your going to be married?

JIM. Well, the cat's not out of the bag at the warehouse yet. (Picks up his hat from the telephone table.) You know how they are. They call you Romeo and stuff like that.—It's been a wonderful evening, Mrs. Wingfield. I guess this is what they mean by Southern hospitality.

AMANDA. It was nothing. Nothing at all.

JIM. I hope it don't seem like I'm rushing off. But I promised Betty I'd pick her up at the Wabash depot an' by the time I get my jalopy down there her train'll be in. Some women are pretty upset if you keep them waiting.

AMANDA. Yes, I know all about the tyranny of women! Well, good-by, Mr. O'Connor. (AMANDA puts out her hand. JIM takes it.) I wish you happiness—and good fortune. You wish him that, too, don't you, Laura?

LAURA. Yes, I do, Mother.

JIM (crosses left to LAURA). Good-by, Laura. I'll always treasure that souvenir. And don't you forget the good advice I gave you. So long, Shakespeare! (Up center.) Thanks, again, ladies.—Good night! (He grins and ducks jauntily out by the right.)

AMANDA (faintly). Well, well, well. Things have a way of turning out so badly—. (LAURA crosses to the phonograph, puts on a record.) I don't believe that I would play the Victrola. Well, well—well, our gentleman caller was engaged to be married! Tom!

TOM (off). Yes, Mother?

AMANDA. Come out here. I want to tell you something very funny.

TOM (entering through the right kitchen door to the dining room and into the living room, through the curtains, down center). Has the gentleman caller gotten away already?

AMANDA. The gentleman caller made a very early departure. That was a nice joke you played on us, too!

TOM. How do you mean?

AMANDA. You didn't mention that he was engaged to be married.

TOM. Jim? Engaged?

AMANDA. That's what he just informed us.

TOM. I'll be jiggered! I didn't know.

AMANDA. That seems very peculiar.

TOM. What's peculiar about it?

AMANDA. Didn't you tell me he was your best friend down at the warehouse?

TOM. He is, but how did I know?

AMANDA. It seems very peculiar you didn't know your best friend was engaged to be married!

TOM. The warehouse is the place where I work, not where I know things about people!

AMANDA. You don't know things anywhere! You live in a dream; you manufacture illusions! (TOM starts for the right door.) Where are you going?

Where are you going? Where are you going?

TOM. I'm going to the movies.

AMANDA (*rises, crosses up to* TOM). That's right, now that you've had us make such fools of ourselves. The effort, the preparations, all the expense! The new floor lamp, the rug, the clothes for Laura! All for what? To entertain some other girl's fiancé! Go to the movies, go! Don't think about us, a mother deserted, an unmarried sister who's crippled and has no job! Don't let anything interfere with your selfish pleasure! Just go, go, go—to the movies!

TOM. All right, I will, and the more you shout at me about my selfish pleasures, the quicker I'll go, and I won't go to the movies either. (*Gets his hat from the phone table, slams the door at the right, and exits up the alley at the right.*)

AMANDA (*crosses up to the fire-escape landing, yelling*). Go, then! Then go to the moon—you selfish dreamer!*

[*Music cue No. 18. The interior light dims out.*]

[*Re-enters the living room, slamming the right door.* TOM's *closing speech is timed with the interior pantomime. The interior scene is played as though viewed through soundproof glass, behind the outer scrim curtain.* AMANDA, *standing, appears to be making a comforting speech to* LAURA, *who is huddled on the right side of the day bed. Now that we cannot hear the mother's speech, her silliness is gone and she has dignity and tragic beauty.* LAURA's *hair hides her face until at the end of the speech she lifts it to smile at her mother.* AMANDA's *gestures are slow and graceful, almost dancelike, as she comforts her daughter.*]

[TOM, *who has meantime put on, as before, the jacket and cap, enters down right from off stage, and again comes to the fire-escape landing, stands as he speaks. Mean-time the lights are upon* AMANDA *and* LAURA, *but are dim.*]

TOM. I didn't go to the moon. I went much farther. For time is the longest distance between two places. . . . I left St. Louis. I descended these steps of this fire escape for the last time and followed, from then on, in my father's footsteps, attempting to find in motion what was lost in space. . . . I traveled around a great deal. The cities swept about me like dead leaves, leaves that were brightly colored but torn away from the branches. I would have stopped, but I was pursued by something. It always came upon me unawares, taking me altogether by surprise. Perhaps it was a familiar bit of music. Perhaps it was only a piece of transparent glass. . . . Perhaps I am walking along a street at night, in some strange city, before I have found companions, and I pass the lighted window of a shop where perfume is sold. The window is filled with pieces of colored glass, tiny transparent bottles in delicate colors, like bits of a shattered rainbow. Then all at once my sister touches my shoulder. I turn around and look into her eyes. . . . Oh, Laura, Laura, I tried to leave you behind me, but I am more faithful than I intended to be! I reach for a cigarette, I cross the street, I run into a movie or a bar. I buy a drink, I speak to the nearest stranger—anything that can blow your candles out! —for nowadays the world is lit by lightning! Blow out your candles, Laura. . . . (LAURA *blows out the candles still burning in the candelabrum and the whole interior is blacked out.*) And there my memory ends and your imagination begins. And so—goodby! (*Exit up the alley to the right.*)

[*The music continues to the end.*]

CURTAIN

ARTHUR MILLER

NOT SINCE the early days of Eugene O'Neill has a playwright won such high and immediate acclaim in the American theatre as Arthur Miller. His first play, *The Man Who Had All the Luck*, which opened at the Forrest Theater on Broadway in 1944, failed after a single week. But his second, *All My Sons*, first performed in New York on January 29, 1947, was well received. It was the Drama Critics' Circle choice for the best American play of the season. And *Death of a Salesman*, which began its phenomenal run on February 10, 1949, won both the Critics' Circle award and the Pulitzer Prize. Such a triumph is rare in American stage history, and it is built upon clean and solid literary and dramatic ability.

The author was born in New York City in 1915. He attended the public schools in Manhattan and Brooklyn, and then went on to the University of Michigan where the Avery Hopwood endowment encourages and rewards creative work in poetry, fiction, essay and drama. Arthur Miller won the Hopwood Prize for drama in 1936. His life was not cloistered. He helped support himself by working at various odd jobs which kept him close to the life of the common American man about whom he writes with such startling insight. He was graduated from the University of Michigan in 1938, and in the same year received the Theatre Guild National Award.

Between this academic training and his present professional eminence were several years during which he wrote radio scripts and had an unsatisfactory try at Hollywood, which he described as "swimming in a sea of gumdrops." During the war he was assigned the duty of collecting material for the movie *G. I. Joe*, released in 1945. He also wrote a successful novel titled *Focus* (1945). At the same time he was keenly observing life as it was flowing along through business boom to depression and on into war and its aftermath. He saw its impact upon individual men like Joe Keller and his son Chris, Willy Loman and his sons Happy and Biff, and women like Linda Loman, Kate Keller and Ann Deever. These materials flowed through the crucible of his developing dramatic talent and finally emerged triumphant on the stage in *All My Sons* and *Death of a Salesman*.

They are native American plays. The scene of *All My Sons* is "the backyard of the Keller home in the outskirts of an American town. August of our era." That is to say, almost any American town immediately following World War II. It is not directly about the war, but the stresses and strains of the national effort are dominant in the play and give it some of its emotional impact. Yet they are incidental. Here is a large segment of the very fabric of our society—a household, a neighborhood, a nation, and a world—caught, simplified, intensified and re-created in the turbulent conflict between Joe Keller and his conscience, between two standards of business conduct, between the values of father and sons, between the realism and the dreams of the strong-minded mother Kate.

It brings into sharp focus the ideal integrity of Joe's sons, who fought in the war for things worth dying to preserve, and the rationalization of Joe himself, who would risk compromise with that integrity to advance the living standards and worldly prestige of his family. The characters who act out this tragedy are firm and vital, and their speech is fresh with the idiom of their own backyard. The action is tight and tense, even crowded, and the total effect is powerful. In general development it conforms to the age-old demands of high tragedy. The delicate balance of the moral law has been upset by Keller's deed of shame. Forces are then let loose through his sons to expiate the sin and bring a sad new equilibrium to the house of Keller.

Many of the qualities, and something of the same milieu were carried over into the more spectacular success, *Death of a Salesman*. Few plays have had heaped upon them so many superlatives by all the front rank newspaper critics. Brooks Atkinson called it "one of the finest dramas in the whole range of the American Theatre"; Richard Watts, Jr., "something to make strong men weep and think"; John Chapman, "unforgettable . . . all is right and noth-ing is wrong"; John Mason Brown, "overpowering"; and Ward Morehouse, "poignant, shattering and devastating."

The dramaturgy is more complex than in *All My Sons*, though the effect in both is one of simplicity. There are many superficial resemblances between the two plays, and their titles might have been reversed without seriously distorting their respective themes. The drama, however, is more fully centered upon the central character of the salesman than upon Joe Keller, and Willy Loman's poor sons are the product of his own wayward and shallow philosophy of life rather than stalwart examples of the moral law against which he has sinned, as in *All My Sons*. The two plays may well be read together, along with Arthur Miller's piece in the *New York Times* (February 27, 1949) in which he expounds his view that the "tragic flaw" is the protagonist's "inherent unwillingness to remain passive in the face of what he conceives to be a challenge to his dignity, his image of his rightful status."

These plays represent the best achievement of the newer generation of playwrights whose voices are just beginning to be heard in the post-war theatre.

ALL MY SONS

CHARACTERS

FRANK LUBEY

JOE KELLER

DR. JIM BAYLISS

SUE BAYLISS, *his wife*

LYDIA LUBEY, *Frank's wife*

CHRIS KELLER, *Joe's son*

BERT, *a little boy*

KATE KELLER (MOTHER), *Joe's wife*

ANN DEEVER

GEORGE DEEVER

ACT ONE

SCENE. *The back yard of the Keller home in the outskirts of an American town. August of our era.*

The stage is hedged on right and left by tall, closely planted poplars which lend the yard a secluded atmosphere. Upstage is filled with the back of the house and its open porch, which extends into the yard some six feet. The house is two stories high and has seven rooms. It would have cost perhaps fifteen thousand 10 in the early twenties when it was built. Now it is nicely painted, looks tight and comfortable, and the yard is green with sod, here and there plants whose season is gone.

At the right, beside the house, the entrance of the driveway can be seen, but the poplars cut off view of its continuation downstage. In the right corner, downstage, stands the four-foot-high stump of a slender apple tree whose upper trunk and branches lie toppled 20 beside it, fruit still clinging to its branches.

Downstage left is a small, trellised arbor, shaped like a sea shell, with a decorative bulb hanging from its forward-curving roof. Garden chairs and a table are scattered about. A garbage pail is on the ground next to the porch steps, a wire leaf-burner near it.

As the curtain rises, it is early Sunday morning. JOE KELLER *is sitting in the sun reading the want ads of the Sunday paper, the other sections of which lie neatly on the ground beside him. Behind his back, inside the arbor,* DOCTOR JIM BAYLISS *is reading part of the paper at the table.*

KELLER *is nearing sixty. A heavy man of stolid mind and build, a businessman these many years, but with the imprint of the machine-shop worker and boss still upon him. When he reads, when he speaks, when he listens, it is with the terrible concentration of the uneducated man for whom there is still wonder in many commonly known things, a man whose judgments must be dredged out of experience and a peasantlike common sense. A man among men.*

DOCTOR BAYLISS *is nearing forty. A wry*

*self-controlled man, an easy talker, but with
a wisp of sadness that clings even to his self-
effacing humor.*

They sit reading in peace. In a moment
FRANK LUBEY *enters, from the right, through
a small space between the poplars.* FRANK *is
thirty-two but balding. A pleasant, opin-
ionated man, uncertain of himself, with a
tendency toward peevishness when crossed, but
always wanting it pleasant and neighborly.*
*He rather saunters in, leisurely, nothing to do.
He does not notice* JIM *in the arbor. On his
greeting,* JIM *does not bother to look up.*

FRANK. Hya.

KELLER. Hello, Frank. What's doin'?

FRANK. Nothin'. Walking off my breakfast. (*Looks up at the sky.*) That beautiful? Not a cloud.

KELLER (*looks up*). Yeah, nice.

FRANK. Every Sunday ought to be like
this.

KELLER (*indicating the sections beside him*).
Want the paper?

FRANK. What's the difference, it's all bad
news. What's today's calamity?

KELLER. I don't know, I don't read the
news part any more. It's more interesting in the want ads.

FRANK. Why, you trying to buy something?

KELLER. No, I'm just interested. To see
what people want, y'know? For instance, here's a guy is lookin' for two
Newfoundland dogs. Now what's he
want with two Newfoundland dogs?

FRANK. That is funny.

KELLER. Here's another one. Wanted—
old dictionaries. High prices paid.
Now what's a man going to do with
an old dictionary?

FRANK. Why not? Probably a book collector.

KELLER. You mean he'll make a living
out of that?

FRANK. Sure, there's a lot of them.

KELLER (*shakes his head*). All the kinds of
business goin' on. In my day, either
you were a lawyer, or a doctor, or you
worked in a shop. Now . . .

FRANK. Well, I was going to be a for-
ester once.

KELLER. Well, that shows you; in my
day, there was no such thing. (*Scan-
ning the page, sweeping it with his hand.*)
You look at a page like this you
realize how ignorant you are. (*Softly,
with wonder.*) Psss!

FRANK. Hey, what happened to your
tree?

KELLER. Ain't that awful? The wind
must've got it last night. You heard
the wind, didn't you?

FRANK. Oh yes, I got a mess in my yard
too. (*Goes to the tree.*) Ts, what a pity.
What'd Kate say?

KELLER. They're all asleep yet. I'm just
waiting for her to see it.

FRANK. You know—it's funny.

KELLER. What?

FRANK. Larry was born in November.
He'd been twenty-seven this fall.
And his tree blows down.

KELLER (*touched*). I'm surprised you remember his birthday, Frank. That's
nice.

FRANK. Well, I'm working on his horoscope.

KELLER. How can you make him a horoscope? That's for the future, ain't it?

FRANK. Well, what I'm doing is this, see.
Larry was reported missing on February ninth, right?

KELLER. Yeah?

FRANK. Well, then, we assume that if he
was killed it was on February ninth.
Now, what Kate wants . . .

KELLER. Oh, Kate asked you to make a
horoscope?

FRANK. Yeah, what she wants to find
out is whether February ninth was a
favorable day for Larry.

KELLER. What is that, favorable day?

FRANK. Well, a favorable day for a person is a fortunate day, according to his stars. In other words it would be practically impossible for him to have died on his favorable day.

KELLER. Well, was that his favorable day?—February ninth?

FRANK. That's what I'm working on to find out. It takes time! (*With inner excitement, he moves downstage.*) See, the point is, if February ninth was his favorable day, then it's completely possible he's alive somewhere, because . . .

[*He notices* JIM *now.* JIM *is looking at him as though at an idiot. To* JIM—*with an uncertain laugh:*]

FRANK. I mean it's possible! I didn't even see you.

KELLER (*to* JIM). Is he talkin' sense?

JIM. Him? He's all right. He's just completely out of his mind, that's all.

FRANK. The trouble with you is, you don't believe in anything.

JIM. And your trouble is that you believe in *anything*. You didn't see my kid this morning, did you?

FRANK. No.

KELLER. Imagine? He walked off with his thermometer. Right out of his bag.

JIM (*gets up*). What a problem. He can't look at a girl without taking her temperature. (*Goes to the driveway, looks upstage toward the street.*)

FRANK. That boy's going to be a doctor; he's smart.

JIM. Over my dead body he'll be a doctor. A good beginning, too.

FRANK. Why? It's an honorable profession.

JIM (*looks at him tiredly*). Frank, will you stop talking like a civics book?

[KELLER *laughs.*]

FRANK. Why, I saw a movie a couple of weeks ago, reminded me of you. There was a doctor in that picture . . .

KELLER. Don Ameche!

FRANK. I think it was, yeah. And he worked in his basement discovering things. That's what you ought to do; you could help humanity, instead of . . .

JIM. I would love to help humanity on a Warner Brothers salary.

KELLER (*points at him, laughing*). That's very good, Jim.

JIM (*looks toward the house*). Well, where's the beautiful girl was supposed to be here?

FRANK (*excited*). Annie came?

KELLER. Sure, sleepin' upstairs. We picked her up on the one o'clock train last night. (*To* JIM.) Wonderful thing. Girl leaves here a scrawny kid. Couple of years go by, she's a regular woman. Hardly recognized her, and she was running in and out of this yard all her life. That was a very happy family used to live in your house, Jim.

JIM. Like to meet her. The block can use a pretty girl. In the whole neighborhood there's not a damned thing to look at. (*Enter* SUE, JIM's *wife, from left. She is rounding forty, an overweight woman who fears it. On seeing her,* JIM *wryly adds:*) Except my wife, of course.

SUE (*in the same spirit*). Mrs. Adams is on the phone, you dog.

JIM (*to* KELLER, *going to embrace his wife*). Such is the condition which prevails.

SUE (*brushing him off, laughing, but meaning it*). Don't sniff around me.

JIM. My love, my light . . .

SUE. Go to hell. (*Points to their house, left.*) And give her a nasty answer. I can smell her perfume over the phone.

JIM. What's the matter with her now?

SUE. I don't know, dear. She sounds like she's in terrible pain—unless her mouth is full of candy.

JIM. Why don't you just tell her to lay down?

SUE. She enjoys it more when you tell her to lay down. And when are you going to see Mr. Hubbard?

JIM. My dear, Mr. Hubbard is not sick, and I have better things to do than to sit there and hold his hand.

SUE. It seems to me that for ten dollars you could hold his hand.

JIM (*to* KELLER). If your son wants to play golf tell him I'm ready. (*Going to the left.*) Or if he'd like to take a trip around the world for about thirty years. (*He exits by the left.*)

KELLER. Why do you needle him? He's a doctor, women are supposed to call him up.

SUE. All I said was Mrs. Adams is on the phone.

KELLER. You were a nurse too long, Susie. You're too . . . too . . . realistic.

SUE (*laughing, points at him*). Now you said it!

[*Enter* LYDIA LUBEY *from the right. She is a robust, laughing girl of twenty-seven.*]

LYDIA. Frank, the toaster . . . (*Sees the others.*) Hya. (*To* FRANK.) The toaster is off again.

FRANK. Well, plug it in, I just fixed it.

LYDIA (*kindly, but insistently*). Please, dear, fix it back like it was before.

FRANK (*peeved, going off by the right*). I don't know why you can't learn to turn on a simple thing like a toaster! (*FRANK exits right.*)

SUE (*laughs*). Thomas Edison.

LYDIA (*apologetically*). He's really very handy.

KELLER. Left-handy.

LYDIA. Oh, the wind get your tree?

KELLER. Yeah, last night.

LYDIA. What a pity. Annie get in?

KELLER. She'll be down soon. Wait'll you meet her, Sue, she's a knockout.

SUE. I should've been a man. People are always introducing me to beautiful women. (*To* JOE.) Tell her to come over later; I imagine she'd like to see what we did with her house.

KELLER. Sad. Last night when she got out of the car she looked at your house and . . . she looked sad, y'know?

SUE. Well . . . everything is sad, Joe. See you later. (SUE *exits by the left.*)

LYDIA. Is she still unhappy, Joe?

KELLER. Annie? I don't suppose she goes around dancing on her toes, but she seems to be over it.

LYDIA. She going to get married? Is there anybody . . . ?

KELLER. I suppose . . . say, it's a couple years already. She can't mourn a boy forever.

LYDIA. It's so strange . . . Annie's here and not even married. And I've got three babies. I always thought it'd be the other way round.

KELLER. Well, that's what a war does. I had two sons, now I got one. It changed all the tallies. In my day when you had sons it was an honor. Today a doctor could make a million dollars if he could figure out a way to bring a boy into the world without a trigger finger.

[*Enter* CHRIS KELLER *from the house.*]

LYDIA. Hya, Chris . . .

[FRANK *shouts from off right.*]

FRANK. Lydia, come in here! If you want the toaster to work don't plug in the malted mixer.

LYDIA (*embarrassed, laughs*). Did I . . . ?

FRANK. The next time I fix something don't tell me I'm crazy! Come in here!

LYDIA (*going to the right*). I'll never hear the end of this one.

KELLER (*calling to* FRANK). So what's the difference? Instead of toast have a malted!

[LYDIA *exits laughing.* CHRIS *descends smiling from the porch. He is thirty-two, like his father solidly built, a listener, A man capable of immense affection and loyalty.*]

KELLER. You want the paper? (*Offers the whole paper.*)

CHRIS (*coming down to him*). That's all right, just the book section.

KELLER (*giving him the paper*). You're always reading the book section and you never buy a book.

CHRIS (*sitting, opening the section*). I like to keep abreast of my ignorance.

KELLER. What is that, every week a new book comes out?

CHRIS. Lot of new books.

KELLER. All different.

CHRIS. All different.

KELLER (*shakes his head*). Psss! Annie up yet?

CHRIS. Mother's giving her breakfast in the dining room.

KELLER. See what happened to the tree?

CHRIS (*without looking up*). Yeah.

KELLER. What's Mother going to say?

[*Enter* BERT *from the driveway. He is about six.*]

BERT. You're finally up.

KELLER. Ha! Bert's here! Where's Tommy? He's got his father's thermometer again.

BERT. He's taking a reading . . . but it's only oral.

KELLER. Oh, well, there's no harm in oral. So what's new this morning, Bert?

BERT. Nothin'.

KELLER. Then you couldn't've made a complete inspection of the block. In the beginning, when I first made you a policeman, you used to come in every morning with something new. Now, nothin's ever new.

BERT. Except some kids from Thirtieth Street. They started kicking a can down the block, and I made them go away because you were sleeping.

KELLER. Now you're talkin', Bert. Now you're on the ball. First thing you know I'm liable to make you a detective.

BERT. Can I see the jail now?

KELLER. Seein' the jail ain't allowed, Bert. You know that.

BERT. I betcha there isn't even a jail. I don't see any bars on the cellar windows.

KELLER. Bert, on my word of honor, there's a jail in the basement. I showed you my gun, didn't I?

BERT. But that's a hunting gun.

KELLER. That's an arresting gun!

BERT. Then why don't you ever arrest anybody? Tommy said another dirty word to Doris yesterday, and you didn't even demote him.

KELLER. Yeah, that's a dangerous character, that Tommy. (*Beckons him closer.*) What word does he say?

BERT (*blushing*). Oh, I can't say that.

KELLER. Well, gimme an idea.

BERT. I can't. It's not a nice word.

KELLER. Just whisper it in my ear. I'll close my eyes. Maybe I won't even hear it.

BERT (*on tiptoe, puts his lips to* KELLER'S *ear, then in unbearable embarrassment steps away*). I can't, Mr. Keller.

CHRIS (*looks up*). Don't make him do that.

KELLER. Okay, Bert. I take your word. Now go out, and keep both eyes peeled.

BERT (*interested*). For what?

KELLER. For what! Bert, the whole neighborhood is depending on you. A policeman don't ask questions. Now peel them eyes!

BERT (*mystified, but willing*). Okay.

KELLER. And mum's the word, Bert.

BERT. About what?

KELLER. Just in general. Be v-e-r-y careful.

BERT (*nods in bewilderment*). Okay. (BERT *exits up the driveway.*)

KELLER (*laughs*). I got all the kids crazy!

CHRIS (*smiles, looks up toward the tree*). One of these days, they'll all come in here and beat your brains out. (*He gets up, goes leisurely to the tree, touches the break in the stump.*)

KELLER. What's she going to say? Maybe we ought to tell her before she sees it.

CHRIS. She saw it.

KELLER. How could she see it? I was the first one up. She was still in bed.

CHRIS. She was out here when it broke.

KELLER. When?

CHRIS. About four this morning. (*Indicating the window above them.*) I heard it cracking and I woke up and looked out. She was standing right here when it cracked.

KELLER. What was she doing out here four in the morning?

CHRIS. I don't know. When it cracked she ran back into the house and cried in the kitchen.

KELLER. Did you talk to her?

CHRIS. No, I . . . I figured the best thing was to leave her alone. (*Pause.*)

KELLER (*deeply touched*). She cried hard?

CHRIS. I could hear her right through the floor of my room. (*Slight pause.*)

KELLER. What was she doing out here at that hour? (*An undertone of anger showing.*) She's dreaming about him again. She's walking around at night.

CHRIS. I guess she is.

KELLER. She's getting just like after he died. (*Slight pause.*) What's the meaning of that?

CHRIS. I don't know the meaning of it. (*Slight pause.*) But I know one thing, Dad. We've made a terrible mistake with Mother.

KELLER. What?

CHRIS. Being dishonest with her. That kind of thing always pays off, and now it's paying off.

KELLER. What do you mean, dishonest?

CHRIS. You know Larry's not coming back and I know it. Why do we allow her to go on thinking that we believe with her?

KELLER. What do you want to do, argue with her?

CHRIS. I don't want to argue with her, but it's time she realized that nobody believes Larry is alive any more.

[KELLER *simply moves away, thinking, looking at the ground.*]

CHRIS. Why shouldn't she dream of him, walk the nights waiting for him? Do we contradict her? Do we say straight out that we have no hope any more? That we haven't had any hope for years now?

KELLER (*frightened at the thought*). You can't say that to her.

CHRIS. We've got to say it to her.

KELLER. How're you going to prove it? Can you prove it?

CHRIS. For God's sake, three years! Nobody comes back after three years. It's insane.

KELLER. To you it is, and to me. But not to her. You can talk yourself blue in the face, but there's no body and there's no grave, so where are you?

CHRIS. Sit down, Dad. I want to talk to you.

KELLER (*looks at him searchingly a moment, and sitting. . . .*) The trouble is the goddam newspapers. Every month some boy turns up from nowhere, so the next one is going to be Larry, so . . .

CHRIS. All right, listen to me. (*Slight pause.*) You know why I asked Annie here, don't you?

KELLER (*he knows, but*). . . . . Why?

CHRIS. You know.

KELLER. Well, I got an idea, but . . . What's the story?

CHRIS. I'm going to ask her to marry me. (*Slight pause.*)

KELLER (*nods*). Well, that's only your business, Chris.

CHRIS. You know it's not only my business.

KELLER. What do you want me to do? You're old enough to know your own mind.

CHRIS (*asking, annoyed*). Then it's all right, I'll go ahead with it.

KELLER. Well, you want to be sure Mother isn't going to . . .

CHRIS. Then it isn't just my business.

KELLER. I'm just sayin' . . .

CHRIS. Sometimes you infuriate me, you know that? Isn't it your business, too, if I tell this to Mother and she throws a fit about it? You have such a talent for ignoring things.

KELLER. I ignore what I gotta ignore. The girl is Larry's girl . . .

CHRIS. She's not Larry's girl.

KELLER. From Mother's point of view he is not dead and you have no right to take his girl. (*Slight pause.*) Now you can go on from there if you know where to go, but I'm tellin' you I don't know where to go. See? I don't know. Now what can I do for you?

CHRIS (*gets up*). I don't know why it is, but every time I reach out for something I want, I have to pull back because other people will suffer. My whole bloody life, time after time after time.

KELLER. You're a considerate fella, there's nothing wrong in that.

CHRIS. To hell with that.

KELLER. Did you ask Annie yet?

CHRIS. I wanted to get this settled first.

KELLER. How do you know she'll marry you? Maybe she feels the same way Mother does.

CHRIS. Well if she does then that's the end of it. From her letters I think she's forgotten him. I'll find out. And then we'll thrash it out with Mother. Right? Dad, don't avoid me.

KELLER. The trouble is you don't see enough women. You never did.

CHRIS. So what? I'm not fast with women.

KELLER. I don't see why it has to be Annie. . . .

CHRIS. Because it is.

KELLER. That's a good answer, but it don't answer anything. You haven't seen her since you went to war. It's five years.

CHRIS. I can't help it. I know her best. I was brought up next door to her. These years when I think of someone for my wife, I think of Annie. What do you want, a diagram?

KELLER. I don't want a diagram . . . I . . . I'm . . . She thinks he's coming back, Chris. You marry that girl and you're pronouncing him dead. Now what's going to happen to Mother? Do you know? I don't! (*Pause.*)

CHRIS. All right then, Dad.

KELLER (*thinking* CHRIS *has retreated*). Give it some more thought.

CHRIS. I've given it three years of thought. I'd hoped that if I waited, Mother would forget Larry and then we'd have a regular wedding and everything happy. But if that can't happen here, then I'll have to get out.

KELLER. What the hell is *this*?

CHRIS. I'll get out. I'll get married and live some place else. Maybe in New York.

KELLER. Are you crazy?

CHRIS. I've been a good son too long, a good sucker. I'm through with it.

KELLER. You've got a business here, what the hell is . . .

CHRIS. The business doesn't inspire me.

KELLER. Must you be inspired?

CHRIS. I like it an hour a day. If I have to grub for money all day long, at least at evening I want it beautiful. I want a family, I want some kids, I want to build something I can give myself to. Annie is in the middle 10 of that. Now . . . where do I find it?

KELLER. You mean . . . (*Goes to him.*) Tell me something, you mean you'd leave the business?

CHRIS. Yes. On this I would. (*Pause.*)

KELLER. Well . . . you don't want to think like that.

CHRIS. Then help me stay here.

KELLER. All right, but . . . but don't 20 think like that. Because what the hell did I work for? That's only for you, Chris, the whole shootin' match is for you!

CHRIS. I know that, Dad. Just help me stay here.

KELLER (*puts a fist up to* CHRIS's *jaw*). But don't think that way, you hear me?

CHRIS. I'm thinking that way. 30

KELLER (*lowering his hand*). I don't understand you, do I?

CHRIS. No, you don't. I'm a pretty tough guy.

KELLER. Yeah. I can see that.

[MOTHER *appears on the porch. She is in her early fifties, a woman of uncontrolled inspirations, and an overwhelming capacity for love.*]

MOTHER. Joe? 40

CHRIS (*going toward the porch*). Hello, Mom.

MOTHER (*indicating the house behind her; to* KELLER). Did you take a bag from under the sink?

KELLER. Yeah, I put it in the pail.

MOTHER. Well, get it out of the pail. That's my potatoes.

[CHRIS *bursts out laughing.*]

KELLER (*laughing*). I thought it was garbage. (KELLER *retrieves the bag wryly.*)

MOTHER. Will you do me a favor, Joe? Don't be helpful.

KELLER (*with distaste, lifting out the bag*). I can afford another bag of potatoes.

MOTHER. Minnie scoured that pail in boiling water last night. It's cleaner than your teeth. Give me the bag.

KELLER (*as he gives her the bag*). And I don't understand why, after I worked forty years and I got a maid, why I have to take out the garbage.

MOTHER. If you would make up your mind that every bag in the kitchen isn't full of garbage you wouldn't be throwing out my vegetables. Last time it was the onions.

KELLER. I don't like garbage in the house.

MOTHER. Then don't eat. (*She goes into the kitchen with the bag.*)

CHRIS. That settles you for today.

KELLER. Yeah, I'm in last place again. I don't know, once upon a time I used to think that when I got money again I would have a maid and my wife would take it easy. Now I got money, and I got a maid, and my wife is workin' for the maid. (*He sits in one of the chairs.*)

[MOTHER *comes out on the last line.*]

MOTHER. It's her day off, what are you crabbing about?

CHRIS (*to* MOTHER). Isn't Annie finished eating?

MOTHER (*looking around preoccupiedly at the yard*). She'll be right out. (*Moves.*) That wind did some job on this place. (*Of the tree.*) So much for that, thank God.

KELLER (*indicating the chair beside him*). Sit down, take it easy.

MOTHER (*moving toward the border of plants, downstage, left; she presses her hand to the top of her head*). I've got such a funny pain on the top of my head.

CHRIS. Can I get you an aspirin?

MOTHER (*picks a few petals off the ground, stands there smelling them in her hand, then sprinkles them over the plants*). No more roses. It's so funny . . . (*She sits, then continues.*) . . . everything decides to happen at the same time. It'll be his birthday soon; his tree blows down, Annie comes. Everything that happened seems to be coming back. I was just down the cellar and what do I stumble over? His baseball glove. I haven't seen that baseball glove in a century.

CHRIS. Don't you think Annie looks well?

MOTHER. Fine. There's no question about it. She's a beauty . . . I still don't know what brought her here. Not that I'm not glad to see her, but . . .

CHRIS. I just thought we'd all like to see each other again.

[MOTHER *just looks at him, nodding ever so slightly.*]

CHRIS (*almost as though admitting something*). And I wanted to see her myself.

MOTHER (*her nods halt; to* KELLER). The only thing is I think her nose got longer. But I'll always love that girl. She's one that didn't jump into bed with somebody else as soon as it happened with her fella.

KELLER (*as though that were impossible for* ANNIE). Oh, what're you . . .

MOTHER. Never mind. Most of them didn't wait till the telegrams were opened. I'm just glad she came so you can see I'm not *completely* out of my mind.

CHRIS. Just because she isn't married doesn't mean she's been mourning him.

MOTHER (*with an undercurrent of observation*). Why then isn't she?

CHRIS (*a little flustered*). Well . . . it could've been any number of things.

MOTHER (*directly at him*). Like what, for instance?

CHRIS (*embarrassed, but standing his ground*). I don't know. Whatever it is.

[MOTHER *gets up, pressing her palm to the top of her head.*]

CHRIS. Can I get you an aspirin?

MOTHER (*she goes aimlessly toward the tree*). It's not like a headache.

KELLER. You don't sleep, that's why. You're wearing out more bedroom slippers than shoes.

MOTHER. I had a terrible night. (*She stops moving.*) I never had a night like that.

CHRIS (*goes to her*). What was it, Mom? Did you dream?

MOTHER. More, more than a dream.

CHRIS (*hesitantly*). About Larry?

MOTHER. I was fast asleep, and . . . (*Raising her arm over the audience.*) Remember the way he used to fly low past the house when he was in training? When we used to see his face in the cockpit going by? That's the way I saw him. Only high up. Way, way up, where the clouds are. He was so real I could reach out and touch him. And suddenly he started to fall. And crying, crying to me . . . Mom, Mom! I could hear him like he was in the room. Mom!—it was his voice! If I could touch him I knew I could stop him, if I could only . . . (*Breaks off, allowing her outstretched hand to fall.*) I woke up and it was so funny. . . . The wind . . . it was like the roaring of his engine. I came out here . . . I must've still been half asleep. I could hear that roaring like he was going by. The tree snapped right in front of me . . . and I like . . . came awake. (*She is looking at the tree. She suddenly realizes something, turns with a reprimanding finger shaking slightly at* KELLER.) See? We should never have planted that tree. I said so in the first 10 place; it was too soon to plant a tree for him.

CHRIS (*alarmed*). Too soon!

MOTHER (*angering*). We rushed into it. Everybody was in such a hurry to bury him. I *said* not to plant it yet. (*To* KELLER.) I *told* you to . . . !

CHRIS (*grasping her by the arm*). Mother, Mother! (*She looks into his face.*) The wind blew it down. What significance 20 has that got? What are you talking about? (*He releases her. Unconvinced, she moves from him, and stands stroking her own cheek.* CHRIS *goes to her*). Mother, please . . . Don't go through it all again, will you? It's no good, it doesn't accomplish anything. I've been thinking, y'know—maybe we ought to put our minds to forgetting him. 30

MOTHER. That's the third time you've said that this week.

CHRIS. Because it's not right; we never took up our lives again. We're like at a railroad station waiting for a train that never comes in.

MOTHER (*presses the top of her head*). Get me an aspirin, heh?

CHRIS (*goes to her, smooths her cheek*). And let's break out of this, heh, Mom? I 40 thought the four of us might go out to dinner a couple of nights, maybe go dancing out at the shore.

MOTHER. Fine. (*To* KELLER.) We can do it tonight.

KELLER. Swell with me!

CHRIS. Sure, let's have some fun. (*To* MOTHER.) You'll start with this aspirin. (*He goes up and into the house with new spirit.*)

[*Her smile vanishes.*]

MOTHER (*with an accusing undertone*). Why did he invite her here?

KELLER. Why does that bother you?

MOTHER. She's been in New York three and a half years, why all of a sudden . . . ?

KELLER. Well, maybe . . . maybe he just wanted to see her . . .

MOTHER. Nobody comes seven hundred miles "just to see."

KELLER. What do you mean? He lived next door to the girl all his life, why shouldn't he want to see her again? (MOTHER *looks at him critically.*) Don't look at me like that, he didn't tell me any more than he told you.

MOTHER (*a warning and a question*). He's not going to marry her.

KELLER. How do you know he's even thinking of it?

MOTHER. It's got that about it.

KELLER (*sharply watching her reaction*). Well? So what?

MOTHER. What do you mean, so what? (*Alarmed, she glances toward the house.*) What's going on here, Joe?

KELLER. Now listen, kid . . .

MOTHER (*avoiding contact with him*). She's not his girl, Joe; she knows she's not.

KELLER. You can't read her mind.

MOTHER. Then why is she still single? New York is full of men, why isn't she married? (*Pause.*) Probably a hundred people told her she's foolish, but she's waited.

KELLER. How do you know why she waited?

MOTHER. She knows what I know, that's why. She's faithful as a rock. In my worst moments, I think of her waiting, and I know again that I'm right.

KELLER. Look, it's a nice day. What are you arguing for?

MOTHER. I don't like the way Chris is behaving to her, and you too!

KELLER. I haven't said ten words to her.

MOTHER (*warningly*). Nobody in this house dast take her faith away, Joe. Strangers might. But not his father, not his brother. 10

KELLER (*exasperated*). What do you want me to do? What do you want?

MOTHER. I want you to act like he's coming back. Both of you. (*She moves about.*) Don't think I haven't noticed you since Chris invited her. I won't stand for any nonsense.

KELLER. But Kate . . .

MOTHER. Because if he's not coming back, then I'll kill myself! (*She sobs.*) 20 Laugh. Laugh at me. (*She points to the tree.*) But why did that happen the very night she came back? Laugh, but there are meanings in such things. She goes to sleep in his room and his memorial breaks in pieces. Look at it, look. (*She goes to him.*) Joe . . .

KELLER. Calm yourself.

MOTHER. Believe with me, Joe. I can't stand all alone. 30

KELLER (*stroking her hand helplessly*). Calm yourself.

MOTHER. Only last week a man turned up in Detroit, missing longer than Larry. You read it yourself.

KELLER (*noncommittally*). All right, all right, calm yourself.

MOTHER. You above all have got to believe, you . . .

KELLER (*suddenly stops stroking her hand*). 40 Why me above all?

MOTHER (*to cover herself she touches his hair*). Just don't stop believing . . .

KELLER (*brushing her hand away, but gently*). What does that mean, me above all?

[*Little* BERT *comes rushing down the driveway, at the right.*]

BERT. Mr. Keller! Say, Mr. Keller . . . (*Pointing up the driveway.*) . . . Tommy just said it again!

KELLER (*not remembering any of it*). Said what? . . . Who? . . .

BERT. The dirty word.

KELLER. Oh. Well . . . (*He preoccupiedly flicks his hand to dismiss* BERT.)

BERT. Gee, aren't you going to arrest him? I warned him.

MOTHER (*with suddenness*). Stop that, Bert. Go home.

[BERT *backs up as she advances.*]

MOTHER. There's no jail here.

KELLER (*as though to say, Oh-what-the-hell-let-him-believe-there-is*). Kate . . .

MOTHER (*turning on* KELLER *furiously*). There's no jail here! I want you to stop that jail business!

BERT (*past her to* KELLER). He's right across the street . . .

MOTHER. Go home, Bert!

[BERT *looks at her in astonishment, and at* KELLER, *turns around, and goes up the driveway.*)

MOTHER (*she is shaken; her speech is bitten off, extremely urgent*). I want you to stop that, Joe. That whole jail business!

KELLER (*alarmed, therefore angered*). Look at you. Look at you shaking.

MOTHER (*trying to control herself, moving about, clasping her hands*). I can't help it.

KELLER. What have I got to hide? What the hell is the matter with you, Kate?

MOTHER. I didn't say you had anything to hide, I'm just telling you to stop it! Now stop it!

[ANN *and* CHRIS *appear on the porch.* ANN *is twenty-six, gentle, but despite herself capable of holding fast to what she knows.*]

ANN. Ain't love grand!

[*She leads off a general laugh that is not self-*

conscious because they know one another too well.]

CHRIS (*bringing* ANN *down, with an outstretched, chivalric arm*). How about this kid?

MOTHER (*genuinely overcome with it*). Annie, where did you get that dress!

ANN. I couldn't resist. I'm taking it right off before I ruin it. (*Swings around.*) How's that for three weeks' salary?

MOTHER (*to* KELLER). Isn't she the most . . . (*To* ANN.) It's gorgeous, simply gor . . .

CHRIS (*to* MOTHER). No kidding now, isn't she the prettiest gal you ever saw?

MOTHER (*caught short by his obvious admiration, she finds herself reaching out for a glass of water and aspirin in his hand, and . . .*) I'm just afraid you gained a little weight, didn't you, darling? (*She gulps the pill and drinks.*)

ANN (*disappointed*). It comes and goes. (*She walks left, toward the poplars.*)

KELLER. Look how nice her legs turned out!

ANN. Boy, the poplars got thick, didn't they?

KELLER. Well, it's three years, Annie. We're gettin' old, kid.

[*She parts branches, looks toward* JIM's *yard.*]

MOTHER. How does Mom like New York?

ANN. Why'd they take our hammock away?

KELLER. Oh no, it broke. Couple of years ago.

MOTHER (*with gay, loving sarcasm, at* KELLER). What broke? He had one of his light lunches and flopped into it.

ANN (*she laughs and turns back toward* JIM's *yard*). Oh, excuse me!

[JIM *enters from in front of her.*]

JIM. How do you do. (*To* KELLER.) I found my thermometer . . . don't

ask me where. (*To* CHRIS.) She looks very intelligent.

CHRIS. Ann, this is Jim . . . Doctor Bayliss.

ANN (*shaking* JIM's *hand*). Oh sure, he writes a lot about you.

JIM. Don't believe it. He likes everybody. In Luxembourg he was known as Mother McKeller.

ANN. I can believe it. . . . You know? (*To the others.*) It's so strange seeing him come out of that yard. (*To* CHRIS.) I guess I never grew up. It almost seems that Mom and Pop are in there now. And you and my brother doing algebra, and Larry trying to copy my homework. Gosh, those dear dead days beyond recall.

JIM. Well, I hope that doesn't mean you want me to move out.

SUE (*calling from the left*). Jim, come here! Mr. Hubbard is on the phone!

JIM. I told you I don't want . . .

SUE (*commandingly sweet*). Please, dear!

JIM (*resigned*). All right, Susie, (*Trailing off*) all right, all right . . . (*He takes* ANN's *hand.*) I've only met you, Ann, but if I may offer you a piece of advice—when you marry, never—even in your mind—never count your husband's money.

SUE (*from off*). Jim?

JIM. At once! (*Turns and goes to the left.*) At once. (*He exits by the left.*)

MOTHER. I told her to take up the guitar. It'd be a common interest for them. (*They laugh.*) He loves the guitar.

ANN (*she becomes suddenly lively, grasps* MOTHER's *hands*). Let's eat at the shore tonight! Raise some hell around here, like we used to before Larry went!

MOTHER (*emotionally*). You think of him! (*Hugs* ANN's *head.*) You see? (*Triumphantly.*) She thinks of him!

ANN (*with an uncomprehending smile*). What do you mean, Kate?

MOTHER. Nothing. Just that you . . . remember him, he's in your thoughts.

ANN. That's a funny thing to say; how could I help remembering him?

MOTHER (*it is drawing to a head the wrong way for her; she starts anew; she circles* ANN's *waist, and walks her to a chair, fixing the girl's hair*). Sit down, dear.

[ANN *sits, watching her.*]

MOTHER. Did you hang up your things?

ANN. Yeah . . . (*To* CHRIS.) Say, you've sure gone in for clothes. I could hardly find room in the closet.

MOTHER. No. (*Sits.*) Don't you remember? That's Larry's room.

ANN. You mean . . . they're Larry's?

MOTHER. Didn't you recognize them?

ANN (*a little embarrassed*). Well, it never occurred to me that you'd . . . I mean the shoes are all shined.

MOTHER. Yes, dear.

[*Slight pause.* ANN *can't stop staring at her.* MOTHER *breaks it by clasping her hands comfortably in her lap, and speaking with the relish of gossip.*]

MOTHER. For so long I've been aching for a nice conversation with you, Annie. Tell me something.

ANN. What?

MOTHER. I don't know. Something nice.

CHRIS (*wryly*). She means do you go out much.

MOTHER. Oh, shut up.

KELLER. And are any of them serious?

MOTHER (*laughing*). Why don't you both choke?

KELLER. Annie, you can't go into a restaurant with that woman any more. In five minutes thirty-nine strange people are sitting at the table telling her their life story.

MOTHER. If I can't ask Annie a personal question . . .

KELLER. Askin' is all right, but don't beat her over the head. You're beatin' her, you're beatin' her.

[*They are laughing.*]

ANN (*to* MOTHER). Don't let them bulldoze you. Ask me anything you like. What do you want to know, Kate? Come on, let's gossip.

MOTHER (*to* CHRIS *and* KELLER). She's the only one's got any sense. (*To* ANN.) Your mother . . . she's not getting a divorce, heh?

ANN. No, she's calmed down about it now. I think when he gets out they'll probably live together. In New York, of course.

MOTHER. That's fine. Because your father is still . . . I mean he's a decent man after all is said and done.

ANN. I don't care. She can take him back if she likes.

MOTHER. And you? You . . . (*Shakes her head negatively.*) . . . go out much? (*Slight pause.*)

ANN (*delicately*). You mean am I waiting for him?

MOTHER. Well, no, I don't expect you to wait for him but . . .

ANN (*kindly*). But that's what you mean, isn't it?

MOTHER. . . . Well . . . yes.

ANN. Well, I'm not, Kate.

MOTHER (*faintly*). You're not.

ANN. Isn't it ridiculous? You don't really imagine he's . . .

MOTHER. I know, dear, but don't say it's ridiculous, because the papers were full of it. I don't know about New York but there was half a page about a man in Detroit missing longer than Larry and he turned up from Burma.

CHRIS. He couldn't have wanted to come home very badly, Mom.

MOTHER. Don't be so smart. Why couldn't he of lost his memory?

Or . . . or . . . it could've been a million things. What is impossible that hasn't already happened in this world? Who is smart enough to say what can happen?

CHRIS (*going to her with a condescending laugh*). Mother, you're absolutely . . .

MOTHER (*waving him off*). Don't be so damned smart! Now stop it! (*Slight pause.*) There are just a few things you 10 *don't* know. All of you. And I'll tell you one of them, Annie. Deep, deep in your heart you've always been waiting for him.

ANN (*resolutely*). No, Kate.

MOTHER (*with increasing demand*). But deep in your heart, Annie!

CHRIS. She ought to know, shouldn't she?

MOTHER (*looking at* ANN, *pointing at her*). 20 Don't let them tell you what to think. Listen to your heart. Only your heart.

ANN (*gets up, goes to her*). Why does your heart tell you he's alive?

MOTHER. Because he has to be.

ANN. But why, Kate?

MOTHER. Because certain things have to be, and certain things can never be. Like the sun has to rise, it has to 30 be. That's why there's God. Otherwise anything could happen. But there's God, so certain things can never happen. I would know, Annie —just like I knew the day he (*Indicates* CHRIS.) went into that terrible battle. Did he write me? Was it in the papers? No, but that morning I couldn't raise my head off the pillow. Ask Joe. Suddenly, I knew. I 40 knew! And he was nearly killed that day. Annie, you know I'm right! (*Turns, trembling, going upstage.*)

ANN. No, Kate.

MOTHER (*stands there in silence*). I have to have some tea.

[FRANK *appears from the right, carrying a ladder.*]

FRANK. Annie! (*Coming down.*) How are you, gee whiz.

ANN (*taking his hand*). Why, Frank, you're losing your hair.

KELLER. He's got responsibility. Without Frank the stars wouldn't know when to come out.

FRANK (*laughs. To* ANN). You look womanly. You've matured. You . . .

KELLER. Take it easy, Frank, you're a married man.

ANN (*as they laugh*). You still haberdashering?

FRANK. Why not? Maybe I too can get to be president. How's your brother? Got his degree, I hear.

ANN. Oh, George has his own office now!

FRANK. Don't say. (*Funereally.*) And your dad? Is he . . . ?

ANN (*abruptly*). Fine. I'll be in to see Lydia.

FRANK (*sympathetically*). How about it, does Dad expect a parole soon?

ANN (*with growing ill-ease*). I really don't know, I . . .

FRANK (*stanchly defending her father for her sake*). I mean because I feel, y'know, that if an intelligent man like your father is put in prison, there ought to be a law that says either you execute him, or let him go after a year. Because if you look at your statistics . . .

CHRIS. Want a hand with that ladder?

FRANK (*taking the cue*). That's all right, I'll . . . (*Picks up the ladder.*) . . . I'll finish the horoscope tonight, Kate. (*Embarrassed.*) See you later, Ann, you look wonderful.

[*She nods to him as he exits right. They look at* ANN, *who has not moved.*]

CHRIS (*approaches her*). Don't feel that way, he only asked about him.

ANN (*to all*). Haven't they stopped talking about Dad?

CHRIS. Nobody talks about him any more.

KELLER. Gone and forgotten, kid. Here, sit down.

ANN (*as he seats her*). Tell me. Because I don't want to meet anybody on the block if they're going to . . .

CHRIS. I don't want you to worry about it.

ANN (*to* KELLER). Do they still remember the case? Do they talk about you?

KELLER. The only one still talks about it is my wife.

MOTHER. Because you keep playing policeman with the kids. All their parents hear out of you is jail, jail, jail. (*To* ANN.) I do everything I know to make people forget the damned thing and he . . .

KELLER. Actually what happened was that when I got home from the penitentiary the kids got very interested in me. You know kids. I was (*Laughs.*) like the expert on the jail situation. And as time passed they got it confused and . . . I ended up a detective. (*Laughs.*)

MOTHER. Except that *they* didn't get it confused. (*To* ANN.) He hands out police badges from the Post Toasties boxes.

[*They laugh.*]

ANN (*wondrously at them, happily*). Gosh, it's wonderful to hear you laughing about it.

CHRIS. Why, what'd you expect?

ANN. The last thing I remember on this block was one word—"Murderers!" Remember that, Kate? . . . Mrs. Hammond standing in front of our house and yelling that word . . . ? She's still around, I suppose.

MOTHER. They're all still around.

KELLER. Don't listen to her. Every Saturday night the whole gang is playin' poker in this yard. All the ones who yelled murder takin' my money now.

MOTHER. Don't, Joe, she's a sensitive girl, don't fool her. (*To* ANN.) They still remember about Dad. It's different with him—(*Indicates* JOE.)—he was exonerated, your father's still there. That's why I wasn't so enthusiastic about you coming. Honestly, I know how sensitive you are, and I told Chris, I said . . .

KELLER. Listen, you do like I did and you'll be all right. The day I come home, I got out of my car—but not in front of the house . . . on the corner. You should've been here, Annie, and you too, Chris; you'd 'a' seen something. Everybody knew I was getting out that day; the porches were loaded. Picture it now; none of them believed I was really innocent. The story was, I pulled a fast one getting myself exonerated. So I get out of my car, and I walk down the street. But very slow. And with a smile. The beast. I was the beast; the guy who sold cracked cylinder heads to the Army Air Force; the guy who made twenty-one P-40's crash in Australia. Kid, walkin' down the street that day I was guilty as hell. Except I wasn't, and there was a court paper in my pocket to prove I wasn't . . . and I walked . . . past . . . the porches. Result? Fourteen months later I had one of the best shops in the state again, a respected man again, bigger than ever.

CHRIS (*with admiration*). Joe McGuts.

KELLER (*now with great force*). That's the only way you lick 'em, is guts! (*To* ANN.) The worst thing you did was to move away from here. You made it tough for your father when he gets out, and you made it tough for me. Sure, they play poker, but behind their eyes is that dirty thought—Keller, you were very intimate with a murderer. That's why I tell you, I like to see him move back right on this block.

MOTHER (*pained*). How could they move back?

KELLER. It ain't gonna end *till* they move back! (*To* ANN.) Till people play cards with him again, and talk with him, and smile with him—you play cards with a man you know he can't be a murderer. And the next time you write him I like you to tell him just what I said.

[ANN *simply stares at him.*]

KELLER. You hear me?

ANN (*surprised*). Don't you hold anything against him?

KELLER. Annie, I never believed in crucifying people.

ANN (*mystified*). But he was your partner, he dragged you through the mud . . .

KELLER. Well, he ain't my sweetheart, but you gotta forgive, don't you?

ANN. You either, Kate? Don't you feel any . . . ? I mean I'm just curious.

KELLER. The next time you write Dad . . .

ANN. I don't write him.

KELLER (*struck*). Well, every now and then you . . .

ANN (*a little ashamed, but determined*). No, I've never written to him. Neither has my brother. (*To* CHRIS.) Say, do you feel this way too?

CHRIS. He murdered twenty-one pilots.

KELLER. What the hell kinda talk is that?

MOTHER. That's not a thing to say about a man.

ANN. What else can you say? When they took him away I followed him, went to him every visiting day. I was crying all the time. Until the news came about Larry. Then I realized. It's wrong to pity a man like that. Father

or no father, there's only one way to look at him. He knowingly shipped out parts that would crash an airplane. And how do you know Larry wasn't one of them?

MOTHER. I was waiting for that. (*Going to her.*) As long as you're here, Annie, I want to ask you never to say that again.

ANN. I don't understand. I thought you'd be . . . at least mad at him.

MOTHER. What your father did had nothing to do with Larry. Nothing.

ANN. But we can't know that.

MOTHER (*striving for control*). As long as you're here!

ANN (*perplexed*). But Kate . . .

MOTHER. Put that out of your head!

KELLER. Because . . .

MOTHER (*quickly to* KELLER). That's all, that's enough! (*Places her hand on her head.*) Come inside now, and have some tea with me. (*She turns and goes toward the house.*)

KELLER (*to* ANN). The one thing you . . .

MOTHER (*sharply*). He's not dead, so there's no argument! Now come!

KELLER (*angrily*). In a minute!

[MOTHER *turns and goes into the house.*]

KELLER. Now look, Annie . . .

CHRIS. All right, Dad, forget it.

KELLER. No, she dasn't feel that way. Annie . . .

CHRIS. I'm sick of the whole subject, now cut it out.

KELLER. You want her to go on like this? (*To* ANN.) Now listen. Those cylinder heads went into P-40's only. What's the matter with you? You know Larry never flew a P-40.

CHRIS. So who flew those P-40's, pigs?

KELLER (*with great anxiety, a growing note of plea*). The man was a fool, but don't make a murderer out of him. You got no sense? Look what it does to her! (*To* ANN.) You gotta appreciate what was doin' in that shop in the war. It was a madhouse. Every half hour the Major callin' for cylinder heads, they were whippin' us with the telephone. The trucks were hauling them away hot, damn near. I mean just try to see it human, see it human. All of a sudden a batch comes out with a crack. That happens, that's the business. A fine hairline crack. All right, so . . . so he's a little man, your father, always scared of loud voices. What'll the Major say?—Half a day's production shot. What'll I say? You know what I mean? Human. (*Slight pause.*) So he takes out his tools and he . . . covers over the cracks. All right . . . that's bad, it's wrong, but that's what a little man does. If I could've gone in that day I'd a told him—junk 'em, Herb, we can afford it. But alone he was afraid. But I know he meant no harm. He believed they'd hold up a hundred per cent. And a lot of them did. That's a mistake, but it ain't murder. You mustn't feel that way about him. You understand me? I don't like to see a girl eating out her heart.

ANN (*she regards him a moment*). Joe, let's forget it.

KELLER. Annie, the day the news came about Larry he was in the next cell to mine . . . Dad. And he cried, Annie . . . he cried half the night.

ANN (*touched*). He should have cried all night.

KELLER (*almost angered*). Annie, I do not understand why you . . . !

CHRIS (*breaking in—with nervous urgency*). Are you going to stop it?

ANN. Don't yell at him. He just wants everybody happy.

KELLER. That's my sentiments. I'll call Swanson's for a table. We'll have steaks.

CHRIS. And champagne.

KELLER. Now you're talkin'! Big time tonight, Annie!

ANN. Can't scare me.

KELLER (*to* CHRIS, *pointing at* ANNIE). I like that girl. Wrap her up. (*They laugh. Goes up the porch.*) I want to see everybody drunk tonight. . . . You got nice legs, Annie. (*To* CHRIS.) Look at him, he's blushin'.

CHRIS. Drink your tea, Casanova.

[KELLER *laughs tauntingly, but warmly, pointing at* CHRIS, *and goes into the house.*]

CHRIS. Isn't he a great guy?

ANN. You're the only one I know who loves his parents!

CHRIS. I know. It went out of style, didn't it?

ANN (*with a sudden touch of sadness*). It's all right. It's a good thing. (*She goes to a chair, looks about.*) You know? It's lovely here. The air is sweet.

CHRIS (*hopefully*). You're not sorry you came?

ANN. Not sorry, no. But I'm . . . not going to stay . . .

CHRIS. Why?

ANN. In the first place, your mother as much as told me to go.

CHRIS. Well . . .

ANN. You saw that . . . and then you . . . you've been . . .

CHRIS. What?

ANN. Well . . . kind of embarrassed ever since I got here.

CHRIS. The trouble is I planned on sneaking up on you over a period of a week or so. But they take it for granted that we're all set.

ANN. I knew they would. Your mother anyway.

CHRIS. How did you know?

ANN. From her point of view, why else would I come?

CHRIS. Well . . . would you want to?

(ANN *studies him.*) I guess you know this is why I asked you to come.

ANN. I guess this is why I came.

CHRIS. Ann, I love you. I love you a great deal. (*Finally.*) I love you. (*Pause. She waits.*) I have no imagination . . . that's all I know to tell you. I'm embarrassing you. I didn't want to tell it to you here. I wanted some place with trees around . . . some new place, we'd never been; a place where we'd be brand-new to each other. . . .

ANN (*she touches his arm*). What's the matter?

CHRIS. You feel it's wrong here, don't you? This yard, this chair.

ANN. It's not wrong, Chris.

CHRIS. I don't want to win you away from anything. I want you to be ready for me.

ANN. Oh, Chris, I've been ready a long, long time.

CHRIS. Then he's gone forever. You're sure.

ANN. I almost got married two years ago.

CHRIS. . . . Why didn't you?

ANN. You started to write to me . . . (*Slight pause.*)

CHRIS. You felt something that far back?

ANN. M-hm.

CHRIS. Ann, why didn't you let me know?

ANN. I was waiting for you, Chris. Till then you never wrote. And when you did, what did you say? You sure can be ambiguous, you know.

CHRIS (*he looks toward the house, then at her, trembling*). Give me a kiss, Ann. Give me a . . . (*They kiss.*) God, I kissed you, Annie, I kissed Annie. How long, how long I've been waiting to kiss you!!

ANN. I'll never forgive you. Why did you wait all these years? All I've done

is sit and wonder if I was crazy for thinking of you.

CHRIS. Annie, we're going to live now! I'm going to make you so happy. (*He kisses her, but without their bodies touching.*)

ANN. Not like that you're not.

CHRIS (*laughs*). Why? I kissed you . . .

ANN. Like Larry's brother. Do it like you, Chris.

[*He moves from her.*]

ANN. What is it?

CHRIS. Let's drive some place. . . . I want to be alone with you.

ANN. No . . . what is it, Chris, your mother?

CHRIS. No . . . nothing like that . . .

ANN. Then what's wrong? . . . You've got to tell me, mustn't you? It wouldn't work this way, would it . . . (*Slight pause.*) Even in your letters, there was something ashamed.

CHRIS. Yes. I suppose I've been ashamed. I . . . I don't know how to start to tell you. It's mixed up with so many other things, it goes so far back. You remember I was in command of a company.

ANN. Ya, sure.

CHRIS. Well, I lost them.

ANN. How many?

CHRIS. Just about all.

ANN. Oh gee.

CHRIS. It takes a little time to toss that off. Because they weren't just men. For instance, one time it'd been raining several days and this kid came to me and gave me his last pair of dry socks. Put them in my pocket. That's only a little thing . . . but . . . that's the kind of guys I had. They didn't die; they killed themselves for each other. I mean that exactly; a little more selfish and they'd've been here today. And I got an idea—watching them go down.

Everything was being destroyed, see, but it seemed to me that one new thing was made. A kind of responsibility. Man for man. You understand me?—To show that, to bring that onto the earth again like some kind of a monument, and everyone would feel it standing there, behind him, and it would make a difference to him. (*Pause.*) And then I came 10 home and it was incredible. I . . . there was no meaning in it here; the whole thing to them was a kind of a— bus accident. Like when I went to work with Dad, and that rat race again. I felt . . . ashamed somehow. Because nobody was changed at all. It seemed to make suckers out of a lot of guys. I felt wrong to be alive, to open the bankbook, to drive 20 the new car, to see the new refrigerator. I mean you can take those things out of a war, but when you drive that car you've got to know that it came out of the love a man can have for a man, you've got to be a little better because of that. Otherwise what you have is really loot, and there's blood on it. I didn't want to take any of it. And I guess that in- 30 cluded you.

ANN. And you still feel that way . . .

CHRIS. No . . .

ANN. Because you mustn't feel that way any more.

CHRIS. I want you now, Annie.

ANN. Because you have a right to whatever you have. Everything, Chris, understand that?

CHRIS. I'm glad you feel that way.   40

ANN. To me too. . . . And the money, there's nothing wrong in your money. Joe put hundreds of planes in the air, you should be proud. A man should be paid for that. . . .

CHRIS. Oh Annie, Annie. . . . I'm going to make a fortune for you!

ANN (*laughing softly*). What'll I do with a fortune . . . ?

[*They kiss.*]

CHRIS (*rocking with her*). Believe me, Annie, we'll be fine, fine . . .

[KELLER *enters from the house.*]

KELLER (*thumbing toward the house*). Hey, Ann, your brother . . . (*They step apart shyly.* KELLER *comes down, and wryly.*) What is this, Labor Day?

CHRIS (*waving him away, knowing the kidding will be endless*). All right, all right . . .

ANN (*gaily*). You shouldn't burst out like that.

KELLER. Well, nobody told me it was Labor Day. (*Looks around.*) Where's the hot dogs?

CHRIS (*loving it*). All right. You said it once.

KELLER. Well, as long as I know it's Labor Day from now on, I'll wear a bell around my neck.

ANN (*affectionately*). He's so subtle!

CHRIS. George Bernard Shaw as an elephant.

KELLER. George!—hey, that reminds me, your brother's on the phone.

ANN (*surprised*). My brother?

KELLER. Yeah, George. Long-distance.

ANN (*she is strangely upset*). What's the matter, is anything wrong?

KELLER. I don't know, Kate's talking to him. Hurry up, she'll cost him five dollars.

ANN (*she takes a step upstage, then comes down toward* CHRIS). I wonder if we ought to tell your mother yet. She doesn't seem to . . . I mean I'd hate to argue with her.

CHRIS. We'll wait till tonight. After dinner. Now don't get tense, just leave it to me.

KELLER. What're you telling her?

CHRIS. Go ahead, Ann.

[*With misgivings,* ANN *goes up and into the house.*]

CHRIS. We're getting married, Dad.

[KELLER *nods indecisively.*]

CHRIS. Don't you say anything?

KELLER (*distracted*). I'm glad, Chris, I'm just . . . George is calling from Columbus.

CHRIS (*surprised*). Columbus!

KELLER. Did Annie tell you he was going to see his father today?

CHRIS. No, I don't think she knew anything about it.

KELLER (*asking uncomfortably*). Chris, you . . . you think you knew her pretty good?

CHRIS. What kind of a question . . . ?

KELLER. I'm just wondering. All these years George don't go to see his father. Suddenly he goes . . . and she comes here.

CHRIS (*a frown growing on his face*). Well, what about it?

KELLER. It's crazy, but it comes to my mind. She don't hold nothin' against me, does she?

CHRIS. I don't know what you're talking about.

KELLER. I'm just talkin'. To his last day in court the man blamed it all on me; and this is his daughter. I mean if she was sent here to find out something.

CHRIS (*angered*). Why? What is there to find out?

ANN (*on the phone, from within*). Why are you so excited, George? What happened there?

KELLER (*glancing at the house*). I mean if they want to open up the case again, for the nuisance value, to hurt us.

CHRIS. Dad . . . how could you think that of her?

ANN (*from within*). But what did he say to you?

KELLER. It couldn't be, heh. You know.

CHRIS. Dad, you amaze me . . .

KELLER (*breaking in*). All right, forget it, forget it. (*With great force, moving about.*) I want a clean start for you, Chris. I want a new sign over the plant—Christopher Keller, Incorporated.

CHRIS (*a little uneasily*). J. O. Keller is good enough.

KELLER. We'll talk about it. I'm going to build you a house, stone, with a driveway from the road. I want you to spread out, Chris, I want you to use what I made for you . . . (*He is close to him now.*) . . . I mean, with joy, Chris, without shame . . . with joy.

CHRIS (*touched*). I will, Dad.

KELLER (*with deep emotion*). . . . Say it to me.

CHRIS. . . . Why?

KELLER. Because sometimes I think you're . . . ashamed of the money.

CHRIS (*pained*). No, don't feel that.

KELLER. Because it's good money, there's nothing wrong with that money.

CHRIS (*a little frightened*). Dad, you don't have to tell me this.

KELLER (*with overriding affection and self-confidence now. He grips* CHRIS *by the back of the neck, and with laughter between his determined jaws*): Oh, you're going to have a life now, Chris! We'll get Mother so drunk tonight we'll all get married! (*Steps away, with a wide gesture of his arm.*) There's gonna be a wedding, kid, like there never was seen! Champagne, tuxedos . . . !

[*Breaks off as* MOTHER *comes out, listening to:*]

ANN (*from within*). Well, what did he tell you, for God's sake? All right, come then. Yes, they'll all be here, nobody's running away from you! And try to get hold of yourself, will you? All right, all right, good-by!

[ANN *comes out. She is somber with nervousness. Comes down, and manages an everyday smile as:*]

CHRIS. Something wrong?

ANN. He'll be in on the seven o'clock. He's in Columbus.

KELLER (*carefully*). What is it, your father took sick?

ANN (*mystified*). No, George didn't say he was sick. I . . . (*Shaking it off.*) . . . I don't know, I suppose it's something stupid, you know my brother. . . . (*She turns suddenly toward the house. Then comes to* CHRIS.) Let's go for a drive, or something.

CHRIS (*studies her for a troubled instant, then nods*). Sure—(*To his parents.*) Be back right away.

KELLER. Take your time.

[*A guitar begins to play off left, in* JIM's *house as:*]

MOTHER (*to* ANN). You hear? Sue is playing the guitar. It keeps him in the house. They married too young.

[CHRIS, *sensing her nervousness, her appeal to him, kisses her and, with* ANN, *goes up the driveway and out.* MOTHER *comes down toward* KELLER, *her eyes fixed upon him.*] 30

KELLER (*with his heartbeat in it, softly*). What happened? What does George want?

MOTHER. He's been in Columbus since this morning with Herb. He's gotta see Annie right away, he says.

KELLER. What for?

MOTHER. I don't know. (*She keeps watching him. He moves, looking at the ground, thinking. She speaks with warning.*) He's a lawyer now, Joe. George is a lawyer.

KELLER. So what?

MOTHER. All these years he wouldn't even send a post card to Herb. Since he got back from the war, not a post-card.

10 KELLER (*angering*). So what?

MOTHER (*her tension breaking out*). Suddenly he takes an airplane from New York to see him. An airplane!

KELLER. Well? So?

MOTHER (*trembling*). Why?

KELLER. I don't read minds. Do you?

MOTHER. Why, Joe? What has Herb suddenly got to tell him that he takes an airplane to see him?

20 KELLER. What do I care what Herb's got to tell him?

MOTHER. You're sure, Joe?

KELLER (*frightened, but angry*). Yes, I'm sure.

MOTHER (*she sits stiffly in a chair*). Be smart now, Joe. The boy is coming. Be smart.

KELLER (*leans over her—into her face; desperately*): Once and for all, did you hear what I said? I said I'm sure!

MOTHER (*she nods weakly*). All right, Joe. (*He straightens up.*) Just . . . be smart.

[KELLER, *in hopeless fury, looks at her, turns around, goes up to the porch and into the house, slamming the screen door violently behind him.* MOTHER *sits in the chair downstage, stiffly, staring, seeing.*]

ACT TWO

SCENE *as before. The same evening, as twilight falls.*

As the curtain rises, CHRIS *is discovered at the right, pulling the broken-off tree up the alley, leaving the stump standing alone. He is dressed in good pants, white shoes, but with-*out a shirt. He disappears with the tree up the alley when MOTHER appears on the porch. She comes down and stands at the mouth of the alley watching him. She has on a dressing gown, carries a tray of grape-juice drink in a pitcher, and glasses.*

MOTHER (*calling up to the alley*). Did you have to put on good pants to do that?

[*There is no answer, but the sound of the tree being dragged. She comes downstage and sets the tray on the table. Then looks around uneasily, then feels the pitcher for coolness, then picks up a scrap of paper and crumples it, and sits down. In a moment she gets up nervously with her hands clasped together, and moves about touching the chairs, a bush. . . .* CHRIS *enters from the alley, brushing off his hands.*]

MOTHER. You notice there's more light with that thing gone?

CHRIS. Why aren't you dressing?

MOTHER. It's suffocating upstairs. I made a grape drink for Georgie. He always liked grape.

CHRIS. Well, come on, get dressed. And what's Dad sleeping so much for?

MOTHER. He's worried. When he's worried he sleeps. (*She looks into his eyes.*) We're dumb, Chris. Dad and I are stupid people. We don't know anything. You've got to protect us.

CHRIS. You're silly; what's there to be afraid of?

MOTHER. To his last day in court Herb never gave up the idea that Dad made him do it. If he's coming to reopen the case I won't live through it. We can't go through that thing again.

CHRIS. George is just a damned fool, Mother, how can you take him so seriously?

MOTHER. That family hates us. Maybe even Annie . . .

CHRIS. Oh now, Mother . . .

MOTHER. You think just because you like everybody, they like you! You don't realize how people can hate. Chris, we've got a nice life here, everything was going so nice. Why do you bring them into it? We struggled all our lives for a little something, and now . . .

CHRIS. All right, stop working yourself up. Just leave everything to me.

MOTHER. When George goes home, tell her to go with him.

CHRIS (*noncommittally*). Don't worry about Annie.

MOTHER. Herb is her father too.

CHRIS. Are you going to cut it out? Now come.

MOTHER (*going upstage with him*). You don't realize how people can hate, Chris, they can hate so much they'll tear the world to pieces. . . .

[ANN, *dressed up, appears on the porch.*]

CHRIS. See? She's dressed already. (*As he and* MOTHER *mount the porch, to* ANN.) I've just got to put on a shirt.

ANN (*in a preoccupied way*). Are you feeling well, Kate?

MOTHER (*laughs weakly*). What's the difference, dear? There are certain people, y'know, the sicker they get the longer they live. (*She goes into the house.*)

CHRIS (*softly, touching her nose*). You look nice.

ANN. We're going to tell her tonight.

CHRIS. Absolutely, don't worry about it.

ANN. I wish we could tell her now. I can't stand scheming. My stomach gets hard.

CHRIS. It's not scheming, we'll just get her in a better mood.

ANN. The only one who's relaxed is your father. (*Laughs.*) He's fast asleep.

CHRIS. I'm relaxed.

ANN. Are you?

CHRIS. Look. (*Holds out his hand and makes it shake violently. They laugh. He smacks her fanny.*) Let me know when George gets here.

[*He goes into the house.* ANN *comes down off the porch. She moves aimlessly, and then is drawn toward the tree stump. She goes to it, hesitantly touches the broken top in the hush of her thoughts. From the left,*]

SUE *enters and halts, seeing* ANN. ANN *is not aware of her.*]

SUE. Is my husband . . . ?

ANN (*turns, startled*). Oh!

SUE (*comes toward her, concerned*). I'm terribly sorry.

ANN (*laughs, embarrassed*). It's all right, I . . . I'm a little silly about the dark.

SUE (*looks about*). It is getting dark. 10

ANN. Are you looking for your husband?

SUE. As usual. (*Laughs tiredly.*) He spends so much time here they'll be charging him rent.

ANN. Nobody was dressed, so he drove over to the depot to pick up my brother.

SUE. Oh, your brother's in?

ANN. Ya, they ought to be here any minute now. Will you have a cold 20 drink?

SUE. I will, thanks. (SUE *sits, strangely distressed, as* ANN *goes to the table, pours.*) My husband. Too hot to drive me to the beach. But for the Kellers?—Men are like little boys; for the neighbors they'll always cut the grass.

ANN. People like to do things for the Kellers. Been that way since I can remember. 30

SUE (*with an edge*). It's amazing. I guess your brother's coming to give you away, heh?

ANN (*giving her the drink, burdened*). I don't know. I suppose.

SUE. You must be all nerved up.

ANN. It's always a problem getting yourself married, isn't it? (*She sits.*)

SUE. That depends on your shape, of course. (*She laughs.*) I don't see why 40 you should have had a problem.

ANN. Oh, I had chances.

SUE. I'll bet. It's romantic . . . it's very unusual to me, marrying the brother of your sweetheart.

ANN. I don't know. I think it's mostly that whenever I need somebody to tell me the truth I've always thought of Chris. When he tells you something you know it's so. He relaxes me.

SUE. And he's got money. That's important, you know.

ANN. It wouldn't matter to me.

SUE. You'd be surprised. It changes everything. I married an interne. On my salary. And that was bad, because as soon as a woman supports a man he owes her something. You can never owe somebody without resenting them.

[ANN *laughs.*]

SUE. That's true, you know.

ANN. Underneath, I think the doctor is very devoted.

SUE. Oh, certainly. But it's bad when a man always sees the bars in front of him. Jim thinks he's in jail all the time.

ANN (*deprecating*). Oh . . .

SUE. That's why I've been intending to ask you a small favor, Ann. . . . It's something very important to me.

ANN. Certainly, if I can do it.

SUE. You can. When you take up housekeeping, try to find a place away from here.

ANN. Are you fooling?

SUE. I'm very serious. My husband is unhappy with Chris around.

ANN (*amazed*). How is that?

SUE. My husband is a successful doctor. But he's got an idea he'd like to do medical research. Discover things. You see?

ANN. Well, isn't that good?

SUE. It's fine. For a small monk. Research pays twenty-five dollars a week minus laundering the hair shirt. You've got to give up your life to go into it.

ANN. How does Chris . . . ?

SUE (*gets up; with growing feeling*): Now

don't take it that way. I like Chris. If I didn't, I'd let him know. I don't butter people. But there's something about him that makes people want to be better than it's possible to be. He does that to people.

ANN. Why is that bad?

SUE. My husband has a family, dear. Every time he has a session with Chris he feels as though he's compromising himself by not giving up everything for research. As though Chris or anybody else isn't compromising. It happens with Jim every couple of years. He meets a man and makes a statue out of him.

ANN. Maybe he's right. I don't mean that Chris is a statue, but . . .

SUE. Now darling, you know he's not right.

ANN. I don't agree with you. Chris . . .

SUE. Let's face it, dear. The man is working with his father, isn't he? He's taking money out of that business every week in the year.

ANN. What of it?

SUE. *You* ask me what of it?

ANN. I certainly do ask you. (*Pause. She seems about to burst out.*) You oughtn't cast aspersions like that. I'm surprised at you.

SUE. You're surprised at *me*.

ANN. He'd never take five cents out of that plant if there was anything wrong in it.

SUE. You know that.

ANN. I know it. I resent everything you've said.

SUE (*moving toward her*). You know what I resent, dear?

ANN (*troubled and afraid*). Please, I don't want to argue.

SUE. I resent living next door to the Holy Family. It makes me look like a bum, you understand?

ANN. I can't do anything about that.

SUE. Who is he to ruin a man's life? Everybody knows Joe pulled a fast one to get out of jail.

ANN. That's not true!

SUE. Then why don't you go out and talk to people? Go on, talk to them. There's not a person on the block who doesn't know the truth.

ANN. That's a lie. They're on the best terms with the block. People come here all the time for cards and . . .

SUE. So what? They give him credit for being smart. I do too. I've got nothing against Joe. But if Chris wants people to put on the hair shirt, let him take off his broadcloth. He's driving my husband crazy with that phony idealism of his, and I'm at the end of my rope on it!

[CHRIS *enters the porch, wearing shirt and tie now. She turns quickly, hearing:*]

SUE (*with a smile*). Hello, darling. How's Mother?

CHRIS. I thought George came.

SUE. No, it was just us.

CHRIS (*coming down to them*). Susie, do me a favor, heh? Go up to Mother and see if you can calm her. She's all worked up.

SUE. She still doesn't know about you two?

CHRIS (*laughs a little*). Well, she senses it, I guess. You know my mother.

SUE (*going up to the porch*). Oh, yeah, she's psychic.

CHRIS. Maybe there's something in the medicine chest.

SUE. I'll give her one of everything. (*On the porch.*) Don't worry about Kate; couple of drinks, dance her around a little . . . she'll love Ann. (*To* ANN.) Because you're the female version of him. (*Indicates* CHRIS. CHRIS *laughs.*) Don't be alarmed, I said version. (*As they laugh* SUE *goes into house.*)

CHRIS. Interesting woman, isn't she?

ANN (*moving from him, uneasily*). Ya, she's very interesting.

CHRIS. She's a great nurse, you know, she . . .

ANN (*in tension, but trying to control it*). Are you still doing that?

CHRIS (*sensing something wrong, but still smiling*). Doing what?

ANN. As soon as you get to know somebody you find a distinction for them. How do you know she's a great nurse?

CHRIS. What's the matter, Ann?

ANN. The woman hates you. She despises you!

CHRIS. Hey . . . what's hit you?

ANN (*weakly, sits*). Gee, Chris.

CHRIS. What happened here?

ANN (*she looks at him mystified, alarmed*). You never . . . Why didn't you tell me?

CHRIS. Tell you what?

ANN. She says they think Joe is guilty.

CHRIS (*looks away*). Yes. Well . . . (*Looks at her.*) What of it?

ANN. Why did you say there was no feeling any more?

CHRIS. What difference does it make what they think?

ANN. I don't care what they think, I just don't understand why you took the trouble to deny it. You said it was all forgotten.

CHRIS. I didn't want you to feel there was anything wrong in you coming here, that's all. I know a lot of people think my father was guilty. I suppose I assumed there might be some question in your mind.

ANN. But I never once said I suspected him.

CHRIS. Nobody says it.

[*Pause. Their eyes meet.*]

CHRIS (*attempting a laugh*). What's come over you? All of a sudden you . . .

ANN (*she goes up to him*). I know how much you love him.

CHRIS. Do you think I could forgive him if he'd done that thing?

ANN. I'm not here out of a blue sky, Chris. I turned my back on my father; if there's anything wrong here now . . .

CHRIS. I know that, Ann.

ANN. George is coming from my father, and I don't think it's with a blessing.

CHRIS. You've got nothing to fear from George.

ANN. Tell me that. Just tell me that.

CHRIS (*takes her hands*). The man is innocent, Ann. I know he seems afraid, but he was falsely accused once and it put him through hell. How would you behave if you were faced with the same thing again? Believe me, Ann, there's nothing wrong for you here! Believe me, kid!

ANN (*a hesitation, then she embraces him*). All right.

[*They kiss as* KELLER *appears quietly on the porch. He watches them.*]

KELLER. What is this, still Labor Day?

[*They break and laugh in embarrassment.* KELLER *comes down.*]

KELLER. I got a regular Playland back here.

CHRIS. I thought you were going to shave.

KELLER (*sitting*). In a minute. I woke up, I can't see nothin'.

ANN. You look shaved.

KELLER. Oh no. (*Massages his jaw.*) Gotta be extra special tonight. Big night, Annie. (*Crosses his legs.*) So how's it feel to be a married woman?

ANN (*laughs*). I don't know yet.

KELLER (*to* CHRIS). What's the matter, you slippin'?

CHRIS. The great roué!

KELLER. What is that roué?

CHRIS. It's French.

KELLER. Don't talk dirty.

[*They laugh.*]

CHRIS (*to* ANN). You ever meet a bigger ignoramus?

KELLER. Well, *somebody's* got to make a living.

ANN (*as they laugh*). That's telling him.

KELLER. I don't know, everybody's gettin' so goddam educated in this country there'll be nobody to take away the garbage.

[*They laugh.*] 10

KELLER. It's gettin' so the only dumb ones left are the bosses.

ANN. You're not so dumb, Joe.

KELLER. I know, but you go into our plant, for instance. I got so many lieutenants, majors, and colonels, when I want somebody to sweep the floor I gotta be careful, I'll insult somebody. No kiddin'. It's a tragedy; you stand on the street today 20 and spit, you're gonna hit a college man.

CHRIS. Well, don't spit.

KELLER. I mean to say, it's comin' to a pass. (*He takes a breath.*) I been thinkin', Annie. (*They wait for him. He comforts himself, squints thoughtfully ahead.*) Your brother George. I been thinkin' about your brother George. When he comes I like you to brooch 30 something to him.

CHRIS. Broach.

KELLER. What's the matter with brooch?

CHRIS (*smiling*). It's not English.

KELLER. When I went to night school it was brooch.

ANN (*laughs*). Well, in day school it's broach.

KELLER. Don't surround me, will you? Seriously, Ann . . . You say he's not 40 well . . . George. I been thinkin', why should he knock himself out in New York with that cutthroat competition when I got so many friends here. I'm very friendly with some big lawyers in town. I could do something for George; I like to set him up here.

ANN. That's awfully nice of you, Joe.

KELLER. No, kid, it ain't nice of me. I want you to understand me. I'm thinking of Chris. (*Slight pause.*) See . . . this is what I mean. I ain't got the vocabulary, but this is the thought, see. You're young yet. You get older, you want to feel that you . . . accomplished something. In your life. My only accomplishment is my son. I ain't brainy. That's all I accomplished. What I want to know, Annie, is no matter what happens, my son is my son. That there's nothin' going to come between me and him. You follow me?

ANN. No. Why do you say that?

KELLER. Because . . . face the facts, facts is facts . . . your father hates me. I don't have to tell you to his last day in court he blamed the whole thing on me, that I put him there . . . and the rest of it. You know that.

ANN. Well, he'll say anything.

KELLER. Right. He'll say anything. But let's face it, a year, eighteen months, he'll be a free man. Who is he going to come to, Annie? His baby. You. He'll come old, mad, into your house.

ANN. That can't matter any more, Joe.

KELLER. *Now* you say that, but believe me, Annie, blood is blood. A man harps long enough in your ears and you're going to listen. And . . . my son is in your house and . . . What I'm drivin' at, I don't want that hate to come between us. (*Gestures between* CHRIS *and himself.*)

ANN. I can only tell you that that could never happen.

KELLER. You're in love now, Annie, but believe me, I'm older than you; a daughter is a daughter, and a

father is a father. And it could happen. (*Slight pause.*) What I like to see
you do is this. Your father wouldn't
talk to me. But he'll talk to you and
he'll talk to your brother. I like you
both to go to him in prison and tell
him . . . "Dad, Joe wants to bring
you into the business when you get
out."

ANN (*surprised, even shocked*). You'd have 10
him as a partner?

KELLER. No, no partner. A good job.
(*Pause. He sees she is shocked, a little
mystified. He gets up, speaks more nervously.*) I want him to know, Annie
. . . while he's sitting there I want
him to know that when he gets out
he's got a place waitin' for him. It'll
take his bitterness away. To know
you got a place . . . it sweetens you. 20

ANN (*with an edge of fear, but the stress upon
the reprimand*). Joe, you owe him
nothing.

KELLER. No, no . . . I owe him a good
kick in the teeth, but . . .

CHRIS. Then kick him in the teeth. I
don't want him in the plant, so that's
that. And don't talk like that about
him—people misunderstand you.

KELLER. And I don't understand why 30
she has to crucify the man!

CHRIS. Well, it's her father, if she feels . . .

KELLER. No, no . . .

CHRIS (*almost angrily*). What's it to you?
Why . . . ?

KELLER (*a commanding outburst in high
nervousness*). A father is a father!
(*His hand goes to his cheek.*) I better
. . . I better shave. (*He goes upstage
a few yards, then turns, and a smile is on* 40
his face. Pointing at ANN.) Didn't mean
to yell at you, Annie.

ANN. Let's forget the whole thing,
Joe.

KELLER. Right. (*To* CHRIS.) She's likable.

CHRIS. Shave, will you?

KELLER. Right again.

[*As he turns to the porch,* LYDIA *comes hurrying from her house, at the right.*]

LYDIA (*to* JOE). I forgot all about it . . .
(*Seeing* CHRIS *and* ANN.) Hya. (*To*
JOE.) I promised to fix Kate's hair
for tonight. Did she comb it yet?

KELLER. Always a smile, hey, Lydia?

LYDIA. Sure, why not?

KELLER (*going up the porch*). Come on up
and comb my Katie's hair.

[LYDIA *mounts the porch.*]

KELLER. She's got a big night, make her
beautiful. (*At the door, turns to* CHRIS
and ANN *below.*) Hey, that could be a
song. (*Sings nicely, softly.*) "Come on
up and comb my Katie's hair . . ."
(LYDIA *goes into the house before him.*)
"Oh, come on up 'cause she's my
lady fair." (*To* ANN.) How's that for
one year of night school? (*Sings, going
in.*) "Oh come on up, come on up,
and comb my lady's hair; oh . . ."

[*He is half in the doorway when* JIM *enters
from the driveway.* KELLER *waits there.*
JIM *has been walking fast, now comes to a
halt, an air of excitement on him.*]

CHRIS (*after* JIM *has not ventured to speak,
but only looked at them*). What's the
matter. Where is he?

JIM. Where are the folks?

CHRIS. Upstairs, dressing.

ANN. What happened to George?

JIM. I asked him to wait in the car.
Listen to me now. (*Takes her hand,
walks downstage with her, away from the
house, speaks quietly, with running excitement.*) Can you take some advice?
[ANN *waits.*]

JIM. Don't bring him in here.

ANN. Why?

JIM. Kate is in bad shape, you can't
explode this in front of her.

ANN. Explode what?

JIM. You know why he's here, don't try

to kid it away. There's blood in his eye; drive him somewhere and talk to him alone.

CHRIS (*shaken, therefore angered*). Don't be an old lady.

[*He starts up toward the driveway.* JIM *stops him.*]

JIM. He's come to take her home. (*His eyes meet* CHRIS's.) What does that mean? (*Turns to* ANN.) You know what that means. Fight it out with him some place else.

ANN (*with difficulty, to* CHRIS). I'll drive . . . him somewhere. (*She makes a move to go upstage.*)

CHRIS. No. (*She stops.*)

JIM. Will you stop being an idiot?

CHRIS (*indignantly*). Cut that out! Nobody's afraid of him here.

[*He goes to the driveway and is brought up short by* GEORGE, *who enters there.* GEORGE *is* CHRIS's *age, but a paler man, now on the edge of his self-restraint. He speaks quietly, as though afraid to find himself screaming. An instant's hesitation and* CHRIS *steps up to him, hand extended, smiling. With an attempt at heartiness:*]

CHRIS. Helluva way to do. What're you sitting out there for?

GEORGE. Doctor said your mother isn't well, I . . .

CHRIS. So what? She'd want to see you, wouldn't she? (*Bringing him downstage.*) We've been waiting for you all afternoon.

ANN (*touching his collar*). This is filthy, didn't you bring another shirt?

[SUE *comes out of the house.*]

SUE. How about the beach, Jim?

JIM. Oh, it's too hot to drive.

SUE. How'd you get to the station—zeppelin?

CHRIS. This is Ann's brother, Sue. George—Mrs. Bayliss.

SUE (*takes his hand*). How do you do.

GEORGE (*removes his hat*). You're the people who bought our house, aren't you?

SUE. That's right. Come and see what we did with it before you leave.

GEORGE. I liked it the way it was.

SUE (*to* ANN). He's frank, isn't he?

JIM. No, he's George. (*Takes her hand.*) See you later. (*To* GEORGE, *as he and* SUE *go left.*) Take it easy, fella.

CHRIS (*as* SUE *and* JIM *exit*). Thanks for driving him! How about some grape juice? Mother made it especially for you.

GEORGE (*with forced appreciation*). Good old Kate, remembered my grape juice.

[ANN *goes to pour.*]

CHRIS. You drank enough of it in this house. How've you been, George?—Sit down.

GEORGE (*in a breathless way, he never stops moving*). It takes me a minute. (*He looks around.*) It seems impossible.

CHRIS. What?

GEORGE. I'm back here.

CHRIS. Say, you've gotten nervous, haven't you?

GEORGE. Ya, toward the end of the day. What're you, big executive now?

CHRIS. Just kind of medium. How's the law?

GEORGE (*laughs in a strained way*). I don't know. When I was studying in the hospital it seemed sensible, but outside there doesn't seem to be much of a law. The trees got thick, didn't they? (*Points to the stump.*) What's that?

CHRIS. Blew down last night. We had it there for Larry. You know.

GEORGE. Why—afraid you'll forget him?

CHRIS. What kind of a remark is that?

ANN (*breaking in*). When did you start wearing a hat? (*She goes to him with the glass.*)

GEORGE (*discovers the hat in his hand*). Today. (*Directly at her, his fury almost bursting out.*) From now on I decided to look like a lawyer, anyway. (*Holds it up to her.*) Don't you recognize it?

ANN. Why? Where . . . ?

GEORGE. Your father's. (*Tosses it into a chair.*) He asked me to wear it.

ANN (*out of duty, but fearfully*). . . . How is he?

GEORGE. He got smaller. (*Laughs with his lips shut.*)

ANN. Smaller?

GEORGE. Yeah, little. (*Holds out his hand to measure.*) He's a little man. That's what happens to suckers, you know. It's good I went to him in time— another year there'd be nothing left but his smell.

CHRIS (*with an edge of combativeness*). What's the matter, George, what's the trouble?

GEORGE (*puts down the glass; a smile comes onto his face, a sardonic grin*). The trouble. The trouble is when you make suckers out of people once you shouldn't try to do it twice.

CHRIS. What does that mean?

GEORGE (*to* ANN). You're not married yet, are you?

ANN (*frightened*). George, will you sit down and stop being . . .

GEORGE. Are you married yet?

ANN. No, I'm not married yet.

GEORGE. You're not going to marry him.

ANN (*bridling*). Why aren't I going to marry him?

GEORGE. Because his father destroyed your family.

[*Pause.* ANN *does not move.* CHRIS *begins:*]

CHRIS. Now look, George . . .

GEORGE. Cut it short, Chris. Tell her to come home with me. Let's not argue, you know what I've got to say.

CHRIS. George, you don't want to be the voice of God, do you?

GEORGE. I'm . . .

CHRIS. That's been your trouble all your life, George, you dive into things. What kind of a statement is that to make? You're a big boy now.

GEORGE (*as though "you're damned right"*). I'm a big boy now.

CHRIS. Don't come bulling in here. If you've got something to say, be civilized about it. You haven't even said hello to me.

GEORGE (*as though astonished*). Don't civilize me!

CHRIS. Are you going to talk like a grown man or aren't you?

ANN (*quickly, to forestall an outburst from* GEORGE). Sit down, dear. Don't be angry, what's the matter? (*He allows her to seat him, looking at her.*) Now what happened? You kissed me when I left, now you . . .

GEORGE (*breathlessly, to her alone*). My life turned upside since then. I couldn't go back to work when you left. I wanted to go to Dad and tell him you were going to be married. It seemed impossible not to tell him. He loved you so much. (*Slight pause.*) Annie . . . we did a terrible thing. We can never be forgiven. Not even to send him a card at Christmas. I didn't see him once since I got home from the war! Annie, you don't know what was done to that man. You don't know what happened.

ANN (*afraid*). Of course I know.

GEORGE. You can't know, you wouldn't be here. Dad came to work that day. The night foreman came to him and showed him the cylinder heads . . . they were coming out of the process with defects. There was something wrong with the process. So Dad went directly to the phone and called here and told Joe to come down right away. But the morning passed. No sign of Joe. So Dad called again. By this time he had over a hundred defectives. The Army was screaming for stuff and Dad didn't have anything to ship. So Joe told him . . . on the phone he told him to weld, cover up the crack in any way he could, and ship them out.

CHRIS. Are you through now?

GEORGE. I'm not through now! (*To* ANN.) Dad was afraid. He didn't know if they'd hold up in the air. Or maybe an Army inspector would catch him. But Joe told him they'd hold up, and swore to him . . . swore to him on the phone, Annie, that if anything happened he would take the whole responsibility. But Dad still wanted him there if he was going to do it. But he can't come down . . . he's sick. Sick! He suddenly gets the flu! Suddenly! But he promised to take responsibility. Do you understand what I'm saying? On the telephone you can't *have* responsibility! In a court you can always deny a phone call and that's exactly what he did. They knew he was a liar the first time, but in the appeal they believed that rotten lie and now Joe is a big shot and your father is the patsy. (*He gets up.*) Now what're you going to do? Answer me, what're you going to do—eat his food, sleep in his bed? You didn't even send your own father a card at Christmas, now what're you going to do?

CHRIS. What're *you* going to do, George?

GEORGE. He's too smart for me; I can't prove a phone call.

CHRIS (*gets up*). Then how dare you come in here with that rot?

ANN. George, the court . . .

GEORGE. The court didn't know your father! But you know him. You know in your heart Joe did it.

CHRIS. Lower your voice or I'll throw you out of here!

ANN. George, I know everything you've said. Dad told that whole thing in court and they . . .

GEORGE (*almost weeping*). The court did not know him, Annie! (*Now with deliberation he turns to* CHRIS.) I'll ask you something, and look me in the eye when you answer me.

CHRIS (*defiantly*). I'll look you in the eye.

GEORGE. You know your father . . .

CHRIS (*with growing fear, and therefore anger*). I know him well.

GEORGE. And he's the kind of boss to let a hundred and twenty-one cylinder heads be repaired and shipped out of his shop without even knowing about it?

CHRIS. He's that kind of boss.

GEORGE. And that's the same Joe Keller who never left his shop without first going around to see that all the lights were out.

CHRIS (*with growing fury*). The same Joe Keller.

GEORGE. The same man who knows how many minutes a day his workers spend in the toilet.

CHRIS. The same man.

GEORGE. And my father, that frightened mouse who'd never buy a shirt without somebody along—that man would dare do such a thing on his own?

CHRIS. On his own. And because he's a frightened mouse this is another thing he'd do: throw the blame on somebody else because he's not man enough to take it himself. This is *exactly* what he'd do. He tried it in court but it didn't work, but with a fool like you it works!

GEORGE. Oh, Chris, you're a liar to yourself.

ANN (*deeply shaken*). Don't talk like that!

CHRIS. Tell me, George. What happened? The court record was good enough for you all these years, why isn't it good now? Why did you believe it all these years? (*Slight pause.*)

GEORGE. I had no reason not to believe it. And besides—I thought you believed it. That meant something too, you know. (CHRIS *stops moving.*) But today I heard it from his mouth. From his mouth it's altogether dif-10 ferent than the record. Anyone who knows him, and knows your father, will believe it from his mouth. Your father tricked him. He took everything we have. I can't beat that. But this I can. She's one item he's not going to grab. (*Turns to* ANN.) Get your things. (ANN *stares at him.*) Everything they have is covered with blood. You're not the kind of girl who can 20 live with that.

[ANN *turns her eyes on* CHRIS, *mystified and wondering.*]

CHRIS. Ann . . . you're not going to believe that, are you?

ANN (*she goes to him*). You know it's not true, don't you?

GEORGE. How can he tell you? It's his father.

ANN (*to* GEORGE, *angrily*). Don't, please! 30

GEORGE. *He knows*, Annie . . .

CHRIS. The voice of God!

GEORGE. Then why isn't your name on the business? Explain that to her!

CHRIS. What the hell has that got to do with . . . ?

GEORGE. Annie, add it up. Why isn't his name on it?

CHRIS (*furiously*). Even when I don't own it?

GEORGE. Who're you kidding? Who gets it when he dies? (*To* ANN.) Open your eyes, you know the both of them, isn't that the first thing they'd do, the way they love each other?—J. O. Keller and Son?

[*Pause.* ANN *looks from him to* CHRIS. CHRIS *watches her face, waits.*]

GEORGE. None of these things ever even crossed your mind?

CHRIS. Yes, they crossed my mind. Anything can cross your mind!

GEORGE. I'll settle it. Do you want to settle it or are you afraid to?

CHRIS. . . . What . . . what do you 10 mean?

GEORGE. Let me go up and talk to your father. In ten minutes you'll have the answer. Or are you afraid of the answer?

CHRIS. I'm not afraid of the answer. I know the answer. But my mother isn't well and I don't want a fight here now, and all you're going to do is fight with him.

GEORGE. Let me go to him. 20

CHRIS. You're not going to start a fight here now.

GEORGE (*to* ANN). What more do you want!

ANN (*turns her head suddenly toward the house. Apprehensively*). Someone's coming.

CHRIS (*glances toward the house; to* GEORGE, *quietly*). You won't say anything now.

ANN. Don't, George, not now. You'll go soon. I'll call a cab.

GEORGE. You're coming with me.

ANN. Please, leave it to me. And don't mention marriage, because we haven't told her yet. You understand? Don't . . . (*She sees a plan in his eyes. Alarmed.*) George, you're not going to start anything now!

40 [*Enter* MOTHER *on the porch. She is dressed almost formally, her hair is fixed. They are all turned toward her. On seeing* GEORGE *she raises both hands, comes down toward him, and in a voice meant to indicate her ill-health as well as her compassion for him:*]

MOTHER. Georgie, Georgie. (*She has paused in front of him.*)

GEORGE (*a little abashed—he always liked her*). Hello, Kate.

MOTHER (*she cups his face in her hands*). Georgie. They made an old man out of you. (*Touches his hair.*) Look, you're gray.

GEORGE (*her pity, open and unabashed, reaches into him, and he smiles sadly*). I know, I . . . 10

MOTHER (*shakes her finger at him*). I told you when you went away, don't try for medals.

GEORGE (*he laughs, tiredly*). I didn't try, Kate. They made it very easy for me.

MOTHER (*actually angry*). Go on. (*Taking in* CHRIS.) You're all alike. (*To* ANN.) Look at him, why did you say he's 20 fine? He looks like a ghost.

GEORGE (*relishing her solicitude*). I feel all right.

MOTHER. I'm sick to look at you. What's the matter with your mother, why don't she feed you?

ANN. He just hasn't any appetite.

MOTHER. If he ate in my house he'd have an appetite. (*They laugh.*) I pity your husband! (*To* GEORGE.) Sit 30 down, I'll make you a sandwich.

GEORGE (*taking her hand with an embarrassed laugh*). I'm really not hungry.

MOTHER (*shaking her head*). Honest to God, it breaks my heart to see what happened to all the children. How we worked and planned for you, and you end up no better than us.

GEORGE (*with deep feeling for her*). You . . . you haven't changed, you know 40 that, Kate?

MOTHER. None of us changed, Georgie. We all love you. Joe was just talking about the day you were born and the water got shut off. People were carrying basins from a block away—

(*Laughs.*)—a stranger would think the whole neighborhood was on fire! (*They laugh. She sees the juice. To* ANN.) Why didn't you give him some juice!

ANN (*defensively*). I offered it to him.

MOTHER (*scoffingly*). You *offered* it. (*Thrusting the glass into* GEORGE's *hand.*) *Give* it to him! (*To* GEORGE, *who is laughing.*) Sit down, and drink, and . . . and *look* like something!

GEORGE (*sitting*). Kate, I feel hungry already.

CHRIS (*proudly*). She could turn Mahatma Gandhi into a heavyweight.

MOTHER (*to* CHRIS, *with great energy*). Listen, to hell with the restaurant! I got a ham in the icebox, and frozen strawberries, and avocados and . . .

ANN. Swell, I'll help you!

GEORGE. The train leaves at eight-thirty, Ann.

MOTHER (*to* ANN). You're leaving?

CHRIS. No, Mother, she's not . . .

ANN (*breaking through it, going to* GEORGE *quickly*). You hardly got here; give yourself a chance to get acquainted again.

CHRIS. Sure, you don't even know us any more.

MOTHER. Well, Chris, if they can't stay, don't . . .

CHRIS. No, it's just a question of George, Mother, he planned on . . .

GEORGE (*he gets up—and politely, nicely, for* KATE's *sake*). Now wait a minute, Chris . . .

CHRIS (*smiling and full of command, cutting him off*). If you want to go, I'll drive you to the station now, but if you're staying, no arguments while you're here.

MOTHER (*at last confessing the tension*). Why should he argue? (*She goes to him. With desperation and command and compassion, stroking his hair.*) Georgie and us have no argument. How could we have an argument, Georgie? We all got hit by the same lightning, how can you . . . ? Did you see what happened to Larry's tree, Georgie? (*She has taken his arm, and unwillingly he moves across stage toward it with her.*) Imagine? While I was dreaming of him in the middle of the night, the wind came along and . . .

[*Enter* LYDIA *onto the porch. As soon as she sees him:*]

LYDIA. Hey, Georgie! (*She comes down to him eagerly. She has a flowered hat in her hand.*)

GEORGE (*they shake hands warmly*). Hello, Laughy. What'd you do, grow?

LYDIA. I'm a big girl now.

MOTHER (*taking the hat from her*). Look what she can do to a hat!

ANN (*to* LYDIA, *admiring the hat*). Did you make that?

MOTHER. In ten minutes! (*She puts it on.*)

LYDIA (*fixing it on her head*). I only rearranged it.

GEORGE. You still make your own clothes?

CHRIS (*of* MOTHER). Ain't she classy? All she needs is a wolfhound dog.

LYDIA. You work in one of those big skyscrapers?

MOTHER (*moving her head right and left*). It feels like somebody is sitting on me.

ANN. It's beautiful, Kate.

MOTHER (*she kisses* LYDIA—*to* GEORGE). She's a genius! *You* should've married her. (*They laugh.*) *This* one can *feed* you!

LYDIA (*strangely embarrassed*). Oh, stop that, Kate.

GEORGE (*to* LYDIA). Didn't I hear you had a baby?

MOTHER. You don't hear so good. She's got three babies.

GEORGE (*a little hurt by it—to* LYDIA). No kidding, three?

LYDIA. Yeah, it was one-two-three.

You've been away a long time, Georgie.

GEORGE. I'm beginning to realize.

MOTHER (*to* CHRIS *and* GEORGE). The trouble with you kids is you *think* too much.

[*They laugh.*]

LYDIA. Well, we think too.

MOTHER (*slaps* LYDIA'S *backside*). Yes, but not all the time.

GEORGE (*with almost obvious envy*). They never took Frank, heh?

LYDIA (*a little apologetically*). No, he was always one year ahead of the draft.

MOTHER. It's amazing. When they were calling boys twenty-seven Frank was just twenty-eight, when they made it twenty-eight he was just twenty-nine. That's why he took up astrology. It's all in when you were born, it just goes to show.

CHRIS. What does it go to show?

MOTHER (*to* CHRIS). Don't be so intelligent. Some superstitions are very nice! (*To* LYDIA.) Did he finish Larry's horoscope?

LYDIA. I'll ask him now, I'm going in. (*To* GEORGE, *a little sadly, almost embarrassed.*) Would you like to see my babies? Come on.

GEORGE. I don't think so, Lydia. (*Slight pause.*)

LYDIA (*understanding*). All right. Good luck to you, George.

GEORGE. Thanks. And to you . . . and Frank.

[*She smiles at him, turns, and goes off right to her house.* GEORGE *stands staring in that direction.*]

MOTHER (*reading his thoughts*). She got pretty, heh?

GEORGE (*sadly*). Very pretty.

MOTHER (*as a reprimand*). She's beautiful, you damn fool.

GEORGE (*looks around longingly; and softly, with a catch in his throat*). She makes it seem so nice around here. (*He walks slowly across the stage, looking at the ground as:*]

MOTHER (*shaking her finger, almost weeping*). Look what happened to you because you wouldn't listen to me. I told you to marry that girl and stay out of that goddamned war!

GEORGE (*laughs at himself*). She used to laugh too much.

MOTHER. And you didn't laugh enough. While you were getting mad about Fascism Frank was getting into her bed.

GEORGE (*with a bitter smile, to* CHRIS). He won the war, Frank.

CHRIS. All the battles.

MOTHER (*in pursuit of this mood*). The day they started the draft, Georgie, I told you you loved that girl.

CHRIS (*laughs*). And truer love hath no man.

GEORGE (*laughs*). She's wonderful!

MOTHER. I'm smarter than any of you, and now you're going to listen to me, George. You had big principles, Eagle Scouts the three of you; so now I got a tree, and this one (*Of* CHRIS.) when the weather gets bad he can't stand on his feet. (*Indicates* LYDIA'S house.) And that big dope next door who never reads anything but Andy Gump has three children and his house paid off. Stop being a philosopher. Look after *yourself.* Like Joe was just saying—you move back here, he'll help you get set, and I'll find you a girl and put a smile on your face.

GEORGE. Joe? Joe wants me here?

ANN (*eagerly*). He asked me to tell you, and I think it's a good idea.

MOTHER. Certainly. Why must you make-believe you hate us? Is that another principle—that you have to hate us? You don't hate us, George, not in your heart. I know you, you can't fool me, I diapered you. (*Suddenly, to* ANN.) You remember Mr. Marcy's daughter?

ANN (*laughing*). She's got you hooked already!

[*And* GEORGE *laughs, is excited.*]

MOTHER. You look her over, George; you'll see she's the most beautiful . . .

CHRIS. She's got warts, George.

MOTHER (*to* CHRIS). She hasn't got warts! (*To* GEORGE.) So the girl has a little beauty mark on her chin . . .

CHRIS. And two on her nose.

MOTHER. Will you . . . ? (*As though this destroys the warts—to* GEORGE.) You remember. Her father's the retired police inspector.

CHRIS. Sergeant, George. He looks like a gorilla.

MOTHER. He's a very kind man! (*To* GEORGE.) He never shot anybody!

[*They all burst out laughing as* KELLER *enters onto the porch:*]

KELLER (*as he appears the laughter stops; coming down, with strained joviality*). Well! Look who's here. (*Extending his hand.*) Georgie, good to see ya.

GEORGE (*shakes hands—somberly*). How're you, Joe?

KELLER. So-so. Gettin' old. You comin' out to dinner with us?

GEORGE. No, got to be back in New York.

ANN. I'll call a cab for you. (*She goes up and into the house as:*)

KELLER. Too bad you can't stay, George. Sit down. (*To* KATE.) He looks fine.

MOTHER. He looks terrible.

KELLER. That's what I said, you look terrible, George. (*They laugh.*) I wear the pants and she beats me with the belt.

GEORGE. I saw your factory on the way from the station. It looks like General Motors.

KELLER. I wish it was General Motors, but it ain't, George. (*Crossing his legs easily.*) So you finally went to see your father, I hear.

GEORGE. Yes, this morning. What kind of stuff do you make now?

KELLER. Oh, little of everything. Pressure cookers, an assembly for washing machines. Got a nice, flexible plant now. So how'd you find Dad? 10 Feel all right?

GEORGE (*searching* KELLER, *he speaks indecisively*). No, he's not well, Joe.

KELLER. Not his heart again, is it?

GEORGE. It's everything, Joe. It's his soul.

CHRIS (*beginning to rise*). How about seeing what they did with your house?

KELLER. Leave him be.

GEORGE. I'd like to talk to him.   20

KELLER. Sure, he just got here. That's the way they do, George. A little man makes a mistake and they hang him by the thumbs; the big ones become ambassadors. I wish you'd 'a' told me you were going to see Dad.

GEORGE (*studying him*). I didn't know you were interested.

KELLER. In a way, I am. I would like him to know, George, that as far as 30 I'm concerned, any time he wants he's got a place with me. I would like him to know that.

GEORGE (*he looks at* MOTHER). He hates your guts, Joe. Don't you know that?

KELLER. I . . . imagined it. But that can change, too.

MOTHER. Herb was never like that.

GEORGE. He's like that now. He'd like to take every man who made money 40 in the war and put him up against a wall.

KELLER. He'll need a lot of bullets.

GEORGE. And he'd better not get any.

KELLER. That's a sad thing to hear.

GEORGE (*now with his bitterness dominant*).

Why? What'd you expect him to think of you?

KELLER (*the force of his nature rising, but under control*). A thing can be sad even if you expect it. I expected it because I know your father. And I'm sad to see he hasn't changed. (*He gets up.*) As long as I know him, twenty-five years, that part of him made me sad. The man never learned how to take the blame. You know that, George.

GEORGE (*he does*). Well, I . . .

KELLER. But you do know it. Because the way you come in here you don't look like you remember it. I mean like in 1937 when we had the shop on Flood Street. And he damn near blew us all up with that heater he left burning for two days without water. He wouldn't admit that was his fault either. I had to fire a mechanic to save his face. You remember that.

GEORGE. Yes, but . . .

KELLER. I'm just mentioning it, George. Because this is just another one of a lot of things. Like when he gave Frank that money to invest in oil stock.

GEORGE (*distressed*). I know that, I . . .

KELLER (*driving in, but restrained*). But it's good to remember those things, kid. The way he cursed Frank because the stock went down. Was that Frank's fault? To listen to him Frank was a swindler. And all the man did was give him a bad tip.

GEORGE (*gets up, moves away*). I know those things . . .

KELLER. Then remember them, remember them. (ANN *comes from the house, halts as* KELLER *continues.*) There are certain men in the world who rather see everybody hung before they'll take blame. You understand me, George?

[*They stand facing each other*, GEORGE *trying to judge him*.]

ANN (*coming downstage*). The cab's on its way. Would you like to wash?

MOTHER (*with the thrust of hope*). Why must he go? Make the midnight, George.

KELLER. Sure, you'll have dinner with us!

ANN. How about it? Why not? We're 10 eating at the lake; we could have a swell time.

GEORGE (*looks at* KELLER, *then back to her*). All right. (*To* MOTHER.) Is Lydia . . . I mean Frank and Lydia coming?

MOTHER. I'll get you a date that'll make her look like a . . . ! (*She starts upstage*.)

GEORGE (*laughs*). No, I don't want a 20 date.

CHRIS. I know somebody just for you! (*To* MOTHER.) Charlotte Tanner!

MOTHER. Sure, call her up!

[CHRIS *exits*.]

MOTHER (*to* GEORGE). Come upstairs and pick out a shirt and tie!

GEORGE (*they grow silent at his sudden emotion; he looks around at them and the place*). I never felt at home . . . any- 30 where but here. I feel so . . . (*He nearly laughs, and turns away from them*.) Kate, you look so young, you know? You didn't change at all. It . . . rings an old bell. (*Turns to* JOE.) You too, Joe, you're amazingly the same. The whole atmosphere is.

KELLER. Say, I ain't got time to get sick.

MOTHER. He hasn't been laid up in fifteen years . . . 40

KELLER (*quickly*). Except my flu during the war.

MOTHER. Heh?

KELLER. My flu, when I was sick during . . .

MOTHER (*quickly*). Well, sure . . . (*To* GEORGE.) . . . except for that flu, I mean. (*Pause*. GEORGE *stands perfectly still*. MOTHER, *a little desperately*.) I just forgot it, George. (GEORGE *doesn't move*.) I mean he's so rarely sick it slipped my mind. I thought he had pneumonia, he couldn't get off the bed.

GEORGE. Why did you say he's never . . . ?

KELLER. I know how you feel, kid, but I couldn't help it; I'll never forgive myself, because if I could've gone in that day I'd never allow Dad to touch those heads.

GEORGE. She said you'd never been sick.

MOTHER. I said he *was* sick!

GEORGE (*to* ANN). Didn't you hear her say . . . ?

MOTHER. Do you remember every time you were sick?

GEORGE. I'd remember pneumonia . . .

ANN. Now, George!

GEORGE. Especially if I got it the day my partner was going to patch up cylinder heads! What happened that day, Joe?

[MOTHER *sees* FRANK *coming into the yard holding a sheet of paper*.]

MOTHER. Frank!—did you see George?

FRANK (*extending his hand*). Lydia told me, I'm glad to . . . (*Breaks off in emotion*.) You'll have to pardon me. I've got something amazing for you, Kate, I finished Larry's horoscope.

MOTHER (*desperately*). You'd be interested in this, George! (*Draws* GEORGE *over to* FRANK *while* GEORGE *stares at* KELLER.) It's wonderful the way he can understand the . . .

[CHRIS *enters from the house*.]

CHRIS. Charlotte's on the phone, George, go in and talk to her. (*He notices the sudden tension*.) What's . . . ?

MOTHER (*to* CHRIS). He finished Larry's horoscope!

FRANK. Listen! It's amazing!

ANN (*to* CHRIS). I don't think George wants to go.

GEORGE. You don't think *I* want to go!

ANN (*going to* CHRIS, *addressing* GEORGE). Let me talk to him alone.

CHRIS. What happened now?

MOTHER. Nothing, nothing! (*Quickly, to* FRANK.) What did you find out?

FRANK. Larry is alive! Follow it now, you see the Milky Way . . . ?

CHRIS. Will you stop filling her head with that junk?

FRANK. Is it junk to feel there's a greater power than ourselves?

MOTHER. Listen to him! Maybe you'll change your mind about things. (*To* ANN.) Both of you!

GEORGE (*to* ANN). Can't you understand what she's telling you?

CHRIS. What is she telling her? (*To* MOTHER.) What did you say to her?

MOTHER (*of* FRANK, *avoiding his question*). Chris—he could be right!

CHRIS. Frank, you're going to cut out this nonsense.

FRANK. I've studied the stars of his life, Chris, and I'm not going to argue with you. I'm telling you. He was reported missing on February ninth, but February ninth was his favorable day! You can laugh at a lot of it; I can understand you laughing. But the odds are a million to one that a man won't die on his favorable day. That's known, that's known, Chris! Somewhere in this world your brother is alive!

MOTHER. Why isn't it possible? Maybe you're doing a terrible thing with her! (*A car horn is heard from the street.*) Oh, that's their cab. Will you tell him to wait, Frank? And I want to talk about it with you later.

FRANK. Sure thing.

[FRANK *trots up the alley.* MOTHER *calls after him.*]

MOTHER. They'll be right out, driver!

CHRIS. She is not leaving, Mother.

GEORGE (*to* ANN). She told you to go, get your things.

CHRIS. Nobody can tell her to go.

GEORGE. My darling sister, she told you to go! What are you waiting for now? He was never sick . . .

MOTHER. I didn't say that!

GEORGE. . . . He simply told your father to kill pilots and covered himself in bed!

CHRIS (*to* MOTHER). What's this about?

MOTHER. It just happened to slip my mind that Dad . . .

ANN (*breaking in, to* GEORGE). Go now, I want to see Chris alone.

GEORGE. But she told you to go!

ANN. I . . . I can't go.

GEORGE. But, Annie!

ANN. No . . . (*Of* CHRIS.) . . . he's the only one can tell me, George.

MOTHER. I packed your bag, darling . . .

CHRIS (*shocked*). What?

MOTHER. I packed your bag, all you've got to do is close it.

ANN (*on the verge of weeping*). I'm not closing anything. He asked me here and I'm staying till he tells me to go. Till he tells me!

MOTHER (*of* GEORGE). But if that's how he feels . . .

CHRIS (*suddenly bursting out*). That's all! Nothing more till Christ comes, about the case or Larry; not another word as long as I'm here!

[ANN *has been pressing* GEORGE *up toward the driveway.*]

GEORGE. Say no to them, Annie, somebody's got to say no to them. . . .

ANN (*pleading, yet forcing him, trying to comfort him*). Please, dear, please . . . Don't, George, you mustn't cry, please. . . .

[*They go up the driveway.* CHRIS *turns to* MOTHER.]

CHRIS. What do you mean, you packed her bag? How dare you pack her bag?

MOTHER (*sobbing, she reaches out for him*). Chris . . .

CHRIS (*refusing his mother's embrace*). How dare you pack her bag?

MOTHER. She doesn't belong here.

CHRIS. Then I don't belong here. 10

MOTHER. She's Larry's girl, she's Larry's girl.

CHRIS. And I'm his brother and he's dead, and I'm marrying his girl.

MOTHER. Never, never in this world!

KELLER. You lost your mind?

MOTHER (*violently, pointing into* KELLER's *face*). You have nothing to say!

KELLER (*cruelly*). I got plenty to say! Three and a half years you been 20 talking like a maniac and I'm . . . !

MOTHER (*she smashes him across the face. Everything stops. Her hand remains suspended, trembling. She whispers*). Nothing. You have nothing to say. Now I say. He's coming back. He's on his way. A boat is bringing him. Maybe a plane. He'll walk down the driveway. He'll come and say hello. And then we'll have a wedding, dear; 30 he'll call her back and then she'll come. My boy is on his way, a long way home, and we . . . everybody has got to wait.

CHRIS (*about to weep*). Mother dear, Mother . . .

MOTHER (*shaking her head, absolutely*). Wait, wait . . .

CHRIS. How long? How long!

MOTHER (*rolling out of her*). Till he 40 comes; forever and ever till he comes; he's not dead, darling, till we're all in the ground, till all of us are gone.

CHRIS (*as an ultimatum*). Mother, I'm going ahead with it.

MOTHER. Chris, I've never said no to you in my life, now I say no!

CHRIS. You'll never let him go till I do it.

MOTHER. I'll never let him go and you'll never let him go!

CHRIS. I've let him go a long . . .

MOTHER (*with no less force, but turning from him*). Then let your father go.
[*Pause.* CHRIS *stands transfixed.*]

KELLER (*softly*). She's out of her mind.

MOTHER. Altogether! (*To* CHRIS, *but not facing them.*) Let him go too. Is that possible? Then the boy is alive. God does not do such things; the boy is alive. (*She turns to* CHRIS.) You understand me now? As long as you live that boy is alive. (*She bursts into sobs.*) You understand me? (*Beyond control, she hurries up and into the house.*)
[CHRIS *has not moved.*]

KELLER (*he speaks insinuatingly, questioningly*). She's out of her mind.

CHRIS (*a broken whisper*). Then . . . you did it?

KELLER (*the beginning of a plea in his voice*). He never flew a P-40.

CHRIS. But the others.

KELLER (*insistently*). She's out of her mind. (*He takes a step toward* CHRIS, *pleadingly.*)

CHRIS (*unyielding*). Dad . . . you did it?

KELLER. He never flew a P-40, what's the matter with you?

CHRIS (*still asking, and saying*). Then you did it. To the others.

KELLER (*afraid of him, his deadly insistence*). What's the matter with you? (*Comes nervously closer to him, and, seeing wildness in his eyes.*) What the hell is the matter with you?

CHRIS (*quietly, incredulously*). How . . . how could you do that?

KELLER (*lost, he raises his fists*). What's the matter with you?

CHRIS (*his passion beginning to flow*). Dad

. . . Dad, you killed twenty-one men.

KELLER. What, killed?

CHRIS. You killed them, you murdered them.

KELLER (*as though throwing his whole nature open before* CHRIS). How could I kill anybody?

CHRIS. Dad! Dad!

KELLER (*trying to hush him*). I didn't kill anybody!

CHRIS. Then explain it to me. What did you do? Explain it to me, or I'll tear you to pieces! What did you do, then? What did you do? Now tell me what you did. What did you do?

KELLER (*horrified at his overwhelming fury*). Don't, Chris, don't . . .

CHRIS. I want to know what you did, now what did you do? You had a hundred and twenty-one cracked engine heads, now what did you do?

KELLER. If you're going to hang me, then I . . .

CHRIS. I'm listening, God almighty, I'm listening!

[*Their movements now are those of subtle pursuit and escape.* KELLER *keeps a step out of* CHRIS's *range, as he talks.*]

KELLER. You're a boy—what could I do? I'm in business, a man is in business; a hundred and twenty-one cracked, you're out of business; you got a process, the process don't work you're out of business; you don't know how to operate, your stuff is no good; they close you up, they tear up your contracts, what the hell's it to them? You lay forty years into a business and they knock you out in five minutes—what could I do, let them take forty years, let them take my life away? (*His voice cracking.*) I never thought they'd install them. I swear to God. I thought they'd stop 'em before anybody took off.

CHRIS. Then why'd you ship them out?

KELLER. By the time they could spot them I thought I'd have the process going again, and I could show them they needed me and they'd let it go by. But weeks passed and I got no kickback, so I was going to tell them.

CHRIS. Then why didn't you tell them?

KELLER. It was too late. The paper, it was all over the front page, twenty-one went down, it was too late. They came with handcuffs into the shop, what could I do? (*Weeping, he approaches* CHRIS.) Chris . . . Chris, I did it for you, it was a chance and I took it for you. I'm sixty-one years old, when would I have another chance to make something for you? Sixty-one years old you don't get another chance, do ya?

CHRIS. You even knew they wouldn't hold up in the air.

KELLER. I didn't say that . . .

CHRIS. But you were going to warn them not to use them . . .

KELLER. But that don't mean . . .

CHRIS. It means you knew they'd crash.

KELLER. It don't mean that.

CHRIS. Then you *thought* they'd crash.

KELLER. I was afraid maybe . . .

CHRIS. You were afraid maybe! Almighty God in Heaven, what kind of a man are you? Kids were hanging in the air by those heads. You knew that!

KELLER. For you, a business for you!

CHRIS (*with burning fury*). For me! Where do you live, where have you come from? For me!—I was dying every day and you were killing my boys and you did it for me? I was so proud you were helping us win and you did it for me? What the hell do you think I was thinking of, the goddam business? Is that as far as your mind can see, the business? What is that, the world—the business? What are you made of, dollar bills? What the hell do you mean, you did it for me? Don't you have a country? Don't you live in the world? What the hell are you? You're not even an animal, no animal kills his own, what are you? What must I do to you? I ought to tear the tongue out of your mouth, 10 what must I do?

[*He is weeping, and with his fist he begins to pound down upon his father's shoulder, and* KELLER *stands there and weeps.*]

CHRIS (*with each blow*). What? What! What! What! (*He stumbles away, covering his face as he weeps.*) What must I do, Jesus God, what must I do?

[*He falls into a chair and cries.* KELLER *raises a hand weakly, and comes toward him weeping, saying:*]

KELLER. Chris . . . My Chris . . .

ACT THREE

SCENE *as before.* Two o'clock the following morning. MOTHER *is discovered as the curtain rises, rocking ceaselessly in a chair, staring at her thoughts. It is an intense, slight sort of rocking. A light shows from the upstairs bedroom, the lower-floor windows being dark. The moon is strong and casts its bluish light.* KELLER *stands inside the screen door staring at the right.*

Presently JIM, *dressed in jacket and hat, appears from the left, notices* KELLER, *goes up beside* MOTHER.

JIM. Any news?

MOTHER. No news.

JIM (*he takes another look at her and sits beside her and takes her hand*). You can't sit up all night, dear, why don't you go to bed?

MOTHER. I'm waiting for Chris. (*Withdraws her hand.*) Don't worry about me, Jim, I'm perfectly all right.

JIM. But it's almost two o'clock.

MOTHER. Then it's two o'clock. I can't sleep. (*Slight pause.*) You had an emergency?

JIM (*tiredly*). Somebody had a headache and thought he was dying. (*Slight pause.*) Half of my patients are 40 quite mad. Nobody realizes how many people are walking around loose, and they're as cracked as coconuts. Money. Money-money-money-money. You say it long enough it doesn't mean anything. (*She smiles, makes a silent laugh.*) Oh, how I'd love to be around when that happens.

MOTHER (*shakes her head*). Never. You're so childish, Jim! Sometimes you are.

[KELLER *disappears inside the house.*]

JIM (*looks at her a moment*). Kate. (*Pause.*) What happened?

MOTHER. I told you. He had an argument with Joe. Then he got in the car and drove away.

JIM. What kind of argument?

MOTHER. An argument. Joe . . . he was crying like a child, before.

JIM. They argued about Ann?

MOTHER (*slight hesitation*). No, not Ann. Imagine? (*Indicates the lighted window above.*) She hasn't come out of that room since he left. All night in that room.

JIM (*looks at the window, then at her*). What'd Joe do, tell him?

MOTHER (*she stops rocking*). Tell him what?

JIM. Don't be afraid, Kate. I know. I've always known.

MOTHER. How?

JIM. It occurred to me a long time ago. (*Pause.*)

MOTHER. I always had the feeling that

in the back of his head, Chris . . . almost knew. I didn't think it would be such a shock.

JIM (*gets up*). You don't know your own son. Chris would never know how to live with a thing like that. It takes a certain talent . . . for lying. You have it, and I do. But not him.

MOTHER. What do you mean—he's not coming back?

JIM. Oh, no, he'll come back. We all come back, Kate. These private little revolutions always die. The compromise is always made. In a peculiar way. Frank is right—every man does have a star. The star of one's honesty. And you spend your life groping for it, but once it's out it never lights again. I don't think he went very far. He probably just wanted to be alone to watch his star go out.

MOTHER. Just as long as he comes back.

JIM. I wish he wouldn't, Kate. One year I simply took off, went to New Orleans; for two months I lived on bananas and milk, and studied a certain disease. It was beautiful. And then she came, and she cried. And I went back home with her. And now I live in the usual darkness; I can't find myself; it's even hard sometimes to remember the kind of man I wanted to be. I'm a good husband, Chris is a good son—he'll come back.

[KELLER *comes out on the porch.*]

JIM (*going upstage—to* MOTHER). I have a feeling he's in the park. I'll look around for him. Put her to bed, Joe; this is no good for what she's got. (JIM *exits up the driveway.*)

KELLER (*coming down*). What does he want here?

MOTHER. His friend is not home.

KELLER (*his voice is husky; comes down to her*). I don't like him mixing in so much.

MOTHER. It's too late, Joe. He knows.

KELLER (*apprehensively*). How does he know?

MOTHER. He guessed a long time ago.

KELLER. I don't like that.

MOTHER (*laughs dangerously, quietly, into the line*). What you don't like . . .

KELLER. Yes, what I don't like.

MOTHER. You can't bull yourself through this one, Joe, you better be smart now. This is not over yet.

KELLER (*indicating the lighted window above*). And what is she doing up there? She don't come out of the room.

MOTHER. I don't know, what is she doing? Sit down, stop being mad. You want to live? You better figure out your life.

KELLER. She don't know, does she?

MOTHER. She saw Chris storming out of here. It's one and one, she knows how to add.

KELLER. Maybe I ought to talk to her.

MOTHER. Don't ask me, Joe.

KELLER (*almost an outburst*). Then who do I ask! (MOTHER *remains silent.* KELLER, *asking for confirmation.*) But I don't think she'll do anything about it.

MOTHER. You're asking me again.

KELLER. I'm askin' you! Am I a stranger? (*Slight pause. He moves.*) I thought I had a family here. What the hell happened to my family?

MOTHER. You've got a family. I'm simply telling you that I have no strength to think any more.

KELLER. You have no strength. The minute there's trouble you have no strength!

MOTHER. Joe, you're doing the same thing again. All your life whenever there's trouble you yell at me and ou think that settles it.

KELLER. Then what do I do? Tell me, talk to me, what do I do?

MOTHER. Joe . . . I've been thinking this way. If he comes back . . .

KELLER. He's comin' back, what do you mean "if"? . . . He's comin' back, what do I do?

MOTHER. I think if you sit him down and you . . . explain yourself. I mean you ought to make it clear to him that you *know* you did a terrible thing. (*Not looking into his eyes.*) I mean if he saw that you realize what you did. You see?

KELLER. What ice does that cut?

MOTHER (*a little fearfully*). I mean if you told him that you want to pay for what you did.

KELLER (*sensing . . . quietly*). How can I pay?

MOTHER (*she gets up, nervously*). Tell him . . . you're willing to go to prison. (*Pause.*)

KELLER (*amazed, angering*). I'm willing to . . . ?

MOTHER (*quickly*). You wouldn't go, he wouldn't ask you to go. But if you told him you wanted to, if he could feel that you wanted to pay, maybe he would forgive you.

KELLER (*to her, as though she has spoken for herself too*). He would forgive me! For what?

MOTHER (*moving away*). Joe, you know what I mean.

KELLER. I don't know what you mean! You wanted money, so I made money. What must I be forgiven? You wanted money, didn't you?

MOTHER. I didn't want it that way.

KELLER. I didn't want it that way either! What difference is it what you want? I spoiled the both of you. I should've put him out when he was ten like I was put out, and made him earn his keep. Then he'd know how a buck is made in this world. Forgiven! I could live on a quarter a day myself, but I got a family so I . . .

MOTHER. Joe, Joe . . . it don't excuse it that you did it for the family.

KELLER. It's got to excuse it!

MOTHER. There's something bigger than the family to him.

KELLER. Nothin' is bigger!

MOTHER. There is to him.

KELLER. There's nothin' he could do that I wouldn't forgive. Because he's my son. Because I'm his father and he's my son.

MOTHER. Joe, I tell you . . .

KELLER. Nothin' is bigger than that. And you're going to tell him, you understand? I'm his father and he's my son, and if there's something bigger than that I'll put a bullet in my head!

MOTHER. You stop that!

KELLER. You heard me. Now you know what to tell him. (*Pause. He moves from her—halts.*) But he wouldn't put me away though. . . . He wouldn't do that. . . . Would he?

MOTHER. He loved you, Joe, you broke his heart.

KELLER. But to put me away . . .

MOTHER. I don't know. I'm beginning to think we don't really know him. They say in the war he was such a killer. Here he was always afraid of mice. I don't know him. I don't know what he'll do.

KELLER. Goddamn, if Larry was alive he wouldn't act like this. He understood the way the world is made. He listened to me. To him the world had a forty-foot front, it ended at the building line. This one, everything bothers him. You make a deal, overcharge two cents, and his hair falls out. He don't understand money. Too easy, it came too easy. Yes sir.

Larry. That was a boy we lost. Larry. Larry. (*With an impatient cry.*) Where the hell is he?

MOTHER. Joe, Joe, please . . . you'll be all right, nothing is going to happen. . . .

KELLER (*desperately, lost*). For you Kate, for both of you, that's all I ever lived for . . .

MOTHER. I know, darling, I know . . . 10

[ANN *enters from the house. They say nothing, waiting for her to speak.*]

ANN. Why do you stay up? I'll tell you when he comes.

KELLER (*apprehensively*). You didn't eat supper, did you. (*To* MOTHER.) Why don't you make her something?

MOTHER. Sure, I'll . . .

ANN. Never mind, Kate, I'm all right. (*They're unable to speak to each other.*) 20 I'll go upstairs. (*She starts, then halts.*) I'm not going to do anything about it . . .

MOTHER. Oh, she's a good girl! (*To* KELLER.) You see? She's a . . .

ANN. I'll do nothing about Joe, but you're going to do something for me. (*Directly to* MOTHER.) You made Chris feel guilty with me. Whether you wanted to or not, you've crippled 30 him in front of me. I'd like you to tell him that Larry is dead and that you know it. You understand me? I'm not going out of here alone. There's no life for me that way. I want you to set him free. And then I promise you everything will end, and we'll go away, and that's all.

KELLER. You'll do that. You'll tell him.

ANN. I know what I'm asking, Kate. 40 You had two sons. But you've only got one now.

KELLER. You'll tell him . . .

ANN. And you've got to say it to him so he knows you mean it.

MOTHER. My dear, if the boy was dead, it wouldn't depend on my words to make Chris know it. . . . The night he gets into your bed, his heart will dry up. Because he knows and you know. To his dying day he'll wait for his brother! No, my dear, no such thing. You're going in the morning, and you're going alone. That's your life, that's your lonely life. (*She starts for the house.*)

ANN. Larry is dead, Kate.

MOTHER. Don't speak to me.

ANN. He crashed off the coast of China, February ninth. His engine didn't fail him, but he died. I know.

[MOTHER *stops moving.*]

MOTHER. How . . . how did he die . . . ?

[ANN *is silent.*]

MOTHER. How did he die? You're lying to me. If you know, how did he die?

ANN. I loved him. You know I loved him, don't you? Would I have looked at anyone else if I wasn't sure? That's enough for you.

MOTHER (*moving on her*). What's enough for me? What're you talking about?

ANN. You're hurting my wrists.

MOTHER. What are you talking about?

[*Pause.* ANN *looks at* JOE.]

MOTHER. Joe, please go in the house . . .

KELLER. Why should I . . . ?

MOTHER. Go, dear. (*She goes to him, caresses his cheek, and leads him upstage.*) Go.

KELLER (*glancing at* ANN). I'll lay down. I'm tired. Lemme know when he comes. (KELLER *goes into the house.*)

ANN. Sit down . . . go on . . .

[MOTHER *sits slowly.*]

ANN. First you've got to understand. When I came, I didn't have any idea that Joe . . . I had nothing against him or you. I came to get married. I hoped . . . (*She brings out a letter from her pocket.*) So I didn't bring this to hurt you. I thought I'd show it to you only if there was no other way to settle Larry in your mind.

MOTHER. What is that?

ANN. He wrote me a letter just before he . . .

MOTHER. Larry?

ANN (*extending the letter*). I'm not trying to hurt you, Kate. You're making me do this, now remember you're . . .

[MOTHER *takes the letter.*]

ANN. Remember.

[MOTHER *reads.*]

ANN. I've been so lonely, Kate . . . I can't leave here alone again.

[*A long, low groan comes from* MOTHER's *throat as she reads.*]

ANN. You made me show it to you. You wouldn't believe me. I told you a hundred times—why didn't you believe me?

MOTHER. Oh, my God . . .

ANN (*with pity and fear*). Kate, please, please . . .

MOTHER. Oh, my God, my God . . .

ANN. Oh, Kate dear, I'm so sorry . . .

[CHRIS *enters from the driveway. He seems exhausted.*]

CHRIS. What's the matter . . . ?

ANN. Nothing, darling. Where were you? . . . You're all perspired . . .

[MOTHER *doesn't move.*]

ANN. Where were you?

CHRIS. Just drove around a little. I thought you'd be gone.

ANN. Where do I go? I have nowhere to go.

CHRIS (*to* MOTHER). Where's Dad?

ANN. Inside lying down.

[MOTHER *has crumpled the letter in her hand.*]

CHRIS. Sit down, both of you. I'll say what there is to say.

MOTHER. I didn't hear the car . . .

CHRIS. I left it in the garage.

MOTHER. Chris, you look so . . . (*Takes his hand.*) You smashed your watch?

CHRIS. Against the steering wheel. I had a little accident. It's nothing, just a fender . . . I wasn't looking. Mother . . . I'm going away. For good. (*To* ANN *alone.*) I know what you're thinking, Annie. It's true. I'm yellow. I was made yellow here. In this house. Because I've suspected my father and I did nothing about it. If I knew the night I came home what I know now, he'd be in the district attorney's office by this time, and I'd have brought him there. Now if I look at him, all I'm able to do is cry.

MOTHER. What are you talking about? What else can you do?

CHRIS. I could jail him! I tell it to you with your teary eyes. I could jail him, if I were human any more. But I'm like everybody else now. I'm practical now. You made me practical.

MOTHER. But you have to be.

CHRIS. The cats in that alley are practical, the bums who ran away when we were fighting were practical. Only the dead weren't practical. But now I'm practical, and I spit on myself. I'm going away. I'm going now.

ANN. I'm coming with you . . .

CHRIS. No, Ann, I can't make that.

ANN. I don't ask you to do anything about Joe. I swear I never will!

CHRIS. Yes you do. In your heart you always will.

ANN. Take me with you. No one will understand why you're . . .

CHRIS. Maybe a few . . . in some hospital somewhere, there's a few will understand.

ANN. Then do what you have to do!

CHRIS. Do what? What is there to do? I've looked all night for a reason to make him suffer . . .

ANN. There is reason!

CHRIS. What? Do I raise the dead when I put him behind bars? Then what'll

I do it for? We used to shoot a man who acted like a dog, but honor was real there, you were protecting something. But here? This is the land of the great *big* dogs, you don't love a man here, you eat him. *That's* the principle, the only one we really live by.—It just happened to kill a few people this time, that's all. The world's that way; how can I take it out on him? What sense does that make? This is a zoo, a zoo!

ANN (*to* MOTHER). Why are you standing there? *You* know what he's got to do! —Tell him!

MOTHER (*clutching the letter tighter*). Let him go.

ANN. I won't let him go, you'll tell him . . . !

MOTHER (*warning*). Annie . . . !

ANN. Then I will!

[KELLER *enters from the house.* CHRIS *sees him, goes up to the house, and starts past* KELLER.]

KELLER (*worn, brokenhearted*). What the hell is the matter with you? (CHRIS *halts and is silent.*) What's the matter with you? (CHRIS *remains silent.*) I want to talk to you.

CHRIS. I've got nothing to . . .

KELLER (*he pushes him toward the steps of the porch*). I want to talk to you!

CHRIS. Don't do that, Dad. I'm going to hurt you if you do that.

KELLER (*quietly, with a break in his voice*). Go down.

CHRIS (*after an instant*). There's nothing to say, so say it quick.

[CHRIS *comes down from the porch.* KELLER *then comes down, walks past him.*]

KELLER. Exactly what's the matter? Without the philosophy involved. What's the matter? You got too much money? Is that what bothers you?

CHRIS (*with an edge of sarcasm*). It bothers me.

KELLER. Then what's the difficulty? When something bothers you you either get used to it or you get rid of it. If you can't get used to it, then throw it away. You hear me? Take every cent and give it to charity, throw it in the sewer. Does that settle it? In the sewer, that's all. (CHRIS *is silent.*) What's the matter, you think I'm kidding? I'm tellin' you what to do; if it's dirty, then burn it. It's your money, that's not my money. I'm a dead man, I'm an old dead man, nothing's mine. Well, talk to me!— What do you want to do!

CHRIS (*trembling*). It's not what I want to do. It's what you want to do.

KELLER. What should I want to do? (CHRIS *is silent.*) Jail? You want me to go to jail? (CHRIS's *eyes filling with tears, he remains silent.* KELLER, *himself near weeping.*) What're you crying for? If you want me to go say so, don't cry! Is that where I belong?—Then tell me so! (*Slight pause.*) What's the matter, why can't you tell me? (*Furiously.*) You say everything else to me, say that! (*Slight pause.*) I'll tell you why you can't say it. Because you know I don't belong there. Because you know! (*He is moving around* CHRIS, *jerkily, with growing emphasis and passion, and a persistent tone of desperation.*) If my money's dirty there ain't a clean nickel in the United States. Who worked for nothin' in that war? When they work for nothin', I'll work for nothin'. Did they ship a gun or a truck outa Detroit before they got their price? Is that clean? Nothin's clean. It's dollars and cents, nickels and dimes; war and peace, it's nickels and dimes, what's clean? The whole goddam country is gotta go if I go! That's why you can't tell me.

CHRIS. That's exactly why.

KELLER. Then . . . why am *I* bad?

CHRIS. I don't call you bad. *I* know you're no worse than most, but I thought you were better. I never saw you as a man. I saw you as my father. (*Almost breaking.*) I can't look at you this way, and I can't look at myself!

[*He turns quickly and goes directly toward the porch. On this movement* ANN *goes quickly to* MOTHER, *snatching the letter from her hand, and starts for* CHRIS. MOTHER *instantly rushes to intercept her.*]

MOTHER. Give me that!

ANN. He's going to read it! (*She gets away from* MOTHER *and thrusts the letter into* CHRIS's *hand as:*)

MOTHER (*grasping for it in* CHRIS's *hand*). Give it to me, Chris, give that to me!

CHRIS (*looking from her to* ANN, *holding the letter clenched in his fist; looking from one to the other*). What . . . ?

ANN. Larry. He wrote that to me the day he died . . .

KELLER. Larry?

MOTHER. Chris, it's not for you. Give it to me, please. . . . (*He unlocks her fingers from his wrist. In terror she backs from him as he starts to read.*) Joe . . . go away. . . .

KELLER (*mystified, frightened*). Why'd she say, Larry, what . . . ?

MOTHER (*she desperately pushes him toward the alley, glancing at* CHRIS). Go to the street . . . ! (*He is resisting her, starting to speak; she leaves him and starts alone toward the driveway.*) Jim! Where's Jim . . . ! (*As she passes* CHRIS, *a little weeping laugh escapes him. She stops.*) Don't . . . (*Pleading from her whole soul.*) Don't tell him. . . .

CHRIS (*deadly quiet, through his teeth to his father*). Three and one-half years . . . talking, talking. Now you tell me what you must do. . . . This is how

he died, now tell me where you belong.

KELLER (*backing, now in deadly fear*). Chris, a man can't be a Jesus in this world!

CHRIS. I know all about the world. I know the whole crap story. Now listen to this, and tell me what a man's got to be! (*Reads.*) "My dear Ann . . ." You listening? He wrote this the day he died. Listen, don't cry . . . listen! "My dear Ann: It is impossible to put down the things I feel. But I've got to tell you something. Yesterday they flew in a load of papers from the States and I read about Dad and your father being convicted. I can't express myself. I can't face the other men . . . I can't bear to live any more. Last night I circled the base for twenty minutes before I could bring myself in. How could he have done that? Every day three or four men never return and he sits back there "doing business." I can't face anybody . . . I don't know how to tell you what I feel. . . . I'm going out on a mission in a few minutes. They'll probably report me missing. If they do, I want you to know that you mustn't wait for me. I tell you, Ann, if I had him here now I I could kill him.

[KELLER *grabs letter from* CHRIS *and reads. Pause.*]

CHRIS (*after a long pause*). Now blame the world. Do you understand that letter?

KELLER (*almost inaudibly, staring*). I think so. Get the car. I'll put on my jacket.

[*He turns and seems about to fall.* MOTHER *reaches out quickly to support him.*]

MOTHER (*with a pleading, lost cry*). Joe . . .

KELLER (*with complete self-disgust*). No, let me go; I want to go. . . . I'm sorry, Kate.

MOTHER. You're so foolish. Larry was your son too, wasn't he? You know he'd never tell you to do this!

KELLER (*indicating the letter*). What is this if it isn't telling me? Sure, he was my son. But I think to him they were all my sons. And I guess they were, kid . . . I guess they were. (*Quietly, to* CHRIS.) I'll be down . . . in a minute. (*He turns and goes into the house.*)

MOTHER. He'll stay if you tell him to. Go to him!

CHRIS. Mother, he's got to go.

MOTHER. You both gone crazy? (*She presses* CHRIS *to go into the house.*) Tell him to sleep!

CHRIS. No, Mom.

MOTHER. God in Heaven, what is accomplished if he goes?

CHRIS. I thought you read that!

MOTHER. The war is over, didn't you hear?—It's over!

CHRIS. Then what was Larry to you, a stone that fell into the water? It's *not* enough to be sorry. Larry didn't kill himself so you and Dad would be "sorry"!

MOTHER. What more can we be?

CHRIS (*with all his power, beyond all restraint*). You can be better! Once and for all you can know now that the whole earth comes in through those fences; there's a universe outside and you're responsible to it, and if you're not, you threw your son away, because that's why he died! He's got to go, and I'm . . .

[*A shot is heard from the house. They leap in shock.*]

CHRIS. Find Jim! (*He rushes into the house.*)

[ANN *runs off, toward* JIM's *house.* MOTHER *has not moved. Facing the house:*]

MOTHER (*over and over*). Joe . . . Joe . . . Joe.

[CHRIS *comes out of the house.*]

CHRIS (*apologetically*). Mother . . .

MOTHER. Sssh.

[CHRIS *comes to her, trying to speak. Weeping, she embraces him.*]

CHRIS (*going to her arms*). I didn't mean that he . . . (CHRIS *breaks into a sob.*)

MOTHER. Sssh. Sssh . . . Don't, don't, dear; you mustn't take it on yourself. Forget now. Live.

[*She moves from him, and as she mounts the porch he hears the growing sound of her weeping. She goes inside. Alone, he comes erect, moves away from the sound, does not turn to it, as the curtain falls.*]

CURTAIN

THOMAS HEGGEN

O N THE EVENING of February 18, 1948, *Mister Roberts* opened at the Alvin Theatre in New York. Its success on stage was huge and instantaneous. With Henry Fonda in the title role as Lieutenant Roberts, the play impressed both critics and audience with its gusto and masculine humor. As it was projected across the footlights, its humor infected the spectators, obscuring other and more serious values so notable in the book upon which it was based and not entirely absent from the script of the play. Brooks Atkinson characterized it as "a gusty, ribald and sentimental yarn about some brawling seamen in an American rustbucket on the Pacific. . . . The lines are hilarious." And Irwin Shaw considered it "one of the funniest plays ever seen on the American stage."

The play does bubble and roar with much laughter and rowdyism. That quality is certainly one of its merits; and we can do with some merriment in drama and in life. At the same time, just below the tinkling frivolity of the surface, we cannot miss the deep undertone of troubled life. With the slightest shift in emphasis this undertone could have become dominant. The laughter of the play is always about to dissolve in the pathos of lonely men caught in a world upheaval too vast and too complex for them to understand. They are condemned to insufferable boredom, sailing "from Tedium to Apathy and back," with an occasional run "to Monotony and Ennui." Month on month, year after year, far from the zones of action "in the back areas of the Pacific," they sweat it out while the war and life itself passes them by.

These sketches, loosely woven into a unit, first appeared as a short novel in 1946. In this form it has sold close to a million copies. The author was born at Fort Dodge, Iowa, December 23, 1919, and was found dead under mysterious circumstances in his apartment in New York, May 19, 1949. While he was a student in journalism at the University of Minnesota he revealed exceptional talent as a columnist and a writer of both comic and tragic sketches. Following his graduation in 1941 he enlisted in the Navy. He spent much of his four years of war service on duty in the Pacific Theater, emerging with the rank of Lieutenant. Unlike Mr. Roberts of the play, he was in action aboard an assault transport in the campaigns against Guam, Peleliu, Iwo Jima, and Okinawa. He saw a good deal of the war. In the long hours of watch, alone amidst the crowd of restless men cooped below, he had plenty of time and talent for meditating on the strange turn of fate which had picked them up from all parts of America and brought them together on the Pacific. Here each man was only one infinitesimal part of a stupendous war operation. His individual role in it was so insignificant that he felt lost in the petty, day by day details of loading cargo, swabbing decks, and scraping rust. Heggen came out with a sea bag of distilled experience and an urge to share it.

What did it all mean to each of them?

325

Clearly it meant something different in each case.

For the career Captain it means the chance of a lifetime to advance in rank, and he would sacrifice any member of the crew to that ambition.

For Doc it means an ironic acceptance of things as he finds them, an almost cynical detachment from the issues of the war.

For Ensign Pulver it is a personal adventure which has lost its glamour, and he is preoccupied with keeping out of danger and squeezing out of his cramped existence as much relief from tedium as he can manage.

For Mannion and Insigna, miserably thrown together aboard ship, it is reduced to the small dimensions of personal hatred of each other, of fisticuffs and vulgar personal abuse.

For Mister Roberts it is one uninterrupted struggle with the Captain to get transferred from this cargo bucket to the fighting ships. He left medical school to go into the war. He went with high purpose to engage in combat, only to find himself a captive of his captain, "a lousy spectator," only half alive, while the great conflict itself sweeps on around him. Throughout the play he is consumed with resentment against his fate, performing his distasteful duty with distinction, and exhausting every means to get into the fight.

These are typical of the ship's company. For the purpose of the play the action is highly compressed. It centers on the extracurricular activities of a dozen men who vent their discontent and boredom on the one tangible object which they can hate and make war upon—the Captain. Since they cannot directly and personally attack this enemy of theirs, they assault the scrawny palm tree he potted in a five gallon can, which he keeps by his cabin door and waters as if he were performing a religious rite. They have as much joy and release in destroying the palm tree as they would have in blowing up a Japanese destroyer with a torpedo.

The high quality of the play results from the accuracy and vitality of the portraits of these men. This is the way such men behave and talk. This is the way they make adjustments to an almost intolerable existence, detached from normal life and held together by external compulsion. This is how they make that life bearable, and, at times, amusing. Heggen catches and conveys their vulgarities, ribaldries, horseplay, and rebellion, and also their loyalties and comradeship. The episodes of the play were never concentrated on any one ship, but there is no incident that did not happen, or might not have happened, aboard some unit of the fleet. The result is both hilarious and disturbing.

The stage version of *Mister Roberts* was prepared by Joshua Logan, native of Texarkana, who gained distinction in dramatics while he was a student at Princeton. He spent eight months on a scholarship with the Moscow Art Theatre, and directed a half-dozen hits on Broadway. He served in the war as a captain with the Air Forces intelligence. In recent seasons he has directed *Annie Get Your Gun*, *South Pacific*, and other successes. The original sketches of *Mister Roberts* should be read along with the dramatization to relish the expert skill with which the same material is transferred from one medium to the other.

MISTER ROBERTS

CHARACTERS

(in order of appearance)

CHIEF JOHNSON	SCHLEMMER
LIEUTENANT (JG) ROBERTS	REBER
DOC	ENSIGN PULVER
DOWDY	DOLAN
THE CAPTAIN	GERHART
INSIGNA	PAYNE
MANNION	LIEUTENANT ANN GIRARD
LINDSTROM	SHORE PATROLMAN
STEFANOWSKI	MILITARY POLICEMAN
WILEY	SHORE PATROL OFFICER

SEAMEN, FIREMEN, AND OTHERS

SCENE: *Aboard the U. S. Navy Cargo Ship* AK601, *operating in the back areas of the Pacific.*

TIME: *A few weeks before V-E Day until a few weeks before V-J Day.*

Note: In the United States Navy, all officers below the rank of Commander are addressed as "Mister."

ACT ONE

SCENE I

The curtain rises on the main set, which is the amidships section of a Navy cargo ship. The section of the ship shown is the house, and the deck immediately forward of the house. Dominating center stage is a covered hatch. The house extends on an angle to the audience from downstage left to upstage right. At each side is a passageway leading to the after part of the ship. Over the passageways on each side are 20-millimeter gun tubs; ladders lead up to each tub. In each passageway and hardly visible to the audience is a steep ladder leading up to a bridge. Downstage right is a double bitt. At the left end of the hatch cover is an opening. This is the entrance to the companionway which leads to the crew's compartment below. The lower parts of two king posts are shown against the house. A life raft is also visible. A solid metal rail runs from the stage right and disappears behind the house. Upstage center is the door to the CAPTAIN's cabin. The pilothouse with its many portholes is indicated on the bridge above. On the flying *bridge are the usual nautical furnishings, a searchlight, and two ventilators. Over the door is a loudspeaker. There is a porthole to the left of the door, and two portholes to the right. These last two look into the* CAPTAIN's *cabin.*

The only object which differentiates this ship from any other Navy cargo ship is a small scrawny palm tree, potted in a five-gallon can, standing to the right of the CAP- 10 TAIN's *cabin door. On the container, painted in large white letters, is the legend:* "PROP.T OF CAPTAIN, KEEP AWAY."

At rise, the lighting indicates that it is shortly after dawn. The stage is empty and there is no indication of life other than the sound of snoring from below.

CHIEF JOHNSON, *a bulging man about forty, enters through the passageway upstage left. He wears dungaree shirt and pants and a chief petty officer's cap. He is obviously* 20 *chewing tobacco, and he starts down the hatchway, notices the palm tree, crosses to the* CAPTAIN's *door cautiously, peering into the porthole to see that he is not being watched, then deliberately spits into the palm-tree container. He wipes his mouth smugly and shuffles over to the hatch. There he stops, takes out his watch and looks at it, then disappears down the hatchway. A shrill whistle is heard.* 30

JOHNSON (*off stage—in a loud singsong voice which is obviously just carrying out a ritual*). Reveille . . . Hit the deck . . . Greet the new day . . . (*The whistle is heard again.*) Reveille . . .

INSIGNA (*off stage*). Okay, Chief, you done your duty—now get your big fat can out of here!

[JOHNSON *reappears at the head of hatchway calling back.*] 40

JOHNSON. Just thought you'd like to know about reveille. And you're going to miss chow again.

STEFANOWSKI (*off stage*). Thanks, Chief. Now go back to bed and stop bothering us.

[*His duty done,* JOHNSON, *still chewing, shuffles across the stage and disappears. There is a brief moment of silence, then the snoring is resumed below.*

[*After a moment,* ROBERTS *enters from the passageway at right. He wears khaki shirt and trousers and an officer's cap. On each side of his collar he wears the silver bar indicating the rank of lieutenant (junior grade). He carries a rumpled piece of writing paper in his left hand, on which there is a great deal of writing and large black marks indicating that much has been scratched out. He walks slowly to the bitt, concentrating, then stands a moment looking out to the right. He suddenly gets an idea and goes to the hatch cover, sitting, and writing on the paper.* DOC *enters from the left passageway.* DOC *is between thirty-five and forty and he wears khakis and an officer's fore-and-aft cap; he wears medical insignia and the bars of a lieutenant (senior grade) on his collar. A stethoscope sticks out of his hip pocket. He is wiping the sweat off his neck with his handkerchief as he crosses above the hatch cover. He stops as he sees* ROBERTS.]

DOC. That you, Doug?

ROBERTS (*wearily, looking up*). Hello, Doc. What are you doing up?

DOC. I heard you were working cargo today so I thought I'd get ready. On days when there's any work to be done I can always count on a big turnout at sick call.

ROBERTS (*smiles*). Oh yeah.

DOC. I attract some very rare diseases on cargo days. That day they knew you were going to load five ships I was greeted by six more cases of beriberi —double beriberi this time. So help me, I'm going down to the ship's library and throw that old copy of *Moby Dick* overboard! (*He sits on the hatch cover.*)

ROBERTS. What are you giving them these days for double beriberi?

DOC. Aspirin—what else? (*He looks at* ROBERTS.) Is there something wrong, Doug?

ROBERTS. I've been up all night, Doc.

DOC. What is it? What's the matter?

ROBERTS. I saw something last night when I was on watch that just about knocked me out.

DOC (*alarmed*). What happened?

ROBERTS (*with emotion*). I was up on the 10 bridge. I was just standing there looking out to sea. I couldn't bear to look at that island any more. All of a sudden I noticed something. Little black specks crawling over the horizon. I looked through the glasses, and it was a formation of our ships that stretched for miles! Carriers and battleships and cans—a whole task force, Doc!

DOC. Why didn't you break me out? I've 20 never seen a battleship!

ROBERTS. They came on and they passed within half a mile of that reef! Carriers so big they blacked out half the sky! And battlewagons sliding along —dead quiet! I could see the men on the bridges. And this is what knocked me out, Doc. Somehow—I thought I was on those bridges—I thought I was riding west across the Pacific. I 30 watched them until they were out of sight, Doc—and I was right there on those bridges all the time.

DOC. I know how that must have hurt, Doug.

ROBERTS. And then I looked down from our bridge and saw our Captain's palm tree! (*Points at the palm tree, then bitterly:*) Our trophy for superior achievement! The Admiral John J. 40 Finchley award for delivering more tooth paste and toilet paper than any other Navy cargo ship in the safe area of the Pacific. (*Taking a letter from his pocket and handing it to* DOC.) Read this, Doc—see how it sounds.

DOC. What is it?

ROBERTS. My application for transfer. I've been rewriting it ever since I got off watch last night.

DOC. Oh God, not another one!

ROBERTS. This one's different—I'm trying something new, Doc—a stronger wording. Read it carefully.

[DOC *looks for a moment skeptically, then, noticing the intensity in his face, decides to read the letter.*]

DOC (*reading*).

"From: Lieutenant (jg) Douglas Roberts

To: Bureau of Naval Personnel

16 April 1945

Subject: Change of Duty, Request for . . ."

(*He looks up.*) Boy, this is sheer poetry.

ROBERTS (*rises nervously*). Go on, Doc.

DOC (*reads on*). "For two years and four months I have served aboard this vessel as Cargo Officer. I feel that my continued service aboard can only reduce my own usefulness to the Navy and increase disharmony aboard this ship."

[*He looks at* ROBERTS *and rises.* ROBERTS *looks back defiantly.*]

ROBERTS. How about *that!*

DOC (*whistles softly, then continues*): "It is therefore urgently requested that I be ordered to combat duty, preferably aboard a destroyer."

ROBERTS (*tensely, going to* DOC). What do you say, Doc? I've got a chance, haven't I?

DOC. Listen, Doug, you've been sending in a letter every week for God knows how long . . .

ROBERTS. Not like this . . .

DOC. . . . and every week the Captain has screamed like a stuck pig, *dis*approved your letters, and forwarded them that way. . . .

ROBERTS. That's just my point, Doc. He *does* forward them. They go through the chain of command all the way up to the Bureau. . . . Just because the Captain doesn't . . .

DOC. Doug, the Captain of a Navy ship is the most absolute monarch left in this world!

ROBERTS. I know that.

DOC. If he endorsed your letter "approved" you'd get your orders in a minute . . .

ROBERTS. Naturally, but I . . . (*Turns away from* DOC.)

DOC. . . . but "disapproved," you haven't got a prayer. You're stuck on this old bucket, Doug. Face it!

ROBERTS (*turns quickly back*). Well, grant me this much, Doc. That one day I'll find the perfect wording and one human guy way up on top will read those words and say, "Here's a poor son of a bitch screaming for help. Let's put him on a fighting ship!"

DOC (*quietly*). Sure . . .

ROBERTS (*after a moment*). I'm not kidding myself, am I, Doc? I've got a chance, haven't I?

DOC. Yes, Doug, you've got a chance. It's about the same chance as putting your letter in a bottle and dropping it in the ocean. . . .

ROBERTS (*snatching the letter from* DOC). But it's still a chance, goddammit! It's still a chance!

[ROBERTS *stands looking out to sea.* DOC *watches him for a moment, then speaks gently:*]

DOC. I wish you hadn't seen that task force, Doug. (*Pauses.*) Well, I've got to go down to my hypochondriacs. (*He goes off slowly through passageway.*)

[ROBERTS *is still staring out as* DOWDY *enters from the hatchway. He is a hardbitten man between thirty-five and forty and is wearing dungarees and no hat. He* stands by the hatchway with a cup of coffee in his hand.)

DOWDY. Morning, Mister Roberts.

ROBERTS. Good morning, Dowdy.

DOWDY. Jeez, it's even hotter up here than down in that mess hall! (*He looks off.*) Look at that cruddy island . . . smell it! It's so hot it *already* smells like a hogpen. Think we'll get out of here today, sir?

[ROBERTS *takes* DOWDY's *cup as he speaks and drinks from it, then hands it back.*]

ROBERTS. I don't know, Dowdy. There's one LCT coming alongside for supplies . . . (*Goes to the hatchway, looks down.*) Are they getting up yet?

DOWDY (*also looking down the hatch*). Yeah, they're starting to stumble around down there—the poor punchdrunk bastards. Mister Roberts, when are you going to the Captain again and ask him to give this crew a liberty? These guys ain't been off the ship for over a year except on duty.

ROBERTS. Dowdy, the last time I asked him was last night.

DOWDY. What'd he say?

ROBERTS. He said "No."

DOWDY. We gotta get these guys ashore! They're going Asiatic! (*Pause.*) Will you see him anyhow, Mister Roberts —just once more?

ROBERTS. You know I will, Dowdy. (*Hands* DOWDY *the letter.*) In the meantime, have Dolan type that up for me. (*He starts off to the right.*)

DOWDY (*descending the hatchway*). Oh, your letter. Yes, sir!

ROBERTS (*calling over his shoulder*). Then will you bring a couple of men back aft? (*He exits through the passageway.*)

DOWDY. Okay, Mister Roberts. (*He disappears down the hatchway. He is heard below.*) All right, you guys in there. Finish your coffee and get up on deck.

Stefanowski, Insigna, off your tails
. . .

[*After a moment the center door opens and
the* CAPTAIN *appears, wearing pajamas
and bathrobe and his officer's cap. He is
carrying water in an engine-room oil can.
He waters the palm tree carefully, looks at
it for a moment tenderly, and goes back
into his cabin. After a moment,* DOWDY'S
voice is heard from the companionway and 10
*he appears followed by members of the
crew.*]

DOWDY. All right, let's go! Bring me
those glasses, Schlemmer. (SCHLEM-
MER *exits by the ladder to the bridge.
Other men appear from the hatchway.
They are* INSIGNA, STEFANOWSKI, MAN-
NION, WILEY, REBER, *and* LINDSTROM
—*all yawning, buttoning pants, tucking in
shirts, and, in general, being comatose.* 20
*The men do not appear to like one another
very much at this hour—least of all* IN-
SIGNA *and* MANNION.) All right, I got
a little recreation for you guys. Stefanowski, you take these guys and
get this little rust patch here. (*He
hands* STEFANOWSKI *an armful of scrapers
and wire brushes, indicating a spot on the
deck.* STEFANOWSKI *looks at the instruments dully, then distributes them to the* 30
men standing near him. SCHLEMMER *returns from the bridge, carrying four pairs
of binoculars and a spyglass. He drops
them next to* INSIGNA, *who is sitting on
the hatch.*) Insigna, I got a real special
job for you. You stay right here and
clean these glasses.

INSIGNA. Ah, let me work up forward,
Dowdy. I don't want to be around
this crud Mannion.   40

MANNION. Yeah, Dowdy. Take Insigna
with you!

DOWDY. Shut up, I'm tired of you two
bellyaching! (*Nodding to the others to
follow him.*) All right, let's go, Reber
. . . Schlemmer.

[DOWDY, REBER, *and* SCHLEMMER *leave
through the passageway at the right. The
others sit in sodden silence.* LINDSTROM
wanders slowly over to INSIGNA. *He picks
up the spyglass and examines it. He holds
the large end toward him and looks into it.*)

LINDSTROM. Hey, look! I can see myself!

STEFANOWSKI. Terrifying, ain't it?

[INSIGNA *takes the spyglass from him and
starts polishing it.* LINDSTROM *removes his
shoe and feels inside it, then puts it back
on.*]

MANNION (*after a pause*). Hey, what time
is it in San Francisco?

INSIGNA (*scornfully*). When?

MANNION. Anybody ask you? (*Turns to*
WILEY.) What time would it be there?

WILEY. I don't know. I guess about midnight last night.

STEFANOWSKI (*studying the scraper in his
hand*). I wonder if you could get sent
back to the States if you cut off a
finger.

[*Nobody answers.*]

INSIGNA (*looking off stage*). Hey, they got
a new building on that island. Fancy
—two stories . . .

[*Nobody shows any curiosity.*]

MANNION. You know, I had a girl in
San Francisco wore flowers in her
hair—instead of hats. Never wore a
hat . . .

[*Another sodden pause.*]

INSIGNA (*holding the spyglass*). Hey, Stefanowski! Which end of this you look
through?

STEFANOWSKI. It's optional, Sam. Depends on what size eyeball you've got.

[INSIGNA *idly looks through the spyglass at
something out to the right. Another pause.*]

INSIGNA. Hey, the Japs must've took
over this island—there's a red and
white flag on that new building.

MANNION. Japs! We never been within
five thousand miles of a Jap! Japs!
You hear that, Wiley?

WILEY. Yeah, smart, ain't he?

MANNION. Japs! That's a hospital flag!

INSIGNA. Anybody ask you guys? (*Nudging* LINDSTROM *and pointing to the other group.*) The goldbrick twins! (*Looks through the spyglass.*) Hey, they got a fancy hospital . . . big windows and . . . (*Suddenly rises, gasping at what he sees.*)

STEFANOWSKI. What's the matter, Sam?

INSIGNA. Oh my God! She's nekkid!

STEFANOWSKI. *She!*

INSIGNA. Taking a shower . . . in that bathroom . . . that nurse . . . upstairs window!

[*Instantly the others rush to the hatch cover, grab the binoculars, and stand looking out to the right.*)

WILEY. She's a blonde—see!

LINDSTROM. I never seen such a beautiful girl!

MANNION. She's sure taking a long time in that shower!

WILEY. Yeah, honey, come on over here by the window!

INSIGNA. Don't you do it, honey! You take your time!

STEFANOWSKI. There's another one over by the washbasin—taking a shampoo.

INSIGNA (*indignantly*). Yeah. But why the hell don't she take her bathrobe off! That's a stupid goddamn way to take a shampoo!

[*For a moment the men watch in silent vigilance.*]

STEFANOWSKI. Ah-hah!

WILEY. She's coming out of the shower!

MANNION. She's coming over to the window! (*A pause.*) Kee-ri-mi-ny!

[*For a moment the men stand transfixed, their faces radiant. They emit rapturous sighs. That is all.*]

LINDSTROM. Aw, she's turning around the other way!

MANNION. What's that red mark she's got . . . there?

INSIGNA (*authoritatively*). That's a birthmark!

MANNION (*scornfully*). Birthmark!

INSIGNA. What do you think it is, wise guy?

MANNION. Why, that's paint! She's sat in some red paint!

INSIGNA. Sat in some red paint! I'm tellin' you, that's a birthmark!

MANNION. Did you ever see a birthmark down there?

INSIGNA (*lowers his spyglass, turns to* MANNION). Why, you stupid jerk! I had an uncle once had a birthmark right down . . .

WILEY. Aww!

[INSIGNA *and* MANNION *return quickly to their glasses.*]

STEFANOWSKI (*groaning*). She's put her bathrobe on!

MANNION. Hey, she's got the same color bathrobe as that stupid bag taking the shampoo!

[*The four men notice something and exclaim in unison.*]

INSIGNA. Bag, hell! Look at her now with her head out of the water . . .

LINDSTROM. She's just as beautiful as the other one . . .

STEFANOWSKI. They look exactly alike with those bathrobes on. Maybe they're twins.

MANNION. That's my gal on the right— the one with the red birthmark.

INSIGNA. You stupid crud, the one with the birthmark's on the left!

MANNION. The hell she is . . .

[MANNION *and* INSIGNA *again lower their glasses.*]

INSIGNA. The hell she ain't . . .

WILEY. Awwww!

[MANNION *and* INSIGNA *quickly drop their argument and look.*]

STEFANOWSKI. They're both leaving the bathroom together. . . .

[*The men are dejected again.*]

LINDSTROM. Hey, there ain't no one in there now!

STEFANOWSKI (*lowering his glasses*). Did you figure that all by yourself? (*He looks through his glasses again.*)

MANNION (*after a pause*). Come on, girls, let's go!

WILEY. Yeah. Who's next to take a nice zippy shower?

INSIGNA (*after a pause*). They must think 10 we got nothing better to do than stand here!

LINDSTROM. These glasses are getting heavy!

STEFANOWSKI. Yeah. We're wasting manpower. Let's take turns, okay? (*The others agree.*) All right, Mannion, you take it first.

[MANNION *nods, crosses, and sits on the bitt, keeping watch with his binoculars. The* 20 *others pick up their scrapers and wire brushes.*]

INSIGNA (*watching* MANNION). I don't trust that crud.

LINDSTROM. Gee, I wish we was allowed to get over to that island. We could get a closer look.

STEFANOWSKI. No, Lindstrom. They'd see us and pull the shades down.

LINDSTROM. No they wouldn't. We could 30 cover ourselves with leaves and make out like we was bushes—and sneak up on them—like them Japs we seen in that movie . . .

[*He starts to sneak around in front of the hatch, holding his wire brush before his face.* STEFANOWSKI *hears a noise from the* CAPTAIN'S *cabin and quickly warns the others.*]

STEFANOWSKI. Flash Red! (*The men im-* 40 *mediately begin working in earnest as the* CAPTAIN, *now in khaki, enters. He stands for a moment looking at them, and then wanders over to the group scraping the rust patch to inspect their work. Then, satisfied that they are actually working, he starts*

toward the passageway. He sees MANNION, *sitting on the bitt, looking through his glasses and smiling. The* CAPTAIN *goes over and stands beside him, looking off in the same direction.* STEFANOWSKI *tries frantically to signal a warning to* MANNION *by beating out code with his scraper.* MANNION *suddenly sees the* CAPTAIN *and quickly lowers his glasses and pretends to clean them, alternately wiping the lenses and holding them up to his eyes to see that they are clean. The* CAPTAIN *watches him suspiciously for a moment, then he exits by the ladder to the bridge.* STEFANOWSKI *rises and looks up the ladder to make certain the* CAPTAIN *has gone.*) Flash White! (*He turns and looks at* MANNION.) Hey, Mannion. Anyone in there yet?

MANNION (*watching something happily through the glasses*). No, not yet!

INSIGNA (*picks up the spyglass and looks, and rises quickly*). Why, you dirty, miserable cheat!

[*Instantly all the men are at the glasses.*]

LINDSTROM. There's one in there again.

STEFANOWSKI. The hell with her—she's already got her clothes on!

INSIGNA. And there she goes! (*Slowly lowers his glass, turning to* MANNION *threateningly.*) Why, you lousy, cheating crud!

MANNION (*idly swinging his glasses*). That ain't all. I seen three!

STEFANOWSKI. You low-down Peeping Tom!

LINDSTROM (*hurt*). Mannion, that's a real dirty trick.

INSIGNA. What's the big idea?

MANNION. Who wants to know?

INSIGNA. *I* want to know! And you're damn well going to tell me!

MANNION. You loud-mouthed little bastard! Why don't you make me?

INSIGNA. You're damn right I will. Right now!

[*He swings on* MANNION *as* LINDSTROM *steps clumsily between them.*]

LINDSTROM. Hey, fellows! Fellows!

INSIGNA. No wonder you ain't got a friend on this ship . . . except this crud Wiley.

[*He jerks his head in the direction of* WILEY, *who stands behind him on the hatch cover.* WILEY *takes him by the shoulder and whirls him around.*]

WILEY. What'd you say?

STEFANOWSKI (*shoving* WILEY). You heard him!

[MANNION *jumps on the hatch cover to protect* WILEY *from* STEFANOWSKI. INSIGNA *rushes at* MANNION *and for a moment they are all in a clinch.* LINDSTROM *plows up on the hatch and breaks them apart. The men have suddenly formed into two camps* —MANNION *and* WILEY *on one side,* IN- 20 SIGNA *and* STEFANOWSKI *facing them.* LINDSTROM *is just an accessory, but stands prepared to intervene if necessary.*]

MANNION (*to* WILEY). Look at them two! Everybody on the ship hates their guts! The two moochingest, no-good loud-mouths on the ship!

[STEFANOWSKI *starts for* MANNION, *but* IN-SIGNA *pulls him back and steps menacingly toward* MANNION.]

INSIGNA. Why, you slimy, lying son of a bitch!

[*Suddenly* MANNION *hits* INSIGNA, *knocking him down. He jumps on* INSIGNA, *who catches* MANNION *in the chest with his feet and hurls him back.* WILEY *and* STEFAN-OWSKI *start fighting with* LINDSTROM, *attempting to break them apart.* MANNION *rushes back at* INSIGNA. INSIGNA *side-steps* MANNION'S *lunge and knocks him to the* 40 *deck.* INSIGNA *falls on him. They wrestle to their feet and stand slugging. At this point* ROBERTS *and* DOWDY *run on from the passageway.* ROBERTS *flings* INSIGNA *and* MANNION *apart.* DOWDY *separates the others.*]

ROBERTS. Break it up! Break it up, I tell you!

[INSIGNA *and* MANNION *rush at each other.* ROBERTS *and* DOWDY *stop them.*]

DOWDY. Goddamn you guys, break it up!

ROBERTS. All right! What's going on?

INSIGNA (*pointing at* MANNION). This son of a bitch here . . .

ROBERTS. Did you hear me?

MANNION (*to* INSIGNA). Shut your mouth!

DOWDY. Shut up, both of you!

INSIGNA. Slimy son of a bitch!

[*Picks up a scraper and lunges at* MANNION *again.* ROBERTS *throws him back.*]

ROBERTS. I said to cut it out! Did you hear me? (*Wheels on* MANNION.) That goes for you too! (*Includes the entire group.*) I'm going to give it to the first one who opens his mouth! (*The men stand subdued, breathing hard from the fight.*) Now get to work! All of you! (*They begin to move sullenly off to the right.*) Mannion, you and the rest get to work beside Number two! And, Insigna, take those glasses way up to the bow and work on them! Stefanowski, keep those two apart.

STEFANOWSKI. Yes, sir.

[*The men exit.* ROBERTS *and* DOWDY *look after them.*]

DOWDY (*tightly*). You seen that, Mister Roberts. Well, last night down in the compartment I stopped three of them fights—worse than that. They've got to have a liberty, Mister Roberts.

ROBERTS. They sure do. Dowdy, call a boat for me, will you? I'm going ashore.

DOWDY. What are you going to do?

ROBERTS. I just got a new angle.

DOWDY. Are you going over the Captain's head?

ROBERTS. No, I'm going around his end —I hope. Get the lead out, Dowdy.

[*He exits left as* DOWDY *goes off right and the lights fade out.*]

[*During the darkness, voices can be heard over the squawk box saying:*]

Now hear this . . . now hear this. Sweepers, man your brooms. Clean sweep-down fore and aft. Sweep-down all ladders and all passageways. Do *not* throw trash over the fantail.

Now, all men on report will see the master-at-arms for assignment to extra duty.

Now hear this . . . now hear this. Because, in violation of the Captain's orders, a man has appeared on deck without a shirt on, there will be no movies again tonight—by order of the Captain.

SCENE II

The lights dim up, revealing the stateroom of PULVER *and* ROBERTS. *Two lockers are shown, one marked "Ensign F. T. Pulver," the other marked "Lt. (jg) D. A. Roberts." There is a double bunk along the bulkhead at the right. A desk with its end against the bulkhead at the left has a chair at either side. There is a porthole in the bulkhead above it. Up center, to the right of* PULVER'S *locker, is a washbasin over which is a shelf, and a medicine chest. The door is up center.*

An officer is discovered with his head inside ROBERTS' *locker, throwing skivvy shirts over his shoulder as he searches for something.* DOLAN, *a young, garrulous, brash yeoman second class, enters. He is carrying a file folder.*

DOLAN. Here's your letter, Mister Roberts. (*He goes to the desk, taking a fountain pen from his pocket.*) I typed it up. Just sign your old John Henry here and I'll take it in to the Captain . . . then hold your ears. (*No answer.*) Mister Roberts! (PULVER'S *head appears from the locker.*) Oh, it's only you, Mister Pulver. What are you doing in Mister Roberts' locker?

PULVER (*hoarsely*). Dolan, look in there, will you? I know there's a shoe box in there, but I can't find it.

[DOLAN *looks in the locker.*]

DOLAN. There ain't no shoe box in there, Mister Pulver.

PULVER. They've stolen it! There's nothing they'll stop at now. They've broken right into the sanctity of a man's own locker.

[*He sits in the chair at the desk.*]

DOLAN (*disinterested*). Ain't Mister Roberts back from the island yet?

PULVER. No.

DOLAN. Well, as soon as he gets back, will you ask him to sign this baby?

PULVER. What is it?

DOLAN. What is it! It's the best damn letter Mister Roberts writ yet. It's going to blow the Old Man right through the overhead. And them big shots at the Bureau are going to drop their drawers too. This letter is liable to get him transferred.

PULVER. Yeah, lemme see it.

DOLAN (*handing the letter to* PULVER). Get a load of that last paragraph. Right here.

PULVER (*reading with apprehension*). ". . . increase disharmony aboard this ship . . ."

DOLAN (*interrupting gleefully*). Won't that frost the Old Man? I can't wait to jab this baby in the Old Man's face. Mister Pulver, you know how he gets sick to his stomach when he gets extra-mad at Mister Roberts—well, when I deliver this letter I'm going to take along a wastebasket! Let me know when Mister Roberts gets back.

[DOLAN *exits.* PULVER *continues reading the letter with great dismay. He hears* ROBERTS *and* DOC *talking in the passageway, off stage, and quickly goes to his bunk and hides the letter under a blanket. He goes to the locker and is replacing skivvy shirts as* ROBERTS *and* DOC *enter.*]

ROBERTS. . . . so after the fight I figured I had to do something, and do it quick!

DOC. What did you do over on the island, Doug?

ROBERTS (*sitting in the chair and searching through the desk drawer*). Hey, Frank, has Dolan been in here yet with my 10 letter?

PULVER (*innocently*). I don't know, Doug boy. I just came in here myself.

DOC. You don't know anybody on the island, do you, Doug?

ROBERTS. Yes. The Port Director—the guy who decides where to send this ship next. He confided to me that he used to drink a quart of whisky every day of his life. So this morning when 20 I broke up that fight it came to me that he might just possibly sell his soul for a quart of Scotch.

PULVER (*rises*). Doug, you didn't give that shoe box to the Port Director!

ROBERTS. I did. "Compliments of the Captain."

DOC. You've had a quart of Scotch in a shoe box?

ROBERTS. Johnny Walker! I was going 30 to break it out the day I got off this ship—Resurrection Day!

PULVER. Oh my God! It's really gone! (*He sinks to the bunk.*)

DOC. Well, did the Port Director say he'd send us to a Liberty Port?

ROBERTS. Hell, no. He took the Scotch and said, "Don't bother me, Roberts. I'm busy." The rummy!

PULVER. How could you do it!

DOC. Well, where there's a rummy, there's hope. Maybe when he gets working on that Scotch he'll mellow a little.

PULVER. You gave that bottle to a goddamn *man!*

ROBERTS. Man! Will you name me another sex within a thousand miles . . . (PULVER, *dejected, goes up to the porthole.*) What the hell's eating you anyhow, Frank?

[DOC *crosses to the bunk. He sees two fancy pillows on the bottom bunk, picks up one, and tosses it to* ROBERTS. *He picks up the other.*]

DOC. Well, look here. Somebody seems to be expecting company!

ROBERTS. Good Lord!

DOC (*reads the lettering on his pillowcase*). "*Toujours l'amour* . . . Souvenir of San Diego . . . Oh you kid!"

ROBERTS (*reading from his pillowcase*). "Tonight or never . . . Compliments of Allis-Chalmers, Farm Equipment . . . We plow deep while others sleep." (*He looks at* DOC, *then rises.*) Doc—that new hospital over there hasn't got nurses, has it?

DOC. Nurses! It didn't have yesterday!

PULVER (*turning from the porthole*). It has today!

DOC. But how did you find out they were there?

PULVER (*trying to recall*). Now let me think . . . it just came to me all of a sudden. This morning it was so hot I was just lying on my bunk—thinking . . . There wasn't a breath of air. And then, all of a sudden, a funny thing happened. A little breeze came up and I took a big deep breath and said to myself, "Pulver boy, there's women on that island."

ROBERTS. Doc, a thing like this could make a bird dog self-conscious as hell.

40 PULVER (*warming up*). They just flew in last night. There's eighteen of them —all brunettes except for two beautiful blondes—twin sisters! I'm working on one of those. I asked her out to the ship for lunch and she said she was kind of tired. So then I got kind of

desperate and turned on the old personality—and I said, "Ain't there anything in the world that'll make you come out to the ship with me?" And she said, "Yes, there is, one thing and one thing only—— (*Crosses to* ROBERTS, *looks at him accusingly.*) A good stiff drink of Scotch!" (*He sinks into the chair.*)

ROBERTS (*after a pause*). I'm sorry, Frank. 10 I'm really sorry. Your first assignment in a year. (*He pats* PULVER *on the shoulder.*)

PULVER. I figured I'd bring her in here . . . I fixed it up real cozy . . . (*Fondling the pillow on the desk.*) . . . and then I was going to throw a couple of fast slugs of Scotch into her and . . . but, hell, without the Scotch, she wouldn't . . . she just wouldn't, 20 that's all.

ROBERTS (*after a pause*). Doc, let's make some Scotch!

DOC. Huh?

ROBERTS. As naval officers we're supposed to be resourceful. Frank here's got a great opportunity and I've let him down. Let's fix him up!

DOC. Right! (*He goes to the desk.* ROBERTS *begins removing bottles from the medi-* 30 *cine chest.*) Frank, where's the rest of that alcohol we were drinking last night?

PULVER (*pulling a large vinegar bottle half filled with colorless liquid from the wastebasket and handing it to* DOC). Hell, that ain't even the right color.

DOC (*taking the bottle*). Quiet! (*Thinks deeply.*) Color . . . (*With sudden decision.*) Coca-Cola! Have you got any? 40

ROBERTS. I haven't seen a Coke in four months—no, by God, it's five months!

PULVER. Oh, what the hell! (*He rises, crosses to his bunk, reaches under the mattress of the top bunk, and produces a bottle of Coca-Cola. The others watch him.* DOC *snatches the bottle.* PULVER *says apologetically:*) I forgot I had it.

[DOC *opens the bottle and is about to pour the Coca-Cola into the vinegar bottle when he suddenly stops.*]

DOC. Oh—what shade would you like? Cutty Sark . . . Haig and Haig . . . Vat 69 . . .

PULVER (*interested*). I told her Johnny Walker.

DOC. Johnny Walker it is! (*He pours some of the Coca-Cola into the bottle.*)

ROBERTS (*looking at the color of the mixture*). Johnny Walker Red Label!

DOC. Red Label!

PULVER. It may look like it—but it won't taste like it!

ROBERTS. Doc, what does Scotch taste like?

DOC. Well, it's a little like . . . uh . . . it tastes like . . .

ROBERTS. Do you know what it's always tasted a little like to me? Iodine.

DOC (*shrugs as if to say "Of course" and rises. He takes a dropper from a small bottle of iodine and flicks a drop into the bottle*). One drop of iodine—for taste. (*Shakes the bottle and pours some in a glass.*)

PULVER. Lemme taste her, Doc!

DOC (*stops him with a gesture*). No. This calls for a medical opinion. (*Takes a ceremonial taste while the others wait for his verdict.*)

PULVER. How about it?

DOC. We're on the right track! (*Sets the glass down. Rubs his hands professionally.*) Now we need a little something extra —for age! What've you got there, Doug?

ROBERTS (*reading the labels of the bottles on the desk*). Bromo-Seltzer . . . Wildroot Wave Set . . . Eno Fruit Salts . . . Kreml Hair Tonic . . .

DOC. Kreml! It has a coal-tar base! And it'll age the hell out of it! (*Pours a bit of Kreml into the mixture. Shakes the bottle solemnly.*) One drop Kreml for age. (*Sets the bottle on the desk, looks at his wrist watch for a fraction of a second.*) That's it! (*Pours a drink into a glass.* PULVER *reaches for it.* ROBERTS *pushes his arm aside and tastes it.*)

ROBERTS. By God, it does taste a little like Scotch!

[PULVER *again reaches for the glass.* DOC *pushes his arm aside and takes a drink.*]

DOC. By God, it does!

[PULVER *finally gets the glass and takes a quick sip.*]

PULVER. It's delicious. That dumb little blonde won't know the difference.

DOC (*hands the bottle to* PULVER). Here you are, Frank. Doug and I have made the Scotch. The *nurse* is your department.

[PULVER *takes the bottle and hides it under the mattress, then replaces the pillows.*]

PULVER (*singing softly*). Won't know the difference . . . won't know the difference. (DOC *starts to drink from the Coca-Cola bottle as* PULVER *comes over and snatches it from his hand.*) Thanks, Doc. (*Puts the cap on the bottle and hides it under the mattress. Turns and faces the others.*) Thanks, Doug. Jeez, you guys are wonderful to me.

ROBERTS (*putting the bottles back in the medicine chest*). Don't mention it, Frank. I think you almost deserve it.

PULVER. You do—really? Or are you just giving me the old needle again? What do you really think of me, Doug —honestly?

ROBERTS (*turning slowly to face* PULVER). Frank, I like you. No one can get around the fact that you're a hell of a likable guy.

PULVER (*beaming*). Yeah—yeah . . .

ROBERTS. But . . .

PULVER. But what?

ROBERTS. But I also think you are the most hapless . . . lazy . . . disorganized . . . and, in general, the most lecherous person I've ever known in my life.

PULVER. I am not.

ROBERTS. Not what?

PULVER. I'm not disorganized—for one thing.

ROBERTS. Have you ever in your life finished anything you started out to do? You sleep sixteen hours a day. You pretend you want me to improve your mind and you've never even finished a book I've given you to read!

PULVER. I finished *God's Little Acre*, Doug boy!

ROBERTS. I didn't give you that! (*To* DOC.) He's been reading *God's Little Acre* for over a year! (*Takes a dog-eared book from* PULVER'S *bunk.*) He's underlined every erotic passage, and added exclamation points—and after a certain pornographic climax, he's inserted the words "well written." (*To* PULVER.) You're the laundry and morale officer and I doubt if you've ever seen the laundry.

PULVER. I was down there only last week.

ROBERTS. And you're scared of the Captain.

PULVER. I'm not scared of the Captain.

ROBERTS. Then why do you hide in the passageway every time you see him coming? I doubt if he even knows you're on board. You're scared of him.

PULVER. I am not. I'm scared of myself —I'm scared of what I might do to him.

ROBERTS (*laughing*). What you might do to him! Doc, he lies in his sack all day long and bores me silly with great moronic plots against the Captain and he's never carried out one.

PULVER. I haven't, huh.

ROBERTS. No, Frank, you haven't. What happened to your idea of plugging up the line of the Captain's sanitary system? "I'll make it overflow," you said. "I'll make a backwash that'll lift him off the throne and knock him clean across the room."

PULVER. I'm workin' on that. I thought about it for half an hour—yesterday.

ROBERTS. Half an hour! There's only one thing you've thought about for half an hour in your life! And what about those marbles that you were going to put in the Captain's overhead—so they'd roll around at night and keep him awake?

PULVER. Now you've gone too far. Now you've asked for it. (*Goes to his bunk and produces a small tin box from under the mattress. Crosses to* ROBERTS *and shakes it in his face. Opens it.*) What does that look like? Five marbles! I'm collecting marbles all the time. I've got one right here in my pocket! (*Takes a marble from his pocket, holds it close to* ROBERTS' *nose, then drops it in the box. Closes the box.*) Six marbles! (*Puts the box back under the mattress, turns defiantly to* ROBERTS.) I'm looking for marbles all day long!

ROBERTS. Frank, you asked me what I thought of you. Well, I'll tell you! The day you finish one thing you've started out to do, the day you actually put those marbles in the Captain's overhead, and then have the guts to knock on his door and say, "Captain, I put those marbles there," that's the day I'll have some respect for you— that's the day I'll look up to you as a man. Okay?

PULVER (*belligerently*). Okay!

[ROBERTS *goes to the radio and turns it up. While he is listening,* DOC *and* PULVER *exchange worried looks.*]

RADIO VOICE. . . . intersecting thirty miles north of Hanover. At the same time, General George S. Patton's Third Army continues to roll unchecked into Southern Germany. The abrupt German collapse brought forth the remark from a high London official that the end of the war in Europe is only weeks away—maybe days . . .

[ROBERTS *turns off the radio.*]

ROBERTS. Where the hell's Dolan with that letter! (*Starts toward the door.*) I'm going to find him.

PULVER. Hey, Doug, wait! Listen! (ROBERTS *pauses at the door.*) I wouldn't send in that letter if I were you!

ROBERTS. What do you mean—*that* letter!

PULVER (*hastily*). I mean any of those letters you been writin'. What are you so nervous about, anyway?

ROBERTS. Nervous!

PULVER. I mean about getting off this ship. Hell, this ain't such a bad life. Look, Doug. We're a threesome, aren't we—you and Doc and me? Share and share alike! Now look, I'm not going to keep those nurses all to myself. Soon as I get my little nursie organized today, I'm going to start working on her twin sister—for you.

ROBERTS. All right, Frank.

PULVER. And then I'm going to scare up something for you too, Doc. And in the meantime you've got a lot of work to do, Doug boy—improvin' my mind and watching my grammar. And speaking of grammar, you better watch your grammar. You're going to get in trouble, saying things like "disharmony aboard this ship!" (ROBERTS *looks at* PULVER *quickly.* PULVER *catches himself.*) I mean just in case you ever said anything like "disharmony aboard this ship" . . . or

. . . uh . . . "harmony aboard this ship" or . . .

ROBERTS. Where's that letter?

PULVER. I don't know, Doug boy . . . (*As* ROBERTS *steps toward him, he quickly produces the letter from the blanket.*) Here it is, Doug.

ROBERTS (*snatching the letter*). What's the big idea!

[ROBERTS *goes to the desk, reading and preparing to sign the letter.* PULVER *follows him.*]

PULVER. I just wanted to talk to you before you signed it. You can't send it in that way—it's too strong! Don't sign that letter, Doug, please don't! They'll transfer you and you'll get your ass shot off. You're just running a race with death, isn't he, Doc? It's stupid to keep asking for it like that. The Doc says so too. Tell him what you said to me last night, Doc—about how stupid he is.

ROBERTS (*coldly, to* DOC). Yes, doc, maybe you'd like to tell me to my face.

DOC (*belligerently*). Yes, I would. Last night I asked you why you wanted to fight this war. And you said: "Anyone who doesn't fight it is only half alive." Well, I thought that over and I've decided that's just a crock, Doug —just a crock.

ROBERTS. I take it back, Doc. After seeing my task force last night I don't even feel half alive.

DOC. You are stupid! And I can prove it! You quit medical school to get into this thing when you could be saving lives today. Why? Do you even know yourself?

ROBERTS. Has it ever occurred to you that the guys who fight this war might also be saving lives . . . yours and mine, for instance! Not just putting men together again, but *keeping*

them together! Right now I'd rather practice that kind of medicine— Doctor!

DOC (*rising*). Well, right now, that's exactly what you're doing.

ROBERTS. What, for God's sake!

DOC. Whether you like it or not, this sorry old bucket does a necessary job. And you're the guy who keeps her lumbering along. You keep this crew working cargo, and more than that— you keep them *alive*. It might just be that right here, on this bucket, you're deeper and more truly in this war than you ever would be anywhere else.

ROBERTS. Oh Jesus, Doc. In a minute you'll start quoting Emerson.

DOC. *That* is a lousy thing to say!

ROBERTS. We've got nothing to do with the war. Maybe that's why we're on this ship—because we're not good enough to fight. (*Then quietly, with emotion.*) Maybe there's some omniscient son of a bitch who goes down the line of all the servicemen and picks out the ones to send into combat, the ones whose glands secrete enough adrenalin, or whose great-great-grandfathers weren't afraid of the dark or something. The rest of us are packed off to ships like this where we can't do any harm.

DOC. What is it you want to be—a hero or something?

ROBERTS (*shocked*). Hero! My God, Doc! You haven't heard a word I said! Look, Doc, the war's way out there! I'm here. I don't want to be here—I want to be out there. I'm sick and tired of being a lousy spectator. I just happen to believe in this thing. I've got to feel I'm *good* enough to be in it—to *participate!*

DOC. Good enough! Doug, you're good enough! You just don't have the opportunity. That's mostly what physical heroism is—opportunity. It's a reflex. I think seventy-five out of a hundred young males have that reflex. If you put any one of them—say even Frank Thurlowe Pulver here —in a B-29 over Japan, do you know what you'd have?

ROBERTS. No, by God, I don't.

DOC. You'd have Pulver the Congressional Medal of Honor winner! You'd have Pulver who, singlehanded, shot down twenty-three attacking Zeros, then with his bare hands held together the severed wing struts of his plane, and with his bare feet successfully landed the mortally wounded plane on his home field. (PULVER *thinks this over.*) Hell, it's a reflex. It's like the knee jerk. Strike the patella tendon of any human being and you produce the knee jerk. Look. (*He illustrates on* PULVER. *There is no knee jerk. He strikes again—still no reaction.*)

PULVER. What's the matter, Doc?

DOC. Nothing. But stay out of B-29's, will you, Frank?

ROBERTS. You've made your point very vividly, Doc. But I still want to get into this thing. I've got to get into it! And I'm going to keep on sending in these letters until I do.

DOC. I know you are, Doug.

ROBERTS (*signs the letter. Then to* DOC): I haven't got much time. I found that out over on the island. That task force I saw last night is on its way to start our last big push in the Pacific. And it went by me, Doc. I've got to catch it. (*He exits.*)

PULVER (*after a pause*). Doc, what are you going to give Doug on his birthday?

DOC. I hadn't thought of giving him anything.

PULVER. You know what? I'm gonna show him he's got old Pulver figured out all wrong. (*Pulls a small cardboard roll from under the mattress.*) Doc, what does that look like?

DOC. Just what it is—the cardboard center of a roll of toilet paper.

PULVER. I suppose it doesn't look like a firecracker.

DOC. Not a bit like a firecracker.

PULVER (*taking a piece of string from the bunk*). I suppose that doesn't look like a fuse.

DOC (*rising and starting off*). No, that looks like a piece of string. (*He walks slowly out of the room.* PULVER *goes on:*)

PULVER. Well, you just wait till old Pulver gets through with it! I'm going to get me some of that black powder from the gunner's mate. No, by God, this isn't going to be any peanut firecracker—I'm going to pack this old thing full of that stuff they use to blow up bridges, that fulminate-of-mercury stuff. And then on the night of Doug's birthday, I'm going to throw it under the Old Man's bunk. Bam—bam—bam! (*Knocks on* ROB-ERTS' *locker, opens it.*) Captain, it is I, Ensign Pulver. I just threw that firecracker under your goddamn bunk.

[*He salutes as the lights fade out.*]

[*In the darkness we hear the sound of a winch and shouted orders:*]

LCT OFFICER. On the *AK*—where do you want us?

AK VOICE. Starboard side, up for'd— alongside number two!

LCT OFFICER. Shall we use our fenders or yours?

AK VOICE. No, we'll use ours! Stand off till we finish with the barge!

SCENE III

The curtain rises and the lights dim up on the deck. ROBERTS *stands on the hatch cover.* SCHLEMMER, GERHART, *and another sea-*

man are sitting on the hatch cover. They are tired and hot. A cargo net filled with crates is disappearing off right. Off stage we hear the shouts of men working cargo. Two officers walk across the stage. Everyone's shirt is wet with perspiration.

ROBERTS (*calling through a megaphone*). Okay—take it away—that's all for the barge. On the LCT—I'll give you a bow line.

LCT OFFICER (*off stage*). Okay, Lieutenant.

ROBERTS (*to the crew*). Get a lineover!

DOWDY (*off stage*). Yes, sir!

REBER (*off right*). Heads up on the LCT!

ROBERTS. That's good. Make it fast.

[PAYNE, *wearing the belt of a messenger, enters from the companionway as* DOWDY *enters from the right.*]

PAYNE. Mister Roberts, the Captain says not to give this LCT any fresh fruit. He says he's going to keep what's left for his own mess.

ROBERTS. Okay, okay. . . .

PAYNE. Hold your hat, Mister Roberts. I just saw Dolan go in there with your letter. (*He grins and exits as* ROBERTS *smiles at* DOWDY.)

DOWDY. Here's the list of what the LCT guy wants.

ROBERTS (*reading rapidly*). One ton dry stores . . . quarter-ton frozen food . . . one gross dungaries . . . twenty cartons tooth paste . . . two gross skivvy shirts . . . Okay, we can give him all that.

DOWDY. Can these guys take their shirts off while we're working?

ROBERTS. Dowdy, you know the Captain has a standing order . . .

DOWDY. Mister Roberts, Corcoran just passed out from the heat.

ROBERTS (*looks at the men, who wait for his decision*). Hell yes, take 'em off. (DOWDY *exits.* SCHLEMMER, REBER, *and*

the seaman remove their shirts, saying "Thanks, MISTER ROBERTS" *and exit right.* ROBERTS *calls through the megaphone.*) LCT, want to swap movies? We've got a new one.

LCT (*off stage*). What's that?

ROBERTS. *Charlie Chan at the Opera.*

LCT (*off stage*). No, thanks, we've seen that three times!

ROBERTS. What you got?

LCT (*off stage*). Hoot Gibson in *Riders of the Range.*

ROBERTS. Sorry I brought the subject up.

DOWDY (*entering from the right*). All set, Mister Roberts.

LCT (*off stage*). Lieutenant, one thing I didn't put on my list because I wanted to ask you—you couldn't spare us any fresh fruit, could you?

ROBERTS. You all out?

LCT (*off stage*). We haven't seen any for two months.

ROBERTS (*to* DOWDY). Dowdy, give 'em a couple of crates of oranges.

DOWDY. Yes, sir.

ROBERTS. Compliments of the Captain.

DOWDY. Aye aye, sir. (*He exits.*)

ROBERTS (*to* LCT). Here comes your first slingload! (*There is the grinding sound of a winch. With hand signals* ROBERTS *directs the placing of the slingload. Then he shouts:*) Watch that line!

[DOWDY's *voice is heard off stage.*]

DOWDY. Slack off, you dumb bastards! Slack off!

[PAYNE *enters.* ROBERTS *turns to him sharply.*]

ROBERTS. What!

PAYNE. The Captain wants to see you, Mister Roberts.

DOWDY (*off stage*). Goddammit, there it goes! You've parted the line!

ROBERTS. Get a fender over! Quick! (*To* PAYNE.) You go tell the Captain I'm busy! (PAYNE *exits.* ROBERTS *calls off stage:*) Get a line over—his bow's coming in!

REBER (*off stage*). Heads up!

GERHART (*off stage*). Where shall we secure?

DOWDY (*off stage*). Secure here!

ROBERTS. No. Take it around the bitt!

DOWDY (*off stage*). Around the bitt!

ROBERTS. That's too much! Give him some slack this time! (*Watches in-* 10 *tently.*) That's good. Okay, let's give him the rest of his cargo.

GERHART (*entering quickly and pointing toward the companionway*). Flash Red!

[*He exits. The* CAPTAIN *enters, followed by* PAYNE *and* DOLAN.]

CAPTAIN. All right, Mister! Let's have this out right here and now! What do you mean—telling me you're busy!

ROBERTS. We parted a line, Captain. 20 You didn't want me to leave the deck with this ship coming in on us?

CAPTAIN. You're damn right I want you to leave the deck. When I tell you I want to see you, I mean *now*, Mister! I mean jump! Do you understand?

[*At this point a group of men, attracted by the noise, crowd in. They are naked to the waist. They pretend they are working, but actually they are listening to the* CAP- 30 TAIN'S *fight with* ROBERTS.]

ROBERTS. Yes, Captain. I'll remember that next time.

CAPTAIN. You're damn right you'll remember it! Don't *ever* tell me you're too busy to see me! Ever! (ROBERTS *doesn't answer. The* CAPTAIN *points to the letter he is carrying.*) By God, you think you're pretty cute with this letter, don't you? You're trying to get 40 me in bad with the Admiral, ain't you? Ain't you?

ROBERTS. No, I'm not, Captain.

CAPTAIN. Then what do you mean by writing "disharmony aboard this ship"?

ROBERTS. Because it's true, Captain.

[*The men grin at each other.*]

CAPTAIN. Any disharmony on this ship is my own doing!

ROBERTS. That's true too, Captain.

CAPTAIN. Damn right it's true. And it ain't gonna be in any letter that leaves this ship. Any criticism of this ship stays on this ship. I got a reputation with the Admiral and I ain't gonna lose it on account of a letter written by some smart-aleck college officer. Now you retype that letter and leave out that disharmony crap and I'll send it in. But this is the last one, understand?

ROBERTS. Captain, every man in the Navy has the right to send in a request for transfer . . . and no one can change the wording. That's in Navy regs.

CAPTAIN (*after a pause*). How about that, Dolan?

DOLAN. That's what it says, sir.

CAPTAIN. This goddamn Navy! I never put up with crap like that in the merchant service. All right, I'll send this one in as it is—*dis*approved, like I always do. But there's one thing I don't have to do, and that's send in a letter that ain't been written. And, Mister, I'm tellin' you here and now —you ain't gonna write any more. You bring one next week and you'll regret it the rest of your life. You got a job right here and, Mister, you ain't *never* going to leave this ship. Now get on with your work. (*He looks around and notices the men. He shouts:*) Where are your shirts?

ROBERTS. Captain, I . . .

CAPTAIN. Shut up! *Answer me, where are your shirts?* (*They stare at him.*) Get those shirts on in a goddamn quick hurry.

[*The men pick up their shirts, then pause, looking at* ROBERTS.]

ROBERTS. Captain, it was so hot working cargo, I . . .

CAPTAIN (*shouting louder*). I told you to shut up! (*To the men.*) I'm giving you an order—get those shirts on!

[*The men do not move.*]

ROBERTS (*quietly*). I'm sorry. Put your shirts on.

[*The men put on their shirts. There is a pause while the* CAPTAIN *stares at the* 10 *men. Then he speaks quietly.*]

CAPTAIN. Who's the captain of this ship? By God, that's the rankest piece of insubordination I've seen. You've been getting pretty smart playing grab-ass with Roberts here . . . but now you've gone too far. I'm givin' you a little promise—I ain't never gonna forget this. And in the meantime, every one of you men who disobeyed my standing order and ap- 20 peared on deck without a shirt— every one—is on report, do you hear? On report!

ROBERTS. Captain, you're not putting these men on report.

CAPTAIN. What do you mean—I'm not!

ROBERTS. I'm responsible. I gave them permission.

CAPTAIN. You disobeyed my order?   30

ROBERTS. Yes, sir. It was too hot working cargo in the sun. One man passed out.

CAPTAIN. I don't give a damn if fifty men passed out. I gave an order and you disobeyed it.

LCT (*off stage*). Thanks a million for the oranges, Lieutenant.

CAPTAIN (*to* ROBERTS). Did you give that LCT fresh fruit?

ROBERTS. Yes, sir. We've got plenty, Captain. They've been out for two months.

CAPTAIN. I've taken all the crap from you that I'm going to. You've just got yourself ten days in your room. Ten days, Mister! Ten days!

ROBERTS. Very well, Captain. Do you relieve me here?

CAPTAIN. You're damn right, I relieve you. You can go to your room for ten days! See how you like that!

LCT (*off stage*). We're waiting on you, Lieutenant. We gotta shove off.

[ROBERTS *gives the megaphone to the* CAPTAIN *and starts off. The* CAPTAIN *looks in the direction of the* LCT, *then calls to* ROBERTS:]

CAPTAIN. Where do you think you're going?

ROBERTS (*pretending surprise*). To my room, Captain!

CAPTAIN. Get back to that cargo! I'll let you know when you have ten days in your room and you'll damn well know it! You're going to stay right here and do your job! (ROBERTS *crosses to the crew. The* CAPTAIN *slams the megaphone into* ROBERTS' *stomach.* PULVER *enters around the corner of the house, sees the* CAPTAIN, *and starts to go back. The* CAPTAIN *sees* PULVER *and shouts:*) Who's that? Who's that officer there?

PULVER (*turning*). Me, sir?

CAPTAIN. Yes, you. Come here, boy. (PULVER *approaches in great confusion and can think of nothing better to do than salute. This visibly startles the* CAPTAIN.) Why, you're one of my officers!

PULVER. Yes, sir.

CAPTAIN. What's your name again?

PULVER. Ensign Pulver, sir.

[*He salutes again. The* CAPTAIN, *amazed, returns the salute, then says for the benefit of* ROBERTS *and the crew:*]

CAPTAIN. By God, I'm glad to see one on this ship knows how to salute. (*Then to* PULVER.) Pulver . . . oh yes . . . Pulver. How is it I never see you around?

PULVER (*terrified*). I've wondered about that myself, sir.

CAPTAIN. What's your job?

PULVER (*trembling*). Officer in charge of laundry and morale, sir.

CAPTAIN. How long you been aboard?

PULVER. Fourteen months, sir.

CAPTAIN. Fourteen months! You spend most of your time down in the laundry, eh?

PULVER. Most of the time, sir. Yes, sir.

[ROBERTS *turns his face to hide his laughter.*]

CAPTAIN. Well, you do a good job, Pulver, and . . . you know I'd like to see more of you. Why don't you have lunch with me in my cabin today?

PULVER. Oh, I can't today.

CAPTAIN. Can't? Why not?

PULVER. I'm on my way over to the hospital on the island. I've got to go pick up a piece . . . of medical equipment.

ROBERTS (*calling over*). Why, I'll take care of that, Frank.

CAPTAIN. That's right, Roberts. You finish here and you go over and fetch it.

ROBERTS. Yes, sir. (*He nods, and turns away grinning.*)

CAPTAIN (*to* PULVER). Well, how about it?

PULVER. This is something I've got to take care of myself, sir. If you don't mind, sir.

CAPTAIN. Well, some other time then.

PULVER. Yes, sir. Thank you, sir.

CAPTAIN. Okay, Pulver.

[*The* CAPTAIN *baits another salute from* PULVER, *then exits.* PULVER *watches him go, then starts to sneak off.*]

ROBERTS (*grinning and mimicking the* CAPTAIN). Oh, boy! (PULVER *stops uneasily.* ROBERTS *salutes him.*) I want to see more of you, Pulver!

PULVER (*furiously*). That son of a bitch! Pretending he doesn't know me!

[*He looks at his watch and exits.* ROBERTS *turns laughing to the crew, who are standing rather solemnly.*]

DOWDY (*quietly*). Nice going, Mister Roberts.

SCHLEMMER. It was really beautiful the way you read the Old Man off!

GERHART. Are you going to send in that letter next week, Mister Roberts?

ROBERTS. Are we, Dolan?

DOLAN. You're damn right we are! And I'm the baby who's going to deliver it!

SCHLEMMER. He said he'd fix you good. What do you think he'll do?

REBER. You got a promotion coming up, haven't you?

SCHLEMMER. Yeah. Could he stop that or something?

DOLAN. Promotion! This is Mister Roberts. You think he gives a good hoot in hell about another lousy stripe?

ALL. Yeah.

GERHART. Hey, Mister Roberts, can I take the letter in next week?

DOLAN (*indignantly*). You can like hell! That's my job—isn't it, Mister Roberts?

GERHART. Can I, Mister Roberts?

ROBERTS. I'm afraid I've promised that job to Dolan.

DOLAN (*pushing* GERHART *away*). You heard him. (*To* ROBERTS.) We gotta write a really hot one next week.

ROBERTS. Got any asbestos paper?

[*He starts off, the men follow happily as the lights fade out.*]

SCENE IV

The lights come up immediately on the main set. REBER *and* GERHART *enter from the right passageway. As they get around the corner of the house, they break into a run.* REBER *dashes off through the left passageway.*

GERHART (*excitedly, descending the hatchway*). Hey, Schlemmer! Schlemmer!

[MISS GIRARD, *a young, attractive, blonde Army nurse, and* PULVER *enter from the right passageway.*]

MISS GIRARD. Well, Mannion. I wouldn't take that bet if I were you, because you'd lose a hundred bucks. (*To* PULVER.) Come on, Harmless.

[*She exits, followed by a bewildered* PULVER. *The men watch her off.* STEFANOWSKI *throws his cap on the ground in anger.*]

MANNION (*to* INSIGNA). You loud-mouthed little bastard! Now you've gone and done it! 10

ROBERTS. Shut up! Insigna, how did you . . .

INSIGNA. We seen her taking a bath.

LINDSTROM. Through these glasses, Mister Roberts! We could see everything!

STEFANOWSKI (*furious*). You heard what she said—she's going to hang some curtains.

MANNION. Yeah . . .

LINDSTROM. Gee, them nurses was pretty 20 to look at. (*He sighs. There is a little tragic moment.*)

ROBERTS. She's got a ten-minute boat ride. You've still got ten minutes.

WILEY. It wouldn't be any fun when you know you're going to be rushed.

LINDSTROM. This was the first real good day this ship has ever had. But it's all over now.

ROBERTS. Well, maybe you've got time 30 then to listen to a little piece of news. . . . (*He reads from the paper in his hands.*) "When in all respects ready for sea, on or about 1600 today, the *AK601* will proceed at ten knots via points X-Ray, Yolk, and Zebra to Elysium Island, arriving there in seven days and reporting to the Port Director for cargo assignment." (*Emphatically.*) "During its stay in Ely- 40 sium, the ship will make maximum use of the recreational facilities of this port."

[*The men look up in slow surprise and disbelief.*]

STEFANOWSKI. But that means liberty!

LINDSTROM. That don't mean liberty, Mister Roberts?

ROBERTS. That's exactly what it means!

INSIGNA (*dazed*). Somebody must've been drunk to send us to a Liberty Port!

[ROBERTS *nods.*]

LINDSTROM. Has the Old Man seen them orders?

ROBERTS. He saw them before I did.

[*Now the men are excited.*]

WILEY. Elysium! Where's that?

MANNION. Yeah! Where's that, Mister Roberts?

[*The men crowd around* ROBERTS *as he sits on the hatch.*]

ROBERTS (*reading from a guidebook*). "Elysium is the largest of the Limbo Islands. It is often referred to as the 'Polynesian Paradise.' Vanilla, sugar, cocoa, coffee, copra, mother-of-pearl, phosphates, and rum are the chief exports."

INSIGNA. Rum! Did you hear that? (*He gooses* LINDSTROM.)

LINDSTROM. Cut that out! (DOLAN *gooses* INSIGNA.)

INSIGNA. Cut that out!

MANNION. Shut up!

ROBERTS. "Elysium City, its capital, is a beautiful metropolis of palm-lined boulevards, handsome public buildings, and colorful stucco homes. Since 1900, its population has remained remarkably constant at approximately 30,000."

INSIGNA. I'll fix that!

[*The men shout him down.*]

ROBERTS. That's all there is here. If you want the real dope on Elysium, there's one man on this ship who's been there.

STEFANOWSKI. Who's that?

MANNION. Who?

ROBERTS. Dowdy!

[*The men run off wildly in every direction, shouting for* DOWDY. *The call is taken up all over the ship.* ROBERTS *listens to them happily, then notices a pair of binoculars. He looks toward the island for a moment shrugs, and is lifting the binoculars to his eyes as the lights fade out.*]

SCENE V

During the darkness we can hear the exciting strains of Polynesian music.

The lights come up slowly through a port- 10 *hole, casting a strong late-afternoon shaft of light onto motionless white figures. It is the enlisted men's compartment below decks. Except for a few not yet fully dressed, the men are all in white uniforms. The compartment is a crowded place with three-tiered bunks against the bulkheads. Most of the men are crowded around the porthole, downstage left. The men who cannot see are listening to the reports of* INSIGNA, *who is standing on a* 20 *bench, looking out the porthole. The only man who is not galvanized with excitement is* DOWDY, *who sits calmly on a bench, downstage center, reading a magazine*—True Detective.

GERHART (*to* INSIGNA). What do you see now, Sam?

INSIGNA. There's a lot of little boats up forward—up around the bow. 30

PAYNE. What kind of boats?

INSIGNA. They're little sort of canoes and they're all filled up with flowers and stuff. And there's women in them boats, paddling them . . .

PAYNE. Are they coming down this way?

INSIGNA. Naw. They're sticking around the bow.

STEFANOWSKI. Sam, where's that music coming from?

INSIGNA. There's a great big canoe up there and it's all filled with fat bastards with flowers in their ears playing little old git-tars. . . .

SCHLEMMER. Why the hell can't we go up on deck? That's what I'd like to know!

LINDSTROM. When are we going ashore! That's what I'd like to know!

[INSIGNA *suddenly laughs.*]

PAYNE. What is it, Sam?

INSIGNA. I wish you could see this . . .

[CHIEF JOHNSON *enters, looking knowingly at the men, shakes his head, and addresses* DOWDY.]

JOHNSON. Same story in here, eh? Every porthole this side of the ship!

DOWDY. They're going to wear themselves down to a nub before they ever get over there. . . .

LINDSTROM (*takes a coin from his pocket and thrusts it at* INSIGNA). Hey, Sam, here's another penny. Make them kids down below dive for it.

INSIGNA (*impatiently*). All right! (*Throws the coin out the port.*) Heads up, you little bastards! (*The men watch tensely.*)

LINDSTROM. Did he get that one too?

INSIGNA. Yeah. . . .

[*The men relax somewhat.*]

LINDSTROM. Them kids don't ever miss!

INSIGNA. Hey, Dowdy—where's that little park again? Where you said all the good-looking women hang out?

DOWDY. For the last time—you see that big hill over there to the right . . .

INSIGNA. Yeah.

DOWDY. You see a big church . . . with a street running off to the left of it.

INSIGNA. Yeah.

DOWDY. Well, you go up that street three blocks . . .

INSIGNA. Yeah, I'm there.

DOWDY. That's the park.

INSIGNA. Well, I'll be damned. . . .

LINDSTROM. Hey, show me that park, Sam?

[*The other men gather around* INSIGNA, *asking to see the park.*]

INSIGNA (*the authority now*). All right, you bastards, line up. I'll show you where the women hang out.

[*The men form a line and each steps up to the porthole, where* INSIGNA *points out the park.*]

JOHNSON (*to* DOWDY). Smell that shoe polish? These guys have gone nuts!

DOWDY. I went down to the ship's store the other day to buy a bar of soap and, do you know, they been sold out for a week! No soap, no Listerine, no lilac shaving lotion—hell, they even sold 10 eighteen jars of Mum! Now these bastards are bootlegging it! They're gettin' ten bucks for a used jar of Mum!

[REBER, *wearing the messenger's belt, enters. The men greet him excitedly.*]

STEFANOWSKI. What's the word on liberty, Reber? Is the Old Man still asleep?

MANNION. Yeah, what's the word?

REBER. I just peeked in on him. He's 20 snoring like a baby.

GERHART. Jeez, how any guy can sleep at a time like this!

INSIGNA. I'll get him up! I'm going up there and tap on his door! (*Picks up a heavy lead pipe.*)

DOWDY (*grabbing* INSIGNA). Like hell you are! You're going to stay right here and pray. You're going to pray that he wakes up feeling good and decides 30 he's kept you guys sweating long enough!

MANNION. That's telling the little crud!

[INSIGNA *and* MANNION *threaten each other.*]

REBER. Hey, Lindstrom. I got good news for you. You can take them whites off.

LINDSTROM. I ain't got the duty *tonight?*

REBER. That's right. You and Mister Roberts got the duty tonight—the twelve to four watch. The Exec just 40 posted the list . . .

[*He is interrupted by the sound of static on the squawk box. Instantly all the men turn toward it eagerly.*]

DOLAN (*on the squawk box*). Now hear this! Now hear this!

WILEY. Here we go! Here we go!

STEFANOWSKI (*imitating the squawk box*). Liberty . . . will com-mence . . . immediately!

GERHART. Quiet!

DOLAN (*on the squawk box*). Now hear this! The Captain's messenger will report to the Captain's cabin on the double!

REBER. My God! He's awake! (*He runs out.*)

PAYNE. Won't be long now!

WILEY. Get going, Mannion! Get into those whites! We're going to be the first ones over the side!

MANNION. Hell, yes! Give me a hand!

[*Now there is a general frenzy of preparation—the men put the last-minute touches to shoes, hair, uniforms.*]

GERHART (*singing to the tune of "California, Here I Come"*).

Ee-liss-*ee*-um, here I come! . . .
Ta-ta-ta-ta-*ta*-da-tah . . .

SCHLEMMER (*to* GERHART). Watch where you're going! You stepped on my shine!

INSIGNA. Schlemmer . . . Stef . . . Gerhart . . . come here! (*These men gather around him.* LINDSTROM *remains unhappily alone.*) Now listen! Stefanowski and me are going to work alone for the first hour and a half! But if you pick up something first . . . (*Produces a small map from his pocket.*) We'll be working up and down this street here . . .

[*They study the map. Now the squawk box is clicked on again. All the men stand rigid, listening.*]

DOLAN (*on the squawk box*). Now hear this! Now hear this! The Captain is now going to make a personal announcement.

[*Sound of the squawk-box switch.*]

CAPTAIN (*on the squawk box*). Goddammit, how does this thing work? (*Sound of the squawk-box switch again.*) This is the Captain speaking. I just woke up from a little nap and I got a surprise. I found out there were men on this ship who were expecting liberty. (*At this point the lights start dimming until the entire scene is blacked out. The speech continues throughout the darkness. Under the* CAPTAIN's *speech the strains of Polynesian music can be heard.*) Now 10 I don't know how such a rumor got around, but I'd like to clear it up right now. You see, it's like this. Because of cargo requirements and security conditions which has just come to my personal attention there will be no liberty as long as we're in this here port. And one other thing—as long as we're here, no man will wear white uniforms. Now I would like to 20 repeat for the benefit of complete understanding and clearness, *No liberty.* That is all.

SCENE VI

The lights come up on the CAPTAIN's *cabin. Against the left bulkhead is a settee. A chair is placed at the center. Up center is the only door. The* CAPTAIN *is seated behind his desk, holding a watch in one hand and 30 the microphone in the other, in an attitude of waiting. Just over the desk and against the right bulkhead is a ship's intercommunication board. There is a wall safe in the right bulkhead. After a moment there is a knock on the door.*

CAPTAIN. Come in, Mister Roberts. (*As* ROBERTS *enters the* CAPTAIN *puts the microphone on the desk.*) Thirty-eight 40 seconds. Pretty good time! You see, I been expectin' you ever since I made my little announcement.

ROBERTS. Well, as long as you're expecting me, what about it—when does this crew get liberty?

CAPTAIN. Well, in the first place, just kinda hold your tongue. And in the second place, sit down.

ROBERTS. There's no time to sit down. When are you going to let this crew go ashore?

CAPTAIN. I'm not. This wasn't my idea —coming to a Liberty Port. One of my officers arranged it with a certain Port Director—gave him a bottle of Scotch whisky—compliments of the Captain. And the Port Director was kind enough to send me a little thank-you note along with our orders. Sit down, Mister Roberts. (ROBERTS *sits.*) Don't worry about it. I'm not going to make trouble about that wasted bottle of Scotch. I'll admit I was a little pre-voked about not being consulted. Then I got to thinking maybe we oughta come to this port anyway so's you and me could have a little talk.

ROBERTS. You can make all the trouble you want, Captain, but let's quit wasting time. Don't you hear that music? Don't you know it's tearing those guys apart? They're breakable, Captain! I promise you!

CAPTAIN. That's enough! I've had enough of your fancy educated talk. (*Rises, goes to* ROBERTS.) Now you listen to me. I got two things I want to show you. (*He unlocks the wall safe, opens it, and takes out a commander's cap with gold braid "scrambled eggs" on the visor.*) You see that? That's the cap of a full commander. I'm gonna wear that cap someday and you're going to help me. (*Replaces the cap in the safe, goes back to* ROBERTS.) I guess there's no harm in telling you that you helped me get that palm tree by working cargo. Now don't let this go to your head, but when Admiral Finchley gave me that award, he said, "You got a good cargo officer, Morton; keep him at it, you're going places." So I went out and bought that hat. There's nothing gonna stand between me and that hat— certainly not you. Now last week you wrote a letter that said "disharmony aboard this ship." I told you there wasn't going to be any more letters. But what do I find on my desk this 10 morning . . . (*Taking a letter from the desk.*) Another one. It says "friction between myself and the Commanding Officer." That ain't gonna go in, Mister.

ROBERTS. How are you going to stop it, Captain?

CAPTAIN. I ain't, you are. (*Goes to his chair and sits.*) Just how much do you want this crew to have a liberty any- 20 how? Enough to stop this "disharmony"? To stop this "friction"? (*Leans forward.*) Enough to get out of the habit of writing letters ever? Because that's the only way this crew is ever gonna get ashore. (*Leans back.*) Well, we've had our little talk. What do you say?

ROBERTS (*after a moment*). How did you get in the Navy? How did you get on 30 our side? You're what I joined to fight *against*. You ignorant, arrogant, ambitious . . . (*Rises.*) . . . jackass! Keeping a hundred and sixty-seven men in prison because you got a palm tree for the work *they* did. I don't know which I hate worse—you or that other malignant growth that stands outside your door!

CAPTAIN. Why, you goddamn . . . 40

ROBERTS. How did you ever get command of a ship? I realize that in wartime they have to scrape the bottom of the barrel, but where the hell did they ever scrape you up?

CAPTAIN (*shouting*). There's just one thing left for you, by God—a general court-martial.

ROBERTS. That suits me fine. Court-martial me!

CAPTAIN. By God, you've got it!

ROBERTS. I'm asking for it!

CAPTAIN. You don't have to ask for it, you've got it now!

ROBERTS. If I can't get transferred off here, I'll get court-martialed off! I'm fed up! But you'll need a witness. Send for your messenger. He's down below. I'll say it all again in front of him. (*Pauses.*) Go on, call in Reber! (*The* CAPTAIN *doesn't move.*) Go on, call him. (*Still the* CAPTAIN *doesn't move.*) Do you want me to call him?

CAPTAIN. No. (*He walks upstage, then turns to* ROBERTS.) I think you're a pretty smart boy. I may not talk very good, Mister, but I know how to take care of smart boys. Let me tell you something. Let me tell you a little secret. I hate your guts, you college son of a bitch! You think you're better than I am! You think you're better because you've had everything handed to you! Let me tell you something, Mister—I've worked since I was ten years old, and all my life I've known you superior bastards. I knew you people when I was a kid in Boston and I worked in eating places and you ordered me around. . . . "Oh, busboy! My friend here seems to have thrown up on the table. Clean it up, please." I started going to sea as a steward and I worked for you then . . . "Steward, take my magazine out to the deck chair!" . . . "Steward, I don't like your looks. Please keep out of my way as much as possible!" Well, I took that crap! I took that for years from pimple-faced bastards who weren't good enough to wipe my nose! And now

I don't have to take it any more!
There's a war on, by God, and I'm
the captain and you can wipe my
nose! The worst thing I can do to
you is to keep you on this ship! And
that's where you're going to stay!
Now get out of here!

[*He goes to his chair and sits.* ROBERTS
*moves slowly toward the door. He hears
the music, goes to the porthole and listens.*
Then he turns to the CAPTAIN.]

ROBERTS. Can't you hear that music,
Captain?

CAPTAIN. Yeah, I hear it. (*Busies himself
at the desk, ignoring* ROBERTS.)

ROBERTS. Don't you know those guys
below can hear it too? Oh my God.

CAPTAIN. Get out of here.

[*After a moment,* ROBERTS *turns from the
porthole and slumps against the* CAPTAIN's
locker. His face is strained.]

ROBERTS. What do you want for liberty,
Captain?

CAPTAIN. I want plenty. You're through
writin' letters—ever.

ROBERTS. Okay.

CAPTAIN. That's not all. You're through
givin' me trouble. You're through
talkin' back to me in front of the
crew. You ain't even gonna open
your mouth—except in civil answer.
(ROBERTS *doesn't answer.*) Mister Roberts, you know that if you don't take
my terms I'll let you go out that door
and that's the end of any hope for
liberty.

ROBERTS. Is that all, Captain?

CAPTAIN. No. Anyone know you're in
here?

ROBERTS. No one.

CAPTAIN. Then you won't go blabbin'
about this to anyone ever. It might
not sound so good. And besides I

don't want you to take credit for
gettin' this crew ashore.

ROBERTS. Do you think I'm doing this
for credit? Do you think I'd *let* anyone know about this?

CAPTAIN. I gotta be sure.

ROBERTS. You've got my word, that's all.

CAPTAIN (*after a pause*). Your word. Yes,
you college fellas make a big show
about keeping your word.

ROBERTS. How about it, Captain? Is it a
deal?

CAPTAIN. Yeah. (ROBERTS *picks up the
microphone, turns on a switch, and thrusts
the microphone at the* CAPTAIN.) Now
hear this. This is the Captain speaking. I've got some further word on
security conditions in this port and
so it gives me great pleasure to tell
you that liberty, for the starboard
section . . .

ROBERTS (*covering the microphone with his
hand*). For the entire crew, goddammit.

CAPTAIN. Correction: Liberty for the
entire crew will commence immediately.

[ROBERTS *turns off the microphone. After a
moment we hear the shouts of the crew.*
ROBERTS *goes up to the porthole. The*
CAPTAIN *leans back on his chair. A song,
"Roll Me Over," is started by someone
and is soon taken up by the whole crew.*]

ROBERTS (*looking out the porthole. He is
excited and happy*). Listen to those
crazy bastards. Listen to them.

[*The crew continues to sing with increasing
volume. Now the words can be distinguished:*

Roll me over in the clover,
Roll me over, lay me down
And do it again.]

THE CURTAIN FALLS

ACT TWO

SCENE I

The curtain rises on the main set. It is now 3:45 A.M. The night is pitch-black, but we can see because of a light over the head of the gangway, where a temporary desk has been rigged; a large ship's logbook lies open on this desk. A small table on which are hospital supplies is at the left of the door.

At rise, ROBERTS, DOC, LINDSTROM, 10 JOHNSON, *and four* SEAMEN *are discovered on stage.* LINDSTROM, *in a web belt, is writing in the log.* ROBERTS *is standing with a pile of yellow slips in his hand; he wears the side arms of the Officer of the Deck.* JOHNSON *and a* SEAMAN *are standing near the hatchway, holding the inert body of another* SEAMAN, *who has court plaster on his face. Two more* SEAMEN *lie on the hatch cover, where* DOC *is kneeling, bandaging one 20 of them. As the curtain rises we hear the sound of a siren off right. Everyone turns and looks—that is, everyone who is conscious.*

LINDSTROM. Here's another batch, Mister Roberts—a whole paddy wagon full. And this one's an Army paddy wagon.

ROBERTS. We haven't filed away this batch yet. (*To* DOC.) Hurry up, Doc. 30

JOHNSON (*to* DOC, *indicating the body he is carrying*). Where do we put number twenty-three here, Doc? Sick bay or what?

DOC. Just put him to bed. His condition's only critical.

JOHNSON (*carrying the* SEAMAN *off*). They just roll out of their bunks, Doc. Now I'm stacking 'em on the deck down there—I'm on the third layer already. 40

VOICE (*off stage*). Okay, Lieutenant! All set down here! You ready?

ROBERTS. (*calling off stage—and giving a hand signal*). Okay! (*To* DOC.) Here they come, Doc! Heads up!

SHORE PATROLMAN'S VOICE (*off stage*). Lieutenant!

ROBERTS. Oh, not you again!

SHORE PATROLMAN'S VOICE (*off stage*). I got a bunch of real beauties for you this time.

ROBERTS (*calling off stage*). Can they walk?

SHORE PATROLMAN'S VOICE (*off stage*). Just barely!

ROBERTS (*calling*). Then send 'em up.

LINDSTROM. Man, oh man, what a liberty! We got the record now, Mister Roberts! This makes the seventh batch since we went on watch!

[*The sound of a cargo winch and a voice off stage singing the Army Air Corps song are heard.* ROBERTS *is looking off stage.*]

ROBERTS (*signaling*). Looks like a real haul this time. Schlemmer, look out!

LINDSTROM. Schlemmer, look out!

ROBERTS. Okay, Doc. (DOC *and* ROBERTS *lift the two bodies from the hatch cover and deposit them farther upstage. At this moment, the cargo net appears, loaded with bodies in once-white uniforms, and leis. Riding on top of the net is* SCHLEMMER, *wearing a lei and singing "Off We Go into the Wild Blue Yonder."*) Let her in easy . . .

LINDSTROM. Let her in easy . . .

[*The net is lowered onto the hatch cover and* LINDSTROM *detaches it from the hook. All start untangling bodies.*]

ROBERTS. Well, they're peaceful anyhow.

[*At this point a* SHORE PATROLMAN *enters from the gangway.*]

SHORE PATROLMAN (*handing* ROBERTS *a sheaf of yellow slips*). For your collection. (*Points down the gangway.*) Take a look at them.

ROBERTS (*looks off stage*). My God, what did they do?

SHORE PATROLMAN. They done all right,

Lieutenant. Six of them busted into a formal dance and took on a hundred and twenty-eight Army bastards. (*Calls off.*) All right, let's go!

[STEFANOWSKI, REBER, WILEY, PAYNE, *and* MANNION, *with his arm around* IN-SIGNA, *straggle on—a frightening sight—followed by a* MILITARY POLICEMAN. INSIGNA'S *uniform is torn to shreds.* MAN-NION *is clad in a little diaper of crepe* paper. *All have bloody faces and uniforms. A few bear souvenirs—a Japanese lan-tern, leis, Army caps, a Shore Patrol band, etc. They throw perfunctory salutes to the colors, then murmur a greeting to* ROBERTS.]

MILITARY POLICEMAN. Duty officer?

ROBERTS. That's right.

MILITARY POLICEMAN (*salutes*). Colonel Middleton presents his compliments to the Captain and wishes him to know that these men made a sham-bles out of the Colonel's testimonial dinner-dance.

ROBERTS. Is this true, Insigna?

INSIGNA. That's right, Mister Roberts. A shambles. (*To* MANNION.) Ain't that right, Killer?

MANNION. That's right, Mister Roberts.

ROBERTS. You men crashed a dance for Army personnel?

MANNION. Yes, sir! And they made us feel unwelcome! (*To* INSIGNA.) Didn't they, Slugger?

ROBERTS. Oh, they started a fight, eh?

WILEY. No, sir! *We* started it!

STEFANOWSKI. We finished it too! (*To* MILITARY POLICEMAN.) Tell Mister Roberts how many of you Army bas-tards are in the hospital.

MANNION. Go on.

MILITARY POLICEMAN. Thirty-eight sol-diers of the United States Army have been hospitalized. And the Colonel himself has a very bad bruise on his left shin!

PAYNE. *I* did that, Mister Roberts.

MILITARY POLICEMAN. And that isn't all, Lieutenant. There were young ladies present—fifty of them. Colonel Mid-dleton had been lining them up for a month, from the finest families of Elysium. And he had personally guar-anteed their safety this evening. Well, sir . . .

ROBERTS. Well?

MILITARY POLICEMAN. Two of those young ladies got somewhat mauled, one actually got a black eye, six of them got their clothes torn off and then went screaming off into the night and they haven't been heard from since. What are you going to do about it, Lieutenant?

ROBERTS. Well, I'm due to get relieved here in fifteen minutes—I'll be glad to lead a search party.

MILITARY POLICEMAN. No, sir. The Army's taking care of that end. The Colonel will want to know what pun-ishment you're going to give these men.

ROBERTS. Tell the Colonel that I'm sure our Captain will think of some-thing.

MILITARY POLICEMAN. But . . .

ROBERTS. That's all, Sergeant.

MILITARY POLICEMAN (*salutes*). Thank you, sir. (*He goes off.*)

SHORE PATROLMAN. Lieutenant, I been pretty sore at your guys up till now —we had to put on ten extra Shore Patrolmen on account of this ship. But if you knew Colonel "Chicken" Middleton—well, I'd be willing to do this every night. (*To the men.*) So long, fellows!

[*The men call "So long."* SHORE PATROL-MAN *exits, saluting* ROBERTS *and the quarter-deck.*]

ROBERTS. Well, what've you got to say for yourselves?

STEFANOWSKI (*after a moment*). Okay if we go ashore again, Mister Roberts?

ROBERTS (*to* LINDSTROM). Is this the first time for these guys?

LINDSTROM (*showing the log*). Yes, sir, they got a clean record—they only been brought back once.

ROBERTS. What do you say, Doc?

[*The men turn eagerly to* DOC.]

DOC. Anybody got a fractured skull?

MEN. No.

DOC. Okay, you pass the physical.

ROBERTS. Go down and take a shower first and get into some clothes.

[*The men rush to the hatchway.*]

STEFANOWSKI. We still got time to get back to that dance!

[*As they descend hatchway,* INSIGNA *pulls the crepe paper from around* MANNION *as he is halfway down the hatchway.*]

ROBERTS. How you feeling, Doc?

DOC. These alcohol fumes are giving me a cheap drunk—otherwise pretty routine. When do you get relieved, Doug? (*Takes a box from the table and gestures for the men to remove the table. They carry it off.*)

ROBERTS. Soon as Carney gets back from the island. Any minute now.

DOC. What are you grinning like a skunk for?

ROBERTS. Nothing. I always grin like a skunk. What have you got in the box?

DOC (*descending the hatchway—holding up a small packet he has taken from the box*). Little favors from the Doc. I'm going to put one in each man's hand and when he wakes up he'll find pinned to his shirt full instructions for its use. I think it'll save me a lot of work later on. (*His head disappears.*)

LINDSTROM. I wish Gerhart would get back here and relieve me. I've got to get over to that island before it runs out of women.

[DOLAN *enters from the gangway.*]

DOLAN. Howdy, Mister Roberts! I'm drunk as a goat! (*Pulls a goat aboard.*)

Show him how drunk I am. Mister Roberts, when I first saw her she was eatin', and you know, she just eat her way into my heart. She was eatin' a little old palm tree and I thought to myself, our ship needs a mascot. (*He points out the palm tree to the goat.*) There you are, kid. Chow!

[ROBERTS *blocks his way.*]

ROBERTS. Wait a minute . . . wait a minute. What's her name?

DOLAN. I don't know, sir.

ROBERTS. She's got a name plate.

DOLAN. Oh, so she has . . . her name is . . . (*Reads from the tag on the goat's collar.*) . . . Property Of.

ROBERTS. What's her last name?

DOLAN. Her last name . . . (*Reads again.*) . . . Rear Admiral Wentworth.

[*An approaching siren is heard off stage.*]

ROBERTS. Okay, Dolan, hit the sack. I'll take care of her.

DOLAN. Okay, Mister Roberts. (*Descends the hatchway.*) See that she gets a good square meal.

[*He points to the* CAPTAIN's *palm tree and winks, then disappears.* GERHART *enters from the gangway.*]

LINDSTROM. Gerhart!

[LINDSTROM *frantically removes his web belt and shoves it at* GERHART.]

GERHART. Okay, okay—you're relieved.

LINDSTROM (*tosses a fast salute to* ROBERTS *and says in one breath*): Requestpermissiontogoashore! (*He hurries down the gangway.*)

[*A* SHORE PATROLMAN *enters from the gangway.*]

SHORE PATROLMAN. Lieutenant, has one of your men turned up with a . . . (*Sees the goat and takes the leash.*) Oh, thanks. (*To the goat.*) Come on, come on, your papa over there is worried about you. (*Pulls the goat down the gangway.*)

GERHART. Where's your relief, Mister Roberts?

ROBERTS (*sitting on the hatch*). He'll be along any minute. How was your liberty, Gerhart?

[GERHART *grins. So does* ROBERTS. DOC *enters from the hatchway*.]

DOC. What are you looking so cocky about anyway?

ROBERTS. Am I looking cocky? Maybe 10 it's because for the first time since I've been on this ship I'm seeing a crew.

DOC. What do you think you've been living with all this time?

ROBERTS. Just a hundred and sixty-seven separate guys. There's a big difference, Doc. Now these guys are bound together. You saw Insigna and Mannion. Doc, I think these guys are 20 strong enough now to take all the miserable, endless days ahead of us. I only hope I'm strong enough.

DOC. Doug, tomorrow you and I are going over there and take advantage of the groundwork that's been laid tonight. You and I are going to have ourselves a liberty.

[PULVER *enters slowly from the gangway and walks across the stage.* DOC *calls* 30 ROBERTS' *attention to him*.]

ROBERTS. Hello, Frank. How was your liberty?

[PULVER *half turns, shrugs, and holds up seven fingers, then exits. A* SHORE PATROL OFFICER *enters from the gangway and calls off stage. He speaks with a Southern accent*.]

SHORE PATROL OFFICER. That's your post and that's your post. You know 40 what to do. (*He salutes the quarter-deck, then* ROBERTS.) Officer of the deck? (ROBERTS *nods. The* SHORE PATROL OFFICER *hesitates a moment*.) I hope you don't mind, but I've stationed two of my men at the foot of the gangway.

I'm sorry, but this ship is restricted for the rest of its stay in Elysium. Your Captain is to report to the Island Commander at seven o'clock this morning. I'd recommend that he's there on time. The Admiral's a pretty tough cookie when he's mad, and he's madder now than I've ever seen him.

ROBERTS. What in particular did this?

SHORE PATROL LIEUTENANT. A little while ago six men from your ship broke into the home of the French Consul and started throwing things through the plate-glass living-room window. We found some of the things on the lawn: a large world globe, a small love seat, a lot of books, and a bust of Balzac—the French writer. We also found an Army private first class who was unconscious at the time. He claims they threw him too.

ROBERTS. Through the window?

SHORE PATROL LIEUTENANT. That's right! It seems he took them there for a little joke. He didn't tell them it was the Consul's house; he said it was a—what we call in Alabama—a cathouse. (ROBERTS *and* DOC *nod*.) Be sure that your Captain is there at seven o'clock sharp. If it makes you feel any better, Admiral Wentworth says this is the worst ship he's ever seen in his entire naval career. (*Laughs, then salutes*.) Good night, Lieutenant.

ROBERTS (*returning the salute*). Good night.

[*The* SHORE PATROL LIEUTENANT *exits down the gangway—saluting the quarter-deck*.]

GERHART. Well, there goes the liberty. That was sure a wham-bam-thank you, ma'am!

DOC. Good night. (*He exits through the left passageway*.)

GERHART. But by God it was worth it. That liberty was worth anything!

ROBERTS. I think you're right, Gerhart.

GERHART. Hunh?

ROBERTS. I think you're right.

GERHART. Yeah.

[*He smiles.* ROBERTS *looks over the log.* GERHART *whistles softly to himself "Roll Me Over" as the lights slowly fade out.*]

[*During the darkness we hear* JOHNSON *shouting:*]

JOHNSON. All right, fall in for muster. Form two ranks. And pipe down.

SCENE II

The lights come up, revealing the deck. Morning sunlight. A group of men, right and left, in orderly formation. They are talking.

JOHNSON. 'Ten-shun!

[*The command is relayed through the ship. The* CAPTAIN *enters from his cabin, followed by* ROBERTS. *The* CAPTAIN *steps up on the hatch cover.* ROBERTS *starts to fall in with the men.*]

CAPTAIN (*calling to* ROBERTS *and pointing to a place beside himself on the hatch cover*). Over here, Roberts. (ROBERTS *takes his place at the left of the* CAPTAIN.) We're being kicked out of this port. I had a feeling this liberty was a bad idea. That's why we'll never have one again. We're going to erase this blot from my record if we have to work twenty-four hours a day. We're going to move even more cargo than we've ever moved before. And if there ain't enough cargo work, Mister Roberts here is gonna find some. Isn't that right, Mister Roberts? (ROBERTS *doesn't answer.*) Isn't that right, Mister Roberts?

ROBERTS. Yes, sir.

CAPTAIN. I'm appointing Mister Roberts here and now to see that you men toe the line. And I can't think of a more honorable man for the job. He's a man who keeps his word no matter what. (*Turns to* ROBERTS.) Now, Roberts, if you do a good job —and if the Admiral begins to smile on us again—there might be something in it for you. What would you say if that little silver bar on your collar got a twin brother some day? (ROBERTS *is startled. The* CAPTAIN *calls off stage.*) Officer of the deck!

OFF STAGE VOICE. Yes, sir!

CAPTAIN (*to* ROBERTS). You wasn't expectin' that, was you? (*Calling off stage.*) Get ready to sail!

OFF STAGE VOICE. Aye aye, sir!

CAPTAIN. You men are dismissed!

JOHNSON. Fall out!

[*The men fall out. Some exit. A little group forms downstage.*]

CAPTAIN. Wait a minute! Wait a minute! Roberts, take these men here back aft to handle lines. And see that they work up a sweat. (ROBERTS *and the men look at him.*) Did you hear me, Roberts? I gave you an order!

ROBERTS (*carefully*). Yes, Captain. I heard you.

CAPTAIN. How do you answer when I give an order?

ROBERTS (*after a pause*). Aye aye, sir.

CAPTAIN. That's more like it . . . that's more like it! (*He exits into his cabin.*)

STEFANOWSKI. What'd he mean, Mister Roberts?

ROBERTS. I don't know. Just what he said, I guess.

GERHART. What'd you let him give you all that guff for?

DOLAN (*stepping up on the hatch, carrying a file folder*). Because he's tired, that's why. He had the mid-watch last night. Your tail'd be dragging too if you had to handle all them customers.

ROBERTS. Come on. Let's get going. . . .

DOLAN. Wait a minute, Mister Roberts. Something come for you in the mail this morning—a little love letter from the Bureau. (*Pulls out a paper from the file folder.*) Get a load of this! (*Reads.*) "To All Ships and Stations: Heightened war offensive has created urgent need aboard combat ships for experienced officers. (*He clicks his teeth and* 10 *winks at* ROBERTS.) All commanding officers are hereby directed to forward with their endorsements all applications for transfer from officers with twenty-four months' sea duty." (ROBERTS *grabs the directive and reads it.* DOLAN *looks at* ROBERTS *and smiles.*) You got twenty-nine months—you're the only officer aboard that has. Mister Roberts, the Old Man is hanging 20 on the ropes from the working-over the Admiral give him. All he needs to flatten him is one more little jab. And here it is. Your letter. I typed it up. (*He pulls out a triplicate letter from the file cover—then a fountain pen, which he offers to* ROBERTS.) Sign it and I'll take it in——

MANNION. Go on, sign it, Mister Roberts. He'll take off like a bird.   30

DOLAN. What're you waitin' for, Mister Roberts?

ROBERTS (*handing the directive back to* DOLAN). I'll want to look it over first, Dolan. Come on, let's get going.

DOLAN. There's nothing to look over. This is the same letter we wrote yesterday—only quoting this new directive.

ROBERTS. Look, Dolan, I'm tired. And 40 I told you I wanted——

DOLAN. You ain't too tired to sign your name!

ROBERTS (*sharply*). Take it easy, Dolan. I'm not going to sign it. So take it easy! (*Turns to exit right, finds himself blocked by the crew.*) Did you hear me? Let's get going! (*Exits.*)

STEFANOWSKI. What the hell's come over him?

[*They look at one another.*]

INSIGNA. Aye aye, sir—for Christ's sake!

MANNION (*after a moment*). Come on. Let's get going.

DOLAN (*bitterly*). "Take it easy . . . take it easy!"

[*The men start to move off slowly as the lights fade out.*]

[*During the darkness we hear a radio. There is considerable static.*]

AMERICAN BROADCASTER. Still, of course, we have no official word from the Headquarters of the Supreme Allied Command in Europe. I repeat, there is no official announcement yet. The report that the war in Europe has ended has come from only one correspondent. It has not been confirmed by other correspondents or by SHAEF headquarters. But here is one highly intriguing fact—that report has not been denied either in Washington or in SHAEF headquarters in Europe. *It has not been denied.* Right now in those places the newsmen are crowded, waiting to flash to the world the announcement of V-E Day.

SCENE III

The lights come up on ROBERTS' *and* PULVER'S *cabin.* DOC, *at the desk, and* PULVER, *up in his bunk, are listening to the radio.*

PULVER. Turn that damn thing off, Doc. Has Doug ever said anything to you about wanting a promotion?

DOC. Of course not. I doubt if he's even conscious of what rank he is.

PULVER. You can say that again!

DOC. I doubt if he's even conscious of what rank he is.

PULVER. That's what I said. He doesn't even think about a promotion. The only thing he thinks about is the war news—up in the radio shack two weeks now—all day long—listening with a headset, reading all the bulletins. . . . Anyone who says he's bucking for another stripe is a dirty liar.

DOC. Who says he is, Frank?

PULVER. Insigna, Mannion, and some 10 of the other guys. I heard them talking outside the porthole. They were talking loud on purpose so I could hear them—they must've guessed I was lying here on my bunk. What's happened to Doug anyway, Doc?

DOC. How would I know! He's spoken about ten words to me in as many days. But I'm damn well going to find out.

PULVER. He won't talk, Doc. This morning I followed him all around the room while he was shaving. I begged him to talk to me. I says, "You're a fellow who needs a friend and here I am." And I says, "What's all this trouble you're having with the crew? You tell me and I'll fix it up like that." And then I give him some real good advice—I says, "Keep 30 your chin up," and things like that. And then do you know what he did? He walked out of the room just as though I wasn't here.

[*There is a knock on the door.*]

DOC. Come in.

[DOWDY *enters.*]

DOWDY. Doc, Mister Pulver—could we see you officers a minute?

DOC. Sure. (GERHART *and* LINDSTROM 40 *enter, closing the door.*) What is it?

DOWDY. Tell them what happened, Gerhart.

GERHART. Well, sir, I sure don't like to say this but . . . Mister Roberts just put Dolan on report.

LINDSTROM. Me and Gerhart seen him.

PULVER. On report!

GERHART. Yes, sir. Tomorrow morning Dolan has to go up before the Captain—on account of Mister Roberts.

LINDSTROM. On account of Mister Roberts.

GERHART. And we was wondering if you officers could get him to take Dolan off report before . . . well, before . . .

DOC. Before what, Gerhart?

GERHART. Well, you see, the guys are all down in the compartment, talking about it. And they're saying some pretty rough things about Mister Roberts. Nobody just ever expected to see him put a man on report and . . .

20 LINDSTROM. He ain't gonna turn out to be like an officer, is he, Doc?

DOWDY. Lindstrom . . .

LINDSTROM. Oh, I didn't mean you, Doc . . . or even you, Mister Pulver!

DOC. That's all right, Lindstrom. What was this trouble with Dolan?

DOWDY. This letter business again!

GERHART. Yes, sir. Dolan was just kiddin' him about not sending in any more letters. And all of a sudden Mister Roberts turned just white and yelled, "Shut up, Dolan. Shut your goddamn mouth. I've had enough." And Dolan naturally got snotty back at him and Mister Roberts put him right on report.

LINDSTROM. Right on report.

[ROBERTS *enters.*]

PULVER. Hello, Doug boy. Aren't you listening to the war news?

DOWDY. All right, Doctor. We'll get that medical storeroom cleaned out tomorrow.

[DOWDY, GERHART, *and* LINDSTROM *leave.*]

PULVER. We thought you were up in the radio shack.

ROBERTS (*to* PULVER). Don't you want to go down to the wardroom and have a cup of coffee?

PULVER (*jumping down from the bunk*). Sure. I'll go with you.

ROBERTS. I don't want any. Why don't you go ahead?

PULVER. Nah. (*He sits back on the bunk. There is another little pause.*)

ROBERTS. Will you go on out anyway? I want to talk to Doc.

PULVER (*rising and crossing to the door*). All right, I will. I'm going for a cup of coffee. (*Stops, turns, and gets his cap from the top of the locker.*) No! I'm going up to the radio shack. You aren't the only one interested in the war news. (*He exits.*)

ROBERTS (*with emotion*). Doc, transfer me, will you? (DOC *looks at him.*) Transfer me to the hospital on this next island! You can do it. You don't need the Captain's approval! Just put me ashore for examination—say there's something wrong with my eyes or my feet or my head, for Christ's sake! You can trump up something!

DOC. What good would that do?

ROBERTS. Plenty! I could lie around that hospital for a couple of weeks. The ship would have sailed—I'd have missed it! I'd be off this ship. Will you do it, Doc?

DOC. Doug, why did you put Dolan on report just now?

ROBERTS (*angrily*). I gave him an order and he didn't carry it out fast enough to suit me. (*Glares at* DOC, *who just studies him.* ROBERTS *rises and paces at right.*) No, that's not true. It was the war. I just heard the news. The war was ending and I couldn't get to it and there was Dolan giving me guff about something—and all of a sudden I hated him. I hated all of them. I was sick of the sullen bastards staring at me as though I'd sold them down the river or something. If they think I'm bucking for a promotion—if they're stupid enough to think I'd walk ten feet across the room to get anything from that Captain, then I'm through with the whole damn ungrateful mob!

DOC. Does this crew owe you something?

ROBERTS. What the hell do you mean by that?

DOC. You talk as if they did.

[ROBERTS *rises and crosses to his bunk.*]

ROBERTS (*quietly*). That's exactly how I'm talking. I didn't realize it but that's exactly the way I've been feeling. Oh Jesus, that shows you how far gone I am, Doc. I've been taking something out on them. I've been blaming them for something that . . .

DOC. What, Doug? Something what? You've made some sort of an agreement with the Captain, haven't you, Doug!

ROBERTS (*turns*). Agreement? I don't know what you mean. Will you transfer me, Doc?

DOC. Not a chance, Doug. I could never get away with it—you know that.

ROBERTS. Oh, my God!

PULVER (*off stage*). Doug! Doc! (*Entering.*) Listen to the radio, you uninformed bastards! Turn it up!

[ROBERTS *reaches over and turns up the radio. The excited voice of an announcer can be heard.*]

ANNOUNCER. . . . this broadcast to bring you a special news flash! The war is over in Europe! *The war is over in Europe!* (ROBERTS *grasps* DOC's *arm in excitement.*) Germany has surrendered unconditionally to the Allied Armies. The surrender was signed in a schoolhouse in the city of Rheims . . .

[ROBERTS *stands staring.* DOC *turns off the radio. For a moment there is silence, then:*]

DOC. I would remind you that there's still a minor skirmish here in the Pacific.

ROBERTS. I'll miss that one too. But to hell with me. This is the greatest day in the world. We're going to celebrate. How about it, Frank?

PULVER. Yeah, Doug. We've got to celebrate! 10

DOC (*starting to pull the alcohol from the wastebasket*). What'll it be—alcohol and orange juice or orange juice and alcohol?

ROBERTS. No, that's not good enough.

PULVER. Hell no, Doc! (*He looks expectantly at* ROBERTS.)

ROBERTS. We've got to think of something that'll lift this ship right out of 20 the water and turn it around the other way.

[PULVER *suddenly rises to his feet.*]

PULVER (*shouting*). Doug! Oh, my God, why didn't I think of this before! Doug! Doc! You're going to blow your tops when you hear the idea I got! Oh Jesus, what a wonderful idea! It's the only thing to do. It's the only thing in the whole world to 30 do! That's all! Doug, you said I never had any ideas. You said I never finished anything I started. Well, you're wrong—tonight you're wrong! I thought of something and I finished it. I was going to save it for your birthday, but I'm going to give it to you tonight, because we gotta celebrate . . .

ROBERTS (*waves his hands in* PULVER's *face* 40 *for attention*). Wait a minute, Frank! What is it?

PULVER. A firecracker, by God. (*He reaches under his mattress and pulls out a large, wobbly firecracker which has been painted red.*) We're gonna throw a firecracker under the Old Man's bunk. Bam-bam-bam! Wake up, you old son of a bitch, IT'S V-E DAY!

ROBERTS (*rising*). Frank!

PULVER. Look at her, Doc. Ain't it a beauty? Ain't that the greatest handmade, hand-painted, hand-packed firecracker you ever saw?

ROBERTS (*smiling and taking the firecracker*). Yes, Frank. That's the most beautiful firecracker I ever saw in my life. But will it work?

PULVER. Sure it'll work. At least, I think so.

ROBERTS. Haven't you tested it? It's got to work, Frank, it's just got to work!

PULVER. I'll tell you what I'll do. I'll take it down to the laundry and test it—that's my laboratory, the laundry. I got all the fixings down there—powder, fuses, everything, all hid behind the soapflakes. And if this one works, I can make another one in two minutes.

ROBERTS. Okay, Frank. Take off. We'll wait for you here. (PULVER *starts off.*) Be sure you got enough to make it loud. What'd you use for powder?

PULVER. Loud! This ain't a popgun. This is a firecracker. I used fulminate of mercury. I'll be right back. (*He runs out.*)

ROBERTS. Fulminate of mercury! That stuff's murder! Do you think he means it?

DOC (*taking the alcohol bottle from the wastebasket*). Of course not. Where could he get fulminate of mercury?

ROBERTS. I don't know. He's pretty resourceful. Where did he get the clap last year?

DOC. How about a drink, Doug? (*He pours alcohol and orange juice into two glasses.*)

ROBERTS. Right! Doc, I been living with a genius. This makes it all worth while—the whole year and a half he spent in his bunk. How else could you celebrate V-E Day? A firecracker under the Old Man's bunk! The silly little son of a bitch!

DOC (*handing* ROBERTS *a drink*). Here you are, Doug. (DOC *holds the drink up in a toast.*) To better days!

ROBERTS. Okay. And to a great American, Frank Thurlowe Pulver . . . Soldier . . . Statesman . . . Scientist . . .

DOC. Friend of the Working Girl . . .

[*Suddenly there is a tremendous explosion.* DOC *and* ROBERTS *clutch at the desk.*]

ROBERTS. Oh my God!

DOC. He wasn't kidding! That's fulminate of mercury!

CAPTAIN (*off stage*). What was that?

[ROBERTS *and* DOC *rush to the porthole, listening.*]

JOHNSON (*off stage*). I don't know, Captain. I'll find out!

[*We hear the sounds of running feet.*]

ROBERTS. Doc, we've got to go down and get him.

DOC. This may be pretty bad, Doug.

[*They turn to start for the door when suddenly a figure hurtles into the room and stops. For a moment it looks like a combination scarecrow and snowman, but it is* PULVER—*his uniform tattered; his knees, arms, and face blackened; he is covered with soapsuds and his eyes are shining with excitement.* ROBERTS *stares in amazement.*]

PULVER. Jeez, that stuff's terrific!

DOC. Are you all right?

PULVER. I'm great! Gee, you should've been there!

ROBERTS. You aren't burned—or anything?

PULVER. Hell no. But the laundry's kinda beat up. The mangle's on the other side of the room now. And there's a new porthole on the star-board side where the electric iron went through. And I guess a steam line must've busted or something— I was up to my neck in lather. And soapflakes flyin' around—it was absolutely beautiful!

[*During these last lines,* DOC *has been making a brisk, professional examination.*]

DOC. It's a miracle. He isn't even scratched!

PULVER. Come on down and see it, Doug. It's a Winter Wonderland!

CAPTAIN (*off stage*). Johnson!

ROBERTS. Quiet!

JOHNSON (*off stage*). Yes, sir.

CAPTAIN (*off stage*). What was it?

JOHNSON (*off stage*). The laundry, Captain. A steam line must've blew up.

PULVER (*explaining*). Steam line came right out of the bulkhead. (*He demonstrates.*) Whish!

CAPTAIN (*off stage*). How much damage?

JOHNSON (*off stage*). We can't tell yet, Captain. We can't get in there—the passageway is solid soapsuds.

PULVER. Solid soapsuds. (*He pantomimes walking blindly through soapsuds.*)

CAPTAIN (*off stage*). Tell those men to be more careful.

ROBERTS (*excitedly*). Frank, our celebration is just getting started. The night is young and our duty's clear.

PULVER. Yeah? What're we gonna do now, Doug?

ROBERTS. Get cleaned up and come with me.

PULVER. Where we goin' now, Doug?

ROBERTS. We're going down and get the rest of your stuff. You proved it'd work—you just hit the wrong target, that's all. We're going to make another firecracker, and put it where it really belongs.

PULVER (*who has slowly wilted during* ROBERTS' *speech*). The rest of my stuff was—in the laundry, Doug. It all went up. There isn't any more. I'm sorry, Doug. I'm awful sorry.

ROBERTS (*sinks into a chair*). That's all right, Frank.

PULVER. Maybe I can scrounge some more tomorrow.

ROBERTS. Sure.

PULVER. You aren't sore at me, are you, Doug?

ROBERTS. What for?   10

PULVER. For spoilin' our celebration?

ROBERTS. Of course not.

PULVER. It was a good idea though, wasn't it, Doug?

ROBERTS. Frank, it was a great idea. I'm proud of you. It just didn't work, that's all. (*He starts for the door.*)

DOC. Where are you going, Doug?

ROBERTS. Out on deck.

PULVER. Wait'll I get cleaned up and 20 I'll come with you.

ROBERTS. No, I'm going to turn in after that. (*To* PULVER.) It's okay, Frank. (*He exits.*)

[PULVER *turns pleadingly to* DOC.]

PULVER. He was happy there for a minute, though, wasn't he, Doc? Did you see him laughing? He was happy as hell. (*Pause.*) We gotta do something for that guy, Doc. He's in bad shape. 30 What's the matter with him anyhow, Doc. Did you find out?

DOC. No, he wouldn't tell me. But I know one thing he's feeling tonight, and that's panic. Tonight he feels his war is dying before he can get to it. (DOC *goes to the radio and turns up volume.*)

PULVER. I let him down. He wanted to celebrate and I let him down. (*He drops his head.*)

[ANNOUNCER'S VOICE *on radio comes up as the lights fade out.*]

[*During the darkness and under the first part of Scene IV we hear the voice of a British broadcaster:*]

BRITISH BROADCASTER. . . . we hope that the King and the Queen will come out. The crowds are cheering—listen to them—and at any second now we hope to see Their Majesties. The color here is tremendous—everywhere rosettes, everywhere gay, red-white-and-blue hats. All the girls in their summer frocks on this lovely, mild, historic May evening. And although we celebrate with joyous heart the great victory, perhaps the greatest victory in the history of mankind, the underlying mood is a mood of thanksgiving. And now, I believe, they're coming. They haven't appeared, but the crowd in the center are cheering madly. Handkerchiefs, flags, hands waving—*Here they come!* First, Her Majesty the Queen, has come into view. Then the King in the uniform of an Admiral of the Fleet. The two Princesses standing on the balcony—listen to the crowd—— (*Sound of wild cheering.*)

[*This broadcast continues throughout the blackout and the next scene. Several times the station is changed, from a broadcast of the celebration in San Francisco to the speaker in New York and the band playing "The Stars and Stripes Forever" in Times Square.*]

SCENE IV

The lights dim up on the main set. It is a few minutes later, and bright moonlight. The ship is under way—this is indicated by the apparent movement of the stars, slowly up and down. A group of men are sitting on the hatch cover in a late bull session. They are INSIGNA, MANNION, DOLAN, *and* STEFANOWSKI. GERHART *stands over them; he has obviously just returned from some mission for the group.*

GERHART. I'm telling you, that's all it was. A steam pipe busted in the laundry—they're cleaning it up now. It ain't worth going to see.

[*The others make way for him and he sits down beside them.* INSIGNA *cocks his head toward the sound of the radio.*]

INSIGNA. What the hell's all that jabbering on the radio now?

MANNION. I don't know. Something about the King and Queen . . .

[*The men listen for a moment without curi-* 10 *osity; then, as the radio fades, they settle back in indolent positions.*]

INSIGNA. Well, anyhow, like I was telling you, this big sergeant in Elysium was scared to fight me! Tell 'em how big he was, Killer.

MANNION. Six foot seven or eight . . .

STEFANOWSKI. That sergeant's grown eight inches since we left Elysium. . . . Did you see me when I swiped 20 that Shore Patrol band and went around arresting guys? That Shore Patrol Lieutenant said I was the best man he had. I arrested forty-three guys. . . .

MANNION (*smiles at* DOLAN, *who is looking depressed*). Come on, Dolan, don't let him get you down.

INSIGNA. Yeah, come on, Dolan.

[ROBERTS *enters. He looks at the men, who* 30 *have their backs turned, hesitates, then goes slowly over to them.*]

GERHART (*idly*). What was them croquette things we had for chow tonight?

[STEFANOWSKI *looks up and notices* ROBERTS. *Instantly he sits upright.*]

STEFANOWSKI. Flash Red!

[*The men sit up. There is an embarrassed silence.*] 40

ROBERTS. Good evening. (*The men smile politely.* ROBERTS *is very embarrassed.*) Did you hear the news? The war's over in Europe.

MANNION (*smiling*). Yes, sir. We heard.

STEFANOWSKI (*helping out the conversation*).

Sure. Maybe somebody'll get on the ball out here now. . . .

[DOLAN *rises, starts down the hatchway.*]

ROBERTS. Dolan, I guess I kind of blew my top tonight. I'm sorry. I'm taking you off report.

DOLAN. Whatever you want, sir. . . . (*He looks ostentatiously at his watch and yawns.*) Well, I guess I'll hit the old sack. . . . (*He goes down the hatchway.*)

MANNION. Yeah, me too . . .

INSIGNA. Yeah . . .

GERHART. It's late as hell.

STEFANOWSKI. I didn't realize how late it was. . . .

[*All the men get up, then go down the hatchway.* ROBERTS *stands looking after them. Now the radio is heard again.* ROBERTS *goes to the hatchway and sits listening.*]

SPEAKER. . . . Our boys have won this victory today. But the rest is up to you. You and you alone must recognize our enemies: the forces of ambition, cruelty, arrogance and stupidity. You must recognize them, you must destroy them, you must tear them out as you would a malignant growth! And cast them from the surface of the earth!

[*The end of the speech is followed by a band playing "The Stars and Stripes Forever."* ROBERTS' *face lights up and a new determination is in it. He repeats the words "malignant growth." The band music swells. He marches to the palm tree, salutes it, rubs his hands together, and as the music reaches a climax, he jerks the palm tree, earth and all, from the container and throws it over the side. Then, as the music continues, loud and climactic, he brushes his hands together, shrugs, and walks casually off left singing the tune to himself.*

[*For a moment the stage is empty. Then the lights go up in the* CAPTAIN'S *cabin. The door to the* CAPTAIN'S *cabin opens and the* CAPTAIN *appears. He is in pajamas and* bathrobe, and in one hand he carries his watering can. He discovers the empty container. He looks at it, then plunges into his cabin. After a moment, the General Alarm is heard. It is a terrible clanging noise designed to rouse the dead. When the alarm stops, the CAPTAIN's voice is heard, almost hysterical, over the squawk box.]

CAPTAIN. General Quarters! General Quarters! Every man to his battle station on the double! 10

[JOHNSON, in helmet and life jacket, scurries from the hatchway into the CAPTAIN's cabin. WILEY enters from the right passageway and climbs into the right gun tub. Now men appear from all directions in various degrees of dress. The stage is filled with men frantically running everywhere, all wearing helmets and life preservers.]

INSIGNA (appearing from the hatchway). 20 What happened? (He runs up the ladder and into the left gun tub. PAYNE enters from the left and starts to climb up to the left gun tub.) Get the hell out of here, Payne. This ain't your gun—your gun's over there!

DOLAN (also trying to climb the ladder with PAYNE). Over there . . . over there . . .

[PAYNE crosses to the right gun tub.] 30

REBER (entering from the hatchway). What the hell happened?

SCHLEMMER. Are we in an air raid?

PAYNE. Submarine . . . must be a submarine!

GERHART. Hey, Wiley, what happened?

DOWDY (calling to someone on a life raft). Hey, get away from that life raft. He didn't say abandon ship! 40

[During the confusion, STEFANOWSKI, bewildered, emerges from the hatchway and wanders over to the right gun tub.)

STEFANOWSKI. Hey, Wiley, Wiley—you sure you're supposed to be up there?

WILEY. Yeah.

STEFANOWSKI (crossing to the left gun tub). Hey, Sam. Are you supposed to be up there?

INSIGNA. Yeah, we was here last year!

STEFANOWSKI. Hey, Dowdy. Where the hell's my battle station?

DOWDY. I don't know where your battle station is! Look around!

[STEFANOWSKI wanders aimlessly about. WILEY, in the gun tub right, is receiving reports of battle readiness from various parts of the ship.]

WILEY. Twenty-millimeters manned and ready. (Pause.) Engine room manned and ready. (Pause.) All battle stations manned and ready.

STEFANOWSKI (sitting on a corner of the hatch). Yeah, all but mine. . . .

JOHNSON'S VOICE (in the CAPTAIN's cabin). All battle stations manned and ready, Captain.

CAPTAIN'S VOICE. Give me that thing.

JOHNSON'S VOICE ("on mike"—that is, speaking directly into the squawk-box microphone; "off mike" means speaking unintentionally into this live microphone). Attention . . . Attention . . . The Captain wishes to . . .

CAPTAIN'S VOICE (off mike). Give me that thing! (On mike.) All right, who did it? Who did it? You're going to stay here all night until someone confesses. You're going to stay at those battle stations until hell freezes over until I find out who did it. It's an insult to the honor of this ship, by God! The symbol of our cargo record has been destroyed and I'm going to find out who did it if it takes all night! (Off mike.) Johnson, read me that muster list!

JOHNSON'S VOICE (reading the muster list off mike). Abernathy . . .

CAPTAIN'S VOICE. No, not Abernathy . . .

MANNION (against background of CAPTAIN's voice). Symbol of our cargo record? What the hell's that?

JOHNSON'S VOICE. Baker . . .

CAPTAIN'S VOICE. No . . .

[STEFANOWSKI *rises, sees the empty container, kneels, and ceremoniously bows to it.*]

DOWDY (*against background of* CAPTAIN'S *voice*). For God's sake, Stefanowski, find some battle station!

JOHNSON'S VOICE. Bartholomew . . . Becker . . . Billings . . . Carney . . . Daniels . . . Dexter . . . Ellison . . . Everman . . . Jenkins . . . Kelly . . . Kevin . . . Martin . . . Olsen . . . O'Neill . . .

[STEFANOWSKI *points to the empty container.* DOWDY *sees it and spreads the news to the men on the left.* SCHLEMMER *sees it and tells the other men. Now from all parts of the ship men enter and jubilantly look at the empty container. Bits of soil fly into the air as the men group around the empty can.*]

CAPTAIN'S VOICE. No, not O'Neill . . .

JOHNSON'S VOICE. Pulver . . .

CAPTAIN'S VOICE. No, not Pulver. He hasn't the guts . . .

JOHNSON'S VOICE. Roberts . . .

CAPTAIN'S VOICE (*roaring, off mike*). Roberts! He's the one! Get him up here!

JOHNSON'S VOICE (*on mike*). Mister Roberts will report to the Captain's cabin on the double!

[*The men rush back to their battle stations.*]

CAPTAIN'S VOICE. Get him up here, I tell you! Get him up here. . . .

JOHNSON'S VOICE (*on mike*). Mister Roberts will report to the Captain's cabin on the . . .

CAPTAIN (*off mike*). Give me that thing. (*On mike.*) Roberts, you get up here in a goddamn quick hurry. Get up here! Roberts, I'm giving you an order—get the lead out of your pants.

[ROBERTS *appears from the left passageway and, walking slowly, enters the* CAPTAIN'S *cabin. The men move on stage and* LINDSTROM *gets to a position on the ladder where he can look through the porthole of the* CAPTAIN'S *cabin.*]

ROBERTS' VOICE. Did you want to see me, Captain?

CAPTAIN'S VOICE. You did it. You did it. Don't lie to me. Don't stand there and lie to me. Confess it!

ROBERTS' VOICE. Confess what, Captain? I don't know what you're talking about.

CAPTAIN'S VOICE. You know damn well what I'm talkin' about because you did it. You've double-crossed me— you've gone back on your word!

ROBERTS' VOICE. No I haven't, Captain.

CAPTAIN. Yes, by God, you have. I kept my part of the bargain! I gave this crew liberty—I gave this crew liberty, by God, but you've gone back on *your* word.

[DOWDY *takes off his helmet and looks at the men.*]

ROBERTS' VOICE. I don't see how you can say that, Captain. I haven't sent in any more letters.

[DOLAN, *on the gun-tub ladder, catches* INSIGNA'S *eye.*]

CAPTAIN'S VOICE. I'm not talkin' about your goddamn sons-a-bitchin' letters. I'm talkin' about what you did tonight.

ROBERTS' VOICE. Tonight? I don't understand you, Captain. What do you think I did?

CAPTAIN. Quit saying that, goddammit, quit saying that. You know damn well what you did. You stabbed me in the back. You stabbed me in the back . . . aaa . . . aa . . .

JOHNSON'S VOICE. Captain! Get over to the washbasin, Captain!

CAPTAIN'S VOICE. Aaaaaaa . . .

INSIGNA. What the hell happened?

DOLAN. Quiet!

JOHNSON (*on mike*). Will the Doctor please report to the Captain's cabin on the double?

[DOC *appears from the left, pushing his way through the crowd, followed by two* MEDICAL CORPSMEN *wearing Red Cross brassards and carrying first-aid kits and a stretcher.* DOC *walks slowly; he is idly attaching a brassard and smoking a cigarette. He wears his helmet sloppily.*]

DOC. Gangway . . . gangway . . .

DOWDY. Hey, Doc, tell us what's going on.

DOC. Okay. Okay.

[*He enters the* CAPTAIN'S *cabin, followed by the* CORPSMEN, *who leave the stretcher leaning against the bulkhead. The door closes. There is a tense pause. The men gather around the cabin again.* LINDSTROM *is at the porthole.*]

REBER. Hey, Lindstrom, where's the Old Man?

LINDSTROM. He's sittin' in the chair—leaning way forward.

PAYNE. What's the Doc doin'?

LINDSTROM. He's holdin' the wastebasket.

REBER. What wastebasket?

LINDSTROM. The one the Old Man's got his head in. And he needs it too. (*Pause.*) They're helpin' him over to the couch. (*Pause.*) He's lying down there and they're takin' off his shoes. (*Pause.*) Look out, here they come.

[*The men break quickly and rush back to their battle stations. The door opens and* ROBERTS, DOC, *and the* CORPSMEN *come out.*]

DOC (*to the* CORPSMEN). We won't need that stretcher. Sorry. (*Calls.*) Dowdy! Come here.

[DOWDY *comes down to* DOC. *He avoids* ROBERTS' *eyes.*]

ROBERTS. Dowdy, pass the word to the crew to secure from General Quarters.

DOC. And tell the men not to make any noise while they go to their bunks. The Captain's resting quietly now, and I think that's desirable.

ROBERTS. Pass the word, will you, Dowdy?

DOWDY. Yes, Mister Roberts.

[*He passes the word to the crew, who slowly start to leave their battle stations. They are obviously stalling.*]

DOC (*to* ROBERTS). Got a cigarette? (ROBERTS *reaches into his pocket and offers* DOC *a cigarette. Then he lights* DOC's *cigarette.* DOC *notices the men stalling.*) Well, guess I'd better get back inside. I'll be down to see you after I get through.

[*He enters the cabin and stands there watching. The men move off stage, very slowly, saying "Good night, Mister Roberts," "Good night, sir." Suddenly* ROBERTS *notices that all the men are saying good night to him.*]

DOLAN (*quietly*). Good night, Mister Roberts. (ROBERTS *does not hear him.*) Good night, Mister Roberts.

ROBERTS. Good night, Dolan.

[DOLAN *smiles and exits down the hatch.* ROBERTS *steps toward the hatch, removes his helmet, looks puzzled as the lights fade out.*]

[*During the darkness, over the squawk box the following announcements are heard:*]

FIRST VOICE. Now hear this . . . Now hear this . . . C, E and S Divisions and all Pharmacist's Mates will air bedding today—positively!

SECOND VOICE. There is now available at the ship's store a small supply of peanut brittle. Ship's store will be open from 1300 to 1315.

THIRD VOICE. Now, Dolan, yeoman second class, report to the radio shack immediately.

SCENE V

The lights come up on the stateroom of ROBERTS *and* PULVER. PULVER *is lying in the lower bunk.* DOC *is sitting at the desk with a glass and a bottle of grain alcohol in front of him.* ROBERTS *is tying up a sea bag. A small suitcase stands beside it. His locker is open and empty.* WILEY *picks up the sea bags.*

WILEY. Okay, Mister Roberts. I'll take these down to the gangway. The boat from the island should be out here any minute for you. I'll let you know. 10

ROBERTS. Thanks, Wiley.

WILEY (*grinning*). That's okay, Mister Roberts. Never thought you'd be taking this ride, did you? (*He exits with the bags.*)

ROBERTS. I'm going to be off this bucket before I even wake up.

DOC. They flying you all the way to the *Livingston?*

ROBERTS. I don't know. The radio dis- 20 patch just said I was transferred and to travel by air if possible. I imagine it's all the way though. They're landing planes at Okinawa now, and that's where my can is probably running around. (*Laughs a little.*) Listen to me, Doc—my can!

PULVER (*studying the map by* ROBERTS' *bunk*). Okinawa! Jeez, you be might-y careful, Doug. 30

ROBERTS. Okay, Frank. This is *too* much to take, Doc. I even got a destroyer! The *Livingston!* That's one of the greatest cans out there.

PULVER. I know a guy on the *Livingston.* He don't think it's so hot.

DOLAN (*entering; he has a file folder under his arm*). Here you are, Mister Roberts. I typed up three copies of the radio dispatch. I've got to keep a copy 40 and here's two for you. You're now officially detached from this here bucket. Let me be the first.

ROBERTS. Thanks, Dolan. (*They shake hands.* ROBERTS *takes the papers and looks at them.*) Dolan, how about these

orders? I haven't sent in a letter for a month!

DOLAN (*carefully*). You know how the Navy works, Mister Roberts.

ROBERTS. Yeah, I know, but it doesn't seem . . .

DOLAN. Listen, Mister Roberts, I can tell you exactly what happened. Those guys at the Bureau need men for combat duty awful bad and they started looking through all the old letters and they just come across one of yours.

ROBERTS. Maybe—but still you'd think . . .

DOLAN. Listen, Mister Roberts. We can't stand here beating our gums! You better get cracking! You seen what it said there, "Proceed immediately." And the Old Man says if you ain't off of here in an hour, by God he's going to throw you off!

ROBERTS. Is that all he said?

DOLAN. That's all he said.

ROBERTS (*grinning at* DOC). After fighting this for two years you'd think he'd say more than that . . .

CAPTAIN'S VOICE (*off stage*). Be careful of that one. Put it down easy.

DOC. What's that?

DOLAN. A new enlarged botanical garden. That's why he can't even be bothered about you today, Mister Roberts. Soon as we anchored this morning he sent Olsen over with a special detail—they dug up two palm trees. . . . He's busy as a mother skunk now and you know what he's done—he's already set a twenty-four-hour watch on these new babies with orders to shoot to kill. (*To* PULVER.) That reminds me, Mister Pulver. The Captain wants to see you right away.

PULVER. Yeah? What about?

DOLAN. I don't know, sir. (*To* ROBERTS.) I'll be back to say good-by, Mister

Roberts. Come on, Mister Pulver. (*He exits.*)

PULVER (*following* DOLAN *out*). What the hell did I do with his laundry this week?

[ROBERTS *smiles as he starts putting on his black tie.*]

DOC. You're a happy son of a bitch, aren't you?

ROBERTS. Yep. You're happy about it too, aren't you, Doc?

DOC. I think it's the only thing for you. (*Casually.*) What do you think of the crew now, Doug?

ROBERTS. We're all right now. I think they're nice guys—all of them.

DOC. Unh-hunh. And how do you think they feel about you?

ROBERTS. I think they like me all right . . . till the next guy comes along.

DOC. You don't think you're necessary to them?

ROBERTS (*sitting on his bunk*). Hell no. No officer's necessary to the crew, Doc.

DOC. Are you going to leave this ship believing that?

ROBERTS. That's nothing against them. A crew's too busy looking after themselves to care about anyone else.

DOC. Well, take a good, deep breath, Buster. (*He drinks some alcohol.*) What do you think got you your orders? Prayer and fasting? Sending in enough Wheatie box tops?

ROBERTS. My orders? Why, what Dolan said—one of my old letters turned up . . .

DOC. Bat crap! This crew got you transferred. They were so busy looking out for themselves that they took a chance of landing in prison for five years—any one of them. Since you couldn't send in a letter for transfer, they sent one in for you. Since they knew the Captain wouldn't sign it

approved, they didn't bother him— they signed it for him.

ROBERTS. What do you mean? They forged the Captain's name?

DOC. That's right.

ROBERTS (*rising*). Doc! Who did? Which one of them?

DOC. That would be hard to say. You see, they had a mass meeting down in the compartment. They put guards at every door. They called it the Captain's Name Signing contest. And every man in this crew—a hundred and sixty-seven of them—signed the Captain's name on a blank sheet of paper. And then there were judges who compared these signatures with the Captain's and selected the one to go in. At the time there was some criticism of the decision on the grounds that the judges were drunk, but apparently, from the results, they chose well.

ROBERTS. How'd you find out about this, Doc?

DOC. Well, it was a great honor. I am the only officer aboard who does know. I was a contestant. I was also a judge. This double honor was accorded me because of my character, charm, good looks, and because the medical department contributed four gallons of grain alcohol to the contest. (*Pauses.*) It was quite a thing to see, Doug. A hundred and sixty-seven guys with only one idea in their heads—to do something for Mister Roberts.

ROBERTS (*after a moment*). I wish you hadn't told me, Doc. It makes me look pretty silly after what I just said. But I didn't mean it, Doc. I was afraid to say what I really feel. I love those bastards, Doc. I think they're the greatest guys on this earth. All of a sudden I feel that there's something wrong—something terribly wrong—about leaving them. God, what can I say to them?

DOC. You won't say anything—you don't even know. When you're safely aboard your new ship I'm supposed to write and tell you about it. And at the bottom of the letter, I'm supposed to say, "Thanks for the liberty, Mister Roberts. Thanks for every- 10 thing."

ROBERTS. Jesus!

[PULVER *enters, downcast.*]

PULVER. I'm the new Cargo Officer. And that's not all—I got to have dinner with him tonight. He *likes* me!

[*There is a polite rap on the door.*]

DOC. Come in. (*Enter* PAYNE, REBER, GERHART, SCHLEMMER, DOLAN, *and* IN-SIGNA, *all carrying canteen cups except* 20 INSIGNA, *whose cup is in his belt. He carries a large red fire extinguisher.*) What's this?

INSIGNA. Fire and rescue party. Heard you had a fire in here.

[*All are looking at* ROBERTS.]

ROBERTS. No, but—since you're here—I . . .

INSIGNA. Hell, we got a false alarm then. Happens all the time. (*Sets the ex-* 30 *tinguisher on the desk.*) In that case, we might as well drink this stuff. Give me your glass, Mister Roberts, and I'll put a head on it—yours too, Doc. I got one for you, Mister Pulver. (*He fills their glasses from the fire extinguisher.*)

ROBERTS. What's in that, a new batch of jungle juice?

INSIGNA. Yeah, in the handy, new, port- 40 able container. Everybody loaded?

[*All nod.*]

DOLAN. Go ahead, Sam.

INSIGNA (*to* ROBERTS). There's a story going around that you're leaving us. That right?

ROBERTS (*carefully*). That's right, Sam. And I . . .

INSIGNA. Well, we didn't want you to get away without having a little drink with us, and we thought we ought to give you a little sort of going-away present. The fellows made it down in the machine shop. It ain't much but we hope you like it. (REBER *prompts him.*) We all sincerely hope you like it. (*Calls off stage.*) All right, you bastards, you can come in now.

[*Enter* LINDSTROM, MANNION, DOWDY, *and* STEFANOWSKI. MANNION *is carrying a candy box. He walks over to* ROBERTS *shyly and hands him the box.*]

ROBERTS. What is it?

SCHLEMMER. Open it.

[ROBERTS *opens the box. There is a deep silence.*]

PULVER. What is it, Doug?

[ROBERTS *holds up the box. In it is a brass medal shaped like a palm tree, attached to a piece of gaudy ribbon.*]

LINDSTROM. It's a palm tree, see.

DOLAN. It was Dowdy's idea.

DOWDY. Mannion here made it. He cut it out of sheet brass down in the machine shop.

INSIGNA. Mannion drilled the words on it too.

MANNION. Stefanowski thought up the words.

STEFANOWSKI (*shoving* LINDSTROM *forward*). Lindstrom gets credit for the ribbon from a box of candy that his sister-in-law sent him. Read the words, Mister Roberts.

ROBERTS (*with difficulty*). "Order . . . order of . . ." (*He hands the medal to* DOC.)

DOC (*rises and reads solemnly*). "Order of the palm. To Lieutenant (jg) Douglas Roberts for action against the enemy, above and beyond the call of duty on the night of eight May 1945." (*He passes the medal back to* ROBERTS.)

ROBERTS (*after a moment—smiling*). It's very nice, but I'm afraid you've got the wrong guy.

[*The men turn to* DOWDY, *grinning.*]

DOWDY. We know that, but we'd kinda like for you to have it anyway.

ROBERTS. All right, I'll keep it.

[*The men beam. There is an awkward pause.*] 10

GERHART. Stefanowski thought up the words.

ROBERTS. They're fine words.

[WILEY *enters.*]

WILEY. The boat's here, Mister Roberts. I put your gear in. They want to shove off right away.

ROBERTS (*rising*). Thanks. We haven't had our drink yet.

REBER. No, we ain't. 20

[*All get to their feet.* ROBERTS *picks up his glass, looks at the crew, and everyone drinks.*]

ROBERTS. Good-by, Doc.

DOC. Good-by, Doug.

ROBERTS. And thanks, Doc.

DOC. Okay.

ROBERTS. Good-by, Frank.

PULVER. Good-by, Doug.

ROBERTS. Remember, I'm counting on 30 you.

[PULVER *nods.* ROBERTS *turns to the crew and looks at them for a moment. Then he takes the medal from the box, pins it on his shirt, shows it to them, then gives a little gestured salute and exits as the lights fade out.*]

[*During the darkness we hear voices making announcements over the squawk box.*] 40

FIRST VOICE. Now hear this . . . now hear this . . . Sweepers, man your brooms. Clean sweep-down fore and aft!

SECOND VOICE. Now hear this! All men put on report today will fall in on the quarter-deck—and form three ranks!

THIRD VOICE. Now hear this! All divisions will draw their mail at 1700— in the mess hall.

SCENE VI

The lights come up showing the main set at sunset. DOC *is sitting on the hatch, reading a letter.* MANNION, *wearing side arms, is pacing up and down in front of the* CAPTAIN's *cabin. On each side of the door is a small palm tree in a five-gallon can—on one can is painted in large white letters,* KEEP AWAY; *on the other,* THIS MEANS YOU. *After a moment,* PULVER *enters from the left passageway, carrying a small packet of letters.*

PULVER. Hello, Mannion. Got your mail yet?

MANNION. No. I've got the palm-tree watch.

PULVER. Oh. (*To* DOC.) What's your news, Doc?

DOC. My wife got some new wallpaper for the living room.

[PULVER *sits on the hatch cover.* DOWDY *enters wearing work gloves.*]

DOWDY. Mister Pulver, we'll be finished with the cargo in a few minutes.

PULVER. How'd it go?

DOWDY. Not bad. I've got to admit you were right about Number Three hold. It worked easier out of there. Mister Pulver, I just found out what the Captain decided—he ain't going to show a movie again tonight.

PULVER. Why not?

DOWDY. He's still punishing us because he caught Reber without a shirt on two days ago. You've got to go in and see him.

PULVER. I did. I asked him to show a movie yesterday.

DOWDY. Mister Pulver, what the hell good does that do us today? You've got to keep needlin' that guy—I'm tellin' you.

PULVER. Don't worry. I'll take care of it in my own way.

DOWDY (*going off, but speaking loud enough to be heard*). Oh God, no movie again tonight.

[*He exits.* PULVER *starts looking at his packet of mail.*]

PULVER (*looking at the first letter*). This is 10 from my mother. All she ever says is stay away from Japan. (*He drops it on the hatch cover.*) This is from Alabama. (*Puts it in his pocket and pats it. Looks at the third letter.*) Doc! This is from Doug!

DOC. Yeah? (PULVER *rips open the envelope.*) What does he say?

PULVER (*reading*). "This will be short and sweet, as we're shoving off in 20 about two minutes . . ." (*Pauses and remarks:*) This is dated three weeks ago.

DOC. Does he say where he is?

PULVER. Yeah. He says: "My guess about the location of this ship was just exactly right." (*Looks up.*) That means he's around Okinawa all right! (*Reads on and chuckles.*) He's met Fornell. That's that friend of mine 30 . . . a guy named Fornell I went to college with. Listen to this: "Fornell says that you and he used to load up your car with liquor in Omaha and then sell it at an indecent profit to the fraternity boys at Iowa City. How about that?" We did too. (*Smiles happily.*) "This part is for Doc." (DOC *gestures for him to read it.*) "I've been aboard this destroyer for two weeks 40 now and we've already been through four air attacks. I'm in the war at last, Doc. I've caught up with that task force that passed me by. I'm glad to be here. I had to be here, I guess. But I'm thinking now of you, Doc, and

you, Frank, and Dolan and Dowdy and Insigna and everyone else on that bucket—all the guys everywhere who sail from Tedium to Apathy and back again—with an occasional side trip to Monotony. This is a tough crew on here, and they have a wonderful battle record. But I've discovered, Doc, that the most terrible enemy of this war is the boredom that eventually becomes a faith and, therefore, a sort of suicide—and I know now that the ones who refuse to surrender to it are the strongest of all.

"Right now, I'm looking at something that's hanging over my desk: a preposterous hunk of brass attached to the most bilious piece of ribbon I've ever seen. I'd rather have it than the Congressional Medal of Honor. It tells me what I'll always be proudest of—that at a time in the world when courage counted most, I lived among a hundred and sixty-seven brave men.

"So, Doc, and especially you, Frank, don't let those guys down. Of course I know that by this time they must be very happy because the Captain's overhead is filled with marbles and . . ." (*He avoids* DOC's *eyes.*) . . . "Oh, hell, here comes the mail orderly. This has to go now. I'll finish it later. Meanwhile you bastards can write too, can't you?
                              "Doug"

DOC. Can I see that, Frank?

[PULVER *hands him the letter, looks at the front of his next letter, and says quietly:*]

PULVER. Well, for God's sake, this is from Fornell!

DOC (*reading* ROBERTS' *letter to himself*). ". . . I'd rather have it than the Congressional Medal of Honor." I'm glad he found that out. (*He looks at* PULVER, *sensing something wrong.*)

What's the matter? (PULVER *does not answer*.) What's the matter, Frank?

[PULVER *looks at him slowly as* DOWDY *enters*.]

DOWDY. All done, Mister Pulver. We've secured the hatch cover. No word on the movie, I suppose.

DOC (*louder, with terror*). Frank, what is it?

PULVER. Mister Roberts is dead. (*Looks at the letter*.) This is from Fornell. . . . They took a Jap suicide plane. It killed everyone in a twin-forty battery and then it went on through and killed Doug and another officer in the wardroom. (*Pause*.) They were drinking coffee when it hit.

DOWDY (*quietly*). Mister Pulver, can I please give that letter to the crew?

DOC. No. (*Holding out* ROBERTS' *letter*.) Give them this one. It's theirs. (DOWDY *removes his gloves and takes the letter from* DOC *and goes off*.) Coffee . . .

[PULVER *gets up restlessly*. DOC *stares straight ahead*. PULVER *straightens*. He seems to grow. He walks casually over to* MANNION.]

PULVER (*in a friendly voice*). Go on down and get your mail. I'll stand by for you.

MANNION (*surprised*). You will? Okay, thanks, Mister Pulver.

[MANNION *disappears down the hatch. As soon as he exits* PULVER *very calmly jerks the rooted palms, one by one, from their containers and throws them over the side.* DOC *looks up to see* PULVER *pull the second tree.* DOC *ducks as the tree goes past him. Then* PULVER *knocks loudly on the* CAPTAIN's *door*.)

CAPTAIN (*off stage. His voice is very truculent*). Yeah. Who is it?

PULVER. Captain, this is Ensign Pulver. I just threw your palm trees overboard. Now what's all this crap about no movie tonight?

[*He throws the door open, banging it against the bulkhead, and is entering the* CAPTAIN's *cabin as*]

THE CURTAIN FALLS

STUDENTS' BIBLIOGRAPHY OF MODERN DRAMA

T HE number of books on modern drama has grown to huge proportions. The
subject has had so many points of interest, and it has been so dynamic over a
period of sixty years, that it has called forth hundreds of articles, studies, and books
on every aspect of drama and the theatre. Many of these works served a useful
purpose but were outmoded by the onrush of the movement. Others have been
superseded by later, more complete treatises. The following list is a beginner's
guide to the most helpful books on the drama, the playwrights, and the theatre.

BIBLIOGRAPHY

ANDERSON, MAXWELL. *The Essence of Tragedy*. Washington, 1939.

BENTLEY, ERIC. *The Playwright as Thinker*. New York, 1946.

BLOCK, ANITA. *The Changing World in Plays and Theatre*. Boston, 1939.

BROWN, JOHN MASON. *Broadway in Review*. New York, 1940.

—— *The Modern Theatre in Revolt*. New York, 1929.

—— *Two on the Aisle: Ten Years of the American Theatre in Performance*. New York,
1938.

CAGEY, EDMOND M. *Revolution in American Drama*. New York, 1947.

CLARK, BARRETT H. *Eugene O'Neill, The Man and His Plays*. New York, 1929 and 1936.

—— *A Study of the Modern Drama* (Revised ed.) New York, 1936.

—— and Freedley, George (ed.). *A History of Modern Drama*. New York, 1947.

DICKINSON, THOMAS H. *An Outline of Contemporary Drama*. Boston, 1927.

FLEXNER, ELEANOR. *American Playwrights: 1918–1938*. New York, 1938.

GASSNER, JOHN. *Masters of the Drama*. New York, 1940.

GILDER, ROSAMOND. *A Theatre Library*. A Bibliography of One Hundred Books Relat-
ing to the Theatre. New York, 1932.

GORELIK, MORDECAI. *New Theatres for Old*. New York, 1941.

HAMILTON, CLAYTON MEEKER. *The Theory of the Theatre*. (Consolidated ed.) New York,
1939.

ISAACS, EDITH J. R. *The Negro in the American Theatre*. New York, 1947.

KRUTCH, JOSEPH WOOD. *The American Drama Since 1918*. New York, 1939.

MANTLE, ROBERT BURNS. *Contemporary American Playwrights*. New York, 1939.

O'HARA, FRANK HURBURT. *Today in American Drama*. Chicago, 1939.

QUINN, ARTHUR HOBSON. *A History of the American Drama from the Civil War to the
Present Day*. New York, 1936.

SKINNER, RICHARD DANA. *Eugene O'Neill, A Poet's Quest*. New York, 1935.

SOBEL, BERNARD. *The Theatre Handbook and Digest of Plays*. New York, 1940.

WINTHER, SOPHUS KEITH. *Eugene O'Neill, A Critical Study*. New York, 1934.